LINCOLN CHRISTIAN UNIVERSITY

ZONDERVAN
HANDBOOK TO THE
HISTORY OF CHRISTIANITY

ZONDERVAN
HANDBOOK TO THE
HISTORY OF CHRISTIANITY

JONATHAN HILL

ZONDERVAN®

ZONDERVAN.com/
AUTHORTRACKER
follow your favorite authors

ZONDERVAN®

Zondervan Handbook to the History of Christianity

Copyright © 2006 by Jonathan Hill

Published by Lion Publishing Plc. Mayfield House, 256 Banbury Road, Oxford OX2 7DH, England

www.lionhudson.com

This edition published by special arrangement with Lion Publishing by Zondervan, *Grand Rapids, Michigan 49530*

Library of Congress Cataloging-in-Publication Data
    Hill, Jonathan.
        Zondervan handbook to the history of Christianity : a comprehensive global survey of the growth,
    spread, and development of Christianity / Jonathan Hill.
        p. cm.
        Includes bibliographical references and index.
        ISBN-13: 978-0-310-26270-1
        ISBN-10: 0-310-26270-4
        1. Church history. I. Title.
    BR150.H55 2006
    270–dc22
    2006009459
    CIP

This edition printed on acid-free paper.

All Scripture quotations, unless otherwise indicated, are taken from the *Holy Bible: New International Version®*. NIV®. Copyright © 1973, 1978, 1984 by International Bible Society. Used by permission of Zondervan. All rights reserved.

The website addresses recommended throughout this book are offered as a resource to you. These websites are not intended in any way to be or imply an endorsement on the part of Zondervan, nor do we vouch for their content for the life of this book.

All rights reserved. No part of this publication may be reproduced, stored in a retrieval system, or transmitted in any form or by any means—electronic, mechanical, photocopy, recording, or any other—except for brief quotations in printed reviews, without the prior permission of the publisher.

Printed in Singapore

06 07 08 09 10 11 12 • 10 9 8 7 6 5 4 3 2 1

CONTENTS

126762

TIMELINE OF CHRISTIAN HISTORY

c.30 Execution of Jesus of Nazareth.

c.49 Council of Jerusalem establishes that Christians do not have to be Jewish.

c.50–c.64 Paul writes letters to different churches.

c.64 First persecution of Christians, under Nero. Deaths of Peter, Paul, and James the Just.

c.66–c.95 Probable dates of the four Gospels.

70 Destruction of the Temple in Jerusalem.

c.90 Council of Jamnia marks break between Christianity and Judaism.

c.95 Persecution under Domitian.

c.107 Ignatius of Antioch writes to seven churches.

c.180 Irenaeus of Lyons writes On the so-called gnosis.

c.190 Osrhoene becomes the first officially Christian state.

c.230 Origen of Alexandria writes On first principles.

250 Persecution under Decius.

303–11 Persecution under Diocletian and Galerius.

c.310s–370s Persecutions in Persia under Shapur II.

313 Edict of Milan legalizes Christianity.

325 Council of Nicaea condemns Arianism.

330 Constantinople founded as the Christian capital of the Roman empire.

c.330 Pachomius writes the first Rule for a Christian monastery.

381 Council of Constantinople condemns Arianism again.

380s Emperor Theodosius effectively establishes Christianity as the official religion of Rome.

393 A council at Hippo establishes the canon of the Bible.

417 Pope Innocent I condemns Pelagius.

c.426 Augustine of Hippo completes City of God.

431 Council of Ephesus condemns Nestorius.

c.433 Patrick lands in Ireland and converts King Laoghaire.

451 Council of Chalcedon condemns Eutyches.

484 Roman synod excommunicates Acacius of Constantinople over the Henoticon, marking the first official break between the two churches.

c.500 Pseudo-Dionysius writes The mystical theology.

c.530 Benedict of Nursia writes his Rule.

537 Dedication of new cathedral of Hagia Sophia, Constantinople.

553 Second Council of Constantinople condemns the 'Three Chapters'.

590 Gregory the Great becomes Pope.

627 Emperor Heraclius conquers Ctesiphon and restores the 'True Cross' to Jerusalem.

630s Persia, Egypt, Armenia, and Levant conquered by Muslims.

652 Christian Makuria and Muslim Egypt agree the baqt treaty.

664 Synod of Whitby decrees that England will use Roman, not Celtic, rites.

680 Third Council of Constantinople condemns monotheletism.

725 Emperor Leo III begins crackdown on icons.

c.780 Stele of Xian records the state of the Chinese church.

787 Second Council of Nicaea authorizes use of icons in worship.

c.800 Book of Kells produced in Ireland.

843 'Restoration of orthodoxy' in Byzantium confirms legitimacy of icons.

845 Emperor Wu-tsang closes Chinese monasteries.

858 Pope Nicholas I condemns Photius of Constantinople, marking the second official break between the two churches.

864 Baptism of Khan Boris I of Bulgaria.

878 Treaty of Wedmore forces Vikings in England to convert to Christianity.

910 Cluniac order founded.

966 Prince Mieszko I of Poland baptized.

988 Prince Vladimir of the Rus baptized.

1051 Kiev-Pechersk Lavra founded in Kiev.

1054 'Great Schism' between Roman Catholic and Orthodox churches.

1075 Pope Gregory VII issues the Papal decree.

1084 Carthusian order founded.

1095 Pope Urban II preaches the First Crusade.

1098 Cistercian order founded.

1099 Crusaders capture Jerusalem.

1128 Knights Templar founded.

1145 Pope Eugenius III preaches the Second Crusade.

1180 Pope Alexander III condemns the Waldensians.

1187 Saladin captures Jerusalem.

1198 Innocent III becomes Pope.

1204 Third Crusade results in sacking of Constantinople and the establishment of a Latin patriarchate.

1210 Francis of Assisi founds the Franciscan order.

1215 Fourth Lateran Council defines Catholic beliefs and practices, including transubstantiation.

1216 Dominic de Gusmán founds the Dominican order.

1242 Montsegur, citadel of the Cathars, destroyed.

1242 Alexander Nevsky defeats the Teutonic Knights at the Battle of Lake Peipus, to keep Russia Orthodox.

1261 Byzantines recapture Constantinople.

1273 Thomas Aquinas leaves his Summa theologiae unfinished.

c.1280 Kebre Negast compiled in Ethiopia.

1305 Pope Clement V moves the Papacy to Avignon.

1314 Knights Templar suppressed.

1330s–40s Amda Siyon of Ethiopia conquers Ifat and imposes Christianity there.

1338 Gregory Palamas writes Triads in defence of the holy hesychasts.

1368 Fall of the Yuan dynasty brings the Chinese church to an end.

1377 Pope Gregory XI condemns John Wycliffe.

1380s Persecutions under Tamerlane almost destroy the Church of the East.

1387 'Great Schism' begins between the Avignon and Roman Papacies.

1414 Council of Constance resolves 'Great Schism', restores Papacy to Rome, and condemns Jan Hus.

1438 Council of Basle (later Ferrara, Florence, and Rome) briefly reunites Roman Catholic and Orthodox churches.

1453 Fall of Constantinople to the Ottomans.

1474 Marsilio Ficino writes Platonic theology.

1483 Spanish Inquisition set up.

1491 Nzinga Nkuvu (João) of Congo is baptized.

1498 Portuguese establish contact with Indian Christians.

1509–43 Mvemba Nzinga (Afonso) establishes Christianity throughout Congo.

1513 Requirement imposed upon Conquistadors in the Americas, requiring that they give a cursory explanation of Christianity to natives.

1517 Martin Luther nails his 'Ninety-five theses' to the church door in Wittenberg.

1520 Portuguese establish contact with Ethiopia.

1521 The Diet of Worms condemns Martin Luther.

1534 Act of Supremacy makes King Henry VIII head of the Church of England.

1537 Pope Paul III condemns the enslavement of native Americans.

1540 Ignatius Loyola founds the Society of Jesus.

1542 Francis Xavier arrives in India and begins preaching there.

1545–63 Council of Trent re-affirms Catholic doctrine in the face of Protestantism.

1549 Francis Xavier arrives in Japan and begins preaching there.

1552 Thomas Cranmer publishes the second edition of the Book of common prayer.

1553 Jesuits establish a mission at Luanda, Angola.

1559 John Calvin publishes the definitive edition of Institutes of the Christian religion.

1561 Cathedral of the Intercession of the Virgin on the Moat (known as St Basil's Cathedral) completed in Moscow.

1565 Augustinian missionaries arrive in the Philippines.

1569 Ukraine is given to Poland and Catholicized.

1571 The 'Thirty-nine articles' established as the doctrine of the Church of England.

1577 Teresa of Avila publishes The interior castle.

1583 Matteo Ricci enters China.

1596 Eastern-rite Ukrainian Catholic Church established.

1596 Persecutions of Christians in Japan begun.

1598 King Henry IV of France issues the Edict of Nantes, permitting freedom of worship to the Huguenots.

1599 Synod of Diamper attempts to Catholicize the Malabar Christians in India.

1603 Matteo Ricci completes The true doctrine of the Lord of heaven.

1609 Jesuits gain control of Paraguay and establish the first of the 'Thirty Missions'.

1611 A team of scholars commissioned by King James I of England produce the Authorized Version of the Bible in English.

1615 New basilica of St Peter's completed in Rome.

1618 The Synod of Dort condemns Arminianism and defines orthodox Calvinism.

1619 Feodor Romanov is enthroned as Filaret, patriarch of Moscow.

1620 'Pilgrim Fathers' land at Plymouth Rock and establish a Puritan society.

1622 Pope Gregory XV creates the Congregation for the Propagation of the Faith.

1633 Emperor Fasilidas expels Jesuits and other Catholic missionaries from Ethiopia.

1639 Japan closes its borders to westerners, driving Christianity underground.

1645 Pope Innocent X bans the Chinese rites.

1649–60 England becomes a Commonwealth, with Puritanism dominant in the church.

1652 Nikon becomes patriarch of Moscow and begins his controversial reforms.

1667 Ukraine is divided between Poland and Russia, bringing the Catholic Enlightenment to Russia.

1672 Thousands of Huguenots are killed in the Bartholomew's Day massacre in France.

1673 Test Act in England bans non-Anglicans from all establishment posts.

1674 Catholic hierarchy officially established in New France.

1682 The French clergy issue a Declaration of Gallicanism.

1685 King Louis XIV of France revokes the Edict of Nantes.

1688 King James II of England is deposed, partly because of his increasing support of Roman Catholicism.

1721 Tsar Peter the Great of Russia replaces the patriarchate of Moscow with a Holy Synod.

1724 Emperor Yongzeng of China bans Christianity.

1728 William Law publishes *A serious call to a devout and holy life*.

1730 Matthew Tindal publishes *Christianity as old as creation*.

1739 John Wesley breaks with the Moravians in Britain and founds what will become the Methodists.

1740 George Whitefield arrives in America and preaches the new revivals.

1742 Pope Benedict XIV confirms the banning of the Chinese rites.

1750 Jesuits expelled from Paraguay.

1754 Methodist missionaries arrive in Antigua and begin the first systematic preaching to West Indian slaves.

1755 The Lisbon earthquake causes many to question the goodness of God.

1764 Voltaire publishes the *Philosophical dictionary*.

1773 Pope Clement XIV suppresses the Jesuits.

1774–77 Gotthold Lessing publishes fragments by Hermann Reimarus casting doubt on the authenticity of the New Testament.

1786 Virginia passes Thomas Jefferson's bill guaranteeing complete religious liberty.

1790s Persecutions against Christians begin in Korea.

1792 Colonists from North America arrive in Sierra Leone to establish a new Christian colony there.

1792–94 The National Convention in France attempts to replace Catholicism with Deism.

1796 The London Missionary Society sends the first missionaries to Tahiti.

1799 Friedrich Schleiermacher publishes *On religion: speeches to its cultured despisers*.

1799 William Carey arrives in Serampore and begins to preach there.

1807 Robert Morrison arrives in China and begins to preach there.

1807 G.W.F. Hegel publishes *Phenomenology of spirit*.

1809 Napoleon invades the Papal States and forces Pope Pius VII into exile.

1814 Pope Pius VII restores the Jesuits.

1819 Pomare II of Tahiti is baptized.

1820s *Mfecane* migrations in southern Africa help to spread Christianity into the interior.

1821 Robert Moffat arrives in Kuruman and sets up a mission station.

1830 Friedrich Schleiermacher publishes the second edition of *The Christian faith*.

1830 Joseph Smith founds the Church of Christ, later the Church of Jesus Christ of Latter-day Saints.

1833–41 Publication of *Tracts for the times* by the leaders of the Oxford Movement.

1835 David Strauss publishes *The life of Jesus critically examined*.

1835–43 Thousands of Boers head north from Cape Town in the Great Trek, bringing the Reformed faith with them.

1836 Synod at Mavelikara rejects interference by the British in the Malankara Church.

1846 Pius IX becomes Pope.

1847 Rosendo Salvado establishes the monastery of New Norcia in Australia and preaches to the Aborigines.

1850s Persecutions against Christians in Vietnam reach a peak.

1854 Pope Pius IX defines the doctrine of the immaculate conception of the Blessed Virgin Mary.

1858 Keshab Chandra Sen joins the Brahmo Sabha and pushes for a universal religion combining Jesus' teachings with those of Hinduism.

1860 An argument about Darwinism, involving Thomas Huxley and Samuel Wilberforce, takes place in Oxford.

1864 Samuel Crowther becomes the first black Anglican bishop.

1865 Bernard Petitjean rediscovers the *Kakure Kirishitan* of Japan.

1870 First Vatican Council condemns the *Syllabus of errors* and affirms Papal infallibility.

1871 'Old Catholics' establish their own church, rejecting the First Vatican Council.

1872 Te Kooti establishes the Ringatu church in New Zealand.

1873 The passing of the 'May Laws' begins the *Kulturkampf* in Germany.

1878 Emperor Yohannes IV of Ethiopia calls the Council of Borumeda to establish Christological orthodoxy.

1883 Christianity legalized in Korea.

1889 Christianity legalized in Japan.

1899 Plenary Council for Latin America calls for reforms in the Latin American Catholic Church.

1900 'Boxers' kill many foreigners and Christians in Beijing.

1901 Charles Parham reports manifestations of the Holy Spirit in his Bible study class in Kansas, initiating Pentecostalism.

1901 Uchimura Kanzō founds the Nonchurch movement in Japan.

1902 Gregorio Aglipay founds the Philippine Independent Church.

1903 P.L. Le Roux founds the Zionist Apostolic Church, one of the first AICs.

1907 Great Revival at P'yŏngyang helps spread Christianity in both Korea and China.

1910 World Mission Conference in Edinburgh marks the start of the modern ecumenical movement.

1910–15 *The fundamentals* are published in the United States, defining the typical doctrines of fundamentalism.

1917 The Russian Orthodox Church restores the patriarchate of Moscow.

1917 New Mexican constitution clamps down on Catholicism.

1918 Tahupotiki Wiremu Ratana has a series of visions, leading to the establishment of the Ratana Church in New Zealand.

1920s–30 Russian Orthodox Church increasingly persecuted.

1926 Pope Pius XI ordains the first six indigenous Chinese bishops of modern times.

1927–29 Cristero Rebellion in Mexico.

1929 Lateran Pacts establish Vatican City as an independent state.

1932–68 Karl Barth publishes *Church Dogmatics*.

1933 Adolf Hitler agrees a concordat with the Catholic Church, and has the German Protestant churches united into a Nazi-dominated Reich Church.

1934 German Confessing Church founded in opposition to Nazism.

1936 Italians conquer Ethiopia and begin intermittent persecutions of the Ethiopian Orthodox Church.

1936–37 Many Russian Orthodox clerics die in Joseph Stalin's 'Great Purge'.

1937 Persecutions begin against Catholic priests in Germany.

1937 Pope Pius XI condemns both communism and Nazism.

1939 Congregation for the Propagation of the Faith decrees that Chinese rites are compatible with Catholicism.

1941 United Church of Christ formed as the only officially recognized Protestant body in Japan.

1943 Joseph Stalin legalizes the Russian Orthodox Church.

1945–47 Communist governments are installed in most eastern European countries, which oppress the churches there to varying degrees.

1948 Establishment of a communist government leads to clampdown on Christianity in North Korea.

1950 Pope Pius XII defines the doctrine of the physical assumption of the Blessed Virgin Mary.

1950 Chinese Christian Manifesto appears, leading to the establishment of the Three-Self Patriotic Movement.

1954 Establishment of a communist government in North Vietnam leads to many Christians fleeing south.

1955 Trevor Huddleston publishes *Naught for your comfort*.

1959–64 Nikita Krushchev clamps down on the Russian Orthodox Church.

1962–65 The Second Vatican Council restates Catholicism for the modern age.

1966–69 Cultural Revolution in China sees persecution against Christians and all churches closed.

1971 Gustavo Gutiérrez publishes *Theology of liberation*.

1978 John Paul II becomes Pope.

1978 Bharat Christian Church created as a federation of Indian churches.

1979 Jerry Falwell forms the Moral Majority, initiating a period of political influence for right-wing Christianity in the United States.

1980 China Christian Council created, as churches are gradually reopened there.

1981 President Anwar Sadat of Egypt briefly outlaws the Coptic Church.

1984 Pope John Paul II performs the first canonization outside Rome, in Seoul.

1985 Institute for Contextual Theology in South Africa issues the *Kairos Document*.

1989–91 Collapse of communism in most of eastern Europe leads to new freedom for the churches there.

1990 Catholicism legalized in Cambodia.

1992 The Church of England ordains its first female priests.

1994 The 'Toronto Blessing' is reported at Toronto Airport Vineyard Christian Fellowship.

2003 Bernard Law resigns as Catholic archbishop of Boston over allegations of covering up paedophilia among the priesthood.

2003 Gene Robinson becomes Episcopalian bishop of New Hampshire in the US, drawing deep controversy over his active homosexuality.

2005 German Cardinal Joseph Ratzinger is elected as the new Pope.

2006 The general synod of the Church of England, led by the archbishop of Canterbury, apologizes for benefiting from slavery up to 1834.

INTRODUCTION

Palestine, c. AD 30: an obscure Jewish
preacher, the latest in a line of charismatic
religious figures, is executed by the Roman
authorities. His followers scatter. The wider
world pays no attention whatsoever.

The early twenty-first century:
approximately a third of the world's
population – some two billion people – are
estimated to be followers of that preacher.
Typing his name into the most popular
search engine on the Internet brings up well
over 100 million hits. More books have been
written about him than about any other
person in history.

How did a group of scared peasants from
a backwater of the Roman empire, followers
of an executed criminal, become the largest
religion on the planet? The story of
Christianity, its transformation from an illegal
sect to the religion of emperors, kings and
presidents, and its spread across the globe, is
an endlessly fascinating one. This book offers
an overview of these extraordinary two
thousand years. It is written to be accessible
to readers without any background in the
subject, but the hope is that it will also
contain plenty of interest to those who are
already familiar with much of the story.

It is a story not just of how Christianity
has changed the world, but of how the world
has changed Christianity. In these pages, we
will meet persecuted pacifists, sword-wielding
monks, Arabian courtiers, glossy American
televangelists, feudal Japanese warlords,
medieval African kings, Enlightenment-era
European philosophers, nomads of the
Mongolian steppes, and many more –
Christians one and all. Christianity has
spread to virtually every culture on earth, and
people from each culture have understood or
re-interpreted the Christian message in their
own way. And so we have aimed to tell not

simply what Christians did and where they
went, but how Christianity itself has adapted
to different peoples and cultures – even as
Christians seek to remain true to the same
message of Jesus, however differently they
have understood it.

The history of Christianity is such a vast
subject that no one book can hope to do
justice to its scope and complexity. This book
is intended as a sort of bird's-eye view of the
main contours. It is divided into seventeen
chapters, each one describing a different
period of Christian history; along the way,
text boxes highlight especially important
figures or themes. The first thirteen chapters
(and the sections within each chapter) are
arranged mostly chronologically, to create a
single narrative from the time of Jesus up to
the modern day – although occasionally a
more thematic arrangement has been used to
clarify matters. The last four chapters all
describe the history of the church in the past
hundred years or so, each one focusing on a
different part of the world.

Perhaps inevitably, the history of
Christianity in Europe forms the dominant
theme for much of the book. Christianity
began in the Middle East, and in recent
decades it has seen its greatest growth in
Africa. Yet for much of the intervening period,
it was in Europe that it grew and developed
most dramatically, and European-style
Christianity has proven far more determined
and effective at spreading overseas than the
versions of Christianity that developed
elsewhere. In the past, this fact has
sometimes led to Europeans and Americans
almost entirely overlooking non-European
forms of Christianity, with Asia and Africa
depicted as passive receivers of the religion of
European or American missionaries, rather
than as the homes of ancient, thriving, and

independent Christian traditions. In this book, we have aimed to reflect the importance of these non-European traditions while acknowledging the role of Europeans in spreading Christianity in later centuries – and the role of non-Europeans in creatively interpreting the message that they heard.

The book does not presuppose any prior knowledge of Christian history or theology. There is a glossary to help those unfamiliar with any technical terms that may crop up. There is also a bibliography, with chapter-by-chapter suggestions for further reading for those who wish to delve more deeply into some of the subjects sketched here. It is our hope that this *Handbook* will inspire many – whether or not they are Christians themselves – to do exactly that. For while the history of Christianity is by turns violent, inspiring, shocking, tragic, comic, or just plain bizarre, it is certainly never dull.

Manuscript from Hradcany Castle, Prague, showing Christ reigning as king in the heavenly Jerusalem.

CHAPTER 1

CHRISTIAN BEGINNINGS

How did Christianity begin? Some of the people we will meet later in this book argued that, because Christianity taught the truths of God, it was as old as time itself. Others insisted that Christianity as we know it was an invention of the emperor Constantine (c. AD 274–337) and had virtually nothing to do with Jesus himself. But, to most historians, Christianity had its origins in the movement started by the surviving disciples of Jesus of Nazareth, a Jewish preacher from Galilee who was executed by the Romans in around AD 30.

THE SETTING

THE ROMAN EMPIRE

It was a striking fact, and one not lost upon later Christians, that Jesus was born just as the Roman empire was coming into existence. The city of Rome, which had gradually expanded its power across the Italian peninsula and beyond, had until recently been a republic. By the beginning of the first century AD, Rome had defeated its rivals, Carthage and the Greek states, and controlled more or less the entire coastline of the Mediterranean Sea, as well as Gaul, conquered by the brilliant but ruthless Julius Caesar.

The first real Roman emperor was Caesar's nephew, Octavian, a man at least as remarkable as his famous uncle. Caesar's murder in 44 BC saw further civil war, which Octavian won – defeating Mark Antony and his lover, Cleopatra, and adding Egypt to the Roman domains in the process. Taking the name Caesar Augustus, he essentially created the government and structures of the Roman empire, although he refused to call himself by any title other than *princeps* ('first'). He was careful to maintain the forms of the old republic, with the senate retaining nominal control of the state. But elections to the senate were rigged by Augustus, it was filled with his men, and it concerned itself with

his business. Although the senate remained, the emperor ruled. This meant that, under some of Augustus's more intemperate successors, being a senator could be a very dangerous business.

Augustus reorganized the civil service, issued new laws, commissioned new works of art, endorsed the traditional religion of Rome, and generally set the former republic on a firmly imperial footing. Under Caesar Augustus, the whole of modern-day Spain and France were subdued, as well as the Balkans and North Africa.

The emperor was far more than simply the 'first' among equals. In 12 BC, Augustus followed Julius Caesar's lead in becoming *pontifex maximus*, the chief priest of the traditional Roman religion: there was thus an official union of state and religion, both of which were personified in the one man, the emperor. Augustus also endorsed the cult of Julius Caesar, which regarded him no longer as a mere man but as a god. Augustus himself was formally deified after his death in AD 14. From then on the emperors were all officially gods, even

Marcus Aurelius, Stoic philosopher and Roman emperor (reigned AD 161–180), depicted in the Piazza del Campidoglio, Rome.

during their lifetimes. Quite what this actually meant is hard to tell: probably some people genuinely believed their emperor was divine, whilst others regarded this as simply a patriotic sentiment that did not really mean anything substantial. Sometimes the emperor was believed to be under the influence of a divine spirit who guided his actions: in this case, it was 'Caesar's genius' to which the devout paid homage.

PALESTINE

The Jews had lived in Palestine, at the eastern end of the Mediterranean Sea, for many centuries. But it had been a long time since they had been truly independent. In the sixth century BC, they had been conquered and transported by the Babylonians for fifty years in a traumatic period known as the Babylonian exile. Since then they had been dominated by first the Persians (who built a powerful empire to the east) and then the Seleucids, a dynasty founded in the wake of the conquests of the Macedonian general Alexander the Great. They had rebelled against the Seleucids in the second century BC, but in the first century BC they were conquered by the Roman general Pompey. From then on, Palestine was part of the Roman empire.

Most of the country was devoted to agriculture, which was made difficult by its hot and dry weather. In the north, Galilee enjoyed a wetter and milder climate. Here the Jordan flowed into and out of a large lake called the Sea of Galilee, which was the basis for a fishing industry. Most of the people worked the land, either on small farms of their own or as tenant farmers on the property of large landowners.

Ruling it all was first the Hasmonean dynasty and then the Herodian one. Palestine was not literally 'occupied' by the Romans. On the contrary, their policy was to allow the local king to administer his kingdom as a client ruler. The Romans did not really want to rule Palestine or to tax it to death – indeed, they may even have made a net loss from the place. Their interest was in having a stable and friendly

area near the frontier with Persia, Rome's perennial rival, protecting the more important regions of Egypt and Syria. They wanted to do the minimum required to keep it that way, which meant leaving most local affairs to a local king. From 37 BC to 4 BC this king was Herod the Great, a domineering personality who devoted vast quantities of money and resources to great building projects and the founding of new cities. As a client of Rome, Herod had to pay tribute to the emperor and defer to him on matters of foreign policy, but otherwise he had a largely free hand. After Herod's death, Caesar Augustus divided Palestine among his sons, who ruled as 'tetrarchs' in much the same way as Herod had done. The son who ruled Judea (the southern region of Palestine, containing Jerusalem) proved incompetent. In AD 6 he was removed and the Romans ruled this part of Palestine directly, via an official called the prefect. Being prefect of Judea was a rather thankless job. The Romans regarded this country as an appalling backwater inhabited by insane barbarians with a strange religion, and it was not a desirable place to be. Moreover, the prefect had very few troops – only a few thousand, not nearly enough to police the area properly. He therefore spent most of his time at Caesarea, a Romanized city on the coast, and left the day-to-day running of Judea and Jerusalem to the Jewish high priest, who acted almost as prime minister, setting taxes, dealing with law and order and so on.

JUDAISM

At the heart of Jewish culture was the Jewish religion, its basic faith perhaps best summed up in the speech that farmers made when dedicating their early crops to God, as laid down in Deuteronomy 26:5–9:

A wandering Aramean was my ancestor; he went down into Egypt and lived there as an alien, few in number, and there he became a great nation, mighty and populous. When the Egyptians treated us harshly and afflicted us, by imposing hard labour on us, we cried to the Lord, the God of our ancestors; the Lord heard our voice and saw our affliction, our toil, and our oppression. The Lord brought us out of Egypt with a mighty hand and an outstretched arm, with a terrifying display of power, and with signs and wonders; and he brought us into this place and gave us this land, a land flowing with milk and honey.

Deuteronomy is the last book of the Pentateuch, five books also known collectively as the Torah. Probably written at around the time of the Babylonian exile in the sixth century BC, they told the following story. The 'wandering Aramean' was Abraham, who left the Sumerian city of Ur (in modern Iraq) for the land of the River Jordan. God made a covenant with him, promising that his descendants would become a great people and live in this land. But his family moved to Egypt, where their descendants did become numerous, becoming 'Israel', that is, the Jews. Here they were enslaved; but God rescued them in the great event known as the exodus, described in the second book, of that name. Not only did he lead them out of Egypt and into the Promised Land, Palestine, he also gave them the Law, a large set of regulations about how to worship the one God and how to live together as a society. The Law was summed up in the Ten Commandments which God wrote directly onto tablets of stone and gave to Moses. Although his death is described near the end of Deuteronomy, Jews believed that Moses was the author of all five books. The subsequent history of the Jews was told in other books, which recounted how, under a succession of kings, they either adhered to or fell away from fidelity to the Law and the worship of the one God. God therefore sent a series of prophets to recall Israel to the true religion. These books formed the basis of the Jewish scriptures, although at the time of Jesus there was no 'official' view of which books were authoritative and which were not. Some of them would later form part of what Christians would call 'the Old Testament'.

This, then, is what Jews believed about their history, a history that was intimately tied up with God. The Jews believed they were chosen by God as a special people, and he not only spoke to them through the Law and the Prophets but acted on their behalf at key moments such as the exodus. Bad events, such as the Babylonian exile, might be interpreted as divine displeasure, perhaps resulting from the people's infidelity. They believed that God had an abiding covenant with them, according to which the land of Palestine was theirs. Their side of the covenant was to keep the Law. As a sign of this covenant, Jews were circumcised, something that set them apart from other people and was regarded as one of their key characteristics – in the New Testament we often find the terms 'the circumcised' and 'the uncircumcised' to refer to Jews and non-Jews respectively.

Not only was the land of Palestine given to Abraham's descendants by God, but its capital, Jerusalem, was a holy city. Jerusalem was home to the Temple, one of the most remarkable buildings in antiquity. Originally built on King Solomon's orders centuries earlier, it was rebuilt and restored by Herod the Great in the first century BC and was absolutely central to Jewish religion. The Pentateuch set out a number of sacrifices and other rituals, which were to be performed at this single, central location. God himself was believed to inhabit its central precinct, the Holy of Holies, and the only person who could enter this was the high priest, and that only once a year. The Temple employed a small army of priests, and all Jews had to pay a special tax to keep it running. Vast sums flowed in and out of the Temple, and some people even used it as a sort of bank to keep their money in. The Temple guards not only protected this wealth but policed the city of Jerusalem. So the Temple was not simply the centre of Jewish religion – it was the centre of political, economic and social life too. The regular festivals that were celebrated throughout the year centred on it. At Passover in particular, tens of thousands of people would pack into

Now the Temple was built of stones that were white and strong, and each one was twenty-five cubits long, eight cubits high, and about twelve wide; and the whole structure… could be seen by those who lived in the countryside for many miles… [The lintels] were adorned with embroidered veils, with purple flowers, and interwoven pillars. Over these, but under the crown-work, was spread out a golden vine, with its branches hanging down from a great height, whose size and fine workmanship amazed the spectators, to see what vast materials there were, and with what great skill the workmanship was done. [Herod] also encircled the entire Temple with very large cloisters, of appropriate size; and he spent more money on them than had been done before, until it seemed that no-one else had so greatly adorned the Temple as he had done. There was a large wall around both the cloisters, which was itself the most prodigious work that was ever heard of by man.

Josephus, *Antiquities*, c. AD 94

A model of the Temple of Herod the Great in Jerusalem.

Jerusalem, forcing the prefect to move there from Caesarea and borrow troops from Syria to keep the peace. The Temple extended its presence throughout Palestine in the persons of the priests, who worked in Jerusalem part-time and spent the rest of their time back home, working as teachers or judges and essentially running their local areas. These priests came from certain priestly families, making them a special social class as well as a religious one.

There were Jews outside Palestine as well. In fact, by Jesus' day there were more Jews outside it than inside it. The members of this 'diaspora' were obviously more remote from the Temple – though they still had to pay the Temple tax – and so they developed an alternative institution called the synagogue. A synagogue was not a place of worship or sacrifice but one of learning and study. It was used for reading the Pentateuch and giving instruction, as well as for communal prayers and even meals. It seems that many non-Jews – known as Gentiles – also visited synagogues, though of course they were not full members of the community. They were sympathetic to Judaism and interested in learning more about it – for many Gentiles throughout the Roman empire greatly respected the Jewish religion, with its strong monotheism and its impressive moral code. In the first century AD, synagogues also appeared throughout Palestine, as a kind of supplement to the Temple-based cult.

However, Judaism was far from being a monolithic religion, identical everywhere you went. There were many variations on the same theme, even within Palestine, and the religion developed enormously (as we shall see) throughout the first century AD. Rather than thinking of Christianity as peeling off, as it were, from a static 'Judaism', we should think of Judaism as redefining itself quite radically throughout the first century, a process that produced (among other things) Christianity.

Many Jews, to varying degrees, hoped for a great divine intervention. Although they were mostly not governed by Rome directly, they still regarded themselves as living under the rule of a foreign, non-Jewish force. Many thus hoped that God would intervene and deliver them from these foreigners, just as, they believed, God had intervened in history many times before to deliver his people. Some Jews went further than this: they hoped not simply for a political miracle but for the coming 'kingdom of God', a really decisive and ultimate intervention on God's part. The worldly order would be swept away and God would rule the world directly. Most Jews probably believed this would happen at some distant time in the future; some were particularly keen to see it happen soon.

Related to this was 'messianism', the hope that God would raise up some great human leader to usher in the kingdom. The word 'messiah' means 'anointed one' and appears relatively rarely in the Old Testament; it referred to this kind of special leader. Other figures appear in some writings in association with the coming of the kingdom: one was the mysterious 'Son of Man' in the book of Daniel. Different groups believed different things about these leaders of the end times. Some anticipated a 'Son of Man' and some the 'messiah'; sometimes he was understood in priestly terms and sometimes he was more of a warrior or king. The Dead Sea Scrolls talked about two messiahs, one a priest and one a king, accompanying the coming kingdom of God.

In addition to this, there were a number of different parties within Judaism. We have already seen the role that the priests played in Jerusalem and elsewhere: they were the 'official' leaders of Judaism and acted as general teachers and experts. They were rivalled by a group called the Pharisees, who were mostly laymen. Like the priests (and a few Pharisees were priests), they specialized in studying the Law and applying it to everyday life. To help with this they had evolved a large body of traditions. For example, the Law forbade work on the Sabbath, the seventh day of the week: the Pharisees therefore set out what they thought counted as 'work' to explain the rule more clearly. Different schools of thought competed within

Pharisaism over how severe or liberal the interpretations should be. These elucidations were developed for their own use and were not intended to be normative for anyone else, since the Pharisees had no formal authority over others. However, the Pharisees were extremely popular, since most people respected their attempt to think through the Law and apply it to everyday life.

The priests and the Pharisees were the most important groups that Jesus and the first Christians alike had to contend with. In addition, there were others, such as the Sadducees, who denied that the dead would ever rise again (the Pharisees believed that the resurrection of all people would be one of the signs of the end of the world). There were also the Essenes, who like the Pharisees were an unofficial party of both priests and laymen who studied and interpreted the Law. However, the Essenes generally interpreted the Law in a much more severe way than the Pharisees, extending its rules where possible. They

One of the caves at Qumran in which the Dead Sea Scrolls were discovered.

I saw one like a Son of Man coming with the clouds of heaven. And he came to the Ancient One and was presented before him. To him was given dominion and glory and kingship, that all peoples, nations, and languages should serve him. His dominion is an everlasting dominion that shall not pass away, and his kingship is one that shall never be destroyed.

Daniel 7:13–14

also formed communities, the most famous of which was that at Qumran near the Dead Sea. This was a sort of monastery of those who wished to dedicate their lives to following the Law as perfectly as possible, and who also believed that the coming of the kingdom of God was imminent. They regarded themselves as the only really faithful Jews, and had nothing to do with the Temple because they thought that the current priests defiled it. This group was associated with the Dead Sea Scrolls, a large collection of religious texts discovered dramatically in a cave near Qumran in 1947. These scrolls have taught scholars an enormous amount about apocalyptic Judaism in the first century AD, although it is unlikely that anything in them has any direct bearing upon either Jesus or Christianity.

THE FIRST CHRISTIANS

In around AD 30, Jesus of Nazareth, a preacher from Galilee with a reputation for miracle-working, was executed on the outskirts of Jerusalem. He had made a nuisance of himself, causing a disturbance in the Temple. The high priest could not tolerate this, as it happened during Passover, when vast numbers of pilgrims were in Jerusalem and tempers were high. He had therefore been arrested by the guards of the high priest and condemned to death. This order had been ratified by the Roman prefect, Pontius Pilate, since the high priest did not have the power to order an execution. Jesus therefore suffered the Roman punishment of crucifixion, and he died relatively quickly. This, and almost everything else we know about Jesus, is described in the four 'Gospels', books describing what Jesus did which were written by the Christians later, and which are known as 'Matthew', 'Mark', 'Luke' and 'John' since these are the figures traditionally thought to have written them.

Jesus had a number of disciples, pre-eminent among whom was an inner circle called 'the twelve', who accompanied him during his ministry in Galilee and on his

Euangelio (that we call 'gospel') is a Greek word, and it signifies good, merry, glad and joyful tidings, that make a man's heart glad, and make him sing, dance and leap for joy.

William Tyndale, c.1494–1536

Jesus

He was born in an obscure village. Mostly he worked as a carpenter, but he became a travelling preacher. During his short life he never had his own home or raised a family. While he was still a young man, people grew to hate him. He ended up in the hands of his enemies and was put on trial and, although innocent, was found guilty. He was sentenced to death and died on a cross between two thieves. One friend had pity on him and placed his bruised body in a borrowed tomb…

The life-story of Jesus of Nazareth, when set out in this way, cannot explain how a major world religion began. Yet take away the story of this mysterious figure from the ancient world and there is no Christianity. So what do we know about Jesus' life? And why do Christians see it as so significant?

For greater details on Jesus' life we must turn to the four accounts of Jesus known as the 'canonical Gospels' (Matthew, Mark, Luke and John). To be sure, there are other non-Christian sources which mention Jesus in passing, thereby confirming that Jesus was a historical person. For example, the Roman historian Tacitus (c. AD 55–120) recounts that Jesus 'underwent the death penalty in the reign of Tiberius, by sentence of the procurator Pontius Pilate' (*Annals* 15:44); and Josephus, a Jewish historian (writing c. AD 90), says much the same, describing Jesus as a 'wise man', a 'teacher', a 'worker of incredible deeds' and the one who brought into existence the 'tribe of the Christians'.

But we are most indebted, not unnaturally, to those writers who consciously chose to write up Jesus' story. If we take their accounts at face value, the outline of Jesus' life looks something like this:

■ he was born in Bethlehem (10 km or 6 miles south of Jerusalem) around 6 BC – the monk who worked out the dates in the sixth century got the year slightly wrong! – and was raised in the tiny village of Nazareth in the hills of western Galilee

■ he started his public, itinerant ministry around Lake Galilee when in his young 30s (soon after his cousin John had called people to be 'baptized' in the River Jordan) and quickly gathered around him a special group of twelve men (his 'disciples', later known also as the 'apostles')

■ his reputation as a teacher and healer spread far and wide, with many seeing him as inspired uniquely with God's Spirit or as a prophet (similar to Old Testament prophets such as Elijah)

■ he certainly seemed to have extraordinary powers over disease and natural forces, even raising one or two people from death

■ his own teaching was focused on the long-awaited kingdom of God, announcing that through his ministry God was becoming king in a dramatic new way

■ drawing on images from the Old Testament, he identified himself as 'the Son of Man' (in the book of Daniel this figure was a glorious one who represented God's people before God's throne); but he also gave clear hints that he was the Suffering Servant (foretold in Isaiah) and the long-awaited king or 'messiah'

■ although he had been there before, he eventually set out purposefully towards Jerusalem, presenting a prophetic and royal challenge to the city and its leaders, and performing a symbolic act in its Temple (turning over the tables, which pointed to his own authority over the Temple and its imminent destruction)

■ one of his disciples (Judas Iscariot) then betrayed him to the religious authorities; they arrested him after midnight in the garden of Gethsemane, tried him on various charges and then presented him the next morning before the Roman governor, who ordered his execution by crucifixion

■ all this seems to have been foreseen and even intended by Jesus; he had spoken of his approaching 'hour', had attempted on three occasions to warn his friends that he would be 'rejected and killed', and on the evening before his death he had taken some bread and wine (an integral part of the traditional Passover celebrations) and given them a wholly new meaning: they were his body and his blood.

Put like this, these ingredients (most of which are largely uncontested by modern scholars) indicate that there may be more to this 'solitary life' than we first imagined: if Israel's God was becoming king through Jesus, who then was Jesus? Where did he get his evident authority from – in word and deed? And why did he seemingly orchestrate his own death? What could that possibly achieve?

And what happened 'on the third day' after his death? Christians are those who are convinced that the story did not end here, but instead that Jesus was raised from the grave by the power of God. All the Gospels

end with this dramatic resurrection-claim: Jesus came back from the dead and in due course returned to God in heaven, where (as the Creeds say) he is seated in glory at the 'right hand of the Father'.

The earliest creed (or 'confession') amongst the first Christians was 'Jesus is Lord' and they spread this 'good news' around the world. In the light of his resurrection they now began to unpack the true identity of this Jesus: not just the messiah and the king of Israel, but one greater than Abraham, Moses and David; not just the Suffering Servant, but the lamb of God and the true high priest; indeed not just a human being, but someone who could be identified with the very God of Israel as his 'Son', as his eternal and pre-existent 'Word', as the 'Lord of Glory'. In a Jewish culture, rooted in ardent monotheism, these claims for Jesus were extraordinary – and remain so. They point us to the 'incarnation' as the hallmark of the Christian church: the belief that in Jesus, God himself has come amongst us.

And, if so, then Jesus' death takes on a new meaning – as the moment when God gave himself to meet us at our point of deepest need, as the place where divine judgment was removed and the door opened to God's mercy and forgiveness – 'God shows his love for us in that while we were yet sinners Christ died for us' (Romans 5:8). Now perhaps we understand why the poem concludes:

> … *Nearly two thousand years have*
> *passed. Yet he still remains the figure*
> *at the very heart of the human race.*
> *All the kings, rulers and powers*
> *that have ever been,*
> *all the armies that have ever fought,*
> *indeed nothing since time began,*
> *has had so great an effect upon*
> *humanity as has that*
> *one solitary life.*
> 'ONE SOLITARY LIFE', AUTHOR UNKNOWN

PETER WALKER

Christ on the Cross, from the wall of the San Marco Monastery, Florence, by the Italian Dominican painter Fra Angelico (1387–1455).

As they entered the tomb, they saw a young man, dressed in a white robe, sitting on the right side; and they were alarmed. But he said to them, 'Do not be alarmed; you are looking for Jesus of Nazareth, who was crucified. He has been raised; he is not here. Look, there is the place they laid him. But go, tell his disciples and Peter that he is going ahead of you to Galilee; there you will see him, just as he told you.' So they went out and fled from the tomb, for terror and amazement had seized them; and they said nothing to anyone, for they were afraid.

Mark 16:5–8

fateful trip to Jerusalem. The sources disagree over their names, which may mean that there were actually more than twelve of them. The number twelve was highly significant to Jews, since it brought to mind the twelve tribes which had once made up the nation of Israel, so it is possible that Jesus talked about 'the twelve' in a symbolic sense even while their number fluctuated. During Jesus' trial and execution, most of them scattered. His closest friend, Peter, denied that he even knew him. Jesus was buried in a tomb donated by a sympathizer, Joseph of Arimathea. However, a couple of days later, some claimed to have seen Jesus, risen from the dead. There was a new spirit of hope among the disciples.

THE RESURRECTION

What had happened? The question of the resurrection appearances is one of the most vexed in the study of the early Christians, if only because the sources seem very hard to interpret. Jesus died in Jerusalem, and Luke's Gospel insists that Jesus appeared to his disciples there and told them not to leave. In Matthew, it seems that they left Jerusalem and saw him back home in Galilee. Again, according to Matthew, Jesus first appeared to his mother and to Mary Magdalene, one of his disciples. In John, he first appeared to Mary Magdalene alone. In Luke, the women did not meet the risen Jesus at all, only reported that his grave was empty, and Peter ran there to see this for himself. In John, Peter was accompanied by an unnamed 'beloved disciple' who beat him to the tomb. Paul, the most important Christian missionary of the first century, tells a different story again in his first letter to the Corinthian church, and his account was written years, perhaps even decades, before any of the Gospels:

He appeared to Cephas [Peter], then to the twelve. Then he appeared to more than five hundred brothers and sisters at one time… Then he appeared to James, then to all the apostles. Last of all… he appeared also to me.

1 Corinthians 15:5–8

That dramatic-sounding appearance to five hundred people at once is not mentioned in any other source. And equally puzzling is what the disciples saw. The Gospels all recount the story of Jesus' female disciples discovering his tomb empty, suggesting that Jesus had physically got up and walked away: other Gospel passages describe the risen Jesus as touching people and eating, although he can also appear in locked rooms or conceal his appearance to those who should be able to recognize him, suggesting that he was not simply a normal person who had recovered. But the earlier Paul (again in 1 Corinthians) does not mention the story of the empty tomb. This is odd, given that he is arguing that the resurrection was real and did happen, which suggests that he did not know about the empty tomb, or at least did not regard it as evidence for the resurrection. Moreover, Paul lists himself as one of those who saw the risen Lord, but the account of this event in the book of Acts states that Paul only saw a light from heaven and heard a voice, not that he met a physical person. Paul also insists that resurrection involves being changed from a physical body into a spiritual one, the meaning of which is not easy to establish – for it suggests that the risen Jesus had a body, but was somehow not physical at the same time.

Whatever actually happened to Jesus, and whatever the disciples saw, it is certain that they believed they had seen the risen Jesus, even if they could not quite agree on who had seen him and what had happened. Many of them would later die for this belief. This basic fact – the fact of the 'resurrection experiences' – is the event that started Christianity.

PENTECOST

The precise history of how this group of excited disciples set up the first Christian communities is hard to determine, for reasons that will become clearer shortly. But the disciples also believed not only that God had raised Jesus from the dead

Herod's family tomb in Jerusalem. The entrance was sealed by a stone in the same way as the tomb in which Jesus was laid.

but that the spirit of God, or of Jesus, was with them. In John's Gospel, the risen Jesus gives this Holy Spirit to his disciples directly, by breathing on them. A different story appears in the book of Acts, a history of the early church written by the same author as the Gospel of Luke, probably in the 80s of the first century. Acts states that the risen Jesus left his disciples after forty days, and they received God's Holy Spirit shortly afterwards, during the Jewish festival of Pentecost, which gave them both spiritual strength and the miraculous ability to speak foreign languages. Empowered in this way, according to Acts, Peter spoke to the crowds who had gathered in Jerusalem for Pentecost like this:

You that are Israelites, listen to what I have to say: Jesus of Nazareth, a man attested to you by God with deeds of power, wonders, and signs that God did through him among you, as you yourselves know – this man, handed over to you according to the definite plan and foreknowledge of God, you crucified and killed by the hands of those outside the law. But God raised him up, having freed him from death, because it was impossible for him to be held in its power…

Therefore let the entire house of Israel know with certainty that God has made him both Lord and Messiah, this Jesus whom you crucified.
Acts 2:22–24, 36

THE CHRISTIAN COMMUNITY

The book of Acts tells us that 3,000 people joined the disciples as a result of Peter's speech, and that in the days that followed they set up a remarkable community:

Awe came upon everyone, because many wonders and signs were being done by the apostles. All who believed were together and had all things in common; they would sell their possessions and goods and distribute the proceeds to all, as any had need. Day by day, as they spent much time together in the Temple, they broke bread at home and ate their food with glad and generous hearts, praising God and having the goodwill of all the people. And day by day the Lord added to their number those who were being saved.
Acts 2:43–47

When the day of Pentecost had come, they were all together in one place. And suddenly from heaven there came a sound like the rush of a violent wind, and it filled the entire house where they were sitting. Divided tongues, as of fire, appeared among them, and a tongue rested on each of them. All of them were filled with the Holy Spirit and began to speak in other languages, as the Spirit gave them ability.
Acts 2:1–4

23

As we shall see later in this book, this idyllic account would be highly influential over later Christian social reformers. But how accurate is it? The truth is that there has been enormous disagreement over how to reconstruct the history of the very first Christians. Our main sources are the book of Acts and the letters of Paul. But certain disagreements between them mean that scholars have to choose which is the more reliable at certain points. As a result, there is much uncertainty and disagreement over what actually happened – for example, how many times did Paul visit Jerusalem? He says three; Acts says five. Did the first Christians really live quite as the author of Acts suggests or is this a later idealization written fifty years after the event? Although details such as these are rather blurred, we can still piece together a general picture and outline of the first years of what would become known as Christianity.

There is good reason to think that Peter's speech, as described in the book of Acts and quoted earlier, does reflect the beliefs of the first Christians. They interpreted Jesus' resurrection as, above all, a vindication of his message and person. Jesus had been sent by God after all, and his message of the coming kingdom of God was right. They also believed that Jesus was the messiah, the great leader that many Jews thought would one day come – although, as we saw earlier, different Jews had different notions of what 'messiah' meant. The Greek word for 'messiah' is 'christos' (or 'Christ') and this is why Jesus' followers would become known as 'Christians' and Jesus himself would be referred to as 'Christ', almost as if it were literally his name. The presence of the messiah, of course, was further confirmation that the coming of the kingdom of God was imminent.

Moreover, at this stage the Christian community was still part of the Jewish one. The passage about their daily life quoted above mentions that they met frequently at the Temple. But they were also a distinct group – the reference to 'breaking bread' together probably suggests not a formal ceremony but the act of eating meals together. Even today, sharing meals is a way of bonding socially and creating a sense of group identity. This was even more the case in antiquity, and especially in Judaism – for the most important annual event of a Jewish family was the Passover meal itself. In this way the Christian community became a 'church'. The Greek word for 'church' actually means 'assembly', and in the New Testament it is generally used to refer to the individual communities – so there was one church in Jerusalem, one in Antioch and so on. For the whole of the first century, Christians met not in purpose-built buildings but in each other's houses, or, later, houses that had been converted into meeting places. So the sense of 'church' as a kind of building, a Christian equivalent to the Jewish synagogue, had not yet developed.

All of this was set in Jerusalem. What was going on elsewhere? We know even less about this. The author of Luke and Acts states that, after Jesus' resurrection, all his disciples stayed in Jerusalem, where they received the Holy Spirit and formed the first Christian community as described above. But according to Matthew's Gospel, after Jesus' resurrection they all went home to Galilee. John's Gospel even has them returning to their lives as fishermen. If they did indeed bring their message to Galilee in this way, nothing is known of what became of it. The book of Acts suggests that Christianity became dispersed throughout Palestine as a result of persecutions against the Christians in Jerusalem, who fled, carrying the message with them.

DIVISIONS AND DISAGREEMENTS

The first Christians, then, were Jews who believed that God had raised Jesus from the dead, thereby vindicating his message. But Acts 6:1–6 hints at a more complex group, describing a dispute between 'the Hellenists' and 'the Hebrews'. Who were these 'Hellenists'? Were they Jews from the diaspora rather than from Palestine? Were they Jewish Christians who wanted the group to dissociate itself more from mainstream Judaism? Or were they non-Jews, that is, Gentiles, who also believed in Jesus? Nobody knows. The following chapter of Acts gives a clue, though, in the story of Stephen. A prominent Christian, Stephen is taken before the high priest and told to explain himself. The speech Stephen gives, according to Acts, is highly critical of the Jews: he retells their story from Abraham onwards, stressing how the Jews had always misunderstood or rejected God's prophets, a process that culminated in their rejection of Jesus. Furious at this speech, members of the council drag Stephen outside and stone him to death, thereby making him the first Christian martyr.

The view attributed to Stephen here is one critical of the Jews, blaming them for rejecting God's message and for killing Jesus. And this split which was beginning to form between Judaism and Christianity (and, perhaps, between Judaism-minded Christians and those who wanted to take things in a different direction) was epitomized in the career and thought of the most significant figure of the early church, Paul of Tarsus.

By the time Paul was writing, in the 50s of the first century, Christianity had spread well beyond not simply Jerusalem but Palestine itself. The book of Acts suggests that one of the major centres of Christianity was Antioch, the leading city of the eastern Roman empire – indeed, Acts claims that it was here that the believers were first called 'Christians' (earlier in the book they are referred to as followers of 'the Way'). This spread of Christianity meant that it was no longer simply a subset of Judaism: on the contrary, Gentiles were converting too. It is likely that many, if not most, of these people were those Gentiles, sympathetic to Judaism, whom we saw earlier. For example, when Paul preached to Gentiles, he may usually have done so not simply by speaking to random crowds but by going to synagogues and talking to the Gentiles who visited them.

Acts 11 describes Peter coming under criticism for associating with non-Jewish Christians: he defends his actions by describing a vision in which God told him that he could make clean what before had been profane, and also by retelling how the Holy Spirit had come upon the Gentiles as he preached to them, just as it had upon the disciples at Pentecost. The issue led to an event known as the Council of Jerusalem, sometime in the late 40s or early 50s. At this council Paul travelled to Jerusalem to meet with the leaders there, especially Peter and James. It was decided that Paul should continue his missions to the Gentiles, and that they should not be forced to become Jews before becoming Christians; meanwhile, Peter would continue his missions to the Jews.

But there were tensions. In his letter to the Galatians, Paul writes that after this council, Peter came to Antioch and 'I opposed him to his face, for he stood self-condemned'. Acting under James' influence, Peter was now refusing to eat with Gentiles. And most of the letter to the Galatians is concerned with a related problem. Many in the Galatian church had apparently become convinced that it was essential to be circumcised – that is, to become a Jew – before becoming a Christian. Paul was completely opposed to them and insisted that 'in Christ Jesus neither circumcision nor uncircumcision counts for anything: the only thing that counts is faith working through love'.

The degree to which the first-century church was divided over this and related issues is very hard to tell. Some historians have argued that the divisions were far greater than they might appear from a casual reading of the evidence, and that there was complete schism between Paul and the pro-Gentiles on the one hand, and Peter and James and the pro-Judaism party on the other; and that, because Paul's party won, the surviving documents were written in a biased way to paper over the cracks. Of course, such a view rather begs the question, because there is no evidence other than those surviving documents. It may be that, while the divisions did run deeper than books such as Acts might suggest, they were not quite on such a dramatic scale. Certainly

[Paul was] a man small in size, with meeting eyebrows and a rather large nose, bald-headed, bow-legged, strongly built, full of grace; for at times he looked like a man, and at times he had the face of an angel.

The Acts of Paul,
c. AD 160

A theology of mission: Paul

One man dominates the picture of first-century Christianity like no other, save Jesus himself. Indefatigable missionary, forthright debater, theologian of extraordinary originality – the genius of Paul would shape Christianity for the next 2,000 years.

The main sources for Paul's life and thought are the book of Acts, whose second half is dominated by accounts of his travels, and Paul's own letters, which dominate the New Testament itself. The two sources are not always easy to reconcile, but both agree that Paul came from Tarsus, a city in Anatolia not far from Antioch. He was probably born at around the same time as Jesus, although he never met him. Paul was one of the Jews of the diaspora, a strict Pharisee, and his name was Saul ('Paulos' was the Greek form of this name, and it was understandable that he preferred this version, since 'saulos' in Greek means a provocative wiggle of the hips!). He was a skilled manual worker, probably a tentmaker, but he also studied in Jerusalem under Gamaliel, one of the leading Pharisee teachers.

Both Acts and his own letters confirm that in the early days of Christianity Paul hated the new religion. In fact he was a leading figure in the attempt on the part of the Jewish authorities to suppress it. Acts describes him as present at the death of Stephen, guarding everyone's coats and approving while they stoned the martyr. But, while travelling to Damascus in the course of these activities, Paul had an extraordinary experience: according to Acts 9, he was temporarily blinded by a celestial light and heard the voice of Jesus. According to his own account, he met Jesus himself. The church's worst enemy had become a Christian.

Almost immediately Paul began to preach about Jesus, first in Arabia and Damascus, where he escaped arrest by being let down out of a window in a basket, before going to Jerusalem to meet the apostles and then returning to Tarsus, apparently for several years. After this, beginning probably in the mid-40s, Paul began what are often called three great missionary journeys. In reality, they were one long journey back and forth throughout the eastern empire, a journey that probably ended only with Paul's imprisonment and death. Each of the three main legs of the journey took him through Anatolia, before passing through Jerusalem and Antioch; the second and third also saw Paul travelling down the Greek peninsula. Major cities that he visited included Athens, Corinth, Ephesus, Thessalonica and Philippi. After the third leg of the journey Paul was attacked by a mob outside the Temple in Jerusalem and arrested. Pleading his rights as a Roman citizen, Paul was taken to Rome for trial and put in prison. And there our early sources fall silent.

Paul apparently hoped to be released and extend his work in the western empire, and some later traditions indicated that he did just that, making it all the way to Spain or even Britain. However, it seems more likely that he was executed for his faith in Rome, in the early to mid-60s.

Paul was accompanied in his work by various companions, notably Timothy, Titus, Barnabas, and his physician, Luke. During his travels he supported himself by the labour of his hands. He spoke to churches that had already been established, but increasingly he founded new churches – presumably as time went by he became more effective at speaking. He was concerned not only to win converts for Christ, but also to raise money for the church in Jerusalem: this 'collection' was important since it symbolized the unity of all the churches. After he left his churches, he wrote letters to them, urging them to keep the faith. Some (not all) of these letters survive, and they make up a major part of the New Testament. Thirteen letters bear Paul's name, although most modern scholars agree that at least some are not his work. Those which are almost universally accepted as genuine are the letter to the Romans, two to the Corinthians, one to the Philippians, one to the Galatians, the first one to the Thessalonians, and the shorter, personal note to Philemon.

Paul's letters testify to his theological concerns, which arose directly from his experiences as a preacher. Many of his ideas were worked out as responses to pastoral or theological problems raised by his congregations, but the touchstone for everything he wrote was the role of Christ in the history of salvation. Paul was convinced that the God who sent Christ was the God of the Jews, and that salvation came through him – but what role did this leave for the Jewish Law and the Jewish people? Paul never abandoned his conviction that the Jews were God's chosen people, but in different letters he tried different ways of reconciling this with his faith in Christ. He expressed more clearly than any other New Testament writer the centrality of the death and resurrection of Christ. Indeed, Paul was convinced that Christ was a living reality in his own life and in that of all Christians. He urged the Roman Christians, for example, to 'not be conformed to this world, but be transformed by the renewing of your minds, so that you may discern what is the will of God – what is good and acceptable and perfect' (Romans 12:2). This notion that Christians should live a different kind of life, one that was an example to others, would resonate for centuries.

Paul has sometimes been called the true founder of Christianity, obliterating the original message of Jesus and the apostles with his own distinctive religion, especially his emphasis on the person of Christ instead of his teaching. We should be wary of such claims. In his lifetime, Paul was just one of a number of Christian missionaries: the spread of the religion during this period was certainly not solely due to his efforts. In his letter to the Galatians, Paul goes to considerable effort to stress his equality with the apostles (even calling himself an apostle), indicating that many people did not see him as so important. It is only with hindsight that Paul looms so large, mainly because of the enormous influence of his letters. These letters were apparently collected, edited and circulated among the churches after his death, and they became a great inspiration for them. Paul's theology would become the starting point for most Christian theology in the years to come. In particular, his letter to the Romans, in which his ideas were worked out most fully, would be a major influence on theologians from Augustine to Luther to Barth. Paul was not simply the first great Christian writer: he has remained as a constant and living influence upon the church for nearly two millennia.

JONATHAN HILL

The apostle Paul, by the Cretan–Spanish artist El Greco (1541–1614).

I handed on to you as of first importance what I in turn had received…

1 Corinthians 15:3

Since many have undertaken to set down an orderly account of the events that have been fulfilled among us, just as they were handed on to us by those who from the beginning were eyewitnesses and servants of the word, I too decided, after investigating everything carefully from the very first, to write an orderly account for you, most excellent Theophilus, so that you may know the truth concerning the things about which you have been instructed.

Luke 1:1–4

it seems that the people against whom Paul directed his ire were not Peter and James so much as more extreme, unnamed individuals who possibly influenced them. More important perhaps is the question of just how many of the other controversies that we hear of from this period and shortly afterwards were connected to this basic problem of Jews and Gentiles. We hear of disagreements over church discipline, different opinions about the person of Jesus and so on – did these all derive from the Jew–Gentile divide, suggesting that it continued to fester throughout the first century? Or was that issue pretty much laid to rest after the 50s by the decisions of the Jerusalem conference and Paul's fiery condemnation of the extreme Judaizers? Again, nobody really knows the answers to these questions.

CHRISTIAN WRITINGS

The faith of the first Christians was passed on by word of mouth. The book of Acts represents the apostles as going out and preaching to people, either individuals or large crowds. Less is said of what kind of instruction was given within the communities, after people had made their initial commitment. Presumably they were taught in the same way, through speech. By this method the teachings of the Christians, and their memories of Jesus, were passed on and shaped by the needs of the community.

The growth of the movement meant that eventually this was not enough, and Christians began to put pen to paper. The earliest known Christian writings are the letters of Paul, written in the AD 50s; other letters by various Christian leaders, some anonymous, also survive. And there are the Gospels, the accounts of Jesus' ministry, which were written by Christians who wanted to preserve the memories of Jesus that had been handed down through the community. These writings form the bulk of what would become known as the 'New Testament', and in the next chapter we shall see how they became compiled and were regarded as authoritative by later

Christians. They are by far the most important source of our knowledge of Jesus and the early church.

There are also other Christian works, which never made it into the New Testament, including plenty of gospels, complete or surviving only in fragments, which claim to describe Jesus and his ministry, but which are evidently almost completely fictional. (The 'Gospel of Peter', for example, expands on the canonical accounts of Jesus' death by describing the vigil of the soldiers who were sent to guard his tomb.) It is generally agreed that virtually nothing in these books is of any value when it comes to reconstructing the life or death of Jesus himself. Most seem to have been written later than the four 'canonical' Gospels, and to have been partly based upon them. On the whole, the early Christians showed fairly good sense in deciding which books to put in the New Testament and which ones to leave out. But these 'non-canonical' works are very valuable in shedding light on what some Christian groups believed, especially where these beliefs were at odds with what would later become accepted as correct Christian doctrine. Together, all the early writings allow us to reconstruct what those first Christians believed.

THE FAITH OF THE CHRISTIANS

LIVING IN THE LAST DAYS

As we have seen, the Christians believed that God had raised Jesus from the dead; but this was not all. They also anticipated that he would return soon. Jesus had talked about the kingdom of God and, since he had been vindicated by his resurrection, this meant that the kingdom was on its way. Moreover, the Christians were convinced that Jesus was the messiah, meaning that he would come back with the kingdom. Jesus had also spoken of himself as the 'Son of Man', which had similar connotations, although apparently the

Christians hardly ever referred to Jesus by this title.

The earliest Christian writing to survive, Paul's first letter to the Thessalonian church, testifies to this conviction. The letter was written in around AD 50, partly to address concerns raised by the deaths of some members of the community. Evidently, the others had not anticipated that anyone would die before Jesus came back with the kingdom. Paul reassured his readers that the dead Christians would not miss out, since they would be raised just as Jesus had been:

> For the Lord himself, with a cry of command, with the archangel's call and with the sound of God's trumpet, will descend from heaven, and the dead in Christ will rise first. Then we who are alive, who are left, will be caught up in the clouds together with them to meet the Lord in the air; and so we will be with the Lord forever.
>
> 1 Thessalonians 4:16–18

Clearly, Paul expected to be alive when this happened. According to Mark 13:30, Jesus himself had said that 'this generation will not pass away until all these things have taken place'. Yet the years passed, and the Lord did not return. It seems that the Christians began to tell each other that at least some of the first generation would still be alive when Jesus returned. The last chapter of John's Gospel mentions a rumour among the later churches that one disciple in particular would still be alive – but evidently he had died by the time this passage was written, because in it the author is at pains to point out that in fact Jesus made no such prediction. Thus the first generation did die, and still Jesus did not return.

Little wonder, perhaps, that some people jeered at the Christians, saying, 'Where is the promise of his coming? For ever since our ancestors died, all things continue as they were from the beginning of creation!' This mockery is reported in 2 Peter, thought by many scholars to be the last book of the New Testament to be written,

perhaps in the early second century. By this stage many Christians had given up expecting Jesus to appear very soon, though they still expected him to come at some point. The author explains the reasoning:

> But do not ignore this one fact, beloved, that with the Lord one day is like a thousand years, and a thousand years are like one day. The Lord is not slow about his promise, as some think of slowness, but is patient with you, not wanting any to perish, but all to come to repentance. But the day of the Lord will come like a thief, and then the heavens will pass away with a loud noise, and the elements will be dissolved with fire, and the earth and everything that is done on it will be disclosed.
>
> 2 Peter 3:8–10

As this suggests, the faith of the Christians survived the non-appearance of Jesus surprisingly well. This was, in part, because their faith also focused on the question of who Jesus actually was, quite apart from his role in bringing the kingdom of God. This issue is generally called 'Christology', that is, the study of Christ, and, as we shall see in the later chapters of this book, it has been a central concern of Christianity ever since those first days.

FAITH IN CHRIST

We have seen the Christians' conviction, from the outset, that Jesus was the messiah – although, since different people had different views on what that meant, this did not in itself say a great deal about him. He was also 'Lord', a term that carried greater meaning than it might have for most people today. It indicated that Jesus was exalted, for the word 'Lord' was generally reserved for God or for those associated with divinity – God himself in the case of Jews or Caesar in the case of most Roman citizens. To call Jesus 'Lord', as the writers of the New Testament did repeatedly, indicated that he was at the very least closely associated with God and came as his envoy.

There was a sense that, after his

resurrection, God had not simply vindicated Jesus but glorified him. Thus, in the opening words of his letter to the church at Rome, Paul reproduces what appears to be an early formula of faith, referring to:

> …the gospel concerning [God's] Son, who was descended from David according to the flesh and was declared to be Son of God with power according to the spirit of holiness by resurrection from the dead, Jesus Christ our Lord…
>
> Romans 1:3–4

This implies what has sometimes been called a 'two-stage' Christology – that is, it distinguishes between who Jesus was during his life and who he was after his resurrection. Paul suggests that it was after the resurrection that Jesus was 'declared' to be the Son of God. It is important to note that, although 'Son of God' has become a common title for Jesus, it was rather vague in a Jewish context. It meant only someone blessed or favoured by God, not necessarily a person somehow metaphysically related to him or literally his son.

Other texts give more of a sense of Jesus' post-resurrection exaltation in heaven. Consider this passage from the letter to the Colossians:

> He is the image of the invisible God, the firstborn of all creation; for in him all things in heaven and on earth were created, things visible and invisible, whether thrones or dominions or rulers or powers – all things have been created through him and for him. He himself is before all things, and in him all things hold together. He is the head of the body, the church; he is the beginning, the firstborn from the dead, so that he might come to have first place in everything. For in him all the fullness of God was pleased to dwell, and through him God was pleased to reconcile to himself all things, whether on earth or in heaven, by making peace through the blood of his cross.
>
> Colossians 1:15–20

Long ago God spoke to our ancestors in many and various ways by the prophets, but in these last days he has spoken to us by a Son, whom he appointed heir of all things, through whom he also created the worlds. He is the reflection of God's glory and the exact imprint of God's very being, and he sustains all things by his powerful word.

Hebrews 1:1–3

This growing understanding of Jesus' post-resurrection nature accompanied a relative downplaying, at least in some quarters, of the life of Jesus before his death. Paul, for example, has an enormous amount to say about Christ, understood in a cosmic way as in the passage above or, even more, as a present reality to Christians – but has hardly anything to say about what Jesus did or said during his lifetime. This accompanied another new emphasis, which was not just on Jesus' resurrection, but on his death. In Romans 6, we find Paul telling his readers:

> Do you not know that all of us who have been baptized into Christ Jesus were baptized into his death? Therefore we have been buried with him by baptism into death, so that, just as Christ was raised from the dead by the glory of the Father, so we too might walk in the newness of life. For if we have been united with him in a death like his, we will certainly be united with him in a resurrection like his.
>
> Romans 6:3–5

On this view, Jesus' death was not simply an unpleasant but necessary prelude to his resurrection; on the contrary, it was just as important as his resurrection, with immediate consequences for all Christians. Jesus died not simply as a condemned criminal, but in order to save his people. Christians, in Paul's view, were those who in some mystical way participated in Jesus' death, with the promise one day to participate in his resurrection. Through Jesus, it seemed, Christians had the promise to beat death just as he had. And more – Jesus was a present reality to Christians. Paul told the Galatians that 'I have been crucified with Christ; and it is no longer I who live, but it is Christ who lives in me.'

A number of images developed to express these ideas. Paul described Jesus' death as a sacrifice, referring to the system of sacrifices in Judaism: just as they were believed to remove the people's sins and to bring God and his people together, so too Jesus' death had accomplished the same thing. The author of the anonymous letter to the Hebrews develops this theme at length. In his view, Jesus is both perfect sacrifice and perfect high priest at the same time. His sacrifice on the cross was made once for all, but he still intercedes on his followers' behalf with God in heaven. John's Gospel expresses the same idea: at the start of the Gospel, John the Baptist describes Jesus as 'the Lamb of God who takes away the sin of the world', while, at the end of the Gospel, Jesus dies at precisely the moment that the lambs were sacrificed for the Passover feast. Mark's Gospel, meanwhile, offers a slightly different image: there, Jesus himself states that 'the Son of Man came not to be served but to serve, and to give his life as a ransom for many'. The problem of how, precisely, this worked, and to whom Jesus offered this ransom, would exercise Christian minds for centuries to come.

The stress on Jesus' role as saviour, through his death and resurrection, meant that the message of his imminent return was no longer the main belief of the Christians. Not that the two were intrinsically opposed – Paul, for example, often seen as the architect of this 'cross-centred' theology, still referred to Jesus as 'Christ', stressing his messianic role, and saw his resurrection as the prototype for the future resurrection of all humanity. Paul has sometimes been criticized for directing attention away from the life and teachings of Jesus to a more mystical religion revolving around the godlike 'Christ', one focused upon his saving death, a concept almost entirely absent from the speeches of the disciples described in the book of Acts. This is rather unfair. Paul believed that the Christ whom he had seen and whom he wrote about was identical with Jesus who lived and died: indeed, this was the heart of his message.

Later, or perhaps at the same time in different places, Christology developed further. Christians began to think of Jesus in his earthly life in the same terms as he now was in his exalted life. In place of the 'two-stage' Christology, there was more of a sense of continuity in Jesus' nature throughout his career. John's Gospel, probably written in the closing years of the first century, expresses this view quite clearly. The figure of Jesus in this Gospel is more serene than the Jesus of the other Gospels and his message is primarily about himself, rather than about the coming kingdom of God, which is what he talks about in the other Gospels. Moreover, the famous opening words clearly teach that Jesus not only existed before his birth in Palestine but was exalted and close to God even then:

In the beginning was the Word, and the Word was with God, and the Word was God. He was in the beginning with God. All things came into being through him, and without him not one thing came into being. What has come into being in him was life, and the life was the light of all people. […] And the Word became flesh and lived among us, and we have seen his glory, the glory as of a father's only son, full of grace and truth.
John 1:1–4, 14

So we have a shift towards a sense of Jesus not simply as a human being who died and was raised to exaltation, but as a being closely associated with God from the beginning of time who came down to earth before returning to his original place by God's side. We can call it a belief in the 'incarnation', the belief that Jesus was a divine being incarnate, that is, made flesh. Much of the rest of John's Gospel explores this idea: Jesus speaks of God as 'the Father' and himself as 'the Son'. The Son is presented as the authentic agent of the Father, so that Jesus can say, 'Whoever has seen me has seen the Father… Do you not believe that I am in the Father and the Father is in me?'

Some Christians went still further than this and denied that Jesus was really human at all. On this view, known as Docetism, he was actually a divine being sent by God who only appeared to be human, and he did not really suffer and die on the cross. This view was condemned by other Christians, who insisted that, whatever else Jesus may have been, he was certainly human and really did suffer and die. The

[Jesus] was continent, enduring all things. Jesus digested divinity; he ate and drank in a special way, without excreting his solids. He had such a great capacity for continence that the nourishment within him was not corrupted, for he did not experience corruption.

Valentinus, a second-century Gnostic docetic, quoted by Clement of Alexandria, *Stromateis* 3.59

31

letters attributed to John (though they are actually anonymous) apparently attack this teaching a number of times.

This, then, is more or less how the New Testament leaves the question of Jesus' identity. Rather than make a concerted effort to provide a clear picture, its authors present a patchwork of different images and ideas: Jesus is the Word who is with God at the beginning, the messiah who brings the kingdom of God, the Son who is close to the Father, the high priest who intercedes with God, the sacrifice who takes away the sins of the world. As a rule, the New Testament authors are content with this and generally shy away from stating explicitly that Jesus really was God. In the next two chapters, we shall see how that claim became more explicit and gave rise to new questions. For how could Jesus be God if he was not identical with the Father, given the basic Jewish belief in monotheism? And how could anyone be both God and a human being? These questions would dominate the church for centuries.

THE 'NEW ISRAEL'

The early Christians were convinced that all of this was in line with historic Judaism. To put it another way, everything that Jesus did and was fulfilled the Jewish scriptures. Thus, in the first sentence of his letter to the Romans, Paul insists that the Christian message was 'promised beforehand through [God's] prophets in the holy Scriptures'. He told the Corinthians that 'Christ died for our sins in accordance with the Scriptures'. In Luke's Gospel, the risen Christ meets two disciples who, not recognizing him, tell him their fears for the future now that their master had gone. Jesus chides them:

Then he said to them, 'Oh, how foolish you are, and how slow of heart to believe all that the prophets have declared! Was it not necessary that the Messiah should suffer these things and then enter into his glory?' Then beginning with Moses and all the prophets, he interpreted to them the things about himself in all the Scriptures.
Luke 24:25–27

Certain key passages of the scriptures were now understood as prophecies about Jesus (even passages not previously regarded as prophecies at all). Psalm 22, which Jesus himself apparently quoted at the moment of death, was seen as a prophecy of his death and the circumstances surrounding it. Isaiah 53, which speaks of a 'suffering servant', was interpreted in the same way. Since Jesus was the messiah, he was the culmination of the hopes of the Jewish people, and the subject of all the prophecies about a glorious future. To put it another way, Christianity was fulfilled Judaism – and Judaism was, as it were, Christianity waiting to happen. The Christian church was the 'new Israel' and the heir to the promises God made to Abraham and the Jews in the Old Testament. Paul, musing on the fact that far more Gentiles than Jews had become Christians, commented in his letter to the Roman church:

It is not as though the word of God had failed. For not all Israelites truly belong to Israel, and not all of Abraham's children are his true descendants... it is not the children of the flesh who are the children of God, but the children of the promise are counted as the descendants.
Romans 9:6–7a, 8

However distant Christianity and Judaism would grow as religions, there would always be this notion – on the part of the Christians – that they were the true inheritors of the promises God made to the Jews. Thus, Christianity was deeply rooted in Judaism, and Christians believed fervently in the unity of God's saving actions throughout history, beginning with Abraham and culminating in Christ. The 'Father' of whom Jesus spoke was identical with the God of Abraham. Some Christians would later deny this and try to cut Christianity adrift from its Jewish foundations. The mainstream church would always reject such attempts.

LIFE IN THE CHURCH

THE CHRISTIAN RITES

Right from the start, Christians had a set of rituals that distinguished them from other Jews. The two most important were inherited directly from the life of Jesus. The first was baptism. The origins of baptism are rather obscure, having their roots in some Jewish practices, but Jesus had begun his career by being baptized by John the Baptist, a slightly earlier preacher from Galilee who had made a big impact by calling upon people to repent of their sins. As a sign of this repentance, he would baptize them, that is, ritually wash them, in the River Jordan. According to John 3:22, Jesus himself, after leaving John, had baptized people. Thus, the Christians did the same thing. According to the book of Acts, Peter followed up his speech on the day of Pentecost with a call to 'repent, and be baptized every one of you in the name of Jesus Christ so that your sins may be forgiven'. Through baptism, it was thought, believers came to share the one Holy Spirit and form a single, united community. In 1 Corinthians 12:13, Paul wrote, 'For in the one Spirit we were all baptized into a single body – Jews or Greeks, slaves or free – and we were all made to drink of one Spirit.' According to Matthew 28:19, believers would be baptized 'in the name of the Father and of the Son and of the Holy Spirit'. Baptism therefore marked the believer's faith in God, in Jesus and in the Holy Spirit which guided the church.

If baptism marked the beginning of the Christian life, the Eucharist (from a Greek word meaning 'giving thanks') kept it going and by the end of the first century was the central Christian ritual. The Eucharist was a re-enactment of the Last Supper, Jesus' final meal with his closest disciples on the night before his death. Two main descriptions of this are found in the New Testament: one in the Gospels of Matthew, Mark and Luke (it is omitted in John) and an earlier account in 1 Corinthians, where Paul writes:

For I received from the Lord what I also handed on to you, that the Lord Jesus on the night when he was betrayed took a loaf of bread, and when he had given thanks, he broke it and said, 'This is my body that is for you. Do this in remembrance of me.' In the same way he took the cup also, after supper, saying, 'This cup is the new covenant in my blood. Do this, as often as you drink it, in remembrance of me.' For as often as you eat this bread and drink the cup, you proclaim the Lord's death until he comes.

1 Corinthians 11:23–26

It seems likely, though not certain, that this re-enactment was distinct from the 'breaking of bread' that we saw mentioned in the book of Acts earlier. That was apparently a meal, but the Eucharist seems to have been more formal than that, an act of worship which involved eating only a small amount.

Go therefore and make disciples of all nations, baptizing them in the name of the Father and of the Son and of the Holy Spirit.

Matthew 28:19

Christian baptism, depicted on a third-century sarcophagus in Rome.

Paul's description of the Last Supper, with its solemn cadences and use of repetition, sounds like a formula that had already been used for some time at the Eucharist itself. Yet it does not seem to have been a formal 'service' that would be familiar to modern Christians. We hear of no set prayers that were to accompany the ritual or even whether prayers were said or hymns sung at all. We do not know if the Eucharist was celebrated at the kinds of meetings mentioned by Paul in 1 Corinthians 14:26: 'When you come together, each one has a hymn, a lesson, a revelation, a tongue, or an interpretation.' We do not know how often these rather chaotic-sounding meetings occurred – perhaps every day, or perhaps only once a week, as a number of passages in Acts and Paul alike suggest. It may have been that Christians worshipped together every day but reserved the Eucharist for the first day of the week. For the Christians did meet on this day, apparently from an early date. The Jewish Sabbath was the last day of the week, Saturday; but Jesus had been raised from the dead on the first day, Sunday. The Christians therefore called it 'the Lord's Day' and met then, perhaps for a communal meal; this would have mirrored the communal meal that Jewish families shared at the start of every Sabbath. It is possible that the Christians also continued to attend the synagogue on Saturdays; we do not know for sure.

This was the start of Christian 'liturgy', a word originally meaning 'work for the people', that is, anything done for the community. In the Jewish diaspora it had taken on the meaning of work done for God, specifically praise and worship, and this is how the first Christians used it too. It came to refer not so much to individual or private prayer as to communal services. These certainly involved singing as well as teaching. Colossians 3:16 instructs its readers to 'teach and admonish one another in all wisdom; and with gratitude in your hearts sing psalms, hymns and spiritual songs to God'.

LEADING THE COMMUNITY

Who led these services? Once again, we do not really know. There was certainly a kind of Christian leadership from the earliest days, but it is uncertain to what extent it corresponded to what we would recognize as a 'priesthood' and it is also uncertain how uniform it was between different churches. At the top of the pile were the apostles. 'Apostle' means someone who is sent, so these were the people 'sent' by Jesus – that is, the original leaders of the Christians. It is sometimes assumed that the apostles were identical with 'the twelve' who had formed Jesus' inner circle, but this is not necessarily the case. In his account of the resurrection appearances which we saw earlier, Paul distinguished between these two groups – and he also regarded himself as an apostle, although he had never known Jesus before his death. It seems that the apostles were those who regarded themselves as charged by Jesus personally, after his resurrection, with spreading the Christian message. Their leaders were primarily Peter and James, Jesus' brother. This James, probably the most important Christian leader of his day, is traditionally known as 'James the Just' to distinguish him from another disciple named James, the brother of John. James the Just, despite being Jesus' brother, apparently did not follow him during his lifetime and therefore does not appear in the Gospels. Having converted to Christianity after his brother's death, though, James took the leadership of the church at Jerusalem. Paul's description in Galatians of his disagreement with Peter and James about Gentiles suggests that, whether or not James was officially senior to Peter, he certainly acted like it: the weaker Peter vacillated in his views and changed them to match James's. In Acts 15, meanwhile, James is represented as giving the final decision on this matter at the Council of Jerusalem.

The other dominant apostle was Peter, by far the most prominent of Jesus' disciples in the Gospels and apparently

Jesus' closest friend (although in John's Gospel an unnamed 'beloved disciple' is more prominent). Peter's name was actually Simon, but in Matthew 16 Jesus gives him the nickname 'Rock', that is, Cephas (in Aramaic) and Peter (in Greek). In the Gospels Peter often acts as the general spokesman for all the disciples, and he clearly takes a leading role in the book of Acts – giving, for example, the speech on the day of Pentecost that we saw earlier. In Galatians, Paul states that after learning about Christianity in Damascus he went to Jerusalem specifically to see Peter. Slightly later traditions state that Peter left Jerusalem at some unspecified time and went to Rome, where (again, for an uncertain length of time) he led its Christian community.

In addition to James and Peter, John, the brother of the other James and also a prominent character in the Gospels, was apparently a leading figure at Jerusalem. Behind these three were the other apostles and beneath them there were other leaders. In Acts 6 we are told that the twelve apostles named seven men to help distribute the community's money to the needy members. These seven, including Stephen, were chosen by the community, and we are told that they stood before the apostles, who prayed and laid hands on them. It therefore seems that there was some kind of notion of 'ordination', that is, the bestowing of spiritual authority from one leader to another.

But what role did all these people

Peter, depicted in a ninth-century mosaic.

play? They would certainly have had a pastoral function, encouraging their communities, giving advice and so on. Stephen and 'the seven' apparently helped to run the community, taking money and food around while the apostles did mission work, preaching to the unconverted. These two basic activities seem to be the main ones of the early Christian leaders. There is no evidence that they led the liturgical services, whether the Eucharist or those of praise and hymn-singing. However, there is reason to think that they conducted baptisms. Given that they led missionary work, and that those who converted were apparently often baptized on the spot, this would have naturally fallen within their remit.

There is some difficulty over what titles we should use for the early Christian leaders. A number of words are used in the New Testament to describe Christian leaders, mainly 'bishop' (from 'episcopos', a word meaning 'overseer') and 'presbyter' (literally, 'old man'). These are usually used in the plural, implying that each community had a number of leaders rather than a single one. They are also, at different places, called 'pastors' (that is, shepherds) and 'stewards'. So the traditional view, that James was 'the' bishop of Jerusalem, while Peter was 'the' bishop of Rome, seems not to be quite right. There was probably not any such formal structure at this stage, although evidently figures such as James and Peter were pre-eminent among the leaders in their communities. As time went on, this became the norm, with a single dominant leader being in charge of the lesser ones. He would be the 'bishop' and they would be the 'presbyters'. We shall see how this process came about in the next chapter.

THE SPREAD OF CHRISTIANITY

Paul's missionary journeys around the Roman empire were enormously successful. He founded churches in cities around the northern rim of the Mediterranean Sea, and encouraged others that sprang up without his help, above all that of Rome, where we know there was a Christian community in the early 50s. Other missionaries were enjoying similar success, although less is known about their activities. Christianity was becoming more than simply a Jewish sect – and this coincided with a new period of terrible crisis for Judaism itself.

CHURCH AND SYNAGOGUE

In AD 66 the Jews broke out in revolt against the rule of Rome. The First Jewish War was the result, a war which proved a disaster for the Jews. The imperial forces crushed them and, in AD 70, destroyed the Temple. Its treasures were carted off to Rome in triumph.

Given the role the Temple played in Jewish religion and society, this was clearly a critical moment for Judaism. The priests who had previously led the people suddenly had no role; the sacrifices which had been carried out every day to bind the people to God ceased. To many it seemed the end times must be near – indeed, Jesus himself had apparently predicted the Temple's destruction as a sign of the end times.

A group of Jewish scribes and scholars fled Jerusalem for Jamnia, a town on the coast. Here, they set about rethinking their faith. It has traditionally been supposed that these scholars were Pharisees, and this may well be true, since the kind of Judaism they preserved revolved around the keeping of the Law in everyday life – rather than the bits about sacrifices – and the study of the Law, the better to understand how to do this. The form of Judaism that resulted from this is what is now known as 'rabbinical' Judaism, meaning that it revolved around the teaching of rabbis, learned scholars who devoted themselves to the study of the ancient texts and to commenting upon them. These rabbis would, in the years to come, produce the

The taking of Jerusalem by Titus (detail), by a fifteenth-century artist of the Flemish School.

I am speaking the truth in Christ – I am not lying; my conscience confirms it by the Holy Spirit – I have great sorrow and unceasing anguish in my heart. For I could wish that I myself were accursed and cut off from Christ for the sake of my own people, my kindred according to the flesh. They are Israelites, and to them belong the adoption, the glory, the covenants, the giving of the law, the worship, and the promises; to them belong the patriarchs, and from them, according to the flesh, comes the Messiah, who is over all, God blessed for ever.

Romans 9:1–5

Mishnah, a huge series of commentaries upon the Law and other associated writings. Officially, the system of sacrifices was never actually abolished or superseded – its abandonment was forced by the destruction of the Temple – but the rise of rabbinical Judaism was, in essence, the beginnings of Judaism as we know it today. From this time on, Judaism would be much more monolithic than it had been in Jesus' day.

In around AD 90, a council was held at Jamnia to settle a number of questions. One issue was the canon of scripture: until this time, the Jews had had no fixed set of holy books, but had generally regarded anything that seemed sufficiently ancient as authoritative. Now, though, the rabbis of Jamnia set out a list of books they considered scriptural. They were to be read in Hebrew, not the Greek translation used by most Christians. Moreover, the rabbis apparently approved an alteration to the *Amidah*, also known as the 'Eighteen Benedictions', a set of prayers which was said in all synagogues. Different versions of the new prayer have been recorded in different traditions, but the version known as the 'Palestinian' one reads:

And for apostates let there be no hope; and may the insolent kingdom be quickly uprooted, in our days. And may the Nazarenes and the heretics perish quickly; and may they be erased from the Book of Life; and may they not be inscribed with the righteous.

This council represents the most decisive point in the growing rift between Jews and 'Nazarenes', that is, the followers of Jesus of Nazareth. Relations had been deteriorating long before this, though. We saw earlier how Stephen was killed by a Jewish mob for his Christian faith and his attack on 'unbelieving' Jews; and the book of Acts testifies to a series of persecutions by the Jewish authorities on the burgeoning Christian movement in Jerusalem and elsewhere. Paul, before his

experience of the risen Christ, was one of the most merciless Jewish persecutors of Christians. A major incident occurred in the early AD 60s with the death of James, leader of the church at Jerusalem. James's fate seems to have been not dissimilar to that of his brother, Jesus. Together with some of his companions, he was brought before the high priest and his advisers and condemned as a breaker of the Law. Different sources give different accounts of his death: we are told, variously, that he was stoned to death, thrown from a tower of the Temple, beaten to death with a club or pushed down a flight of stairs. Evidently, where Jesus was legally executed by the Roman prefect, James was lynched. But both brothers had been condemned by the high priest and killed, thirty years apart.

It is hardly surprising that Christians became increasingly bitter about the situation and came to characterize non-Christian Jews as their opponents. Different books of the New Testament, written at different times, testify to the developing situation. In Paul's letters we find anguish about the Jews' failure to recognize Christ, not bitterness towards them – on the contrary, Paul states in Romans 9 that he wishes he could be condemned if it would save them.

The Gospels, written a couple of decades later, tell a rather different story. Arguments between Christians and non-Christian Jews evidently led to greater interest in how Jesus himself, during his lifetime, had handled such situations, and so in the Gospels we find many stories of Jesus debating with other Jews. Most of his interlocutors are Pharisees – unsurprising given the rise of Pharisee-style Judaism during this period. And the different Gospels apparently reflect different attitudes. For example, most scholars believe that Mark's Gospel was written first, and here we find a mixture of positive and negative characterizations of Pharisees. Matthew's Gospel is far more negative, culminating in its famous chapter 23, a long diatribe against the

Pharisees, denounced as 'hypocrites', 'children of hell' and a 'brood of vipers'. This Gospel is often thought to have been written at around the time that the Christians – at least those Matthew knew – were redefining themselves as a separate group from Judaism. Relations between the two groups were at their worst, hence the bitterness that comes across in his Gospel. John's Gospel, by contrast, was probably written shortly after the introduction of the new *Amidah* in the synagogues, and here we find that Jesus' opponents are generally just 'the Jews', with little attempt to distinguish between Pharisees, priests, and the rest; and the debates about the Law and Sabbath observance that punctuate the other Gospels are missing. It seems that by this time the Christians that the author of John's Gospel knew had finally split away completely from Judaism. The debates between the two were, for him, a dead issue, and he was not interested in reproducing that kind of material in his work. For him, 'the Jews' were apparently a fairly homogenous group who were largely hostile to Jesus and who were not critically engaged with, except to be denounced.

CHRISTIANITY IN THE EMPIRE
Caesar Augustus (63 BC–AD 14) ruled the Roman empire for forty years – a long time by any standards, but especially for antiquity. The average lifespan in Rome at this time was only forty. When he died, few people could have remembered a time when Rome was a republic. But his successors were inevitably weaker men. His stepson and heir, Tiberius, was a paranoid recluse who ordered vast numbers of persecutions of those he believed were plotting against him. His successor, Gaius – known as Caligula – was even worse, apparently spiralling into complete insanity. Worst of all was Nero (AD 37–68), who turned degenerate decadence into an art form. According to the legend, when Rome burned in a terrible fire in AD 64, the emperor cared so little for the people that

he simply played his lyre and sang.

It was now that the Roman authorities began to target the Christians. Very little is known of the initial persecution, which apparently took place under Nero in the AD 60s. We do not know precisely why Nero singled out the Christians, although presumably they were regarded as members of a subversive organization. Similarly, we do not know whether a law was passed making Christianity illegal or whether the supposed subversiveness of the religion was considered sufficient justification for the clampdown. Nero blamed the fire of Rome upon the Christians and executed many of them for it, which suggests that he did not have a law banning Christianity *per se* but simply found an excuse for the persecution.

We do not know how many Christians died in this persecution, although presumably it cannot have been very many, simply because there were not that many Christians around yet – the religion was still a very minor sect in the grand scheme of things. One person who probably died at this time was Peter. He certainly died for his faith, as the first letter of Clement, written in the AD 90s, states, as does John's Gospel, although neither gives the circumstances. Tradition records that, just as Peter guided the Christian community at Rome, so too he died there. A rather unlikely story tells that he was crucified, but upside down, at his own request, since he did not feel worthy of dying in exactly the same way as Jesus. He is supposed to have been executed and also buried on Vatican Hill, a graveyard by the River Tiber. Paul probably died in the same persecution and tradition claims he was beheaded near the Via Ostia, to the south of the city. The fact that these two great Christian leaders both died in Rome helped to make that city all the more significant to Christians in years to come. This period probably also saw the development of the first Christian symbols, used to communicate the faith secretly, that we shall see in the next chapter.

To kill the rumours, Nero charged and tortured some people hated for their evil practices – the group popularly known as 'Christians'… Their deadly superstition had been suppressed temporarily, but was beginning to spring up again – not now just in Judea but even in Rome itself where all kinds of sordid and shameful activities are attracted and catch on. First those who confessed to being Christians were arrested. Then, on information obtained from them, hundreds were convicted, more for their anti-social beliefs than for fire-raising. In their deaths they were made a mockery. They were covered in skins of wild animals, torn to death by dogs, crucified or set on fire – so that when darkness fell they burned like torches in the night… As a result, although they were guilty of being Christians and deserved death, people began to feel sorry for them.

Tacitus, *Annals* 15.44, early second century

Nero's paranoia rivalled that of Tiberius. Eventually his attempts to execute anyone he suspected of opposing him led to widespread revolt among the aristocracy. In AD 68 Nero was deposed, fled and killed himself – stating as he did so, pretentious to the last, 'I feel an artist dying in me.' After a period known as 'the year of the four emperors' – which should give some idea of the political chaos of this time – everything settled down with Vespasian, a general acclaimed as the new emperor by his troops. He was succeeded by Titus and then Domitian, who ruled from AD 81 to 96. There is some evidence of intermittent persecution of the Christians during this time, but it is unknown how severe or widespread it was.

During this period, Christianity continued to spread around the empire. The Roman province of Asia (Anatolia, the region between the Black Sea and the Mediterranean, where Turkey is today) became an important Christian centre, with Ephesus being home to a major church that traced its foundation to John the apostle. It is highly likely that Christianity also became established at Alexandria, which rivalled Antioch as the greatest city in the Roman east. Alexandria was already home to a thriving Jewish community and was renowned for its philosophers and scientists. Tradition credits Mark, a companion of Peter and traditionally thought to be the author of Mark's Gospel, with bringing Christianity to the city, although we only begin to hear anything of a church at the end of the second century.

As this suggests, Christianity within the Roman empire was very much an urban religion. In Acts we read of Paul and other missionaries travelling from city to city to spread the word, and we hear of churches growing in the big population centres of the empire, but there is virtually no mention of rural Christians despite the fact that Peter and many of his companions were Galilean fishermen. It seems too that the members of these churches tended to be members of the lower classes. Writing to the Corinthian church, Paul commented, 'Consider your own call, brothers and sisters: not many of you were wise by human standards, not many were powerful, not many were of a noble birth.' The book of Philemon is a short letter written by Paul to a Christian about his slave, also a Christian. As we shall see in the next chapter, Christians were, as a rule, rather looked down upon by the rich, the aristocratic, and the intellectual.

The Christians still met in houses, although as the churches grew it seems likely that they would have converted houses into dedicated meeting places rather than meet in each other's homes. The earliest building that we know was used for Christian worship is in Dura-Europos on the Euphrates. It was a large house that was converted into a Christian meeting place in the early third century. About a hundred people could fit into the main room, which also contained a baptistery, a bath for baptizing people. And where the very first generation of Christians would have spoken Aramaic, the language of Jesus and of Galilee, soon the lingua franca of the Christians was Greek, the language of the eastern empire. The whole of the New Testament is written in Greek, and even the Christians in Rome and elsewhere in the west apparently spoke it, rather than Latin, the language of the western empire.

BEYOND THE EMPIRE

The faith spread beyond the borders of the Roman empire. Indeed, one of the major centres of Christianity in the early centuries was Edessa (modern Urfa), the capital of a small kingdom called Osrhoene in northern Syria. Osrhoene had been independent since the second century BC and was ruled by its own dynasty of kings, descended from Assyrians who had founded the kingdom centuries earlier. In AD 216, however, Osrhoene would be incorporated into the Roman empire, and Edessa would become a frontier city of the empire.

A curious legend about the coming of Christianity to this area dates back at least to the fourth century. King Abgar V of Osrhoene, we are told, became seriously ill.

Let us set before our eyes the illustrious apostles. Peter, through unrighteous envy, endured not one or two, but numerous labours, and when he had finally suffered martyrdom, departed to the place of glory due to him. Owing to envy, Paul also obtained the reward of patient endurance, after being seven times thrown into captivity, compelled to flee, and stoned. After preaching both in the east and west, he gained the illustrious reputation due to his faith, having taught righteousness to the whole world, and come to the extreme limit of the west, and suffered martyrdom under the prefects. Thus was he removed from the world, and went into the holy place, having proved himself a striking example of patience.

1 Clement, c. AD 96

Nero, from the workshop of the Belgian Florentine painter Johannes Stradanus (1523–1605).

The Zoroastrian Towers of Silence in Yazd, Iran. Zoroastrians would leave their dead at the top of the towers to be consumed by vultures. The practice was banned in Iran in 1970 but continues today among the Parsis of India.

However, he heard about Jesus, at that time preaching and healing in Galilee. He sent emissaries to Jesus, asking him to come to Edessa and cure him. Jesus received the message and wrote a polite reply to Abgar, explaining that he was unable to come since he had work to do in Jerusalem; however, he did heal the king at a distance and promise to send disciples later to bring Christianity to Edessa. This he did, sending an apostle named Addai (the otherwise fairly obscure Thaddeus, one of the twelve), who evangelized the kingdom.

In reality, nothing is known of how Christianity reached Edessa. The religion probably arrived at some time in the second century, perhaps under King Abgar VIII (which might explain the confusion with his earlier namesake), but it still seems likely that Osrhoene was the first state anywhere to make Christianity its official religion. And the city was more significant than even this might suggest. It was a trading city of critical importance. The great road to the east, along which came silk and

other trade items from faraway China, passed through Edessa before going on to Persia and then to the Orient. Thus, Edessa was the main gateway to the east. The arrival of Christianity here practically guaranteed that the religion would spread further – at least to Persia, which at this time was in the hands of the Parthians – and indeed Edessan Christianity became typical of the whole region. The language of Edessa, a dialect of Aramaic which became known as 'Syriac', was to be the language of Christianity in the Middle East for centuries.

The Parthians, who ruled Persia at this time, came from east of the Caspian Sea. Here the main religion was Zoroastrianism, which had been founded (perhaps around 1200 BC) by Zoroaster, sometimes known as Zarathustra, a mysterious figure but an immensely important one. No one knows for sure when he lived, possibly around the same time as Homer, possibly centuries earlier. He probably lived in what is now Iran, or perhaps Afghanistan, and preached his new faith, often thought of as a dualistic religion, involving two great gods – a good god of light and an evil god of darkness. The symbol of the good god is fire, and Zoroaster urged his followers to lead good lives and throw their lot in with the good god. He believed that in the future, the good god would be triumphant and would reward his followers by raising them from the dead and ushering in a new age of immortality and light. So despite its dualist reputation, it might be more accurate to see Zoroastrianism as a monotheistic religion like Judaism and Christianity, since the good god was regarded as more powerful than the evil one. Certainly Zoroastrianism seems to have had some of the doctrines associated with monotheistic religions – such as life after death, judgment and so on – before either Christianity or Judaism did. That would make Zoroaster himself one of the most influential figures ever to live.

Zoroastrianism was the dominant religion in Persia, but Judaism was also an important element there. In fact, it seems likely that in Jesus' day there were more Jews in Persia than anywhere else. Many had remained there after the Babylonian exile, when in the sixth century BC the Jews were enslaved in Babylon; many more, perhaps, were descendants of the 'lost' ten tribes of Palestine, who had been conquered and dispersed by the ancient Assyrians. Whatever the truth, many Persian Jews were doing well: the silk trade with China, which passed through Persia, was dominated by Jewish merchants. It seems likely that Christianity first came to Persia through these Jewish communities, which mostly spoke Aramaic. Another tradition, known from the third century, was that the apostle Thomas brought Christianity to the Parthians. However it got there, by the end of the second century Christianity was well established in Persia, although we know little about how the Persian Christians lived during this period.

CHAPTER 2

THE YOUNG CHURCH

The era of the apostles – the first leaders of the Christian church – was over by the end of the first century AD. The era from the second to the fifth or sixth centuries is often known as that of 'the Church Fathers' – those Christians who were the first to inherit an established religion, but who still had an enormous amount of work to do in understanding and interpreting it. It was during this period that Christianity took a form that we might recognize today, with established doctrines, liturgy, and church hierarchies. Much of this development occurred during the second and third centuries, when Christianity was still illegal.

THE ROMAN EMPIRE

Christianity emerged in a 'client state' of the Roman empire, a marginal country only nominally under Roman control. Yet it spread and flourished, and found its sense of identity, within the Roman world. What was this world like?

With the death of Vespasian's son Domitian in AD 96, the empire entered its greatest age, in a period known as the time of 'the five good emperors'. These were Nerva, Trajan, Hadrian, Antoninus Pius, and Marcus Aurelius, all of whom ruled wisely until Marcus Aurelius's death in AD 180. At Trajan's death in AD 117, the Roman empire had reached its greatest extent. His successors sensibly chose not to try for further military conquests, but used the army to maintain order in the territories they already ruled and prevent incursions from outside. This meant that money was not wasted on pointless military adventures, and the empire prospered.

The *pax Romana* or 'Roman peace' that the empire claimed to bring was not simply a PR-friendly title given by arrogant conquerors to an empire seized by force. The Mediterranean world really did enjoy an age of peace and plenty under the Roman empire, at least in the age of Augustus and under the five good emperors. Within that vast empire, there were few wars, and security was guaranteed by the imperial legions. The Romans brought unprecedentedly high living standards to their subject peoples.

Perhaps one of the most striking things that the Romans did was not treat people simply as 'conquered'. On the contrary, the aim was to break down the barriers between conquerors and conquered through a process of Romanization. Those who lived in the empire were amalgamated into it, which meant that on the one hand everyone became basically Roman, and on the other the definition of 'Roman' was broadened. You could be from virtually any ethnic background and still be 'Roman'. Anyone could climb up through the Roman civil service or other professions, and so after the time of Augustus we find army officers, generals, local governors, and even senators in the city of Rome itself, who were not from Italy or the heartlands of the old republic. Throughout the empire, cities were transformed into centres of Roman culture and new cities were founded to promote Roman culture. These cosmopolitan cities acted as cultural melting pots, although the people of the countryside were often much more culturally conservative and preserved beliefs and traditions from pre-imperial times for far longer.

The Roman culture that was spread in this way was basically Hellenistic culture in a new form. Hellenism (Greek culture)

Every moment think steadily as a Roman and as a man to do what you have to do with perfect and simple dignity, and feeling of affection, and freedom, and justice; and to give yourself relief from all other thoughts. And you will give yourself relief, if you do every act of your life as if it were the last, putting aside all carelessness and emotional rebellion against the commands of reason, and all hypocrisy, and self-love, and discontent with what you have been given.

Marcus Aurelius,
Meditations II, AD 167

had spread throughout the eastern Mediterranean with the Hellenistic dynasties established in the fourth century BC after the conquests of Alexander the Great. When the Romans overthrew the Hellenistic dynasties in the second century BC and later, they took over the Greek culture and continued to endorse it. Whilst the official language of the empire was Latin, the language of Rome, spoken throughout the west, Greek was also extensively used, especially in the east. In imperial times all educated Romans, whether from east or west, would have spoken both languages.

The Romans believed in many gods, each of whom had his or her own personality and characteristics and represented particular aspects of life; Venus, for example, was the goddess of love. Honouring and respecting these gods was important, partly because they were believed to have influence over human affairs, and partly because they were the gods of the empire and thus had patriotic value. Worshipping the Roman gods was part of what it was to be Roman. Cities would hold regular festivals, which would involve honouring the locally favoured gods. Most public entertainments, such as sporting events or plays, began with an acknowledgment of the gods – rather like the national anthem being played at certain sporting events today. The gods were consulted through divination, and people might visit an oracle for this purpose.

CHRISTIANITY IN THE EMPIRE

This, then, was the world in which Christianity would flourish, and flourish it did by the end of the first century AD. The persecutions by Nero and Domitian had been half-hearted at best: they probably regarded Christians as convenient scapegoats, rather than having some fervent desire to eradicate the religion. It had, it seems, spread to the whole of the Roman empire, and beyond, into the small independent states to the east and even to Persia.

There is a great deal we do not know about how Christianity developed in this period. However, it seems clear that it was a primarily urban religion. Just as the Roman empire itself was based around great cities which acted as conduits and

The Pont du Gard, near Nimes, France. An example of the imagination and skill of Roman architects and builders.

Already there is the fragrance of blessedness on you, you who will soon be enlightened. Already you are gathering the spiritual flowers, to weave garlands of heaven. Already the fragrance of the Holy Spirit has breathed on you. Already you have gathered around the entrance to the king's palace – may the king also lead you in! The blossom has appeared on the trees – may the fruit also be found to be perfect!

Cyril of Jerusalem, addressing catechumens, *Catechetical lectures*, c. AD 348

Will it be lawful [for a Christian] to occupy himself with the sword, when the Lord declares that he who uses the sword will perish by the sword? And shall the son of peace, for whom it will be unfitting even to go to law, be engaged in a battle?… And shall he carry a flag, too, that is a rival to Christ?

Tertullian, *On the garland*, early third century

reservoirs of Roman culture, so too Christianity spread by the same means. Most Christian communities were based in these cities, and, as a rule, the larger and more important the city, the larger and more important the Christian community there. Christians from lesser cities instinctively deferred to those from greater ones – at least in theory – an attitude we see as early as Paul's letter to the Christians in Rome.

BECOMING A CHRISTIAN

As before, people who converted to Christianity were baptized. First, however, the new believer would be properly instructed in the beliefs and practices of Christianity. These 'beginner' Christians were the 'catechumens' (from the Greek meaning 'oral handing down', that is, teaching by word of mouth) and the way in which they were instructed developed as time went on. In his *First apology*, published in the middle of the second century, the Christian writer Justin Martyr (c. AD 100–165) gives us a valuable insight into how people were admitted into the church in Rome:

As many are persuaded and believe that what we teach and say is true, and undertake to be able to live accordingly, are instructed to pray and to entreat God with fasting, for the remission of their sins that are past, we praying and fasting with them. Then they are brought by us where there is water, and are regenerated in the same manner in which we were ourselves regenerated. For, in the name of God, the Father and Lord of the universe, and of our Saviour Jesus Christ, and of the Holy Spirit, they then receive the washing with water.

So there were clear requirements before someone could be baptized: praying, fasting, a commitment to live a moral life and understanding of Christian beliefs. It is not clear from Justin how formal this process was or how long it was expected to take.

As time went on, it became increasingly codified. In around AD 215 Hippolytus (d. c. AD 236), an important Christian writer in Rome, described quite an elaborate catechumenate. It began with an assessment of the candidate's suitability, which was apparently quite a thorough process. If a slave wished to become a Christian, his or her master would be consulted. Once the background checks were passed, the candidate's job was assessed. A number of professions were considered incompatible with Christianity. These included anything to do with prostitution, anything to do with magic or divination and anything to do with the theatre or with games (because of the association with pagan religion). Military commanders and magistrates were not eligible to join, because their jobs involved ordering executions, something the Christians were opposed to. A soldier could join provided he vowed never to execute anyone, even if ordered, and painters or sculptors could join, provided they vowed never to make an idol. After the candidate's lifestyle and job had been checked, he or she would spend three years being taught Christian beliefs (although good candidates could be fast-tracked). This was done at the morning services, where the catechumens were present, although they could not fully participate.

Other churches apparently provided more formal Christian education. This was especially the case in Alexandria, where a 'school' for the catechumens was founded in the late second century. Here, a Christian teacher would expound to his hearers the doctrines of the Christian religion, just as a Platonist or Stoic philosopher would explain the doctrines of his philosophy to his hearers. By AD 190, the Alexandrian school was being run by the famous teacher Clement, who believed that three years was the minimum time a catechumen should spend under him. The teaching might, of course, require written materials as supplements; and by the fourth century we find some Christian writers producing works apparently intended for this purpose – the most famous being Cyril of Jerusalem's *Catechetical lectures*. Shortly afterwards, Augustine's *Enchiridion* seems designed for a similar purpose. In later years, catechisms typically took question-and-answer form, reflecting their oral use.

Having – at last – thoroughly learned the religion, the catechumen would expect to be baptized and become a full member of the Christian community. Baptisms were generally 'saved up' and performed en masse at either Pentecost or Easter (the annual celebration of Jesus' resurrection). These, then, were apparently the main festivals in the Christian year, other Jewish festivals not being retained. The book of Acts already speaks of entire households being baptized, but the first explicit mention of children and infants being baptized is in the writings of the Latin Christian author Tertullian in AD 206. The reasoning, presumably, was that baptism represented initiation into the Christian community: it allowed a person to be included. Thus it would be unreasonable to exclude children of those who were included themselves.

Nevertheless, there was also a trend in the opposite direction, to delay baptism. This was because the powers of the ceremony were taken increasingly seriously. Paul had written in Romans 6:3, 'Do you not know that all of us who have been baptized into Christ Jesus were baptized into his death?' Thus, it was believed that baptism washed away the new believer's sins, and he was expected to live correctly thereafter. The church took a very dim view of those who sinned after they had been baptized. The usual stance was that one major lapse after baptism was permitted and the sinner could be readmitted to communion after a suitable time of penitence; after that they had 'used up' their chance. Many people, anxious that they might still have a lot of sinning to do, therefore chose to defer baptism, in order to minimize the chances of falling afterwards. It was not unusual to wait until death was near. Delayed baptism was especially common among those in

professions thought intrinsically unchristian, such as soldiers, who might wish to wait until they had killed their last opponent or criminal before being baptized into a religion that condemned all killing.

LEADING THE COMMUNITY

Those who ministered to the Christian communities had to have been baptized, of course, and deferred baptism is one reason why we sometimes hear of people being baptized and consecrated as a priest on a single day. But we know little of how the institution of the priesthood and the other orders of ministry evolved. We have already seen the confusion of terminology in the New Testament on this matter, and this continued into the second century. Ignatius of Antioch, writing in AD 107, repeatedly stressed the power of the 'bishop'. He understood the church as divided into a

Clement of Alexandria, in a twelfth-century Byzantine fresco.

Appoint for yourselves bishops and deacons worthy of the Lord, meek men, not avaricious, who are honest and approved, for their ministry to you is that of the prophets and teachers. So do not despise them, for they are your honourable men, just like the prophets and teachers.

The *Didache* 15, probably second century

strong Christian community, 3rd century
town with Christian congregations
border of Roman empire, 3rd century

0   600 km
0   400 miles

The church in the
third-century
Roman empire.

Danube

Black Sea

THESSALONICA ✝ ✝ PHILIPPI ✝ NICAEA

✝ CAESAREA

SMYRNA ✝ EDESSA ✝
EPHESUS ✝ ✝ COLOSSAE ✝ ICONIUM
CORINTH ✝ ✝ ATHENS TARSUS ✝
PATMOS ✝ ✝ MILETUS LYSTRA ✝ ✝ DERBE
✝ ANTIOCH

Mediterranean Sea

Crete

✝ SALAMIS
PAPHOS ✝

CAESAREA ✝
JERUSALEM ✝
ALEXANDRIA ✝ BETHLEHEM ✝

Nile

As for the Eucharist, hold it like this. First, with the cup: 'We give you thanks, our Father, for the holy Vine of David your child, which you made known to us through Jesus your child. To you be glory for ever.' And with the broken bread: 'We give you thanks, our Father, for the life and knowledge which you made known to us through Jesus your child. To you be glory for ever.' And after you have been satisfied with the food, give thanks like this: 'We give you thanks, holy Father, for your holy Name which you made to dwell in our hearts, and for the knowledge and faith and immortality which you made known to us through Jesus your child. To you be glory for ever. Lord, remember your church, to deliver it from evil and make it perfect in your love, and gather it in its holiness from the four winds to the kingdom that you have prepared for it. For yours is the power and the glory for ever. Let grace come, and let this world pass away. Hosannah to the God of David! If anyone be holy, let him come! If anyone be not, let him repent! Maranatha! Amen.'

The *Didache* 10, probably second century

number of communities, one in each city, and each one owed complete allegiance to its bishop. As he put it, writing to the Smyrneans, 'Wherever the bishop is, there let the people be, for there is the Catholic Church' – the first appearance of the term 'Catholic Church', meaning the whole body of Christians.

Yet in the *Didache*, an anonymous document apparently written some time in the second century which describes the life and organization of the church, the bishop is regarded as subject to 'prophets' and 'teachers'. It seems likely that church organization developed in different ways and at different rates at different places. By the end of the second century, a roughly uniform system had settled into place of bishops, priests and deacons. The bishop was the head of the church in a particular city. In theory, he was the one who performed baptisms and celebrated the Eucharist. But he could delegate these functions to the priests, who were there to help him. They in turn were assisted by the deacons, who could not perform baptisms or the Eucharist, and were therefore 'lay' or unordained. Notably, those in formal positions of authority seem always to have been men. However, at this stage there were many women in the congregations – something that contrasted strongly with some of the mystery cults (Mithraism banned women from worship altogether). This went back to the first century, when Paul had apparently had many female converts – his letters abound with female names. In the second century, we hear of female prophets – the most well known being those of the Montanists – and many female martyrs. But little is known of what distinctively female contribution they made to church life, since they were not church leaders and few wrote anything. As the surviving literature presents it (almost entirely written by men), the great female saints of the early centuries are mostly either martyrs or play supporting roles to men, such as Gregory of Nyssa's sister Macrina, Augustine's mother Monica and Jerome's

fellow hermit Paula. In the fourth century, a number of theologians, principally Ambrose of Milan and, above all, Jerome, would develop a fundamentally misogynistic view of women, regarding them as basically a flawed version of men, there to tempt men and to be avoided. For, they argued, Adam would never have sinned had Eve not urged him on – and was not Adam created first anyway? This view would be inherited by the Middle Ages, though it would also be combined with an idealization of the female, characterized by the meek, obedient and ever-virgin Mary, mother of Jesus.

THE CHRISTIAN LIFE

One task of church leaders was to oversee the liturgical celebrations which lay at the heart of the Christian community. At this time these were still fairly simple. The Eucharist was celebrated every Sunday morning with a relatively straightforward set of prayers. In Justin Martyr's day there was apparently no set form of words for this, apart from the repetition of Jesus' words of institution over the bread and wine, and the celebrant would simply speak to the best of his ability. Worshippers would pray standing, with their arms upraised. There would be a reading from the 'memoirs' of the apostles. Other meetings were held early on other days, before work began. Like the Eucharist, these concluded with a collection of food and clothes to help needy Christians. Not for some centuries would this be replaced by a collection of money. On Wednesday and Friday, according to the *Didache*, they would fast.

By the early third century, according to Hippolytus of Rome, the services had become a little more complex and standardized. They would feature readings from both the Old and the New Testaments – read by different people – and the bishop, who presided over the service, would give a short speech on what they had just heard. Prayers would be offered on behalf of the Christian community, and also on behalf of those in need, and for the Roman empire and its emperor.

Ignatius of Antioch

In the early years of the second century, Ignatius, bishop of Antioch, was arrested and taken to Rome to suffer martyrdom in the Coliseum. In the course of his travels, this lively and energetic man met and wrote to other Christian communities. In his seven letters to the communities at Ephesus, Magnesia, Tralles, Rome, Philadelphia and Smyrna and to Polycarp of Smyrna he was primarily concerned with three issues: the unity of the church as lived in communion with the bishop and fostered in the Eucharist, the danger of heresy, and the glory of martyrdom.

For Ignatius (d. c. AD 107) the unity of the church was of supreme importance because this unity consisted of Christ (the head) and his body. This unity was first of all founded upon a unity of faith – all believed in the one true gospel (thus his concern for heresy which destroys the unity of faith). It was the bishop, as the earthly presence of Christ and successor to the apostles, who is the foundation of this present unity, for he is the authentic teacher and defender of the gospel and the pastor who oversees the proper care and harmony of all the faithful. The fullest expression and fostering of this unity, 'a symphony of minds in concert', is found in the Eucharist, for there the local faithful, in union with the bishop, gather to hear the gospel and to come into communion with Christ by receiving his risen body and blood, which is 'the medicine of immortality'.

The greatest heresy that faced Ignatius was Docetism (from the Greek word *dokesis* meaning 'to seem'), which held that the Son/Word of God only 'seemed' or 'appeared' to take on human flesh, but actually did not. Thus all that pertained to Jesus' humanity – birth, eating, suffering, dying and so on – was only apparent and not real. The Docetists argued that, if the Son/Word was truly God, he could not truly assume human flesh; for to do so would jeopardize and destroy his divine nature. God could not actually suffer and die.

In response to this, first, Ignatius argued that Jesus, being the true Word of the Father, was the full revealer of the Father. He speaks from the Father's

'silence' and the Word as the Father's 'mouthpiece'. As such Jesus is truly God. Ignatius calls Jesus God on fourteen occasions and on eight of these actually refers to him as *ho theos*, 'the God' – in Greek, names are preceded by the definite article. This is very surprising at such an early date, since the New Testament seems very hesitant to call Jesus simply 'God'.

Second, what is also surprising, Ignatius is one of the first, if not the first, to use 'the communication of idioms', that is, the predicating of divine and human attributes of one and the same person. He can speak of 'divine blood' or 'the passion of my God'. This is a very strange use of language. God does not have blood. God cannot suffer. However, if God becomes man, then God does have blood, and he can suffer, not as God but as man. This is why Ignatius used such language. It allowed him to express boldly and even scandalously, contrary to the Docetists, the truth of the incarnation. To the Ephesians Ignatius could write about Jesus in a marvellous, poetic fashion:

> Very Flesh, yet Spirit too;
> Uncreated, and yet born;
> God-and-Man in One agreed,
> Very-Life-in-Death indeed,
> Fruit of God and Mary's seed
> At once impassible and torn
> By pain and suffering here below:
> Jesus Christ, whom as our Lord
>   we know.

Ignatius's main argument for upholding the truth of the incarnation is based on the doctrine of salvation. If the Son of

Removing the heart of St Ignatius, by the Italian Florentine painter Sandro Botticelli (1445–1510). The picture reflects the legend that, after his death, Ignatius's heart was found to have Jesus' name inscribed upon it.

God only pretended to be a man, if his 'human' life were a mere charade and thus his birth, baptism, suffering and death were simply pantomime, then our salvation is a mere pretence and counterfeit. It has no reality either.

This leads to Ignatius's third concern, the glory of martyrdom. Ignatius pointedly told the church at Tralles that, when he arrives in Rome, he will be eaten by real lions with real teeth. He will shed real blood. He will actually suffer and truly die. If Jesus only pretended to shed blood and only feigned suffering and death, then he (Ignatius) is the most to be pitied. He is but a fool. Moreover, it is in becoming a martyr that one fully proclaims the gospel by imitating Jesus himself. Equally, martyrdom fulfils what takes place in baptism in that one dies and rises with Christ and so fully becomes an authentic Christian. Lastly, martyrdom is the living out of the Eucharist, for there, in receiving the body and blood of Christ, we are conformed into his likeness and thus in laying down one's life for Christ one is fully conformed into the true likeness of Christ.

THOMAS WEINANDY

We are equally forbidden to wish ill, to do ill, to speak ill, to think ill of all men. The thing we must not do to an emperor, we must not do to anyone else.

Tertullian, *Apology*, AD 197

The world is soaked with mutual blood; and murder, which in the case of an individual is admitted to be crime, is called a virtue when it is committed wholesale in the name of the state… A gladiatorial combat is being prepared that blood may delight the lust of cruel eyes… Man is killed for the pleasure of man, and to be able to kill is a skill, is an employment, there is sin in the midst of the laws themselves, there is wickedness in the midst of the statutes, and innocence is not preserved where it is defended.

Cyprian of Carthage, *Letter to Donatus*, c. AD 246

These frequent communal services helped to create unity among the Christians. Until the late second century most Christians were from the working classes, even slaves. It is easy to see the attraction, to people whom society looked down upon, of belonging to an organization whose members loved and helped each other. According to Tertullian, outsiders would, on seeing how the Christian community worked, say in amazement, 'See how they love one another!' It was well known that Christians called each other 'brother' and 'sister', and that the bonds between them were stronger than those with non-believing family members. Tertullian's contemporary Minucius Felix wrote about his dead Christian friend, Octavius, commenting that they had been so close that you would have thought they shared a single mind.

In addition to their communal activities, devout Christians would have their own private devotions. Tertullian wrote a whole book, *On prayer*, in which he advised his readers to pray kneeling (except on Sundays) and silently. It was usual for Christians to follow the practice of Daniel in Daniel 6:10 and pray once when getting up, once at noon, and once before going to bed; it was also customary to pray before getting in the bath, presumably because it was reminiscent of baptism. Some followed the advice of Psalm 119:164 and prayed seven times a day – the origin of the seven daily services read by monks in the Middle Ages.

The Christians lived austere lives by the normal standards of the day, striving to avoid what they regarded as immorality or idolatry. This meant they could participate in virtually no public entertainments, either at the theatre or at the circus. Tertullian wrote a scorching denunciation of the immorality of all such activities in his work *On the spectacles*, which he ended with a now notorious passage describing the future return of a vengeful Christ, who would torture the athletes and actors, thereby providing the Christians with the best entertainment of all.

The Christians inherited the moral standards of both Judaism and traditional Roman mores, especially in sexual ethics. Promiscuity was an increasingly common feature of Roman life and it was attacked by pagan Roman commentators such as the second-century satirist Juvenal and by Christians alike. Divorce was frowned upon, especially remarriage – although those who remarried were allowed to participate in church life providing they completed a standard period of prayer and fasting. Similarly, marriages to non-Christians were allowed, but severely frowned upon. As for sex outside marriage, that was also condemned by some Christian moral writers – but really they disapproved of sex in general and usually did not bother to distinguish between marital and non-marital sex. They all believed that the purpose of sex was the procreation of children, and it should not be engaged in for pleasure. Many married Christian couples lived together chastely. Children, conversely, were valued, and abortion was universally condemned by Christians. They also condemned the old Roman practice of 'exposition', where an unwanted baby was left ('exposed') on a hillside to take its chances.

THE CATACOMBS

One of the Christian developments during this period, now world-famous, was the excavation of catacombs, tunnels and caves near Rome. These were primarily places to bury the dead and were used by pagans, Jews and Christians alike. But by the third century the Christian burials were outnumbering the others. The Christians, who believed in the future resurrection of the dead, did not practise cremation as pagans often did. Moreover, most Christians were still fairly poor. They could not afford normal burial plots, and so a lack of space led them to resort to digging caves instead. The early burials here were correspondingly simple: the dead were wrapped in white cloths and laid directly in the niches carved from the rock, without coffins, just as Jesus himself had been.

The Catacomb of Sts Peter and Marcellinus, under Rome.

There was a sense that the catacombs were a holy place. If they were founded out of financial pressure, they developed out of religious motives. They became extremely extensive. Most catacombs began with a stairway dug down to a depth of 12 metres (40 ft) or more, which would then open out into the narrow galleries with several layers of niches on either side. Other passages would lead out from these galleries, leading to more, and stairs would lead down to deeper levels – sometimes a total of three or four. The catacombs contained literally millions of bodies, and it has been estimated that if all the passages were laid out in a straight line, they would extend further than the length of Italy. Most of this was dug by the Christians themselves, working by lamplight, carrying the rock and soil to the surface in bags. In the catacombs the dead all lay as if in a vast dormitory. For that was, of course, what it was to the Christians, who believed that they would all rise together at Jesus' return. The use of the catacombs, remote from the city, where all the dead lay together, reaffirmed the Christians' sense of themselves as a community set apart, whose members were all in it together. Little wonder that rooms were set aside for holding occasional services or remembering the dead – for the Christians, like most Romans of this time, probably shared meals to remember the dead.

The catacombs also offer the first extensive collection of Christian art, for the Christians painted images onto the walls of the tombs and the chambers, just as the pagans and Jews did in their

Graffiti on a wall in the Catacombs of St Sebastian, Rome, using two popular Christian symbols, a fish and an anchor.

Fish-born, divine children of a heavenly father, drink with heartfelt reverence God's waters, the source of immortality to mortals. Eat as a hungry man eats of the Fish you hold in your hands.

Pectorius, author of a third-century inscription at Autun in France

Just thinking about this silly teaching [the resurrection of the dead] makes my head feel funny! Many people have died at sea, or their bodies have been eaten by wild animals and birds. How will their bodies rise? Or let's take an example to test this little doctrine, so innocently advanced. A man was shipwrecked. The hungry fish feasted on his body. But the fish were caught, cooked, and eaten by some fishermen, who had the back luck to be attacked by ravenous dogs, who killed and ate them. When the dogs died, vultures feasted on them. How will the body of the shipwrecked man be put back together, when it has been absorbed by other bodies of different kinds?

Porphyry, *Against the Christians* (quoted in Macarius Magnes, *Apocritus*), c. AD 270

catacombs. Jesus occurs frequently, as you would expect; he is generally represented as a young, beardless Roman. His youth is not only historically accurate (Jesus was probably in his early thirties when he died) but testifies to the youthfulness of the faith: Jesus is a young god, come to replace the old Roman cults. He is often portrayed as a healer, laying his hands or a staff on the sick and the dying, or as the Good Shepherd, carrying a sheep on his shoulders, to represent the way he carries the believer's soul.

Other common symbols are the dove, representing the Holy Spirit, the anchor, representing the steadfastness of the dead person, and the phoenix, the mythical resurrecting bird which, since the late first century, had been used by Christians as an image of the resurrection. There was also the fish, a more cryptic symbol. The Greek word for fish, *icthos*, was used as an acrostic: its letters stood for the Greek for 'Jesus Christ, Son of God, Saviour'. It is not certain whether this was the origin of the fish symbol, or whether the Christians co-opted this traditional religious symbol and reinterpreted it. Finally, the Chi-Rho symbol also appeared, the first two letters of the name Christos in Greek, *X* and *P*, superimposed on each other. Images such as these enabled the Christians to record their faith and to testify to the faith of the dead, but were hard for outsiders to understand.

THE CHRISTIAN PROBLEM

The Christians, one might think on the basis of all this, were blameless members of society, the kind of people the authorities would want to encourage. But the authorities were not happy about them at all. Why was this?

The Christians were subject to considerable ridicule from the educated classes, who laughed at their doctrines – especially the doctrine of the resurrection of all people at the end of time. Platonists mocked this as a crude misunderstanding of their own belief in the immortality of the soul. To many, Christianity was a 'barbarian philosophy', a garbled imitation of real philosophy for the weak-minded. Some time in the second half of the second century, a Platonic philosopher named Celsus wrote a sustained attack on Christianity called *The true doctrine*, in which he also tried to discredit the figure of Jesus himself. For example, he repeated the story, which was common among pagans and also Jews, that Jesus' mother had been raped by a Roman soldier named Panthera, and Jesus was the product. Scornful though Celsus's attacks were, Christianity was gradually becoming more intellectually respectable. Christian intellectuals such as Justin Martyr and Clement of Alexandria (c. AD 150–c. 215), were writing increasingly sophisticated defences of their beliefs. And, in the third century, Celsus's book was answered by

Origen Adamantius (c. AD 185–c. 254), a figure of considerably greater intellectual weight even than most pagan philosophers.

More worryingly from the Christians' point of view, there was a lot of popular suspicion and misunderstanding about what they did. It was generally believed that their services involved incestuous orgies, a belief apparently partly inspired by the fact that Christians called each other 'brother' and 'sister'. It was said that the Christians would attach the lead of a dog to the lamp and wait for it to pull it over, plunging the room into darkness: this was the cue for the orgy to begin. Worse, it was said that the Eucharist really did involve eating flesh and drinking blood – that the Christians would murder children (sometimes, sadistically, tricking recruits into doing so unknowingly) and then consume them. To many people, simply calling oneself a 'Christian' was equivalent to admitting to such acts.

Moreover, Christians were thought to be unpatriotic. Though the notion of what it meant to be 'Roman' was quite flexible, one non-negotiable element was paying homage to the gods of Rome. But the Christians did not do this. By the middle of the second century, many people concluded that the ills of the empire were caused by the gods' anger at the Christians, who were denounced as irreligious. Lucian, writing from Pontus in around AD 170, described the area as 'full of atheists and Christians'. Despite the fact that Christians routinely prayed for the emperor, they were believed to be working against him. It became increasingly common for ordinary people to report Christian activity to the state, and the state generally regarded evidence of Christian profession as enough to condemn someone, without bothering to investigate whether they really murdered children as well.

Yet there was not, as a rule, active state persecution against the Christians. Most of the 'five good emperors' were not too bothered about them (although Marcus Aurelius did not like them). Persecution,

when it happened, was conducted by provincial rulers. A fascinating example has been preserved in the letters of Pliny the Younger, governor of Bithynia in the early second century. He wrote to the emperor Trajan explaining his procedure: if someone were denounced to him as a Christian, he would arrest them, question them, give them several chances to renounce their faith, and if they proved obstinate, execute them. The emperor wrote back commending Pliny, and stating that Christians should not be actively sought out for this treatment, but any that turned up should be dealt with as Pliny had done.

Little wonder that Christian writers appeared who tried to defend their religion. These writers, known as the Apologists (since 'apology' can mean 'defence'), are important sources for our knowledge of Christian beliefs and practices of the time. One of the most famous was Justin Martyr. He argued that the authorities should not condemn people simply on the basis of the name 'Christian' but should look into each case and see if they really committed any atrocities. Justin was executed for his pains, hence the nickname 'Martyr'. Another, more strident voice at the end of the second century belonged to the Latin writer Tertullian, who came from Carthage in North Africa. He was probably a lawyer before his conversion and expertly picked holes in the official policy. If Christians really committed these crimes and deserved death, he sneered, why did the authorities adopt the 'don't ask, don't tell' policy of Trajan?

Still, Trajan's policy did mean long periods of relative calm, during which, although Christianity remained illegal, little was done against it. During these times, it was sometimes possible to be openly Christian and suffer no ill harm: thus, during the long period of quiet in the first half of the third century, we find Origen, the most famous Christian leader of his day, invited to meet the mother of the emperor and discuss Christian ideas with her. Raised a Christian, given the best education available at the hothouse of learning that

If the river Tiber reaches the walls, if the river Nile does not rise to the fields, if the sky does not move or the earth does, if there is famine, if there is plague, the cry is at once: 'The Christians to the lion!' What – all of them to one lion?

Tertullian, *Apology*, AD 197

was Alexandria, Origen dominated both the church and the intellectual world of his day; in years to come, pagan writers would lament the fact that such a brilliant man was a Christian!

But the calm was interspersed with periods of trouble, when either zealous local governors or emperors themselves tried to get rid of the Christians. One of the worst occurred in AD 249, when the emperor Decius came to power and began the first really systematic attempt to wipe out the Christians. Everyone in the empire was ordered to make a sacrifice to the gods; those who did so were issued with a certificate. Anyone who refused was put to death. Many Christians refused and were killed; many others gave in, sacrificed and were released. Still more managed to compromise by acquiring forged certificates stating that they had made the sacrifice when they had not. Meanwhile, prominent church leaders were tortured in the hope of forcing them to recant their faith; the authorities deliberately tried to avoid killing them, recognizing that martyrs only encouraged the growth of Christianity. Origen, who only a few years earlier had been feted at court, was tortured and released to die in obscurity; the bishops of both Rome and Jerusalem died in prison. The persecutions continued under Decius's successor, Valerian, who was at war with Persia and suspected the Christians of disloyalty. But Valerian's son, Gallienus, emperor from AD 260 to 268, decreed that the Christians could worship as they wished, and another long period of calm resulted.

The worst persecution of all took place half a century later, between AD 303 and 311, undertaken by the emperor Diocletian and, after his abdication in AD 305, by his successor (and the more fanatical anti-Christian) Galerius. A series of edicts was passed, banning the Christian scriptures, arresting all clergy and finally forcing all Christians to sacrifice to the gods on pain of death. Enormous numbers of Christians died, especially in the eastern half of the empire. But this was the last great persecution of Rome. It ended as Galerius, on his deathbed, decided he needed all the supernatural help he could get and ordered that the Christians should pray to their God for the emperor's health. God, on this occasion, was not forgiving, and Galerius perished soon after.

The persecutions had failed. They had even proved counterproductive. As usually happens, state persecution of a group simply produced a siege mentality and greater determination among those being persecuted. Those who perished were celebrated as 'martyrs', a word meaning 'witnesses' to the faith. They played an important role in the spread of Christianity, as many non-Christians were impressed by their courage. Tertullian famously commented that 'the blood of Christians is seed', often misquoted as 'the blood of the martyrs is the seed of the church', and he himself is sometimes thought to have been converted after seeing the bravery of Christians killed in the circus. Eusebius, writing in the early fourth century, describes the death of a Christian woman named Potamiana a century earlier in Egypt. She was killed by boiling pitch, but the soldier who carried out the execution, Basilides, was so moved by her death that he converted to Christianity and was executed himself a couple of days later.

From around the middle of the second century, it became increasingly common to celebrate the 'birthdays' of martyrs – that is, the anniversaries of their deaths. The places where they fell were honoured, as were their remains. Accounts of their deaths were written which proved very inspirational. One famous story tells of the death of Polycarp, bishop of Smyrna, in the AD 160s. Ordered to honour Caesar's genius and renounce Christ, the old man replied, 'For eighty-six years I have been his servant, and he has done me no wrong. How can I blaspheme my King, who saved me?'

The historian Eusebius preserved a graphic account of persecution, written in Gaul in the late second century:

First, [the arrested Christians] endured nobly the injuries inflicted by the people – shrieks and blows and draggings and thefts and stonings and imprisonments – all the things which a furious mob love to inflict on their enemies. Then, being taken to the forum by the tribune and the city authorities, they were examined in the presence of all the people, and having confessed, they were imprisoned until the arrival of the governor… the soon-to-be-witnesses were obviously ready, and finished their confession eagerly. But some seemed unprepared and untrained, still weak, and unable to endure such a trial. About ten of these proved abortions [denying their faith], causing us great grief and terrible sorrow… And some of our heathen servants were also arrested, as the governor had commanded that all of us should be examined publicly. Led astray by Satan, afraid of the tortures which they saw the saints endure, and egged on by the soldiers, they falsely accused us of Thyestean banquets [cannibalism] and Oedipodean intercourse [incest], and of deeds which are not only unlawful for us to mention or think of, but which we cannot believe anyone ever committed. When these accusations were reported, all the people raged against us like wild animals… [The arrested Christians suffered] confinement in the dark and most loathsome parts of the prison, having their feet stretched to the fifth hole in the stocks, and other outrages… A great many were suffocated in prison, being chosen by the Lord for this manner of death, so that his glory could be shown in them… Maturus, Sanctus, Blandina, and Attalus were led to the amphitheatre to be thrown to the wild animals, and to give to the heathen public a show of cruelty… Both Maturus and Sanctus… endured again the customary running of the gauntlet and the violence of the wild beasts, and everything which the furious people called for or desired, and at last, the iron chair in which their bodies being roasted tormented them with the fumes… [Attalus] was led around the amphitheatre with a notice carried in front of him, on which was written in the Roman language 'This is Attalus the Christian,' and the people were filled with hatred towards him… when Attalus was placed in the iron seat, and the fumes rose from his burning body, he said to the people in the Roman language, 'Look! What you are doing now is eating up men, but we do not eat men, or do any other wicked thing.'… [Blandina,] after the scourging, after the wild beasts, after the roasting seat, was finally enclosed in a net, and thrown before a bull. And having been tossed about by the animal, but feeling none of the things which were happening to her, on account of her hope and firm hold upon what had been entrusted to her, and her communion with Christ, she also was sacrificed. And the heathen themselves said that never among them had a woman endured so many and such terrible tortures.

Another account told of the death of Cyprian, bishop of Carthage, who was beheaded in AD 258 during the Valerian persecution. It described how the very last thing that the martyr saw was a pile of cloths under the block on which he was to die, placed there by other Christians to catch his blood when he was decapitated. Those bloodstained cloths would become precious relics, for the Christians believed that God was with the martyrs, and their remains were holy. The remains of those who died were generally bought from the executioners at great cost. Many were laid to rest in the catacombs, and these graves would be especially holy places. By the fourth century many of the martyrs' graves in the catacombs had become crypts, that is, small chapels or churches built around the tomb, where the faithful could come and pray in the presence of the martyr.

HELLENISTIC CULTURE

The rise of the cult of the martyrs was not the only way in which Christianity was changed by the Roman world. More subtle changes were also taking place, as the religion assimilated elements of Roman culture – a culture that had already assimilated much of the older Hellenistic culture.

If apostles and martyrs while still in the body can pray for others, when they ought to be thinking about themselves, how much more must they do so after they have won their crowns, overcome, and triumphed? One lone man, Moses, wins pardon from God for six hundred thousand armed men [Exodus 32:30], and Stephen, the follower of his Lord and the first Christian martyr, begs forgiveness for his persecutors [Acts 7:59–60]. So when they have entered life with Christ, will they have less power than before? The apostle Paul says that two hundred and seventy-six souls were given to him in the ship [Acts 27:37]. So when, after his death, he has begun to be with Christ, must he shut his mouth, and be unable to say a word for those who throughout the whole world have believed in his Gospel?… In fact the saints are not called dead – they are said to be sleeping.

Jerome on the intercession of saints and use of relics, *Against Vigilantius*, AD 406

HELLENISTIC PHILOSOPHY

The Greeks had pioneered the philosophical and scientific approach to the world, especially during the golden age of Athens in the fourth century BC. That was the time of Socrates, his student Plato, and *his* student Aristotle. Plato had founded a school just outside Athens called the Academy, a kind of high-level aristocratic think-tank. Here, after the master's death, the 'Platonists' developed a system of philosophy based upon his thought. This system revolved around the distinction between the physical world and the spiritual. Platonic philosophers urged people to look beyond what their senses perceived, to use their minds rather than their eyes, and come to know spiritual reality. They believed that the physical world was only a kind of pale reflection of this higher, more real world.

Platonism also developed the idea that the physical world was actively run by the spiritual world. They suggested a 'World Soul', a sort of divine being, which controlled the whole world in the way that the human soul controlled the body. For Platonists also believed in a soul, a part of the human being which belonged to the higher world and which would go there after the death of the body. Some Platonists distinguished between the World Soul and a higher God, the ultimate cause of everything else.

Another important school of thought,

A fifteenth-century depiction of Troy, the setting of Homer's *Iliad*.

which developed after Plato's time, was Stoicism. The Stoics – named after the stoa or portico in Athens where they used to argue with each other – were most renowned for their ethics, which were strict. They believed that true happiness comes only through virtue, not through pleasure or wealth. Unlike the Platonists, they did not believe that anything non-physical could exist, but they still believed in God; they just thought God was physical. They also believed in something like the World Soul, although they called it the 'Logos', which means 'principle' as well as 'word', and they thought this Logos permeated the world like a thin fire.

HELLENISTIC RELIGION

Philosophies such as Platonism and Stoicism functioned like religions in some ways. They sought to explain human nature and its place in the world, and they talked about God and salvation, as well as about how to lead a moral life. But there were more popular cults as well, many inherited from the Greeks. The cults of the Greek gods revolved around a set of stories that were told about them and about the human beings they interacted with. The most important of these stories were found in the works of Homer and Hesiod, two Greek poets of great antiquity, whose writings formed what were essentially the scriptures of Greek religion.

In the time of Plato and Aristotle and later, in the Hellenistic age, these works were treated as genuine history and mythology. Their authors were believed to have been divinely inspired and the gods had spoken through them, playing their voices as a human musician might play a flute. They remained enormously important in the Roman empire. Latin-speaking writers reworked their myths, and in the Greek-speaking part of the empire, Homer and Hesiod continued to be taught at school, together with other great works of the past. They were taught not simply as great literature – although students were encouraged to master the difficult style of the poets and imitate it – but as moral instruction. The divinely-inspired Homer had, it was believed, captured in his work all ethics as well as the truth about the gods. Since Homer's work contains remarkably graphic battle scenes, as well as unedifying behaviour on the part of the heroes and gods alike, this presented problems. Many people argued that Homer intended his work to be taken allegorically. For example, a writer of the first century AD named Heraclitus (not to be confused with an earlier Greek philosopher of this name) wrote a defence of Homer, showing how each story could be interpreted. So when, in *The Odyssey*, we read of the goddess of love, Aphrodite, committing adultery with the god of war, Ares, we are meant to see this as a lesson on how love can overcome war. Evidently, there was criticism of Homer from less traditionally-minded people: indeed, the philosopher Heraclitus had declared that Homer should have been punished, not praised, for his morally reprehensible work.

OTHER RELIGIONS IN THE EMPIRE

The Romans liked to mix different local cults or integrate them into their own religion. In the first and second centuries AD, this resulted in a huge variety of religious philosophies and cults swirling around the Roman empire, which could be combined in interesting ways. Some of these ideas came from outside the imperial borders. One of the most important religions at this time was Zoroastrianism. As we saw in the first chapter, Zoroastrianism was the religion of the Parthians as it had been of the Persians before them, so in Hellenistic and imperial times alike the ideas of Zoroastrianism filtered over the border and became current in the Roman world.

Ideas from even further afield were known in the Roman empire, especially from India. Quite how much influence Indian philosophy and religion really had on the Roman world is hard to tell: it seems that 'India' was little more than an exotic name which was not very well known in detail. Apollonius of Tyana, a popular religious philosopher of the first century AD, was said to have studied with the brahmans of India; Plotinus, the last great philosopher of pagan antiquity, was said to have joined the imperial armies on their expeditions east in the early third century AD in order to learn Indian wisdom. But we are not told precisely what either of them learned from these adventures, and it may be that their biographers simply invented such details to add an air of exotic mystique to their heroes. Clement of Alexandria, a Christian writer at the end of the second century AD, was the first westerner to mention Buddha – but he tells us nothing of his doctrines.

The native religion of Rome, together with the religions of the Greeks and of other cultures that were assimilated into the empire, as well as these foreign and exotic ideas, all mingled in the great cosmopolitan cities of the empire. New cults were born. In the first and second centuries AD, these included the 'mystery cults', so called because these religions all involved complex rites and rituals, and claimed to possess secret knowledge that only those in the know could access. Initiates looked for a life beyond the current one. And in the spirit of Hellenistic syncretism, it was quite possible to be a member of several of these cults at once. Perhaps the best known of these religions today is Mithraism, based around the worship of a Zoroastrian god named Mithras. There were seven levels of knowledge that a Mithrain could hope to achieve, but little is known of what they actually believed or what rites they practised. Another important mystery religion was a complex of rituals known as the Eleusian mysteries, associated with the town of Eleusis near Athens. These rites involved feasting, fasting, special liturgical celebrations, and mystic rituals so secret that revealing them to outsiders was punishable by death. More dramatic rites were involved in the cult of Cybele, originally a Phrygian goddess, whose cult spread throughout the empire. In this religion, castrated priests led the faithful in wild orgies with loud music and frenzied shrieking – the Roman equivalent of a heavy metal concert, perhaps.

The authorities regarded the mystery cults with suspicion. Adherence to the traditional religion of Rome was very important, so worshippers of the mystery cults might not be good, reliable Romans. The state often tried to crack down on the mystery religions, banning their more extreme celebrations – although the religions themselves were generally not banned.

THE HELLENIZING OF CHRISTIANITY

By the second century, Christianity existed primarily within the larger Hellenistic world, rather than within the more parochial Jewish one. The presence of non-Jewish Christian churches throughout the cities of the Roman empire meant that

Christians were moving in the sort of religious landscape we have just been looking at, instead of within the thought world of Judaism. Christianity inevitably changed accordingly.

We have already seen the beginnings of this change in the last chapter, as Christianity became an urban religion, rather than a rural one, whose believers spoke primarily Greek, rather than Aramaic. Christianity remained a predominantly Greek-speaking religion for a long time. Even in the western, Latin-speaking half of the empire, including Rome, most churches seem to have been made up mainly of people who spoke Greek as their first language. No doubt there were Latin-speakers too, and indeed it seems that parts at least of the Bible were translated into Latin in this period; but it was not until around the year AD 200 that Latin Christian writers began to appear.

THE DECLINE OF JEWISH CHRISTIANITY
At the same time, Christianity became finally divorced from Judaism. Quite how this happened is hard for us to tell, but several factors seem to have been involved. The first was the great success in the early years of the Christian missions to the Gentiles, coupled with the relative failure of those to the Jews; by the end of the first century AD, there were far more Gentile Christians than there were Jewish ones. Another factor was the rapidly changing nature of Judaism during this period. As we saw in the last chapter, the destruction of the Temple in AD 70 led to the rise of the Pharisaic party within Judaism and the condemnation of Christianity by AD 90.

If the Jews were hostile to the Christians, the Christians were happy to return the favour. Paul's subtle discussions of the role of the Law in Christian theology gave way to simpler condemnations of anything associated with Judaism. Thus, the readers of Titus 1:10 (a letter traditionally attributed to Paul, but now commonly thought to have been written years after his death) were warned against 'many rebellious people, idle

talkers and deceivers, especially those of the circumcision'. Ignatius of Antioch, writing to the church in Magnesia in AD 107, stated that 'it is monstrous to talk of Jesus Christ and to practise Judaism'. The Christian community was the 'New Israel', with whom God had made a New Covenant; there was thus no longer a place for the Old Israel.

Yet the original mission to the Jews had had at least some success. Even at the end of the first century there were people who were both Jewish and Christian, or at least who regarded themselves as such. What happened to them? This subject is one of the biggest mysteries in the history of early Christianity. Their voices apparently fell silent and although there are some clues a definitive answer is yet to be found. It seems likely that some of the heretical views attacked by Christians in the second and third centuries, such as Ebionism (which we shall look at shortly), were Jewish Christian in origin. Thus, the Jewish Christians apparently continued to exist as a fading, minority voice within Christianity in the empire. Outside it, they may have done better. There were many Jews in Persia

A nineteenth-century depiction of the Eleusian mysteries.

and the origins of Christianity in that area are rather obscure; it may well be that Jewish Christianity flourished there. Intriguingly, there are some cases where Christianity has gone Jewish again. The best example is Ethiopia, where, as we shall see in Chapter 4, Hellenistic-style Christianity arrived in the fourth century in a country that already had a large Jewish population. What resulted was a Christianity that was highly influenced by Judaism, but which did not have historical roots in the 'original' Jewish Christian movement. The same could be said of modern 'Messianic Judaism', whose members regard themselves as Jews – and are culturally completely Jewish – but who believe in Jesus as the messiah.

INSTITUTIONS AND RITES

As Christianity was becoming less Jewish, so it was becoming more Hellenistic. The rapid spread of the religion throughout the empire even within the first century meant that it quickly became part of the philosophical melting pot that was Hellenism. In some ways Christianity came to resemble Roman religion. For example, where the Romans honoured different gods and virtues, the Christians venerated those who died in the faith. The martyrs were not worshipped, of course, but their psychological role to Christians was probably not unlike that of the various gods to pagans.

A more vexed question is the development of Christian rites, especially the Eucharist. How did this become a liturgical event, a church service, rather than a formalized meal? We do not really know, only that it did. Justin Martyr, writing in the middle of the second century to a non-Christian audience, explained that Christians would meet early in the morning – especially on Sundays, the Lord's Day – to share this service. He also reported that, when Jesus' words of institution were repeated, the bread and wine were changed, and gained the power of spiritually nourishing the recipient. This attitude is also found in Ignatius, some decades earlier, for whom the Eucharist was

'the medicine of immortality'.

Many have argued that the way in which the Eucharist became the central service for Christians, a rather mysterious 'rite' to which only the initiated (those who had been baptized) were welcome, closely paralleled the mystery religions. Some of the paraphernalia of the mystery cults became used by the Christians: white robes for people being baptized, candles and so on. Baptisms were conducted during the night before Easter Day, another 'secretive' practice similar to the initiation rites of the mystery religions. Like those of the mystery cults, the Christian rites became associated with special places. Just as the mystery religions used holy temples or other locations, so too the Christians, by the third century, were using purpose-built churches – rather than people's houses – to hold their services. There was a corresponding sense that these churches were holy, that the tables upon which the Eucharist was celebrated were altars, and that the ceremony had special powers.

Nevertheless, it is important to recognize that, although many practices were taken from the mystery religions, the basic rites themselves – baptism and Eucharist – came ultimately from Judaism, via the life of Jesus himself. However Hellenized they may sometimes have become, they were not Hellenistic in origin.

HELLENISTIC THEOLOGY

There was more development in what Christians believed, as the categories of Hellenistic philosophy began to determine the way Christians thought. The great figure most associated with this shift was the apologist Justin Martyr, a philosopher of the Platonic school who converted to Christianity. Even after his conversion, Justin regarded himself as a professional philosopher and continued to wear the distinctive cloak of that profession. He discussed the issues of the day with other philosophers and students in Rome, where he promoted Christianity as a philosophical alternative to Platonism, Stoicism and the rest. This attitude was in itself enormously

In a herald's voice I cry: Let peoples of every nation come and receive the immortality that flows from baptism. This is the water that is linked to the Spirit, the water that irrigates Paradise, makes the earth fertile, gives growth to plants, and brings forth living creatures. In short, this is the water by which a man receives new birth and life, the water in which even Christ was baptized, the water into which the Holy Spirit descended in the form of a dove.

Hippolytus of Rome (attrib.), *Sermon on Epiphany*

important. But the content of Justin's teaching also showed signs of significant development compared to New Testament times. Where Paul had preached about Christ, Justin seems to have been more interested in God and how he relates to the world. In this he was greatly influenced by both the Platonists and the Stoics. From them both he inherited the idea of the 'Logos' or World Soul, a kind of second God, who acts as an intermediary between the high God and the world. The Logos, in Justin's view, is like the ray of light from the sun, distinct from the sun but inseparable from it. The Logos is the power of God active on earth. But the Logos is also Christ. It was as the Logos that Christ existed before his life on earth, and as the Logos he now orders and runs the universe.

This emphasis on the heavenly Logos, on his relationship with God the Father and with the physical world, meant a corresponding lack of emphasis on the earthly Jesus and his life and death. Shortly after Justin's death in AD 165, a follower of his named Athenagoras wrote a *Plea for the Christians* in which he managed to present the ideas of Christianity without mentioning the names 'Jesus' or 'Christ' at all! Both Justin and Athenagoras were writing for non-Christian audiences, and they were arguing that Christianity was a reasonable religion which fitted in well with Hellenistic philosophy. That might account, to some degree, for the way in which they presented it. Yet an even more striking example of this 'Hellenizing' of Christianity is a Roman lawyer named Marcus Minucius Felix, writing in around AD 200. His defence of Christianity is largely a defence of monotheism and of the Christian lifestyle and, remarkably, he *denies* that Christians worship a man named Jesus! It is not clear what we should make of this, except that there was evidently a great deal of variety in belief among Christians of this period.

In fact, this variation of beliefs, and the attempts of educated Christians to present their views to a sceptical world, were the beginnings of what we now recognize as Christian theology.

An imaginative engraving of Justin Martyr by Michael Burgh.

HERESY, ORTHODOXY, AND THE BIRTH OF THEOLOGY

We saw in the last chapter how disputes and disagreements arose in the church in the first century. The end of the New Testament period did not see this situation calm down. On the contrary, it became worse. In the second century, there were a number of differing voices within the broad tradition of Christianity – and they were on a collision course.

THE NEW PROPHECY
One important movement was Montanism, which was founded in the second half of the second century by a Phrygian named Montanus. Shortly after becoming a Christian, Montanus believed he was given a new revelation, which appointed him as the leader of the church in its final days before the reappearance of Christ. His main disciples were two prophetesses named Prisca and Maximilla,

I confess that I both boast and with all my strength strive to be found a Christian; not because the teachings of Plato are different from those of Christ, but because they are not in all respects similar.

Justin Martyr, Second Apology 13, c. AD 156

who spoke with what their followers believed was the voice of the Holy Spirit. The movement's followers therefore called it the 'New Prophecy'; 'Montanism', like many labels of this period, was applied by their opponents. The Montanists did not preach any particular doctrines that anyone objected to, but other Christians were disturbed by the ecstatic, wild demonstrations that accompanied the prophecies. They were not always happy about the prominence of women in the movement, either.

Most of the Montanist prophecies were concerned with morality, and they taught a very strict way of living. They were harsher than most Christians to those who failed to live up to the standard, and they denied that post-baptismal sin could be forgiven at all. Many people were attracted by the movement and it spread beyond Anatolia, where it originated, to the whole empire. It proved especially popular in Africa. Here, as elsewhere, it developed an ecclesiastical structure of its own, with its own priests and bishops working as rivals to the mainstream ones. Mystical rites were celebrated in secret, apparently based partly on standard Christian ones but also on imitating the ecstatic trances of the prophetesses. Thus, the movement began to resemble the pagan mystery religions. The death of Montanus and his prophetesses, and the non-reappearance of Christ, did not harm the movement's vitality, and it was still in existence – as a minor, secretive cult – in the sixth century.

EBIONISM

Although the Montanists agreed with other Christians in doctrine, many groups did not. One major disagreement was over the nature of Jesus. Was he human, God or something else? The Docetists, who denied Jesus' true humanity, were still around, and they were joined by their opposite number, the Ebionites. These people were condemned primarily because they regarded Jesus simply as a human being and nothing more, but there seems to have been more to them than that.

Their name comes from the Aramaic for 'poor' – those to whom Jesus had promised the kingdom of God. Judging by the fragments that remain of their writings, the Ebionites regarded themselves as Jews who believed in Jesus. Before Jesus, Judaism had revolved around sacrifices in the Temple; now, they believed, it was to revolve around obeying the Law in the light of the teaching of Jesus. They seem to have regarded Paul – and the Gentile form of Christianity which he founded – as a heretical movement. Here, then, we have what seems to be a group descended from the 'original' Jewish Christians, increasingly marginalized by 'mainstream' gentile Christianity. It existed mainly on the eastern fringes of the empire, around Jerusalem and perhaps in Persia; and very little is known of it. The Ebionites were still around in the fourth century, but as far as most Christians were concerned, they were a minor, heretical sect.

GNOSTICISM

Without doubt the biggest and most controversial movement within Christianity in the post-New Testament period was Gnosticism. There is enormous disagreement between scholars over practically everything to do with Gnosticism: where it came from, when it was around, even what, precisely, it was. This in itself shows that it was a very vague movement. Unlike Montanism, which was a single sect, the Gnostics were not one group but a whole host of movements with similar views or ideas. They came in different varieties and strengths, and it seems that some were very similar to 'mainstream' Christianity and existed within Christianity, whilst others were so alien they were not really Christians at all but followers of a separate religion.

Although different Gnostics believed different things, a basic conviction common to them all was dualism. They believed in two principles of good and evil, intrinsically opposed. Moreover, these were made concrete in two great divisions of reality – the physical and the spiritual. The physical world was evil, and the spiritual world was good. It seems likely that this basic view owed much to Zoroastrianism and perhaps something to Platonism.

This belief entailed a number of other distinctive doctrines. First, they needed to explain how such an evil world came to exist. The good God could not have created it. Therefore, some believed in a lesser God, an ignorant or evil one, called the 'Demiurge' or 'Creator', who fashioned the physical world. Some developed an elaborate mythology to explain how this creator and matter came to exist in the first place. Valentinus, an extremely influential Gnostic who lived in the first half of the second century, believed that the spiritual world contained thirty-one deities, arranged in a hierarchy from the highest God of all, 'Bythos' or 'Depth', ranging down to 'Sophia' or 'Wisdom'. Sophia rebelled, dissatisfied with her position at the bottom of the divine scale; she was restored, but her 'Passion' was purged from her and cast out. Out of this Passion emerged matter and the Demiurge, who, unaware of the spiritual world, believed himself to be God, and made the physical world. This ignorant Creator was the 'God' of the Old Testament, a different being from the loving Father of the New Testament.

Bizarre stories? Certainly – but they were intended to tell the truth about human nature. We are created out of imperfect 'Passion', cast out of heaven – and so we are flawed, but we still retain a spark of our heavenly origins. Gnostics such as Valentinus believed that salvation consisted of escaping from the evil, physical world and returning that spiritual spark to the divine realm. This could only really happen after death, but many Gnostics believed they could start the process now by living ascetic, austere lives, involving themselves with matter as little as possible. Others reasoned that, if the material world is evil, it doesn't really matter what you do to it, and so they lived as libertines with no moral rules at all.

The word 'gnostic' meant 'one who knows', and Gnosticism was about secret knowledge. Valentinus believed that only some people have the spiritual spark and the chance of salvation, and so only they could be taught these doctrines. Gnosticism was a secret religion with esoteric knowledge and an inner core of initiates – thus, again we see what may have been the influence of the mystery religions. Some Gnostics believed that these secret teachings came from Jesus. But who was he? Clearly not both God and a physical human being, because the good God could not touch evil matter. Some Gnostics were therefore Docetics, denying that Jesus was material at all. Others distinguished between the man Jesus and the spiritual being Saviour, who spoke through him. As messiah, Jesus had been sent by the Old Testament God – who was the ignorant Creator. But if you listened to him carefully, you could hear the message of the divine Saviour, sent by the real, higher God.

THE FOUNDATION OF ORTHODOXY

Many – both Christians and pagans – were shocked by ideas such as these. One who opposed them was a late second-century Christian from Anatolia, Irenaeus, who later moved to Lyons in what is now France. Here he encountered Gnosticism, and in around AD 180 he wrote a very long book describing and attacking it. Irenaeus hated pretty much everything to do with Gnosticism. He hated the way it denigrated the material world, in which he believed God took an active interest. He hated the way it split Christ up or refused to recognize his true humanity. He hated the way Gnostics distinguished between the Old Testament God and the New Testament God, and how this meant that they could not see the importance of history. Christianity, he believed, must be rooted in its Jewish past. God had been working in Old Testament times, and the church was the embodiment of his promises to Abraham and his family.

I said to the Saviour, 'Lord, will all the souls be brought safely into the pure light?' He replied, 'Great things have come into your mind, for it is hard to explain them to anyone except those from the immovable race. Those on whom the life-giving Spirit will come down with power will be saved. They will become perfect and worthy of greatness, and they will be purified there from all evil. Then they will think of nothing but incorruption, which will occupy all their thoughts from then on, without anger or envy or jealousy or desire for anything. They are not affected by anything apart from being in the flesh, which they put up with while they look forward to the time when the receivers of the body will meet them. For they endure all things and keep going under all things, so that they may finish the good fight and inherit eternal life.'

From the *Apocryphon of John*, a Gnostic Gospel of the second century AD

The apostles received for us the Gospel from our Lord Jesus Christ, and our Lord Jesus Christ received it from God… [The apostles] appointed bishops and deacons, and gave a rule of succession, so that when they had fallen asleep, others, who had been approved, might succeed to their ministry.

1 Clement, c. AD 96

Irenaeus of Lyons, in a mosaic from the sixth-century Hagia Sophia, Istanbul.

Irenaeus represented what we might call 'mainstream', non-gnostic Christianity. In opposition to the Gnostics' claims of a secret tradition, handed down only by 'those in the know', Irenaeus argued that the church's beliefs are quite open and accessible to all. In making this claim, Irenaeus was setting out the standards of what would become orthodoxy.

Tertullian, who lived a few years later, did much the same thing, although not in opposition to the Gnostics. Irenaeus and Tertullian agreed that the Christian faith originated with Jesus. He had taught the truth to his followers, particularly the twelve apostles; and after Pentecost these apostles and other disciples had spread the good news throughout the world, founding churches as they went. There they taught the gospel as Jesus had taught it to them; and they ordained ministers and bishops to continue the work after they had died. And this had continued down ever since. Thus, there was an unbroken chain of tradition from Jesus to the present day. This idea, the 'apostolic principle', was a central concern of the church fathers, and it would continue to be extremely important in later centuries.

This meant that there was a standard against which beliefs could be tested. As Tertullian put it in his *Prescription against the heretics*:

It is clear that all doctrine which agrees with the apostolic churches – those moulds and original sources of the faith – must be considered true, as undoubtedly containing what those churches received from the apostles, the apostles from Christ, Christ from God. And all doctrine must be considered false which contradicts the truth of the churches and apostles of Christ and God.

A Christian philosophy: Origen

The Egyptian philosopher, theologian, and biblical exegete Origen (c. AD 185–254) was the most influential of all the early Christian Greek-speaking theologians, and the architect of most of the substructure of Christian dogma and biblical theology in the late antique period.

When Origen was seventeen, in AD 202, a severe persecution broke out in Alexandria and his father was executed. To offset the ruination of his family, the young Origen received the lowly appointment as a catechist from the local church. At the same time, he followed advanced courses in philosophy with some of the leading intellectuals of his day and began to develop his own school, living an ascetical life as a philosopher–sage. Later his ascetical life was rumoured to be the result of a decision to have himself castrated. It was a story reported a century after his death by Eusebius, bishop of Caesarea, but it is highly unlikely, as Origen himself speaks of those who interpret the Gospel text on castration (Matthew 19:12) in a literal way as little better than fools.

Origen's guiding star in his intellectual life was the belief that the highest goals of philosophy were reconcilable with the mysterious plan of the divine wisdom (the Logos) and that, in the sacred scriptures, the gift of revelation and the human quest for enlightenment would meet. And so, from the beginning of his studies in philosophy, Origen deliberately channelled all his ideas through a complex system of symbolic biblical exegesis, setting out rules of interpretation that would be massively influential on all Christians who followed. Origen's approach was governed by the notion that the scripture was a single reality, a coherent corpus emanating from one mind, that of the Divine Logos. Its apparent multiplicities were but the masking of the eternal revelation under the illusory appearances of history and relative conditions. A text, therefore, had several layers of meaning. For Origen, those who stayed only with the literal meaning of the biblical text were unenlightened souls who had not realized that Jesus gave some of his teaching in the valleys and some on mountain tops. Only to the latter disciples, those who could ascend the mountains, did Jesus reveal himself transfigured (see Mark 9).

In AD 212 Origen travelled to Rome and heard the theologian Hippolytus lecture. It was the first of many tours and book-buying expeditions. He began to receive government invitations to present philosophical discourses, and his fame as a thinker extended far beyond Christian circles, making him the first truly international philosopher the Christian movement could boast of. Back in Alexandria he published *On first principles*, ambitiously designed as an introductory summary of Christian faith, with a vast scope, trying to relate how the Christian worldview embraces cosmology, philosophy and religion. His book attempts to offer a definitive answer to the major issues raised by all other schools before him. But the local bishop, Demetrius, began to grow suspicious of the young theologian.

These tensions led to Origen's permanent departure from Alexandria in AD 231. He was adopted by the learned bishops of Jerusalem and Caesarea, where he established a new advanced school, one of the first examples of Christianity's embrace of higher education as part of its role in establishing a new civilization. At Caesarea Origen finished his greatest work, the *Commentary on the Gospel of John*, and his most influential writing, the *Commentary on the Song of Songs*.

In c. AD 249 the accession of the emperor Decius unleashed a new storm of hostility against the Christians of Palestine. Origen was sought out, and the Roman governor ordered him to be tortured carefully (so he would not die before denying the faith). He was set in the iron collar and stretched over 'four spaces' (ratchet marks in the rack) which would more or less have permanently crippled him. His courage and fidelity, however, outlasted his persecutors' efforts, and in the subsequent peace, in AD 253, he was taken into convalescence by the church, and spent a year dying. Eusebius tells us that the old man's primary anxiety was that he would have time to finish a series of encouraging letters, so that those who had suffered losses in the persecution would not be left 'uncomforted'. Sadly these last works have not survived. He died aged 69 with a martyr's honour, if not a martyr's crown. If he had possessed that status formally his works might not have suffered the depletions that have reduced them over the centuries. His writings were ordered to be burned in the sixth century, but even so a massive amount has survived, and his influence can be felt in almost all aspects of Christian dogma, spirituality, exegesis, and not least in the desire to connect faith and philosophy in day-to-day Christian living.

JOHN MCGUCKIN

A page from the
Codex Sinaiticus.

possessed writings by the apostles and their immediate disciples which expressed the rule of faith in written form. Justin Martyr wrote that the Christians regularly read 'the memoirs of the apostles' when they met: evidently it was believed that this would help to keep the congregation on the straight and narrow. By the time of Tertullian, Christians regarded these writings as equivalent in importance to the Jewish scriptures. Tertullian talked of 'two testaments which are divine scripture', and his contemporary Clement of Alexandria was the first to talk about 'the New Testament', referring to this collection of apostolic writings. Where the Hebrews had appealed to a single collection of old writings, the Christians – the new Israel, as they believed themselves to be – had two collections, the Old and the New Testaments. Together, the two collections would make up the Christian Bible (so called from the Greek word for 'book').

They were not quite sure which books were part of this written canon, though. Irenaeus was clear that there were four Gospels which described Jesus' life. These are the four Gospels we know, and Irenaeus attributed them to Matthew, John (followers of Jesus in his lifetime) and Mark and Luke (followers, respectively, of Peter and Paul). It seems, though, that these attributions originated in the middle of the second century at the earliest; and the texts themselves are anonymous. Most modern scholars do not think that Irenaeus' attributions are correct. Many other gospels were used as well, especially by the Gnostics, but Irenaeus and most Christians rejected them as fictional (an assessment with which modern scholars do agree). The letters of Paul were also regarded as part of the canon, as were letters attributed to other apostles, especially Peter and John. The first letter of Clement of Rome (an important leader there in the closing years of the first century) was widely used, as was a work called *The Shepherd*, attributed to one Hermas, and a letter attributed to Paul's follower Barnabas. But there was no universal standard. In the Syriac-speaking

Therefore, the guarantee of correct belief was the authenticity of the tradition from Jesus via the apostles. Irenaeus agreed. In his *Against heresies*, Irenaeus identified certain churches as bearing this apostolic tradition most clearly. In his eyes, the church of Rome, which had been taught by both Peter and Paul, was the greatest of these, and he commented that 'it is a matter of necessity that every church should agree with this church, because of its primary authority'.

What the apostles had handed down was sometimes known as the 'rule of faith' or the 'canon' (a Greek word meaning 'measuring stick'). Beliefs could be held up to this measuring stick and compared. On this view, Gnosticism in its various forms failed the test, because it did not match the doctrines which had been handed down in the church of Rome and other apostolic foundations such as Jerusalem (James the Just), Ephesus (John) and Antioch (Paul).

THE ROLE OF SCRIPTURE
But the rule of faith was not simply an oral tradition. By the time of Irenaeus and Tertullian, Christians believed that they also

churches, most Christians read not the four canonical Gospels but a book by the second-century theologian Tatian called the *Diatesseron*, a compilation of the four Gospels into a single narrative. And another approach was taken by a man named Marcion, who was active in Rome in the middle of the second century. Marcion believed that the Old Testament God had been evil, different from the New Testament God – a belief shared by Gnostics, although Marcion appears to have held no other Gnostic views. Marcion therefore thought that Christianity should purge itself of all Jewish influence. The only apostolic writings he would accept were the Gospel of Luke and some of Paul's letters, all edited to remove anything 'Jewish'.

The canon of the New Testament as we know it was not generally agreed until the fourth century, although the most important writings, the Gospels and most of the letters, were fairly universally used by the time of Tertullian. The first list giving precisely the 27 books that we know as the New Testament was given by the bishop of Alexandria, Athanasius, in a letter to his flock of AD 367. Athanasius regarded the other books, such as *The Shepherd* of Hermas and the letter of 1 Clement, as useful books, but not part of the canon. His list was approved by councils at Hippo in AD 393 and Carthage in AD 397, so that is the time when the canon of the New Testament became 'official'.

Athanasius also lived at approximately the same time as a certain copy of the New Testament writings was made, which contained all the books Athanasius listed as well as Barnabas and Hermas. This manuscript still exists. Known as the *Codex Sinaiticus*, it is the oldest complete copy of the New Testament in existence. A slightly older version, known as the *Codex Vaticanus*, also contains most of the Old Testament, but lacks some of the New. Today the *Codex Vaticanus* is held by the Vatican in Rome, while the *Codex Sinaiticus* can be seen at the British Library in London. Manuscripts like these, and even older (though less complete) ones, enable scholars to be sure that the text of the Bible that we have today is the same as that used by the early church.

Why were these writings considered important? Effectively, the church fathers had a two-pronged approach to the New Testament. On the one hand, they were authoritative simply because they were believed to be the writings of the apostles. In other words, they were part of the 'rule of faith', not the source of it, to be consulted in conjunction with the current teaching of the apostolic churches. Thus Tertullian, in his *Prescription against the heretics*, argued that heretics did not simply misinterpret the scriptures – they actually had no right to be reading them at all, because they did not read them in accordance with the teaching of the churches. The scriptures, Tertullian bullishly concluded, were the property of the churches and of orthodox Christians like himself, and the heretics were trespassing on them. Such an attitude could be gleaned from the New Testament itself, for 2 Peter 1:20 stated that 'no prophecy of scripture is a matter of one's own interpretation' – that is, you cannot simply sit down, read the Bible and draw your own conclusions. You have to read it in light of the teachings of the church, with which it forms a unity.

On this understanding, the writings of the New Testament drew their intrinsic authority from their connection to the apostles, and the criterion for whether a book should be part of the canon was whether it had really been written by an apostle or immediate disciple. For example, there was much disagreement even as late as the fourth century over the book of Revelation. Some believed this was the work of the apostle John and they included it in the canon; others denied it was his work and they excluded it. Dionysius, bishop of Alexandria in the third century, studied the language and ideas of Revelation and compared them to the Gospel of John. He concluded that it was not by the same author – a conclusion with which most modern scholars agree, for much the same reasons – and he therefore

My son, you should diligently concentrate on reading the sacred Scriptures. I say again, concentrate! For we who read the things of God need to work hard, to avoid saying or thinking anything rash about them. As you concentrate on studying the things of God, in a faithful way that pleases him well, knock at its locked door, and the gatekeeper will open it for you, as Jesus says, 'The gatekeeper opens the gate for him' [John 10:3]. And concentrating in this way on divine study, with unfaltering trust in God search for the meaning of the holy Scriptures, which so many people have missed. Don't be satisfied with knocking and seeking, for prayer is the one thing that is indispensable for knowing the things of God. The Saviour told us this, and said not just, 'Knock, and the door will be opened for you; search, and you will find,' but also, 'Ask, and it will be given to you' [Matthew 7:7].

Origen, *Letter to Gregory the Wonderworker*, c. AD 235

excluded it from the canon. However, this text was eventually included as the last book of the New Testament. The anonymous letter to the Hebrews posed another problem. Some people believed that Paul had written it, but there was no consensus on the matter; this book was thus regarded with some suspicion, and was only rarely used in the western church until after the fourth century, when it did make it into the canon after all.

At the same time as this 'historical' approach to the New Testament, there was what we might call a 'spiritual' one. Many Christians believed that these writings were not simply records of the beliefs of the first Christians – they were records of God himself. The first Christians, like the Jews, believed that God spoke through scripture; as 2 Peter 1:21 put it, 'no prophecy ever came by human will, but men and women moved by the Holy Spirit spoke from God'.

This was applied to the Jewish scriptures as well as to the New Testament, and the Christians who rejected the views of the Gnostics and Marcion claimed that the same God who inspired the New Testament had inspired what came to be regarded as the Old Testament. The Christians invariably read the Old Testament in a Greek translation known as the Septuagint, which had been made by Jewish scholars at Alexandria in the second or third century BC. This meant that there was less uncertainty among Christians over which books were in the Old Testament compared to the New, since the Septuagint was a standard translation of a particular set of books – the Pentateuch, the Prophets, and other ancient Jewish works. But this was a sticking point between Christians and Jews. As we saw in the previous chapter, the Council of Jamnia had decided that Jews would read their scriptures in Hebrew, and some regarded the Septuagint as an unreliable translation. Also, the canon established at Jamnia did not quite correspond to the books in the Septuagint. The Septuagint contained several extra books, which the church continued to use, but some Christians regarded as a kind of

supplement to the Old Testament rather than really part of it. Origen, for example, consulted with Jewish rabbis on this matter and concluded that the extra books – known as 'deuterocanonical' or 'of the secondary canon' – were not exactly canonical, although they were still to be used with profit. However, by the late fourth and early fifth centuries, Popes Damasus and Innocent I determined that the deuterocanonical books were fully part of the Old Testament canon. From this time on into the Middle Ages, the books were generally regarded as part of the canon, although there were always some who were uneasy about using them because of their absence from the Jewish canon. It should be noted that the order of the texts in the Christian Old Testament, which ends on Malachi's stern prophecy of a curse on those who do not recognize the prophet Elijah who is to come (Malachi 4:5–6), differs from that of the Hebrew Bible, which rounds off at 2 Chronicles 36:23 with a call to go up to the Temple of the Lord in Jerusalem.

Meanwhile, the Christians defended their use of the Septuagint in the first place, and generally thought that the divine inspiration had occurred when this translation was made, rather than to the original Hebrew authors. In the fourth century, when the Christian scholar Jerome translated the Old Testament into Latin, he was greatly criticized by many (including Augustine) for doing so from the Hebrew instead of from the Septuagint.

For just as Hellenistic religion held that the gods had spoken through Homer and Hesiod, and that truth about the divine and the ethical could be found in their works, so too the Christians increasingly believed the same thing about their own sacred books, the Septuagint and the New Testament. Some believed that God had spoken through the authors as if he were playing an instrument (just as traditionalist pagans held about Homer and Hesiod), whilst others believed that the authors had retained their own personalities and had had some say over what they wrote.

A representative of this latter approach was Origen, the most important theologian of the third century. Origen was devoted to scripture, both Old and New Testaments, and believed that progress in the Christian life was directly related to progress in reading and understanding scripture. But there was much in the Bible that was not very edifying. The Old Testament was full of long and boring lists of genealogies or priestly garments, as well as accounts of bloody battles. Moreover, some canonical books contradicted others, or contained stories that were intrinsically hard to believe, at least for a philosophically inclined Alexandrian. What was to be made of this? Origen took exactly the same approach as the Hellenistic traditionalists: he appealed to allegory. What the scriptural authors tell us is always true and they cannot be mistaken or contradict each other; but there are different kinds of truth. Scripture has an 'obvious' meaning, the plain sense of the text on first reading; but it has deeper meaning as well. Where the plain sense seems inadequate or wrong, Origen tells us that we need to look for the 'spiritual' sense.

The procedure was identical to that used by pagans when reading Homer, and there is something slightly comic about Origen's book *Against Celsus*, which dealt with the criticisms that this pagan opponent of Christianity had made a century earlier. Both Celsus and Origen ridicule their opponents for venerating violent and immoral ancient writings, whilst defending their own through allegory. It is as if neither side realized that they were both behaving in exactly the same way, except to different collections of texts.

CHAPTER 3

CHRISTIAN ROME

The second and third centuries saw Christianity grow slowly but steadily throughout the Roman empire, despite the best efforts of a number of emperors to stop it. But it was still a minority concern. By the end of this period, no more than perhaps one Roman in ten was a Christian, and there was still no official position on what they were to believe. All this was to change during the momentous fourth century, possibly the most extraordinary hundred years that the church would ever experience. By the end of it Christianity would have changed forever.

THE CONVERSION OF CONSTANTINE

He said that about noon, when the day was already beginning to decline, he saw with his own eyes the trophy of a cross of light in the heavens, above the sun, and bearing the inscription: CONQUER BY THIS. At this sight he himself was struck with amazement and his whole army also, which followed him on this expedition and witnessed the miracle.

This story is taken from *The life of Constantine* by Eusebius of Caesarea, a Christian writer and historian who lived in the first half of the fourth century. It describes one of the most important events in western history: the moment when Constantine the Great (c. AD 274–337), a powerful general who had been proclaimed Caesar by his troops, embraced Christianity. It was a fateful moment, just before the Battle of the Milvian Bridge near Rome in AD 312, as the general prepared to face his rival for the imperial throne. As he later told the story to Eusebius personally, he was pondering which gods he should ask for assistance in the forthcoming battle, when he saw the sign of the cross in the sky. Constantine took the celestial advice, marched under the sign of the cross and won a resounding victory to become the first Christian Roman emperor.

Could anything more unexpected have happened to the church? Just a couple of years earlier it had been buckling under the harshest persecutions ever, under the emperors Diocletian and Galerius. But now, Constantine and his eastern co-ruler, Licinius, issued the Edict of Milan, officially ending all persecution and allowing freedom of religion throughout the empire. Christianity was not made the official religion of the empire, but Constantine promoted the faith, and now it would flourish like never before.

It is hard to imagine what it must have been like for the church at this time. Many regarded the sudden reversal in its fortunes as a sign that the end of time must be approaching – the triumph of Christ must be at hand for the Roman emperor himself to have become his servant. The final book of Eusebius's *Ecclesiastical history*, an account of the church from its early days to his own time, consists of nothing but rapturous praises to God and to the emperor for ushering in this new age. And in a *Panegyric to Constantine*, delivered on the thirtieth anniversary of the emperor's accession, the same author praised him as an earthly image of the divine monarchy, halfway between heaven and earth:

Our emperor, like the radiant sun, illuminates the most distant subjects of his

---

We have determined, with sound and upright purpose, that no-one at all should be denied the liberty to choose and follow the religious observances of the Christians. Each person shall be given the freedom to devote his mind to whatever religion he thinks best for himself, so that in everything God (whom we worship freely from our hearts) may show us his usual care and favour.

The Edict of Milan, AD 313

empire through the presence of the Caesars, as with the far piercing rays of his own brightness… Invested as he is with a semblance of heavenly sovereignty, he directs his gaze above, and frames his earthly government according to the pattern of that Divine original, feeling strength in its conformity to the monarchy of God.

Constantine – who became sole ruler of the empire after defeating Licinius in AD 324 – was one of the greatest emperors in Rome's history. He reformed the army, revitalized the economy, and generally saw to it that the empire, which had been in danger of falling apart through a combination of debased currency, corruption, political instability and external threats, survived. His attitude to Christianity, though, is unclear and remains controversial. As we shall see in this chapter, Constantine seems to have been more concerned for religious unity than for doctrinal accuracy. Did his faith in the Christian God really go beyond an opportunistic belief that here was a source of military, political and perhaps metaphysical power? Famously, Constantine was not baptized until he lay on his deathbed – although as we have seen, this was quite common at the time, especially for those in the military. Pagan gods remained on the coins until AD 320, and the emperor retained the old pagan title of *pontifex maximus*. Meanwhile, however, his armies continued to march under the Christian Chi-Rho sign. Sunday was made a holiday, and soldiers had to attend church parades.

Most strikingly of all, the emperor founded a new imperial capital in the east. Known as New Rome, this city was built on the site of an ancient town called Byzantium, on the west coast of the Bosphorus, the channel linking the Black Sea to the Mediterranean. The city was provided with all the amenities of Roman civilization – a forum, a basilica, public baths and the rest, as well as the trappings of the imperial court. But unlike in Old Rome, there were no temples. Indeed, Constantine decreed that no pagan rites would ever be performed in his new capital.

Instead, churches were built. New Rome was a potent symbol of the new empire; an empire whose centre of gravity was shifting eastwards into the Greek-speaking half of the Mediterranean, and which was built upon the worship of the Christian God, not of pagan deities. New Rome was usually known as Constantinople – 'the city of Constantine' – and by the end of the fourth century it was not only the imperial capital but the largest and most culturally vibrant city in the eastern empire. It would remain the most important Christian city in the world for over a thousand years.

Constantine's dream, by the Italian painter Piero della Francesca (d. 1492). The painting shows an angel telling Constantine of his victory at Milvian Bridge, the night before the battle.

Christianity had, as it were, come out of the closet, even if Christians were still in the minority. There was to be no more worshipping in converted houses or hiding underground, although the Roman catacombs now became more popular as a place of pilgrimage. People came to pay their respects to the great heroes of the past – for the end of persecution meant there were no new martyrs. Meanwhile, a new kind of church appeared – the basilica. In the empire a 'basilica' was a large hall, used as a sort of town hall and courthouse in one. It consisted of a long hall, possibly with side aisles separated from the main part (the 'nave') by pillars. Shortly after his conversion, Constantine turned an old palace in Rome – known as

the Lateran Palace, which belonged to his wife – into a church. This church, sometimes known as the 'Golden Basilica' because of the treasures that were lavished upon it, followed the style of these basilicas quite closely. The cathedral is still there, now known as St John Lateran; although it has been rebuilt frequently over the centuries it remains the Catholic cathedral of Rome. Constantine also began a new church, St Peter's basilica, in the same style. At its heart was the tomb believed to be that of Peter himself.

In addition to basilicas, new kinds of buildings appeared – baptisteries, for conducting baptisms, and *martyria*, shrines to the martyrs. In contrast to the basilicas, these buildings were normally round, in the style of old pagan temples – indeed,

The basilica of St John Lateran, Rome. The modern baroque-style façade was designed by the Florentine architect Alessandro Galilei (1691–1736) in the 1730s.

martyria were often built on the site of old temples, as the church encouraged people to shift their allegiances from the old gods to the martyrs. Later, attempts to combine these two styles – the long basilica and the round baptistery or *martyrion* – would produce the remarkable achievements of Byzantine architecture.

Basilica churches sprang up through the empire, and the earlier house churches, or churches built in the style of houses, quickly fell out of use. State sponsorship of Christianity led to far more people joining the church, so the buildings became correspondingly larger to fit them all in. These churches also helped to define further the roles of the clergy and the laity within the Christian community. At the east end of the basilica (churches were always built facing east, the direction from which Christ was expected to return) was the sanctuary, where the priest performed the Eucharist and other services. The congregation, seated in the aisles to the side of the nave, would watch: thus there was a psychological separation between the two. The nave itself would be occupied by a choir. Beyond the sanctuary was the 'apse'. If this was a bishop's church, this is where he would sit, surrounded by his priests, who sat on a semicircular bench called a synthronon. Such a church would be called a 'cathedral' (from the Greek word for 'seat'). The fact that the sanctuary was between the bishop and the congregation was symbolic, for it meant that the holy mysteries were performed in the middle of the Christian community – just as Christ himself had lived in the midst of human society.

Bishops, meanwhile, became more important figures, both in their congregations and in society. They could now use the imperial post, previously restricted to state business. Growing congregations meant that the bishop was no longer a simple pastoral leader of a small group, as he had been in the past; in a large city he was more like a head of a modern corporation, in charge but delegating most of the actual running of the organization to lesser figures.

The bishop of a particularly large city – a metropolis – was known as a metropolitan. The Council of Antioch, held in AD 341, stated that a metropolitan had authority over his neighbouring bishops, but it was not always clear at this stage which bishops *were* metropolitans – there wasn't a clear 'set' of metropolitan sees (a 'see' or 'diocese' is the area under the control of a bishop). This would, however, have developed by the fifth century. By the sixth century, metropolitans were also commonly referred to as archbishops. Their special authority was represented by the 'pallium', a sort of scarf sent to them personally by the patriarch of Rome.

For above the metropolitans or archbishops were the patriarchs, the most important bishops of all. Again, it was not quite clear which bishops counted as patriarchs, at least at first, but everyone agreed on three – at Rome, Alexandria and Antioch. These cities, it should be noted, were all associated with important apostles, and so they also determined correct doctrine, according to the 'apostolic principle' of the 'rule of faith' that we saw in the last chapter. A patriarch could claim authority over lesser bishops who were geographically nearby. By the early fourth century, the patriarch of Alexandria regarded himself as primary over other Egyptian bishops, as well as those of Cyrenaica. Meanwhile, the patriarch of Rome was being seen as senior over his colleagues in Italy and much of the west. Antioch was in charge of the eastern churches, from Syria onwards. Almost all the bishops in the system were urban administrators, although there were a few given the task of overseeing rural Christian communities. These, known as *chorepiscopi*, were also subject to the ruling bishop of the area.

As church architecture and organization evolved to fit the new situation of the church in society, so too did Christian art. Until this point, Christians had conceived of art primarily as a means of communication, of

I think there's no need to go into details now about the length and breadth of the building, its indescribable splendour and majesty, and the brilliance of the work, with its lofty towers reaching the heavens, and the expensive cedars of Lebanon above them... Why would I need to describe the clever architectural planning and the perfect beauty of each part, when what the eye sees makes what the ear hears unnecessary? For when [Paulinus, the bishop] had finished the temple, he gave it high thrones in honour of those who preside, and also with seats arranged in an orderly way throughout the whole building. Finally, he placed in the middle the holy of holies, the altar, and so that the people couldn't get at it, he surrounded it with wooden lattice-work, covered with detailed and artistic carvings, making a wonderful sight for those who saw it.

Eusebius, describing the new cathedral at Tyre, dedicated c. AD 314, *Ecclesiastical history* 10 conveying their ideas to each other. Since the religion was officially proscribed and subject to intermittent clampdowns, there was relatively little Christian art, and what there was existed mainly in hidden catacombs. Now, however, things changed radically. Churches remained relatively unadorned on the outside, but inside they were lavishly decorated. Painted frescos covered the walls, as did rich mosaics, often featuring extensive use of gold, whilst floors were made of marble. The objects used in worship, such as the cup and the plate used in the Eucharist, might now be made of silver or gold and richly ornamented. Enriched by generous donations from the emperor and from other nobles, and exempt from paying taxes, the church could afford this sort of thing for the first time. But it had important spiritual meaning too. The Christians inherited from the Platonists a deep faith in the power of beauty to lead the mind to God. The rich furnishings of the great basilicas were intended to create a spiritual atmosphere, one that felt holy and set apart: here, worshippers could truly believe themselves caught up to heaven.

Another consequence of the fourth-century revolution was the emergence of pilgrimage. Constantine's mother, Helena, was also a Christian, and she devoted time to excavating Jerusalem in the hope of uncovering the places where Jesus spent his last days. And indeed, a number of sites were identified as those where Jesus held the Last Supper, was executed, rose from the dead and so on. So where Christians had already developed a sense of the holiness of time – for God intervened in history to save his people, and was the unseen force behind all history, as Irenaeus had insisted – they now developed one of the holiness of place, focusing on those places on earth where God had most clearly been active. There arose the desire to travel and visit those places, and by the end of the fourth century pilgrimages to Jerusalem were not uncommon. Some Christians disapproved of this, since they felt that God should properly be worshipped spiritually without regard to place (and also because such journeys necessitated men and women coming into close proximity), but the phenomenon would be an important element of Christianity in the years to come.

In modern times many people, both Christian and non-Christian, have deplored the transformation of the fourth-century church. It has even been said, with some exaggeration, that the conversion of Constantine was the worst thing that ever happened to Christianity. The riches and power that the church acquired practically overnight sit uneasily with the poverty of Jesus and the simplicity of his message, it is said, whilst the association of bishops with emperors led to complacency, corruption and a distorted worldview. Of course, that is something of a caricature: bishops did not suddenly become corrupt toadies, and neither did they start executing those whom they thought heretical, as is sometimes mistakenly charged. Certainly, imperial acceptance changed the church, but it also changed the empire. The church, in part, became the conscience of the empire. Christians retained a special place in their hearts for the poor; indeed, one of the most distinctive features of Christianity in a Roman context was the way it almost venerated the lowest class of society, 'the poor', as specially deserving of praise and help. In traditional Roman society, it was the duty of the rich to help their city, to leave endowments to help their fellow citizens; the notion that the poor deserved more help than anyone else was novel. So, too, was the notion that strangers and foreigners should be cared for. But the fourth century saw the construction not only of magnificent basilicas but also of houses known as *xenodocheia* ('houses for strangers') – hostels for travellers and for the poor and hungry. By the end of the fourth century, one of the main functions of the church was as the imperial welfare system; for

Just as one understands the Greek historians better when one has seen Athens, or the third book of Virgil when one has sailed to Troas or Sicily... so we also understand Scripture better when we have seen Judea with our own eyes, and discovered what still remains... That is why I took care to travel through this land.

Jerome, *On Chronicles*, preface, c. AD 380

until then there had been virtually no welfare system at all.

Strikingly, this welfare system extended to a kind of early version of legal aid. Constantine created an institution known as the 'episcopal audience', whereby bishops could act as civil judges in local disputes. The system was a great success, since it not only helped free up time in the official legal system but was very effective, as most bishops did their best to be fair and scrupulous, and on the whole did a good job. Many people converted to Christianity simply so they could bring their cases to the bishop instead of to the magistrate – and the service was, of course, free, unlike the services of conventional lawyers.

However, there was indeed a price to be paid for official acceptance. Church and state were becoming closely intertwined. The church enjoyed the protection and patronage of the emperor, but in return it would have to deal with the authority of the emperor. That was a new problem for Christianity, and it would be brought to the fore in a remarkable way in the other major event of the fourth century that would mark Christianity forever: the Arian crisis.

Two pheasants, from a fourth-century mosaic floor in the crypt of the basilica of Aquileia, Italy.

77

St Augustine in
debate with
St Ambrose, in a
mural by Benozzo
Gozzoli.

THE ARIAN CONFLICT

ARIUS

In AD 320 Alexander, bishop of Alexandria, held a council of local bishops in which he condemned the views of Arius (c. AD 250–336), a popular presbyter in the Alexandrian church. He wrote a circular letter to the other patriarchs explaining his actions.

Arius had been denounced for his views on the relationship between God and Christ. It will be remembered that, in the second century, Christian theologians such as Justin Martyr had used the old 'Logos' idea – ultimately taken from pagan philosophy – to try to express this relationship. Christ was the 'Logos', a sort of quasi-God who functions as God's agent. This had formed the basis for the development of what would become the doctrine of the Trinity. Origen had maintained this basic approach when he talked of the Father, the Son and the Holy Spirit: he had taught that the Father is the greatest of the three, and the Spirit the least. The Trinity was thus a sort of hierarchy. He also believed that the Son and the Spirit are generated by the Father eternally, which set him apart from the views of earlier writers such as Justin and Tertullian, who both thought there was a moment in time – shortly before the creation of the universe – when the Father actually generated the Son.

All these ideas were therefore floating about at the start of the fourth century, and none had been made 'official' – for no mechanism for making doctrines official had yet developed. In some ways, Arius represented something of a throwback to Justin's day. He believed that there was a time when the Son had come into being, and that the Son was definitely lower than the Father. However, he went further than Justin. Whilst the third-century theologians had been clear that the Son is God (in at least some sense), Justin had been a bit vague on the issue. Arius was not. He believed that the Son was not divine: he was a creature like any other. Certainly he was the greatest creature of all – a sort of mighty archangel – but he was not God. This, in his view, was the being who was incarnate in Jesus.

THE COUNCIL OF NICAEA

Arius, who regarded himself as a theological conservative, appealed against his condemnation. From his exile in Palestine he wrote songs expressing his views, which proved remarkably popular. The emperor Constantine called for a council of all bishops throughout the world to settle the matter. It met at Nicaea, across the Bosphoros from Constantinople, in AD 325. Constantine himself was present, as were – according to tradition – 318 bishops, mostly from the eastern, Greek-speaking half of the empire. These bishops agreed that the condemnation of Arius was fair, and they also agreed on a new statement of faith in the light of the affair:

We believe in God the Father almighty,
maker of all things, visible and invisible.
And in one Lord Jesus Christ,
the only-begotten of the Father,
that is, begotten of the substance of the Father,
God from God, light from light, true God
* from true God,*

Portrait of Arius, by the fourteenth-century Italian artist Andrea di Buonaiuto.

begotten, not made,
of the same substance as the Father,
through whom all things were made, in
heaven and earth;
who for us humans and our salvation came
down, took flesh, and was made human,
suffered and rose again on the third day,
ascended into heaven,
and will come to judge the living and the
dead.
And in the Holy Spirit.

This 'symbol' of Nicaea would become one of the most important Christian texts ever to be produced, the basis for the 'Nicene Creed' which is still recited in churches today. The creed is similar in form to another text, the 'Apostles' Creed', which was developing at around the same time. This summary of the faith appeared at some point in the first centuries of Christianity, certainly by the fourth century. Although never authoritative in quite the same way as the Nicene Creed, it has always been used extensively, especially in the western churches.

At the same time, the bishops condemned anyone who said that there was a time when the Son did not exist – one of Arius's key doctrines. In modern times, a number of wild claims have been made about the Council of Nicaea, often by conspiracy theorists hoping to show that Christianity as we know it was an invention of the emperor Constantine. We are told, for example, that the bishops were severely divided over the question of Arius, and the pro-Arius faction was silenced only by force on the emperor's orders; that Arius himself was beaten; and that at this council, Constantine decreed which books should be considered part of the Bible, effectively rewriting the history of the early church. In fact, the ancient sources tell us that only seventeen bishops supported Arius at the sessions, and by the end their number had been reduced to two. Arius was questioned at length, but there is no evidence that he was mistreated. The council did consider a number of other issues, including some of church organization and the date of Easter, but not the question of the canon of

scripture, which was settled half a century later. And although Constantine chaired the opening session and the final vote, he seems to have been absent from the intervening discussions and to have made few positive contributions beyond a plea for unity.

That might have been the end of it. But Arius continued to make a noise, and he had supporters. The emperor became convinced that they spoke for the majority of the church, and that at Nicaea he had been hoodwinked by a minority partisan group. In AD 336, he ordered the church to reverse the condemnation of Arius. Suddenly the church had a new and unprecedented problem. Instead of persecuting the church, the emperor was telling it what to do. Constantine was the sole master of the Roman empire and, as far as he was concerned, this made him the sole master of the church too; he even called himself a 'bishop'.

The immediate problem was solved by the timely death of Arius, which occurred in a remarkably grotesque fashion at a public toilet in Constantinople, where he suffered an unpleasant haemorrhage. Constantine himself died the following year.

THE CRISIS DEEPENS
The great Constantine was dead. His attitude – and the problems he posed to the church – lived on. His sons were named (confusingly) Constantine II, Constans and Constantius, and in a dramatic move Constantine had split the empire among them. Constantine II inherited the western part of the empire, Constans the middle and Constantius the east. All three had been raised as Christians, were apparently quite devout and continued to sponsor Christianity and try to discourage pagan practices. In AD 340 Constantine II went to war against Constans and was killed, his territory being absorbed into Constans's: therefore there were two emperors to contend with, Constans and Constantius. This was an enormously significant development, for the territory of Constans was the Latin-speaking, western half of the empire while that of Constantius was the

The novel ideas that [Arius and his followers] teach, contrary to the Scriptures, are these: God was not always a Father, but there was a time when God was not a Father. The Word of God did not always exist, but came into being from things that did not exist, for God, who exists, made him that did not exist, out of that which did not exist. So there was a time when he did not exist, for the Son is a created thing, a work. And he is not similar in nature to the Father. He is not the true, natural Word of the Father. He is not his true Wisdom. Rather, he is one of the made, created things, and is called 'Word' and 'Wisdom' by a misuse of language… The Father cannot be described by the Son, since the Word does not either know or see the Father perfectly. In fact, the Son doesn't know his own nature as it really is.

The teaching of Arius, reported by Alexander of Alexandria, *Deposition of Arius* c. AD 321

Greek-speaking, eastern half. Although officially a single domain, the Roman empire had started down the irrevocable path of division into two quite distinct civilizations.

Meanwhile, the theological dispute had moved into a new phase. Arius was dead, but many people – including many bishops – had similar views to his. Their opponents labelled them all 'Arians' as if they were simply followers of the dead heretic, but they did not necessarily agree with him entirely, and many denied that they had any connection to him: after all, how could a bishop be a disciple of a mere presbyter? New theologians appeared, with new arguments for the shared conviction that the Son was not God. Aetius, a brilliant logician, pointed out that God is intrinsically uncaused: if a thing is created by someone else it cannot be God. But the Son is begotten of the Father. How, then, can the Son be God?

At the same time, a new generation of anti-Arians was also moving into the fray. The most prominent was Athanasius (c. AD 296–373), who became bishop of Alexandria in AD 328, was deposed for misconduct in AD 335 (probably on charges invented by those who did not like him), and spent most of his episcopate either in exile or in hiding. He wrote many books against his opponents even while he was on the run. Athanasius's answer to the Arians was that being begotten did not entail being

Gregory of Nazianzus, from a fourteenth-century mosaic in St Mark's Cathedral, Venice.

Athanasius, Hilary and Gregory of Nazianzus

In that period of sixty or so years that separated the Council of Nicaea (AD 325) from the Council of Constantinople (AD 381), Athanasius, Hilary and Gregory of Nazianzus played a decisive role.

Athanasius was present at the Council of Nicaea as a young deacon in the entourage of the patriarch of Alexandria, Alexander, whom the council upheld against his priest Arius. Athanasius succeeded Alexander in AD 328. The authority of the bishop of Alexandria was extensive, covering the whole of Egypt, and Nubia and Libya besides; he needed a certain ruthlessness to be effective, and Athanasius did not fail in this. In his own eyes Athanasius was bishop of Alexandria for nearly fifty years – until his death in AD 373 – though during this time he was deposed, both by church synod and emperor, and was expelled from his see five times, on the first two occasions (AD 335–37, 339–46) spending his exile in the west. These periods in the west were important, for they enabled him to establish links with Latin Christians, generally more inclined to support Nicaea. He also harnessed the new monastic movement in Egypt to his purposes,

forming a close relationship with Antony the Great, the greatest of the early hermits, whose *Life* he probably wrote. At the heart of Athanasius's commitment to the Nicene faith was his conviction that God saves humankind personally by himself becoming a human being in Jesus of Nazareth.

Hilary was elected bishop of Poitiers in about AD 350, when he was about 35, and remained bishop until his death in AD 367/8. Like Athanasius, he was exiled by the imperial authorities, spending AD 356–60 in Phrygia. There he became an expert on the issues surrounding the Council of Nicaea, though he reveals the surprising information that until he went into exile he 'had never heard the Nicene creed' (*On the synods*, 91). On his return to the west, Hilary became the most prominent and articulate supporter of Nicaea. His most important treatise, perhaps written in exile, is a substantial work in twelve books called *On the Trinity*, which sums up his understanding of the Nicene faith. Hilary emphasizes the mystery of God and regards human formulations of doctrine as only necessary to prevent the misunderstandings found in the heretics; his presentation of the relationship of the Father and the Son in the one Godhead is worked out through careful consideration of the biblical witness of both the Old and the New Testaments.

Gregory of Nazianzus belongs to the final triumph of the Nicene faith at the Council of Constantinople. Born in

Cappadocia around AD 330, he was a scholar and a poet, drawn to a life of prayer and study. He was appointed bishop (of Sasima, a small town he never made his home) in around AD 372, until he was later called by the emperor Theodosius I to Constantinople to minister to the small Nicene congregation there. In Constantinople, Gregory preached a set of five sermons on 'theology' (that is, the doctrine of the Trinity), the fame of which led to Gregory being given the title (otherwise only given to John the Evangelist) of 'the Theologian'. In these sermons he presents, with consummate rhetorical skill, the Christian understanding of the Trinity, and also of the incarnation of the Son. Like Hilary, he stresses the mystery of God, lying far beyond our human understanding. Like Athanasius, he sees the Nicene faith presenting a vision of the ultimate destiny of human kind as 'becoming God', for which he coined the term *theosis*, 'deification'. He was deposed (for having been translated from another see) by the council that affirmed the faith he had defended, and spent the remaining years of his life in prayer and study on his family estates.

ANDREW LOUTH

Bear in mind that the very heart of a faith that saves is belief not just in God, but in God as Father; not just in Christ, but in Christ as the Son of God; in him, not as a created being, but as God the Creator, born of God.

Hilary of Poitiers, On the Trinity 1.17, c. AD 360

created (as the symbol of Nicaea suggested) and therefore the Son could be one without being the other, and so he *could* be God. But the thrust of his position was that the Son *must* be God. Like most Christian thinkers of this period, Athanasius believed that Jesus saved people primarily through who he was. Irenaeus, nearly two centuries earlier, had taught that in Christ divinity and humanity meet. Through him, divinity is introduced into humanity, and it spreads, almost like a benign infection, restoring what was lost in Adam. Athanasius's point was therefore simple: how could this happen if Jesus were not really God?

Constans, emperor of the west, apparently agreed with this sort of viewpoint. In this he seems to have been in accordance with the spirit of his domain: most Arians, of whatever kind, were in the eastern, Greek-speaking half of the empire. There were plenty in the west, but on the whole the movement seems to have been weaker there. Good Latin-speaking theologians wrote against them, but to relatively little effect. Hilary of Poitiers, one important anti-Arian writer, tried to be even-handed and to treat the Arians fairly, but seems to have made relatively little impact. Another, a philosopher named Marius Victorinus, wrote brilliant works against the Arians, but they were so complex that no one could understand them!

Constantius, in contrast to his brother, was an out-and-out Arian. Under his rule, leading anti-Arians such as Athanasius were routinely deposed and replaced by Arian yes-men. It is hard for us now to tell to what extent Constantius's views reflected those of most Christians. Certainly the people of Alexandria seem to have largely opposed Arianism. They supported Athanasius, and on one occasion his unfortunate successor, George the Cappadocian, was lynched by a mob who murdered him by the curious method of tying him to a camel and burning it. Elsewhere in the east, however, Arianism seems to have been strong. Many easterners were extremely suspicious of Latin-speaking theologians; they suspected that all western

Christians denied that there were any real distinctions between the Father and the Son, so that they were really the same person appearing in different guises. The word 'Sabellian' – after a third-century theologian who denied distinctions in the Trinity – was thrown about.

Further attempts were made to find a solution. New councils were called, particularly after AD 350, when Constans was killed by a usurper. Constantius quickly gained control of the entire Roman empire, and set about holding councils in both eastern and western halves to try to silence anti-Arian sentiments. Most of the councils were Arian to varying degrees. The key statement of Nicaea that Father and Son were *homoousios* – the key word around which the controversy revolved, meaning 'of the same substance' – was either ignored or banned. Bishops were expected to sign new creeds that were suggested instead. At the Council of Milan in AD 355 the bishops started tussling with each other; Constantius, who had been hiding behind a curtain, suddenly burst in with a sword and forced them to sign the creed he wanted. 'This is against the canon!' protested one bishop. 'I am the canon!' replied the emperor.

Evidently Constantius, like his father, regarded the church as essentially another department of the state, there to obey him. Yet was the emperor really the head of the church? That bishop at Milan obviously thought not, but there was little he could do about it. The emperor held all the cards. In practice most Christians of this period seem not to have thought about the issue too hard. If they liked how the emperor handled the church, they praised him to high heaven as God's anointed; if they did not like his policies, they condemned him as a vicious monster. Whether he technically had the *right* to implement ecclesiastical policies, good or bad, seems not to have concerned them so much. But the nature of church and state, and the relative power of the two, would be a big issue for the future. The approach of Constantius is often called 'Caesaropapism' – literally, treating the emperor like the pope, that is, the head of the church. In modern times this has also been known as 'Erastianism', putting the church subject to the state.

THE CRISIS RESOLVED

Constantius died in AD 361, initiating a new period of political instability. He was succeeded first by his cousin, Julian, a complex man who has fascinated people for centuries, for he tried, ambitiously, to de-Christianize the empire. At this time it was still customary, on the death of an emperor, for political factions to kill many potential rivals for the throne. On the death of Constantine the Great, Julian's family, including his father, Constantine's brother, had been killed: Julian therefore harboured a grudge against those who had done this, who had been – at least, so they said – Christians. As a student at Athens, Julian was initiated into the Eleusian mysteries. And as emperor, he did his best to reinstate the worship of the traditional gods and cause as much trouble as possible for the Christians. Rather than persecute the Christians, however, he did this by declaring that all bishops previously exiled by Constantius could return home. He hoped that this would cause immense confusion, and indeed it did – but it also helped the anti-Arian cause.

Julian died in battle against the Persians in AD 363, ending both the dynasty of Constantine and the bold but brief attempt to repaganize Rome. For renouncing his Christian upbringing, Julian has been known to history as 'the Apostate' (an apostate being someone who defects from Christianity). He was succeeded by his head general, Jovian, who died after eight months (apparently suffocated by a smoky fire in his tent) to be succeeded by another general, Valentinian. The empire was divided once more, as Valentinian took control of the west and made his brother Valens emperor of the east. Valentinian was a soldier who spent most of his time rebuilding the army and repelling the barbarians, and he did not dabble in ecclesiastical matters. Valens also spent most of his time fighting, but

he continued the pro-Arian policies of Constantius. Valentinian died in AD 375 and was succeeded by his sons Gratian and the infant Valentinian II, between whom the west was divided. Gratian was a supporter of Nicene Christianity, which meant that he did not get on with his uncle Valens. The constant battles with the barbarians were still going on, and Valens died in battle in AD 378. Gratian took the opportunity to appoint a retired soldier named Theodosius (c. AD 346–395) to the eastern throne. Theodosius I was also a Nicene. For the first time, both emperors opposed Arianism.

Theodosius proved to be a wise choice. He fought the Goths and negotiated peace with them. And in AD 381 he called yet another council to settle the Arian issue. This was the Council of Constantinople, presided over by Gregory of Nazianzus, a major anti-Arian writer from Cappadocia in Anatolia. Gregory had been the closest friend of Basil, metropolitan of Caesarea, an extremely prominent churchman and opponent of Arianism who had died a couple of years previously. One of the first things that happened at the council was that Gregory's Arian opponents managed to have him removed as president on procedural grounds, but this was their only success. The council found in favour of the Council of Nicaea, and overruled all the councils that had been held since AD 325. A new version of the creed of Nicaea was issued, which reaffirmed the *homoousios* and even extended it to the Holy Spirit, meaning that the Spirit, like the Son, was officially divine too.

In the face of this and the strong emperor Theodosius, Arianism largely melted away within the empire. It was a gradual process, and Theodosius came under much pressure from the Arians whose churches he was closing. Even in the west, Ambrose, bishop of Milan, was still fighting Arianism in the AD 390s. But to all intents and purposes it had become a dead issue. This was especially so after AD 394. A usurper named Eugenius had taken the western throne: although nominally a Christian, his rule was supported

I am a servant of the sovereign Sun... I think, in fact, that the Sun (if what the wise tell us is true) is the common father of all mankind; for as it is very properly said [by Aristotle], 'Man and the Sun generate man.'... This deity presides over the city of Rome, and because of this, not only does Jupiter, the celebrated father of all things, reside in its tower, together with Minerva, and Venus, but Apollo also resides on the Palatine hill, together with the Sun himself, who, as everyone knows, is one and the same with Apollo.

Julian the Apostate, *Oration to the Sovereign Sun*

We believe in... the Spirit, the holy, lordly, and life-giving one, who comes forth from the Father, who is worshipped and glorified together with the Father and the Son, who spoke through the Prophets.

From the creed of the First Council of Constantinople (according to the canons of Chalcedon), AD 381

Antony of Egypt, from a mosaic in the Monastery of St Bishoi, Egypt.

On his death the empire was divided once more, between his sons, and the division would now prove permanent.

THE MONKS

It is easy to get dazzled by the dramatic history of the fourth century. The conversion of Constantine and the Arian controversy were the 'big' events of the time. But not all Christians were involved in these. For many, Christianity offered a safe spiritual haven, where they could pursue the vision of God in tranquillity.

ANTONY OF EGYPT

The first key figure in this movement was Antony. Antony was a rich young Egyptian, but he came from the countryside, not the city of Alexandria. Evidently, by the late third century, Christianity was spreading from the big cities into the rural areas. Antony spoke not Greek but Coptic, the language of these rural Egyptians, and apparently he visited Alexandria only twice in his long life. One day he heard a sermon on the commandment to sell and give to the poor: Antony did just that and left his village to live by himself. First he spent fifteen years living among tombs, but then he decided this was not extreme enough and moved to an abandoned fort in the middle of the desert, where he lived on scraps that well-wishers threw over the walls for him.

What was Antony trying to do? He wanted to escape the world of human society and be alone with God. He did not live in his self-denying way for the sake of it, but because he believed that possessions, family – or anything else that people prize, other than God – actually get in the way of loving God. Paradoxically, his success was also his failure. For Antony became so famous that people began to flock to his fort to see this holy man, and he was obliged to abandon his ideal of solitude and come out and teach them. Eventually, he left the desert to set up a community at Mount Colzim near the Red Sea, where he remained for forty years. He died in AD 356, at the age, supposedly, of 105.

by many pagan aristocrats and also many barbarians, who were by now an important element in the military. In AD 394 Theodosius invaded and met Eugenius at the River Frigidus. The usurper was killed, and his barbarian hordes were dispersed. In the eyes of posterity, this was the last military stand of paganism. A Christian emperor had defeated a pagan horde and reunited the empire. At the same time Theodosius was enacting legislation that effectively outlawed pagan practices. The triumph of Christianity was complete: it had become the state religion of the Roman empire, all other faiths were proscribed, and zealous Christians began destroying pagan temples.

Whilst the triumph of Nicene Christianity was now assured, the future of the empire was not. Theodosius the Great died in AD 395, having ruled a united empire for under a year. He was the last man ever to do so.

THE DESERT FATHERS

The life of Antony was an enormous inspiration to others: none other than Athanasius wrote his biography, and it was widely read. Despite the triumphs of the church which were taking place within his lifetime, many people felt tired of society. There was a common feeling among many that the Roman empire was exhausted, that it was nearing its end. The social world, and even the natural world, that had existed for so long was in its old age. In the third century, Cyprian had dealt with an argument from a pagan that the woes of the empire were due to the unpatriotic Christians by responding that the decline of the empire was part of a natural process of cosmic degeneration. According to Cyprian, harvests were getting smaller, summers were getting cooler and even mines were returning fewer minerals. The world was in its old age.

Little wonder that others sought to turn away and focus on God alone. Many thousands, from all over the empire, emulated Antony by going to the desert. This was not only a sensible choice for anyone wanting to get away from society: it also had symbolic value. The Bible often depicts the desert as a place of trial and testing, where God can be found through the purging of sins. It was in the desert that the Hebrews wandered for forty years; it was here that Saul chased David and was reconciled to him; it was here that Jesus fasted for forty days after his baptism and was tempted. With the conversion of Constantine, there were no more martyrs: no longer could the devout long for a baptism of blood. The desert lifestyle came to replace martyrdom as the ideal for those radically commited to Christ: the hermits came to regard themselves as dead to the world (as Colossians 3:3 suggests), living out a new kind of martyrdom.

These hermits lived in the deserts throughout the Middle East, especially in Egypt, Syria and Palestine, and so they are known as the 'desert fathers'. Stories of their holiness, their deeds, and their wise sayings were written down in a number of collections, which help us to reconstruct their lifestyles and their beliefs. Most of them lived in the Egyptian desert, just like Antony. At first, many lived as he had, as true hermits, trying to escape the company of others, which they regarded as inevitably leading to temptations which they would be too weak to resist. But other lifestyles quickly developed. Many lived together, hoping to strengthen and encourage each other in their common goal of seeking God. A major figure in this development was Pachomius, a pagan soldier who served in Constantine's army in Egypt in AD 313 and became converted to Christianity when he met the hermits who were already there. In the AD 320s, Pachomius returned to Egypt to become a hermit himself, but he was joined by a large number of people and decided to write a set of rules for the community. His plan was for the group to be largely self-sufficient. The members would work at a number of trades, sell their produce and pool the money for the benefit of all. They would even have their own fishing boats on the Nile. This meant that they would have less time for private meditation and prayer – but the members were encouraged to go beyond the letter of Pachomius's rule.

Pachomius died in AD 346, by which time there were eleven communities following his rule, including two for women (the hermits had very strong views on not mixing the sexes). Each one consisted of a group of huts surrounded by a wall, but by the end of the fourth century some housed all the members in a single large building. Pachomius's simple plan of regulating a community of like-minded people had started the monastic movement. His communities were the first true monasteries, and his followers the first Christian monks. The word 'monk' comes from the Greek *monachos* (meaning 'alone'): a 'monk' was someone who sought solitude to be alone with God.

In the future, monasteries would develop into quite rigid communities where everyone prayed and ate together, following set rules. But for much of late antiquity the most common way of life was

You are truly blessed because you do not have the cares of this world. I was born to kingship, and the affairs of my empire are a constant concern to me. Each day I dine on the richest meats and cakes and the finest wines are poured into my goblet. And yet, today mere bread and water have satisfied me as no sumptuous feast ever has.

The verdict of the Roman emperor after visiting a monk, according to a story of the desert fathers

The demon of listlessness, which is also called the noondam demon, is worse than all others. It attacks a monk at about 10:00 am and whirls the soul round and round till about 2:00 pm. It begins by making a man notice miserably how slowly the sun moves, or does not move at all, and that the day seems to have become fifty hours long. Then it makes the man look frequently out of the window or leave his cell to look at the sun and see how long it is till 3:00 pm. It makes him look around to see if some of the brothers are about. Then it makes him angry about the place and his way of life itself and his work, adding that there is no more love among the brothers – no-one will come to comfort him. If someone has offended him, the demon reminds him of it to increase his anger. Then it makes him long to be somewhere else, where he could find some job that would be easier and more profitable.

Evagrius Ponticus, the most important theologian of the Egyptian desert, c. AD 345–99, *Praktikos*

a halfway house between true solitude and a monastery. The monks would spend most of their time alone in their huts (or 'cells'), coming together to eat or attend services; they were not bound by strict rules. It was more informal than true monasticism, but still provided some kind of structure for those unable to master the self-discipline required for a life like Antony's.

One of the largest communities like this was at Nitria, a large hill a couple of days' journey south of Alexandria – another symbolic location, since holy mountains also figure in the Bible. The community was founded by a monk named Amoun in around AD 330, and in its prime must have been like a bustling town. A traveller named Palladius, who visited it, wrote that there were 5,000 monks there. Most of these monks lived alone in one- or two-roomed cells made of mud bricks: when a new monk arrived, the others would help him build his cell, a task which could be accomplished in a day. Some of the cells were quite remote, so that monks might have to walk several miles to the imposing central church, where communal services were held. Near the church was a large guest house. Visitors could stay for as long as they liked, but after a week they would have to help out with the tasks of the community.

Meals were taken outdoors at large tables and the food on offer was remarkably healthy. Bread was the staple, and Nitria apparently had seven bakeries. Dipped in olive oil, and served with generous helpings of fish and lentils, this proved more than sufficient for the monks' needs. There was also plenty of wine at Nitria. The only thing they really lacked was fruit, and the stories of the desert fathers testify that the thought of fresh, juicy fruit seems to have tantalized them more than the lustful visions one might expect.

THE MONASTIC IDEAL

Life at Nitria may sound quite idyllic, but the monks were not there to relax. They were there to focus on God. They believed

that, to do this, they must reduce their dependence on – and desire for – material things. This is sometimes misunderstood to mean a distaste for the body, or even a belief that it does not matter. On the contrary, the monks understood well that bodily things matter. But the body had to become holy just as the soul did. Thus, the monks sought to regulate their lives, aiming to eat and sleep less. They especially believed that drinking water represented spiritual laxity, and encouraged each other to do with less. One monk is said to have told a disciple: 'For twenty years I have never had as much bread, water or sleep as I wanted. I weighed my bread, measured my water and snatched a little sleep leaning against a wall.'

The desert fathers believed that God could be found only through tranquillity and stillness. They inherited from Platonism a conviction that passion was something that disturbed the soul, like ripples on a pond. They therefore sought to attain *apatheia* (literally, 'passionlessness'), a state of mind so serene that they could at last focus on God. This was the aim of their sometimes severe training. One famous monk, John of Lycopolis, told a group of visitors:

Everyone who has not renounced the world fully and completely but chases after its attractions suffers from spiritual instability. His preoccupations, being bodily and earthly, distract his mind through the many enterprises in which he is engaged. And then, absorbed in his struggle against the passions, he cannot see God… The will of those who seek God must be free from all other concerns. For Scripture says, 'Be still and know that I am God.'

The task was not easy. The stories of the desert fathers speak of a continual onslaught by demons, who apparently spent their time trying to tempt the monks in various ways. Evidently, the monks believed very firmly in a spirit world, which was even more real to them than the physical desert in which they lived.

NEW DISPUTES

The monastic movement would remain extremely important in Christianity for many centuries, and remains central to some churches today. But it would also be a source of conflict. Monasteries would become large and powerful, and their leaders, the 'abbots' (a word taken from the word for 'father' used by the desert monks), could in some cases be extremely important figures. There was thus a potential clash between the monastic system and the bishops. Moreover, the monastic ideal was itself controversial. To what extent were all Christians called to live like these monks? This question was the source of new disputes in this period.

JOVINIANISM

The first of these disputes involved a man named Jovinian, who lived in Rome towards the end of the fourth century. He had been a monk but gave up the severe lifestyle, and became a vocal critic of ascetic practices. In particular, Jovinian attacked those who believed that a life of virginity was better than a married life. He said that it is no better to fast than it is to eat, and that in heaven everyone is rewarded equally. Unfortunately, one of those who disagreed with him was the writer, spiritual director, and generally bad-tempered scholar Jerome. Jerome was a major figure at the time, but a controversial one: he praised the state of virginity to such a degree that many felt that he was going too far and teaching that sex is intrinsically evil. Like many people, Jerome stressed the virginity of Mary, Jesus' mother. It was commonly believed by this stage that Mary had remained a virgin all her life, and that the siblings of Jesus mentioned in the Gospels were Joseph's children by an earlier marriage. It was even believed that she preserved her 'virginity in parturition', meaning that Jesus was born in a miraculous fashion that left Mary physically unchanged. But Jovinian denied this too.

Jovinian was condemned at a synod in Rome in AD 390 and vanished into obscurity. Jerome was careful to tone down his ascetic advice after this, but nevertheless the church had, essentially, chosen to endorse the sort of approach of the desert fathers: those who abstain from worldly things in order to focus on God are living the Christian life in a more authentic manner than those who do not. That is not to say that it is wrong not to do so – only that it is not so good. They agreed with Jesus' pronouncement in Luke 10:38–42 that, although one could lead a normal life and be a Christian, still, leaving everyday life to contemplate the Lord is to choose 'the better part'.

PELAGIANISM

Jovinian was gone, but the issue was not settled, for now a new teacher appeared and stirred up controversy. If Jovinian had been judged too lax, Pelagius was judged too severe. Pelagius, a Briton, arrived in Rome at the end of the fourth century, and he did think an ascetic lifestyle was important. He was not a monk, but he lived a very austere life and became highly respected as a spiritual teacher. He wrote a number of books, some of which survive and which make him the earliest extant British author.

Pelagius was shocked by what he found at Rome. Now that Christianity was the official religion of the empire, congregations had swelled enormously, but the dedication and fervour of the faithful had been diluted. He felt that people were lax. But worse, people justified moral looseness theologically. Some theologians were arguing that human beings, since Adam, are intrinsically sinful. 'Original sin' meant not only that people have a tendency to do wrong but that they cannot help doing it. Moreover, everything takes place within God's providence. If God determines that you will be saved and live a moral life, you will do so – but if he does not, you cannot do it by yourself. Therefore, why try?

These ideas were associated with Augustine (AD 354–430), the bishop of Hippo in North Africa, who was making a name for himself as a great writer and

We can never start down the path of virtue unless we have hope as our guide and companion, and if every effort made to look for something is cancelled out by despair of ever finding it... the Lord of justice wanted man to be free to act, without being forced. This is why he left him free to make his own decisions and put before him life and death, good and evil, and he will be given whatever pleases him.

Pelagius, *Letter to Demetrias*, AD 413

Augustine

Aurelius Augustinus or Augustine (which means 'little emperor') was the greatest father of the western church. He was born in AD 354 in Thagaste, a Roman-style town (today Souk-Ahras in Algeria) when the Roman province of 'Africa' was at the height of its prosperity. His mother, Monica, was a deeply committed Christian.

Augustine was educated first in Thagaste and then, from the age of eleven, in Madauros (modern Mdaourouch). He loved Latin but never mastered Greek and, like many boys, preferred games to books. When he was fifteen, his parents sent him to university at Carthage, but not before he had been back home in Thagaste for a year, running wild with the local youths. His famous prayer, 'Grant me chastity, but not yet' (*Confessions*, 8.7.17) may have been coined at this time.

In Carthage Augustine joined the Manichees, a gnostic sect which offered escape from the corrupt realm of matter to the pure realm of the spirit. He was a member for nine years and converted many friends, but became disillusioned by the narrow superstition and hypocrisy he encountered. He also met a woman who became his partner for fifteen years. In his writings Augustine never divulges her name, but they lived together faithfully and had a much-loved son, Adeodatus ('gift of God') who died at the age of seventeen.

As a student, Augustine read Cicero's *Hortensius*, which introduced him to philosophy and opened up the idea of loving wisdom and truth rather than merely conjuring words. Frustrated by disruptive students, Augustine sailed for Rome in AD 383 and became professor of rhetoric at the imperial court in Milan. Here he came under the influence of Bishop Ambrose (c. AD 339–397), a distinguished preacher and scholar, who helped Augustine to read the Bible with understanding and introduced him to the neoplatonist synthesis of Christian doctrine and Greek philosophy. Monica joined her son in Milan, dismissing his partner in preparation for a wealthy marriage to further his career.

In the late summer of AD 386, torn by conflicting ideals and temptations, Augustine was wrestling with his thoughts in a garden. Hearing a child's voice chanting '*Tolle lege*' ('Pick up and read'), he opened Paul's letter to the Romans and read at random: 'Put on the Lord Jesus Christ and make no provision for the flesh, to satisfy its desires.' From this point Augustine accepted a life of discipline and self-denial – although it was always, for him, a life lived with others in community. He was baptized by Ambrose in Milan cathedral, together with his son, at sunrise on Easter Day AD 387.

Returning to Thagaste, Augustine intended to live the rest of his life in a religious community based on his family home. Events overtook him when, in AD 391, while visiting the prosperous port of Hippo Regius (modern Annaba), the local congregation seized him to become their priest. He accepted ordination and in AD 396 he succeeded as bishop of Hippo.

Augustine's life now took on the public and hard-working concerns of defining and defending the Christian faith, serving the church in teaching and preaching, and undertaking pastoral, administrative and judicial responsibilities. Despite incessant labours and much travel, he achieved an enormous output of books, commentaries, sermons, pamphlets and letters.

Augustine of Hippo, by the fourteenth-century Italian artist Nicoletto Semitecolo, from the church of Maria dei Servi, Venice.

Foremost among Augustine's writings are: *Confessions* (AD 397–401), a unique record of his life and spiritual journey, presented as a prayer; *The City of God* (AD 413–27) in which he wrestles with the issues raised by the fall of Rome to the barbarians in AD 410; and the monumental *On the Trinity* (AD 399–419). His gifts to the church include his affirmation of the goodness of creation (as opposed to the 'matter is evil' stance of the Manichees), the essential unity and future perfection of the church (as distinct from the 'separate for purity now' of the Donatists) and the necessity of grace (as distinct from the 'self-perfection' of Pelagius). Augustine's definition of evil as the absence of good, and sin as the abuse of free will, are key points in any debate on the problem of evil.

In AD 429 barbarian Vandals crossed to Africa at the straits of Gibraltar and laid siege to Hippo. During this siege, on 28 August AD 430, Augustine died at the age of seventy-six.

ANDREW KNOWLES

profound spiritual teacher. Augustine, of course, did not approve of loose living, and his theology was intended to emphasize the grace of God, not the sinfulness of man. But that is not how Pelagius saw it. Instead, Pelagius taught that human beings are not intrinsically sinful. When Adam sinned, he set a bad example to those who came after; this did not mean they had to follow it. People have free will and can choose whether to sin or not. In theory they can live without sin – after all, in Matthew 5:48, Jesus tells us to 'be perfect', and he could hardly do that if it were impossible. Pelagius therefore stressed people's responsibility to live properly. He felt that living a normal, worldly life was incompatible with real Christianity. Christians were called to live differently, to be set apart. In other words, Pelagius approved of the kind of lifestyle of the desert fathers, but he felt that all Christians should live like this. Anything less was disobeying the commandment to 'be perfect', a commandment that he believed we are all capable of obeying.

Pelagius got into serious trouble for this. First, Jerome attacked him for his belief that it is possible to lead a perfect life. Augustine, meanwhile, was horrified by Pelagius's emphasis on free will. He thought that Pelagius was saying that human beings save themselves through living right, rather than through relying on God's grace in Christ.

Pelagius left Rome after it was sacked by barbarians in AD 410 and travelled around the empire. He and Augustine wrote books attacking each other, in which they argued over the nature of grace. Pelagius said it is external to the person: God's grace consists of giving us free will and the good examples of Christ and the saints. Augustine said it is internal to the person: God's grace means he actually works inside us, as it were, and makes us do what is right. A number of councils were held, which found in favour of Augustine. Pelagius seems to have meekly accepted their ruling and disappeared into obscurity. But some of his disciples refused to lie down. They

continued to attack the doctrines of Augustine more stridently than Pelagius ever had. In particular, Pelagianism proved very popular in Gaul (now France). Here, debates over the nature of grace continued for some centuries.

SCHISM

We saw in the last chapter why these doctrinal disputes, such as the Pelagian controversy or the Arian crisis, aroused such strong feelings. But this period also saw a number of disputes which had virtually no doctrinal element to them. For one reason or another, groups of Christians broke away from the mainstream church and set up their own, with their own bishops, own church buildings and so on. The Montanists, who we met in the last chapter, were one such 'schismatic' sect ('schism' means 'break'). Another were the Novatians. They originated in the AD 250s, when a priest at Rome, Novatian, rejected the legitimacy of the new bishop and had himself appointed instead. He was condemned, but had many supporters, who set up a rival church structure not only at Rome but throughout the empire. The Novatians continued to exist as a rival sect until the end of the sixth century. They believed they were the true church and everyone else was in schism from them, not vice versa. One fourth-century Novatian bishop of Constantinople was once asked if he was dismayed by the fact that there were two bishops in his diocese. He replied simply, 'There aren't.'

A more problematic schism existed in North Africa, where a rival church, known as the Donatist Church, was more popular than the mainstream one. This church had its origins in the great persecution of Christians at the start of the fourth century. Many Christians had given in to the persecution and renounced their faith. They were known as *traditors*, from a word meaning 'to hand over' (since they handed over the scriptures to be burned). This is where the word 'traitor' comes from. But when the persecution ended, many wanted to return to the church. In North Africa,

The 'Lady of Carthage', a fourth- or fifth-century image of a woman thought to be a Donatist.

The Church is called Catholic or universal because it has spread throughout the entire world, from one end of the earth to the other. Again, it is called Catholic because it teaches fully and unfailingly all the doctrines which ought to be brought to people's knowledge, whether concerned with visible or invisible things, with the realities of heaven or the things of earth. Another reason for the name Catholic is that the Church brings under religious obedience all classes of men, rulers and subjects, learned and unlettered. Finally, it deserves the title Catholic because it heals and cures unrestrictedly every type of sin that can be committed in soul or in body, and because it possesses within itself every kind of virtue that can be named.

Cyril of Jerusalem,
Catechetical lectures,
c. AD 348

some felt that the *traditors* had completely lost God's grace. They were no longer Christians, and those who were priests were no longer priests. When they were allowed back into the church, the rigorists refused to accept their legitimacy and split off, setting up their own church structure. They became known as the Donatists, after a charismatic leader in the early years.

Groups such as the Novatians and Donatists were anathema to mainstream Christians. It was universally believed that there could be only one church. This did not mean simply one body of believers who might be divided into different administrative groups – on the contrary, one church meant one church structure. This was essential to the principle of apostolic succession, and therefore to the guarantee of doctrinal purity, but it had a more mystical dimension too. The church, it was felt, was the body of

Christ: therefore it could not be broken. Cyprian, the African martyr of the third century who was revered by Donatists and Catholics alike, had stated that outside the church there is no salvation – even for a martyr. Augustine, who wrote at length against the Donatists, stressed this point repeatedly, insisting that those who cut themselves off from the church were simply damning themselves. By 'the church', Augustine meant the Catholic Church, the single, mainstream church from which these schismatic groups had split off.

Just like the earlier Christians, the theologians of Augustine's age believed in a holistic 'rule of faith', a combination of the teaching of scripture and the traditions of the church. These all supported and reinforced each other. Focusing on one without attending to the other would be unthinkable.

THE EMPIRE CRUMBLES

In AD 410 an event occurred that sent shockwaves through the Mediterranean world. The city of Rome itself was invaded and sacked by Alaric the Visigoth and his barbarian hordes. Not in nearly eight centuries had Rome been attacked like this, and the psychological effect it had on the empire was not unlike that suffered by the USA after the terrorist attacks of 11 September 2001. Clearly, the world was changing. Many blamed the recent conversion of the empire to Christianity, and suggested that the traditional gods of Rome were angry; this argument led Augustine to respond with one of the greatest works of Christian literature, *The city of God*.

Rome had been fighting the 'barbarians' for as long as the empire had existed, but in recent years the problem had become far worse. 'Barbarian' meant anyone who did not speak Latin or Greek (from the 'barbarbar' sound of foreign languages to the classical ear). The third century, in particular, had seen renewed attacks from the Germanic peoples to the north of the western empire. Their homelands were getting crowded, and the people began to move into new lands, many of which were within the imperial borders. The Franks and the Alamanni, who lived on the Rhine, and the Goths, on the Danube, were on the move, and the Romans could do little about it because they were also fighting the Persians to the east. For a while it looked as if the empire might collapse from the pressure on these two fronts: the AD 250s saw the Franks crossing the Rhine, the Alamanni invading northern Italy, and the Goths moving into Greece. But Rome held them off. In the AD 270s the emperor Aurelian recognized the threat and made it his priority, successfully seeing off the invasions and earning the title 'restorer of the world' in the process. Strong emperors after him, notably Diocletian and Constantine, kept the empire together. A new military system called the Tetrarchy was established, which put the political and bureaucratic system of the empire on a military footing. And, crucially, many barbarians were now allowed to settle in the empire. Peace treaties with their chieftains granted land within the imperial borders, and many barbarians joined the Roman army. The first stage of the *Völkerwanderung*, the 'migration of the people', had been tamed.

The second and more serious stage began a century later. For reasons that are not well understood even now, the Huns, a central Asian people, began to move west. The Huns, who may have been related to the Xiong people in what is now Kazakhstan, were fearsome, horse-mounted warriors, armed with powerful composite bows, and it seems that no one could stand up to them. They moved west into the lands of the Ostrogoths (the eastern Goths), who in their turn began to move west too. One by one, barbarian peoples began to move once more, like a row of dominos. Goths, desperate to escape the Huns, streamed over the borders of the empire in the Balkans. Visigoths (the western Goths) headed west, invaded northern Italy, and sacked Rome. Vandals, Alamanni, and others crossed the Rhine as they fled west, and moved across Gaul and even into Spain. The emperors could do little about it. Troops were moved and battles fought, but this just opened up gaps elsewhere in the defences. In AD 407, troops were withdrawn from Britain to fight barbarians who were invading Gaul. The withdrawal was intended to be temporary, but the troops never returned, and yet more barbarians – Saxons, Jutes and others – sailed over the North Sea and invaded the unprotected Romano-British.

More treaties were made with the barbarians, allowing them to settle within the imperial borders – but this time there were far more barbarians. Where, once, Rome had conquered other peoples and incorporated them into its empire and its culture, now the foreigners were starting to eat the empire from the inside out. Instead of 'Romanization' there was 'barbarianization'. The peoples of the

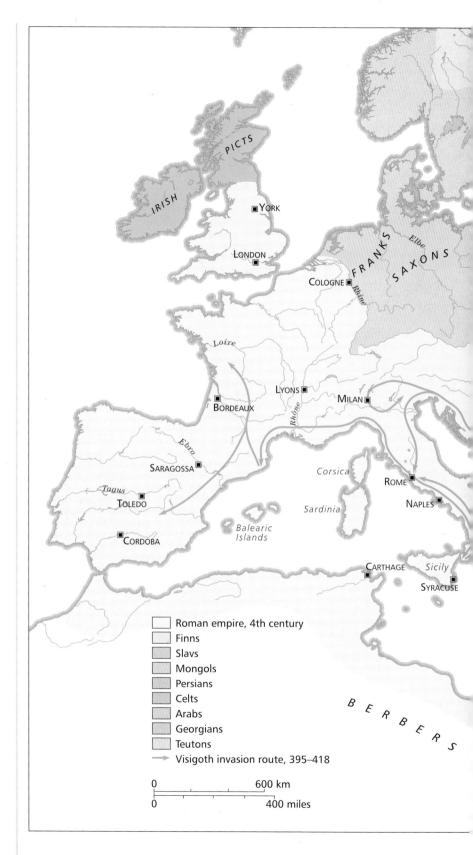

PICTS

IRISH

YORK

LONDON

COLOGNE

FRANKS

SAXONS

Elbe

Rhine

Loire

LYONS

MILAN

BORDEAUX

Rhône

Ebro

SARAGOSSA

Corsica

ROME

Tagus

TOLEDO

Sardinia

NAPLES

Balearic
Islands

CORDOBA

CARTHAGE

Sicily

SYRACUSE

Roman empire, 4th century
Finns
Slavs
Mongols
Persians
Celts
Arabs
Georgians
Teutons
Visigoth invasion route, 395–418

0		600 km
0		400 miles

B E R B E R S

FINNS

SLAVS

OSTROGOTHS

HUNS

VISIGOTHS

Danube

Black Sea

ALANS

ABASGIANS

LAZICA

IBERIA

ARMENIANS

ALONICA

■ CONSTANTINOPLE ■

■ NICAEA

■ CAESAREA

■ EDESSA

NISIBIS ■

■ ATHENS

■ EPHESUS

Cyprus

■ ANTIOCH

Euphrates

PERSIAN EMPIRE

Crete

editerranean Sea

■ DAMASCUS

CTESIPHON ■

CYRENE

JERUSALEM ■

ALEXANDRIA ■

Nile

ARABS

Western Europe in
the last days of
Rome.

The cupbearers brought us a cup, following the custom of the country, so that we could pray before we sat. After sipping from the cup, we sat down on the chairs that lined the walls of the room on either side. Attila sat in the middle, on a couch. Attila's attendant came in first with a dish of meat, and behind him came the other attendants with bread and food, which they put on the tables. A splendid meal, on silver plates, had been prepared for us and the barbarian guests, but Attila ate only meat from a wooden plate. He showed self-restraint in everything else, too. His cup was wooden, while the guests had goblets of gold and silver. His clothes were also simple, aiming only to be clean. The sword by his side, the buckles of his Scythian shoes, and the bridle of his horse were not covered in gold or jewels or anything expensive, like those of the other Scythians... When evening came, torches were lit, and two barbarians came in front of Attila and sang songs they had written, celebrating his victories and great deeds of war.

Prisces of Panium, *Byzantine history*, c. AD 475, describing a feast at Attila's court

empire, especially in the west, were increasingly barbarian in culture. The Visigoths, for example, were allowed to settle in southern Gaul, around Toulouse. Cooperation between the Romans and the barbarians did help to stem the invasions. The most dangerous barbarian of the fifth century was Attila, who united the Hunnish tribes into a terrifying war machine and rampaged throughout eastern Europe. Attila the Hun ruled an empire larger than that of Rome, from modern Germany to the steppes of central Asia, and his attacks went as far as Constantinople, northern Italy, and even central Gaul. He was held back only by the combined might of the Roman and Visigothic kings, before dying in AD 453, apparently of a nosebleed in his sleep – a curious way to go for the most notorious barbarian king of all time.

We will see more of the barbarians and the way they took over Roman and Christian culture in chapter 6. For now, we need to bear in mind that this process was going on throughout the late fourth century and the whole of the fifth. By the end of the fifth century, the western half of the Roman empire barely existed any more. It had simply crumbled away, dissolving into a number of smaller barbarian kingdoms, which sought to maintain imperial-style order to varying degrees. From this time on, the Roman empire would survive only in the east, with its capital at Constantinople. The eastern Roman empire is often called the Byzantine empire, after the old town of Byzantium where Constantinople was built, but the name is rather vague. Its inhabitants always called themselves 'Romans', even after Rome was lost and no one spoke Latin any more – 'Byzantine' is a name used by historians. And it is not clear when it is useful to stop talking about the Roman empire and start talking about the Byzantine empire. Some might put the origins of the Byzantine empire as early as Constantine, with his Christianizing of the empire and founding of Constantinople; others might put it after Justinian, who ruled in the sixth century and temporarily reconquered much of the West. However

one chooses to define it, though, this was an age of transition, when the old world of antiquity was fading and it was not clear what new age would replace it. Eastern emperors, based at Constantinople, continued to claim authority over the western territories, but that increasingly became meaningless in practice. Many people found this hard to accept. Rome had stood firm for over a thousand years. Its empire had ruled the lives of millions for nearly five centuries. Now it had fallen, virtually within a single generation. What could possibly take its place?

THE CHRISTOLOGICAL CONTROVERSY

While all this was going on, the church was becoming embroiled in yet another doctrinal controversy, one that would prove more long-lasting and divisive than even the Arian crisis of the previous century. Where the Arian row had been over the nature of the Trinity, and the relation of the second Person to the first, this one was over the person of Jesus himself, and how he (as a human being) related to the second Person of the Trinity (now acknowledged by everyone to be fully divine). However, where Arianism had been a live issue throughout the empire, this new problem was confined to the eastern Mediterranean and the Middle East, where the empire was still a political reality. It was therefore the first theological issue facing the Byzantine empire.

In its first stage, the controversy was a dispute between the two most powerful churchmen of the East. One was Cyril (AD 376–444), patriarch of Alexandria, and the other Nestorius (d. after AD 451), patriarch of Constantinople. Both were strong men, bad at compromise, and the dispute was partly political. In AD 381 the Council of Constantinople had declared that the bishop of Constantinople was a patriarch, just like those in Rome, Alexandria, and Antioch; and moreover he

Cyril of Alexandria

One cannot understand fully the Christology of Cyril of Alexandria (AD 376–444) unless one grasps the controversy between him and Nestorius. The controversy began in AD 428 when the new patriarch of Constantinople, Nestorius, was asked if it was appropriate to call Mary *Theotokos* – Mother of God. Nestorius responded that the title was doubtful, because it implied that the Son of God changed in becoming man, and more specifically that he underwent human experiences that were incompatible with his immutable and impassible divinity. God could not only not be born, he could not be said to truly hunger, thirst, suffer and die.

Cyril, the patriarch of Alexandria, vehemently protested. Following his predecessor, Athanasius, Cyril saw the title *Theotokos* as accentuating the truth that the Son of God actually did become man and so could not only be truly born of Mary, but could also truly hunger, thirst, suffer and die.

Thus Cyril was, and in many ways remains, the theologian of the incarnation. He believed that, if we are truly to be saved, the Son of God actually had to become man, rather than just dwell in a man or be joined to a man. Taking his inspiration from the Creed of Nicaea, Cyril perceived that the Son who is 'one in being with the Father' is the same Son who 'became incarnate' of the Virgin Mary and so was 'crucified… under Pontius Pilate, suffered, and was buried'.

Cyril frequently used the phrases 'the one nature of the Incarnate Word' and 'one Incarnate nature of the Word of God'. What he meant by 'one nature' is that Christ is one reality or one being, just as a man, though composed of body and soul, is one being or reality. This one reality or being is 'the Incarnate Word'. For Cyril the act of incarnation, the 'becoming', is not the mixing or confusing of natures, but the one Son taking on a new mode of existence, that is, as man. To speak of 'one Incarnate nature' or 'one nature of the Word Incarnate' is simply, for Cyril, to state that Christ is one reality or being and the one reality or being that is Christ is the Son existing as incarnate – as man.

While the above was clear to Cyril, it was obviously not so clear to others. In the course of the controversy Cyril clarified his understanding of the incarnation in a most remarkable manner. Commenting on the phrases that the Word 'was incarnate' and 'made man', Cyril wrote:

We do not mean that the nature of the Word was changed and made flesh or, on the other hand, that he was transformed into a complete man consisting of soul and body, but instead we affirm this: that the Word personally united to himself flesh, endowed with life and reason, in a manner mysterious and inconceivable, and became man.

This is what took place in the womb of Mary. The Holy Spirit simultaneously brought into being a human nature and substantially united it to the person of the Son so that the Son actually came to exist as man. Traditionally this type of union came to be termed 'the hypostatic union'. The person of the Son came to exist as man.

Thus for Cyril, while Son of God as God could not be born of Mary, yet because the Son came to exist as man in Mary's womb, he could rightly be said to be born of Mary, and Mary could rightly be said to be the Mother of God. Moreover, while the Son of God could not hunger, thirst, suffer and die as God, yet, because he actually came to exist as a man, the Son of God could actually be said to truly hunger, thirst, suffer and die as a man.

Both Nestorius and Cyril wrote to Pope Celestine. In August AD 430 the pope held a synod in Rome at which the title *Theotokos* was upheld and Nestorius was condemned. Moreover, in AD 431 an ecumenical council was held at Ephesus. It was a very messy affair, but it affirmed Cyril's understanding of the creed of Nicea and accepted his *Second Letter to Nestorius* as an authentic expression of the faith.

THOMAS WEINANDY

Cyril of Alexandria, from a church in Nagoricino, in the Former Yugoslav Republic of Macedonia.

I urge you now, as a brother in the Lord, to preach the word of teaching and the doctrine of the faith to the people with complete accuracy. Bear in mind that scandalizing even the least of those who believe in Christ exposes a person to the unbearable indignation of God. And what care and skill is needed when so many people are harmed, so that we can give the healing word of truth to those who seek it!

Cyril of Alexandria, *Second Letter to Nestorius*, AD 429

I was summoned by Cyril who had assembled the council, even by Cyril who was chairing it. Who was judge? Cyril. And who was the accuser? Cyril. Who was bishop of Rome? Cyril. Cyril was everything… What need was there for a council, when this man was everything?

Nestorius, *The Bazaar of Heraclides*, c. AD 455, on the council of Ephesus

was the second most important, after Rome. This reflected Constantinople's new status as the leading city of the east, despite the fact that no apostle had ever been there. The people of Alexandria were not happy about that at all. But there were important theological issues at stake too, for Cyril identified Jesus with the pre-existent Son, whereas Nestorius – so it seemed – thought Jesus was a kind of composite person 'made' of the Son and a human being. Much of the controversy revolved around the concept of 'nature', which at this time was poorly defined. Nestorius insisted that Christ had two 'natures', while Cyril, branding this as belief in two Christs, said he had only one.

Cyril did manage to patch things up with the Antiochene theologians before his death in AD 444. He was succeeded by Dioscorus, who was evidently keen to maintain the tradition of fighting with Constantinople. The next round in the battle concerned an elderly and highly respected abbot named Eutyches, who ran a big monastery near the eastern capital. Eutyches had taken Cyril's teaching to extremes. He not only denied that there were two natures in Jesus after his birth, but argued that his single nature was purely divine: his divinity swallowed up his humanity, as it were, so that the Jesus that Christians now pray to is not human at all. Flavian, the new patriarch of Constantinople, condemned Eutyches. Dioscorus, eager to protect his natural ally Eutyches, condemned Flavian. He even held a council at Ephesus to do it, just as Cyril had against Nestorius. This was in AD 449.

The western church stepped into the fray. Leo, bishop of Rome, wrote a famous letter to Flavian known as the *Tome* (although it is not really very long) in which he approved of the condemnation of Eutyches. In his *Tome*, Leo spoke of the two natures of Christ, one divine, and one human. He taught that even after the incarnation Christ retains these two natures, but he remains a single person, identical with the second Person of the Trinity. Where Nestorius had apparently thought of a 'nature' as a kind of 'thing' or

substance, Leo was clear that a 'nature' is something that a substance possesses: it is simply a way of describing that substance. Thus, Christ could have two natures whilst remaining only a single person. Here, then, was a middle way between Nestorianism and Eutycheanism.

To sort out the row once and for all, in AD 451 Emperor Theodosius II called yet another council, at Chalcedon, across the Bosphorus from Constantinople. This council read and approved of Leo's *Tome*, but it also approved of some of Cyril's letters too, thereby hoping to mollify moderates in both parties. The extremists were all condemned, though. Nestorius had been condemned twenty years earlier at Ephesus, and now Eutyches joined him on the rapidly growing roster of heretics. The council issued a new creed, supposedly simply an elucidation of the Creed of Nicaea over a century earlier. This creed agreed with Cyril that Christ was one person, identical with the pre-existent Son, but it also agreed with Leo that after the incarnation he possessed two distinct natures, one human and one divine.

But the hoped-for lasting solution to the christological controversies had not quite been achieved. Instead of uniting under the Creed of Chalcedon, many people around the eastern Mediterranean simply had a new thing to hate. Those who revered the memory of Cyril – and there were many, especially in Egypt – noted that he had never approved of the formula 'two natures' in Christ, and refused to accept Chalcedon. Leo of Rome, in particular, was a bogeyman to them. These people were known as the 'Monophysites' – the 'one-nature' people – and in the next chapter we shall see what happened to them, and how for the next two centuries the eastern church continued to pull itself apart over these issues.

In the West, Chalcedon was seen as something of a triumph. Ever since the fifth century, the western church has accepted as normative the teaching of the four great councils of the patristic age –

known as 'ecumenical' councils, since they represented the consensus of the whole church at that time. These councils are Nicaea (AD 325), Constantinople (AD 381), Ephesus (AD 431) and Chalcedon (AD 451). The Eastern church, as we shall see in chapter 5, would go on to hold another three councils regarded by them as equally important, making seven in all, but in the West the latter three have never been accepted as on an equal footing with the first four. Of those, Nicaea is especially significant – as the first, and the one that produced the original Nicene Creed. Chalcedon is especially significant as the last, which ratified the teaching of the first three and set out the classical understanding of the person of Jesus and his relationship to God. This council also published a slightly longer version of the Nicene Creed, which it attributed to the Council of Constantinople. This is the version of the creed that is generally known today and repeated in churches every week. One other move was significant: Chalcedon pronounced the bishop of Jerusalem to be a patriarch, like those of Rome, Constantinople, Alexandria and Antioch.

CHAPTER 4

AFRICA, THE MIDDLE EAST AND THE MISSIONS EAST

If the fourth century had seen Christianity transformed, the fifth saw it splinter. We have already seen how the religion had spread throughout both the Roman and Persian empires, as well as into smaller, associated states in the Middle East. The churches in these different regions were already distinct in a number of ways, not least in language – Latin in the western empire, Greek in the eastern, and Syriac in Edessa, Syria and Persia. Now, with the christological controversy that was started by Cyril and Nestorius, these churches began to move apart doctrinally as well. In this chapter we focus on the churches outside the Roman (or Byzantine) empire. Since many were still within the Byzantine empire for the first couple of centuries, we shall trace some of the history of Byzantium too.

THE MONOPHYSITE MOVEMENT AND THE BYZANTINE EMPIRE

The Council of Chalcedon was, to put it mildly, not popular among most Egyptians. It had deposed their patriarch, Dioscorus, and overruled his council of AD 449 (known to its opponents as the 'robber council'). On top of that, Chalcedon's adoption of the 'two natures' formula was, as far as they were concerned, nothing less than Nestorianism. It was a direct insult to the saintly Cyril of Alexandria, who had never accepted such a formula. There was

no way the Egyptians were going to kowtow to Proterius, Dioscorus's official replacement. Instead, they elected their own patriarch, Timothy Aelurus – 'the Cat'. Shortly afterwards, Proterius was murdered by a mob (a common fate for unpopular patriarchs of the city), leaving 'the Cat' as the sole claimant to the Alexandrian throne.

Timothy got his nickname not only because of his small physical stature, but also because he was a wily manipulator, able to navigate his way through the political quagmire into which he had been dropped. He believed it should be possible to work out some kind of moderate Monophysitism, opposing the hated Council of Chalcedon and its 'two natures' whilst conceding that Eutyches had gone too far. In this he was not alone. Peter the Fuller, a tanner from Constantinople who had become a monk, was a vocal advocate of the same approach. He had powerful friends, including the Byzantine emperor Zeno, who was said to possess the improbable distinction of having been born with no kneecaps. Zeno appointed Peter bishop of Antioch. These two – the Fuller and the Cat – were the brains behind moderate Monophysitism. In AD 475 there was a coup at Constantinople and Zeno was replaced by the emperor Basiliscus. He issued a statement, drafted by Peter and Timothy, condemning Chalcedon and endorsing Monophysitism.

The following year, Zeno regained power. Basiliscus was out and so were Timothy and Peter. But Zeno evidently thought that, whilst their loyalty had been suspect, their ideas were sound and in AD 482 he issued his famous *Henoticon*, an imperial decree which aimed to bring closure to the whole christological debate. It upheld the teachings of the first three ecumenical councils (the ones everyone agreed with) and completely ignored those of both AD 449 and AD 451 (the ones everyone was arguing about). Likewise, there was no mention of natures or persons, although both Nestorius and Eutyches were condemned.

The *Henoticon*, which was endorsed by Acacius, Peter's replacement as patriarch of Constantinople, was moderately successful. But for those who upheld the doctrines of Chalcedon, it was unacceptable. It went too far in the view of Calendio, who had replaced Peter the Fuller at Antioch; and it was also condemned in the West – not that this meant much to those in the East, of course. After all, the westerners did not even have an emperor any more.

By contrast, the *Henoticon* did not go far enough for the Monophysite majority in Egypt. They wanted Chalcedon to be officially struck from the records. Many in Syria agreed with them. Their spokesman was the great Severus of Antioch, who came from Pisidia but was educated at Alexandria. He spent many years at Constantinople arguing against the Council of Chalcedon, until in AD 512 the bishop of Antioch was deposed by a Monophysite synod headed by Philoxenus of Mabbug. Severus replaced him. Like other moderate Monophysites, Severus regarded himself as a disciple of Cyril of Alexandria, and he attacked extreme Monophysitism just as much as he did Chalcedonianism.

Attitudes were clearly hardening. So far, the debate had been held within the one church. No one had split off, like the Donatists two centuries earlier. But the two sides were increasingly loath to have anything to do with each other. In AD 536 the Byzantine emperor Justinian began to crack down on the Monophysites. He exiled Severus of Antioch and banned his books. Many Monophysites therefore now began to wash their hands of the established church, and set up their own

ecclesiastical structures. The authorities hunted them down, and many were killed. A point of no return had been reached, and it was clear that the Monophysites were going to go their own way, never to be reconciled with the Chalcedonians and official Byzantine orthodoxy. One of their rallying slogans was, 'I do not communicate with the synod,' meaning, of course, the Council of Chalcedon and its supporters. In their minds, Chalcedon had become synonymous with heresy, with imperial meddling in religion and with state oppression.

A key figure in this was Jacob Baradaeus – 'saddle-man' – so-called because he dressed in horse cloth as part of his ascetic lifestyle. Born in around AD 500 in Gamawa, on the Euphrates, Jacob was educated at Nisibis, within the territory of the Persians, before moving to Constantinople.

Unfortunately, as Jacob was becoming well known as a Monophysite holy man, the emperor Justinian began his clampdown on Monophysitism. Jacob Baradaeus became a man on the run. Now the Monophysite bishop of Edessa, he travelled throughout Syria, supporting and encouraging the new Monophysite Church. His travels made him into a figure of legend. According to the stories, he travelled throughout the entire known world, consecrating 120,000 priests, including 90 bishops. Just what Jacob really did remains shrouded in mystery, as does his strange death in AD 578 in Alexandria, where he was trying to unite the Syrian Monophysites with the Egyptian ones. Whatever the truth, Jacob is the great hero of the Syrian Church to this day, which has always been known as the Jacobite Church in his honour.

In Egypt, meanwhile, the same thing was happening. Those Egyptians who were ethnically Coptic were generally Monophysites, but many Greek-speakers were Chalcedonian. They were contemptuously known by the Coptic majority as 'Melkites' (from the Aramaic word for 'king'), because they were the

How can it not be obvious to everyone that the Only-Begotten, being God by nature, has been made man – not by an external or non-essential connection, but by a real union, ineffable and beyond comprehension? And so he is understood as One and Only, and everything that is said of him is appropriate, being said of one person. For the Incarnate nature of the Word himself, after the union, is conceived as one.

Cyril of Alexandria, *Five tomes against Nestorius*, c. AD 435

Limestone stela from the sixth century listing monks belonging to the Monophysite Church.

emperor's lackeys, protected by Justinian and his successors. By the end of the sixth century, there were two churches throughout Egypt, the popular Monophysite Church, which increasingly spoke Coptic, and the more Greek-oriented Melkite Church. There were even two rival patriarchs of Alexandria.

For a while it looked as if there might be some peace between them – from an unlikely source, al-Moundhir, ruler of the Ghassanid Arabs. The Ghassanids, originally from the southern Arabian peninsula, had migrated north, united a number of tribes and carved out a small but important kingdom in the desert east of the River Jordan. They controlled much of what is modern-day Syria, Palestine and Jordan and were therefore significant players in Middle Eastern politics, although their ruler, the phylarch, governed only by permission of the Byzantine emperor.

No Arabs were Muslims yet, of course; the Prophet Muhammad was about ten years old when these events were taking place. The Ghassanids were Monophysite Christians and had played an important role in allowing Monophysitism to flourish in their territories. Indeed, al-Moundhir's predecessor, al-Harith, had personally sponsored Jacob Baradaeus's consecration as bishop of Edessa. The Byzantine emperor Tiberius II thought that the Ghassanids might prove valuable allies in the never-ending struggle against Persia. Al-Moundhir was entertained at Constantinople and even allowed to call himself king of the Arabs. The pressure against the Monophysites was relaxed as this prominent Monophysite was courted by the emperor himself. Unfortunately, the truce collapsed. A Byzantine army, attacking Persia in AD 580, discovered that a key bridge had been destroyed. Al-Moundhir was blamed and exiled. The Arabic phylarchy over which he had ruled was broken up, and many of its members allied with the Persians instead. In fact, the Arabs were enormously hurt by this event, which they regarded as treachery on the part of the Byzantines. Christianity among the Arabs declined accordingly, and

Pseudo-Dionysius the Areopagite

The 'Dionysian' works were first cited amid the christological disputes of AD 520–40, initially during a colloquy at Constantinople in AD 532. The corpus consists of three treatises (*The celestial hierarchy*, *The ecclesiastical hierarchy*, *The divine names*), the brief *Mystical theology* and ten *Letters*. Despite occasional questions over its authenticity, the Dionysian writings were for many centuries considered apostolic and thus highly authoritative. Only in 1895 was there firm documentation that they date from the late fifth or early sixth century. Perhaps nothing more about the author's identity will ever be proven.

The celestial hierarchy begins with the method for interpreting symbols, whether biblical or liturgical. It presents the angelic hierarchy in three triads, a distinctively Dionysian pattern: seraphim, cherubim and thrones; dominions, powers and authorities; principalities, archangels and angels. *The ecclesiastical hierarchy*, similarly, presents the rites and

orders of a Christian community.

The longest work in the corpus is *The divine names*. Chapter one introduces the basic point, that the scriptures can praise God by many names, some more appropriate than others, and yet they also by a 'wise silence' state that God is actually beyond every name and thus ineffable and unknowable. With Chapter 3, *The divine names* discusses its first specific name for God, the 'good', as well as light, love and beauty. Chapters 5–7 treat the divine names of being, life and wisdom, among others. Chapter 13 culminates the work with a discussion of the names perfect and one, leading to the subject of union with God.

Only five pages long, *The mystical theology* begins by advising 'Timothy' that he should ascend above sense perception and conceptual achievement towards union with the One who is beyond perception and conception. The use of affirmation and negation in this ascent is illustrated by the story of Moses entering the cloud or the 'darkness of unknowing' on Mount Sinai. Chapter 4 negates every category of sense perception; God is 'not a material body, and hence has neither shape nor form, quality, quantity or weight.' Chapter 5 goes 'higher' to negate every type of concept regarding

God, even the very titles of *The divine names*; God is 'not greatness or smallness… neither one nor oneness, divinity nor goodness… nor even sonship or fatherhood.' Finally, no affirmations suffice, and the Godhead even transcends all denials.

Translated into Latin by John (the Scot) Eriugena in the ninth century, 'Dionysius' profoundly influenced medieval theology and spirituality. From Hugh of St Victor's appropriation in the twelfth century come both the scholastic interest by Albert the Great and especially Thomas Aquinas as well as the mystical interpretations by Richard of St Victor, Bonaventure, *The cloud of unknowing* and many others. Even the Gothic architecture of Saint-Denis in Paris, named for this same legendary author-become-missionary, is sometimes attributed to the Areopagite's theory of uplifting illumination.

PAUL ROREM

the Monophysites within the Byzantine empire lost their freedom to worship. The truce was over, and under the emperor Maurice the persecutions against Monophysites began again with renewed vigour.

THE MONOPHYSITES AND THE MIDDLE EASTERN WARS

The fortunes of the Monophysites during this period waxed and waned according to who ruled them. The end of the sixth century and the beginning of the seventh was a time of great flux and uncertainty in the Middle East.

What proved to be the endgame in the centuries-long struggle between Rome and Persia began in AD 602, when Maurice was overthrown by a general called Phocas (AD 547–610). Phocas – if the hostile accounts of his rule are true – was possibly the worst emperor in Byzantine history. He

slaughtered thousands of opponents in an effort to maintain his rule. Worse, the Persian king, Chosroes II, had been a friend of Maurice and now used this coup as an excuse to end his peace treaty with Byzantium and march west. Enormous swathes of land were conquered as the Persians moved across Syria, the Holy Land, Egypt and Anatolia. By AD 608 they had reached Chalcedon, and were encamped within sight of Constantinople itself. In these conquered territories, the Persians expelled all Chalcedonian Christians, for they shared the religion of the Byzantines. The Monophysites, however, were largely tolerated, since they hated the Byzantine emperor and were therefore to be encouraged. Egypt was an exception, where Monophysite Coptic monks were massacred as the Persian troops advanced in AD 620.

Byzantium was plunged into crisis and civil war. From the chaos emerged Heraclius

Painted enamel
plaque from the
Mosane School
depicting Heraclius
and the vision of
Ezekiel.

(c. AD 575–641), a soldier from North Africa who seized power and killed the wretched Phocas in AD 610. The empire was in tatters, and Heraclius spent his first twelve years as emperor rebuilding and reorganizing the army. The Persians were not idle during this time: in AD 614 they sacked Jerusalem and carried off what were believed to be the relics of the 'true cross' to Ctesiphon, their capital (near modern-day Baghdad, in Iraq). The Byzantines were outraged. Those relics had been placed there three centuries earlier, they thought, by Helena, the sainted mother of Constantine himself. Accordingly, in AD 622, having built up his forces, Heraclius launched an almighty assault against the Persians. This was not simply another Roman-Persian conflict. It was a holy war, one whose object was the retrieval of the 'true cross'. In effect, it was the first Crusade. The Byzantine forces even destroyed Zoroastrian fire temples as they advanced. Heraclius himself – the first Roman emperor for centuries to ride at the head of his army – was the prototype for all the crusading kings of the Middle Ages.

The campaign, though often brutal, would be remembered as the stuff of legend. Like a new Alexander, the golden-haired Heraclius led his armies to victory after victory. At the River Sarus the emperor himself won the battle by leading a heroic gallop over the bridge and routing the enemy. At Nineveh

the Persian general challenged Heraclius to single combat, a traditional Middle Eastern method of resolving battles. The emperor stepped forward and decapitated his opponent with a single blow. By AD 627 Chosroes II had fled, the 'true cross' was recaptured and Byzantium was victorious. Heraclius returned to Constantinople as the most popular Roman emperor perhaps since Caesar Augustus himself. The 'true cross' was reverentially returned to its resting place in Jerusalem.

From the viewpoint of the Monophysites, the recapture of most of the Middle East by Byzantine forces was not the disaster it might have been. Although a Chalcedonian, Heraclius was amenable to Monophysitism and in AD 638 he issued a document known as the *Ekthesis* which sought to find a new way of reconciling them to the church. This suggested that, although Christ had two natures, he had only one will. However, as we shall see in the next chapter, this doctrine proved highly controversial among Chalcedonians and was ultimately condemned and dropped.

But all of this was increasingly irrelevant as far as most of the Monophysites were concerned. A remarkable new development was about to take place, one which absolutely no one had foreseen – the rise of Islam and the Arab conquests, which would have dramatic consequences for the Monophysites.

MONOPHYSITISM OUTSIDE THE EMPIRE

THE ARMENIAN CHURCH

Armenia, a mountainous area lying between the Roman and Persian empires, clung onto its precarious independence with tenacity. Christianity had come here at the end of the third century, and King Tiridates had converted in around AD 301 – which meant that Armenia had been officially Christian before Rome, a source of great pride to the Armenians. Indeed, the head of the Armenian church, the catholicos, acted almost as the king's prime minister. The catholicos generally came from Cappadocia, since it had been Cappadocians who had brought Christianity to Armenia in the first place; and so Christianity here had quite a Greek feel to it. Nevertheless, at this stage Christianity had not yet penetrated the whole country. This rugged region bred rugged warriors, and the Armenians loved to hear tales of their national heroes; the Christian religion did not sit easily with this.

In AD 363 Rome was forced to cede large territories to Persia, a concession that included a promise not to intervene if Persia invaded Armenia. Persia promptly did just that, and the Armenian church lost contact with the Cappadocian church. Instead, it became more influenced by Syria, which was after all much closer geographically. A key figure in the establishment of a national Armenian church was Mesrob Mashtotes, an Armenian who lived in the early fifth century and who worked hard to bring Christianity to those areas of Armenia that had not yet converted. In so doing, Mesrob translated much of the Bible into Armenian, devising a new alphabet for this purpose, since no Armenian alphabet yet existed.

For a while, Nestorianism (the predominant form of Christianity in Persia, as we shall see shortly) was strong in Armenia, but the influence of Syria prevailed and the church became largely Monophysite. Throughout the fifth century, the Persians did their best either to force the Armenians to unite with the Nestorian Christians in Persia or to eradicate Christianity there entirely, but they always failed. Indeed, their attempts helped to reinforce the religion. In AD 451 many Armenian nobles fought and died at the battle of Avarair, rather than have Zoroastrianism imposed upon them; in the hands of later Armenian writers, the '1,036 martyrs' of this battle would be remembered as Christian warrior heroes and the faith for which they died would be inextricably linked to national pride. In AD 506 a council was held at Dvin, in eastern Armenia, which rejected Nestorianism and endorsed the *Henoticon* of the emperor Zeno as well as the writings of Timothy Aelurus. Here, then, the moderate Monophysitism of 'the Cat' became official orthodoxy.

If the Armenian church was a bastion of Monophysitism in the east, then even greater Monophysite powers were rising in the south. Beyond Egypt, for centuries to come, Monophysitism was to flourish in the ancient lands of Nubia and Ethiopia.

ETHIOPIA

The people of Ethiopia were culturally and ethnically close to those of Arabia, which was only just on the other side of the Red Sea, and especially to Saba (now Yemen). In fact the ancient Yemenite civilization of Saba, also known as Sheba, played a key part in the ancient myth of the Ethiopians' origins. According to the story, the queen of Sheba once visited King Solomon of Israel (as recorded in the Bible, in 1 Kings 10). The Ethiopian legend adds that, while there, the exotic queen and the fabulously wealthy king had a son, Manelik – who, we are told, went on to found the Axumite empire in Ethiopia. The Axumites at one time possessed the largest navy on earth. They were the only African civilization south of Egypt to develop writing, and the city of Axum itself was one of the most splendid in the ancient world.

This civilization believed passionately in its close links with the ancient Israelites. The Axumites were Jews and believed that Manelik had brought the religion with him

Do not be afraid of the great numbers of the heathen; do not turn and run from the fearsome swords of mortal men; because if the Lord grants us victory, we shall destroy their might so that the cause of righteousness might be exalted. And if the time has come for us to meet a holy death in this battle, let us accept it with joyful hearts, without staining our valour and bravery with cowardice... Stand firm by our resolute General, who shall never forget your valiant deeds. Gallant warriors! ... Our Commander is not a man, but the Commander-in-chief of all martyrs. Fear is a sign of doubt. We repudiated doubt a long time ago; let fear also disappear from our hearts and minds.

The speech of Vardan of Armenia to his troops on the eve of the battle of Avarair, AD 451, recounted by Yeghishé, *History of Vardan and the Armenian war*, c. AD 465

I armed myself with the power of the Lord of the Land and fought on the Takkaze at the ford of Kemalke. And thereupon they fled and stood not still, and I pursued the fugitives twenty-three days slaying them and capturing others and taking plunder from them, where I came; while prisoners and plunder were brought back by my own people who marched out; while I burnt their towns, those of masonry and those of straw, and seized their corn and their bronze and the dried meat and the images in their temples and destroyed the stocks of corn and cotton; and the enemy plunged into the river Seda, and many perished in the water, the number I know not, and as their vessels foundered a multitude of people, men and women were drowned.

Inscription of Ezana of Axum, c. AD 325

The relic chapel of the church of Saint Mary of Zion, at Axum, Ethiopia. It is claimed to hold the original ark of the covenant.

from Israel. In fact, many believed that Judaism had flourished in Ethiopia even before it had reached Israel – for, it was said, when Moses led the Hebrews out of Egypt, some of them had gone south instead of east. Ethiopia was therefore a holy land, the land of God himself.

Where Pharisaic Judaism became the norm in Europe and the Middle East after the first century AD, it never reached Ethiopia. So the Jews there based their religion solely on the Torah and never developed a rabbinical law. The close connection that they believed existed between their religion and that of ancient Israel took political form in the person of the king, who, it was believed, could trace his family tree all the way back to King Solomon. And it took tangible form in the ark of the covenant, which, it was thought, Solomon had given to Manelik for safekeeping. It was believed to reside on the shores of Lake Tana, the source, in the Ethiopian highlands, of the Blue Nile.

It was here that, in the fourth century AD, a young Syrian named Frumentius was shipwrecked, together with his brother Aedesius. Both were welcomed into the court of King Ezana of Axum, and Frumentius rose to become regent for Ezana's son. He later left for Egypt, where he

visited the patriarch, Athanasius. He felt that the Ethiopians, with their strong sense of Jewish history, would be amenable to a Christian mission, and he asked Athanasius to appoint a bishop for them. Athanasius therefore made Frumentius himself bishop, and sent him back to Axum to preach to the Ethiopians.

The mission was extremely successful and Frumentius, later often known in Ethiopia as 'Kasate Berhan' or 'Revealer of the Light', is remembered as the apostle of the region. Ethiopia had already been the first African nation to mint its own coins; now those coins showed the cross. By the sixth century, Christianity was strongly entrenched throughout the country, although Judaism still remained strong in many areas. Indeed, Ethiopian Christianity always retained a strong Jewish flavour, with the survival of customs such as circumcision and Sabbath observance. The church also retained its links with Egypt, since the head of the Ethiopian Church, the abana, was always sent from Alexandria. But it quickly developed its own identity, speaking Ge'ez, a tribal tongue which supplanted Greek as the official language of Axum. Things developed further with the arrival in around AD 500 of the 'nine saints', possibly a large group of Monophysite refugees from Syria, fleeing Byzantine persecution. This group preached throughout the country and translated the Bible into Ge'ez.

Perhaps as a result of this, Christianity in Ethiopia took on a Monophysite character, rejecting the Council of Chalcedon. It seems to have been a relatively moderate kind, though, modelled after people like Severus of Antioch – for the Ethiopian Church always condemned Eutyches as well as Nestorius. This may have been one of the factors which allowed Ethiopia at this period to have good relations with the Byzantine empire, for the emperor Justinian hoped that Ethiopia might provide a useful trading link to India which bypassed the Persians. Byzantine accounts of Ethiopian court life at this period tell us that the Ethiopian king wore only a gold-

embroidered, linen loincloth and a turban, but was shaded by a domed umbrella covered with golden jewellery and he travelled everywhere in a chariot pulled by four elephants, surrounded by bodyguards and musicians, especially drummers.

The 'nine saints' and their followers also helped to give Ethiopian Christianity its strongly monastic character. They built many monasteries, including the famous Debre Damo, built on the site of an old pagan shrine. Like many monasteries in the country, Debre Damo was built on an almost unclimbable mountain top, accessible only with the aid of a copper cable.

The church was defined in part by its liturgy, and it had a complex and rich liturgical tradition from an early date. St Yared, who lived in the sixth century, is credited with the composition and compilation of an enormous number of hymns and chants for use at set times of the year and in praise of particular saints – as well as the invention of the Ethiopian system of musical notation. This developed quite independently from the European

system and was considerably more complex, involving a combination of letters from the Ge'ez alphabet (of which there are over 250) and a system of dots, dashes and squiggles. This was used to write down songs much like Gregorian chant in Europe – sung without musical accompaniment, with free-flowing rhythms determined by the text rather than by a musical beat.

THE NUBIAN KINGDOMS

Many people in the West are surprised to learn that Ethiopia's neighbour Sudan also had a thriving Christian civilization in antiquity and the Middle Ages. In the West virtually nothing was known of this lost age until the 1960s, when an emergency series of archaeological excavations along the Upper Nile Valley – in an area soon to be dammed and flooded – revealed just what had once existed there.

By late antiquity, this vast region, known generally as Nubia, had seen successive powers rise and fall. The most recent was Meroe, a civilization whose power was finally broken by Ezana of Axum, who invaded it in the middle of the fourth

The interior of an Axumite church at the mountain-top monastery of Debre Damo in northern Ethiopia

century AD. On the ruins of the old, new kingdoms arose, based around the Nile. The northernmost kingdom was Nobatia, in the south of what is now Egypt, based around the city of Faras. To the south of this was Makuria, with its capital at Dongola, and finally there was Alwah (or Alodia), whose seat of power was Soba, near modern-day Khartoum.

Christianity first came to these kingdoms – or to their predecessor, Meroe – at some unknown time in late antiquity, presumably filtering up the Nile from Egypt. Acts 8:27 speaks of the baptism of an important eunuch from the Meroean court at the

hands of the apostle Philip. He is described there as 'Ethiopian', but is in fact probably Nubian – 'Ethiopia' was used by many ancient writers to mean anywhere south of Egypt. But the full-scale evangelizing of the area began only in the AD 540s, when the Byzantine emperor Justinian and his wife Theodora sent rival missions there. Justinian sent Chalcedonian missionaries and Theodora sent Monophysite ones, reflecting their rather pluralistic household; Theodora's missionaries got there first, and Christianity in Nubia therefore became predominantly Monophysite. Christianity became popular first at the royal courts,

From inscriptions in these we know that the language of the Nubian Christians was a mixture of Greek and Old Nubian, which was written in Coptic letters. Their churches were built of bricks in a kind of local variation on the Byzantine style, the most striking feature of which was the 'skewed vault'. This involves making a long, narrow roof out of what is essentially a series of brick arches, but each arch literally leans on the one before it, as if someone had pushed them all over like a row of dominoes.

THE CHURCH OF THE EAST

The Council of Chalcedon had split Christendom into three. In the middle were those who accepted Chalcedon, who became the orthodox majority in Byzantium. On one side were the Monophysites, as we have seen. On the other was the Nestorian Church, which rejected Chalcedon (and Ephesus before it) for condemning Nestorius. The heartlands of this faith lay outside the Christian Roman empire, in Persia.

We saw in the first chapter how Christianity came to Persia in the time of the Parthian empire, following the great trade route east that led through Edessa. The church's numbers had been swelled again in the third century when King Shapur I invaded the Roman empire and temporarily captured large areas (he even captured the Roman emperor Valerian and imprisoned him for the rest of his life!). Thousands of Christians were enslaved and brought back to Persia.

In the centuries that followed, the fortunes of war meant that life was not always easy for these eastern Christians. One of the principal cities of the area was Nisibis, an important centre of Christian activity and scholarship. Until AD 363 Nisibis was in Roman hands, as a frontier town, but in that year the Romans were forced to give it back to Persia. Rather than submit to Persian rule, many Christians fled

and spread only slowly, if at all, out into the surrounding countryside. In fact, it seems likely that Christianity remained a largely urban religion of the nobility throughout all the centuries of Christian Nubia.

Even now, little is known of the early Nubian churches. This is, of course, partly because they ultimately perished; but few documents remain from the period, and the fact that Nubia was so culturally remote from the Mediterranean world means that few descriptions of it survive. What we do know of Nubian Christianity comes mainly from archaeology and the study of the church buildings which still dot the landscape there.

west. Among them was Ephraim the Syrian, an extremely important Christian hymn-writer and poet, who would later be considered one of the fathers of the Syrian church, and who settled in Edessa.

Those who remained beyond Rome's control followed a different hierarchical structure from the westerners. In the late third century, Papa, bishop of Ctesiphon, the Persian capital, had insisted on his own supremacy throughout the region. Quite how he managed it is unclear, but Papa is regarded as the first catholicos or head of the Church of the East – although it seems that at the time he regarded himself only as a metropolitan. Theologically, Papa's church seems to have been little different from the church in the Roman empire. One major difference was that Arianism never spread here. The Persian Church therefore completely avoided the huge storm of the Arian controversy which dominated the fourth century. Unfortunately, it was at that time undergoing an even worse crisis of its own. In the third century, the Parthian empire was taken over by the Sassanids, who established what might be called a neo-Persian empire. The Parthians had been quite tolerant of Christianity, and the first Sassanids continued this policy, but under King Shapur II, who ruled for a remarkable seventy years from AD 309 to 379, there were intermittent but cruel persecutions. Shapur was keen to establish religious unity under Zoroastrianism and had little time for a religion that was now endorsed by Constantine, emperor of his hated enemy, the Roman empire. Many thousands of Christians were killed. The names of 16,000 of them are still remembered by the Church of the East, and they are still prayed for seven times a day.

After this, things improved somewhat for the church. Shapur's successors were keen to put relations with Rome on a better footing. Not only did the persecutions cease, but Christian bishops were sometimes used to accompany diplomatic missions west. There were closer relations with the Roman Christians, ratified at a great council in Ctesiphon in AD 410, held

Human beings know what is behind them, but in front of them is infinity. And for those who seek the Lord, evening and morning is more than enough. Their road goes a long way, but it is close at hand as they travel along it.

Babai the Great
(AD 569–628), abbot
of the Mar Abraham
monastery on Mt Izla

under the metropolitan Isaac. This council officially accepted the faith of the Council of Nicaea and also agreed to follow the calendar of the Roman church.

A NESTORIAN CHURCH?

The church had its own organization, and at the same time it had a thriving theological centre at Edessa, just across the border in the Roman empire. Ephraim and others had fled Nisibis to find sanctuary here, and in the AD 420s and 430s a new series of persecutions in Persia led to another wave of Christian refugees to Edessa. Under its energetic bishop, Rabbula, who directed its church between AD 411 and 435, Edessa became a hotbed of theological activity. Just as Christianity itself had once passed through Edessa to Persia, so too theological developments in the Roman empire passed into Persia via the same route. In particular, the works of Theodore of Mopsuestia, a revered Antiochene theologian, were translated into Syriac and eagerly read by the theologians of Edessa.

Unfortunately, Theodore was closely associated with Nestorius – or, more accurately, the slightly later Nestorius apparently taught doctrines little different from Theodore's. Indeed, the two had apparently been cousins. Those who venerated Theodore saw no reason to condemn Nestorius. Edessan delegates, including Rabbula, were present at the Council of Ephesus in AD 431, at which Cyril of Alexandria secured the condemnation of Nestorius, and they opposed the decision. Rabbula later changed his mind, becoming a strong supporter of Cyril and even burning the books of Theodore of Mopsuestia. But his attempt to reverse the theological direction of Edessa came to nothing. His successor, Ibas, was more in tune with popular feeling in Edessa and even translated some of Theodore's books into Syriac.

The situation could not last. The emperor Zeno, who was trying to reconcile the Monophysites to the Chalcedonians, could have no time for the Nestorians. After

Ibas's death in AD 457, Zeno closed the theological school of Edessa. The Nestorian theologians fled east to the relative safety of the Persian empire, leaving Edessa in the hands of Chalcedonians and Monophysites. Nestorianism was a dead issue in the Byzantine empire: the Chalcedonians and Monophysites could agree on that, at least. But under the Persians it would flourish.

First, a new school was set up at Nisibis, a copy of the old one at Edessa. One of the leading figures in this was 'Narsai the leper' – so-called by his theological enemies – who worked closely with the bishop of Nisibis, Barsumas. At its height, this new school was said to have been training 800 priests at a time, not only to minister to their own flock but to go as missionaries throughout Persia and even beyond. Nisibis became the intellectual capital of the Middle East, with courses revolving around the works of Theodore of Mopsuestia, together with those of Aristotle and Galen. The school was almost monastic in tone: students lived in solitary cells, where they memorized much of the Bible and learned a thoroughly Nestorian faith. Narsai argued that Christ had had two natures and also two substances, united in a single person. He also declared that Nestorius himself had been a good man who had been unfairly treated by political enemies.

But does it really make sense to call Narsai a 'Nestorian'? Like most Persian theologians, he regarded Theodore of Mopsuestia, not Nestorius, as his main authority. Moreover, although Narsai emphasized the two natures of Christ, he also stressed the unity of Christ. If to be a Nestorian is to split Christ into two people, then Narsai was not a Nestorian – but then neither, really, was Nestorius. In any event, those outside Persia labelled him, and his church, 'Nestorian'. The Persian church resisted this label, and has done ever since: in recent times it has been known as 'the church of the East'. Yet the more pejorative label has stuck. This was especially so after a pair of synods in the AD 480s. The first, at Beth Lapat, seems to have endorsed the work of Theodore of Mopsuestia. The second and more important, at Ctesiphon, produced a new christological creed, stressing the completeness and distinction of the two natures in Christ. The Persian authorities also encouraged this direction: they were happy to protect the Persian church as long as it was at theological loggerheads with the Byzantines.

Where, once, the Persian church had been dominated by refugees or slaves, it was now an important and respected institution. Many Christians were wealthy or important: many of the lucrative pearl fisheries of the Persian Gulf, for example, were in Christian hands. One of the most famous Christians of the early seventh century AD was Yazdin of Kirkuk, a minister at the court of King Chosroes II, who was in charge of taxes and booty stolen during the wars with Byzantium. Indeed, it was he who had taken possession of the 'true cross' when it was taken from Jerusalem. Yazdin was known as 'defender of the church in the manner of Constantine and Theodosius', but unlike some prominent Christians his faith gave him no need to fear for his life: Chosroes's favourite wife was also a Nestorian.

The threat of persecution was never far away, though. More wars between Byzantium and Persia in the AD 540s saw further attacks on Christians. The church was held together during this difficult period by the catholicos, Mar Aba I. This brilliant man had once been a prominent Zoroastrian, but he had converted to Christianity and studied not only in Nisibis but throughout the Roman empire on a series of extensive travels. He founded his own school in Ctesiphon and brought about a number of reforms throughout the church. But his brilliance was his downfall: his former colleagues among the Zoroastrians could not abide him, and the wars of the AD 540s gave them the opportunity they sought to have him deposed and forced into exile.

By the end of the sixth century, then, the Persian church was firmly established with a thriving theological tradition and a strong ecclesiastical organization: the

God is silence, and in silence is he sung and glorified by means of that psalmody and praise of which he is worthy.

Abraham of Nathpar
(c. AD 600)

Eastern spirituality, from Ephraim the Syrian to Isaac of Nineveh

The Christians of Syria and Mesopotamia brought to their new faith a cultural and religious heritage which was distinct from that of the Greek world, both in its central genius and in its Semitic expression.

Among the earliest surviving Syriac works is the *Acts of Thomas* (third century). This work reveals the fundamental framework of Syriac spirituality, a tri-partite economy of salvation in which the 'first man' lost his primordial robe of glory (one aspect of which was celibacy), thus initiating the age of the 'old man': the 'new man' has his robe restored through baptism.

Ephraim the Syrian (AD 306–73) towers over all subsequent history of Syriac theology and spirituality. His writings cover several genres, from hymns to Bible commentaries and refutations of Marcionites and Manichaeans, but it is in his poetry that the spiritual genius of Ephraim is most evident. His spirituality and theology gloried in allegory and typology. The 'wood of the cross' is not just wood, but connected in Ephraim's mind to the wood of Noah's saving ark and the wood of the tree of knowledge in the garden of Eden: through one Adam died, through another Noah was rescued, and through the third Christ gave life. This springs from a deep spiritual awareness of the connectedness of all things as part of the divine plan. God speaks to us through metaphor because, though the newly baptized Christian has his robe of glory restored by Christ, like infants we cannot attain to full understanding.

Many of the greatest works of Syriac spiritual literature were written in the monastic context, either by or for monks. The *Book of steps*, an anonymous late fourth century work of Eastern Syriac origin, distinguishes two levels or grades of Christian, 'the upright' and 'the perfect'. The former are the ordinary faithful (fed on milk), while the latter commit themselves to a higher ideal of

Ephraim the Syrian, in a fresco from the Kanalon Monastery, Thessaly, Greece.

celibacy/chastity and poverty (fed on solid food).

In Philoxenus of Mabbug (d. AD 523) we meet another major figure, whose works are among the most appealing in Syriac spirituality. The themes of body and spirit, self-emptying and childhood recur, with special emphasis on baptism as new birth. Those who pursue the spiritual life must be simple and childlike, not questioning the divine will, but accepting it, as a child accepts the instruction of parents.

Our brief survey ends with Isaac of Nineveh (later seventh century church of the East), perhaps the most profound and impressive of all the Syriac ascetical writers, whose system is based on the now traditional distinction between stages in the spiritual life: of the body (turning from created things), of the soul (transformation from within) and of the spirit (contemplation of the divine). His vision of the divine mercy is astonishingly modern, containing uninhibited insights into the nature of God's love for his creation, a love which is boundless, excludes any idea of requital for sin and encompasses all creation, saints and sinners, animals and even demons. For Isaac there is no eternal punishment after death, since such a concept is incompatible with his notion of a loving God: hell is but a kind of purgatory, part of God's loving purpose which will lead mysteriously to a final resolution. Isaac is a mystic for our time, ready to embrace all creation in the divine plan, to underpin a Christian environmentalism and to deal theologically with our central cultural belief in ultimate redemption.

JOHN HEALEY

catholicos of Ctesiphon was now recognized as the fifth patriarch, ranking alongside Rome, Alexandria, Constantinople and Antioch (the Persians didn't recognize Jerusalem as having a patriarch, since that had been established at the unacceptable Council of Chalcedon). More theological schools were opened in the early seventh century. The church of the East was strong enough to send missionaries beyond the Persian borders.

MISSIONS TO THE EAST

The famous school at Nisibis existed in large part to train missionaries. The great learning that its students imbibed was intended to make them great preachers, and it seems to have been extremely effective. Since the days of Edessa's primacy, the church of the East had been sending missionaries east, to complete the evangelization of the Persians and beyond. By the seventh century, however, this process was largely complete and the missionaries looked further east. The great Silk Road provided a ready-made highway: Chinese power was expanding west, and trade with both Persia and Byzantium increased. By the middle of the sixth century, Persian diplomats regularly took the six-month journey to Hsian-fu, China's western capital (modern Chang'an, near Xi'an).

CENTRAL ASIA

Central Asia at this time was populated mostly by nomadic or semi-nomadic tribes. The homeland of the Huns, who had migrated into Europe in the fifth century, had been here; here too were the origins of the Avars, the Petchenegs, the Magyars and other peoples who would follow them in subsequent centuries – all fearsome horse warriors. The Silk Road passed through these lands on its way to distant China.

Christians had already travelled along the Silk Road, although very little is known of what they did. We do know that in AD 552 two enterprising Persian monks succeeded in smuggling silkworms out of China, hoping to set up silk production on their own. That led to a contract with the Byzantine emperor Justinian and the establishment of a Roman silk industry in Constantinople, but not the spread of Christianity in China. More important was the expansion of Persian power itself towards the east. In the sixth century, great strides forward were made in agriculture throughout Mesopotamia, and the Persian kings sought to settle people in the newly fertile areas to consolidate their power there. Christian captives were seized in raids on the Roman empire and transported en masse to the new habitations. They did well here, and more Christian settlements appeared further and further east, well into central Asia. In AD 549, the Huns of Bactria asked the Nestorian patriarch to send them a bishop. Merv, meanwhile, an oasis on the southern edge of the Kara-kum Desert and an eastern border city of the Persian empire, became something of a centre of central Asian Christianity. It had its own metropolitan: one of these bishops, Elijah, directed major missions to what is now Turkestan. Christian communities appeared throughout the area that is now Iran and Afghanistan, and also what is now Uzbekistan. The city of Samarkand, in particular, governed at various times by the Arabs, the Turks and the Mongols, had its own bishop.

Not a great deal is known of the central Asian church during this period, but it seems to have spread quickly and abundantly. The further east it spread, the more Syriac was replaced by local languages, such as Sogdian, the language of Samarkand. In the twentieth century, many Christian manuscripts – from a variety of periods and locations, and written in a variety of languages – were found in Turkestan, with a particularly rich haul coming from Shuipang. And there was a monastery at the Turfan oasis, in China. For the Nestorian Church spread beyond central Asia into China itself.

THE EARLY CHINESE CHURCH

In AD 635 a monk named Alopen arrived at Hsian-fu, with books and images. The

As a lamb goes silently to be slaughtered so [Ye Su] was silent, not proclaiming what he had done, for he had to bear in his body the punishment of the Law. Out of love he suffered so that what Adam had caused should be changed by this. While his Five Attributes passed away, he did not die but was released again after his death. Thus is it possible for even those who fail to live after death. Through the holy wonders of the Messiah all can escape becoming ghosts. All of us are saved by his works. You don't need strength to receive him, but he will not leave you weak and vulnerable, without qi.

The Jesus Sutras

emperor allowed him to preach his 'luminous religion' and found a monastery, and also commissioned him to translate into Chinese the books he had brought with him. Whether anything came of this literary endeavour is unknown, but a Syriac monastery was founded in Chang'an (now Xi'an) in AD 638.

The mission grew. In AD 642 the first Christian texts were translated into Chinese, and in the latter half of the seventh century we are told that monasteries were built in all of the prefectural capitals of the empire – although it seems intrinsically unlikely that there really were monasteries in all AD 360 or so prefectures. The 'Persian religion', as the Chinese called it, was growing, especially in the north of China. We know nothing of how the authorities, or indeed anyone else, viewed it, but the paucity of sources alone indicates that Christianity made relatively little impact during this period.

Desperately little is known of this early Chinese church. It seems to have been spread largely by foreigners; the monastery in Chang'an, for example, was inhabited only by Syriac-speaking monks. It seems that Christianity in China was largely a foreign import which foreigners were permitted to follow, rather than something which any Chinese themselves were likely to believe in. The monasteries were known as Ta-Tsin monasteries, after the Chinese name for Byzantium – evidently, the distinctions between Orthodox and Nestorian churches eluded the Chinese. Nevertheless, the number of churches and their apparent success indicate that at least some Chinese must have been converted. Certainly, some Chinese were sympathetic to the western religion. Kuo Tzu-i, an important general and official in the late eighth century, donated large sums for the building of churches.

Much of what we do know of this period comes from a stele, or stone monument, made in Chang'an in AD 781 and rediscovered in 1625 (before which date, the existence of the early Chinese church

had been completely forgotten). It was one of a number of stelae made for the churches in the provincial capitals, and names many priests and their bishop – all, apparently, foreigners.

Even more remarkable than this stele was the discovery, in 1907, of a huge stash of religious documents in a cave near Dunhuang. Most were Buddhist, Confucian and Taoist, but a few called themselves the 'Jesus Sutras', scrolls written by members of the early Chinese church. Strikingly, one of the scrolls identifies itself as being written in AD 641, one of the first known uses by any church of the AD dating system. The scrolls teach what are recognizably Christian doctrines, featuring fairly loose translations of plenty of material from the Gospels, especially the teaching of 'Ye Su' (Jesus). But it is influenced by Taoism to varying degrees and often sounds rather peculiar to ears used to western Christianity.

The Chinese church did not flourish. Something of a death blow was dealt to it in the ninth century, when under the emperor Wu-tsang a new persecution of Christians was initiated. All monks of foreign religions were ordered to return to their normal lifestyles. The emperor was primarily clamping down on Buddhist monks, who were exempt from taxes, and Christianity seems to have been condemned by association with the older religion. Many churches and monasteries were razed to the ground, and the church was largely eradicated, even while Buddhism recovered.

THE MONGOLS AND THE YUAN DYNASTY

Christianity apparently disappeared completely from China for over two hundred years. In the eleventh century, Nestorian missions to the country resumed, with a Christian community appearing in Guangzhou. These Christians had come not from the Persian heartlands of the church but from central Asian Nestorian communities, now migrating into China itself. They were Mongols, another nomadic group of peoples of central Asia. Like many of their predecessors from this region, they were extremely able mounted warriors. They were unified and led by Temuchin, more commonly known as Genghis Khan, who in 1206 led his mounted warriors out of Mongolia and set about carving out the largest land-based empire of all time. As we shall see in Chapter 8, the Mongols expanded west with terrifying speed, conquering much of Russia, but Genghis Khan was even more interested in capturing northern China. By 1241 the whole of this immense area had fallen to the Mongols.

The Mongolian conquests greatly damaged the church in many areas. Merv, seat of a Nestorian metropolitan and centre of Muslim learning, was destroyed, killing a million people, and Samarkand too was

pillaged. But some of the Mongols were themselves Christians, converted during the spread of the Nestorian church into central Asia after the Arabian conquests. Christian tribes allied with the Mongols included the Kerait, who lived on the River Orkhon and who had converted to Nestorianism in the early eleventh century, and also the Öngüt, from what is now Inner Mongolia. Some of these groups successfully combined Christianity with the traditional nomadic Mongolian lifestyle, using movable tents as churches. The prince of the Kerait had a special mare whose milk he drank, in the Mongol style – but he blessed it first with a cross.

With the conquest of northern China in the thirteenth century, many of these Nestorians were put in charge of local administration. In 1264, Genghis Khan's

A Chinese Nestorian tablet, from the Forest of Stelae Museum, Xi'an.

grandson, Kublai Khan, moved his capital to Beijing, and soon afterwards took the name Yuan. The Mongolian khan had become a Chinese emperor, and the Yuan dynasty had been founded. Kublai Khan was keen to promote religious debate in his great realm and, in addition to the Nestorians already present, Buddhists, Muslims, Hindus and (as we shall see later) Catholics were encouraged to send missionaries. There was a Nestorian metropolitan of Beijing, and apparently another in Chang'an, as well as a bishop in Tatung. Once again, it seems that conversions among indigenous Chinese were very rare – although, as with the earlier Nestorian Church in China, very little is known about the Mongolian Christians there. Moreover, they were destined to make as little long-term impact. In 1368, the Yuan dynasty fell, and the indigenous Ming dynasty that replaced it the following year had little interest in Christianity. Without the support of the Yuan, the church seems to have collapsed once again, and all the missionaries left.

THE MALABAR CHURCH

The Church of the East had more success slightly closer to home, in India. The apostle Thomas was credited with bringing Christianity to Persia; by the fourth century he was also believed to have brought it to India. There is no good evidence that Thomas actually came to India, but it is possible: there was trade between Alexandria and the western coast of the subcontinent throughout the days of the Roman empire and even afterwards. An enterprising apostle could easily have voyaged with a merchant to exotic climes to spread the good news. However, whatever the truth of this legend, Christianity seems to have arrived in force in India somewhat later. Again, quite when and how this happened is unclear. Records exist of missions in the fourth century, on the part of the Persian church, in particular one led by a certain Thomas Kinayi. No one knows who this Thomas was – he could have been a missionary, but he could equally have

been a refugee or a trader who allowed missionaries to travel with him; he could have been hoping to bring Christianity to the Indians for the first time or he could have been planning to offer aid to an already existing church there. Whatever the truth, there seems to have been some kind of Syriac-speaking Christian community in India after his day, in the fifth century, because successive catholicoi sent communications to them. By the sixth century, there were strong Christian communities in both India and Sri Lanka.

These churches were mostly along the southern part of the western coast of India, the Malabar Coast, and so the early Indian church is sometimes known as the Malabar church. Most of the churches were in what is now the state of Kerala, on the southern tip of the subcontinent. As with the Chinese church of this time, not much is known about it. In particular, it is not known whether it existed primarily for immigrants, foreigners and merchants – as the Chinese church appears to have done – or whether there was a successful mission to the Indians themselves. The main centres of Christian activity seem to have been Quilon (modern Kollam), a trading

city on the coast, and Cranganur, to the north. And the Christians appear to have done well for themselves. According to some official copper plates from the ninth century, the Christians were allowed to sit on carpets and ride elephants – activities normally restricted to the aristocracy – and they had their own merchants' guild, which was in charge of other merchants as well. Evidently the Christians had a reputation for honesty, since they were also put in charge of scales and weights, making them the official customs officers. The church was also given low-caste families as slaves. Quite what happened to them is unknown, but it is reasonable to suppose that they were baptized and eventually absorbed into the Christian community.

In addition to this contemporary evidence, traditions and oral history recorded by Europeans in the sixteenth century add to our picture of Christian life in ancient India. The Christians acted much like normal Hindu aristocrats. In addition to riding around on elephants, they practised old Indian customs such as feeding newborn babies a mixture of honey and gold, taking ritual cleansing baths and marrying in the Hindu style. Similarly, men and women lived separately, in accordance with Hindu views on purity. The Christians dressed like upper-caste Hindus – but with crosses woven into their hair. Here, then, we have a remarkable story of people who were culturally Indian but retained their distinctive Christian faith. Indeed, these Christians seem to have got on well with the Hindu majority. They even believed – very unusually for this time – that Hindus could be saved through their own religion.

During this time we hear of another influx of Christians to Malabar, led by two missionaries named Sapor and Prot; again, we do not know their purposes in coming to a church that certainly already existed. But whether the Persian church really founded the Malabar church or not, it certainly dominated it. The Persian catholicos apparently claimed spiritual authority over Christians in India as well as those in Persia, and the Indian Christians seem to have been quite happy with this arrangement. The catholicos exercised his authority through a local metropolitan, who was generally sent from Persia; these metropolitans tended not to speak the local languages, so the Indian church was actually administered by a native

A twelfth-century frieze of Indian elephants.

archdeacon. Known as 'the prince and head' of the Indian church, the archdeacon's post was hereditary, and in the eyes of the secular authorities he was responsible for the Christian community – rather like the Jewish high priest in the days of Pontius Pilate. However, the archdeacon ruled via a synod called the *yogam*, made up of both clerical and lay representatives of the Indian church. At the local level, the *yogam* was represented by *palliyogams*, smaller versions of the synod which controlled local parish affairs.

NESTORIANS IN INDONESIA

There is evidence that Nestorian Christians sailed even further than India, setting up churches as they went. A seventh-century Persian account of south-east Asia testifies to churches along the west coast of Sumatra, in what is now Indonesia; some of these churches were dedicated to the Virgin Mary. Virtually nothing is known of these churches or the communities who built them; presumably, like the early churches in China and India, they were built for Persian traders and merchants living in distant lands. Yet these communities seem to have lasted for some considerable time. An Italian traveller in the mid-fourteenth century encountered Nestorians in Java, and we know of a Nestorian bishop consecrated at Palembang, in eastern Sumatra, in 1502. However, by the seventeenth century, these presumably scattered communities of Nestorians seem to have more or less completely died out.

THE COMING OF ISLAM

While Christianity was spreading to China and India, major developments in the Middle East were overturning the established political and religious order. The rise of Islam was one of the most remarkable and unexpected events in history, one with profound implications for Christianity.

It was the last thing anyone might have

expected from the Arabian peninsula. This area, mostly desert, was inhabited by a number of nomadic tribes. Most followed local polytheistic cults, but some were Jewish, and some were Christian, mainly as a result of missions by the Persian church, although it seems there were also Monophysites as well, such as the Ghassanids. As far as Byzantium and Persia were concerned, Arabia was interesting only because it produced frankincense, an important resource for Christian rituals.

There were no large settlements in Arabia, except for some on the Red Sea coast, primarily Mecca. Mecca possessed a great shrine called the Ka'ba, a black building which incorporated in its structure a mysterious black stone, revered since ancient times, and possibly a meteorite. Many Arabs who knew Jewish or Christian legends believed that the Ka'ba had originally been built by Adam, the first man, and later restored by Abraham, the first Jew.

Here, in around AD 610, a trader from Mecca named Muhammad felt called by God to deliver a new message. Preaching an uncompromising monotheism, Muhammad denounced polytheism and gathered a group of followers. Forced to leave Mecca for Medina in AD 622 (the starting date of the Muslim calendar), he subsequently united Medina, marched on Mecca with a huge army and captured it without a struggle. The Muslim conquests had begun.

Muhammad's new religion was called Islam, from a word meaning 'submission', referring to the need to submit to God; a 'Muslim' is one who submits. By the time Muhammad died in AD 632, the whole of the Arabian peninsula had been united under Islam. Muhammad himself would be honoured as 'the Prophet', the last and greatest in a long line of messengers that the Muslims believed had been sent by God throughout history.

After Judaism and Christianity, Islam was the third great monotheistic religion. And they were all closely related. The Muslims believed that, while the Jews were descended from Abraham through his son Isaac, they

O followers of the Book! do not exceed the limits in your religion, and do not speak lies against Allah, but the truth; the Messiah, Isa [Jesus] son of Marium [Mary] is only an apostle of Allah and His Word which He communicated to Marium and a spirit from Him; believe therefore in Allah and His apostles, and say not, Three. Desist, it is better for you; Allah is only one God; far be it from His glory that He should have a son, whatever is in the heavens and whatever is in the earth is His, and Allah is sufficient for a Protector.

The Qur'an 4.171

The Ka'ba in Mecca, depicted in an eighteenth-century ceramic tile.

themselves were descended from his other son, Ishmael. Moreover, they honoured Jesus as a prophet, although not as divine; neither could they accept the Christian doctrine of the Trinity, which they felt compromised strict monotheism. However, it seems that the Christianity of the Arabian peninsula may have influenced Muhammad. There was a tradition that he had a Monophysite teacher called Sergius Bahira. Moreover, there are similarities between early Islam and early Jewish Christianity. It may be that some Jewish Christians, cast out by the mainstream church in the Roman empire, retreated to Arabia, where they never developed the doctrines of Jesus' divinity or the Trinity. A common title for Muhammad himself was 'the seal of the prophets', a term he is said to have used himself. But the earliest known appearance of this phrase is Christian: it was used by Tertullian to describe Christ.

Whatever the links may have been between early Christianity and early Islam, the Muslims were relatively tolerant to both Jews and Christians living in their lands. The rule was that all non-Muslims had to accept Islam, but Jews and Christians were recognized as *Dhimmi*, 'people of the Book', who were sufficiently close to Islam to be allowed to continue to practise their own religion. However, they had to pay a special tax, known as the *jizya*, for this privilege.

Once Muhammad had unified the Arabs, they proceeded to sweep out of Arabia in an astonishing series of conquests. They were led in this endeavour by the Prophet's father-in-law, Abu Bakr, the first caliph (or 'successor' of Muhammad). Under Abu Bakr, and then the second caliph, Umar Farooq, the Muslims invaded the Persian territories. First Egypt and Armenia fell in AD 639, and then Persia itself was attacked. Exhausted by the recent wars with Heraclius, the Persians were barely able to muster a defence against the brilliant cavalry of the Muslims, and their ancient empire was crushed with ease.

The Byzantines, probably not really understanding the nature of the threat which now faced them, sent an army in AD 635 to attack the Arabs: blinded by a sandstorm, it was completely wiped out. Damascus was taken, and in AD 638 Jerusalem itself fell. The 'true cross', so recently rescued from the Zoroastrians, was now in the hands of the Muslims. The story of mighty Heraclius had turned from adventure to tragedy. Old and ailing, no longer the golden hero of former days, he became increasingly paranoid, convinced that divine favour had left him and his people and moved to the followers of Muhammad instead. He died, depressed, in AD 641, with the condemnation of his *Ekthesis* by the pope the final blow.

The Muslims, meanwhile, conquered their way through the rest of the Middle East and North Africa. Some differences began to arise within Islam, most notably a dispute over the legitimacy of the early caliphs (collectively known as the Umayyad dynasty). Those who believed that a different line should have ruled became known as Shia Muslims; the majority, who accepted the Umayyads, became known as Sunnis. This division still exists today.

THE CHURCH OF THE EAST UNDER ISLAM
The first Christian church to find itself under the rule of the Prophet was the 'Nestorian' Church of the East, based mainly in Persia, the first great power to fall before the Arabian armies. Much of the eastern part of this church, in central Asia, also fell within the Arabian domains: Merv, one of the most important eastern Christian cities, was conquered by the Muslims in AD 646, becoming their base of operations for further conquests.

But the Church of the East did quite well under the Muslims – better, in some ways, than it had under the Zoroastrians. Even though the Muslims had conquered Persia, they were greatly outnumbered by Christians. For the first couple of centuries after the conquests, Islam was confined mostly to the great cities such as Damascus and Basra (in the south of what is now Iraq), where the conquerors built splendid mosques. Beyond these cities, Muslims were

If you want to spend your life in peace, abandon the foolish faith which you learned in your childhood. Deny the man Jesus, and turn to the great God whom I worship, the God of our father Abraham. Dismiss your army, and send the troops back to their own places. I shall make you a great prince in that region. I shall send governors to your city to examine all the treasures, and shall order that they be divided into four parts: three parts will go to me, and one part to you. I shall give you as many troops as you need, and take in tribute as much as you can pay. Otherwise, how can that Jesus, whom you call Christ – who was unable to save himself from the Jews – possibly save you from me?

Letter from a Muslim leader to emperor Constans II of Byzantium, c. AD 651, in Sebeos of Armenia, *History* 36, c. AD 661 far outnumbered by Christians. Much of the civil service and local government remained in their hands, even in Damascus: the theologian John of Damascus came from a family of Christian tax collectors here. There were tens of millions of Christians in Persia, in over two hundred dioceses. This was not a small schismatic 'rump' but a major church in its own right, even not counting its daughter churches in China and Malabar. Many new monasteries were founded in the seventh century, including the famous monastery of Mar Mari at Ctesiphon. And it seems that under a succession of treaties with the Arab rulers (dating back, it was claimed, to an agreement between the bishop of Nadjran and Muhammad himself) monks were exempt from the *jizya*. The theological school of Nisibis prospered, and under the beneficent rule of Catholicos Ishoyahb III it expanded to became a major centre of other studies too, including philosophy, law, medicine and music.

Moreover, this period saw something of an explosion in the copying of manuscripts and the writing of new ones. Ishoyahb's successor, Giwargis I, produced a huge anthology of the sayings of the Egyptian monks, entitled *Paradise of the Fathers*. And his successor, Henanisho I, wrote a copious amount on theology and spirituality, including commentaries on Aristotle.

In AD 750 the Umayyad caliphate fell, partly because of its continued failure to conquer Constantinople, and was replaced by the Abbasid caliphate. The new caliph, al-Mansur, founded a new capital at Baghdad in AD 764. His regime took a more hands-on approach to its Christian subjects. Al-Mansur and his successors often interfered with the election of the catholicos, and were not above locking him up when the occasion called for it. Indeed, the late eighth century and the early ninth century saw a series of persecutions of the Christians, partly in response to wars with the Christian Byzantine empire. Many Persian Christians fled the Arab lands to find sanctuary in the Byzantine empire – where, of course, they found themselves regarded as Nestorian heretics.

Throughout this period, the Church of the East was guided by the strong hand of Catholicos Timotheos I, who ruled from AD 780 to 823. Timotheos recognized that restoring good relations with the caliphate was essential if the church was to survive, and he moved his seat from Ctesiphon, the old Persian capital, to Baghdad. Here, his considerable diplomatic skills enabled him to win the confidence of the caliph al-Mahdi and he was allowed to rebuild churches. Timotheos also oversaw a period of rejuvenated mission east, in which he even anticipated sending a bishop to Tibet. He engaged in theological discussions with the caliph too, helped by his own considerable learning, in philosophy as well as theology; he was quite capable of citing Aristotle in his letters. Notably, Timotheos spoke Arabic with the caliph, and was apparently bilingual in this language and Syriac, the traditional language of the church. Arabic seems to have increasingly elbowed Syriac out of the way throughout the ninth century, until the Christians all spoke the language of their conquerors.

Timotheos was helped in his endeavours by a realization on the part of the caliphate that the Persian Christians were not quite the same as the Byzantine ones. Al-Mahdi interrogated a Byzantine prisoner and learned what the Persian emperors had known before him: that the Byzantines regarded the Persian Christians as Nestorian heretics, hardly Christians at all. Clearly, then, the Persian church was something to be encouraged after all. Nevertheless, a healthy spirit of debate throve between the two religions. Apologists for each side wrote refutations of the other. Just how healthy this debate was tended to vary according to the views of the current caliph. Some were friendly to the Christians, whilst others were suspicious of them and their apparent ability to infiltrate positions of power. There were Christian aristocrats, riding expensive horses and wearing expensive clothes. Many high-ranking physicians, at the court of the caliph and elsewhere, were Christians, and some of them handed down their position from father to son. The skill of these Christian doctors was an important element in

Verily, you are communities of Nubia enjoying the guarantee of Allah and of his messenger, Muhammad, the Prophet, with the condition that we shall not wage war against you or declare war against you, or raid you, as long as you abide by the stipulations in effect between us… You are to look after the safety of any Muslim or one of our allies who lodges in your territories or travels in them until he leaves… You are to look after the mosque which the Muslims have built in the courtyard of your capital, and you are not to prevent anyone from worshipping in it… Incumbent upon us hereby is the pact of God and his agreement and his good faith, and the good faith of his messenger Muhammad. And incumbent on you towards us is the utmost observance of the good faith of the Messiah and that of the disciples and of any of the people of your religion and community whom you revere. God be the witness of this between us.

From the baqt, as reported by al-Maqrizi, History of Egypt, fifteenth century

winning the trust of their Muslim rulers.

Not only that, but the Christians played a major role in transmitting the culture of the past to the Muslims. Many devoted their time to translating Greek classics, especially the works of the great philosophers, into first Syriac and then Arabic. A major figure in this was Hunain ibn Ishaq, who lived in the late ninth century, and who was the personal physician to the caliph, an expert on problems of the eye, as well as a Christian deacon. He translated over 250 Greek works, concentrating on the medical writings of Galen, and he co-opted his son and grandson into the great task as well. Note his Arab-sounding name – by this time, well-to-do Christians had adopted Arabic naming conventions as well.

Without people like Hunain ibn Ishaq, Islam would never have become a religion of philosophy and advanced theology, as it did in the later Middle Ages. But still, Hunain's time was waning. Despite the strength of the Church of the East, it weakened as time passed. The Muslims collected fewer and fewer taxes from the church, indicating diminishing numbers. Forcing people to convert to Islam was discouraged, since it was felt that adherence to a religion should be through personal conviction. Indeed, sometimes conversion at all was discouraged, since it was feared that Christians might convert to Islam simply to avoid paying the jizya, and that was a poor motivation. Nevertheless, the numbers of Christians steadily fell, as was perhaps inevitable. Despite their tolerated status, Christians were necessarily second-class citizens, as the infliction of the jizya symbolized. The eastern reaches of the church suffered especially. Sogdiana – the region around Samarkand – which had previously had a strong Christian community, declined.

Things changed in the thirteenth century, with the rise of the Mongols to the east. As we saw earlier, some Mongols were Christian already. Their rulers were not much bothered about religion and they mostly tolerated Christians, along with adherents of other faiths, within their realms. Indeed, some Christians were extremely influential within the new Mongol empire. Mongke, who became Great Khan in 1250, sent his brother Hulagu to lead the campaigns in the Middle East; Hulagu was greatly in awe of his wife, Doquz-Khatun, who was a Christian and reportedly hoped for the conversion of the Mongols. The Mongols conquered much of the Arabian territory in the Middle East, including Baghdad, Nisibis, and Edessa. Many regarded the Mongols as liberators, saving the church from its Muslim overlords, and the Nestorian catholicos was even able to occupy the now vacant caliph's palace in Baghdad. But the Mongols overreached themselves. In 1260, they were defeated by the Mamluks of Egypt, who reconquered Syria, and who were much less well disposed towards the Christians.

Worse was to come, once again from central Asia. The late fourteenth century saw the rise of a new warlord, Timur Lenk (Timur the Lame), normally remembered as Tamerlane. A Turkicized Mongol and a Muslim, Tamerlane declared himself khan and proceeded to conquer another great empire in the region, based around his home city of Samarkand. Most of central Asia and Mesopotamia fell in just a few short years, and Tamerlane was merciless in his destruction of all who opposed him, either militarily or in matters of faith. The Church of the East was thrown into disarray, coming close to extinction throughout the new empire. Tamerlane's empire, and the 'Dark Ages' of the Church of the East, lasted for a century before dissolving, but his heirs would go on to found the Mughal empire in India. The strength of the Church of the East was shattered: it survived, but only as small, scattered communities.

NUBIA IN THE AGE OF ISLAM
The Nubian kingdoms survived for centuries through a combination of cultural strength, military determination, skilful diplomacy and sheer luck. In AD 641 the Arabs, fresh from their conquest of Egypt, attacked the two northernmost Nubian kingdoms, Nobatia and Makuria. The Nubians sued for peace and the Muslims withdrew – for they regarded this land as poor and its people as

hostile, not worth occupying, at least compared to the Egyptians. An uneasy standoff was the result.

After this, Nobatia and Makuria merged into a single kingdom, centred on the city of Dongola. As a result, the Nubians were more united, both religiously and politically. In fact, Makuria was powerful enough to invade Egypt in AD 745 and release the patriarch of Alexandria, who had been imprisoned. However, relations between the Christian Nubian kingdoms and the Muslim powers to the north throughout this period were based on the *baqt*, literally a pact, a basic agreement to recognize the other party's right to exist. Egypt had the upper hand in this pact, since Makuria had to provide them with a regular levy of slaves, and they were also charged to maintain and protect the mosque in Dongola. Alwah, meanwhile, appears to have been outside the terms of the *baqt*, but that state was in relatively little danger from Egypt since Makuria lay between them. In AD 836, when he was still only co-ruler with his father, Georgios I of Makuria visited Baghdad – seat of the Abbasid caliphate – and reaffirmed the *baqt* with them as well.

So, although there was intermittent warfare between Makuria and Egypt, none of it was very serious. Under the *baqt*, Makuria became remarkably powerful and developed a close bond between church and state, modelling itself to some degree on Byzantium. Indeed, the kings were traditionally priests, thereby creating a kind of 'caesaropapism' technically more extreme even than that of Byzantium, and they apparently modelled themselves on the great Christian Roman emperors. Merkurios, who ruled in the early eighth century, was styled 'the new Constantine', and oversaw a major programme of palace and church building. In Faras he built a great cathedral in the Nubian style, the ruins of which are still impressive today. The walls are still adorned with extensive and beautiful frescos, a particular feature of Nubian churches and cathedrals.

Monasteries appear to have played an important role in Nubian Christianity. Two are known at Dongola, and there is a well-known one at Qasr el-Wizz. These monasteries were not large, at least compared to contemporary monastic foundations in Byzantium and Europe. About twenty to fifty monks seems to have been the norm. They consisted of a compound protected by an encircling wall and a number of buildings within. It may well have been that monasteries provided accommodation for others, in the Byzantine tradition of the hospice for travellers and the sick. Small bedrooms and chapels apparently dedicated for this purpose have been discovered in some Nubian monasteries.

Nubia spread its cultural and military influence beyond its borders. The patriarch of Alexandria was still regarded as the spiritual leader of all Nubian Christians, but he was protected by the Nubian king. Georgios I, who ruled from AD 860 to 920, was regarded as not only the king of Makuria, but the spiritual protector of all Christians in Nubia and Egypt alike. To the south, the Nubian

Marianus, bishop of Faras (d. 1037), from a fresco in the cathedral of Faras, former capital of Nobatia.

kingdom of Alwah was apparently prospering, and its rulers enjoyed close family links to the rulers of Makuria – although no cities or towns of any size are known other than the capital, Soba. Makuria, by contrast, was much more extensive, with many towns outside the capital, Dongola, and a high population in and near its second city, Faras.

Life, it seems, was not at all bad in medieval Nubia. People were fairly healthy and lived fairly long lives by the standards of the time – indeed, some evidently lived to advanced ages, since we know that Petros, bishop of Faras, died at 93. Perhaps the biggest health problem was self-inflicted – like the Ethiopians, the Nubians retained many features of Judaism in their Christianity, including circumcision, and they also carried out the practice of female circumcision. Still, the wine flowed freely in Dongola, where we are told that there were many taverns, often better built than the houses, and where the people sang heartily. Of course, our sources for this information are Muslim, and therefore teetotal, so they may have rather overemphasized the rowdiness of their toping neighbours.

Things looked good, but this did not last. In the later Middle Ages the Egyptians had the upper hand and Makuria waned. The Sunni Ayyubid dynasty, which took power in Egypt in the twelfth century, had less interest in the historic *baqt*. The shipments of grain stopped arriving. In 1272 David, king of Makuria, launched an incredibly unwise attack on the town of Aidhab, on the coast of the Red Sea. Egyptian recrimination was inevitable and, with it, economic and political freefall. Makuria survived – just – as a political entity, but after 1316 it was officially Muslim. Later in this century, plague struck Egypt, killing enormous numbers of people, and Nubia appears to have been affected as well.

The death throes of the kingdom lasted for two centuries, as political control over the provinces collapsed and the ecclesiastical structure decayed. The state infrastructure collapsed and the people changed from an urban, agriculturally-based way of life to a rural, nomadic one. It seemed that although the church had been powerful, closely allied to the state, it was not sufficiently ingrained in the people. It had remained an urban, court religion and had not penetrated to the countryside.

The final nail in the coffin of Nubian Christendom came in the sixteenth century, when the Funj people, who lived to the south, converted to Islam and invaded. Alwah fell, followed by what remained of the provinces of Makuria. At the same time, the Ottomans were conquering Egypt and pushing south. Caught between these two pincers of Islamic military might, what remained of Nubian Christianity perished together with Nubian political independence.

ETHIOPIA IN THE AGE OF ISLAM

The Ethiopians fought against the Muslims for many years, especially in naval wars on the Red Sea. At first they had great success. Ethiopian corsairs ravaged the Arabian coastline and some Muslims even feared the Christians would capture Mecca. However, by the early eighth century the Muslims had regained control of the areas taken by the Ethiopians, had driven the Christian ships out of the Red Sea and had captured or destroyed their coastal towns. The peoples to the east and south of Ethiopia were all converted to Islam, but fortunately for the Ethiopians remained largely divided among themselves. The most important of these groups were Yifat, in the hills between Ethiopia and the Red Sea coast, and Adal, further east.

Abandoning their old capital of Axum and its port city of Adulis, the Ethiopians moved largely into the mountainous plateau that dominated their country. Their monasteries doubled as fortresses and safe houses, refuges for the most precious objects of Ethiopian civilization. Fortunately, despite occasional skirmishes with Yifat and Adal, relations with these new sultanates were generally not bad. A tradition among the Muslims held that the

Prophet himself had blessed Ethiopia, where some of his followers had found shelter, and forbade Muslims from declaring holy war against it in perpetuity. Thus, the coastal sultanates were largely content to pay tribute to the more powerful Ethiopian empire, and the trade routes between Ethiopia and the sea remained open, although in Muslim hands.

But more troubles beset the Ethiopians. In the late tenth century, the country was invaded by a savage people led by a fierce warrior queen, who burned churches and smashed religious artefacts. Scholars disagree over the identity of these people and their queen, but Ethiopian legend identifies her as Yodit (or Judith), a Jewish leader, who hated Christianity and sought to return the country to its ancestral faith. Under her brilliant command, we are told, Axum was looted, the Christian dynasty was overthrown, and Yodit herself seized the throne and ruled for forty years. How true the story is, and whether Yodit was a single person, a dynasty, or even existed at all is now unknown. She and her people are just as likely to have been pagans as Jews. Perhaps Yodit is as legendary as the queen of Sheba, an 'evil' queen to balance that 'good' queen; a demonizing of the Jewish and the female alike by later reactionary Christian myth-makers.

NEW DYNASTIES, NEW WARS
Whatever the details, continual war with tribes both outside and inside the borders of the Christian kingdom saw the overthrow of the old 'Solomonic' dynasty. A new dynasty arose from the Agew peoples, whose lands the Ethiopians had conquered, but who had never been completely culturally assimilated. They spoke their own language, although they did accept Christianity quickly. From them came the Zagwe dynasty, whose most famous member was King Lalibela, who ruled in the early thirteenth century. Lalibela was painfully aware that he was not descended from King Solomon, like the old rulers of Ethiopia, so he did his best to create a new founding myth: it was said, for example,

that the Zagwe kings were descended from Moses. Meanwhile, Lalibela sought to consolidate his claim to the Christian kingship by founding a new capital, Roha, in the mountains, by a river he renamed Jordan. Here the king commissioned a remarkable monument: a series of eleven churches carved directly out of the rock. Some were cut from cliff-faces, whilst others were created by digging great pits or wells in the plateau and literally cutting around the shape of the church, so that it stood in a great sunken courtyard, its roof level with the ground. Passages, tunnels, and caves linked the churches in an underground maze of rock. These remarkable churches still stand, and are often called the eighth wonder of the world; Roha itself has been renamed Lalibela, after the king who tried to create a new Jerusalem in the African highlands.

But the Zagwe squabbled among themselves and could not hold the empire together. The king of the province of Shewa, Yekuno Amlak, declared independence, and in 1270 he murdered the Zagwe emperor Yitbarek in front of the altar of a parish church and took his crown. Fortunately, the new Shewan dynasty quickly discovered that they too were descended from Solomon after all, and everyone was happy. A new and more detailed version of the old Solomonic origins legend was compiled, called the *Kebre Negast,* which described the birth of the legendary Manelik, son of Solomon, and helped to cement the authority of the Shewan dynasty. It also described how God gave custody of the ark of the covenant to Manelik, symbolizing the passing of his favour from the Hebrews to the Ethiopians.

An important figure associated with the restoration of the Solomonic line was Takla Haymanot, the 'Tree of the Faith'. This revered man was supposedly a descendant of Zadok, high priest of Jerusalem, who had crowned King Solomon himself. Takla Haymanot had been appointed a deacon at the precocious age of fifteen, and later rose to become effectively the head of the Ethiopian church. It was he who had

Thus has God made for the king of Ethiopia more glory, and grace, and majesty than for all the other kings of the earth, because of the greatness of Zion, the Tabernacle of the Law of God, the heavenly Zion. And may God make us perform his spiritual pleasure, and deliver us from his wrath, and make us share his kingdom. Amen.

The *Kebre Negast,* 117, thirteenth century

The roof of
St George's Church,
Lalibela. The church
and its surrounding
courtyard are carved
directly out of the
ground; to enter,
the visitor must
descend through a
series of tunnels
and stairways in the
rock.

persuaded Yekuno Amlak to seize power: thus, the descendant of Zadok had anointed the descendant of Solomon.

Whether it had anything to do with the restoration of the Solomonic line or not, things began to go better in Ethiopia – just as they were starting to go worse for Makuria to the north-west. Amda Siyon, who was emperor between 1314 and 1344, symbolized a new sense of Ethiopian strength. He reorganized the agricultural and social system of the country, creating something close to the European feudal system, whereby the emperor owned the whole land but leased it to local lords, whose responsibility it was to ensure that the land was worked and to provide troops when necessary. Amda Siyon engaged in a series of wars with the sultanates of Yifat and Adal, which had finally broken the edict of Muhammad and declared holy war against Ethiopia. The emperor conducted a brilliant campaign, capturing large swathes of territory and subduing it with his feudal system. At the same time, the Ethiopian church aggressively evangelized these lands which only a few years before had been waging jihad against them. Abuna Yakob, who became head of the Ethiopian church in 1337, sent large numbers of monks throughout these territories to preach to the people. Many were attacked or killed, but their mission was successful, and Christianity became firmly established throughout the lowlands of Ethiopia as well as the highlands.

THE SABBATARIAN CONTROVERSY
This period of expansion of the Ethiopian church coincided with new divisions within it. An abbot named Abba Ewostatewos started to speak out against what he saw as moral and spiritual laxity within the church. He believed that the increasing interdependence of church and state would inevitably expose the church to worldly influences and weaken it, and he pointed to the trading of slaves to Egypt and Arabia as evidence of this. Indeed, Ewostatewos argued that the church should return to its

Jewish roots and taught that the Law of the Old Testament continued to be binding on Christians. He and his followers kept the Sabbath and refused to pay tribute to the government.

Church and state authorities alike denounced Ewostatewos and his teachings. Ewostatewos himself was exiled to the Holy Land, and then to Armenia, where he died in 1352, and his followers – the Sabbatarians, also known as the 'Ayhud', a derogatory term for Judaizing Christians – were persecuted back home. They were banned from holy orders, cast out of monasteries and even driven out of towns. Some of them banded together and founded new settlements in the north-east of the country, where they practised a Jewish form of Christianity so extreme that in some cases it seems to have reverted to Judaism proper. More moderate Sabbatarians persisted throughout the country, and their enthusiastic preaching won them many followers. They refused to rejoin the church, setting up an ecclesiastical structure of their own outside the clerical orders.

In 1436 the emperor Zara Yakob conceived of an ingenious way to end the schism in his country when the old abuna died. He asked Alexandria to send not one but two replacements, who he asked to act as ecclesiastical reformers. He hoped that if these abunas could study the situation in Ethiopia and report back to Alexandria, the patriarch there might decree that Sabbath observance was permitted. Then the Sabbatarians would no longer have any reason to be in schism from the orthodox, and unity could be re-established with both camps in the one church. He never secured this decree from Alexandria, but the two abunas did conclude that Sabbath observance was to be permitted. In 1450, the Sabbatarians accepted the ruling and agreed to take clerical orders within the Ethiopian Orthodox Church, thereby ending the schism.

The event was significant not only because of the end of the schism, but because of the emperor's role. He had

In the case of Mary, it is impossible to count her miracles and wonders, for it seems to me that they are more than the sand of the seashore and the stars of the sky. Mary is praised in the praise accorded to a dual virginity, for upon her have appeared perfectly, without blemish, the glory of the virginity of mind and the glory of the virginity of body.

Emperor Zara Yakob, *Revelation of the miracle of Mary*, fifteenth century mediated between the two sides, and the effect was that the emperor was increasingly seen as the protector of the church – just as the king of Makuria had once been, to the north-west.

However, no sooner had Ethiopia overcome these internal problems than new threats from outside arose. In the early sixteenth century the coastal sultanates rose again under the burgeoning power of Adal, and from them emerged a mighty military leader, Ahmad ibn Ibrahim al-Ghazi, known to his enemies and posterity as Grañ, 'the Left-handed'. Under his leadership, the Adal sultanate would bring Ethiopia to its knees in the 1520s. As we shall see in Chapter 10, Christian civilization in Africa would survive this crisis only through the scarcest of good fortune.

CHAPTER 5

THE BYZANTINE EMPIRE

Rome had fallen, but New Rome, the city of Constantinople, stood firm. Here, the vision of Constantine – of a perfect Christian state, with the emperor presiding over civil and religious life – was realized. As western Europe degenerated into squabbling barbarian kingdoms, and the Middle East and North Africa fell to the followers of the Prophet, Byzantium stood as a bastion of Christian civilization.

BYZANTIUM AND THE ORTHODOX CHURCH

Christ enthroned between the Byzantine emperor Constantine Monomachus (reigned AD 1042–55) and the empress Zoe, in a mosaic from Hagia Sophia, Istanbul.

From the founding of Constantinople by Constantine the Great in AD 330 to the fall of the city to the Ottomans in 1453, the Byzantine empire endured for 1,123 years and 18 days. Over such a vast time span there was inevitably great change, both social and political, yet the degree of cultural uniformity throughout that time is

striking. That was due, in large part, to the central role that Christianity played in the empire.

EMPERORS, CHURCHES AND HEAVEN ON EARTH

Perhaps the most obvious element of this role was the near-perfect union of church and state, above all in the person of the emperor. The tendency of 'caesaropapism', pioneered by Constantine and his sons, was taken further than ever before. The emperor was regarded as Christ's regent on earth. In the Golden Hall, the imperial throne room, a magnificent icon of Christ in majesty towered over the throne itself. Nearby was an icon of the Virgin Mary, the protector of the city of Constantinople. From AD 641 onwards, each new emperor would be crowned in the cathedral of Hagia Sophia by the patriarch of Constantinople and acclaimed by the people with the words 'God gave you to us. God will guard you'; a Eucharist would follow. The emperor played a key role in the great religious ceremonies of the empire. Indeed, although he could not perform any of the sacraments, the emperor was regarded as having the office of a priest.

Quite what all this meant was not always clear. In general, the emperor was regarded as the protector of the faith: he called church councils and enacted laws against heretics. Theological decisions, by contrast, were the task of the bishops, above all the four patriarchs of Constantinople, Antioch, Alexandria and Jerusalem, particularly the patriarch of Constantinople, the first among equals, known as the ecumenical patriarch – that is, the leader of the Orthodox Church. But the line between the emperor's authority and that of the patriarch was not always clearly drawn. Patriarchs were elected by other bishops, but after the sixth century the final choice lay with the emperor, and on some occasions emperors chose none of the candidates suggested by the bishops. To add to the confusion, the political system of the Byzantine empire was enormously complex, based upon a complicated court and bureaucracy – indeed, we still use the word 'byzantine' to mean an incomprehensibly dense political or legal system. This was especially so in later years, and the emperor Constantine VII Porphyrogenitus, who ruled in the tenth century, wrote an extraordinary book describing the rituals that the court had to perform throughout the year, all in a sumptuous detail that would put Gormenghast to shame. Patriarchs might move in this court world as readily as they did in the ecclesiastical

world. Emperors sometimes chose various court officials to act as close advisers or, in effect, prime ministers, especially if they were away campaigning. Sometimes, the ecumenical patriarch might be the one so appointed.

If Constantine was regarded as the originator and founder of the Christian Roman empire, its greatest emperor after the fall of Rome itself, and the model for all subsequent emperors, was Justinian the Great, whom we have already met. Born in AD 482, Justinian was a Thracian and always spoke Greek with a foreign accent. His uncle, Justin, was a general who became emperor in AD 518. He quickly made his nephew one of his closest advisers, and Justinian became the true power behind the throne. Thus he remained until AD 527, when Justin died and Justinian succeeded him. He shared his throne with his wife, Theodora, a woman at least as remarkable as her

Justinian the Great, emperor of Byzantium (reigned AD 527–65), depicted in a mosaic in the Basilica of San Vitale, Italy. It is sometimes claimed that this mosaic originally represented Theodoric, king of the Ostrogoths (reigned AD 488–526), but was altered after Justinian's forces conquered Italy.

First, the rebels completely changed their hairstyles. They cut it differently from other Romans – letting the moustache and beard grow as long as they could, like the Persians, and cutting their hair short at the front of the head to the temples, and letting it hang in untidy lengths at the back, like the Massageti. They called this strange combination the Hun haircut. Then they decided to wear the purple stripe on their togas, and swaggered about in clothes that suited their social superiors – for it was only by ill-gotten money that they could afford such finery... Almost all of them openly carried steel from the start, and during the day they hid their two-edged daggers along the thigh, under their cloaks. They gathered in gangs as dusk fell, and robbed those who were better than them in the open forum and in the narrow alleyways, grabbing from passers by their cloaks, belts, gold brooches, and whatever they were carrying. They killed some people after robbing them, so that they could not tell anyone what had happened.

The 'Blues', according to Procopius of Caesarea, *Secret history*, c. AD 550

husband; since she was a former actress and circus performer (and, it was said, prostitute), Justin had had to change the law to allow his nephew to marry her. Strong-willed and charismatic, she captivated her powerful husband. Justinian was nothing if not audacious: not content with warring upon the Persians in the traditional manner, he sent his brilliant general Belisarius to reconquer much of the western half of the old Roman empire, successfully capturing North Africa and Italy, although many areas were devastated in the wars.

Despite the centrality of Christianity to Byzantium, there seems always to have been a certain savagery to the empire. The belief of the early church that Christianity and killing were fundamentally incompatible had long since been abandoned in Byzantium, just as it had in western Europe. The conversion of Rome to Christianity in the fourth century had led to a rapid re-interpretation of warfare as potentially undertaken in the service of God: the Christian soldier could fight for his emperor safe in the belief that the emperor's cause was that of God. The Persian campaigns of Heraclius in the AD 620s were just one dramatic consequence of this pragmatic U-turn on the part of the church. Capital punishment, too, was now no longer regarded as unchristian; the main remnant of the church's earlier opposition to the practice was that priests could not order an execution or carry one out, an injunction that remained in force in western Europe too. In addition to 'lawful' violence such as this, Byzantium was often at the mercy of lawless acts of savagery. Throughout its history, emperors were routinely murdered, often by those they trusted, and their killers would become emperor themselves despite, often, having no dynastic claim to the throne at all. The people themselves could be prone to violence, often associated with the 'demes'. These organizations, which have no real modern parallel, were like a cross between football supporters' clubs, political parties and street gangs. There were two main ones – the 'Blues' and the

'Greens' – in addition to the less powerful 'Reds' and 'Whites' (all named after the colours of the chariot teams they supported); and they were based around the Hippodrome, the main sporting venue and centre of social life in Constantinople. The demes could inspire riots, between the four groups or in unison against unpopular emperors or their policies. On one famous occasion in AD 532, one such riot at the Hippodrome, which lasted a week and destroyed many buildings in the city, almost scared the emperor Justinian into fleeing the capital, until his wife Theodora persuaded him to stay. Until then both Justinian and Theodora had supported the Blues, but the rioters were put down savagely. Some 30,000 people were killed.

Justinian used the destruction this had caused as the occasion to start a new building programme. He was already addicted to the creation of splendid public monuments, such as the magnificent Great Palace with its Bronze Gate. But by far his most famous monument was the church of Hagia Sophia – the 'Holy Wisdom' – in the capital. Originally built by Constantius in AD 360 and rebuilt in AD 415, this had been a standard basilica-type church which was destroyed by the rioters of AD 532. Justinian was determined to build something much bigger and more ambitious, to a completely new design. He hired the two best architects of the day – Anthemius of Tralles and Isidore of Miletus – and told them not to worry about expense. They did not disappoint. A team of 10,000 workmen laboured for five years to construct the vast square church, surmounted by an enormous dome – the largest the world had ever seen. At its completion Justinian is said to have declared, 'Solomon, I have surpassed you!' Its square-round design was ultimately inspired by the baptisteries and *martyri*, first seen in the fourth century, which preserved the basic plan of pagan temples. The dome, as a feature of ecclesiastical design, had only recently been invented; so one of this size – 31 metres (103 ft) across, 50 metres (163 ft) high, and supported by an

The interior of Hagia Sophia, Istanbul.

[Inside Hagia Sophia, you can see] the fresh green from Carystus, and many-coloured marble from the Phrygian range, in which a rosy blush mingles with white or shines bright with flowers of deep red and silver. There is a wealth of porphyry too, powdered with brilliant stars, that once weighed down the boats of the broad Nile. You may see an emerald green from Sparta, and the glittering marble with the undulating veins which the tool has worked from the deep bosom of the Iassian hills, showing slanting streaks of blood-red and livid white… Stone too there is that the Libyan sun, warming with his golden light, has nurtured from the dark clefts of the Moorish hills, of crocus colour sparkling like gold.

Paul the Silentiary, *Description of Hagia Sophia*, AD 562

innovative system of arches and vaults – was a truly radical step forward. The general design of this church, especially its dome, would be copied for centuries, creating the distinctive Byzantine style of architecture.

Inside, the cathedral was finished with vast quantities of gold, marble and precious stones imported from the furthest reaches of the known world. In addition to this there was a 15-metre (50-ft) solid silver iconostasis – the screen before the altar – which itself was covered in gold and jewels. All this was not just for show. It was intended to express the glory of God and the beauty of his worship. In AD 555 the historian Procopius, in his *On the buildings*, commented:

> [Hagia Sophia] is remarkably full of light and sunshine. You would say that the place is not lit by the sun from outside, but that the rays are produced within itself, there is so much light poured into this church… When you enter this building to pray, you feel that it is not the work of human power… The soul, lifting itself to the sky, realizes that here God is close, and that he delights in this, the home he has chosen.

To the Byzantines, the church on earth was a reflection of the church in heaven: to enter a cathedral such as Hagia Sophia was to be transported closer to God. To the Byzantine mind, heaven and earth could meet at certain well-defined points. A church service in Hagia Sophia, perhaps featuring a procession of priests with the emperor at its head, was an obvious such point. In the earlier years of the empire the really grand services were held throughout the whole city of Constantinople, as the procession, headed by the emperor, marched through, holding services at special locations along the way. After the sixth century these celebrations of the city's life and faith were discontinued, and all the processions were held inside the church itself.

Thus there developed a greater understanding of the church building itself as the place where God was most present.

Where shall I begin to lament the deeds of my wretched life? What first-fruit shall I offer, O Christ, for my present lamentation? But in Thy compassion grant me release from my falls.

Andrew of Crete, *Great Canon*, early eighth century

In addition to being dazzled by the golden mosaics, a member of the congregation would find the very air itself conveying beauty and holiness, as incense hung in a dense mist throughout the church. The building was a reflection of heaven. The seventh-century theologian Maximus the Confessor claimed that the building symbolized the whole of creation, just as the whole of creation was there to praise God's glory:

> God's holy church is itself a symbol of the sensible world, since it possesses the divine sanctuary as heaven and the beauty of the nave as earth. Likewise the world is a church since it possesses heaven corresponding to a sanctuary, and for a nave it has the adornment of the earth.

The music also expressed the beauty of heaven. It was sung by the priests and people together, without accompaniment, like the 'plainsong' that was also developing in the western church. The liturgy, in general, was a complex web of elements, mostly drawn from the Bible. For example, an extremely popular element in later years was the 'canon', invented by Andrew of Crete in the eighth century. A 'canon' was a cycle of nine odes, reflecting the nine canticles or songs of the Old Testament. Andrew's *Great Canon* was basically a patchwork of biblical texts arranged in this way on the theme of repentance. Orthodox churches still sing this canon twice every Lent, making it one of the most often-recited long poems ever written.

Within the service, and outside it too, there were particular points where heaven and earth came together most closely. The sacraments – or 'mysteries', as they were known in the East – were examples of this. In contrast to the time of Constantine, in Byzantine times everyone was baptized as a baby, and confirmed at the same time (known as chrismation, because the baby was anointed with chrism, that is, oil). The Eucharist was central to church services, the central mystery of the liturgy, and the focal point of the union of human and divine. Another such focal point was the icon, developed in the sixth and seventh centuries. Icons were highly stylized portraits of Christ or the saints, intended to focus the mind of the viewer upon their subject and encourage imitation of their virtues. Many believed that icons served not simply as reminders of Christ or the saints but as extensions of their being, so that to look upon an icon was, in some way, to look upon what it represented. They were literally windows into heaven. Some believed that icons could even work miracles. To paint an icon was a deeply spiritual task, and artists would fast and spiritually prepare themselves before creating one. Their value as beautiful works of art was also important, since like the liturgy they represented the notion, which eastern Christianity had imbibed from Platonism and made its own, that God is the supreme beauty and is therefore known through the contemplation of beauty. The more beautiful the icon or the church, the closer it takes you to God.

All of this expressed the fundamental point of Christianity for the Byzantines, which was the incarnation. It was in Jesus Christ, above all, that heaven and earth met, for in him God and humanity were perfectly united. In Christ, heaven and earth had met perfectly, showing that such a thing was possible; this meant that the divine liturgy did not simply imitate heaven but really brought it to earth. The icons did not simply portray the presence of God in people's lives – they enabled it. This helps to explain the role that the Virgin Mary played in Byzantine religion, since as the mother of Jesus her womb was the place where God and man had met. The Virgin was regarded as the special protector of the city of Constantinople, and on more than one occasion its safe deliverance from besieging forces was believed to be the result of her direct intervention. The role of the incarnation in the church also helps to explain the incredibly drawn-out debates about the person of Christ and the relation of the human and divine in him. Rows between Chalcedonians and Monophysites were so heated because people recognized that they struck at the very heart of the faith.

THE MONASTERIES
Monasticism played a central role in Byzantine religion, just as it had in the life of the fourth-century church. Indeed, Byzantine monasticism was simply a continuation of the same movement. There never developed the different 'orders' of monasteries that appeared in the Middle Ages in western Europe. But there was still great variation in the ways that monasticism expressed itself. The style associated with Pachomius of Egypt, where everyone lived and worked together, remained very popular. There were a number of monasteries within cities that followed this pattern, which operated as large 'houses'. By the mid-sixth century there were seventy in Constantinople alone. Often such monastic houses were established with money provided by rich private individuals, or even emperors. Other monasteries followed the pattern of the desert fathers and were semi-communal, with monks living in separate cells and coming together only at weekends. These could also exist within cities. Most of these monasteries were quite small, with between three and twenty monks; sometimes, a small monastery would have been much like a family, with just a few monks living closely together. But a large one would have its own stables and kitchens, as well as its own chapel and dining room; it might own agricultural land and also a library and scriptorium for copying books. The ever-increasing size and complexity of the liturgy required an endless supply of service books of one kind or another, and these largely came from the monasteries: reading was compulsory for monks in such houses.

Some holy men became famous and could wield a spiritual authority that overruled even the highest political authority. There was a notable occasion in the AD 470s, when the emperor Basiliscus issued a statement endorsing Monophysitism. The horrified patriarch, Acacius, arranged for the intervention of Daniel Stylites, a hermit who lived on top of a pillar in Constantinople itself. This strange lifestyle had been pioneered by Symeon Stylites, a fifth-century Syrian who had spent thirty years on top of a pillar, and it had become quite popular in Syria. The pillars were typically about 18 metres (60 ft) high and surmounted by a small platform with a rail, so that the hermit didn't have to stand all the time. They were major tourist attractions, and crowds would flock to see the holy men standing, arms outstretched in imitation of Christ on the cross. Daniel, one of these pillar saints living in the capital

itself, was enormously revered. He came down from the pillar – an unprecedented event – and went directly to the palace to confront the emperor. Aware that he could not realistically disobey this revered man, Basiliscus duly rescinded his decree.

Certain monasteries or groups of monasteries also became famous. One developed in the Meteora region of northern Greece. Where the Pindus Mountains give way to the plains of Thessaly, great rock pillars rise up from the plains; and upon these, in the fourteenth century, monasteries began to appear – some so inaccessible that in the morning the monks had to be lowered in nets to work the fields, and pulled back up again in the evening. More famous still were the monasteries of Mount Athos, a rocky peninsula in northern Greece. Monks came

Meteora, Greece

here throughout the early Middle Ages, until by the middle of the eleventh century there were some 7,000 of them, in a number of monasteries. Here, the monks sought to escape the rather exhausting pace of life in the city and focus on contemplating God. Many followed the spiritual path set out by John Climacus ('John of the Ladder'), an enormously popular writer of the early seventh century. His *Ladder of perfection* described a progression from an active life to a contemplative one, suggesting that one climbs the ladder to God by eradicating vice and adopting virtue. But the ladder of perfection can be climbed only slowly. It is a difficult process and one that should be entered into realistically. However, the growing awareness of God that it produces makes it easier as one goes on, and it

becomes increasingly apparent that all the work is really being done by God himself in his grace. The final goal of this is contemplation of God in love. Many found John's work deeply inspiring, and his work is still appointed to be read every Lent in Orthodox monasteries, making him among the most read spiritual writers of the church.

John Climacus anticipated in some ways a form of mysticism associated with Mount Athos and known as 'hesychasm', from a word meaning 'quiet'. Hesychasm developed, in part, from the quest for *apatheia* or passionlessness that we saw in Chapter 3. Monks sought to attain this state through mastery of the mind and body alike, conceived as a unity. They used breathing techniques and repetitive prayers to achieve a state of self-hypnosis, whereby

If you pass judgement on another you brazenly usurp God's prerogative; if you condemn another, you destroy your own soul.

John Climacus, *Ladder of perfection*, early seventh century

the mind would become completely cleared of thoughts and, it was believed, able to see God. A prayer known as the 'Jesus prayer' (first described by John Climacus) was used, which in its basic form was simply 'Jesus, son of God, have mercy on me, a sinner.' The form of words varied and sometimes was nothing more than the name 'Jesus', repeated over and over again. Chanted in time with the monk's own breathing, the prayer would almost lose all meaning – but this was precisely the intent, since they sought a state of mind empty of thoughts, into which God might move.

Although its roots lay much earlier, hesychasm became especially popular and well known in the thirteenth and fourteenth centuries. Controversial in some parts, it was championed by Gregory Palamas, the leading theologian of the later Byzantine period. It would later be influential in Russian spirituality.

CHRIST ON EARTH AND CHRIST IN PAINT: THE CONTROVERSIES

The role of the monasteries, and indeed the very nature of Byzantine faith, was challenged in the seemingly interminable dispute which dogged the Byzantine church for centuries. This was the perennial argument about the nature of Christ and, specifically, the relation of the divine to the human in him. We saw in Chapter 3 how this issue was first debated by Cyril and Nestorius, and in the last chapter we saw its outcome from the point of view of the Monophysites and Nestorians who found themselves out of communion with Constantinople – for the Byzantines were, for the most part, staunch supporters of Chalcedon. But the Byzantine church itself continued to be wracked by these disputes and their aftermath.

THE THREE CHAPTERS
In the AD 540s the emperor Justinian I decided to try to entice the Monophysites back to the Chalcedonian fold by proving to them that Chalcedonians were not really Nestorians in disguise. This he hoped to do by condemning the works of three famous theologians who were revered by the Nestorians – Theodore of Mopsuestia, Theodoret of Cyrrhus and Ibas of Edessa. All three had been dead for a century, so there was considerable unease about condemning them – in the past, councils had been called only to deal with the living. However, Justinian got his way (as usual) and in AD 553 the Second Council of Constantinople duly condemned 'the three chapters', extracts from the works of the three theologians. Of course, the Monophysites were not duped by this and continued to hate Chalcedon as much as they had ever done. All it accomplished was to increase the antagonism that the Nestorians – mostly living in Persia, as we saw in the last chapter – felt towards the Byzantine church. As if it had not been enough to depose the harmless Nestorius a century earlier, they felt, the iniquitous Byzantines had now condemned the revered Theodore of Mopsuestia!

The 'three chapters affair' was, from the point of view of Byzantine orthodoxy, a failure, since it had not led to the reconciliation of the Monophysites, but it did no particular harm (the outraged Nestorians were all heretics and foreigners anyway). Indeed, the Second Council of Constantinople was accepted as the Fifth Ecumenical Council. Much more harmful was the next major attempt to woo the Monophysites back, eighty years later, which led to the Monotheletism controversy.

MONOTHELETISM
Monotheletism was the unfortunate brainchild of Sergius, patriarch of Constantinople in the early seventh century. A good friend of the emperor Heraclius, and the son of Syrian Jacobites, Sergius was extremely keen to reconcile Chalcedonians and Monophysites. He believed that the key concern of Monophysites was that Christ should have

a single 'will' or faculty of volition, and this was why they insisted that Christ had only one nature. But why, reasoned Sergius, should there be a 'will' in every 'nature'? He therefore suggested that Christ had two natures (in accordance with Chalcedon) but only one 'will', located in his person (which everyone agreed he had only one of). The idea proved amenable to the emperor Heraclius, and in AD 638 he issued his famous decree called the *Ekthesis*, in which he imposed the doctrine of Monotheletism – that is, 'one will' – upon the church. Sergius died some months afterwards.

Monotheletism was controversial right from the start. Sergius had intended the doctrine to mean that the human and the divine in Christ cooperated perfectly, to the extent that it was not cooperation at all but the single act of a single person. Many Byzantine theologians agreed with him. But many others interpreted it as saying that Christ had a divine will which simply overrode his humanity. That is, Christ was a divine person masquerading as a human being: he was not really properly human. This was how most people in the West interpreted the doctrine. They had no sympathy whatsoever with Monophysitism and regarded this new doctrine as Monophysitism in disguise. Pope John IV condemned it in AD 641 – the final blow to Heraclius, already sinking into black depression in the face of the Muslim conquests. He died soon after and was succeeded by Constans II Pogonatus, who issued a decree called the *Typus*, which banned all discussion of will in Christ, and which was completely ignored. Bishops and monks continued to argue with each other about it, and in AD 649 Pope Martin I held a council at the Lateran Palace which condemned Monotheletism again, together with the *Typus*. Relations between East and West cooled considerably. The pope sheltered a number of anti-Monothelite theologians from Byzantium, who had fled to the West. Their leader was Maximus, a monk who had once been Heraclius's personal secretary. Maximus was convinced that Monothelitism was nothing less than a denial of the reality of the incarnation, *the* central doctrine of Orthodox faith. For, he argued, to have a will is part of human nature: a creature with no human will is not really human. Therefore, Christ must have had a human will and a divine will, distinct from each other, but acting in perfect harmony.

In AD 653 Constans II, sick of having imperial theological policy mocked by this upstart monk and the Roman bishop alike, had them both arrested and brought to Constantinople. The pope and Maximus were imprisoned and tortured. Martin was exiled to Cherson, where, ill and weak from lack of food, he died shortly afterwards. Maximus was exiled to Bizya, but he survived and continued to speak out against Monotheletism. So he was brought back to Constantinople in AD 662 and tried again. This time the punishment was harsher: his tongue was ripped out and his right hand cut off to prevent him spreading his views any further by speech or writing. He was taken around the city so everyone could see what had been done to him, and then exiled to Lazica, where he died soon afterwards.

Nevertheless, support for Monotheletism was waning. The intransigent opposition of Rome to the doctrine was one reason; another was the fact that recent years had seen most of the Monophysites come under Muslim rule, so there was less motive to try to win them back. The policy had succeeded in reconciling some Monophysites, but most of them simply hated Chalcedon so much that nothing would ever persuade them to back it. In AD 668 Constans II was murdered in his bath, removing the final obstacle to the reversal of the policy. In AD 680 the emperor Constantine IV Pogonatus called the Third Council of Constantinople, which condemned Monotheletism and endorsed the view of Maximus that Christ had had two wills, one human and one divine, acting in

It was not as naturally God, one substance with God the Father, that the Only Begotten Son gave us grace. It is as having become naturally man in the incarnation, one substance with us, that he gives grace to all who need it.

Maximus the Confessor, *Chapters on knowledge*, seventh century perfect accord. The council would become recognized as the Sixth Ecumenical Council and Maximus himself remembered as 'the Confessor' – one step down from a martyr.

Divisive and tragic in its consequences as the Monotheletism row was, it proved to be simply the opening act for the biggest religious upheaval of the Byzantine empire – the iconoclasm controversy. Very different on the surface, this was actually about much the same issues underneath.

FROM MONOTHELETISM TO ICONOCLASM

The controversy began with the emperor Leo III. By the time he became emperor, in AD 717, things had changed considerably since the days of Justinian. The territory that that great emperor had recaptured in the West had almost entirely been lost: Italy had been devastated by war, and Byzantine rule, with high taxes and religious intolerance, was considerably less popular than the rule of the Ostrogoths which it had displaced. Byzantine rule in Italy did not long outlive Justinian, since the Lombards, another barbarian people who were allowed to settle there, soon established a kingdom of their own. And we saw in the last chapter how the early seventh century witnessed the loss of Byzantine power in the Middle East to the Muslim Arabs. Antioch, Jerusalem, and Alexandria, the great cities of the eastern empire, were all under foreign rule.

THE ISAURIANS

Into all this came Leo III 'the Isaurian', who actually grew up in Thrace and had never been near the Isaurian Mountains. A clerical error led to his nickname, which was also applied to the dynasty he founded. A leading general, he seized the throne in AD 717 during a period of political confusion.

Leo was another remarkable military genius, though his triumphs were less dramatic than those of either Justinian I or Heraclius. As he became emperor, a huge Muslim force of 80,000 men and 1,800

If anyone ventures to represent the divine image of the Word after the Incarnation with material colours, let him be anathema!

Decree of the Council of Hiera, AD 754

warships was beginning to lay siege to Constantinople. The city was relieved by a horde of barbarians from Bulgaria, and Leo capitalized on the Muslims' defeat to recapture the whole of Anatolia from Muslim forces. Rather than press on as Heraclius had done, Leo devoted his reign to consolidating his forces and protecting what had been recaptured. Not for many centuries would the Muslims again threaten the existence of the empire.

Leo's other main preoccupation was with icons. There had already been a major attack on the use of icons in churches – not in Byzantium, but in Persia, by the caliph Iezid II, who reigned from AD 720–724. He ordered the destruction of all Christian images in his domains – not because they were Christian, but because they broke the Qur'an's prohibition of all representational art.

However, in around AD 724, the opposition to the use of icons moved to within the imperial borders. Two bishops from Asia Minor expressed reservations about icons to the patriarch, Germanus, arguing that they were idolatrous. Germanus rebuked them, insisting that the honour paid to images was different from the honour paid to God. Yet there seems to have been a growing feeling of unrest about icons throughout the empire.

This feeling of unrest extended to the emperor. No one really knows quite why Leo decided that icons were wrong, but he did so in AD 725 – although whether he actually issued an edict banning their use is unknown. In the years that followed, increasingly direct action was taken against images – apparently partly as a result of volcanic eruptions in the Aegean, which Leo interpreted as divine impatience. In AD 726 he ordered the removal of a prominent figure of Christ over the Bronze Gate in Constantinople. The soldier who climbed the ladder to do this was rushed by a mob and killed. Leo punished those responsible, and ordered a more wholescale attack on icons throughout the empire. His policy became known as 'iconoclasm' – literally, 'icon-smashing'.

Naturally the policy provoked opposition, led theologically by John of Damascus. Safe to criticize the emperor because he lived in Muslim lands, John argued that icons could be used because they were not *worshipped* (that would indeed be idolatry); rather, they were *venerated*, and through them God was worshipped – just as through the man Jesus, God was genuinely seen and properly worshipped.

For the next couple of years the destruction of icons continued, although it appears not to have been a violent campaign. Nobody died in defence of icons, and by around AD 732 the campaign seems to have ended, Leo apparently being content with what he had achieved.

His son, Constantine V, was far more extreme. He despised those who used icons, and they despised him back – dubbing him 'Copronymus', a name which cannot be translated in polite company. It apparently referred in part to the characteristic smell of the emperor, who loved horses and spent much of his time in stables. However, Constantine's hatred of icons seems to have had something to do with his leanings towards Monophysitism and a dislike of what he regarded as the superstitious veneration of human things. The emperor discouraged the cult of Mary, laughed at the veneration of relics and refused to allow anyone in his presence to prefix 'Saint' to any name, even that of Peter. Like Justinian I, he was an amateur theologian and wrote a number of treatises defending his views.

In AD 754 Constantine V called a council at Hiera near Chalcedon. The 338 bishops who attended condemned the use of icons as idolatry, using an ingenious argument: either icons depicted only Jesus' humanity, separating it from his divinity, in which case they were Nestorian, or they depicted his humanity and divinity as a single image, in which case they were Monophysite. The icon-defenders, including John of Damascus and Germanus of Constantinople, were condemned.

However, no one could agree on whether this council was really a proper ecumenical council like Nicaea and the rest. No patriarchs had been present (Constantine had been careful to invite only his own yes-men). Opposition to iconoclasm grew, and it was centred on the monasteries. The monks had used icons as an integral part of their devotions for well over a century, and they had no intention of giving them up. Their leader was Stephen of the monastery of St Auxentius, who was thrown into prison on trumped-up charges. In AD 761 a monk named Andrew of Crete (not the hymn-writer) was flogged to death for denouncing Constantine V as a new Julian the Apostate, thereby becoming the first martyr for icons. A couple of years later Stephen was dragged from his cell by a mob and killed.

In the face of monastic opposition Constantine V was uncompromising.

Mother of God from Vladimir, an icon from twelfth- or thirteenth-century Constantinople.

Monasteries were raided and their inhabitants flung into prison. Icons were seized and smashed. The emperor went further and initiated a clampdown on monks in general – 'unmentionables' as he called them – irrespective of their views on icons. Monks were forced to marry and the patriarch of Constantinople, a vegetarian, was forced to eat meat and take a wife. Libraries were burned. In AD 766 monks were forced to parade through the Hippodrome holding hands with women. The following year, prayers to the saints and the use of relics were banned. Though partly theologically inspired, it seems that Constantine's persecutions were also partly caused by a growing unease in governmental circles with the monastic movement from a practical point of view. Monasteries were becoming more and more popular – and this as the government was keen to resettle many imperial lands, especially in Anatolia, which had not recovered from the invasions of the Muslims and were underpopulated. It was no good to them if young people were dedicating themselves to a life of chastity on mountaintops. This came, moreover, as the last foothold of Byzantine power in Italy – Ravenna – was finally lost to the Lombards in AD 751. Having lost the West, maintaining a hold over the East was now even more important.

Constantine V died in AD 775 and his cruel persecution died with him: within a few years the monasteries were refilled, and Anatolia remained largely empty. Constantine's son, Leo IV, seems to have shared his views but not imposed them on the people. He died in AD 780, leaving his wife Irene (AD 752–803) as regent for their infant son, and this saw a new phase in the controversy.

THE FEMALE EMPEROR AND THE SECOND COUNCIL OF NICAEA

Little is known of Irene's background, except that her astonishing beauty alone is said to have secured her marriage to Leo IV. She was also an uncompromising advocate of icons – a problem, since the government, church and army were all dominated by Constantine V's appointees, every one of them an iconoclast. An attempt at a military coup was defeated, and Irene purged the army, forcing the ringleaders to become monks and ordaining them against their will.

In AD 784 Irene made her secretary, a layman named Tarasius, patriarch of Constantinople, and laid plans for a council to settle the icon issue. The council opened in AD 786, but it was disrupted by iconoclast troops; Irene sent them away to fight the Muslims, and the council re-convened the following year at Nicaea, where Irene's purges of iconoclasm seem to have worked. Everyone agreed that icons were acceptable after all, and that the Council of Hiera in AD 754 had been a ghastly mistake. The council agreed with John of Damascus that icons were to be not worshipped but venerated. Just as God could be known through the human being Jesus, so too Jesus could be known through the paint and wood of an icon. At last there was a degree of unity in the church, at least in the east – for the western church heard only garbled reports of the council and did not like what it heard.

Irene was forced from power in AD 790 by the army. Her son, Constantine VI, ruled alone – and incompetently – for two years before being ousted in his turn. Irene reclaimed the throne and had Constantine blinded, in the very building where she had once given birth to him. He died soon after from his injuries, leaving his monstrous mother as the first woman to rule the Byzantine empire in her own right. The still-beautiful Irene hoped to cement her rule by marrying Charlemagne, crowned in AD 800 as the new emperor of the West; but the prospect of a western barbarian becoming Byzantine emperor was the final straw to a population already alienated by an increasingly unpopular rule. There was only one emperor, the regent of Christ on earth, and he was in Constantinople; the very notion of a western emperor was in itself little short of blasphemy to the Byzantine mind, let alone the idea of him moving to Constantinople, in all his

Just like the holy and life-giving cross, so too the holy and precious icons, painted with colours, made with little stones or any other materials for this purpose, should be placed in the holy churches of God, on vases and sacred vestments, on walls and boards, in houses and on roads… For each time that we see their representation in an image, each time, while gazing upon them, we are made to remember the originals, we grow to love them more, and we are more induced to worship them.

Decree of the Second Council of Nicaea, AD 787

A fifteenth-century icon representing the Restoration of Orthodoxy.

illiterate uncouthness, and installing himself there! Irene was toppled in another coup in AD 802 and replaced by a palace official who became Nicephorus I (d. AD 811). Irene accepted her fate with dignity and was exiled to Lesbos, where she was allowed to earn a meagre living as a spinner before her death a year later.

THE FINAL PHASE

Irene had been desperately unpopular, and icons were tarnished by association. When an Armenian general, Leo V, seized the throne in AD 813, he tapped into this new and growing iconoclast feeling. The patriarch of Constantinople protested, leading to his deposition, but opposition to the new policy was led by Theodore the Studite, a remarkably cantankerous monk. He and the outgoing patriarch had always hated each other – part of the general resentment between bishops and monks – but they buried the hatchet when it came to icons. Repeatedly imprisoned or exiled, Theodore continued to encourage the icon-loving opposition, writing from his cell not only to supporters in Constantinople but to the pope and others in the West.

The persecution never reached the extremes that it had done under Constantine V. Nobody was killed, at least not under Leo V or his successor, Michael

Because man is made in the image and likeness of God, there is something divine about the act of painting an icon.

Theodore the Studite

II, 'the Stammerer', who was relatively relaxed. Michael's son, Theophilus, who became emperor in AD 829, was harsher, and some defenders of icons were beaten to death under his rule. Two Palestinian monks who led the pro-icon party suffered the peculiar punishment of having twelve lines of abusive poetry tattooed onto their faces. Theophilus died in AD 842, leaving his wife, Theodora, regent for their toddler son.

Like the last female regent, Theodora venerated icons and was said to have kept some secretly under her bed even as her husband was cracking down on their use elsewhere. In AD 843 she held a new council which vindicated the Second Council of Nicaea. That council was now recognized as the Seventh Ecumenical Council. The question of loyalty to the dead emperor was neatly solved by Theodora's insistence that he had repented of iconoclasm on his deathbed and had had an icon held to his lips as he died – hardly likely, but politically expedient.

A service of thanksgiving was held at Hagia Sophia on the first Sunday in Lent. Ever since, the Orthodox Church has marked this day as the Restoration of Orthodoxy. The battle over icons was finally over and, with it, the seemingly endless wrangling over Christology which had begun with Nestorius over four centuries earlier. For this was what the controversy was really about. The iconoclasts had insisted that God could not be represented in material form, that a physical object such as an icon was intrinsically non-holy, and that venerating it was idolatry. The defenders of icons recognized that this logic, if pushed only a bit further, would lead to the denial of the incarnation – for what was Jesus himself, if not God in material form? The role of icons in worship or meditation was, in effect, an extension of the principle of the incarnation. Theodore the Studite had put it neatly: just as the Son is the image of the Father, who is worshipped through him, so too the icon is the image of the Son, who is worshipped through it.

OTHER NATIONS, OTHER CHURCHES

Byzantine religion revolved around the twin poles of church and state, united in the Byzantine mind into a whole – just as the body and the soul, though distinct, were thought to make up a single person. Under such a scheme, it is unsurprising that the Orthodox Church of Byzantium did not get along very well with other churches. If the emperor was the regent of Christ on earth, where did that leave Christians who were not under his rule?

ROME

The history of the relations between Rome and Constantinople was one of increasing distrust and lack of understanding. Whether this was inevitably so is a moot point. After all, most of the time the two sees were in communion with each other, even if they largely ignored each other; and papal legates were present at certain major councils of the East, such as the second and third councils of Constantinople. But there were periods when the two were clearly at loggerheads.

The first formal breach between the western and eastern halves of Christendom was the Acacian schism. The unhappy Acacius himself was patriarch of Constantinople at the time when the emperor Zeno – he of, supposedly, no kneecaps – was trying to reunite Chalcedonians and Monophysites by means of the decree known as the *Henoticon*, as we saw in the last chapter. Acacius supported the *Henoticon*, and for this he was formally deposed by the bishop of Rome, Felix III. Rome had absolutely no sympathy for Monophysitism. Acacius responded by removing Felix's name from the diptychs. These were the official lists of bishops (past and present) who should be prayed for. To remove a name from them was, in effect, to state that they were out of communion with the church. Acacius died in AD 489, and his successors tried to restore the breach; but Rome would not permit it

The *Filioque*

Doctrinal dispute over the *filioque*-clause served as one of the main ingredients in the deterioration of relations between the Eastern churches and the West during the Middle Ages.

The clause marks an addition to the 'Nicene Creed' (of the Council of Constantinople in AD 381), made exclusively and unilaterally in the West. In the East believers declared their faith in the Holy Spirit 'who proceeds from the father', while in the West the Holy Spirit is professed, 'who proceeds from the father *and the Son*' (in Latin: *filioque*). The *filioque* is first attested in statements of faith in the fifth/sixth centuries in Spain. By the ninth century it was commonly used in the Frankish Church and officially adopted at a synod in AD 809. By the time eastern and western churches effectively split in 1054, it was established as part of the western creed and one of the main grievances in the East. In AD 867 the Constantinopolitan patriarch Photius had already condemned it as heretical.

The eastern churches took offence with the insertion of the clause mainly on two grounds. They condemned what they perceived as unilateral action and the assumed authority of the pope in deciding doctrine. The authority of the ancient councils could not be overturned in this way. At the same time, they criticized the theological import of the clause. In the West, following the teaching of Augustine, emphasis is given to the idea that the Trinity appears to human beings as it really is in itself, and also to the strong bonds of unity between the persons of the Trinity. So the Spirit as the mutual bond of love between Father and Son proceeds from both. In the eastern tradition, the unity of the Trinity is founded in the one origin (Greek: *arche*) of the Father. The Son and the Spirit are marked out by their distinct relations to the Father: the Son is begotten of the Father, the Spirit proceeds from him. Gregory Palamas argued that according to God's essence the Spirit proceeds solely from the Father, but, according to his activities, the Spirit's procession could be pronounced to be from the Father through the Son. In a way this distinction can be seen to differentiate between what in the West might be called the immanent Trinity (how the Trinity really is) and the economic Trinity (how it appears to be).

THOMAS GRAUMANN

---

unless *they* removed *Acacius's* name from the diptychs, which they would not do. The schism remained in effect until AD 519, when the patriarch John finally removed not only Acacius's name but those of all his successors from the diptychs.

We have seen how the seventh century saw more discord, with Pope Martin I condemning the Byzantine doctrine of Monotheletism before being abducted and imprisoned. This was cleared up after the Third Council of Constantinople in AD 680, but a further break with Rome occurred in the ninth century, this time concerning Photius, patriarch of Constantinople. Photius was probably the most brilliant man in the Byzantine empire of his day, a great scholar, theologian and professor of philosophy. He was also personally charming, though with a certain robustness: as patriarch, he is said to have challenged the emperor Michael III (an alcoholic) to a drinking contest, beating him by sixty cups to fifty.

Despite being a layman, Photius was made patriarch in AD 858 after a court plot to remove his predecessor, Ignatius, an unintelligent man who was deeply unpopular with aristocrats and intellectuals alike. However, Pope Nicholas I refused to accept that Ignatius had been legally deposed. Indeed, when he heard reports that Ignatius had been imprisoned and tortured, he condemned Photius as a usurper and declared him excommunicated. Photius, safe in Constantinople, returned the compliment.

The dispute between Photius and Nicholas was not simply one of the legitimacy of an ordination. It was, in part, about the evangelization of the barbarian peoples who lay in between Rome and Constantinople. It was in mission that the struggle between these two great branches of Christendom was gathering pace.

AVARS, SLAVS, BULGARS AND MAGYARS

The Byzantine empire was ruled from a city on the Balkan peninsula, but it did not rule the whole of that large peninsula. Thrace and Macedonia, close to hand, were heartlands of the empire, but the status of Illyria to the west – around what is now Albania – was less clear. This area was disputed, politically, with the Lombards and other western barbarian groups; in terms of religion, it was disputed between the patriarchs of Rome and Constantinople.

In the ninth year of the reign of emperor Nicephorus, the emperor himself invaded Bulgaria, hoping to annihilate it... He captured the palace of the Bulgarian ruler, Krum, and set up his camp there. He encountered an army of up to 12,000 hand-picked Bulgars, left behind to guard the palace, and he fought and killed them all... After this, the wretch's spirit and heart became swollen with pride... he said to his companions, 'Look! What righteous things I have accomplished!' ... The army, jumping on the opportunity, plundered mercilessly, burning fields that had not been harvested. They cut the hamstrings of the cows, ripping their tendons from their loins, as they wailed and struggled.

Nicephorus I's invasion of Bulgaria, shortly before his defeat to Krum, *Scriptor Incertus*, ninth century AD

To the north of the Balkans lay the Carpathian basin. This region was invaded by a people known as the Avars in the middle of the sixth century. Under a series of powerful rulers called *qagans*, the Avar mounted warriors conquered much of the northern Balkans. Their assaults culminated in a terrifying siege of Constantinople itself in AD 626, conducted in alliance with the Persians. The failure of this assault, despite the mighty siege towers and the catapults which rained vast rocks upon the city, was attributed to the protection of the Virgin Mary. Sergius, patriarch of the city, walked along the city walls every day, carrying before him an icon of the Virgin. Some swore they had seen her pacing the battlements herself.

By the end of the ninth century, the Avars' power had been effectively neutered by the arrival of more barbarian peoples in the north-eastern part of the Balkan peninsula, to the south of the Danube. In the seventh century, the Slavs took advantage of the Byzantines' preoccupation with Persia to migrate en masse down into the northern Balkans. Ethnically and politically, the whole region was transformed; and Christianity, which had been established there under Roman rule, fizzled out. For the Slavs, like the Avars, were pagans.

The Slavs now stayed more or less where they were and coalesced into a number of kingdoms. Russia and Poland, to the north,

we shall look at in more detail in Chapter 8. Within the Byzantine sphere of influence, another was Moravia, higher up the Danube and therefore right between the Byzantine empire to the south-east and the emerging Frankish superpower to the west. By far the most important of these Slavic countries, from the Byzantine point of view, however, was Bulgaria.

Bulgaria came into being when yet another people, known to modern scholars rather unimaginatively as the Proto-Bulgarians, moved from what is now Turkey into the north-east part of the Balkan peninsula. They mingled with the Slavs and formed a new kingdom. This new power quickly turned on the Byzantines and in AD 680, under Khan Asparuh, the Bulgarians conquered considerable territories throughout the Balkans. They continued to consolidate their power and in AD 807 became even stronger under the mighty Khan Krum, one of the most formidable military leaders the region had ever seen. Krum led a number of skirmishes into Byzantine territory; the Byzantine emperor Nicephorus I responded by invading Bulgaria, destroying Krum's capital and killing enormous numbers of people. Krum's forces counter-attacked, though, and Nicephorus was killed. Krum had the emperor's skull mounted in silver and used it as a drinking cup. In AD 813 Constantinople itself was besieged and the surrounding area sacked. A second,

mightier assault on the Byzantine capital was prevented only when Khan Krum died of a heart attack while he was organizing it.

Finally, one other important group needs to be mentioned, the Magyars, who like the Avars were terrifyingly adept horsemen. In the ninth century they carved out a significant empire centred on the Danube, and were able to demand tribute from the Byzantines and even from the Germanic kings, whom they also harried constantly. This continued until AD 955, when Otto I (of what would shortly become the Holy Roman empire) defeated them near Augsburg. The Magyars made peace with the emerging western empire and became known as the Hungarians. From this time on, Hungary would exist as a kind of buffer state between the Holy Roman empire to the west and the Byzantine empire to the east.

MISSIONS TO EASTERN EUROPE

All of these barbarian powers existed in an uneasy relationship with both Byzantium and the powers of western Europe. The Avars, Magyars and Bulgars alike were sometimes allied to Byzantium, but were sometimes at war with it; sometimes the Byzantine emperor was forced to pay tribute to them, sometimes it was the other way around. By the eighth and ninth centuries, however, all these people were increasingly faced with a major choice. To the west, as we shall see in the next chapter, a new power was rising: the Frankish empire of Charlemagne and his successors. There was pressure to ally with the West, just as there was to ally with the East. And alliance either way would inevitably mean conversion.

The ball was set rolling in AD 862, when Louis the German, grandson of Charlemagne and Frankish ruler of the eastern half of his grandfather's great empire, made an alliance with Bulgaria. Rastislav, prince of Moravia, caught between these two vastly more powerful countries, felt understandably alarmed. He sent ambassadors to Constantinople, hoping to make an alliance of his own. As part of the deal he was willing to invite

Cyril and Methodius.

LEFT The armies of Krum flee the Byzantine forces in an illustration from a medieval chronicle.

missionaries to his country so that his people might share the religion of their new, powerful friends. Photius, patriarch of Constantinople, was delighted by this new opportunity and appointed a friend of his, named Constantine, to the task. Constantine was rather like Photius himself, a brilliant scholar and talented linguist who had succeeded Photius as professor of philosophy in the capital's university. However, he is normally known by the name of Cyril, which he adopted shortly before his death. His first journey had been made in AD 860, together with his brother, Methodius, also a good linguist, to the Khazar empire, which lay to the east, around the Caspian Sea. This mission had little success, though: the Khazar empire had already been converted by Jews who had fled Byzantium a century earlier because of anti-Jewish persecutions by Leo the Isaurian. The Khazar empire was now therefore the only Jewish state in the world, and the disputations of Cyril and Methodius,

The baptism of Boris of Bulgaria, from a twelfth-century Sicilian manuscript of the *Synopsis of histories* by the eleventh-century historian John Skylitzes.

Because the Slavs and Bulgarians did not understand the Scriptures, which were written in Greek, [Cyril and Methodius] considered this the greatest loss… They turned to the Comforter and begged him for the grace to invent an alphabet that could contain the wildness of the Bulgarian language. They asked for the ability to translate the divine Scriptures into that tongue. And indeed, after fasting and praying, punishing their flesh and humbling their spirits, they received what they had longed for.

Theophylact of Ohrid, *Life of St Clement of Ohrid*, c. 1100

northern Balkans, governed by the great Khan Boris I, an extraordinary ruler with a will of iron and a truly fiery temperament. Boris recognized that unifying his people spiritually under Christianity would be a wise move. But he was reluctant to conform to the Christianity of his rivals, the Byzantines, and so he began negotiations with the Franks and Rome to import western Christianity instead. The Byzantines were unhappy about this and declared war on Bulgaria: Boris was unable to muster an effective resistance and accepted baptism by a delegation from Constantinople in AD 864. The Byzantine emperor Michael III was his godfather.

The rest of the Bulgarians were baptized en masse, a process which took about six months. All pagan temples in the country were destroyed or turned into churches. Many *boyars* or noblemen resisted and there was an armed rebellion; Boris I suppressed it brutally, executing all those involved. He also wrote to Constantinople asking for a Bulgarian archbishop. Unwisely, Photius ignored the request, wishing to keep the nascent Bulgarian church under his own control. Boris, who was used to getting his own way, was deeply insulted and wrote instead to Pope Hadrian II, essentially offering to switch allegiance to Rome. The pope seized this chance gratefully and wrote a long and sympathetic reply to the khan, which he sent together with his own legates. Boris was extremely pleased, and the pope's men began the process of Catholicization of the Bulgarians.

Boris, as usual, was still not happy. The pope was no more willing to grant him an archbishop of his own than Photius had been. Things looked more hopeful for him in AD 867, when the Byzantine emperor Michael III was murdered in his bedchamber and replaced by his former

clever though they were, had little effect other than the release of 2,000 Christian prisoners.

Upon their return, the two brothers were put in charge of the new mission to the Moravians. Their first task was to translate some of the scriptures into Slavonic, a difficult task given that the language had no written form. Cyril therefore invented an alphabet for it, based on the Greek alphabet, and he and his brother translated the Gospels and wrote them in the new script. In AD 864 they arrived in Moravia, where they stayed for three years. Again, they had little success. Cyril had made his translations in the form of Slavonic spoken in Bulgaria, and the Moravians could not understand it well. However, the brothers had more success than the western missionaries also penetrating the area at this time, who disapproved of using any form of Slavonic at all. Cyril and Methodius's belief that the Slavonic churches should use Slavonic liturgies was therefore a major step forward, and it would lay the foundations for the future church in this region. In AD 868 they arrived in Rome, where Pope Hadrian II approved the use of the Slavonic liturgy. Here Cyril became a monk and died shortly afterwards.

Meanwhile, the Bulgars were moving towards conversion too. By now the country was the superpower of the friend Basil the Macedonian. Basil, keen to heal the rift with Rome, held a council in AD 870 at which he dismissed Photius and replaced him with his long-time rival, Ignatius. At this council he also listened more sympathetically to Boris's complaints. The request was granted: the Bulgarian church was made autocephalous, that is, self-governing, with an archbishop who was technically under the control of Constantinople but to all practical purposes independent. That annoyed Rome, but there was little that could be done about it. Indeed, the worrying schism between Rome and Constantinople over Photius was largely over. Although deposed, Photius was reconciled to Ignatius, and succeeded him as patriarch when he died in AD 878, receiving – at long last – official recognition from Pope John VIII three years later.

Although religious independence from Constantinople was assured, Boris I was happy to import all the cultural advantages of Christianity. He sent many nobles, including his son, to be educated in Constantinople. Two pupils of Cyril and Methodius, named Naum and Angelarius, arrived and set up schools and monasteries throughout the country. The late ninth and tenth centuries saw a golden age of literature and culture throughout Bulgaria, and art and architecture flourished too. The country developed a strong tradition of hermitage.

Such was Boris's zeal that in AD 889 he abdicated to retire to a monastery. But his son and successor Vladimir tried to re-establish paganism, so the aged Boris burst out of the monastery, removed Vladimir and replaced him with his other son, Simeon, who had been planning to become a bishop. After this eruption, Boris returned again to his monastery, where he died in AD 907. Meanwhile, despite his ecclesiastical ambitions, Simeon turned out to be a strong and aggressive ruler who fought and beat the Byzantines on a number of occasions, forcing them to recognize him under a new title, tsar, that is, emperor of Bulgaria. And in AD 927, the Byzantines were also forced to recognize the archbishop of Preslav (and later Ohrid) as patriarch of the Bulgarian church. That only lasted until 1018, however, when the Byzantines occupied Ohrid and reduced him to a mere autocephalous archbishop again. That was the end of the Bulgarian empire; but in the twelfth century the Bulgarians rebelled and Byzantium was forced to restore independence to them.

A DWINDLING EMPIRE

The ninth century, the age of Photius, was a time of renewal and strength for Byzantium. Not only did the empire recapture land in Italy (under Basil I, 'the Macedonian') and defeat the Bulgarians (under Basil II, 'the Bulgar-slayer'), but there was more book writing, book copying and general literacy than ever before. Leo the Wise, Basil I's son and successor, was an enormously erudite man who wrote poetry and preached his own sermons in Hagia Sophia. As in the West, most people could not read or write; but literacy levels were higher than in the west at this time, thanks to the increasing power of the monasteries. The education on offer at most monasteries was not as good as the new curriculums which would develop in western Europe in the eleventh century, corresponding instead to modern primary school level, but there were many highly educated and well-read people, such as Photius himself. Most importantly, there were more and more monasteries, and they were fuller than ever before. Education and healthcare were largely in their hands – medicine was more advanced in Byzantium than in western Europe, and the monks and nuns alike ran extremely good hospitals – and they enjoyed significant tax breaks. Of course the old problem of underpopulation of the empire's provinces was not helped by their increasing popularity. Indeed, in AD 964, the emperor Nicephorus II Phocas banned the founding of any more monasteries.

The spiritual life of the monks remained rich. The late tenth and early eleventh centuries saw the teaching of Symeon the

Father, that light appeared to me. The walls of my cell melted away and the whole world vanished. I think it was fleeing before his face. I alone remained, in the presence of the light. And father, I do not know if I was still in my body or carried outside it. I completely forgot that I even have a body. I felt such great joy within me – and it is still in me now – great love and also great longing – and I wept streams of tears, just as you see me doing now.

Symeon the New Theologian, *On the mystical life*, early eleventh century

New Theologian (AD 949–1022), an abbot who lost the loyalty of his monks because he tried to force a highly ascetic lifestyle on them. Accused unfairly of heresy, Symeon was exiled to Asia Minor in 1009 and founded a new monastery in a ruined chapel, where he acquired disciples. Indeed, he became so popular that the ecumenical patriarch, Sergius II, offered to bring him back and make him a bishop, but he refused.

Symeon's teaching was rooted in the standard Byzantine theology of incarnation: the closeness of God to his creation and the possibility of becoming united to him through holy living and meditation. In his works Symeon spoke movingly of his own experience of the closeness of God, using the first person to a degree unusual in Greek-speaking theologians.

NEW HERESIES

Yet the church during this time was also hit with new problems. First came the Paulicians, a group who remain poorly understood even today. Their origins are obscure, but it is thought that the first Paulician community was founded in Armenia in the AD 650s by a teacher called Constantine, who renamed himself 'Silvanus', after one of the apostle Paul's disciples. It is not certain who the 'Paul' was from whom they took their name. Doctrinally, they are traditionally regarded as having been rather like the Manichaeans of an earlier age. If this is so, they were dualists, believing in two great powers, one good, one evil. Like the Gnostics, they believed that the material world was basically evil, and so they rejected the use of icons, all the sacraments and priests. However, some Paulicians, perhaps even all of them, may have been not dualists but Nestorians, remnants of the Syriac-speaking church in Armenia (which, it will be remembered, was more sympathetic to Nestorianism before its conversion to Monophysitism in the early sixth century).

Whatever their precise beliefs, the Paulicians did not survive to teach them within the Byzantine empire. In AD 842 an unprecedentedly cruel crackdown was ordered by Theoctistus, a senior minister of the regent Theodora. 100,000 Paulicians were killed for refusing to renounce their faith. Those who survived fled, setting up a miniature state of their own between the Byzantine empire and the Abbasid caliphate. This state, centred on the town of Tephrike on the upper Euphrates, survived for thirty years until Basil I conquered it in AD 872. Fleeing once again, the Paulicians scattered throughout the Middle East. Some made their way to Armenia, whilst others found new lives within the Abbasid lands themselves, serving with distinction in the Muslim armies against Byzantium. Having been dispersed in this way, Paulicianism proved very tenacious: it has been detected in the rise of Catharism in the West, which we shall look at in Chapter 7, and some Paulicians were still around in the Balkans even in the eighteenth century.

Equally important were the Bogomils. First taught by a preacher named Pop Bogomil ('Pop' being a priestly title in the Bulgarian language) in Bulgaria in the mid-tenth century, Bogomilism spread throughout Bulgaria – although it was never very popular, for reasons that might be fairly apparent. Once again, the Bogomils were dualists, believing in a good principle and an evil one, and identifying the physical world as the work of the latter. They were vegetarians and teetotallers, rejecting the use of anything material in church (icons, relics, bread and wine, and so on), and also rejecting marriage. Saints, priests, and sacraments had no role in their religion. It may be that Bogomilism was inspired by Paulician refugees; if Paulicianism was not dualist after all, however, Bogomilism may date further back, as a development of Manichaeism and the Gnosticism of the second century AD. Alternatively, it is possible that it arose independently. Bogomilism spread slowly but surely throughout the Balkan world and into the

Byzantine empire, where it was first noticed in the eleventh century. By the end of that century, there were Bogomils in Constantinople. Their leader there was a monk called Basil, who taught in the capital for forty years, enjoying success among some aristocratic families. He was arrested in around 1100 and burned at the stake, and Bogomilism in Constantinople seems to have died with him. There were still Bogomils in Asia Minor and in the Balkans, who, though small in number, continued to crop up every so often for the next century or so. Some may have fled to Bosnia, Italy and France, and been involved in the founding of Catharism.

NEW ENEMIES, NEW DEFEATS
As the empire reached its greatest strength, it also began to decline. There were still wars with the various barbarians and, after the death of Basil II in 1025, they were no longer going so well for the Byzantines. This period saw the appearance of an alarming new enemy, too – the Seljuk Turks. These were a people from the East who had been associated with the Khazar empire, but in the middle of the eleventh century they moved west and south, conquering Baghdad and setting up their leader, Sultan Tughrul Bey, as protector of the Abbasid caliphate. They then moved against Armenia, at that time ruled by the Byzantines, and conquered it without difficulty in the 1060s. The crunch came at the battle of Manzikert of 1071, when the emperor Romanus IV Diogenes was captured and forced to hand over large areas of land and pay a considerable ransom. By a nasty coincidence, the same year saw the loss of the Byzantine territory in Italy to the Normans. Byzantium was plunged into civil war as the disgraced Romanus, upon his return to the capital, was dethroned, blinded and thrown into a monastery to die. His successors refused to honour the treaty he had made with the Seljuks, with the inevitable consequence that the Turks advanced remorselessly into Byzantine territory, conquering half of Anatolia and setting up a new sultanate

there, known as Rum (after the Arabian name for Rome), with (in a final indignity for the Byzantine church) Nicaea as its capital.

Worse than this – if such a thing could be imagined – was the appalling Fourth Crusade. We shall see more of the crusades in Chapter 7, but this military expedition was ordered by Pope Innocent III against the Muslims who were holding the Holy Land. However, the crusaders lacked the money to get there, and so they were persuaded by Venetian businessmen to attack Constantinople instead. This they did in 1204, conquering the previously impregnable city and pillaging it mercilessly for three days. Forced to produce a justification after the event, the pope declared that the Byzantines had deserved it because they were schismatics. Baldwin of Flanders was crowned as the new Latin king of Constantinople. The surviving inhabitants of the city fled, and no fewer than three governments in exile were formed. The main one was at Nicaea, under the emperor Theodore Lascaris, where a new ecumenical patriarchate in exile was also set up. Back in Constantinople, a Venetian had been installed as the new Latin patriarch of the city, and attempts were made to put the Byzantine church firmly under the papal heel. One Cardinal Pelagius made himself exceptionally unpopular by persecuting all those who did not accept the supremacy of the pope or use only Latin rites in church.

The westerners could not hold Constantinople: they had limited resources and the Bulgars used the opportunity to launch new attacks on the city. In 1261, the emperor Michael VIII Paleologus recaptured Constantinople and restored Byzantine rule. The empire was reborn, but it would never recapture its old glory. Indeed, it was almost at once hit by a new schism, caused by Michael Paleologus's decision to blind John IV Lascaris, a potential rival to the throne, on his eleventh birthday. The patriarch, Arsenius, excommunicated the emperor for this, and was duly deposed. A large faction of the

NORSE

DANES

SWE

PICTS

IRISH

WELSH

MERCIA

■ YORK

LONDON ■

SAXONS

Elbe

COLOGNE ■

Rhine

BRETONS

Loire

FRANKISH KINGDOM

LYONS ■

LOMBARD
KINGDOM

■ BORDEAUX

Rhône

■ MILAN

GALICIA

BASQUES

Ebro

SARAGOSSA ■

Corsica

ROME ■

BENEVENTO

Tagus

TOLEDO ■

UMAYYAD EMIRATE

NAPLES ■

■ CORDOBA

Balearic
Islands

Sardinia

Sicily

CARTHAGE ■

SYR

Byzantine empire,
8th century

Turks

Mongols   Teutons

Magyars   Latins

Slavs   Balts

Finns   Georgians

Celts   Arabs

0   600 km

0   400 miles

F I N N S

B A L T S

V O L G A
B U L G A R S

S L A V S

M A G Y A R S

KHAZAR KHANATE

A V A R S

Danube
D A N U B E
B U L G A R S

Black Sea

ABASGIANS

SALONICA

CONSTANTINOPLE

NICAEA

CAESAREA

EDESSA

NISIBIS

EPHESUS

Euphrates

ATHENS

ANTIOCH

Cyprus

A
B
B
A
S
I
D

C
A
L
I
P
H
A
T
E

CTESIPHON

Crete

DAMASCUS

diterranean Sea

CYRENE

JERUSALEM

A B B A S I D

ALEXANDRIA

Nile

Western Europe in
the eighth century.

153

church broke away, calling themselves Arsenites and refusing to have anything to do with the imperially sanctioned church, now perceived as a soulless puppet of the emperor. The schism remained in place long after both Michael and Arsenius were dead, and was healed only in 1310.

The following century and a half would be dominated by yet another enemy, the Ottoman Turks. Founded by Osman I in the early fourteenth century in the north-eastern part of Anatolia (an area under Seljuk rule), the Ottoman empire quickly expanded and replaced the Seljuks as the dominant power in the area. Where the Seljuks had taken the Byzantines' eastern provinces, the Ottomans set about conquering their western ones. The process began in 1354 when an earthquake destroyed Gallipoli. The enterprising Ottomans immediately sailed there and established a new city in the ruins. By the end of the century, they had conquered more or less the whole of the Balkan peninsula, leaving the Byzantines with little more than Thessalonica and Constantinople itself. This was bad news for the Balkan Christians. The Bulgarians suffered greatly under Ottoman rule: most of the churches and monasteries were destroyed, and countless priests perished. Many Christians fled to neighbouring countries; many more died for their faith as the Ottomans attempted to force them to convert to Islam (an unusual thing for Muslim occupying forces to do).

The Serbian Orthodox Church, meanwhile, had become an important institution in the northern Balkans, with its own patriarchate, located at Peæ, in the south of modern Serbia. Great cathedrals and monasteries were built throughout the kingdom in the thirteenth and fourteenth centuries. But the Ottomans overran the area in 1389, and the Serbian Orthodox Church began to decline. One of the most damaging practices of the Ottomans, from a Christian point of view, was the taking of children and young men, who were enslaved and brought up as Muslims. Educated as the personal property of the sultan, these young men could rise to the highest positions in the civil service or the government. Others were conscripted into the Ottoman army as janissaries. This bled the Serbian church of its youth, and, while the church never died in Serbia, it lost much of its vigour. Many Serbian Christians fled the towns and cities for the mountains, setting up smaller communities based around subsistence farming.

THE LAST DAYS

Increasingly marginalized in the world at large, the Byzantine church became, if anything, ever more glorious. More monasteries were founded than ever before, and bishops played an even more important role at court and as ambassadors for the empire to the West – for the precarious state of the empire had led to greater interest in the possibility of reunion with the Roman church, despite the vivid memories of the terrible behaviour of the crusaders in 1204.

Even more magnificent works of art were produced during this period. The gold and gems of churches such as Hagia Sophia had originally been laid in abstract patterns or simple blocks of colours; since then, artists had progressed to forming images of the saints in these magnificent materials. After the defeat of iconoclasm in the ninth century, vast icons appeared in church interiors, picked out in golden mosaics; and more of these sumptuous works of art, the very apogee of the Byzantine identification of the love of beauty with the love of God, appeared after the restoration of 1261. This, too, was the period when hesychast mysticism became most popular, and when its foremost proponent, Gregory Palamas, was active within both the church and the court.

Yet the end of the empire – and of the church as its members knew it – was inevitable. In 1453, the Ottoman sultan Muhammad II successfully conquered Constantinople, killing the emperor Constantine XI in the process. The remaining outlying districts of the empire in the Peloponnesus and in Trebizond on the northern shore of the Black Sea were

mopped up in the next few years. Constantinople became the Ottoman capital, its churches either destroyed or converted: the mosaics were ripped out of Hagia Sophia itself and, with the addition of minarets, it was turned into a mosque. The Roman empire had finally fallen in the East, nearly a millennium after it had crumbled in the West.

That was not the end of the Byzantine church. As elsewhere, the Muslims were happy to allow Christian subjects freedom of worship, and a patriarch remained at Constantinople, just as, earlier, patriarchs

had remained at Jerusalem and Antioch. But the church was effectively neutered. Based as it had been around the conviction that the emperor was Christ's regent on earth, it inevitably lost much of its distinctiveness once the emperor had been removed. Christians were often subject to discrimination and even pogroms against their communities. New churches could not be built and the ringing of church bells was forbidden. Yet, paradoxically, the patriarch of Constantinople became in some ways more powerful than in the past. The Ottomans regarded all people of a

Christ as Pantocrator (ruler of all), a twelfth-century mosaic in Cefalu cathedral, Sicily.

155

Gregory Palamas

Gregory Palamas (1296–1359) was archbishop of Thessalonica and the most distinguished theologian of the late Byzantine period.

Gregory was born in Constantinople, where his father was a senator and friend of Emperor Andronicus II. Under the emperor's patronage he studied at the University of Constantinople. He was so good at philosophy that at the age of seventeen he was asked to the palace to speak about Aristotle. He made such an impression with his collected words that his teacher, Theodore Metochite, remarked to the emperor, 'Even if Aristotle was present today, undoubtedly he would have praised him also.'

Gregory abandoned his university studies at an early age. Instead, he devoted himself to the study of ascetic literature and noetic prayer, which took him to Mount Athos in 1318, where he was taught the hesychastic way.

In the 1330s and 40s Gregory took part in a theological dispute with Barlaam the Calabrian and Gregory Akindynos, which led him to expound his own teaching. The dispute took place within the context of attempts to unite the churches at that time. In 1334 Franciscus of Cherson and Richard of Bosphorus arrived in Constantinople as the pope's representatives. Initially these two Latin theologians entered into discussions with a westerner representing the eastern church, Barlaam the Calabrian. However, Barlaam was generally influenced by western sensibilities – especially of that of the emerging Renaissance – and by Aristotelian logic. He used a strict dialectical method and scholastic lines of argumentation.

Gregory Palamas became involved in the dialogue, apparently upon friends' persuasion. In 1335 he composed his treatises on the procession of the Holy Spirit, criticizing Barlaam's dialectical method. Instead, Palamas followed a method which he called apodictic, that is, demonstrative, and this gave his work the title *Apodictic treatises*. Gregory considered the Aristotelian dialectical method to be 'words persuaded by human wisdom', completely ineffective in the comprehension of the divine. The divine is 'above dialectic' and 'greater than all mind and reason'. God is not made up of abstract philosophical concepts and logical definitions. Theology does not examine 'by reason what is beyond reason', but is manifested and granted by God, who is the giver of theology.

Palamas considers it vital that theology is not a consequence of dialectic, but the pure truth, preserved in the divine wisdom of the fathers. These fathers relied on the eye-witness and ear-witness of the disciples and apostles to live out and preach this truth. The apostles were taught everything directly by Christ, 'the truth himself, who was God before all ages, and became for us a theologian'.

While discussing theological method, the subject of

> It is not just a 'God' who transcends beings, but something more than God; the greatness of the one who transcends everything is not only higher than all positive descriptions, but also higher than all negative ones; it transcends all greatness that you could think of.
>
> Gregory Palamas, *Triads* II 3.8, fourteenth century

Gregory Palamas, a nineteenth-century icon of the Russian School.

the difference in ascetic practice also arose. When Barlaam learnt about the psychosomatic techniques of the eastern hesychasts he opposed them. This obliged Gregory Palamas to write nine books, *In defence of the holy hesychasts*. He insisted that the vision of divine light by the individual human person is directly connected with his *theosis* (becoming divine), and it is the surest conviction of this. This vision is the fruit of *ascesis* (self-discipline) and ceaseless prayer. Gregory maintains that *theosis* and the vision of divine light begins in this present life and is fulfilled in the life of the kingdom. This, the vision of divine light, which the hesychasts spoke of, although not perfect in this present life and not bearing the fullness of the vision of the age to come, is nevertheless possible and real. This teaching on the vision of divine light is set out in the *Hagioritic Tome*, which was written by Gregory Palamas in the middle of 1340 and countersigned by twenty-one abbots of Mount Athos.

The vision of divine light is based on the distinction between the divine essence and the uncreated energies of God. The divine essence is self-existent, incomprehensible and incommunicable. The divine energies are attributes of God, the manifestation of God. These energies are distinct from divine essence, and yet are inseparable from it. In his essence, God is absolutely unknown and incommunicable. But his manifestation and communion with humanity comes through the divine energies. The distinction between essence and energies does not introduce a synthesis or addition to Divinity. It simply confirms that God is both known and unknown, communicable and incommunicable.

The teachings of Gregory Palamas are a renewed deliberation about God and human beings, a recapitulation and composition of all the theology of the Greek fathers. In his theology Palamas brings out the connection between historical and suprahistorical, created and uncreated. By participating in divine energies, people can become God by grace – that is, can overcome their created bounds. This prospect starts in the present and is fulfilled in the age to come.

The dynamics and renewal of patristic teaching undertaken by Palamas established him in the consciousness of the East as a doctor of the church. Palamas's theology, due to its dynamism and the combination of theory and practice, found an audience in the Slavic world and also in Romania. Palamite theology flourished especially within the framework of the neo-hesychast movement. St Nicodemus of the Holy Mountain, Paisius Velichkovsky, the starets of Optina and other monastic centres of Russia, and first and foremost, St Seraphim of Sarov, kept the Palamite tradition alive, according to which 'reason is practical, and practice is reasonable'.

Despite the reservations that have occasionally been expressed about Palamas's theology, it is possible that this theology, which is the product of dialogue, could become a serious basis for a new reading of Christian tradition and for the warming of relations between East and West.

CONSTANTINE SCOUTERIS

given religion as a single nation, and so they thought of all the Orthodox Christians within their territories as one and the same, irrespective of which country they had lived in before their subjugation. The patriarch of Constantinople was therefore treated as their spiritual and civil ruler alike, for they were a nation within a nation. This political role for the patriarch meant that the Ottomans often intervened in the election processes, ensuring that a suitable candidate won; patriarchs who did not suit them could easily end up murdered, and indeed few patriarchs during this long period seem to have died a natural death.

The new role of the patriarch of Constantinople marked the end, or at least the subjugation, of the relatively independent churches of Bulgaria, Serbia and elsewhere. Instead of a kind of commonwealth of churches, which had developed over the past few centuries, there was a single Orthodox church within the Ottoman empire, ruled by Constantinople. But there was one big exception to this sudden increase in the dominance of Constantinople over the Orthodox world. One of those daughter churches, nurtured in another great empire that was beginning to rise even as Byzantium fell, never succumbed to the Muslims, and inevitably developed into a great rival and, ultimately, successor to the ancient see. Constantinople, the Second Rome, had fallen, but from now on there would be a Third Rome: the holy city of Moscow, whose fortunes we shall trace in Chapter 8.

CHAPTER 6

A NEW EUROPE

If Christian civilization after the fall of Rome was preserved in Byzantium to the East, things were much worse in the West. The lack of an emperor meant a vast political vacuum, which various competing barbarian kingdoms attempted to fill. Yet during these 'Dark Ages', the Western church grew in strength, setting down roots upon which the glories of medieval Christendom would later be built.

EUROPE AFTER THE EMPIRE

According to the proverb, Rome was not built in a day. It didn't fall in a day, either. How could such a remarkable civilization have fallen into such ruin? We saw the beginnings of the process in Chapter 3, when the migrations of the barbarians into western Europe coincided with political instability and corruption in the empire. The border between the empire and the barbarians became more and more fluid, and less clearly defined. Roman power simply ebbed away, or became diluted, as the barbarians mingled with the Romans or conquered them. Even while much of western Europe was still officially ruled by Constantinople – the capital of the empire since AD 330 – in reality it was being increasingly left to its own devices.

By the end of the fifth century, Roman rule throughout Europe had been effectively replaced by a number of small, competing barbarian kingdoms. Their rise, however, did not necessarily bring with them a reversion to paganism, because many of the barbarians themselves were already Christians. This was thanks to one

The bishop Wulfila [Ulfilas] invents an alphabet, by the German artist Bernhard Rode (1725–97).

of the (usually) unsung heroes of late antiquity, Ulfilas. Born in the early fourth century, Ulfilas was a man between two cultures: his parents were from Cappadocia, in the Roman empire, but they were captured by Visigothic marauders and taken to their territory in eastern Europe, approximately where Romania and Hungary are today. Nevertheless, these Romans, educated in Greek learning, did well in this foreign country, even giving their son a Gothic name. As a young man, Ulfilas was sent to Constantinople, perhaps as an ambassador on behalf of the Goths. While here he was consecrated bishop and charged to return to the Goths and preach to them, which he did for the next half-century or so. His mission was enormously successful. He not only preached verbally to the Goths, but translated the Bible into their language – although until that point their language had never been written down. Ulfilas therefore devised the Gothic alphabet and translated the Bible into it – all except for the books of Kings, we are told, since the Goths were already very warlike and Ulfilas felt that reading the history of the ancient Hebrews' wars would probably not do them much good.

It was partly because of Ulfilas's success in bringing Christianity to the barbarians that the Roman emperors allowed them to settle within the empire. The only problem – and the reason why Ulfilas has not been celebrated as much as other great missionaries of this period – was that he was an Arian. The Goths he converted, therefore, were also Arian. This was not a problem at the time, since the emperors were Arian for much of the fourth century; the fact that the barbarians now shared

their religion made negotiations with them that much easier. But it did mean that after the triumph of Nicene Christianity (within the empire) by the end of the fourth century, there were religious conflicts as the Arian barbarians mingled with, and increasingly came to control, the Nicene citizens of the empire.

ITALY UNDER THE OSTROGOTHS
This was not necessarily a problem. Despite their reputation, in Roman times and ever since, for uncouth savagery, many barbarian peoples were just as civilized as the Romans they conquered or displaced. For example, the Ostrogoths (that is, 'eastern Goths') lived to the north of the Black Sea, but like other barbarian peoples had been displaced from further east by the Huns and wanted to find a permanent home. In AD 488 the eastern emperor, Zeno, allied with the Ostrogoths' king, Theodoric (AD 455–526), and persuaded him to march on Italy. Zeno's plan was that Theodoric should defeat Odoacer, the barbarian king who had conquered Italy. Evidently he thought Theodoric would be easier to get on with. Theodoric

accordingly led his people on a great march west, defeated Odoacer, and set himself up as king of Italy and emperor of the west, taking Ravenna as his capital. Theodoric conquered a considerable area – including not just Italy, but Sicily and south-east France too – and did his best to preserve Roman civilization there. Although a barbarian king, he had been brought up at Constantinople and served as a general in the Roman army. It was under Theodoric that the philosopher Boethius (c. AD 480–524) and the writer Cassiodorus (c. AD 490–580) lived. Theodoric was keen to stay on good terms with the eastern emperor, who regarded him as a sort of provincial sub-ruler, although in reality Theodoric was an independent king. He hoped to unite Roman and barbarian civilization in a new world order which would combine the best of both, and he kept the old Roman civil service intact in his domains as well as commissioning splendid mosaics in churches and other buildings. Indeed, modern visitors to Ravenna generally assume that Theodoric's mosaics, like the others found there, are Roman or

The Last Supper, pictured in a mosaic from the sixth-century church of St Apollinare Nuovo (originally Theodoric's palace chapel), Ravenna, Italy.

Byzantine – for how could a barbarian king be so civilized?

Theodoric displayed a high level of religious tolerance. As an Arian, he regarded himself as a protector of Arianism, the official religion of his kingdom. But he believed that it was wrong to try to force people to believe anything, and so Nicene Christianity also flourished within his domains. However, this peaceful situation was shortlived. Theodoric died in AD 526 and the Byzantine emperor Justinian invaded his kingdom not long after. Although their rule in Italy did not last long, the Byzantines did their best to wipe out the Ostrogoth presence, encouraging the Lombards, another barbarian group, to settle there and displace them. They tried to eradicate all memory of the old king, even reworking many of his mosaics to remove his image from the very walls. All that remained was Theodoric's remarkable mausoleum in Ravenna. And like a select few other great kings and warlords, such as Arthur and Charlemagne, Theodoric lived on in legend. Folk tales still exist about 'Dietrich of Berne', as he became known in the tradition, and in some myths, such as the twelfth-century *Nibelungenlied*, he even became a sort of god-king who led the wild hunt through the winter skies.

Theodoric's desire to mingle barbarian and Roman culture was common among the new powers of western Europe. Take, for example, the Visigoths (that is, the 'western Goths'), who were allowed to settle in south-west Gaul in the early fifth century. In AD 475 their king, Euric, declared himself an independent ruler. He had already been busy for some years carving out an empire. In AD 471 he had moved east from his base at Toulouse and attacked Provence. His troops devastated the countryside, bringing the threat of famine to the whole area. Patiens, bishop of Lyon to the north, responded by organizing a huge relief effort, sending food down the Saône and Rhône rivers to be distributed free to those who needed it. In this time of uncertainty, it was increasingly falling to bishops to look after the civic and temporal needs of their cities as well as their spiritual needs. Indeed, bishops could even be military leaders. During Euric's foray eastwards, he had hit resistance at Clermont. The resistance had been organized by the bishop, Sidonius, who regarded the Visigoths as a threat to Christian faith (since they were Arians) and to Roman culture alike. Sidonius failed to halt the Visigothic advance, but Euric punished him with only a brief period of exile. Perhaps these Visigoths were not so barbaric after all.

SPAIN UNDER THE VISIGOTHS

Indeed, the Visigoths presided over a remarkable survival of Roman culture in Spain. Euric expanded his territory west as well as east, and his successors continued the conquests until Leovigild, who ruled the Visigoths from AD 569 to 586, stamped his authority over the entire Iberian peninsula. Here, the Visigoths appear to have been remarkably keen not to disrupt the normal life of the Hispano–Roman people. They left the governmental structures intact and allowed the people to use the old Roman legal system, even as the Visigoths themselves used their own. They did not attempt to impose their Arian Christianity on the people, and indeed in AD 589 King Reccared converted to the Nicene faith. It is a well-known phenomenon that those who conquer a country often end up being themselves culturally conquered by their new subjects, but it can never have happened quite so strikingly as to the Visigoths in Spain.

Here, as the rest of western Europe fell into uncertainty and strife, it was almost as if the Roman empire had never passed. The main episcopal seat in the kingdom was at Toledo, and successive bishops, having secured the ear of the king, called a series of councils to ensure religious uniformity throughout the kingdom. Scholarship flourished, especially as many scholars and monks left North Africa – where the Vandals were fighting the Byzantines – and settled in Spain.

The most remarkable figure to emerge

[Theodoric] is a man worth knowing, even by those who cannot enjoy being close to him, so well have Providence and Nature cooperated to give him such perfect gifts… He is good-looking, taller than average, but not a giant. His head is round, with curly hair receding a bit from brow to crown… Before dawn he goes with very few attendants for his priests' service. He prays attentively, but, if I may say so privately, I think more out of habit than with real piety. Affairs of state take up the rest of the morning… On ordinary days, his dining table is like that of a normal person. It doesn't groan under the weight of dull, unpolished silver, put there by gasping waiters – the weight is in the conversation rather than on the plates. There is either sensible talk or silence. The hangings used at these times are sometimes purple silk, sometimes just linen… In brief, you will find the elegance of Greece, the good humour of Gaul, the delicacy of Italy, the stateliness of public banquets with the good service of a private table, and everywhere the discipline of a king's house.

Sidonius Apollinaris, *Letter to Agricola* c. AD 454

from this flourishing Christian kingdom was Isidore, who became bishop of Seville in AD 600. He was instrumental in strengthening both the Visigothic monarchy and the Nicene faith in Spain, and in linking the two together. He believed that because the Visigoths had abandoned the heresy of Arianism, they had been divinely ordained as defenders of the church. The fourth council of Toledo, over which Isidore presided in AD 633, stated that the king was appointed by God, and everyone was bound to obey him. For Isidore, this meant that the king had a corresponding duty to rule wisely – and he was not afraid to point this out when necessary.

Yet Isidore apparently spent most of his time in his study. Here he absorbed the classical learning which Rome had bequeathed to Spain, and reproduced it in his own writings. He wrote a history of the world, a history of the Goths, books on Christian doctrine and ethics, works on philosophy and science and his famous *Etymologies*, which ambitiously set out to

Although the Visigoths and their subjects were flourishing in Spain, they had lost their territories in Gaul. This happened in AD 507 when Euric's son, Alaric II, was defeated by Clovis of the Franks. Alaric had no need to be ashamed of this setback, since Clovis was one of the mightiest warlords of the age and his people, the Franks, were destined to play a very important role in European history.

THE FRANKS

The Franks moved from an unknown home into Gaul in the third century and integrated into the Roman empire. In the fifth century, as Roman power ebbed from Gaul, the Frankish king Clovis seized power. He converted to Nicene Christianity in around AD 500 and aimed to assimilate with the old Roman culture rather than replace it. Roman roads and buildings remained in use, chariot races were held and rather bad Latin poetry was written. Clovis was also allied to Theodoric in Italy, who helped him in his wars with the Visigoths.

The body of Isidore of Seville is transported from Chios to Venice, in this fourteenth-century fresco from St Mark's Cathedral, Venice.

present the totality of all knowledge. Inspired by earlier Latin encyclopaedists such as Varro or Pliny the Elder, Isidore's work contained less detail but was much more wide-ranging. It was enormously popular throughout the Middle Ages, and today Isidore has become an unofficial patron saint of the Internet.

Clovis thus founded a new ruling dynasty of Franks in what had once been Roman Gaul – a dynasty which became known as the Merovingian dynasty. But stability never lasted long in the Dark Ages. The law of 'primogeniture', whereby a landowner bequeathed his entire estate to his eldest son, had not yet been developed.

This meant that as soon as anyone managed to build up anything resembling an empire, he died and it was split up again among his sons. This happened when Clovis died in AD 511, and again when his most powerful son, Clotaire I, died fifty years later. Brother fought brother, and kingdoms waxed and waned unpredictably.

The Merovingian age was a dangerous time to be alive. Warfare was sporadic but vicious, conducted by brutal armies with no scruples about burning and pillaging the countryside and slaughtering its inhabitants. A city could change hands from one king to another unpredictably, and in such volatile times, the church was often the most important stable factor in life. Consider, for example, the city of Tours, where a Gallo-Roman nobleman named Gregory became bishop in AD 573. Between then and his death in AD 594, the constant shifting of boundaries as statelets waxed and waned in power meant that Tours passed under the political control of three kings. The city was devastated by war, its cathedral burned to the ground in AD 568. Luckily, Gregory took a firm hand of Tours. He not only had the cathedral rebuilt, but stood up for the people's rights against the shifting political powers and seems to have administered his see with courage and justice.

CELTIC CHRISTIANITY

As the empire crumbled, one country remained untouched by the crisis afflicting the rest of Europe. It was one of the few parts of western Europe that the Romans had never conquered and which therefore survived the fall of Rome relatively unscathed: the island of Ireland.

Ireland in the early Middle Ages was not a single country. It was divided up between various kingdoms and petty warlords, who spent their time warring with each other. But even these were not really kingdoms like those of the new barbarian powers that were rising in mainland Europe. Roman civilization, based around cities, had never reached here, and life in Ireland was still completely rural. Society was organized around *tuatha*, or tribes, who lived in small settlements.

THE CONVERSION OF IRELAND

It was to here that Patrick, a Romano-Briton, was taken by a gang of Irish marauders in the early fifth century. Christianity had come to Britain with the Romans, and it seems to have been fairly well established there by the third century; but the Roman armies had temporarily withdrawn from the island in the opening years of the fifth century in order to deal with a crisis in mainland Europe. Unfortunately for the Britons this crisis had developed into the fall of Rome, and the armies never came back. In AD 410 the emperor Honorius wrote to the Britons, telling them to organize their own defence. Hordes of invaders promptly appeared from across the North Sea – Angles, Saxons and Jutes – who proceeded to set up their own kingdoms in the east, south and centre of the island, either defeating or integrating with the Romano-British population already

Patrick, in an illustration from a fifteenth-century English manuscript.

A monastery should, if possible, be built so that everything needed – water, mill, garden, bakery – is available, so that the monks do not need to wander about outside. For this is not at all good for their souls.

The Rule of St Benedict, mid-sixth century

For thirty-four years he lived and fought upon the island. There was no hour in which he wasn't praying, or reading, or writing, or doing work of some kind. With untiring vigils and fasting, he worked day and night under burdens so heavy that each one seemed too much for human strength. And in all this he was loved by everyone, his face always cheerful, his heart glad with the joy of the divine Holy Spirit.

Adamnan, Life of Columba, late seventh century

there. These new Anglo-Saxon kingdoms were pagan, and Christianity more or less disappeared in what would later become England – one of the very few occasions when Christianity was overwhelmed by paganism. Like the Irish, they spent much of their time jostling for power with each other, engaging in brief but bloody wars. The Romano-British, meanwhile, retreated to the west and north of the island, creating kingdoms in what would become Scotland, Wales and Cornwall. Here, Christianity continued to flourish, in what has been called 'the age of saints'. This was the time of two famous saints – David, who founded monasteries throughout Wales noted for their ascetic severity, and also Gildas, who attacked the practice of ascetic severity if it was done without love, simply to show off.

So this was the religion that Patrick brought to Ireland. Patrick was not the only missionary to the Irish, but he was certainly the most striking personality among them. In AD 433, we are told, he engaged in a kind of magical battle with the pagan druids at Tara, before King Laoghaire, who claimed overlordship of Ireland. Just as in the Old Testament the prophet Elijah triumphed alone over 400 prophets of the pagan god Baal (1 Kings 18:19–40), so too Patrick's prayers overpowered the spells of his opponents, and Laoghaire and his followers converted to Christianity.

A MONASTIC CHURCH

But this was not the Roman empire, where Christianity could spread through imperial edict and where powerful bishops in major cities could play an active role in society and spread the religion that way. There were no cities and not many bishops. Here, instead, Christianity spread slowly through the countryside, and the key figures in its rise were not bishops but monks.

As Christianity spread, the monks came to play a role much like the pagan druids, who had acted as storytellers and judges as well as religious authorities. The monks dressed like the druids, in long white robes, and sported the same haircut – shaved at the front and long at the back, in a kind of extreme, early medieval mullet. The druids had taken part in battles, casting spells from the sidelines, and the monks did the same, but with prayers to God instead. Thus, we are told that Columba, a major figure in the spread of Irish monasticism, was present at the battle of Cul Dreimne in AD 561 (apparently, the saint's prayers were so effective that 3,000 of the enemy were killed compared to only one from his own side). We are told, more reliably, that Columba travelled throughout Ireland founding monasteries. These, and others founded by other much-loved saints, were like whole villages or even small towns, consisting not of single buildings but collections of huts surrounded by a wall. Monasteries were enormously popular, and people flocked to join them. The monastery at Bangor was said to have 4,000 inhabitants – clearly the closest thing Ireland had to a major urban centre, even if that figure is exaggerated. Many of the inhabitants were not monks at all but farmers, carpenters, smiths – all the trades that the community required to operate. The abbots of these monasteries were important people, little different from traditional landowners; they were usually married and their position would be hereditary. In Egypt, monks had fled the towns to find solitude. In Ireland, the towns came to the monks.

The monasteries themselves, meanwhile, became major centres of scholarship. Like their contemporaries in Visigothic Spain and elsewhere in the former empire, the monks of Ireland devoted themselves to copying the great literature of the past – pagan as well as Christian. In so doing, they not only helped to preserve this literature, but developed an extraordinary tradition of calligraphy and manuscript illumination. The beautiful writing of most Irish manuscripts from this period testifies to the effort that went into producing them. A good example is the Cathach or 'Battle

The development of monasteries

When we think of the great images of Christianity in the Celtic lands – the islands of Iona or Lindisfarne, the great illuminated Gospel books, the round towers or the high crosses in Ireland – we should note that in every case we are looking at monastic remains. So how did monasticism come to play such an important role in the lives of Christians, not just in the Celtic lands, but across Europe in the period between the fifth and the tenth centuries?

Monks in Europe
Monasticism was firmly established in the Latin west by the end of the fourth century, and in the writings of John Cassian (c. AD 360–435) it found its first, great, western theorist. Cassian presented his views on monasticism in the context of southern Gaul but in the form of reminiscences of the advice he had heard and the lifestyle he had seen in Egypt and Palestine. His books became daily reading in many monasteries; and when today students of Celtic monasteries note similarity between them and the monks of the desert, they often forget that the early western monks were deliberately imitating their eastern brothers in so far as they read about the desert in Cassian.

The monastic ideal
The monk chose to live a life of discipline within a community under an abbot – this was to root out the evil of pride; it was to be a life of simplicity and work – to root out greed; and it was to be an ordered life lived according to a plan for each day, each week and every year. The purpose of the contemplative life was not only a pursuit of wisdom and holiness, but to offer to God a life of regular praise. Hence the key to the life was 'the work of God' and the regular gatherings during the night and the day to sing the Psalms. Around this daily pattern of prayer was arranged other work (manual and intellectual), business, eating, recreation and sleep.

Rules and disciples
In the early centuries there was a great variety of 'rules' (a law regulating the monastic life and prayer of a monastery) in both east and west. Each monk saw himself as a disciple who, by listening to the rule and following it, became a disciple of the monastery's founder and thus of Christ. Gradually this great variety of rules began to be replaced by a handful of rules linked to prestigious monasteries. The most important was that known today as 'the Rule of St Benedict' (which was a distillation of a more elaborate rule) and which became linked with the abbey of Monte Cassino (south of Rome) founded by Benedict (c. AD 480–550); and so what was destined to be the most influential rule in Europe was attributed to him. By the ninth century this particular rule became so dominant that few groups thought of monasticism in any other way: however, we should remember that there was a far greater variety of forms of monasticism in the west until the ninth century, when 'Benedictinism' became the norm.

Monks and society
Monks saw themselves as at once having fled society and as having established model human communities. This can be seen in the numerous island monasteries – apart, yet close to the larger society. For society monasteries provided a resource of prayer and holiness, whose presence sanctified their region. In turn, the monasteries became repositories of learning, places that ran schools, places that provided pastoral care to the larger church and places that were increasingly called upon to provide specialist clerics (for example, theologians) and candidates for bishops.

Perceptions of monasticism
Today we think of monks as a highly unusual part of the Christian church. In this early period monks were seen as model Christians. Moreover, in Christian cultures which thought of themselves corporately, rather than as simply collections of individual who shared beliefs, monks were a central part of 'the body of Christ' (Ephesians 4:12): its praying heart awake day and night, whose holiness of life made the whole church holy.

THOMAS O'LOUGHLIN

The abbey of Monte Cassino, founded by Benedict of Nursia in AD 529. The abbey was destroyed during World War II and rebuilt according to the original plans.

An illumination from the *Book of Kells*.

Celts had believed certain places or natural features, such as wells or rocks, to be holy and inhabited by spirits. The Christians continued to venerate them, associating them not with spirits but with notable incidents in the lives of saints. The tall stone crosses that are often associated with Celtic religion only started being erected after the Synod of Whitby in the north of England in AD 664, but they seem to preserve elements of ancient beliefs in their design. Similarly, the stone pillars that the Picts made (throughout what is now Scotland) feature strange images, presumably hearkening back to pagan beliefs, that modern scholars cannot decipher.

THE CELTIC MISSIONS

For no sooner had Christianity become established throughout Ireland than Columba was travelling to the British mainland, seeking to bring it to the Picts, a people who had lived in what is now Scotland for many centuries, and who like the Irish had successfully resisted the Romans. The Irish were sending colonists beyond their island at this time anyway – apparently to as far away as the Faroe Islands and Iceland – and the kingdoms they founded in Dalriada (in what is now Scotland) and Dyfed (in Wales) were vital in the dissemination of Irish culture. Irish missionaries appeared in northern England, bringing Christianity to the Anglo-Saxons even as Roman missionaries were arriving in southern England with the same purpose. As the Anglo-Saxons adopted Christianity, they also adopted features of Celtic religion. The great monastery of Lindisfarne, on a little island off the coast of Northumbria, was founded in imitation of Columba's monastery on the island of Iona in the Irish Sea. And the *Lindisfarne Gospels* which were produced there in the early eighth century showed the influence of Celtic manuscript illumination like that of the *Book of Kells*, as well as the Anglo-Saxons' own skill in metalworking and jewellery, transferred to the patterns of the page.

Book', a copy of the Psalms, which according to tradition was written by Columba himself and which was still being used to bless Irish armies in the 1690s. Perhaps most famous of all, though, is the *Book of Kells*, a copy of the Gospels which was probably produced in around AD 800 at the great monastery on the island of Iona (off the coast of what is now Scotland). This manuscript's intricate designs and beautiful illuminations make it one of the outstanding works of art of the early Middle Ages.

Irish Christianity retained some features of Celtic paganism during this period. For example, an important element of Celtic religion had been the anmchara or 'soul friend', where a druid would act as a spiritual adviser to a younger person. The practice continued in the monasteries, where every monk would have his own mentor to help and advise him. And the

Even more dramatic was Columban, not to be confused with the older Columba. Where Columba left Ireland to preach to the Picts, Columban was more ambitious and went to continental Europe. Here, in the late sixth century, he set up a series of monasteries in the Irish style, governed by a rule remarkable in its severity. In Columban's monasteries, forgetting to make the sign of the cross over your spoon before eating would book you a date with the lash. However, the Irish monasteries never really caught on in France. Even Columban's own monasteries later dropped his harsh rules and conformed to the Benedictine Rule which would later become standard, and in this way they were quietly absorbed into mainstream Catholicism.

That would be the fate of the Celtic Church in Ireland and Britain as well, as Christianity in western Europe became increasingly standardized, well organized and more centrally controlled. An essential part of this process was the ever-greater importance of the pope.

THE RISE OF THE PAPACY

THE BISHOPS OF IMPERIAL ROME

The pope's rise to prominence had begun in the days of the Roman empire. Rome had always been important to Christians – not only as the first city of the empire, but as the place where both Peter and Paul had been martyred, according to tradition. As we saw in Chapter 2, the early church placed great faith in the fact that their religion had been passed down from Christ via his apostles. Thus, those churches that had actually been founded by apostles were regarded as normative. In disputes, the decisions of their bishops were especially weighty, because they represented the apostolic foundation.

The Council of Chalcedon had decreed that there were five dioceses with special authority, the seats of the patriarchs – Rome, Jerusalem, Alexandria, Antioch and Constantinople. But, apart from Rome, all of these cities were in the eastern half of the empire. So from the fourth century

St Martin's Cross, a ninth-century monument on Iona.

onwards, as the two halves became increasingly politically and culturally distinct, the easterners had four apostolic sees to appeal to, while the westerners had only one. Rome inevitably became more and more theologically important in the West.

Like so much else, the transformation of the Roman see had its roots in the fourth century. One of the most important Roman bishops in this period was Damasus I, who reigned from AD 366 to 384. Damasus did all the normal things a major bishop of the time did: he intervened in doctrinal disputes and wrote a lot of pious poetry. He was also particularly devoted to the city of Rome, built many churches and monuments there and oversaw the restoration of many others. And Damasus had a high view of his own authority. He referred to Rome as 'the apostolic see', and to himself as *pontifex maximus*. In earlier centuries this had been the title of the chief pagan priest in Rome, until Julius Caesar had taken it over for himself. Since then, it had been applied to the emperor. Now it referred to the bishop of Rome, and that is where the title 'pontiff' comes from. Indeed, Damasus himself cut a fine figure as he travelled Rome in his carriage: he even looked like an emperor.

Damasus argued that the authority of the bishop of Rome had been established by Jesus himself. He appealed to Matthew 16:18–19, where Jesus tells Peter, 'You are Peter, and on this rock I will build my church, and the gates of Hades will not prevail against it. I will give you the keys of the kingdom of heaven, and whatever you bind on earth will be bound in heaven, and whatever you loose on earth will be loosed in heaven.' The name 'Peter' comes from the Greek word for 'rock', so in this passage Jesus gives it to Peter (originally called Simon) as a sort of nickname. But Damasus was the first to argue that, in giving Peter this authority, Jesus also intended it to pass to Peter's successors. Peter went on to become the first bishop of Rome; therefore, every bishop of Rome since had inherited 'the keys of the kingdom of heaven'.

Damasus's ideas were extremely influential: his successor, Siricius, was the first to use the title 'pope', which meant 'father' and had originally applied to the bishops of any of the great apostolic sees. In AD 495 a synod held at Rome was the first known to have hailed the pope (at this time Gelasius I) as 'the Vicar of Christ'. The theological foundations for the power of the papacy had been laid, and in the years that followed the political conditions were also created. There was, increasingly, a lack of strong leadership in Rome. This had begun already before Damasus's time, as the emperors of the western half of the empire generally ruled from Milan, not Rome; but by a century later there was no emperor in the west at all. Leo I, pope from AD 440 to 461, found himself having to take charge of civic matters such as the distribution of grain in Rome, as there was no one else to do it. When Attila the Hun appeared in AD 452 and threatened to attack the city, it was Leo I who had to ride out to his camp and negotiate with him. He successfully prevented Attila from sacking Rome, although his similar negotiations with Genseric and his Vandal hordes three years later went less well.

THE PAPACY AND THE BARBARIANS

As different barbarian kings came and went in Italy and elsewhere in western Europe, the papacy was really the only stable political institution in the area. This was certainly the case with Gregory the Great, who became pope in AD 590. Gregory had already had a career as an important politician in the city, but he had given it up to become a monk. He was apparently not very happy at being thrust back into the limelight – tradition tells that he fled the city hidden in a huge basket in an attempt to avoid being elected pope!

The situation in northern Italy was just as difficult as in Gaul at this time. The main barbarians here, now that the Ostrogoths were gone, were the Lombards, a Germanic tribe who had invaded northern Italy and created a kingdom around Pavia. This kingdom wrestled with the Byzantines for control of the area, whilst Rome remained independent under the control of the papacy. During these centuries, the area around Rome, including the catacombs, was subject to raids and vandalism. The last burials in the catacombs were probably made in Gregory's time or shortly after. The remains of the martyrs were moved into churches in the area, and the catacombs themselves forgotten for a thousand years.

Gregory took charge of Rome's finances, food and water supply, and policing – even using monks as city guards. He worked hard to achieve peace with the Lombards, and raised large sums to ransom prisoners from them. He was an accomplished diplomat, able to compromise when necessary, but completely unbribable. Yet Gregory believed that his main purpose was to help the poor,

Because the primacy of the apostolic see is established by the merit of St Peter, the chief of bishops, by the glory of the city of Rome, and by the authority of a holy council, nobody may attempt anything against its authority without unpardonable presumption.

Emperor Valentinian I,
Decree on papal power,
AD 445

The person who acquires any virtues without humility is like someone carrying powdered spices in the open air.

Gregory the Great

and he reorganized the church's finances to make this more effective. He called himself 'the servant of the servants of Christ', a title that all popes since have taken on.

In addition to all this, Gregory was a reformer and scholar. He reorganized the liturgy of the church, and tradition holds that he compiled or even composed much of the church's liturgical chant – hence the name 'Gregorian chant'. In fact it was probably later churchmen who did this, but Gregory certainly did write many books on theology and on the scriptures – so much so that he is traditionally represented in art as seated at a desk with a dove sitting on his shoulder. The dove is the Holy Spirit, whispering its inspiration into the pope's ear – for Gregory's books were enormously popular for the rest of the Middle Ages. In fact, Gregory often wrote of God's presence as a 'whisper', writing at one point, 'God's mighty whisper fills the universe, seeking a way into every soul.' He was not an original theologian by any means, but he was extremely learned, and in his books he distilled and re-presented the teachings of earlier thinkers in ways that were readily understandable.

Having a man like Gregory on the papal throne could hardly fail to enhance the standing of the papacy, and its temporal power grew slowly but steadily. As we have seen, the absence of the law of primogeniture meant that kingdoms and other realms, painstakingly united through diplomacy or conquest, inevitably divided again upon the death of the ruler. Only the church was exempt from such a problem. The land and money that were given to the church by pious or canny rulers stayed in the church's possession forever, and its power grew. By the time we get to Zacharias, pope from AD 741 to 752, the papacy owned considerable areas of land in Italy, and Zacharias was the chief provider of grain to Rome. He even issued his own coins, one of the first popes to do so. Like Gregory before him, Zacharias played the game of international diplomacy, and played it well – now not simply as a kind of disinterested observer

Gregory the Great. Detail from the fresco by Andrea Delitio in Abruzzi Cathedral.

and arbiter, but as a king among kings – ruler of what was now sometimes called 'the Republic of St Peter'. In AD 781 one of his successors, Hadrian I, set up the papal mint and issued coins with his own name and image on them. Hadrian also allied the papacy to the Frankish kings, and became very close to Charlemagne, whom he dubbed the defender of Rome. It is said that when Charlemagne learned of Hadrian's death in AD 795, the mighty king wept as though he had lost a brother.

It is easy to criticize these popes for their increasing power. Did they, as John Milton put it, 'seek to avail themselves of names, places, and titles, and with these to join secular power, though feigning still to act by spiritual'? As is usually the case, things were a little more complicated than that. These popes had little choice but to wield power in Italy, since no one else was there to do so in any kind of stable way. If no one had organized the distribution of food, the people would have starved. Similarly, the increasing financial resources of the church were used to help people, either by direct distribution to the poor or by the ransoming of prisoners. Only later did the power of the papacy bring about corruption and abuse, as we shall see in the next chapter.

MISSION AND THE SPREAD OF PAPAL POWER

These early medieval popes were also very concerned about mission. Western Europe was still far from fully Christian. As a rule, the further north you went, the more pagan things still were. Once again, Gregory the Great set the standard. He organized missions to Gaul and Sardinia and also sent missionaries to the Jews, hoping to convert them to Christianity. In this, though, Gregory was keen to respect the rights of Jews as citizens. On one occasion he received complaints that a Jewish convert to Christianity had set up a cross and image of Mary in a synagogue. Gregory ordered these Christian objects to be removed, and the synagogue given back to the Jewish leaders.

Most famous was Gregory's mission to England. According to the legend, before becoming pope, Gregory was walking through the slave market of Rome, where he saw some golden-haired boys for sale. (The early Christians had apparently not been opposed to slavery, but in the later empire it had become increasingly common for wealthy Christians to free their slaves as an act of charity. By Gregory's day, slavery was still important to most of western European society, but many Christians were opposed

The church in England

Something of the early history of the church in England is traceable from the names of places honouring those who brought the gospel. Chief among these is St Alban. In the Roman city of Verulamium (today St Albans), Alban was executed for harbouring Christians early in the third century. Christianity, then, existed in England during the Roman period and St Martin's church in Canterbury is believed to have been founded towards the very end of the Roman occupation. Following the end of the Roman occupation, much of Britain was colonized by the pagan Anglo-Saxons; this led to the necessity of new Christian missions to England. The much-heralded evangelization of England in the seventh century was thus effectively a *re-evangelization*. It drew its missionary impetus from two sources, first Pope Gregory the Great's commission to St Augustine and, at almost exactly the same time, Aidan's missionary journey from Iona to Northumbria.

These two missions rested on two very different patterns of church life, which were shaped by the landscape from which they sprang. Augustine's mission, AD 597, was rooted in an urban 'secular' model. Bishops were the focuses of church life and established their cathedrals in key cities. So Augustine, a reluctant missionary, who would have rather remained in the warmer climes of

Burgundy, set up his church in Canterbury alongside the court of King Ethelbert of Kent. This highlights another key element in the re-evangelization of England; it focused on the conversion of royal courts, through whose patronage the gospel could be further spread. Rochester and London were evangelized by missions from Canterbury. Similarly Redwald, king of the east Saxons, was converted by a missionary initiative from Kent; St Felix was the first East Anglian bishop of whom we know and his see city was probably at a Roman station (now underwater) to the east of present-day Felixstowe.

The northern mission was rooted in the Irish/Celtic model. This sprang from the rural, moor-like landscape of Ireland and the Scottish islands. The base here was the monastery and the bishops themselves were monks. King Oswald of the Northumbrians petitioned St Columba, in Iona, to send a missionary to his court. Once again the conversion of the rulers or local kings was central to the pattern of evangelization. Aidan became the friend and counsellor of King Oswald and King Edwin, and his ministry was itinerant throughout the wild countryside of Northumbria, in contrast to the urban pattern deriving from Rome. St Cuthbert, the holy monk, trained under St Boisil (modern St Boswell) at Melrose and, founding his monastery at Lindisfarne, continued this northern mission.

The culture of these two missions was, then, very different and this led to variations in practice; the monastic tonsure varied and they celebrated Easter at different times. As this dispute intensified,

Augustine of Canterbury, in an illustration from a fifteenth-century English manuscript.

in AD 664 King Oswy convened a synod at St Hilda's great monastery at Whitby. Here, under the leadership of the Celtic-trained but Roman sympathizer St Wilfrid, the pattern from the south triumphed, but Ecclesia Anglicana always retained an indigenous independence of spirit, traceable to the Irish/Celtic influence.

In the late seventh century, by a quirk of providence, the Greek bishop Theodore of Tarsus was elected to the see of Canterbury. He was largely responsible for setting up the English parochial system, as we know it.

STEPHEN PLATTEN

to the practice in principle, and the spread of Christianity meant that slavery was almost entirely abolished by AD 1000.) Struck by their appearance, Gregory asked where they were from, and on being told that they were Angles, commented, 'Not Angles, but angels! What a shame that God's grace does not dwell within those beautiful brows.' After becoming pope, he therefore sent a monk from his monastery named Augustine (not to be confused with the great theologian) to their country. Together with forty companions, Augustine arrived in Kent, in south-east Britain, in AD 597. On Christmas Day that year, King Ethelbert of Kent and 10,000 of his subjects were baptized Christians. The first step on the road to the Church of England had been taken.

And the Anglo-Saxons themselves were soon sending missionaries to northern Europe as well. The most famous English missionary was Boniface, who was born in what is now Devon, but who spent much of the early eighth century preaching in what is now the Netherlands and Bavarian Saxony in Germany. This was dangerous work. Whilst Christianity proved popular among many people in these areas, others resented the presence of these missionaries and their foreign religion. Little wonder that Boniface adopted a decidedly no-nonsense approach in his preaching. On one famous occasion, he strode up to a huge tree called the Oak of Thor at Geismar, which was sacred to the pagans, and committed a robust ecumenical act with the aid of a large axe. The favour was returned in AD 754, when he and his travelling companions were ambushed by a group of equally militant pagans and murdered.

As Christianity spread and became consolidated in these areas, the power of the papacy grew – not simply because more people were Christian, but because the kind of Christianity they followed looked more and more to Rome for direction. For example, when Boniface was not advancing the cause of Christ through deforestation, he was helping to set up a proper episcopal system in the newly evangelized regions and reforming the system already in place elsewhere. In AD 742 he played a key role at a council in Francia, which ruled that priests were subject to their bishops and were not allowed to fight in wars or go hunting. At the same time, monasticism was standardized by the recommendation of the Rule of Benedict of Nursia throughout Francia. In all this Boniface was acting as the personal emissary of Pope Gregory III. The Christianity that was becoming established throughout Europe was a Roman Catholic Christianity, a Christianity that was preached and administered at the orders of the pope.

A key event in this process was the Synod of Whitby, held in AD 664 at the orders of King Oswy of Northumbria, another of the warring Anglo-Saxon kingdoms. The Anglo-Saxons were being evangelized by Roman missionaries to the south and Irish missionaries to the north at the same time, but they preached slightly different kinds of Christianity. For one thing, they calculated the date of Easter differently; for another, their monks cut their hair differently. Why on earth did such things matter? In fact, these issues simply represented more fundamental problems. The Catholic monks shaved the crowns of their heads in the stereotypical tonsure haircut that we all know from cartoons. This represented the crown of thorns worn by Christ on the cross. But the Irish retained a pagan haircut, shaving the fronts of their heads. Was such a link to pagan practices acceptable?

Even more divisive was the matter of Easter, the main issue of debate at Whitby. In earlier centuries, different churches had calculated the date of Easter in different ways. In the east, in particular, many churches had followed 'Quartodecimanism', the practice of celebrating Easter on the same day as Passover. This had been condemned by Rome, since it was thought wrong to tie the church's most important festival to Jewish dating. Most churches therefore followed an alternative method of calculating Easter, although it was not

Violence should not be inflicted upon the pagan in order to make him become a Christian.

Pope Nicholas I, *Letter to the Bulgars* AD 866

Christianity and paganism

Most of our information about the religion of those who inhabited northern and western Europe before the missions of the early middle ages comes in the form of missionary literature – intended to glorify the missionary, not document the pagans – or in legal prohibitions enacted after Christianity had become the official religion. The picture we have of paganism is therefore skewed by the nature of the surviving sources. We know about ritual acts such as sacrifices (animal and, less commonly, human), open-air worship of idols and special natural features such as trees and springs, divination and the casting of lots, the celebration of festivals associated with the cycles of the year, and the worship of ancestors. These were all condemned and prohibited by the church.

We know much less about what pagans believed and how they understood the rituals they performed. What does emerge from the evidence is the utilitarian character of paganism. The gods would reward their people – with good harvests, for example, or success in battle – if properly approached. Kings and other leaders consequently played a prominent role in cults. Descent from the gods was widely claimed by rulers. The positioning of the king as a mediator between the supernatural and the human meant that the religious allegiance of his people was within his gift. As leaders of the cult, it was appropriate for rulers, rather than each individual, to make the decision to convert, and this made kings natural targets for missionaries.

Many pagans converted to Christianity peacefully. Other conversions were forced by decree of the king, sometimes with violence. Cult sites were destroyed, holy trees cut down, barrels of holy beer overturned. Some missionaries lost their lives for threatening the gods and customary culture in this way. Missionaries sent by Pope Gregory the Great to England in AD 596, however, were instructed to preserve pagan sites but invest them with Christian meaning. This form of accommodation became crucial in the merging of the new, Mediterranean, religion with traditional Germanic culture. Missionaries faced the difficulty that many aspects of traditional Germanic society had been associated with ritual behaviour and consequently had religious meaning. The task of the missionary was to decide which of these could be retained by converts. Deciding what forms of traditional culture were not 'religious' and could be allowed to survive the conversion was one of the major missionary challenges faced by the church. In the ninth century, for example, the Bulgars asked Pope Nicholas I whether, having converted, they could still wear trousers, pray for rain during a drought or go to war flying horses' tails from their battle standards.

Pre-Christian culture continued, but it was often drained of its pagan significance and made safe for Christian use. In the countryside, rituals of the pre-Christian period continued to be performed, but with Christian ceremony and sacrament. Priests sang masses over herbs used for healing and to exorcize elves; congregations recited the Lord's Prayer and Latin blessings as they buried loaves baked with holy water in the fields. Woden was claimed as the ancestor of English kings many centuries after their conversion to Christianity, but Christ, Noah, and Adam were added to the pedigree. Tales of pre-Christian heroes continued to be popular, even in the most pious society. In the late ninth century, King Alfred memorized them as a child, and his children learned them along with the Psalms.

LESLEY ABRAMS

standardized until the end of the fifth century. Ireland had been evangelized before this time, and the system they used was a different one from everyone else. In the eyes of the Catholic missionaries, this was little different from Quartodecimanism and the Jewish tendency it represented.

The argument at the synod also revolved around how important it was to obey Rome. Those who favoured the Roman customs of Easter and haircuts pointed out that, quite apart from the intrinsic correctness of the Roman customs, the fact that they were Roman was enough to recommend them. The Irish saints were holy and wise, no question – but did they outweigh the authority of the Holy See and of St Peter himself? Faced with that question, King Oswy, who had previously kept the Celtic Easter (whilst his wife kept the Roman one, causing no end of marital strife) decided that he had no intention of seeing St Peter slam the gates of heaven in his face. He ordered the church in his lands to follow the Roman customs. Even in this remote region, the Christian church would be a Catholic church, and it would take its cue from Rome.

With this, the distinctiveness of Celtic Christianity even in Ireland began to fade. Many in Ireland and Wales continued to follow the Celtic customs, but they were gradually replaced by the Roman ones. By the middle of the eighth century, Ireland was part of the greater Catholic Church, a church that was being promoted and protected elsewhere in Europe by increasingly strong kings, even as it was being pressurized on all sides by new threats.

CHRISTIANITY IN THE VICE: THE LATE DARK AGES

One of the most dangerous of the new threats facing Europe as it Christianized was Islamic military expansion, with Muslim armies sweeping all before them in the Middle East and North Africa. In AD 711 the Moorish forces invaded Spain. The Christian kingdom of the Visigoths quickly capitulated to them, and the Umayyad caliphate was established at Cordoba in southern Spain.

AL-ANDALUS AND THE MOZAREBS

Under the Muslims, Spain (or al-Andalus, as it was known, deriving the name from the word 'Vandal') continued to thrive. The Moors brought from Africa irrigation techniques that allowed agriculture to flourish there as never before, and Cordoba itself became the most splendid city in Europe. Half a million people enjoyed paved, well-lit streets, solid houses with marble balconies and dozens of libraries – a level of civilization higher than that of the old Roman empire, even as the rest of western Europe had sunk below it.

As in the other Muslim territories, Christians and Jews were allowed to remain in peace, without being forced to convert, provided they paid their special tax. Christians existed in separate communities, with their own rulers, known as counts – although of course the counts were subject to the caliph. These communities were known as Mozarebs, from a word meaning 'like Arabs', since culturally they were highly influenced by their new masters, speaking Arabic and dressing as the Muslims did. But they retained many customs of the past, maintaining the old ecclesiastical structure of the Visigothic days and using the old liturgy. In the rest of Europe, especially under the Franks, there were increasing efforts to standardize the liturgies and canon laws used by all churches – but the Mozarebs were not part of that world, and so theirs never became standard. This gave Spanish Christianity a quite different flavour from the Catholicism of the rest of Europe.

Although most of Spain now bowed to the caliph, some areas revolted. In AD 750 Galicia, in the north-west of Spain, successfully overthrew Muslim rule and reverted to a Christian state, much as it had been under the Visigoths. This provided a foothold for the beginning of the 'Reconquista', the effort on the part of Christian Europe to drive the Muslims out of Spain – although it would take them another seven centuries to accomplish.

The Mesquita of Cordoba. Originally a mosque built in the eighth century, it was reconsecrated as a cathedral when Ferdinand III of Castille captured Cordoba from the Muslims in 1236.

We – giving over to the oft-mentioned most blessed Pontiff, our father Sylvester the universal pope, as well our palace, as has been said, as also the city of Rome and all the provinces, districts and cities of Italy or of the western regions; and relinquishing them, by our inviolable gift, to the power and sway of himself or the pontiffs his successors – do decree, by this our godlike charter and imperial constitution, that it shall be arranged; and do concede that they shall lawfully remain with the holy Roman church.

The Donation of Constantine, mid-eighth century

Within a couple of decades of conquering al-Andalus, the Moors were setting their sights on the next country – that of the Franks, to the north of the Pyrenees. In AD 732 a mighty army, led by the governor of al-Andalus himself, crossed the mountains into the Loire Valley. The Muslims had entered the very heartlands of Christian Europe. If events played out here as they had done practically everywhere else when troops faithful to the Prophet arrived, Europe would fall and Christianity would dwindle.

It was not to be. Historians today debate the extent to which the Moors could really have conquered France, even if they had won at Poitiers; but the battle still had great symbolic value. Charles Martel was a powerful Frankish warlord who had inherited from his father the title of 'mayor of the palace' (or 'major domo'), a role a bit like that of a prime minister, was helping the Merovingian kings to rule the Franks. But he wasn't very interested in domestic matters. Instead, Charles spent many years fighting and defeating various tribes on the borders of the Frankish lands, and generally extending and consolidating Frankish rule, especially over parts of what is now Germany. It was his fortunate victory over the Moors in AD 732 that earned him the nickname 'Martel' – 'the hammer' – but it was simply the crowning achievement of an extremely successful military career.

THE CAROLINGIANS

Charles Martel died in AD 741. His son Pépin ('the Short') inherited the title 'mayor of the palace', supposedly acting in the name of the Merovingian king Childeric. But Pépin soon brought an end to this charade, deposing Childeric and having himself crowned in his place as Pépin III. Thus ended the Merovingian dynasty, and the Carolingian one began.

The Carolingian age was one of close cooperation between church and state – specifically, the Frankish state. After Charles Martel's incredible victory in AD 732, the Franks felt that God himself had blessed their nation and given them the right to rule, but Pépin III was keen for this to be ratified by the pope and he worked hard at building a good relationship with the papacy. Pope Zacharias endorsed Pépin's claim to the throne. His successor, Stephen II, declared him *patricius Romanorum* – the defender of Rome. Evidently, although Zacharias had been careful to maintain good relations with the Lombards – still the dominant power in northern Italy – Stephen could see which way the wind was blowing. He was well rewarded: in an act known as the 'donation of Pépin', the new Frankish king gave to the pope lands at that time owned by the Lombards, thereby giving the papal states not only greater territories but more legitimacy.

The negotiations were helped by the 'discovery' of a document known as *The Donation of Constantine*. This letter, apparently written in the fourth century by Constantine the Great to the then pope Sylvester, described in magnificent prose the conversion of the famous emperor, and decreed that the pope would in perpetuity enjoy the right to govern much of northern Italy. Popes throughout the Middle Ages would appeal to the authority of *The Donation of Constantine*. It was, of course, a blatant forgery, the work of some eighth-century papal apologist. But it was not until the fifteenth century that this was generally recognized.

By demanding – and receiving – the endorsement of the church, Pépin III helped to increase the church's power. After all, if the great Pépin required the pope's blessing to take the throne, then the pope was clearly a person of note. By the same token, however, Pépin asserted his own authority over the church. The pope gave his endorsement because he had been told to. Moreover, the reforms within the Frankish territories that had been begun by Boniface were still being carried out, and Pépin took control of them. It was the same old story – just as in the fourth-century Roman empire, the secular ruler, having allied himself with the church, expected the church to do as he said. The process had begun with Charles Martel, who had received great support from the church in his campaigns against the pagans and the Muslims. The church lent him money and land to help finance his campaigns. Unfortunately, Charles forgot to give any of it back, making him a target of remarkable hatred from churchmen for many years after his death.

THE AGE OF CHARLEMAGNE

All of these themes came to a head with Pépin III's son, by far the greatest of the Carolingian rulers and probably the most important king of any country in the early Middle Ages – Charles the Great, otherwise known as Charlemagne (d. AD 814). Tall, physically strong, handsome, never seen without his blue cloak and a sword at his side, the king enjoyed physical pursuits – swimming, hunting and riding. He was the very model of an early medieval warrior king.

After co-ruling with his brother for a couple of years, Charlemagne gained the throne for himself in AD 771 when the brother died, and spent the next three decades imitating his grandfather, Charles Martel, and expanding the borders of the Frankish domains. One of the first things he did was smash the power of the Lombards in northern Italy and take their iron crown for himself. He was welcomed in Rome as a liberator. Pope Hadrian I reaffirmed the Frankish king's role as *patricius Romanorum* (protector of the Romans), and the alliance between the Franks and the papacy was strengthened.

Charlemagne took his role as defender of the Christian faith seriously. Indeed, devotion to the church seems to have been one of the most powerful guiding principles of his life. It was even part of the motivation for his conquests. In AD 775 the Saxons, whose territory was still on the borders of the Frankish domains, and who were still largely pagan despite the best efforts of Boniface and others, burned some churches. Charlemagne responded by invading and successfully subjugating the Saxons, holding a church council and ordering that the Saxons must convert to Christianity or die. Evangelization Charlemagne-style was

effective, but it was very brutal. After a Saxon uprising in AD 782 was suppressed, 4,500 of the rebels were beheaded.

Meanwhile, Charlemagne continued the campaigns against the Muslims, turning the tables by crossing the Pyrenees and invading them. This brought him dominion over the Spanish March, in the north-east of Spain. The whole campaign was later shrouded in legend and romance. Turpin, bishop of Rheims, who went on the expedition as the king's secretary, wrote an account of the wars in Spain which stressed the miraculous to an improbable degree: we learn from him that the sun stood still as Charlemagne fought and that city walls

The coronation of Charlemagne by Pope Leo III, in a fourteenth-century French painting.

collapsed at his approach. In the later Middle Ages, these legends became still more embroidered, until they rivalled those of King Arthur for imaginative power, and the tales of mighty Charlemagne and his 'peers' or paladins inspired generations with their romance. The most famous story was the *Song of Roland*, written in the eleventh century, among the greatest pieces of chivalric romance to have come out of the Middle Ages.

By the end of the eighth century Charlemagne had succeeded in carving out

Our task is, with the aid of divine piety, to defend the holy church of Christ with arms… Your task, most holy father, is to lift up your hands to God, like Moses, to aid our troops.

Charlemagne, *Letter to Pope Leo III*, AD 796

a truly impressive empire. The Franks now controlled not only modern France and the Spanish March but Switzerland, the Low Countries (where the Saxons lived), and much of Germany, Austria and Italy. The new empire therefore covered much of what had once been the Roman empire in the west, as well as some areas the Romans had never managed to subdue. A new world order had been created, and it was recognized on Christmas Day, AD 800. On that memorable date Charlemagne attended Mass at St Peter's cathedral in Rome. During the service Pope Leo III crowned him emperor, proclaiming him heir to the Roman caesars, legitimate ruler of Europe. The Byzantine throne at this time was occupied by Irene, who was regarded as illegitimate in the west on account of being a woman: thus Charlemagne and the pope both considered the imperial throne ripe for the taking.

The new regime in much of Europe brought about a standardizing of legal systems. Until this point, different people had used different legal traditions and most of it was unwritten. Charlemagne issued a series of edicts or 'capitularies' designed to harmonize the law where possible, based on Frankish law, whilst still allowing different ethnic groups to use their own laws where there were no serious clashes. The empire was divided into territories, each under the control of a count. The laws were enforced by *missi dominici*, the closest thing Charlemagne had to the FBI. They worked in pairs – each made up of a churchman and a noble – and rode throughout the empire inspecting local government and reforming justice systems.

THE CAROLINGIAN RENAISSANCE
Out of all this came the phenomenon known as the 'Carolingian renaissance'. Charlemagne was illiterate, but he was keen to promote learning (and to learn to read himself), so he imported a number of scholars to his court. Of these scholars the most important was the Anglo-Saxon Alcuin of York (c. AD 730–804). By this time, the Anglo-Saxons were all Christian, and they

Everyone shall live entirely in accordance with God's commands, justly and under a just rule, and everyone shall be ordered to live in harmony with his colleagues in his job or profession.

Charlemagne's Capitulary of the Missi, AD 802

didn't spend quite so much time at war with each other. Instead, a number of powerful kingdoms had coalesced out of the chaos of the pagan Anglo-Saxon world, the greatest of which were Wessex in the south, Mercia in the middle and Northumbria in the north. Northumbria, in particular, was noted for its learning. The great scholar Benedict Biscop had established a famous monastery at Jarrow and Wearmouth and travelled to Rome several times to stock it with books. This library had nurtured the Venerable Bede (c. AD 673–735), a prolific author and historian. Alcuin had taught at the nearby cathedral school in York before being called to the continent to educate Charlemagne's family.

Alcuin wrote many books, including textbooks on a variety of subjects that were mostly compilations from earlier writings. He did work on the liturgy, wrote on theological subjects and produced a revised text of the Vulgate, the Latin Bible, which would become standard. Perhaps more important than these, however, was his role as, essentially, minister for education in Charlemagne's empire. It was at his bidding that the emperor decreed that new schools should be opened in every town under his control, and that all children should be sent to them. For this state education system, parents were asked to pay only what they could afford.

A new wind was blowing through Europe and through the church. The ninth century saw a rise in interest in education, theology and scholarship. More manuscripts were copied and more scholars appeared to study them. A particular effort was made to copy books accurately and a new form of handwriting developed, called 'Caroline minuscule script', which was both elegant and readable. This was the ancestor of our modern lower-case letters. Men such as Alcuin himself, Theodulf of Orléans, Lupus Servatus of Ferrières, and Rabanus Maurus, all leading churchmen or heads of important monasteries, formed a kind of academic society, spending their time writing letters and poetry to each other, swapping books and engaging in

Tradition and innovation in ninth-century theology

Early medieval theology was firmly rooted in the study of the Bible. This desire to understand the Bible and Christian doctrine ensured the survival of scholarship in the post-Roman kingdoms, while the Carolingian Renaissance contributed strongly to the flourishing of theology in the ninth century. The surviving letters of Alcuin and Lupus of Ferrières, among others, reveal their interest in securing copies of rare works and debating knotty theological or linguistic questions. Charlemagne's reforms created many more regional centres of scholarship by the mid-ninth century. Monasteries such as Fulda (in what is now Germany) under the abbot Rabanus Maurus (c. AD 776–856) provided education of the highest quality. The vastly increased copying of manuscripts (approximately 500 surviving manuscripts were copied in Francia in c. AD 500–750, compared with some 7,000 from AD 750–900) made key works widely available, expanding contemporaries' theological and philosophical horizons.

Contemporaries knew that they could not attain the learning and perception of church fathers such as Augustine, Jerome and Ambrose, and sought their authority for all present opinions: 'novelty' was the worst crime of which a scholar could be accused. The best scholars of the day used their authoritative quotations to create new works, by showing how divergent opinions in the authorities could be reconciled, or using them to convey their own views and advance new ideas. The contrasting voices Carolingian scholars found in the church fathers, and the importance attached to establishing and teaching a uniform and correct doctrine, contributed to the active theological debates of the ninth century. Carolingian rulers were closely involved in these debates. For example, marginal comments in the manuscript of the *Caroline Books* preserve Charlemagne's reactions to the text: 'True!'; 'Shrewd!'.

Many debates related to the person and nature of Christ, and scholars explored the orthodox meaning of key words and concepts. Could Christ be described as God's 'adoptive' son, as Felix and Elipandus held? In the debate on the Eucharist between two monks of Corbie, Paschasius Radbertus and Ratramnus, both agreed on Christ's real presence in the Eucharist, but how did this 'reality' relate to its outward form or 'figure' of bread and wine?

In the mid-ninth century the problem of predestination dominated Frankish theological debate. In the AD 840s Gottschalk of Orbais, a controversial monk, began to teach that both salvation and damnation are predestined by God, drawing upon Augustine's later works. Archbishop Hincmar of Rheims, opposing Gottschalk's opinions on practical and pastoral grounds (why do good, or avoid sin, if salvation or condemnation comes regardless of one's crimes or good works?), equally found support in Augustine for the view that God merely *foreknows* damnation. Gottschalk was condemned in AD 849 (and spent his last eighteen years imprisoned), but almost every notable Carolingian scholar produced a work on the subject.

The Carolingian scholars' reading of Augustine and others also equipped them with new methods of theological exploration. John Scotus Eriugena (c. AD 810–877) was most original in his use of the logical techniques Carolingian scholars encountered in Augustine and Boethius. Although Carolingian use of logic cannot compare with that of the scholastic theologians of the late tenth century onwards, the introduction of the tools of logic, together with the great treasure of manuscripts bequeathed to subsequent generations, were perhaps the ninth century's most significant legacies to theology.

ELINA SCREEN

philosophical debate. Spirituality flourished: Amalarius of Metz wrote an influential commentary on the liturgy, interpreting it allegorically, as earlier theologians had interpreted the Bible. For Amalarius, the spiritual life of the church revolved around its communal worship, all forming a single, holistic body of teaching. This view would be influential in the later Middle Ages.

Yet the new Frankish empire and the flowering of civilized pursuits which it engendered was fragile. For one thing, all of this went on in a few monasteries and the imperial court. It didn't make much difference to anyone else. Worse, the empire was politically unstable. Charlemagne died in AD 814, leaving the empire to his only surviving son, Louis 'the Pious', a weak ruler. On Louis's death, in AD 843, the empire was carved up among his three sons. To the west was Aquitaine, the western half of what is now France; to the east was what is now Germany; these two kingdoms spoke different languages, the ancestors of modern French and German. In the middle was Lotharingia, which included Italy. As the generations passed, all three continued to splinter as land was divided among sons or to grow as warlords conquered more territory. Lotharingia dwindled as the western and eastern kingdoms grew and became more distinct. The title of 'emperor' remained, passed from Charlemagne to Louis 'the

Pious', but it was an honorific, squabbled over by competing kings; thus we find a succession of 'emperors' with no empire. It was an inauspicious start to the separate histories of what would one day become France and Germany.

HUNGARY: THE EASTERN BORDER

As we saw in the previous chapter, the rise and spread of Roman Catholicism in the west led inevitably to conflict where it met Byzantine Orthodoxy to the east. Greek and German missionaries clashed in Moravia, and they also clashed in Hungary, the powerful empire that had been founded by the Magyar people. The conversion of Hungary took place mostly under Prince Géza, and then his son, István (or Stephen). Under Géza, Byzantine Christianity slowly but surely seeped through the country. In AD 948 the 'gyula' or prince of the eastern part of the kingdom converted to Orthodoxy, and imported a bishop from Byzantium called Hierotheos. Monasteries were built throughout Hungary. Géza, however, was baptized by Bruno of St-Gallese, a western bishop who was close to Otto II of the Holy Roman empire. Catholic missions began to infiltrate the country.

For Géza this was probably a mostly political choice, as he had decided to ally himself with the west rather than the east; large forced conversions of his nobles took place and, although he ruled his country with a firm hand, it was a cruel one. Civil war followed his death, but his son Stephen defeated his rivals and was crowned king in around AD 1000. Tellingly, he requested coronation from Pope Sylvester II, for Stephen was a devout Catholic. His forty-year reign saw churches and religious foundations spring up throughout the kingdom, a process which coincided with a general ordering of the kingdom: Stephen divided it into counties for administrative purposes, laid out new laws, and generally did all the things expected of a strong medieval monarch of a relatively new country. By the time Stephen died in 1038, Hungary's position was secure as an

important power in central Europe, and the last bastion of Roman Catholicism before the Orthodox lands.

THE VIKINGS

Western Christianity was still in the vice. As it continued to be threatened by the Muslims to the south, a new threat was appearing from the north – the Vikings. These eternally fascinating people were a diverse group from Scandinavia, including Norway, Sweden and Denmark, divided into a number of kingdoms throughout this large area. In fact, the word 'viking' meant a 'pirate' and was applied to all these Scandinavians fairly indiscriminately by other people. The Vikings were pagans, similar in worldview to the Saxons and other north Europeans who had slowly but surely been assimilated into the church. But the Vikings were less easily converted. Missionaries were already active among them in the ninth century, notably the Frankish preacher Ansgar, who as archbishop of Hamburg was put in charge of all missionary activity to the north and travelled throughout Denmark and Sweden. But the Scandinavians remained largely pagan, and in the ninth century, for reasons that remain unclear but may have had something to do with overpopulation in their core territories, they began to migrate.

In AD 793 the first Vikings appeared out of the North Sea on the east coast of Britain, where they sacked Lindisfarne off the Northumbrian coast. More followed, seeking plunder from villages and monasteries. It seems that monasteries and churches were particular targets of the raiders not because they had a pagan grudge against Christianity, but because they were relatively poorly defended and contained plenty of treasure. At first the Vikings conducted only light and opportunistic raids, but the attacks grew more and more serious. By the middle of the ninth century the Vikings were landing in force, with large armies and settlers. In AD 866 a huge Danish army marched on York, where King Aelle of

A seventh-century Viking helmet from Sweden.

Power is never good, unless the one who has it is good.
Alfred the Great

King William… was a man of great wisdom and power… Though stern beyond measure to those who opposed his will, he was kind to those good men who loved God. On the very spot where God granted him the conquest of England he caused a great abbey to be built, and settled monks in it and richly endowed it. During his reign was built the great cathedral at Canterbury, and many others throughout England.
Anglo-Saxon chronicle, 1086

Northumbria was captured and subjected to the hideous fate known as the 'blood eagle' – his ribcage was wrenched open and his lungs flung over his shoulders, like an eagle's wings, while he was still alive. Clearly, these Scandinavians sought nothing less than the complete subjugation of Britain. Even as they were conquering the northern Anglo-Saxons, they were also settling in Scotland and Ireland and in the islands of the north Atlantic, including Iceland. Indeed it is thought they succeeded in making it all the way to North America, even setting up a colony there, although it did not survive.

In England, Christian civilization was saved by King Alfred the Great of Wessex, who resisted the invaders and organized a counter-attack so effective that he defeated the Danes and forced their king, Guthrum, to accept Christian baptism as part of the treaty of Wedmore of AD 878. Indeed, once settled in England, the Vikings seem to have been quite quick to adopt Christianity – more so than the Anglo-Saxons had when *they* were the hostile invaders. The Danes remained in control of the northern part of England, known as the Danelaw, and Alfred ruled a united Anglo-Saxon kingdom to the south. Alfred was another enlightened Christian monarch in the mould of Charlemagne, encouraging Christian learning throughout his domains. Monasteries which had been devastated by the wars were restored and new ones founded. Alfred's noblemen were forced to learn to read or face losing their jobs, and the king himself was a scholar of no mean ability, who translated many works of antiquity and recent centuries into Old English for the benefit of his people.

Although they had been neutralized in England, the Vikings were still causing serious trouble elsewhere. Whilst those from Denmark were settling England and those from Norway were colonizing Scotland and Ireland, people from Sweden were heading east, up the rivers of continental Europe and into eastern

Europe and Russia, where they attacked the people of Kievan Rus, as we shall see in more detail in Chapter 8. Meanwhile, others were raiding the Frankish coasts and sailing up the Seine and other rivers to attack Paris, Orléans, Tours and other cities directly. Even Muslim Spain was not spared the onslaught, with Seville being attacked in AD 844. And the Vikings sailed right round into the Mediterranean to launch assaults on Italy too, while others sailed down rivers from Kiev to launch a rather unwise attack on Constantinople.

Everywhere they could, the Vikings settled. One of their most important strongholds was in north-western France. This was granted to a Viking lord called Rollo in AD 911 by King Charles 'the Simple' of France, in exchange for calling off a raid on Paris. The relationship between the rather weak Carolingian king and the bluff Vikings was symbolized at the ceremony where Rollo, as Charles's new subject, was obliged to kiss the king's foot. Rollo refused to do this, and it was arranged that one of his warriors would do it for him. But the warrior outdid Rollo in audacity: rather than kneel, he simply reached down and lifted Charles's foot to his lips, toppling the king over onto his back.

Rollo and his men took control of a large area to the west of Paris, centred on Rouen. These Viking settlers became known as Normans (since they were men from the north) and their territory was Normandy. The Normans integrated into local culture, speaking French, converting readily to Christianity and accepting the rule of the French king, but they were still a distinct group, owing allegiance to the duke of Normandy. It was one of these dukes, William 'the Bastard', an illegitimate descendant of Rollo, who invaded England in 1066, thereby becoming the more euphonious William 'the Conqueror' and completing the Viking victory over the Anglo-Saxons. Indeed, the Normans were a remarkably expansionist branch of the Viking people: as they were conquering England they

Cefalu cathedral, Sicily. Work on the cathedral began immediately after the Norman warlord Roger II of Sicily founded the town. Roger went on to unite Sicily and southern Italy under Norman rule.

were also settling aggressively in southern Italy. The papacy was not happy about this, but after the Normans defeated the troops of Pope Leo IX in 1053, Rome learned to live with the new political situation. In 1071 the last vestiges of Byzantine control of Italy were overthrown forever and the Normans consolidated their hold on the southern half of the peninsula.

By this time, not only the Normans but all the Scandinavians were converted to Christianity. The trading empire that they established between their settlements would play a major role in the consolidation of Christianity throughout northern Europe. With their conversion and integration into European politics and society, the stage was set for a flowering of western Christianity and civilization that would prove unlike anything that had been seen before.

CHAPTER 7

THE HIGH MIDDLE AGES

If the age of Charlemagne saw Christianity established throughout Europe, the high Middle Ages would see it flourish as never before. Medieval Europe saw the creation of a unified system of belief and worship which would implant Christianity deeply into the European psyche.

MEDIEVAL EUROPE

To any omniscient observer watching world history in the year AD 1000, Europe would not have looked in a very hopeful position. Every time some kind of stability and level of civilization had been reached, such as under Theodoric the Ostrogoth, the Northumbrians or Charlemagne, it had crumbled within decades. Internal dissensions and assaults from outside, such as from the Vikings, had prevented lasting stability and peace. But all this was to change. After AD 1000 conditions in Europe steadily improved – and this time there were no disasters or hostile invasions to wreck the good work. In particular, there were no more migrations and attacks from pagan peoples. More or less everyone in Europe was Christian now. And the eleventh century saw an incredible improvement in almost every area of life in Europe.

THE EMERGENCE OF NATIONS
There was a little more political unity and strength. Otto I of the Franko-Saxons had, in the tenth century, reunified and reorganized the eastern part of Charlemagne's old empire, including the territories of Lotharingia in the middle, and added to it Italy, which he claimed through marriage. He had also succeeded in first quelling and then allying with the Magyars,

or Hungarians, to the east. In AD 962 Otto was crowned emperor, Charlemagne's successor, but for the first time in over a century the title meant something again. From this time on, the title of 'emperor' was handed down the line of rulers of this territory. By the twelfth century their domain was known as the 'Holy Roman empire'. This title is sometimes applied in retrospect, so that we can talk of the Holy Roman empire as a discrete entity from the tenth century onwards. As with the earlier empire of Charlemagne, there was a close alliance between this empire and the papacy – for the Holy Roman emperor was always crowned by the pope.

The region that would become France was not so unified; it was divided into a number of princedoms and dukedoms, the most powerful of whom were the Normans; but they owed at least nominal allegiance to the king, based in Paris. And, while the Holy Roman empire (in modern Germany and Austria) was becoming the strongest political power in Europe, the French were pioneering the social and intellectual advances which would characterize medieval Europe for centuries. While the old Roman ideal of empire was being kept alive to the east, the western Europeans were trying out new ways of governing.

THE FEUDAL SYSTEM
The most important of these was the 'feudal' system, which arose out of precisely this lack of strong central government. Under this system the king literally owned the whole country, but he 'leased' parts of it out to local lords. They also leased parts of their lands to lesser nobles, and so on down to the peasants who worked the land. Contrary to popular

belief, not all peasants were miserable – in fact they had more holidays than most people do today. In England, it was considered just as sinful to fast on a feast day as it was to feast on a fast day.

The feudal system first emerged in what is now France, and it represented a new ideal. Instead of a central imperial government, there would be local government, based on land rights and military service. For part of the 'payment' that the nobles owed the king for the right to run their lands was their oath to go to war if he demanded it. Thus there developed the caste of the mounted knights, although medieval battles were still fought primarily by foot soldiers. Bows and crossbows were more powerful than knights, if used properly, since they could easily pierce mail coats – but their use was limited, partly because the church forbade their employment against Christian armies. Bows, to the medieval mind, were 'weapons of mass destruction' whose use transgressed the normal laws of warfare. Indeed, there was a number of ways the church tried to limit warfare within Europe. One was the 'Peace of God', according to which priests and monks could not participate in warfare or be attacked, and war could not be conducted in consecrated places such as churches. Added to this was the 'Truce of God', according to which no one was allowed to fight on Sundays or church holy days. This originated at the Council of Elne in 1027 and – under threat of excommunication – was applied to the whole of Europe in 1179.

Feudalism worked. It provided a practical system which enabled the countries of western Europe to develop a sense of nationalism. And whether it was down to the feudal system or not, the middle of the eleventh century saw improved agricultural returns, a situation which lasted for decades. More and more areas were farmed, providing more food and of better quality. People were healthier. Skeletons of medieval people reveal that most were taller than their ancestors in earlier centuries – indeed people in the eleventh century were apparently taller and healthier than their descendants in the sixteenth and seventeenth centuries, although life expectancy was considerably lower than today. Contrary to the popular image of the Middle Ages as a time of grubby, stinking peasants, most people were strong with good teeth (they had no toothpaste, but hardly any sugar either). As far as standards of living were concerned, the Middle Ages was something of a high point compared to the subsequent few centuries. As people became economically and medically better off, they throve: the population of Europe rose from 40 million in AD 1000 to 73 million in 1300, after which it began to fall again.

FEUDALISM AND THE CHURCH

Society was structured hierarchically, from the peasants at the bottom to the king at the top, with a place for everyone. Even those who were not technically part of the feudal system, such as freeholders, farmers who actually owned their land and did not owe fealty to a lord, had their place within this society. And this, it was believed, mirrored the divine realm. The hierarchies of human society reflected the hierarchies that had been sketched out by earlier theologians such as Pseudo-Dionysius, and people came to think of God as rather like a feudal monarch, with the angels and the high-ranking churchmen as his vassals, exercising power on his behalf. One of the key Christian writers to develop this idea was Anselm, archbishop of Canterbury, at the turn of the eleventh and twelfth centuries. He sometimes described God as acting like a feudal lord, demanding a certain 'debt' and allegiance of his vassals, and protecting them in turn. Of course, the payment God demands is not labour or military assistance but justice and obeying his commandments.

The church was intrinsically enmeshed in the feudal system as a part of it. For example, a monastery could own land,

It is well known that in this world there are three orders, set in unity: these are working men, praying men, and fighting men. Working men are those who labour for our living. Praying men are those who plead for our peace with God. Fighting men are those who battle to protect our towns and defend our land against an invading army. Now the farmer works to provide our food, and the worldly warrior must fight against our foes, and the servant of God must always pray for us and fight spiritually against invisible foes.

Aelfric of Eynsham, tenth century

This is the debt which man and angel owe to God, and no-one who pays this debt commits sin; but everyone who does not pay it sins. This is justice, or uprightness of will, which makes a being just or upright in heart, that is, in will; and this is the sole and complete debt of honour which we owe to God, and which God requires of us.

Anselm of Canterbury, *Why God became man*, 1098

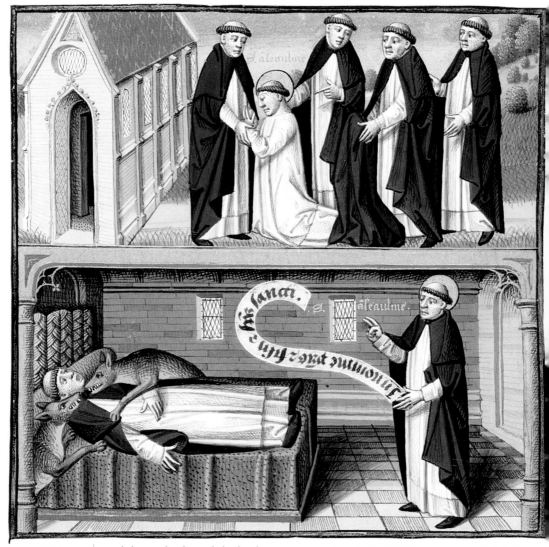

Scenes from the life of Anselm. The lower image depicts an event which supposedly occurred while Anselm was prior of the monastery of Bec. A monk, lying sick in bed, was attacked by two infernal wolves which only he could see. Anselm came in, dispelled the apparition, and heard the monk's confession, absolving him of his sins and allowing him to die in peace.

and those who farmed the land were paying not a local lord but the monastery. Individual churchmen, such as bishops, might be rich landowners in their own right. Religious appointments themselves were granted by lords, just as they granted the right to own or work land. The hoary old issue of the relative powers of state and church was reappearing, and confrontation was inevitable – since the pope was hardly going to allow local warlords to decide who should minister to the flock. But this 'investiture controversy', as it became, was only part of a whole movement of reform and renewal which was sweeping through the church during this time.

SPIRITUALITY, REFORM AND THE PAPACY

THE CLUNIAC MOVEMENT

We can date the beginnings of the new movement of spirituality quite nicely to the year AD 910. That was when William 'the Pious', duke of Aquitaine, paid for the founding of a new monastery at Cluny, 80 kilometres (50 miles) north of Lyons in the east of modern France. Under a succession of strong and wise abbots it was enormously successful. The Rule of St Benedict (which was followed by virtually all monasteries in the west from the eighth century onwards) was observed there with particular integrity and strictness. In an age when standards were evidently slipping in church life, both inside and outside monasteries, this was an important step forward. At Cluny monks were encouraged to develop a personal spirituality, at the same time engaging in common worship and in manual labour. It was a successful combination. The teachings of Cluny spread and daughter monasteries were founded throughout the region. By the end of the eleventh century there were Cluniac monasteries throughout France and the Spanish March and in parts of the Holy Roman empire too.

Cluny had become the second centre of western Christianity after Rome itself, and the magnificence of the abbey itself reflected this. In 1089 the foundations of an immense church were laid; it took forty years to build, and when completed was the largest church in the world at that time. This wonder of the age stood until the French Revolution as a monument to the vision of the monks of Cluny.

An important innovation was that Cluny retained control over its daughter monasteries, whose abbots would be appointed by the abbot of Cluny itself – clearly a very important man. This not only bolstered the power of Cluny but helped to root out corruption in the monasteries; for, before this time, the abbacies of many monasteries had become hereditary, with abbots not only being married but passing their positions to their sons. Cluny helped to bring that to an end, and many other abuses too.

CORRUPTION AND REFORM

For the church, by this time, was not in a great shape. The papacy, in particular, had fallen into appalling disrepute. The powerful popes of the early Middle Ages had by the ninth century given way to weak popes, little more than puppets of foreign rulers. This was the time when, according to later legend, a woman managed to become pope without anyone realizing – the myth of 'Pope Joan' – a picaresque legend, but a wholly untrue one.

Perhaps the low point of the papacy was a notorious incident during the reign of Stephen VI (or VII – Stephens are ambiguously numbered owing to a dispute over whether Stephen II, who reigned for three days, really counted). The creature of one powerful Italian lord, Stephen held a council in AD 897 to try his predecessor, Formosus, who had been allied to a rival lord. However, for some reason known only to himself, Stephen decided that Formosus needed to be there to answer the charges in person. Ignoring the minor detail that his predecessor had been dead for about nine months, Stephen had him disinterred and propped up in a chair at the synod. Formosus was found guilty of all charges (including, ironically, perjury). The body was stripped of his papal robes and the three fingers of his right hand that he would have used to bless people were cut off. The corpse was then dragged through the streets and deposited in a common grave. A couple of days later persons unknown dug him up for a second time and threw him into the Tiber. Stephen was deposed and strangled not long after. His successor, Romanus, lasted a few months

To all who think right, it is clear that God's providence has so provided for certain wealthy men that, if they use their earthly possessions well, they may gain everlasting rewards… I, William, count and duke by the grace of God, carefully considering this, and wishing to provide for my own safety while I still can, believe it advisable – indeed, essential – that from the temporal goods which I have been granted I should give a small portion for the good of my soul.

William 'the Pious', from the charter of Cluny, AD 910

Idleness is the enemy of the soul. Therefore, at fixed times, the brothers should be busy with manual work; and at other times in holy reading.

The Rule of Benedict, mid-sixth century

A seventeenth-century engraving of Cluny Abbey by Pierre Giffart.

Conspectus ecclesiæ Cluniacensis.

before being forced to retire. His successor, Theodore, was pope for only twenty days, but that was long enough to have Formosus dug up for a third time and decently reburied in St Peter's – where he has remained ever since.

Clearly the church could not continue with such shenanigans at the top, but they were still going on well into the eleventh century. This saw the ludicrous spectacle of Benedict IX – a debauched reprobate who became pope in 1032 at the age of twelve and resigned at one point in order to sell the papacy to his godfather (whom he subsequently had deposed). Fortunately, things were to change. Leo IX, who became pope in 1049, had already spent some years trying to reform monasteries, and as pope devoted himself to reforming the clerical system – in particular, stamping out the practice of simony, that is, selling ecclesiastical positions. This, it seems, was rife throughout the church, and Leo travelled throughout Europe trying to crack down on it.

Even more significant was Gregory VII,

pope from 1073 to 1085, one of the most controversial figures of the Middle Ages. Even today, he is alternately venerated as a saint and reviled as one of the most evil men to occupy the papal throne. Gregory, whose original name was Hildebrand, had been a leading light in the reform movement for many years, working as Leo's adviser, and as pope he tried to crack down on the practice of clerical marriage. Priests were supposed to be celibate, according to the Rule of Gregory the Great, but the Rule was broken on a huge scale. Gregory VII brooked no compromise, to a cruel degree. He aimed not simply to stop new priestly marriages but forcibly to dissolve existing ones, and many priests' wives were turfed out, unsupported. He was helped in this by his friend Peter Damian, prior of Fonte Avellana in Italy, and an outspoken critic of all clerical abuses, who was also close to the Cluniac movement. Peter, however, was a better diplomat than Gregory. In 1059 he was sent to Milan to deal with clerical marriages there, and managed to handle the very delicate situation without causing schism or violence.

It is easy to see why Gregory VII was hated by many in Europe – to this day the rumour persists that he attained his position by poisoning all his rivals. He certainly cannot have been easy to get on with. In particular, Gregory sought to rescue the papacy from the position of degrading servitude it had reached under successive warlords of Italy, which he did by proclaiming the rights and dignities of the pope more forcefully than anyone ever had before. The *Papal Decree* of 1075 stated that no one can judge the pope, that the pope alone can appoint and depose bishops, that he can depose kings and emperors, that his rule extends over earthly rulers – who must kiss his feet when they approach him – and that all popes (including himself, naturally) are automatically saints! It will seem to many that Gregory's claims were arrogant and disastrous; equally, they were intended to prevent the papacy being no more than a pawn of powerful warlords. If this was the

Pope Gregory VII with a scribe, in a contemporary illustration.

Medieval religious life

By the late thirteenth century the church had become an increasingly powerful and centralized institution, and the papacy had emerged as a significant political force, capable of challenging kings and emperors. But the church's spiritual and social influence had also grown significantly. This growth was most clearly revealed by changes relating to the sacraments. In the middle of the twelfth century Peter Lombard proposed a tightly organized system with seven sacraments, namely baptism, confirmation, eucharist, matrimony, ordination, penance and extreme unction. Peter's scheme was recognized as orthodox by the Fourth Lateran Council of 1215 because it consolidated the church's thinking on a great number of issues. For instance, matrimony and ordination were presented as mutually exclusive vocational sacraments, strengthening the existing division between secular and ecclesiastical by reinforcing the long-held view that the clergy could not marry. But the scheme also added fresh impetus to a movement that placed the sacraments at the heart of Christian life. Thus infant baptism, which had been challenged by some and was far from widespread, became a universal declaration of orthodoxy.

The church also began to have an increasing effect upon other areas of secular life. From the very beginning the church commemorated events associated with the life of Christ with an annual round of liturgical services, but by the thirteenth century many of these occasions had become important public events, characterized by ecclesiastical processions and other ceremonial displays. As these holy days became important fixtures in the lay calendar, they were soon transformed into secular holidays, the community taking time off work in order to join in the celebrations. The ecclesiastical authorities even began to experiment with liturgical drama – thus initiating a process that would lead to the emergence of the vernacular miracle plays of the twelfth and thirteenth centuries. The period saw a significant rise in the number of hospitals and almshouses, as the church's new-found administrative confidence allowed it to take a more active role in caring for the sick and destitute.

As the church's influence rapidly increased, so too did the expectations of the laity. By the thirteenth century, the demand for miracle plays created tensions that led the church to distance itself from such activities. As a result, they began to be controlled by secular institutions, such as craft guilds, and they slowly changed from liturgical dramas to the mystery play entertainments of the later Middle Ages. Similarly, the demand for education was such that students and teachers began to form their own educational institutions, or universities. The boundaries between ecclesiastical and secular education became ever more blurred as the students increasingly trained as clerks rather than clerics. Book ownership and production provides a particular insight into this shift. Before the emergence of the universities, books tended to be liturgical works, often produced in monasteries for use by monks and clerics. But the universities created a massive demand for non-liturgical texts, which was met by professional scribes, illuminators and binders. There was also an increased demand from wealthy lay people for private devotional books. The thirteenth century saw the appearance of the *Book of Hours*, with readings and prayers for particular hours of the day. This work proved so popular with the laity that it became the most widely produced and lavishly decorated book of the medieval period.

One of the most interesting ways in which the changing relationship between church and laity revealed itself during this period was connected to the growing phenomenon of sainthood. Although saints had tended to be locally revered figures, the church promoted and organized their veneration so effectively that the already busy calendar was soon full of officially sanctioned saints' days. Moreover, the church supported the view that saints were able to act as intercessors between man and God through the medium of prayer. Indeed, it fostered a cult of sainthood that encouraged people to view relics as mystical objects possessing miraculous powers. It was this primitive thinking that effectively underpinned the medieval notion of the pilgrimage, which saw increasing numbers of people set out on journeys to places such as Canterbury, Compostela, Rome and Jerusalem in search of spiritual and physical cures.

JUSTIN CLEGG

A papal seal of Pope Clement II (reigned 1046–47)

only way to prevent a return to the days of corpses in court or pubescent popes, then so be it.

Gregory's pronouncements were also a declaration of war against the practice of investiture, whereby secular rulers appointed bishops and abbots. In the same year that he issued them, the pope deposed and excommunicated no less a person than the Holy Roman emperor, Henry IV, for trying to overrule the papal choice for bishop of Milan. Henry responded by deposing the pope and suggesting that he go and be damned. Gregory secured the allegiance of many lords, and the emperor was forced to visit him in disgrace in 1076 – made to stand barefoot in the snow for three days before being allowed inside to kiss the papal foot. The dispute led to civil war within the empire, which Henry won, taking the opportunity to reclaim his investiture rights. Gregory excommunicated him once again. This time the emperor invaded Italy, appointed a new pope of his own and incarcerated Gregory. The desperate pope called on the Normans of southern Italy for help: they responded, restoring him to power, but sacking Rome in the process. Hated by the emperor, despised by the people of Rome, the pope fled to the Norman lands and died there in 1085.

Yet the reform movement did not die with him. On the contrary, it was going from strength to strength, and historians still refer to subsequent popes as 'Gregorian' depending on how fully they lived up to Gregory's ideals. The investiture controversy was dealt with in 1122 at the Concordat of Worms, which officially ended the practice of secular investiture, but compromised by allowing for secular rulers to have a kind of unofficial input into the process.

With reform went centralization and greater efficiency. The whole of the Middle Ages, and the period that followed, saw the development and crystallization of the curia, the government of the church, with a number of departments (or 'congregations') emerging to help the pope run the church. Pope Leo IX had played an important role in this, surrounding himself with energetic movers and shakers (including the future Gregory VII) to help him run the church. The name 'curia' would come into common use not long after his death in 1054. Another word that came into common usage at this time, or a little later, was 'bull' to refer to a pronouncement from Rome. The word came from *bulla*, a metal plate or boss, from the increasingly magnificent seals that were attached to some of these documents. After the fifteenth century it became usual to distinguish between different varieties of papal pronouncements, and 'bull' came to refer only to documents that were signed by the pope and accompanied by a seal.

An especially important development was that of the office of cardinal. 'Cardinal' (from the Latin for 'hinge') was applied from the fifth century to priests permanently posted at certain Italian churches; they were 'hinges' in the sense of the point at which the church interacted with the people. These 'cardinal priests' were later joined by 'cardinal deacons' of Rome, who ministered to the poor. And, finally, the bishops of the area around Rome came to be called 'cardinal bishops'.

This system, with the three orders of cardinals, was in place by the eleventh century, and in 1139 it was decreed that from then on popes would be elected by the cardinals alone, rather than by all the priests in Rome as had previously happened. Thus, the cardinals were extremely powerful figures, and from the twelfth century they were the primary helpers and advisers of the pope. Throughout the Middle Ages and Renaissance their number gradually increased. It was no longer the case that serving in a particular post made somebody a cardinal – rather, people were named cardinal by the pope on the basis of their personal merits. It became understood that, although there were three orders of cardinals, they had a similar sort of status: thus, even a cardinal deacon became more important than an ordinary bishop. The 'college of cardinals' thus came into being, a unified body within the church. In 1514, Pope Leo X would declare that this college was second in importance to the papacy itself. Cardinals were sometimes called princes, and they regarded kings and emperors as their equals.

The system of cardinals remains central to the Catholic Church today, and the three orders are still in place, although despite their varying titles virtually all cardinals today are bishops. That does not mean that they have a diocese, though; they may also head departments of the Curia or hold other positions of authority within the Vatican. All cardinals are appointed by the pope: he may name a currently serving bishop as a cardinal, or make somebody a bishop and cardinal at the same time.

CARTHUSIANS AND CISTERCIANS
Meanwhile, two new movements were beginning which would also act as an unofficial conscience of the church.

The first was the Carthusian movement, which was founded by a priest and scholar called Bruno, who in 1084 started a little community in the Alps called Chartreuse. Unlike the Cluniac movement, which had developed out of the Benedictine Rule, Bruno's group was completely new, and intended to live a slightly different sort of life, more like that of the early desert fathers. The monks inhabited much smaller communities, and they lived alone, spending most of their time in solitary contemplation or manual work but coming together to sing the liturgy. It was thus a kind of blending of the old ideal of the hermitage with the medieval institution of the communal monastery. Bruno was personally much loved, and Pope Urban II was one of his pupils; he was therefore often dragged unwillingly from his cell to the papal court to offer his advice. After his death, the Carthusian order spread throughout Europe – but slowly. The rather severe form of life that the Carthusians followed made them respected perhaps more than envied.

Much more successful in the twelfth and thirteenth centuries was the Cistercian movement, which grew out of Cluny. It had

The cloisters of the Cistercian abbey of Fontfroide, France.

BERNARDUS·ABBAS·CLARAVALLIS

its origins in Robert, abbot of the Cluniac monastery at Molesme. Unfortunately, Molesme did not live up to the high standards of Cluny. Robert eventually gave up in exasperation and in 1098 started a new monastery with some of his friends at Cîteaux in Burgundy. Here, like the original community of Cluny nearly two centuries earlier, Robert and the others sought to live under a strict interpretation of the Rule of St Benedict. Cîteaux was a secluded area, and they hoped to emulate the desert fathers by retreating from the temptations of the world. Under a rule drawn up by their third abbot, Stephen Harding, the monks of Cîteaux were determined to accept no donations from wealthy patrons, and they worked with their hands to support themselves, believing that honest labour was itself a form of prayer. Private property was banned, and what little they did own was held communally. A simple life was the rule – to such an extent that fires were not allowed, no matter how cold it got – except on Christmas Day.

Cîteaux might have been just a footnote in the history of Christianity had not a very remarkable young man entered the monastery in around 1112. This was Bernard, a nobleman from Dijon, who spent three years in the monastery before leaving to found his own, a daughter monastery, at Clairvaux. Here he remained until his death in 1153, during which time he established himself as probably the most prominent and famous figure in Europe. If the eleventh century was the age of Gregory VII, the twelfth was undeniably the age of Bernard of Clairvaux.

Bernard must have possessed an electrifying personality. Enormously charismatic, he was so successful in persuading people of the benefits of a monastic life that it was said that mothers hid their sons when he was around for fear that they would leave their families to become monks. The basic theme of all the voluminous writings that poured from his pen was remarkably simple: love. Bernard believed that the whole Christian message

and life was summed up in God's infinite love to humanity, and the love that human beings return to God. Knowledge, good deeds, even faith itself were secondary to this initial movement of love. Bernard expressed this conviction with poetic grandeur in his writings, particularly in his meditations on the Old Testament book of Song of Songs, a love poem which, like other Christians before him, Bernard interpreted as an allegory of the love between God and humanity:

Like all larger than life figures, Bernard was controversial. He was drawn – not entirely willingly – into church politics, being called on in 1130 to decide a dispute between two rival claimants to the papacy. People accused him of being a foolish monk meddling in affairs which did not concern him. Yet Bernard's message was always one of moral purity and spiritual closeness to God. When a disciple became Pope Eugene III, Bernard wrote him a book explaining that the church could prosper only if its leader were pure of heart. Bernard always recommended meditation over rash action, and was himself addicted to spiritual contemplation in forests: he claimed that trees could teach you more than books ever could.

However, Bernard continues to be reviled by many today, especially for two actions which might seem to contradict much of his basic message. These were his attempts to condemn the philosopher Peter Abelard, and his preaching of the Second Crusade. We shall see more of both of these later in this chapter. In the meantime, Bernard and his followers were enormously successful in spreading the teachings of Cîteaux. By the time Bernard died, there were well over 350 Cistercian abbeys throughout Europe. The movement even threatened to outstrip the venerable Cluniac order, and there was some rivalry between the two organizations. Like other Benedictine monks, the Cluniacs wore black habits (and were known as 'black monks'), but the Cistercians wore white (and were therefore 'white monks'). And despite the

A medieval image of Bernard of Clairvaux venerating the Virgin Mary with Jesus (top left), and the virtues charity, prudence, and humility (bottom left).

Our food is scanty, our garments rough; our drink is from the stream and our sleep often upon our book. Under our tired limbs there is but a hard mat; when sleep is sweetest we must rise at a bell's bidding… Everywhere peace, everywhere serenity, and a marvelous freedom from the tumult of the world.

Aelred of Rievaulx, a leading Cistercian abbot, *The mirror of charity*, c. 1140

Love is sufficient of itself; it gives pleasure by itself and because of itself. It is its own merit, its own reward. Love looks for no cause outside itself, no effect beyond itself. Its profit lies in the practice. Of all the movements, sensations and feelings of the soul, love is the only one in which the creature can respond to the Creator and make some sort of similar return however unequal though it be. For when God loves, all he desires is to be loved in return. The sole purpose of his love is to be loved, in the knowledge that those who love him are made happy by their love of him.

Bernard of Clairvaux, *On the Canticle*

The Creator of the universe set up two great luminaries in the firmament of heaven; the greater light to rule the day, the lesser light to rule the night. In the same way for the firmament of the universal church…. he appointed two great dignities; the greater to bear rule over souls… the lesser to bear rule over bodies… These dignities are the pontifical authority and the royal power. Furthermore, the moon derives her light from the sun, and is in truth inferior to the sun in both size and quality, in position as well as effect. In the same way the royal power derives its dignity from the pontifical authority; and the more closely it cleaves to the sphere of that authority the less is the light with which it is adorned; the further it is removed, the more it increases in splendour.

Innocent III, *Sicut universitatis conditor*, 1198

wish of mothers to keep Bernard away from their sons, the Cistercians were enormously popular with ordinary people. Their virtues of simple living, hard work and personal morality naturally endeared them to people, as did the determination of their leaders to fight any corruption that still lingered among the higher echelons of the church. The Cistercians – always busy at manual labour – even pioneered new agricultural techniques, and are credited with the first moves towards modern selective breeding of domestic livestock.

INNOCENT III AND THE FOURTH LATERAN COUNCIL

Orders such as the Cluniac and Cistercian movements helped to give the church greater strength and unity of purpose, and set the scene for the thirteenth century, arguably the high point of medieval civilization. The papacy, invigorated and strengthened by the reforms of Gregory VII and his successors, dominated the western church as never before. As the thirteenth century dawned, the papacy was occupied by another remarkable man – Innocent III, probably the most powerful pope of all time. Innocent believed that, as Christ's vicar, the pope had authority over all temporal things. After all, all human actions, in whatever sphere, have spiritual overtones: all human acts are tainted by sin, and therefore theologically significant, and thus fall within the remit of the pope. That meant that he was not only the spiritual master of all Christians, but their political master too. Kings and emperors ruled at his say-so.

Where Gregory VII had attempted to make this vision reality and failed, Innocent III succeeded. He had the good fortune to become pope – in 1198 – as the imperial succession was in dispute, which meant he could wade into the power vacuum and inform the German princes that, while he permitted them to elect their own emperor, the pope had the final word. Dynastic squabbles continued for some years, but the pope's candidate,

Otto of Wittelsbach, was finally crowned in 1209. Otto made the mistake of reneging on his promises to Innocent; the pope duly excommunicated him and arranged for the coronation of a replacement, Frederick II, who gave him Sicily in return. The pope, it seemed, had become the puppet master of European politics. While he was at it, Innocent forced England and France, who were at war, to make peace, since he thought it wrong that Christians should fight each other. One of the most potent weapons Innocent developed was the 'interdict', whereby the pope could simply suspend church operations in an entire country, with the result that no one could be baptized, married or buried. In 1213 Innocent used the threat of this to force King John of England to formally hand over his whole kingdom to the pope, who then handed it back to him to govern. In this way, the king of England became nothing more than the pope's vassal, his strict subordinate according to the feudal system.

We should, of course, be wary. It is easy to get the impression that the pope was the true ruler of Europe and all were at his beck and call. That is the impression that Innocent wished to convey. The reality, as always, was more complex. Innocent did get his candidate onto the imperial throne, but it took him many years. He successfully bullied John of England, but John was a weak man, and his nobles thought his inability to stand up to the pope was pretty pathetic. Innocent III was very powerful, but he was not omnipotent – he was just one among other players in European politics.

Arguably Innocent III's greatest triumph was the Fourth Lateran Council, held in 1215, which sought to stamp Innocent's vision over the entire church – east and west, for armies acting under his decree had (temporarily) conquered Constantinople. The council was intended to bring unity of faith and structure to the church and clear up remaining irregularities. Corruption was tackled, and the practice of priests giving positions to their illegitimate sons addressed. Clerical celibacy was once again to be enforced, priests were forbidden from getting drunk or frequenting bars and strict rules were given for their clothing, which had to be suitably dignified: no more red and green cloaks or expensive gloves. Perhaps more importantly, the faithful were instructed to make private confession to priests at least once a year. The practice was not new, but this council aimed to regulate and make official what had been done for many years: thus confession, and the sacrament of penance, would become more important in the church.

The opening declaration of faith of the Fourth Lateran Council also dealt with the Mass. The word 'Mass' had been used in the west to refer to the Eucharist since the time of Gregory the Great – it derived from the Latin word for 'dismissal', used at the end of the service. The council spoke of the miracle of the Mass, in which the bread and wine were transformed into the body and blood of Christ. There was nothing new about this, except the word used to describe how this occurred: transubstantiation. This idea relied on a distinction, drawn from Aristotle, between the 'substance' of a thing – what it actually is – and its 'properties', or qualities. At the Mass, the substance of the bread and wine change into the substance of Christ's body and blood, but their properties remain the same, which is why they look and taste just as they did before. The use of this Aristotelian terminology was new, but the doctrine was not really substantially different from that of the church fathers.

Apart from this, Innocent also initiated the Fourth Crusade and made war against the Albigenses, actions which we shall see in more detail later, and for which he has been viewed in a dim light in more recent times. One other act was to have enormous consequences for the church: he approved the founding of yet two more religious orders. But these were different from the various monastic movements which had appeared in previous centuries:

these were the mendicant orders, the friars. The Fourth Lateran Council forbade the founding of any more religious orders, as there were already quite enough; the mendicant orders were founded shortly before the council, so they were the last great religious orders of the Middle Ages.

THE FRIARS

The Franciscans arose from the preaching of Francis of Assisi, who petitioned Innocent III for permission to found a new order of *friars minore* or 'lesser brothers' in 1210. Innocent wisely recognized the potential of this ragged band of Italians, and saw that they could become a powerful tool if put in the service of the papacy. Unlike the monks, the Franciscan friars owned nothing and travelled about, begging to support themselves and preaching to the people. Since they did this without requiring the authority of the local bishop, here was a means for the pope to undermine the power of bishops if need be.

Similarly, the Dominicans arose from the disciples of Dominic, who preached to the Albigenses. Like the Franciscans, the Dominicans owned nothing and travelled about, but their emphasis was more on preaching and the maintenance of correct belief. There was thus a strong intellectual streak in their approach, more so than among the Franciscans who were, above all else, devoted to Christ through the practice of poverty. Together, both orders of friars became enormously popular throughout Europe, as they were seen to identify with the poor and outcast. People thronged to listen to their sermons, which were delivered in simple language, often laced with plenty of jokes. They were devoted to helping others and so, whenever there were plagues, the friars could be found nursing the sick. Their popularity was shown in a figure like Anthony of

Praise to you, Lord, through all your creatures, especially through my lord, Brother Sun, who brings the day, and through whom you give light. He is beautiful and radiant in his splendour. He bears your likeness, High One.

Francis of Assisi, *Canticle of the sun*, 1225

A statue of Francis of Assisi.

Padua, an extremely learned but very humble man (for much of his career, no one realized how learned he was, because he was more interested in listening than teaching). Anthony joined the Franciscans in the early thirteenth century, and when circumstances forced him to deliver a sermon, his talent was revealed. Francis himself wrote to him, charging him to teach theology to the brothers. Anthony became nearly as universally loved as Francis himself, and he was declared to be a saint almost immediately after his death in 1231.

At the same time, the traditional monastic orders were suspicious of the friars, as were nobles, who despised their often ragged appearance. There was some rivalry between the two orders, who wore different habits: grey for the Franciscans and white with a black cloak for the Dominicans (hence 'grey friars' and 'black friars'), but their ideal of service and self-denial was an important counterbalance to the theology of power being developed by Innocent III. They would both play major roles in mission. Francis himself travelled to the Middle East to preach to the

Francis and Clare

Francis and Clare of Assisi are among the best known figures in Christendom. In an age which frowned on strong friendships between men and women outside marriage, theirs was a durable bond rooted in a common vision about the poverty endured by Jesus Christ.

International commerce formed the backdrop to the early years of Francis (1181/2–1226). The older son of Pietro di Bernardone, he enjoyed the benefits of a comfortable domestic life in the small city and was destined to join his father as a cloth merchant. But his experiences of civil war as a young man left him disillusioned with the values which had hitherto guided him.

For two years Francis lived as a hermit and repaired churches, until he attended Mass at the Portiuncula, a chapel outside the city. As the priest read the familiar passage of how Jesus had sent out his apostles to preach (Matthew 10), Francis suddenly glimpsed his own vocation. Obeying the gospel literally, he adopted the apostolic life and exhorted the people of Assisi to follow the teachings of Jesus Christ. He began to attract recruits. When the incipient fraternity numbered a dozen, Francis sought approbation from Innocent III. Guido, the bishop of Assisi, vouched for the 'friars' (or 'brothers') and was instrumental in their gaining access to the Roman Curia.

Francis preached in the churches of Assisi, where his fervour and zeal deeply impressed the daughter of Count Favarone Scifi, Clare da Favarone di Offreduccio (c. 1194–1253). She heard Francis's stirring sermons in the cathedral of San Rufino and was persuaded by his message. The outcome of these homilies was a series of clandestine conversations with Francis which led to Clare's determination to follow the gospel to the letter. For the last time she accompanied her family to the cathedral on Palm Sunday of 1211/12, and that night she left home and hurried to the Portiuncula, where her hair was cut off and she made her profession to follow the gospel in poverty, chastity and obedience. Defiantly resisting their family's threats, Clare and her younger sister, Agnes (c. 1197–1253), were settled at San Damiano, where they were joined by other recruits living under Francis's guidance. Francis came to rely on Clare and asked her to pray for guidance about whether he should devote himself to prayer or preaching. He also sent the sick to be blessed by her.

Credited with recovering an emphasis on the poverty of Jesus, Francis and his followers launched new missions throughout Christendom from 1217. Once he had secured papal approbation of the Rule on 29 November 1223, Francis concentrated on prayer and asceticism, culminating in the stigmata, that is, the five wounds borne by the crucified Christ. Dogged by illness and disappointment about the evolution of the order, he gravitated increasingly to San Damiano. Francis's companions indicate the strength of the friendship between the two saints. Francis spent fifty days at San Damiano as he awaited treatment for his eyes and composed the *Canticle of Brother Sun*. He also wrote a song for the sisters in 1224/5. During the last week of his life he was in close contact with Clare and sent her a letter of consolation and blessing. When he died on the evening of 3 October 1226, his body was carried back to San Giorgio, the church in Assisi where Clare had first heard him preach. En route the cortège halted at San Damiano so that Clare might venerate the body of the man whose preaching and example had brought her to religious life.

For the last twenty-seven years of her life Clare fought valiantly for the right to live in absolute poverty, firmly opposing papal plans to invest her with some form of endowment. Gregory IX confirmed her privilege of poverty in 1228. Despite the growing friction among the friars and evidence of relaxations, Clare was an exemplar of evangelical poverty and a focal point of unity. Her Rule was approved by Innocent IV on 9 August 1253. Francis's companions, Leo, Juniper and Angelo, were drawn to her deathbed. Clare died on 11 August 1253 and her requiem Mass was celebrated by Innocent IV, whose instinct was to pronounce her a saint before her burial.

MICHAEL ROBSON

Muslims (and to plead for more humane behaviour from the crusaders), and as we shall see in chapter 10, Franciscan missionaries travelled to China soon afterwards.

And the two great mendicant orders played a central role in the intellectual life of the thirteenth century. Many of their members were leading lights of the new universities, and the houses that the orders founded – for those members who did not wish to travel throughout Europe preaching – became centres of scholarship, for they each had a school to educate new recruits. A new renaissance of scholarship and learning was taking place at the same time, one far more lasting than the earlier one under Charlemagne. And it would produce one of the most important philosophical movements in history: scholasticism.

THE WORLD OF FAITH AND REASON

EARLY SCHOLASTICISM

The first signs of scholasticism appears in the eleventh century, with new teachers such as Berengar of Tours, a controversial figure who travelled from one teaching position to another and denied that the bread and wine in the Eucharist really become the body and blood of Christ. But by common consent, the first real scholastic was Roscelin of Compiègne, who lived in the early years of the twelfth century. Like Berengar, he travelled from post to post before becoming a canon at Compiègne, but he was apparently interested in philosophical problems that were not explicitly religious. In fact, the subject on which Roscelin made his most famous pronouncements was the subject which appears to have fascinated all the scholastics almost to the point of obsession: the problem of universal names. The question was whether there are 'universal things' to which universal names refer; if there are, what are they? And if

there are not, then how do universal names mean anything? The extreme positions in this debate were 'realism', the position that there are indeed real universal objects, and 'nominalism,' the claim that universals are only names and only particular things exist.

Roscelin was a nominalist, and stated that universal terms are nothing other than 'puffs of speech'. For this, he was ridiculed by the man who has since become the most famous thinker of this generation, Anselm of Canterbury. Anselm was a rather sweet soul, who ran away from his home in Italy as a teenager and ended up as archbishop of Canterbury. But he was not cut out for this job, which involved having to stand up to the king of England and engage in political machinations and controversy: disagreement of any kind made him physically ill.

As a philosopher, Anselm was at heart a Platonist, even a Neoplatonist: he was deeply influenced by Augustine. Unlike Roscelin, he believed that universals are indeed real, and that it is possible to prove things about the real world simply by pure thought – even without recourse to revelation. On this basis he built his famous 'ontological' proof for the existence of God, which proves God's existence simply from an analysis of what the word 'God' means.

Anselm used similar methods of logical reasoning – rather than appealing to revelation – to present his doctrine of the atonement. At this stage, most people still believed the old 'ransom' theory, according to which our sin has granted Satan legitimate rights over us, and so Christ saves us either by literally dying as a ransom for us or by tricking the devil into handing us over. Anselm, however, in his book *Why God became man*, rejected the idea that Satan can have rights over anyone. Instead, he suggested that it is God who has a legitimate claim over us: by sinning against him, we have not only disobeyed him but wounded his honour. In the feudal system, to impinge on someone's honour was regarded as a sort of theft, and if the offender was to escape punishment he had to make restitution to

Man was created to see God. By sin, man lost the blessedness for which he was made, and found the misery for which he was not made. He did not keep what was good, even though he could keep it easily. Without God it goes badly for us. Our efforts are in vain without God. Man cannot look for God unless God himself teaches him, or find him unless he reveals himself. God created man in his image so that he might be aware of him, think about him, and love him. The believer does not try to understand so that he may believe, but he believes so that he may understand - for if he did not believe, he would not understand.

Anselm of Canterbury, *Proslogion*, c. 1105

My school grew considerably because of my lectures, and the money and fame I acquired cannot be hidden from you, since everyone talked about it. But prosperity always puffs up the foolish, and worldly comfort paralyses the soul, making it an easy prey to temptations of the flesh. So I, who by now had come to think of myself as the only philosopher left in the world, and who had given up worrying about anything, began to loosen the rein on my desires – although until then I had always lived with perfect self-control. And the more progress I made in lecturing on philosophy and theology, the further I drifted from the practice of the philosophers and the spirit of the saints in the uncleanliness of my life.

Peter Abelard, *History of my misfortunes*, c. 1130

the victim, with interest. If this proved impossible, the thief was punished. Anselm applied this to the relationship between humanity and God, suggesting that, in order to avoid having to punish anyone, God arranges for the 'debt' we have accrued through sin to be paid back to him. The price for this is the death of Christ. Since Christ is man, it is just for him to make the payment, but as he is God, he is able to make the payment, for his death has infinite value. Thus there is no need for God to punish anyone.

Anselm of Canterbury's name is still famous today, but far more well known in the early twelfth century was a teacher named Ansellus. Just to make things confusing, he has always been known as Anselm of Laon. Universally known as 'Master Anselm', he founded a school at Laon (north-east of Paris) which was extremely famous. Here Anselm engaged in the novel activity of lecturing on the Bible, as if it were an academic textbook. To date, scripture had been used primarily for devotional purposes. Now, however, it was to be studied rigorously, and theology was to become an academic subject. That is not to suggest that it was to be critical: indeed, Master Anselm was a theological conservative who made little constructive contribution to the debates of his day and was, to be quite frank, pretty dull. But he was, in a sense, the first academic theologian.

Indeed, medieval theology generally revolved around the study of the Bible, one way or another. This was reflected in the physical Bibles themselves that were produced at this time. By the time of Anselm of Laon, it was customary to make Bibles with commentaries written as glosses in columns next to the main text, in smaller writing. These editions were not illustrated, in contrast to the more spectacular illuminated texts; they were, as it were, 'study' Bibles rather than prestige editions. In this way, people could read the canonical text with the help of some famous commentator, such as Lanfranc of Canterbury or Gregory the Great.

SCHOLASTICISM DEVELOPS

So scholasticism involved arguing about universals and treating theology as a sort of academic subject. It also involved the establishment of new schools in which to do these things. A key figure in this was Peter Abelard, easily the most controversial figure of the mid-twelfth century. According to his own account, Abelard was the most famous man in the world, and little wonder. In an age when many followed philosophical debates as eagerly as they do sporting events today, Abelard was Europe's outstanding mental athlete. No one could defeat him in argument, even his teachers – who included Roscelin and Master Anselm. Moreover, Abelard was good-looking, the best poet of the century and a brilliant musician. He was the golden boy of the age – but like many golden boys, he became arrogant, and ultimately disgraced. He fell in love with his pupil Heloise, but her family disapproved of the union and had Abelard castrated. Distraught, Abelard retired to a monastery, and Heloise to a nunnery. The two of them continued to write to each other, and their letters have become some of the most popular writings of the Middle Ages. The story of Abelard and Heloise has been turned into novels, poems, plays – even operas. Final disgrace, however, came in the form of a mighty clash with the other dominant figure of the day – Bernard of Clairvaux. Bernard objected to Abelard's teachings on the nature of salvation, which (he thought) implied that Christ's death was simply an example for Christians to follow and nothing more. Abelard was forbidden from teaching and confined to a monastery, where he died soon after. Many have been tempted to see the dispute between Peter and Bernard as symptomatic of a greater struggle which was going on in this period – one between the old kind of 'affective' theology, which used the forms of poetry and prayer to kindle love in the individual's soul for God, and the new kind of 'philosophical' theology, which sought to apply logic and dialectic to matters of religion and offer objective descriptions of them. On that slightly simplistic conception,

Abelard and Heloise, from an illustration accompanying a poem by Charles, duke of Orléans (1394–1465).

the two men were chronological contemporaries, but Bernard was a man looking back to the past while Abelard was a herald of things to come.

Abelard made his name as a philosopher, defending a modified version of Roscelin's nominalism extremely ably, but he later decided to retrain in theology, which is why he studied under Master Anselm before founding his own school at Paris. This was a little rude, since there was already a good school at Paris, whose master was William of Champeaux, a friend of Master Anselm. Here, then, was the beginning of a new stage in scholasticism: the notion that a city could support more than one great teacher – perhaps many. Students might gather and swap notes. The foundations of what we would recognize as a university – outgrowing the original confines of a cathedral school to spread across a city and offer a number of courses, taught by a number of masters – were being laid. This was also connected to the increasing urbanization of Europe. Although most people still lived in the countryside and worked the fields, the growing population of Europe meant that there were far more large towns, and the largest were becoming very large indeed.

Officially, the first university was the 'universitas' (or 'whole lot' of scholars) of Bologna, which was recognized by the pope in 1088, when Peter Abelard was eight. Here and at Paris, Oxford and other centres of learning it was largely up to the scholars themselves to organize themselves, and as they pooled resources so the first halls of residence, colleges and teaching facilities evolved. Different universities developed different traditions. Paris specialized in theology. Bologna, meanwhile, specialized in law, and it was the students, rather than the teachers, who actually ran the place – surprisingly well, given how young they were. Universities provided more long-term education than their modern equivalents: students generally enrolled in their teens, or as young as twelve, and could stay there for decades. The status of Master, and the right to lecture on theology, was generally not granted until a scholar reached his mid-30s.

Students at the University of Bologna, by the late fourteenth-century Italian sculptors Jacobello and Pierpaolo dalle Masegne.

THE FLOWERING OF SCHOLASTICISM

So the scholastics spent their time arguing about universals and studying theology as an academic discipline in universities. But in the later twelfth century the final brick of the great edifice of scholastic philosophy was laid: the use of Greek philosophy and, above all, the thought of Aristotle. The story of how Aristotle came to be regarded as an authority by the medieval Christian philosophers is a strange one. Throughout antiquity, and in the early Middle Ages, Christian thinkers preferred Plato and his heirs, and shared the Platonists' disapproval of Plato's illustrious pupil. But Aristotle was especially studied in the east. We saw in chapter 4 how the Persian Christians prospered under Arab rule after the Muslim invasions there, and translated classical texts into Syriac and Arabic. Among these were those of Aristotle, and in this way the Muslims came to know

them. Muslim philosophers appeared who used Aristotle's ideas to express their religion in new ways and, as the Christian west interacted with the Muslim east and south in the Middle Ages, the ideas and then the original texts of Aristotle began to filter back into western Europe, where they had been forgotten for centuries.

Aristotle's works were something of a revelation to the medieval theologians, who were accustomed to devoting their time to explaining the Bible through the lens of the vast body of commentaries and doctrine that they had inherited from the church fathers. Aristotle's logic was already known, but his ethics and metaphysics, which began to appear in Latin translations of Arabic versions in the twelfth and thirteenth centuries, provided new ways to think about the world. Many scholars became extremely excited by Aristotle's ideas and embraced them enthusiastically, while others were highly suspicious. After all, Aristotle contradicted church teaching on a number of points, such as his claim that the world had always existed rather than was created by God. Thus, in 1215 his metaphysical works were banned by the University of Paris, although study of his ethics was encouraged and his logic was mandatory.

Nevertheless, although he was controversial, Aristotle became an established part of the scholastic furniture. Albertus Magnus, or Albert the Great, who taught at Cologne in the mid-thirteenth century, pioneered a cautious but constructive use of Aristotle, and his pupil, Thomas Aquinas, perfected it. Aquinas was

It was necessary for the salvation of humanity that there should be knowledge revealed by God, apart from philosophical knowledge learned through reason. First, because man is directed towards God, as towards something that is beyond his reason... So it was necessary for salvation that certain facts which are beyond human reason should be made known through divine revelation.

Thomas Aquinas *Summa theologiae*, c. 1273

Thomas Aquinas

Thomas Aquinas (c. 1225–74) was perhaps the foremost Christian theologian of the Middle Ages.

Against the will of his parents he joined the newly-founded Dominican order at a young age. Devoted to teaching and learning, the Dominicans quickly became a dominant force at the University of Paris, where Aquinas received his early theological training after studying philosophy with Albertus Magnus in Cologne. Aquinas was foremost amongst those making efforts to assimilate Aristotelian methods and tools into the discussion of Christian theology. The influence of Aristotle and of philosophical methodology remained the distinctive feature of scholastic theology until its slow eclipse by humanism and the Reformation.

In addition to commentaries on both Scripture and many of the works of Aristotle, Aquinas authored various works springing from his teaching and lecturing in the University and two large *Summae* (or systematic treatises of Christian doctrine): the *Summa contra Gentiles*, and the *Summa theologiae*. In the first of these, Aquinas attempted to give an account of the Christian faith relying as little as possible on revelation. He holds that the existence and nature of God, creation, the existence and immortality of the human soul, and humanity's final destiny in the vision of God can all be demonstrated independently of revelation; but he also addresses those aspects of theology that rely on revelation: the Trinity, the incarnation, and grace and the sacraments. The vast *Summa theologiae*, left incomplete at the time of Aquinas's death, contains all of his characteristic teachings. Aquinas holds that God's existence can be shown 'in five ways': God is the first mover, an uncaused cause, a necessary being, a maximally excellent being and a final goal of existence. Anything which is a first mover must be wholly actual and lacking any potentiality (since potentiality is the capacity to be moved by something else). This entails, for Aquinas, that God is wholly non-composite. Thus, God cannot be bodily, since bodily things can always be divided; he cannot be distinct from his existence, because anything that is distinct from its existence is such that its existence requires causing, and God is the uncaused cause. That God is identical with his existence – and that all creatures are distinct from their existence – is perhaps the most characteristic of Aquinas's teachings.

In ethics, Aquinas believed that it is possible to determine how things behave by looking at their natural functions or goals. Since human beings have such natural goals, it is possible to determine how they should behave in order to achieve these goals. This yields natural law, and the virtues – dispositions for behaving well – are acquired by acting in accordance with this law. The theory is perhaps more influential in the Catholic Church today than it was in Aquinas's own day. Aquinas's importance for modern Catholicism was established when Pope Leo XIII, in his encyclical *Aeterni Patris* (1879) enjoined the teaching of Aquinas in Catholic Universities, taking him as the model philosopher/theologian.

Aquinas was first and foremost an academic theologian. But he must have been a man of practical skills too, for in 1265 he was entrusted with the foundation of a new Dominican study house at Rome. He returned to Paris in 1268, but in 1272 was ordered to found another study house in Naples. He continued writing until the end of 1273, when he had some kind of breakdown. He died on 7 March 1274 on his way to the Council of Lyons.

RICHARD CROSS

Gothic splendour.
The west front of
Lincoln Cathedral.

controversial among both Aristotle fanatics (who thought he did not go far enough) and Aristotle sceptics (who thought he went too far), but this compromising approach proved very fruitful. Even those who were less happy about Aristotle, such as Aquinas's friend Bonaventure, the head of the Franciscan order, still quoted him frequently. For all these people, Aristotle was 'the Philosopher', as if none other existed.

Aquinas and other scholastics in the thirteenth century disagreed about much, of course. There were still arguments about universal names, and about other issues: for example, the British philosopher John Duns Scotus attacked Aquinas's claim that all language about God is analogical. But they did agree on a broad vision of how the world worked, one where everything was in its place, and where reason and revelation formed parts of a continuous whole. By the thirteenth century, the universities had established a

standard curriculum of different subjects, all of which were regarded as quite distinct and requiring different methods of inquiry (a notion derived from – who else? – Aristotle). But it was also believed that all the subjects, from mathematics to law to theology to logic, were studying the same basic thing – God and his creation. There could be no disagreements within the one body of truth, whether between the church and the Bible or between the church and natural philosophy (that is, science). All knowledge and study was ultimately directed to God, and the world itself, and everything in it, was there to point people to God. Thus the world was invested with an infinity of mystical meaning, if only one had the insight to understand it.

BUILDINGS AND BEAUTY
Such mystical meaning could be found in medieval art, which developed into something like a complex crossword

The temptation of St Anthony, by the Flemish artist David Teniers the younger (1610–90), is a good example of a painting that uses religious symbolism – for instance, Satan is represented here by an owl.

Flying buttresses radiate from the main structure of Chartres cathedral, France.

puzzle. Everything that medieval artists painted had a meaning. For example, it was believed that panthers had extremely sweet breath with healing qualities. The panther was therefore an image of Christ, the great Healer. Therefore, whenever an artist painted a panther, he was directing the viewer to Christ. Similarly, owls (active in the dark) might represent Satan, chastity could be represented by a lily or a unicorn, and so on. When people of the Middle Ages looked at any kind of art, they did not ask, 'What is this?' – they asked, 'What spiritual lesson is this intended to teach?'

This blending of the physical with the spiritual could also be found in the extraordinary churches which were built in the Middle Ages. Indeed, while it is often thought that the Middle Ages were a time of little technological advance, that is not true – it is simply that some of the most impressive technological advances of the medieval period were made in architecture. Builders found new ways to create ever more ambitious structures and put them in the service of the church. In the eleventh century the greatest churches – such as the abbey church of Cluny –

were built in the Romanesque style, a development of the 'basilica' style of church-building of the fourth century. A Romanesque church had, in addition to the nave, sanctuary and other essential elements, a number of chapels along the sides of the church, as well as towers, crypts and other associated elements. It was a demonstration in stone of the unity of the world and of all things, and these churches were bigger and bolder than anything that had been built before. Massive walls and pillars led the eye upwards to heaven – something that smaller churches achieved with towers.

However, in the later Middle Ages, the Romanesque style gave way to the Gothic. This style was based upon the discovery that great loads could be borne – not by the walls – but by flying buttresses, latticework and other, less solid, structures. The massive walls and pillars of the older churches gave way to thinner walls with large windows, the slab-like ceilings became delicate ribbed vaulting, and flying buttresses shot out like spindly spiders' legs to support the whole thing. These techniques were first used on a large scale when the cathedral of Chartres was

Pictures and ornaments in churches are the lessons and scripture of the laity.
William Durand, thirteenth century

rebuilt after a fire in the late twelfth century. This church, and others built in these ways, were far lighter and airier than the earlier ones. They incorporated large areas of stained glass, which not only featured illustrations of Bible stories or the saints but filled the massive interior with colour and light. The abbey church of St Denis, for example, was rebuilt in the 1130s and 40s in this style, and the abbot, Suger, wrote an account of the work in which he explained that his aim was to use beauty in all its forms to lead the visitor's mind to God. Just as in the Byzantine empire, then, the great cathedrals of medieval Europe were intended to bring the visitor closer to heaven through beauty; in their form they were meant to express the orderliness of the world and of God. The Gothic style also allowed cathedrals to be even bigger than ever before, and there was a kind of competition between different cities to see who could build the tallest. The cathedral of Notre Dame in Paris reached 69 metres (226 ft), while the one in Amiens had a nave (not the tower!) that was over 42 metres (137 ft) high. Beauvais tried to make one with a steeple 153 metres (502 ft) high, but it collapsed while it was being built.

As this suggests, the massive cathedrals were the focus of their cities. They were not just used for religious services: they were the meeting places of the citizens, where they might hire day labourers, buy goods or go to be healed or find a bed in the crypt. These immense structures embodied in their function, as well as in their design, the medieval faith in the unity of all life. There was no real distinction between the holy and the profane: they were parts of the same world, under the same God. Should anyone forget this, the Gothic cathedral would be covered in carvings, bas-reliefs and other works of art representing the teachings of the church in suitably mystical fashion.

CHRISTENDOM AND ITS NEIGHBOURS

Such was the worldview of medieval Christendom: a vision of unity and harmony. Yet the reality fell somewhat short of this ideal. And the medieval Christians had some problems accommodating alternative worldviews.

RELATIONS WITH THE BYZANTINE CHURCH

The first problem was that medieval Christendom was not a unity: it was divided between the eastern and western churches. In chapter 5 we saw how the Byzantine church became increasingly detached from the church of western Europe. The same thing was happening from the opposite point of view, too. Just as the Byzantines largely forgot Latin, so too the westerners largely forgot Greek. There were still Greek scholars in the ninth century – the most notable being the Irish philosopher Eriugena – but these were the exception. More fundamentally than this, however, the westerners could not understand the mind-set of Byzantine Christianity. The result was a series of disruptions in diplomatic relations between the two great Christian blocs.

The first of these was the Acacian schism, which we looked at in chapter 5, as well as the Photian schism. But these procedural disagreements were dwarfed by the growing gulf in doctrine between the two sides. The most famous issue between them was the *filioque*, the western belief that the Holy Spirit proceeded from the Son as well as from the Father, which the Byzantines rejected. Equally divisive was the issue of icons. The Second Council of Nicaea of AD 787 commended the veneration of icons, but inaccurate translations and reports of this council reached western ears, leading them to believe that the Byzantines were forcing their subjects to worship images. This was condemned in the *Books of*

Charles, written for Charlemagne by his chief theologian, Theodore of Orléans, which argued that images could help people focus on what is holy, but they have no intrinsic holiness in themselves. Pope Hadrian I disagreed and he defended the Byzantines: perhaps he had a better idea of what had happened at the council, since he had had legates there on his behalf. In any case, Charlemagne called a council of his own at Frankfurt in AD 794, which condemned the Second Council of Nicaea and its supposed imposition of image-worship.

Given these doctrinal differences, it is perhaps surprising that the great break between the two, when it came, was not really anything to do with doctrine or liturgy at all. The precise history of what became known as the 'Great Schism' is complex, but it culminated in the coincidence of two strong men occupying the thrones of Rome and Constantinople at the same time. The former was Leo IX, the great reforming pope of the early eleventh century, and the latter was Michael Cerularius. Leo spent much of his time opposing the Normans of southern Italy for their cruel treatment of the citizens there, and he joined forces with a Byzantine general to try to force them to act better. Cerularius, who hated the idea of being the pope's inferior, didn't like that. And when Leo banned certain Byzantine practices which were being used in southern Italian churches, Cerularius liked that even less. Cerularius became convinced that only complete independence from Rome could guarantee Byzantine worship and his own authority as patriarch, and he therefore began to retaliate against the Latins in the hope of causing a breach. He banned a number of 'Latin' customs, such as the use of unleavened bread in the Eucharist, which had previously been quite uncontroversial; and he closed all the Latin churches in Constantinople when they refused to obey. Leo, to his credit, tried to calm the situation, and even studied Greek to try to understand Cerularius's arguments better;

unfortunately, the envoy he sent to Constantinople to deal with the situation, Cardinal Humbert, was less open to compromise. In 1054, Humbert placed a papal bull of excommunication on the altar of Hagia Sophia in Constantinople. Leo was already dead, having succumbed to malaria earlier that year; nevertheless he is now remembered as the pope who condemned the entire Orthodox Church.

The 'Great Schism' was, then, only one more incident in a long and painful process of drawing apart; but it is generally taken as the moment when the Roman Catholic and Eastern Orthodox churches officially separated. There were attempts to heal the rift in the years that followed. The most significant occurred between 1438 and 1445, when a lengthy council was held first at Basle in Switzerland, then Ferrara, Florence, and finally Rome. The Byzantine emperor and

Pope Leo IX excommunicating Michael Cerularius, in an illustration from a fifteenth-century Greek manuscript.

In early summer of the year in which Peter and Gottschalk assembled an army and set out, there gathered in a similar way an enormous crowd of Christians from various kingdoms and countries – from France, England, Flanders, and Lorraine… I do not know whether it was by a judgement of the Lord, or by a mistake of the mind, but they rose up cruelly against the Jewish people scattered throughout these cities and mercilessly slaughtered them, especially in Lorraine, claiming that it was the start of their expedition and their duty against the enemies of Christianity.

Albert of Aix on the atrocities committed in Europe during the fervour of the First Crusade, *History of the Crusades* c. 1140

the patriarch of Constantinople both attended, and all the issues dividing the churches were discussed. The Byzantines agreed to accept the westerners' teaching on purgatory, which until that point had been accepted by only some in the East. They also agreed that there was nothing wrong with using unleavened bread in the Eucharist, which had been something of a non-issue anyway. Most amazingly, agreement was reached over the *filioque*. The Latins argued that although they believed that the Spirit comes from the Son as well as the Father, they agreed with the Greeks that the Son gets everything he has and is from the Father – including the ability to send the Spirit. Therefore, the Spirit ultimately comes solely from the Father, as the Greeks believed. By 1439, therefore, the two churches were declared to be officially reunited. Amid much rejoicing, the Byzantine emissaries returned home, but they could not convince the people to accept the decision. The southern Russians, based around Kiev, accepted it, but the northern Russians, who were at this time coalescing around the rising power of Moscow, flatly refused to acknowledge it. The emperor tried to bring order to the situation, but the fall of Constantinople to the Muslims in 1453 rendered any remaining discussion largely academic. The attempt at reunion had succeeded in restoring Kiev to communion with Rome, but that was all. Even this lasted for less than a century.

THE CRUSADES

If relations were strained with the Byzantine Christians, that was nothing compared to relations with the Muslims. In this, at least, the Catholics and the Byzantines were one. Much of the tension revolved around the 'Holy Places', the sites in Jerusalem associated with Jesus, especially the Church of the Holy Sepulchre, where his tomb was said to have been. In 1009 the Fatimid caliph of Cairo, al-Hakim, who controlled Jerusalem at this time, ordered the destruction of the Holy Places. They were subsequently restored, but Christians who travelled on pilgrimage to Jerusalem were treated more and more harshly. In 1070 the Seljuk Turks conquered Jerusalem from the Fatimids, but they did not treat Christians any better.

The Christian response came in 1095. Pope Urban II declared that Muslim dominance of the Middle East in general, and of the Holy Places in particular, had to be brought to an end. The Council of Claremont ratified his decree, and the people responded eagerly. The following year, a series of mighty armies – surrounded by well-wishers – streamed eastwards. By 1098 both Edessa and Antioch had fallen to the crusaders, and the following year Jerusalem itself followed and was put under the Christian rule of Godfrey of Bouillon. The crusade had been a resounding success.

However, things were not as good as they seemed. For one thing, the crusaders acted with remarkable brutality, massacring the inhabitants of the cities they captured and even eating some of them, an act which for many years led Muslims to regard all Europeans (or 'Franks') as cannibals. Moreover, the new crusader states that were established in the Middle East – the Outremer, as they were collectively known – did not last very long. The crusaders built massive fortresses to consolidate their rule, but the Christian kingdom of Edessa was reconquered by the Muslims in 1144.

A second crusade was therefore ordered by Pope Eugene III. His mentor, Bernard of Clairvaux, enthusiastically supported the project. He travelled around France promoting it, and was so successful that people ripped his clothes off his back and tore them into strips, to use as badges. Bernard did not, however, preach indiscriminate hatred against non-Christians: on the contrary, he ordered his listeners not to lynch European Jews, which had happened when the First Crusade was preached.

The Second Crusade duly left for the

Holy Land, where the crusaders besieged Damascus but failed to capture it. Bernard's reputation suffered and he was forced to write a defence of his initial preaching. Worse was to come. A mighty Kurdish general, Salah al-Din, appeared in Egypt, where he repelled forces sent from the crusader state of Jerusalem. Having done this, Salah al-Din quickly became the power behind the caliph's throne in Cairo, overthrowing the Fatimids and establishing a new dynasty, the Ayyubids. Salah al-Din then set off for the Christian Outremer, conquering Jerusalem in 1187.

Salah al-Din would go down in legend as Saladin, the greatest Muslim commander of his age, and, in Christian eyes, the 'good' infidel. He was famously merciful to his defeated foes, and a legend even arose that he had been secretly knighted by King Richard I of England! The Christians regarded Saladin rather as the Allies regarded Rommel in the Second World War – a good man on the wrong side. Nevertheless, this did not stop the Third Crusade from being launched by Pope Gregory VIII in 1189 to retake Jerusalem from him. If the earlier crusades had been the 'people's crusades', with large numbers of pilgrims and well-wishers accompanying the troops, this was the 'kings' crusade'. The Holy Roman emperor, Frederick Barbarossa, went with it, although he drowned on the way. King Philip II of France and King Richard I 'the Lionheart' of England were also present, but they and their knights failed to retake Jerusalem. The Third Crusade, like the second, was a dismal failure. Fortunately, Saladin was willing to make peace with the crusaders, and he guaranteed the safety of Christian pilgrims to Jerusalem.

Clearly, the crusades were becoming less successful, and they reached their nadir with the Fourth Crusade, ordered by Pope Innocent III in 1198. This one never even reached the Muslim Middle East. Instead, the crusaders attacked Constantinople, captured it, massacred the population and installed a Catholic king.

The fact that Constantinople was the capital of the Byzantine Empire and therefore Christian seems not to have deterred them. Although the Catholic rule of the city lasted only fifty years, and Byzantine rule was later re-established, the whole incident was possibly the worst point in the history of deteriorating relations between Catholic and Orthodox churches. It is still a bitter memory for the Orthodox today, and this, even more than the mutual excommunication of 1054, was a huge stumbling block to attempts at reunion for many centuries.

Apart from a private 'crusade' launched by Emperor Frederick II in 1228, who captured Jerusalem and held it for fifteen years, there were no more Christian successes in the Middle East. Instead, the Mumluks, who replaced the Ayyubid dynasty, slowly retook all the ground that had been lost, culminating in Acre, the last crusader outpost, in 1281. The Christian Outremer had lasted for little more than a century and a half. Yet it had great consequences for the nature of Christian civilization back home.

THE CRUSADES AND EUROPE

First, there were other crusades than those to the Middle East. One had already been going on since the days of Charlemagne – the reconquest of Spain from the Muslims there. This was a slow process, but by the thirteenth century the Christian kingdoms of Castille and Aragon had been established in the north and east of the Iberian peninsula. And, as we shall see, other crusades were fought within Christian Europe itself, against heretical groups such as the Cathars and the Hussites.

Equally striking was the rise of the ideal of chivalry, one of the stranger offshoots of Christian religious sentiment. Mail-clad knights were still the most powerful troops on the battlefield, and already in the eleventh century churchmen were urging knights to use their weapons in the service of God. This idea, essentially a measure invented to try to curb what were often

Consider, I pray, and reflect how in our time God has transferred the west to the east. We who were once Occidentals have been turned into Orientals. The person who was a Roman or a Frank is now a Galilean or Palestinian, and the person who lived in Rheims or Chartres now inhabits Tyre or Antioch. We have already forgotten the places where we were born. They have already become unfamiliar to many of us, or at least are not mentioned. Some already have homes and servants here that they have inherited. Some have married not just women of their own people, but Syrians, Armenians, or even Saracens who have received the grace of baptism... Different languages are now made common, and are known to both races, while the faith unites those whose ancestors were strangers.

Fulcher of Chartres on the Crusader states, *Chronicle*, c. 1106

Godfrey of Bouillon leaves for the First Crusade, in an illustration by the fifteenth-century Flemish artist William Vrelant.

violent and lawless men, developed into quite an elaborate system. Just as the feudal system relied on personal vows of loyalty, expressed in rituals and ceremonies, so too the knights started swearing oaths to God and the church at initiation ceremonies. These involved ritual bathing, the wearing of white robes, nocturnal vigils and so on. The ideal arose of chivalry (from the French 'chevalier' or knight): a powerful warrior who served God, fighting evil and protecting the weak. Chivalric romances appeared, applying this ideal to great heroes of the past – most notably King Arthur (and his 'knights of the round table') in Britain and Charlemagne (and his 'paladins') in France. The insistence of the early Christians such as Tertullian that Christian faith and military service were incompatible had been completely overturned.

But it was the crusades that really created the ideal of chivalry. When the crusades were preached, the papacy promised that those who answered the call would receive special privileges: they were let off all penances (since going on crusade was a sort of penance in itself). Thus, crusading was not simply a military activity but a spiritual one as well. But it was a temporary one, and when the crusader states were established, they needed permanent troops to protect them against the Muslims. The chivalric orders of knighthood were duly founded. The three most important of these were the Hospitallers of St John, the Teutonic Knights and the Knights Templar.

The Hospitallers were a monastic order recognized by the pope in 1113 and, as the name suggests, they did run hospitals and hospices for pilgrims to the Holy Land. However, they also acted as guards for pilgrims and for the Holy Places. In 1206 their order was restructured and divided between those who were actually monks and those who were lay knights. They were ruled by a Grand Master. After the fall of Acre in 1291, they retreated to Cyprus and Rhodes, and finally were given Malta in 1530. Here they prospered, hence the alternative name of the Order of Malta. However, they also possessed houses and estates throughout Europe, where people were initiated into the order,

or where the more contemplative knights spent their days in retreat, like monks.

The Teutonic Knights originated during the siege of Acre in 1190, just before the end of the Christian Outremer, in order to run a hospital there to care for German crusaders. They were allowed to stay after the Muslims conquered the city and in 1198 were organized into a military-monastic order along the lines of the Knights Hospitaller. But as their name suggests, the Teutonic Knights were more involved in German affairs, especially in Prussia. In the thirteenth century they were engaged in fighting pagan groups who still existed here. They were successful and conquered a significant area, which they administered themselves as a politically independent country. However, they did not hold it for long: a series of revolts meant that by the end of the fifteenth century the Teutonic Knights were subject to Poland. They held cities that were important to trade in the area, however, and in the fourteenth and fifteenth centuries were involved in the Hanseatic League, a trading confederation around the southern Baltic coast.

By far the most famous of the three great orders were the Knights Templar. They were founded at the same time as the Knights Hospitaller, and for the same reason – to protect pilgrims to Jerusalem. They were initially founded as a band of poor warriors who were given shelter in the remains of the Temple at Jerusalem and accepted alms from pilgrims in exchange for protection. In 1128 they were recognized as a Benedictine monastic order and they even adopted the white habit of the Cistercians, adding to it a large red cross. Like the Hospitallers, the order was divided into fighting knights and non-fighting monks, the 'chaplains', and also 'farmers' who looked after their material needs. The Templars became enormously popular, helped by the preaching of Bernard of Clairvaux, who particularly liked them. The papacy protected them from all financial dues, and they became extremely rich. Their power was demonstrated in the mighty castles they built in the Holy Land, but like the Hospitallers they also possessed properties throughout Europe. They built temples in Paris and London, modelled after those of the Middle East, and their power increased as they diverted resources into money-lending.

Both ecclesiastical and temporal rulers were becoming alarmed at the Templars' power. In 1307 King Philip IV 'the Fair' of France – with the connivance of Pope Clement V – had all Templars in his domains arrested. The charge was heresy and devil-worship, because of the rumours of what the Templars got up to in their initiation ceremonies – which were, of course, secret. Under torture or threat of torture, many Templars, even the Grand Master himself, Jacques de Molay, confessed. The power of the Templars in France was broken, and other European monarchs followed Philip's lead. In 1314 Jacques de Molay was burned at the stake, and the Knights Templar ceased to exist, at least officially. In later years, romantic tales grew up around the Templars. They had known the secret of the Holy Grail; the

[The Knights Templar] have now grown so great that in this order today there are about 300 knights who wear the white cloaks, as well as innumerable brethren. They are said to have great possessions here and abroad, so that there is now no province in Christendom which has not given to these brethren part of its produce. It is said today that their wealth is as great as the treasures of kings…

William of Tyre, *History of deeds done beyond the sea*, c. 1170 order still existed in hiding, complete with secret Grand Masters; their secrets were passed on to the Freemasons; and so on. Such has been the allure of the Knights Templar over the centuries that it can be hard to separate fact from fiction; but, as far as history is concerned, their story ended in 1314.

The fate of the Templars was not unlike that of some other groups in medieval Europe. Whether the Templars really were heretics or not is still hotly debated today; but others existed about whom there is much less doubt. Like the Byzantines and the Muslims, heretics formed another class of people who did not fit into the medieval ideal of society and religion.

HERESY AND ORTHODOXY

The question of orthodoxy and heresy in the Middle Ages is still a heated and divisive one, especially given the contrast with our own, more tolerant times. The important thing to remember is that the medievals were convinced that their view of the world, including the teaching of the church, was 'true'. That is, it accurately described the way things really were, and could be relied upon because it was supported by both revelation and reason. Those who disagreed were mistaken about the facts. Worse, they were endangering themselves and others, because salvation depended upon believing the correct things: after all, only Christ saved, and those who did not believe the right things about Christ, about his Father who sent him, and about the church which was his body on earth, did not know the true Christ and could not be saved. So if the heretics spread their erroneous ideas, they would drag others down with them. The modern notion that people have a 'right' to believe what they like therefore had no place in the Middle Ages – you might as well have suggested that people had a 'right' to run amok with a hatchet. Heresy, to the medieval mind, was even more dangerous than that, because it threatened the welfare of the soul itself.

THE WALDENSIANS

There were a number of movements in the Middle Ages which the church considered heretical. One group were known as the Waldensians, from their founder, Peter Waldo, a rich merchant's son from Lyons who felt guilty about his wealth, especially since it had been amassed at others' expense. At the advice of his priest, he unburdened his conscience by repaying the interest he had demanded from his debtors, giving a sum to his wife to maintain her and leaving the rest to the poor. With a group of friends, called the Poor Men of Lyons, he began to preach the virtues of poverty.

Waldo thus seems to have been a lot like St Francis of Assisi, but he met with less success. In 1179, as Francis would four decades later, he asked permission for his group to be recognized officially as a preaching order – but he was refused. The Waldensians continued to preach anyway,

St George slays the dragon and rescues the princess in this fresco by the Italian painter Altichiero (c. 1330–c. 1390), in the church of San Zeno Maggiore, Verona. The semi-legendary George was held to embody the knightly virtues of chivalry.

since they were convinced that they were biblically commanded to do so, and that preaching was essential to helping people to salvation. This was a serious breach of church law. Any preacher had to be officially permitted to do so by the church, because otherwise people might be preaching anything they liked, including heresy. Waldo and his followers were therefore excommunicated in 1180.

This excommunication was for disobeying the church, not for holding heretical views. But the Waldensians developed new ideas which the church did regard as heretical. They insisted that preaching was the *primary* means of salvation, and that it was more important than the sacraments. Preaching, moreover, could be done by anyone, whether they were priests or not – even women – and they denied that there was any special difference between priest and laity anyway. As the movement progressed, they continued to become more radical, rejecting belief in purgatory and in transubstantiation.

The Waldensian movement spread throughout Europe, and drew upon itself an accordingly harsh clampdown from Rome. The Fourth Lateran Council declared their views heretical in 1215, and in the 1230s the church tried a sort of carrot and stick approach to them. The carrot was the creation of a new order, the Poor Catholics, which was intended to take the best ideas of the Waldensians but remain orthodox, and it had some success in winning them back; by this time there were also the Franciscans who might appeal to them. The stick was the Inquisition, which sought out the leaders of the Waldensians; many were tortured to obtain evidence and executed. The cruel suppression eradicated the Waldensians from their native southern France, but the movement spread into the Alps and Germany and survived there until the Reformation and beyond. Independent Waldensians still exist today in South America.

Although the Waldensians were the clearest group of this nature, there were others who were regarded in similar ways. For example, the early fourteenth century saw a major dispute within the Franciscan order over the role of poverty in the order's life, which crystallized into a row over whether Christ and his disciples had been completely poor, and if so in what way. One group, the Fraticelli, declared that Christ had owned nothing whatsoever, and they split with the rest of the Franciscans, roaming northern Italy trying to bring down the institution of private property altogether. Like the Waldensians, the Fraticelli were condemned. Many were burned.

THE CATHARS

As the Waldensians were being persecuted, a more serious threat to Catholic orthodoxy was flourishing in southern Europe. The Cathar movement was something of a mixed bag, containing a number of different elements, but it was essentially a development of Bogomilism, the Gnostic heresy in eastern Europe that we saw in chapter 5. The basic ideas of the Bogomils were brought to France in the eighth century by missionaries from eastern Europe, and they flourished there. Later, Bogomilism became deeply entrenched in the kingdom of Aragon, in north-east Spain; but on the other side of the Pyrenees it had developed into Catharism. It is likely that both kinds were ultimately inspired by the Gnosticism that we saw in chapter 2.

The word 'Cathar' came from the Greek word meaning 'pure', and the pursuit of purity was central to the Cathar faith. From the Bogomils, they inherited a belief in two great, opposed principles of good and evil. Some Cathars maintained that these two principles were equal and opposite, and these were known as the Albigenses. Some Cathars, however, believed that the good principle was more powerful: they were thus doctrinally closer to orthodox Catholicism. Whilst this mitigated Catharism spread through northern Italy, however, the heartlands of Catharism, in south-west France, were staunchly dualist.

We excommunicate and anathematize every heresy that appears against the holy, orthodox, and Catholic faith which we have explained. We condemn all heretics, whatever names they may go by, for while they have different faces, they are still bound to each other by their tails, because vanity is common to them all.

The Fourth Lateran Council, 1215

The Inquisition

Early European legal systems recognized two main kinds of legal procedure, accusatorial and inquisitorial. Accusatorial procedure, until the thirteenth century the more widely used, required that a party claiming injury or damage had to accuse the person responsible before a court and prosecute his own case. Accusatorial procedure had also been extensively used in the Roman republic. Inquisitorial procedure, in which a single magistrate supervised an entire case, from investigation to judgment and sentencing, developed under the Roman empire, was described in the books of Roman law and re-entered European legal practice in the twelfth and thirteenth centuries.

Inquisitorial procedure had survived the end of the Roman empire, but in very attenuated form. Under Charlemagne (AD 768–814), royal inspectors, *missi dominici*, were sent out to hold inquests about matters of governance throughout the empire. Bishops too, having responsibility for the souls in their dioceses, were empowered to conduct investigations in matters of ecclesiastical discipline. Such inquisition was later justified by God's response to the outcry against Sodom and Gomorrah in Genesis 18:21 and the parable of the rich man who seeks an accounting from his steward in the Gospel of Luke 16:1–7. Bishops could also empanel groups of local Christians as synodal witnesses, responsible for denouncing the offences of their fellow parishoners. This procedure was justified by the exegesis of the Gospel of Matthew 18:15–17, which required fraternal admonition. Neither the early form of inquisitorial procedure nor synodal denunciation was particularly prominent until the late eleventh century.

The great movement of ecclesiastical reform that began in the eleventh century not only distinguished clergy from laity much more categorically, but it also imposed great demands on prelates regarding the discipline of the clergy. Since clergy could now only be disciplined by their clerical superiors, Pope Innocent III (reigned 1198–1216) issued a letter in 1199 stating that there were three kinds of legal procedure available for trying clergy in ecclesiastical courts: accusation,

Coloured French wood engraving of the Inquisition by René de Moraine.

denunciation and inquisition. The problem of clerical discipline thus reintroduced inquisitorial procedure into canon law, originally in the courts of bishops. During the following decades the procedure was also adapted by secular courts.

In canon 8 of the Fourth Lateran Council held in 1215, Innocent III identified inquisitorial procedure as the standard procedure for use in ecclesiastical courts. Now, any offence that fell within ecclesiastical jurisdiction could be tried by inquisitorial procedure.

Besides criminous clergy, another growing concern of churchmen during this period was the apparent spread of heterodox belief and practices among Latin Christians, which was termed heresy. The laws of early Christian Roman emperors had violently condemned heresy, and as these were rediscovered in the course of the twelfth century, they seemed to reinforce theological concerns. Initially, churchmen attempted a pastoral approach to heterodoxy, preaching and teaching orthodox belief, using only excommunication, the occasional confiscation of property and denial of Christian burial to those who remained unrepentant.

In 1199, however, Innocent III issued the letter *Vergentis in senium*, which incorporated earlier legislation against heretics, but it also identified heresy with the crime of treason in Roman law, that is, as treason against God and therefore a capital crime. In a letter of 1207 Innocent stated that ecclesiastically convicted heretics should be turned over to secular courts for punishment, since churchmen were prohibited from shedding blood. In the course of the thirteenth century a number of secular rulers also issued legal codes imposing the death penalty for convicted unrepentant or relapsed heretics.

During the pontificate of Gregory IX (1227–42) the pope began to appoint members of the two new mendicant (begging) orders, the Dominicans and Franciscans, as papal judges-delegate or sub-delegate specifically to serve as *inquisitores hereticae pravitatis*, 'inquisitors of heretical depravity'. Originally such authority expired with the death of the pope who had issued it, but a papal letter issued by Clement IV in 1267 made the commissions permanent, so that in effect one could become a career inquisitor. The same letter dealt with inquisitors' powers over Jews who had converted to Christianity and later reverted to Judaism, as well as over unconverted Jews who had assisted them. In 1252 another papal letter had permitted the use of torture in cases of heresy investigations.

But there was no 'institutional inquisition' before the later fifteenth century. Inquisitors worked in specific areas, some vigorously, others not. Often inquisitors had to work closely with the local bishop and secular authorities, who might as often hinder as assist them. Local resistance, too, might delay their work or postpone it altogether. Although a common investigative and trial procedure unique to inquisitions of heretical depravity slowly grew up, along with a literature of manuals of inquisitorial procedure, not all inquisitors were equally familiar with these. Indeed, the absence of an institutional infrastructure generally served to weaken the status of inquisitors.

The first institutional inquisition was the tribunal formed in the kingdoms of Castile and Aragon under Ferdinand and Isabella with the permission of Pope Sixtus IV in 1478. The purpose of the tribunal, which in 1483 became a Council of State ('The Council of the Supreme and General Inquisition'), was primarily to investigate Jewish converts to Christianity, *converses*, who were suspected of having either reverted to Judaism or remained crypto-Jews all along, of whom there were large numbers in Spain since the pogroms of 1391. In the sixteenth century the Inquisition also dealt with Protestants and increasingly with clerical deviance, and by 1550 there were over twenty inquisitorial tribunals in Spain and the Spanish dependencies, including the Americas. By 1540 there was also a similar Inquisition in Portugal, and in 1561 the Portuguese established an Inquisition at Goa, in India.

In 1542 Pope Paul III (reigned 1534–49) established an Inquisition in Rome along similar lines, which became the *Congregation of the Holy Roman and Universal Inquisition* or *Holy Office* in 1588. It was renamed the *Congregation of the Holy Office* in 1908 and renamed again in 1965 by Pope Paul VI (reigned 1963–78) as the *Sacred Congregation for the Doctrine of the Faith*.

Inquisitorial tribunals were slowly abolished by secularizing states in the eighteenth and nineteenth centuries: Naples in 1746, Venice in 1798, Portugal in 1821 and finally Spain in 1834.

EDWARD PETERS

The Cathars were clearly flourishing in France by the eleventh century, since King Robert 'the Pious' ordered thirteen of them to be burned alive in 1022. But the movement reached its peak in the early thirteenth century. By this stage, much of south-west France was completely Cathar: they were practically an independent civilization flourishing in this region. The area was not subject to the kings of France, but was an independent region, known as Occitania (or simply Oc). The people there spoke Occitan, a language which, like French, had developed from Latin and which is still spoken by some in the area.

The Cathars' greatest stronghold was Montsegur, a dramatic rocky outcrop in the foothills of the Pyrenees. Here, in 1204, two Cathars named Raymond de Mirepoix and Raymond Blasco sought and gained permission to rebuild an old fortress. They were *parfaits* or 'perfect people', members of the inner circle of the Cathar faith. Most Cathars were *croyants* or believers, who were less 'in the know' than the *parfaits*; but they all shared the same devotion to personal purity. Like the Gnostics before them, the Cathars believed that salvation consisted of removing one's attachment to the material world, which is intrinsically evil. Poverty was praised and sex regarded as intrinsically evil. Any children which the Cathars did manage to produce were considered demonic until they could be sufficiently purified in morals and doctrine to join the ranks of the *croyants*. Death, meanwhile, was not feared – indeed it was welcomed as the passage of the soul from the material world to the spiritual. Some extreme Cathars starved themselves to death and were considered great heroes for doing so.

The Cathars had also developed something similar to an ecclesiastical system. They did not believe in priests, but the *parfaits* acted as priests to all intents and purposes, preaching to the *croyants* and holding services. Strikingly, women as well as men could be *parfaits*, although they rarely preached. There were also bishops within the *parfait* circle, but these were all men.

Do you promise that from now on you will eat neither meat nor eggs, nor cheese, nor fat, and that you live only from water and wood, that you will not lie, that you will not swear, that you will not kill, that you will not abandon your body to any kind of luxury, that you will never go by yourself when you can have a companion, that you will never sleep without trousers and shirt, and that you will never abandon your faith for fear of water, fire or any other way of dying?

The question asked of a postulant when being received into the Cathar community, from the Lyon Ritual

The Cathar stronghold of Queribus.

The whole system was not so much a Catholic heresy as an entire alternative church, and the Catholic Church sought to destroy it with every means in its power. Innocent III launched an unsuccessful crusade against it in 1209, but it was not until 1242 that the Cathars' power was broken. A revolt against the French led to a brutal clampdown, and for ten months Montsegur itself was besieged before finally surrendering. Under the terms of the truce, any Cathars who recanted their heresy would be forgiven, but most did not, and many asked specifically to be put to death. Over 200 were burned alive on the field below Montsegur and the Cathar fortress was completely destroyed.

THE DECLINE OF THE MIDDLE AGES

The medieval world reached its apogee in the thirteenth century. In the fourteenth, things began – very gradually – to crumble.

This was partly caused by new upheavals in medieval society. One of the most devastating was the plague known as the Black Death, which swept through Europe in the middle of the fourteenth century and killed around a third of the population. Priests, who ministered to the sick, fared even more badly, with one out of two succumbing. Little wonder that some forms of Christianity in this period took on a more morbid character: this was the age of the Flagellants, for example, who stumbled from town to town, wearing rags, whipping and beating themselves. Another effect was a massive labour shortage throughout Europe. The feudal system, based upon local workforces on local land, buckled under the strain. The drive towards a currency-based economy, which had been fostered by the crusades and the new trade routes east that they opened up, accelerated. A new class of merchants and associated trades, based around the movement of goods and money, appeared. It was the beginning of the rise of the middle classes, whose dominance in society would herald the end of medieval society by the fifteenth century.

At the same time, there was more nationalistic sentiment in Europe. People increasingly regarded themselves as 'English', 'French', 'Italian' and so on. The notion of different states, each with their own monarchs who dealt with each other as approximate equals, had now replaced the old ideal of empire, with different local lords all answering to a single emperor. The Holy Roman empire still existed, but it was now only one country among others, albeit an especially powerful one, a conglomerate of smaller states. The different languages of Europe were quickly emerging; for, while scholars still communicated in Latin, ordinary people spoke in the vernacular, now recognizable as early forms of French, English, German and the rest.

THE AVIGNON CAPTIVITY AND THE GREAT SCHISM

In these changing times, the papacy struggled to keep up, but with disastrous consequences. A succession of popes found themselves at the mercy of European politics and nationalism or even pandering to it. Thus the century began with Boniface VIII, who reigned from 1294 to 1303 and spent most of his time arguing with King Philip 'the Fair' of France, the same king who had attacked the Templars when they threatened his authority. The growing power of France saw the church itself split between pro-French and anti-French factions, and in 1305 the former saw to it that the archbishop of Bordeaux was elected Pope Clement V. Clement had no desire to go to Rome, a hotbed of anti-French sentiment, and instead he made the monumental decision to move the papacy to Avignon. Thus began the 'Avignon captivity' of the papacy, which lasted for most of the century. In 1348, under Pope Clement VI, the papacy would actually purchase Avignon: a splendid palace was built there, employing some five hundred people, draining the papal coffers. Throughout this period, the papacy enjoyed very close links with France and Frenchmen dominated the church. The curia, the government of the church, became more developed and efficient: vast sums flowed in and out of Avignon, with the various departments becoming far more professional. If there was a time when the church became a business, the first true international corporation, it was during the Avignon captivity.

In 1367 Pope Urban V, hoping to reform the church and the papacy, returned to Rome, but he failed to regain control over the city and went back to France after three years. His successor, Gregory XI, tried again in 1377 and successfully remained there until his death in 1378. But the new pope, Urban VI, was too authoritarian for many cardinals: they therefore elected a rival, Clement VII. Such things had happened before, of course, but this time Clement had a ready-made way of avoiding being overthrown: he went to Avignon. Now there were two popes, one in Rome and one in Avignon. The situation is known as the Great Schism (not to be confused with the earlier breach between Rome and Constantinople, which is sometimes given the same name).

The church was horribly split, along national lines. The French and Spanish supported the Avignon pope, while most other people supported the Roman one, and this continued even after Urban and Clement died, with successors being elected in both locations.

The whole situation was an international disgrace and a desperate embarrassment to the church. In 1409, a group of cardinals met at Pisa to address the problem. Neither pope would back down: they therefore declared both deposed and elected a new one to replace them both, Alexander V. The result was predictable. Neither pope accepted deposition, so now there were three popes. Only at the Council of Constance, which met in 1414 and lasted for several years, was the scandal finally laid to rest. At this much larger council, John XXIII (Alexander's successor) and Gregory XII (in Rome) were persuaded to resign, while

The papal palace in Avignon.

Benedict XIII (in Avignon) was deposed and sent back to Spain, where he spent the rest of his life still convinced he was pope. A brand new pope, accepted by everyone, ascended the throne of St Peter as Martin V. The Great Schism was resolved – although a new problem had been created for the future. A council had deposed three popes. Did that mean that councils were superior to popes?

CRITICS AND REFORMERS
As all this suggests, not all was well within the fourteenth-century church. There was considerable criticism of the state of the priesthood and the papacy – and even these institutions themselves – from a number of directions. On the one hand there were groups such as the Waldensians and the Fraticelli, representing an alternative lifestyle; but on the other there were more sophisticated criticisms. Geoffrey Chaucer (c. 1345–1400), the great English poet, offered a satirical look at the contemporary church and society, painting the church as a mixture of genuinely pious clerics and wicked hypocrites or worldly monks. From a quite different point of view, mystic theologians such as Meister Eckhart and his pupil, John Tauler, wrote about an experience of God that could be attained without reference to the worldly church.

A Carthusian named Geert Groote extolled the virtues of an austere lifestyle and bitterly denounced clerical abuses, to such a degree that he lost his licence to preach. Groote died of the plague in 1384, but not before he had founded a community at Deventer in Holland. Here, his followers lived a monastic lifestyle, but without taking any vows, so that they could come and go as they wished. The movement became known as *Devotio Moderna* – the 'Modern Devotion' – and Groote's successor, Florens Radewijns, set up more communities along the same lines, the most famous at Windesheim. They also set up schools, which would educate a number of leading figures of the fifteenth century, including the spiritual writer Thomas à Kempis and the humanist Desiderius Erasmus.

All of these people and movements represented criticism of abuses within the church. But John Wycliffe, who went further and criticized much of the ecclesiastical institution itself, caused an even bigger stir. A priest and lecturer at Oxford University, Wycliffe became prominent in the 1370s. In addition to denouncing all clerical abuses in the church, he insisted that no one in the church had any authority apart from God's grace. If they sinned, they were out of grace with God and lost that authority. Pope Gregory XI condemned these views in 1377, but the outbreak of the Great Schism within a couple of years indicated to many that perhaps Wycliffe had had a point after all.

As the years passed, Wycliffe became more and more radical. First he declared that the source of all Christian doctrine is the Bible, and that it could be read and understood by anyone without the need for the church's interpretation. Then, in 1379, he denied that the bread and wine actually become Christ's body and blood in the Eucharist. As we have seen, Wycliffe was not the first to say this, but his view that the Bible and the church might be at odds was a remarkable new idea that ran quite contrary to the accepted understanding ever since the days of Irenaeus and Tertullian. Under pressure from a papal bull his university, which until then had protected him, cast him out. Remarkably, Wycliffe escaped any further persecution and lived quietly until his death in 1384. His ideas inspired a group in England known as the Lollards – a term of abuse meaning 'mumblers' – who were fiercely persecuted by the church authorities. Among their radical activities was the attempt to translate the Bible into vernacular English, an endeavour which, according to tradition, Wycliffe himself began. In widespread risings in England during the Peasants' Revolt of 1381 the sermons of wandering Lollard preachers fired up already discontented labourers, whose relations with the official church were evident when one mob in London beheaded Sudbury, the archbishop of Canterbury, while other rebels in East Anglia were ruthlessly crushed at the orders of the bishop of Norwich.

On the continent, Wycliffe's ideas were associated with Jan Hus, a priest at the University of Prague in the early fifteenth century. Here, he read the works of Wycliffe and found himself in full agreement: he accordingly began spreading them from the pulpit of his Bethlehem Chapel, a large church decorated with pictures of the pope – in all his finery – next to images of the poverty-stricken Christ. The message was quite clear.

All three popes re-affirmed the condemnation of Wycliffe and condemned Hus into the bargain too. Eventually Hus was summoned to the Council of Constance, which, after deposing the popes, tried him for heresy and burned him to death in 1416. Wycliffe, who had inspired him, was condemned once again; in 1428 his remains would be dug up and burned. But the reform movement did not

We ask God then of his supreme goodness to reform our church, as being entirely out of joint, to the perfectness of its first beginning.

The Lollard conclusions, 1394

John Wycliffe, in an eighteenth-century engraving.

Jan Hus, in a woodcut printed in Nuremberg c. 1530–40. The burning goose and the triumphant swan represent Hus (whose name means 'goose') and Martin Luther.

die there. Back in Bohemia, Hus was a national hero. His followers, the Hussites, though outlawed, fought back. They were lucky enough to have a brilliant general in the person of Jan Zizka, a one-eyed former mercenary who formed an army known as the Taborites, because they were based at Tabor. Most of them were peasants, but Jan Zizka had his forces train with the hoes and rakes they were used to wielding, rather than try to find real weapons, which they could not afford anyway. He recognized that such implements could be deadly when used with skill, and he also used the farm carts and wagons that his troops usually drove almost as mobile fortresses. The Hussites would park their carts in a circle, like US frontiersmen, and fight from behind them. Zizka developed other tricks too – famously putting all the horses' shoes

on backwards, so that the enemy could not track them – and he was the first military commander to use artillery in field battles, rather than simply to attack fortresses. Throughout the 1420s, the Holy Roman emperor, Sigismund, launched a series of crusades against the Hussites, all of which were repelled by Zizka and his ragtag forces. Zizka always commanded his troops in person, even though in 1421 he lost his other eye and was therefore completely blind. Zizka died in 1424, but the Hussites continued to be a fearsome military force: in 1437, one opposing army turned tail and fled simply at the sound of their battle song.

Military actions against the Hussites continued throughout the fifteenth century, and they inevitably dwindled, just like the Waldensians before them. Indeed, they resembled the Waldensians in some ways, with many believing that absolute poverty was required for all Christians. But they continued to survive. One group went largely underground, becoming known as the Moravians, from their place of origin. In centuries to come, they would re-emerge as an important church of the Reformation. For although the Lollards and the Hussites had failed to reform the church, they were only the beginning. New and louder voices would arise a century later, and this time they would not be silenced.

CHAPTER 8

RUSSIA: THE HEIR OF BYZANTIUM

While western Christendom was reaching its apogee in the Middle Ages, another great Christian civilization was developing to the east. The heir of Byzantium, Russia, would be the most powerful guardian of orthodoxy for centuries.

THE CONVERSION OF THE RUSSIANS

Until early medieval times, the Slavic peoples of what is now Russia lived in small, isolated communities, with no larger political structure. This changed in the ninth century with the movement of Scandinavian peoples whom the Slavs called Varyags – essentially the same people as the Vikings who were attacking western Europe at this time, except that these were moving east instead of west. The Varyags conquered much of the vast Russian plain and established their main city at Kiev, in what is now Ukraine. The dominance of this city means that the nation – such as it was – is generally referred to at this time as Kievan Rus. The Varyags and the Slavs alike were all pagans, although they did know something of Christianity, partly from the Christian missions to Scandinavia and partly from contact with Crimean Goths.

These people became officially Christian in the tenth century. As usual, it was a gradual process, and one which accompanied the equally gradual fusing of Varyag and Slavic ethnicity and culture into a single 'Russian' people. A number of churches apparently existed in Kiev by the start of the century. Grand Princess Olga was baptized in AD 954 and visited Constantinople three years later. She also sent an embassy to Otto I in the west, requesting a bishop and priests. But her son Svyatoslav, a powerful warlord who conquered large areas and expanded the power of Kiev throughout the area, oversaw something of a pagan resurgence: in his eyes Christianity was effeminate and unworthy of a warrior king like himself.

VLADIMIR AND THE LINKS TO BYZANTIUM

It was Prince Vladimir, the illegitimate son of Svyatoslav and a concubine, who officially established Christianity in Kiev. Since Vladimir was illegitimate, he was sent to govern Novgorod, far to the north; but this worked in his favour, since the legitimate sons subsequently warred with each other. Vladimir marched south, took

Vladimir's forces attack the heathens in this seventeenth-century Russian illustration.

advantage of the civil war to capture Kiev and installed himself as prince of all the Russians. New roads were built to link the remote towns, as well as forts, and Vladimir tried to modernize the flimsy administrative system of the area. Much of his aim was to fortify the area against raids from mounted barbarians from the east, known as the Petchenegs. Vladimir was successful, and he held legendarily sumptuous feasts to celebrate his victories over them.

Vladimir tried to endorse the pagan religion of the Russians as a state cult, but it seems many Slavs resisted this, preferring traditional Slavic religion. So, pragmatically, he changed policy, instead adopting Christianity as the official religion. According to the later story, he sent emissaries to a number of different countries and chose the religion of the Byzantines on the grounds that it was the most beautiful. It seems, though, that Vladimir also had political reasons for adopting Byzantine Christianity. He was keen to pursue closer relations with Byzantium and even hoped to marry a member of the Byzantine royal family, so conversion to their form of Christianity was an obvious step.

Vladimir was baptized in around AD 988. His nobles – the *boyars* – were baptized too, as were the people of Kiev and the surrounding area. Paganism was officially outlawed and churches were built throughout Vladimir's territories. Naturally, the Christianization of the Russians took a long time. Even a century after Vladimir's conversion the northern cities of Kievan Rus, such as Novgorod, were still largely pagan, and certainly most people in the countryside were. The old festivals in honour of the pagan gods continued to be celebrated. Even two centuries after Vladimir's baptism many families still maintained idols in their homes. Polygamy, a feature of Russian paganism (Vladimir had had five wives, as well as lots of concubines) persisted well into the eleventh century. Many missionaries, especially Bulgarian ones, continued to penetrate the remoter areas of Russia. They had a lot of work to do.

CHRISTIANITY BECOMES ESTABLISHED
Vladimir's son, Yaroslav 'the Wise', did far more to establish Christianity than his father had. He founded the cathedral of St Sophia

Then we went to Greece, and the Greeks took us to the buildings where they worship their God, and we did not know whether we were in heaven or on earth. For on earth there is no such splendour or beauty, and we are at a loss how to describe it. We only know that God dwells there among men, and their service is fairer than the ceremonies of other nations. For we cannot forget that beauty.

The report of Vladimir's envoys, according to *The primary chronicle*

The domes of the St Sophia Monastery at Kiev.

Genghis Khan, in an illustration from a fourteenth-century edition of the *Universal history* by the Persian writer Rashid al-Din Tabib (1247–1318).

That same year, foreigners called Tatars came in countless numbers, like locusts into the land of Riazin...

The Novgorod chronicle, 1238

And in the city they hacked men, women, and children to pieces with their swords. And others were drowned in the river. The priests were all hacked, to the last man, and the whole city was set afire. And all of the riches of Riazin... were taken. The churches of God were plundered and much blood was spilled in the holy altars. And in the whole city not a single person was left alive. All perished, all drank from the same cup of death. Not a single person was left to groan or cry, not fathers or mothers with their children, nor brothers, nor relatives, for all were lying dead. And all this happened to us for our sins.

The Mongols' attack on Riazin in 1237, *The tale of the destruction of Riazin*

in Kiev, where he decreed that the Russian church would be led not simply by an archbishop but by a metropolitan. The first was Theopempt, a Byzantine – and Kievan metropolitans continued to be sent from Constantinople for some time – but the language of the liturgy was Slavic right from the start, not Greek. Thus, the Russian church was conceived as autocephalous – self-running – and as closely linked to Russian national identity.

As in the Byzantine empire, monasticism was a major element of Russian Christianity. We shall see this in more detail later in this chapter, but already in the eleventh century there were major monastic foundations, pre-eminently the famous Kiev-Pechersk Lavra or 'cave monastery' of Kiev, founded by Anthony of the Caves, who spent many years at Mount Athos. Indeed, Russian Christianity inevitably owed a huge debt to Byzantium. The princes of Kiev imported Byzantine architects to build churches and cathedrals; and great stone churches, basilicas and even secular buildings such as palaces began to appear in a region which had previously built things out of wood. Domes and pillars proliferated, as did stone carvings, frescoes and mosaics. The cathedral of St Sophia in Kiev was a particular masterpiece, full of beautiful mosaics and frescoes. The Russians benefited from the fact that other Slavic peoples, such as the Bulgarians, had been converted first. This meant there was already a Slavic alphabet in which to write Russian Bibles, and upon his conversion Vladimir had opened a school to train Russian priests. Literacy did not spread throughout the general population, but the nobles could soon all read, and Slavic translations of Byzantine literature became popular.

In the thirteenth century this gradual improvement in literacy, government and general civilization took a massive knock with the invasions of the Mongols. As we saw in Chapter 4, the Mongols were aggressively expanding south into China, but they spread even more quickly west. By 1222 the Mongols had reached the Russians and defeated them. Genghis

Khan died five years later and divided his vast empire among his sons, under the lordship of Ogodai Khan, who continued the conquest of Russia. Huge numbers of towns were destroyed and vast swathes of the countryside ruined: cities were sacked and monasteries wrecked. Streams of refugees fled the southern cities, including Kiev, for the northern ones of Novgorod and Pskov, which were sufficiently distant to escape the onslaught. By 1243 the conquest was complete. Batu Khan, grandson of Genghis Khan, summoned the Russian princes to his capital, Saray, on the lower reaches of the Volga, and informed them that they could continue to rule their own cities, but from now on they would be paying tribute to a Mongolian overlord.

THE THIRD ROME

THE CHURCH UNDER THE TATARS
The invasions of the Mongols – also known in this part of the world as the Tatars – had been devastating, but their rule was relatively benign and strengthened the church enormously. The Mongols became Muslims in 1313, but they were happy to allow subject peoples freedom of worship. Moreover, local rulers retained the right to govern their people – although tribute had to be sent south-east to the city of Saray, the capital of 'the Empire of the Golden Horde', as the Tatars' empire was known. The dominance of Kiev in the pre-Tatar period was over. In effect, the process of centralization had been reversed, so that Russia was once again a loose federation of city states, in varying degrees of competition with each other – although now they were all more or less directly under the overall rule of the Golden Horde. In the absence of strong government, this meant that the church was the only institution from pre-Tatar days that persisted and was universally respected, by people and conquerors alike. As early as 1263 there was a bishop of Saray itself.

Indeed, the church was getting richer and more powerful throughout this whole

Christianizing the Russians

Christianization of the Russian area coincided with the emergence of a loose confederation of principalities, known as Rus, ruled by princes claiming descent from a common ancestor, Riurik. Rus occupied the territory of present-day Belarus and fragments of Ukraine and Russia bounded on the north and east by the Volga River.

Kiev, as the site of the legendary baptism of Rus under Prince Vladimir in AD 988, emerged as the political centre. The extent of christianization of the population generally was proportional to proximity to the chief city and degree of urbanization; christianization was greater the closer people dwelt to cities and the closer to Kiev these cites were located. Moreover the south half of Rus was christianized more thoroughly and sooner than the north half because there had been scattered Christian believers and churches in that region a full century before Vladimir.

While Prince Vladimir played the historic role of baptizer of the Russians, his son Yaroslav 'the Wise' was their christianizer. During his reign in the mid-1000s construction of cathedrals occurred in major cities: Tmutorokan's cathedral of the Mother of God (1022),

Transfiguration in Chernigov (1035) and Holy Wisdom in Novgorod (1045), culminating in Holy Wisdom of Kiev, echoing the name of the chief cathedral of eastern Christianity, Hagia Sophia of Constantinople, and signifying Rus's allegiance to Greek Christianity. Church administration was organized in at least five dioceses with bishops for supervision of priests and parishes. In Kiev the metropolitan emerged as chief bishop.

Yaroslav's brothers ruled several of the principalities of Rus. Where the population was largely Slavic, as in Pskov under Sudislav, Polotsk under Iziaslav and Chernigov under Mstislav, the church prevailed rather easily in the eleventh century, while other brothers and their successors who ruled non-slavic, mainly Finnic areas, like Murom and Rostov in the east and north, confronted resistance to Christianity.

Monasteries promoted the Christian presence. The premier cloister, Kiev's cave monastery, developed during Yaroslav's reign. Monks dispersed from this site to evangelize and plant monastic centres in other areas, including the Savior monastery in Murom (1096), the Trinity and Archangel monasteries of Ustiug (c. 1200) and Trinity in Vologda (1147).

Yaroslav advanced christianization by recruiting Greek scribes to translate ancient Christian documents into Slavonic, building churches, establishing schools to train clergy and ordering

priests to give instruction in basic literacy. Yaroslav issued a church code that made clergy supervisors of public behaviour. Consequently, Christian priests and monks gave the populace of Rus better training in Christian piety than societies of contemporary western Europe had. More people there were literate and could understand the liturgy and spiritual literature because these were translated into Slavonic, in contrast to the Latin that was largely incomprehensible to the laity of the West.

Recent scholarship rejects the portrayal of Rus by earlier historians as not really christianized but rather possessing a 'dual faith' in which Russians retained traditional paganism that was merely decorated with trappings of Christianity. Orthodoxy became the national religion of the eastern Slavs and played a decisive role in the development of Russian culture.

PAUL STEEVES

period. This process had begun right back in the tenth and eleventh centuries, under Vladimir and his successors. At that time, the church had helped to transform the nature of Russian society, which was changing at this time anyway from a family-based tribal society to a land-based feudal society. The Byzantine church was of course a major landowner, and the programme of church-building in Kiev and beyond meant that the Russian church followed the same pattern. The church bought considerable swathes of land and, whilst it tried to abolish slavery, which was practised in various parts of Kievan Rus at this time, it did encourage the establishment of serfdom, where workers paid landowners in labour for the right to work the land. This system was also evolving in western Europe, as we saw in Chapter 7; but it lasted far longer in Russia, right into the nineteenth century. In Russia, more or less all the land was owned by either the church or the *boyars* (the landed aristocracy) or the city's prince. The Russian church became rich, and it became inextricably intertwined with secular authority. In Novgorod, for example, the archbishop was, by the end of the twelfth century, the effective head of the city: he controlled the treasury and the judicial system and signed the city's charters. Nevertheless, the archbishop was not some all-powerful potentate: he relied on the support of the nobles and, if he lost it, he could be replaced. In 1228, one archbishop was sacked on the pretext of not preventing unwanted rainy weather!

The process of land and wealth acquisition continued throughout the Tatar period. Feudalism became deeply engrained in Russian society and the church increasingly came to view the system, and especially its own role in it, as divinely ordained. On this view, any criticism of feudalism or of the wealth of the church was intrinsically heretical. But there were many such attacks, reflecting dissatisfaction among some people with what they regarded as the church 'selling out' in the interest of money or power. Indeed, many

By the power and will of the Most High and Eternal God and by the majesty and most merciful word of Uzbek... Let no one offend against the cathedral church in Rus of Metropolitan Peter or against his people and his churchmen... If someone violates church property and the metropolitan's property, the wrath of God will be on him, and he will not be excused from our great torture by any excuse and he shall die by terrible execution.

Charter guaranteeing freedom to the church under the Tatars, c. 1313

among the artisan classes and the lower clergy in particular resented the wealth and power of the higher clergy, and some concluded that the ecclesiastical hierarchy should be dismantled altogether. The most famous, and most persistent, were the Strigolniks (or 'Barbers', since one of their most prominent figures was Karp the Barber). The Strigolniks, who first appeared at Novgorod in the middle of the fourteenth century, were rather like extreme early Protestants, but their protest was a combination of theological disagreement and social dissatisfaction. They criticized pretty much everything to do with the established church, including corruption and greed, but also the role of the priesthood and the efficacy of the sacraments. The Strigolniks believed that faith should be approached rationally, and so they rejected the Eucharist as an intrinsically irrational act, and also argued that the Bible and other sources of authority should be questioned or used critically. Some went still further and denied the possibility of resurrection or life after death.

THE THREAT FROM THE WEST

An even more serious threat in the eyes of the Russian church was western Europe, and especially the Catholic Church. If many sermons were preached against the heretical Strigolniks, many more were preached against 'Latiny', which meant not only the Roman Catholic Church but the whole of western European culture. And for their part, unlike the Mongols, the Catholics were clearly not happy with the presence of Orthodox Christianity – officially, since 1054, a schismatic sect – right on their doorstep. In 1210 Swedish troops invaded the territory of Novgorod. The invaders were led by the Teutonic Knights, who, as we saw in Chapter 7, were a major crusading order in the Baltic region. They ruled much of Prussia and devoted a lot of energy to trying to invade Lithuania, a Slavic region on the Baltic coast, which was still pagan.

The knights were a fearsome opponent,

but the defenders of Novgorod were rallied by the young Prince Alexander (1218–63), who told his men: 'God is not in might but in Truth. Some trust in princes and some in horses, but we will call upon the Lord our God.' The Russians did just that, although they were certainly helped by a good supply of both princes and horses. They successfully repelled the Teutonic Knights in a series of battles, first in 1240 at the river Neva (after which the prince was known as Alexander 'Nevsky'), but most decisively, in 1242, on Lake Chud, also known as Lake Peipus, which lies on the border between modern Estonia and Russia. This huge body of water was frozen and the opposing armies fought on the ice itself. The Russians had the upper hand. As the Teutonic Knights turned to flee, their heavier armour suddenly broke the ice. Most of those who had escaped the slaughter were dragged into the freezing water and only a handful returned home. This would not be the last invasion of Russia to be defeated by the cold.

That was the end of the Teutonic Knights' crusade against the Russian Orthodox, and this victory was a major event in the evolution of Russian religious consciousness. Prince Alexander himself became a hero. He did his best to unify the statelets of Russia and to maintain resistance against the westerners, whilst at the same time keeping up good relations with the Mongols – something he managed despite refusing to engage in any pagan practices when visiting Saray. Such a refusal normally carried the death penalty, but the emperor, Khan Batu, Genghis Khan's grandson, was so impressed with Alexander's regal bearing and his Christian conviction that he waived the punishment. For his efforts, Alexander is remembered as one of the principal architects of the Russian state and its church, and since 1547 the Orthodox Church has regarded him as a saint.

After Alexander's death Russia fell into disarray once again. It became prey to a new Catholic threat from the West – Lithuania and Poland. Little is known of Poland before the tenth century, except that the people here were Slavs, as yet still pagan: the Orthodox Christianity of Kievan Rus had not penetrated this far west. Instead, Christianity came from the Catholic west, and in AD 966 Prince Mieszko I was baptized, having married a Czech princess. The conversion of Poland followed the familiar pattern: bishops and preachers were imported, a hierarchy established, and mass baptisms performed. Unusually, though, Mieszko put the whole country in the hands of the pope as a vassal state, a move intended to block the attempts of the Holy Roman empire to dominate it ecclesiastically as well as politically. Poland was therefore a particularly strong bastion of Roman Catholicism, and in the 1380s a marriage between the ruling families of Poland and Lithuania united the two countries. Lithuania quickly Christianized. The result was a large bloc of Slavic Roman Catholicism, extending from the Baltic Sea in the north down to the Carpathian Mountains in the south, right on the border between Catholic Europe and Orthodox Russia. Lithuania and Poland extended their influence east and south, dominating Kiev and the surrounding area. The church in Kiev was now in a curious position. As we saw in Chapter 7, the Council of Florence, held in the 1430s, attempted to reunite the Catholic and Orthodox churches, but no one outside the council accepted it – apart from Kiev. So the people of Kiev were politically under the heel of Catholic Poland, and whilst officially dependent on the patriarch of Constantinople, the metropolitan of Kiev was also in communion with the pope – though the pope and the patriarch were not in communion with each other. This situation lasted until 1569, when Ukraine became part of Poland and officially completely Catholic. The Orthodox Church there began to suffer persecution.

THE RISE OF MOSCOW

As Kiev sank into subjugation, however, a new city was on the rise. The conquests of Alexander Nevsky had meant that the centre of gravity of the Russian state had moved north, first to Novgorod, but then to the emerging power base of Moscow. Moscow had been founded in the twelfth century, and it grew quickly, being situated on major trade routes. Its rise in power corresponded with the decline of the power of the Tatars. The fourteenth and fifteenth centuries saw a number of attempts by successive grand princes of Moscow (as the city's rulers were known after 1329) to throw off the rule of the Tatars for good, but this was not achieved until 1480, under Ivan III (the Great). He united the cities around Moscow (mainly by conquering them and replacing their princes with puppet rulers) and finally refused to pay any tribute to Saray. For once the coup was bloodless – neither Ivan's army nor the khan's would commit itself, but the failure of the Tatars to reinforce their demand for tribute meant that, from this date on, the Russian states were effectively independent of Saray.

They were not independent of Ivan, though, who now claimed rule over all of them. His kingdom stretched from the Black Sea to the Ural Mountains. Moreover, the establishment of Moscow-dominated Russia coincided – more or less – with the fall of Constantinople to the Turks in 1453. Ivan concluded that the role of state protector of the Orthodox Church had passed to him and to seal this claim he married a niece of the last Byzantine emperor. He also adopted the Byzantine insignia of the double-headed eagle to represent Russia. In 1461 a new metropolitan see was established at Moscow. This was all reflected in a new theological viewpoint about the role of the city of Moscow itself. Where Constantinople had stood for over a millennium as the Second Rome, Moscow was now declared to be the third. In 1510, a monk named Philotheus of Pskov wrote:

The Apostolic Church stands no longer in Rome or Constantinople, but in the blessed city of Moscow. She alone shines in the whole world brighter than the sun... All Christian empires are fallen and in their

stead stands alone the Empire of our ruler in accordance with the Prophetical books. Two Romes have fallen, but the third stands and a fourth there will not be.

The Third Rome had barely been recognized as such before its faith was tested with a new and rather unusual controversy. It began in Novgorod, where, in 1470, Michael Olelkovich, prince of Kiev, came to visit. He brought with him a Jewish doctor named Skharia. Skharia met two priests of Novgorod, Alexis and Dionysius, and converted them to Judaism: he convinced them that the doctrines of the Trinity and of Jesus' messianic and divine status were false, and that salvation could be secured only by becoming a Jew. This they did. More priests became converted, even Gabriel, dean of the cathedral of St Sophia. But all this was done in secret.

In 1480 Ivan the Great appointed Alexis and Dionysius deans of two cathedrals in Moscow, where they continued to spread their ideas. Meanwhile, back in Novgorod, the archbishop, Gennadius, discovered what was going on and tried to eradicate the secret society – with difficulty, for many of the Judaizers were nobles. Not all of the Bible had been translated into Slavonic, and so Gennadius completed the translation, hoping to show that the Judaizers' claims to be restoring primitive religion were false. He was supported by Joseph Sanin, abbot of the Volokolamsk monastery, a scholarly man who wrote a book called *The enlightener* against the Judaizers. They were condemned at a council in 1490, but the controversy rumbled on for some years.

ART, ARCHITECTURE AND CHRISTIAN CULTURE

This period also saw a revitalization of Russian art and architecture. A new feature of church design, the 'iconostasis' (or 'icon stand'), appeared. This was a development of the screen which traditionally separated the nave of a church from the sanctuary, but it would now be covered in icons, most often in five rows. Major artists such as the monk

The magnificent gilded iconostasis of the Cathedral of the Transfiguration, Uglich, Russia.

Andrei Rublev and the imported Theophanes the Greek, who both worked in the early fifteenth century, helped to inspire new generations of artists and iconographers. In fact, until well into the seventeenth century, churches were virtually the only place where art of any kind could be found in Russia.

Under Ivan the Great, new churches were built, especially in Moscow, and a distinctive Russian form of architecture developed, inspired by Byzantine architecture, but less like it than the earlier building styles of Kiev. The Russians generally built in wood, to such an extent that their towns consisted of practically nothing else: an English emissary to Moscow in 1588 reported in some amazement that the houses consisted solely of wood, held together with pegs, and even the streets were paved with wooden planks. Indeed, it was possible to purchase prefabricated houses, in plank form, for assembly elsewhere. So now the Russians developed increasingly ambitious styles of wooden churches and even cathedrals which in some ways mimicked the domes and towers of Byzantium. Some churches were essentially long sheds, whilst others were built in an octagonal style, rather like Ethiopian churches. One of the most well-known examples of this kind of church was the Church of St Nicholas at Panilovo, which was built in 1600. It featured a tall tower covered in wooden tiles, surmounted by a small but elegant onion dome; the apse and anteroom jutted off it, so it looked as if this wooden tower had erupted out of a Tyrolean chalet. This church, which looks so remarkable to western eyes, seems to have been quite typical of provincial Russian church architecture in the early modern period; but it burned down in the 1920s. This was a common fate of all-wooden buildings, of course, but fortunately they were cheap to replace.

IVAN 'THE TERRIBLE'

A true centralized Russian state was not achieved until Ivan the Great's grandson, Ivan IV, better known as Ivan Groznyi (which means 'the Awe-inspiring' but is often given as 'the Terrible'). This Ivan came to the throne in 1533 at the age of three. At sixteen he had himself crowned tsar. The title was a corruption of 'caesar', and represented Ivan's claim to be the true successor of the Roman emperors. He governed with the help of a kind of parliament known as the 'zemsky sobor' or 'assembly of the land', with which he set out a new legal code for Russia; he also extended the borders of his domain eastwards, launching a crusade against the Tatars in which he slaughtered them mercilessly. He also conquered Kazan, Astrakhan and Siberia, creating a huge empire; but as time went on he apparently became increasingly unstable. Ivan was convinced that he was appointed by God to rule and therefore anyone who opposed him was a heretic and deserved death. He ordered purges of the Russians, killing thousands, including many priests and representatives of the church, and sending many more into exile in remote parts of his vast realm. He also set up a kind of religious secret police, known as the *Oprichniki*. By 1572 there were 6,000 members of this society, all chosen for their loyalty to the tsar, and their appearance and activities have become the stuff of legend: dressed solely in black, bearing the sign of the broom (for sweeping away heresy) and the dog's head (for snapping at their enemies' heels), the *Oprichniki* had a free reign throughout Ivan's empire, and were able to imprison, torture or kill whomever they liked.

Yet Ivan appears to have been a genuinely pious man, and towards the end of his reign he apparently repented of his cruelty, posthumously forgiving those he had executed and even paying for prayers to be said for their souls. He took the habit of a monk and was buried in it, hoping to find forgiveness for his sins. Ivan was also the man responsible for the most striking example of early modern Russian architecture, St Basil's Cathedral in Moscow. This extraordinary building, next to the Kremlin, was designed by

The exterior of the Cathedral of the Transfiguration (built in 1714) on Kizhi Island. The church features twenty-two cupolas and is built entirely of wood, without a single nail.

Then the Great Prince [Ivan IV] moved into Great Novgorod, into the bishop's palace, and took everything belonging to the bishop… Every day he arose and moved to another monastery. He indulged his wantonness and had monks tortured, and many of them were killed. There are three hundred monasteries inside and outside the city and not one of these was spared. Then the pillage of the city began… Every day the Grand Prince could also be found in the torture chamber in person.

Heinrich von Staden, *The land and government of Muscovy*, 1571

Ivan IV, the Hundred Chapters Council and a new state chur

In 1547 the chief bishop in Muscovy, Metropolitan Makary, conducted the first coronation of a Moscow prince as 'tsar', the teenaged Ivan IV. Thereby, Makary asserted a Russian national claim to the imperial authority of the Christian caesars of Byzantium and Moscow's aspiration to pre-eminence within Orthodoxy. This was in accordance with a formula that was sometimes expressed, although never officially so asserted, that Moscow was the 'third Rome', after the original Rome lapsed into papalism and the second, Constantinople, compromised with papalism in the Florentine unions and was overrun by Muslim Turks (1453) because of it. The pageantry of coronation served as first in a series of events whereby Makary consolidated Moscow's leadership of a well-articulated Slavic Orthodox state and community in the Russian area and proclaimed the autonomy of the Russian Orthodox Church.

At two councils (1547, 1549) Makary guided the church hierarchy to formal recognition of a host of Russians as saints of the entire Russian church. Before these councils Russians gave little attention to formally canonizing any native saints, although a handful of church people and even princes received popular veneration, usually in restricted locales. With Makary's councils the Russian church by orderly procedures, based on documented miracles, declared over three dozen of its own to be saints. Indigenous saints authenticated the claim to be a truly national, or 'local', Orthodox Church.

Makary documented Muscovy's supposed contribution to the Orthodox spiritual heritage in a twelve-volume compendium of all spiritual literature (sermons, saints' lives, sacred history, morality tales) produced by Russians. This was entitled the *Great Monthly Readings*.

Makary also compiled the 'Book of Degrees', which provided Ivan's genealogical history with the goal of proving that he was the only legitimate heir of princely authority derived from Russia's first Orthodox ruler, Princess Olga, and her grandson Vladimir, 'baptizer of the Rus'.

Makary's effort to create a Russian national church culminated in his convening and orchestrating a council of unprecedented importance for Russia. Called the 'Hundred Chapters Council', because the written record of its actions comprised one hundred sections, the assembly provided answers to sixty-nine questions placed by the document into Ivan's mouth, identifying diverse topics for the council to give definitive instructions for comprehensive reform concerning moral and spiritual matters in private, public and church life.

The council, made up of all bishops, monastery superiors and many clergy and nobles of Muscovy, issued opinions on a broad range of matters, including: prohibitions on games of chance, fortune tellers, monastic drunkenness and other vices; shaving men's beards; and directions for church administration and discipline of clergy, organization of popular elementary education and catechetical instruction, and proper forms for painting icons and especially for representing persons of the Holy Trinity. The purport of the council's responses was that monasteries should reform themselves into model communities from which the rest of society would learn to live in accordance with Christian values. Muscovy, as the sole guardian of Christ's truth, was to become the representative of God's kingdom on earth.

A handbook entitled *Household Management*, composed under the guidance of Makary and Ivan, provided detailed instructions about how heads of families should translate the council's instructions into practice. The handbook instructed the husband to train his family in Christian piety by leading morning, evening and midnight prayers and disciplining his wife and children, by physical force, if necessary. The wife, in her turn, was to oversee children

The battle of Kozelsk, when in 1238 the townspeople fought off a much larger Mongol army. The illustration is from a chronicle of Russian history written during the reign of Ivan IV.

and servants in the performance of domestic chores and to assure that they did not indulge in worldly games, music and other frivolity. The patriarchal family was to become a virtual monastic community (except for celibacy) so that all of society would become an extended Christian family with the tsar as father.

The Hundred Chapters Council sought to improve the effectiveness of church rituals. It ordered a careful review of the liturgical books in order to expunge copying errors that had entered the texts to assure that the Russian church had a perfect worship system. It also advised clergy to go beyond the mere repetition of litanies and to read spiritual literature to the faithful in order to achieve 'instruction, enlightenment, true repentance, and good works for every Orthodox Christian'.

Of the council's decision regarding ritual, two questions proved especially fateful: how Christians should make the sign of the cross and sing 'alleluia' in the liturgy. The council decreed that the practice of the west Russian area (Novgorod, Pskov) using two fingers joined to the thumb when crossing oneself and singing three alleluias was incorrect and that any who failed to follow Moscow's pattern of holding the first two fingers outstretched while blessing themselves and intoning only two alleluias were accursed. A century later the whole of Russian society was shaken by a great schism when the church leadership supported by the state reversed these strict requirements.

In the aftermath of Makary's manoeuvres, leaders of Mediterranean Orthodox churches, like Alexandria, Constantinople and Antioch, which had excluded the Muscovite church from their fellowship a century earlier because of its unilateral assertion of autonomy, recognized the Russian church as at least their equal. The patriarch of Constantinople, for example, acknowledged Ivan 'tsar and sovereign of Orthodox Christians of the whole world from East to West and to the seas'.

Subsequent centuries demonstrated that the supposed reform council of 1551 was both an enormous success and a dismal failure in Russian history. Achievement of the council's primary goal of creation, in the Russian area, of a centralized autocracy associated with a compliant church was personified by tyrants including Ivan 'the Terrible', Peter the Great and Joseph Stalin. The vision that this society would be a harmonious and prosperous community of enlightened and pious Christian monks, clergy and faithful was mocked by repeated cruel brutalities and bloody strife.

PAUL STEEVES

Postnik Yakovlev and features the characteristic Byzantine dome taken to a new dimension in the famous, brightly coloured 'onion' domes. According to legend, Ivan blinded Yakovlev to ensure that he would not design anything better for anyone else.

In his relations with the church, Ivan represented the old tendency of caesaropapism. He believed that he was appointed by God to rule both church and state, and that churchmen had no business interfering with anything he did. In 1568, Filipp, the metropolitan of Moscow, made the mistake of criticizing the Oprichniki system; Ivan saw to it that he was deposed, confined to a monastery and murdered.

MONASTICISM AND SPIRITUALITY

THE RUSSIAN MONASTERIES

Byzantine Christianity had always revolved, to some extent, around the monasteries, and this proved true of the new version of Byzantium. Byzantine-style monasticism had come to Russia in the pre-Mongolian period, when it was still Kievan Rus. A key figure in this was Anthony of the Caves, who was really called Antyp and came from near Kiev. However, in the early eleventh century Antyp joined a monastery on Mount Athos, taking the name Anthony, and after many years returned to his homeland. He became a hermit in a cave outside Kiev, where he attracted disciples and formed a new monastery. Strangely, as the monastery grew, the monks decided that they liked their troglodyte lifestyle, and so they excavated more caves until a huge warren of passages, tunnels, crypts and chapels had been created. This was the Kiev-Pechersk Lavra – the 'Kiev cave monastery' ('lavra' being the word for 'monastery') – one of the wonders of the Christian world. Even after the centre of gravity in Russia switched from Kiev to Moscow, the Kiev-Pechersk Lavra continued

The famous onion domes of the cathedral of Basil the Blessed, Moscow.

to be a major site in Russian Christianity. It is still there today, having expanded to three miles of subterranean tunnels, topped with churches and towers with golden domes. Now as then, the monastery operates as a city within a city, employing its own builders, tailors, gardeners, bakers and all the trades required for civilization.

Although unusual in its use of caves, the Kiev-Pechersk Lavra was typical of the early Russian monasteries in being associated with a town. Many of these monasteries actually doubled as fortresses, and princes were careful to site them in strategically sensible positions inside the city or in defensive rings around it.

A new and contrasting monastic movement was associated with Sergius of Radonezh, the Russian answer to Antony of

Egypt. Just as Antony had sought solitude and God in the burning desert of Egypt, so Sergius sought them in the freezing forests beyond Moscow. Born in 1314, during the Tatar period, Sergius sought God not in the monasteries like that of Kiev, which were associated with cities, but alone, in the forest. Just like Antony of Egypt, he lived as a hermit until the inevitable disciples appeared. A monastery dedicated to the Holy Trinity was built. Sergius acquired a reputation for wisdom and holiness, and he was consulted on a variety of different matters. In 1380, for example, Dmitry Donskoy, Prince of Moscow, asked his advice on attacking the Tatars – for this was during the period when Moscow was trying to shake off the Mongolian overlords. Sergius advised war, and Dmitry did indeed

completely uninhabited. As in early medieval Ireland, the monasteries developed into population centres, as normal peasants and artisans set up shop there to provide the monks with their worldly needs. Moreover, many trusted to the charity of the monks if times turned hard. Monasteries attracted towns, and the monasteries themselves became major landowners. Fortunately, much of their wealth was indeed used to feed the hungry when necessary, and they also maintained hospitals and hostels. As in early medieval Europe centuries earlier, the monasteries also had the only libraries and schools of note, and were centres of education and scholarship.

A good example of this process was a monk from Moscow named Cyril of Beloozero. Cyril knew Sergius of Radonezh and rose to become abbot of the Simonov monastery in Moscow. But Cyril was not happy with life so close to the city, and one day in the 1390s heard a voice telling him to leave for the White Lake, somewhere in the distant forests. Cyril obediently left for the forests, taking with him only a single companion who knew the area. He climbed a mountain, from which he could see a huge vista of forest and lakes, but no people whatsoever; and here he settled as a hermit. But other monks turned up, built a church, and founded a monastery. It became the Belozersky monastery, a major centre of northern Russian monasticism, and from here new generations of monks would grow dissatisfied with the communal life and strike out on their own even deeper into the forest.

Other monks penetrated into areas that were already inhabited but not yet Christian. This was especially the case for those who went east rather than north, and in these cases the monks acted as missionaries rather than colonizers. From the fourteenth century well into the sixteenth the same pattern repeated itself over and over again: missionary monks would arrive in an area, build a monastery and translate the Bible and liturgy into the local language. The natives would be

win his battle. By the time he died in 1392, Sergius had become possibly the most popular and beloved man in Russia: today he is the country's patron saint. And he had inspired a new wave of hermits and monks, just as Antony of Egypt had a millennium earlier. They streamed out to the woods, seeking solitude; more and more monasteries were founded, although most were small, with just a handful of monks, and most had no communal rule, but each monk did his own thing as he saw fit. Still, this was too crowded for the more radical seekers of solitude, and so the holy men penetrated further and further into the immense forests, seeking perfect loneliness.

This was a key element in the colonization of some of these remote, northern areas, many of which were

Part of the Pechersk-Lavra monastery at Kiev. Buildings in the complex are joined by a network of underground caves.

converted, the monastery would become established, and in its turn it would send out more monks to the next region. The process took centuries, but in this way Russian Orthodoxy spread inexorably eastwards.

Another remarkable foundation was the Valaam monastery, built on a large number of small islands in Lake Ladoga, the largest lake in Europe, near the modern border with Finland. No one really knows when this unusual monastery was founded, but by the time of Ivan the Great it was known as 'the Great Lavra' and was a bustling community, with hundreds of buildings and homes and its own fishing trade. But this monastery was right in the path of any invading armies from Sweden, and intermittent attempts by the Swedes to attack Russian Orthodoxy meant that it was often razed to the ground and had to be rebuilt. Yet the monastery survived, and in the nineteenth century had over 1,000 monks.

RUSSIAN MYSTICISM

As all this suggests, the monks were a major element in the establishment of Orthodox Christianity throughout Russia. Many of the monks were mystics, and they practised the 'hesychast' methods made famous by Gregory Palamas. Sergius of Radonezh played an important role in the establishment of these methods in Russia.

Although Sergius was the key figure in the spread of Russian monasticism, Russian spirituality was also associated with Nilus of Sora, who lived half a century later. Probably born in Moscow in 1433, Nilus entered the Belozersky monastery founded by Cyril some decades earlier, travelled to Mount Athos to learn hesychast practices, and finally founded a new monastery (or 'skete', a small monastery with just a dozen monks) by the River Sora. He described how the monastery was run in a book called *The tradition of sketic life*. Like earlier monastic writers such as the fourth-century desert fathers, Nilus warned his readers of evil thoughts which would inevitably enter the mind, and the dangers of consenting to

Then the soul has no more prayer and not only loses its movement but itself is led by some other power. The soul is mysteriously captured and finds itself in the incomprehensible which it knows not. This is rightly called contemplation and a form of prayer, but it is not prayer itself. In this case the mind is already above prayer, which is left aside for the better. A person is then in rapture and wholly without desire.

Nilus of Sora, on hesychasm

them. To block them out, he advised the use of hesychastic methods. 'Pray unceasingly' was his motto, and he believed that the repetition, out loud, of the Jesus Prayer, combined with regular breathing, would take the soul to a new state where the clamour of thoughts would recede into the background.

Nilus was enormously influential and his works were read by Russian monks for centuries. In particular, the monks who lived beyond the River Volga – known, reasonably, as the Trans-Volga Elders – were deeply influenced by Nilus. But all was not as calm as the hesychast ideal called for: after Nilus's death, the Trans-Volga Elders were persecuted for heresy. They made the mistake of opposing new features of Russian religious and political life: they did not approve of monasteries owning property, and they did not like the increasing centralization of the Russian state. Their opponents included the Josephites, disciples of Joseph Sanin, who like Nilus had criticized the Judaizers. His monastery had been run on extremely rigid lines: there were rules about what its members wore, what they ate, even where they could sit. Joseph believed that this kind of discipline was required for the spiritual life, and his followers disapproved of the looser, more individualistic approach of Nilus. A number of monks were imprisoned, and Russian monasticism began to move more in the favour of the disciplinarians over the mystics. In the more remote monasteries, in particular, there could be so much emphasis on rigorous lifestyles, with constant fasting, penances and interminable services, that monks never read the Bible or the fathers and never did any contemplation at all.

THE HOLY FOOLS

One rather unusual form of spirituality was that of the *Yurodivi*, the 'holy fools'. They were rather like the Russian church's answer to the mendicant friars of Catholic Europe, although they appeared two centuries later. Taking to extremes Paul's statement in 1 Corinthians 1:27 that 'God chose what is foolish in the world to shame the wise', these people deliberately lived outside the constraints and norms of normal society. All monks did that to some extent, of course, but the *Yurodivi* did not retreat from society: they were highly visible within it, as a kind of critical commentary upon it. They deliberately sought the scorn or ridicule of society and acted bizarrely or insanely. One of the leading representatives of this movement was Basil 'the Blessed', a cobbler's apprentice from Moscow who lived in the late fifteenth and early sixteenth centuries. Haggard in appearance, wearing only a loincloth despite the Muscovite climate, Basil would steal from shops and give to the poor, and he was apparently in the habit of scolding Ivan IV – not normally a recipe for a long life. On one occasion he is said to have presented Ivan with a large steak when he should have been fasting, commenting that, since Ivan was a murderer anyway, he need not bother abstaining from meat. Ivan was deeply in awe of the crazy ascetic, however, and Basil always escaped retribution.

Basil was deeply venerated in his lifetime and after his death in 1552 was buried by the new Cathedral of the Protection of the Mother of God in Moscow. This is the cathedral that is normally known as St Basil's, after the ascetic. The *Yurodivi* movement continued to exist in Russia for many years, and as we shall see, it was really just a prototype for the extremist religious movements that would exist on the fringes of Russian Orthodoxy for centuries. Moreover, Basil himself, and the exaggerated veneration paid to him even by a tyrant like Ivan 'the Terrible', was a prototype for the common figure of the charismatic holy man who would crop up repeatedly in Russian history. The Russians would always venerate men like him, believing them to be specially touched by God. Leo Tolstoy, the great nineteenth-century novelist, recalled a *Yurodivi* called Grisha who had wandered about his parents' estate wearing chains.

EARLY MODERN RUSSIA

Ivan 'the Terrible' died in 1584 and, since he had stabbed his oldest son to death during an argument, he was succeeded by his youngest son, Feodor. Feodor was a weak ruler, although he did preside over one event of significance: in 1589 Moscow was given its own patriarch, finalizing the ascendancy of the city in the Orthodox world. This was the work of Feodor's powerful brother-in-law Boris Godunov, who took advantage of the dire financial straits of the churches in Constantinople and Jerusalem. These churches, under Muslim rule, were more and more dependent on Moscow, and Jeremiah, patriarch of Constantinople, agreed that 'in all the world there is just one pious tsar… it is here that the ecumenical patriarch should be, while in old Tsargrad [Constantinople] the Christian faith is being driven out by the infidel Turks for our sins'. There was talk of simply moving the ecumenical patriarch, Jeremiah himself, from Constantinople to Moscow; instead, he stayed where he was while the metropolitan of Moscow was upgraded to patriarchal status.

THE TIME OF TROUBLES

Feodor's death in 1598 left a power vacuum in the centralized state that his father had created, and for fifteen years Russia was rent by dynastic squabbling, civil war and famine in what became known as 'the Time of Troubles'. The *boyars*, the noble landowners, fought each other for the tsar's throne, and pretenders to the throne appeared and were murdered in swift succession. Poland invaded and captured Moscow and tried to impose its rule on the country. There was endemic poverty and many peasants fled east to set up autonomous communities of their own. The authorities tried to stop this by banning peasant relocation, but the Cossacks, as these groups were known, throve. The state's response was more repression: by the end of the seventeenth century, serfs had regressed to little more than slaves, able even to be bought and sold. As Europe was beginning the Enlightenment, Russia was stuck in a medieval time warp with an oppressive feudal system and very low levels of education. Throughout this time, the Orthodox Church provided the only source of unity and strength for the beleaguered Russian people.

THE GREAT SOVEREIGN

The Poles were successfully expelled and in 1613 the Time of Troubles ended with the election of a new teenage tsar, Michael Romanov (1596–1676), grand-nephew of Ivan IV. His father, Filaret, was the patriarch of Moscow, and he was the real power behind the throne until his death in 1633. For twenty years Russia was effectively ruled by the patriarch: calling himself 'the Great Sovereign', Filaret sat on a throne next to his son and signed all state papers with him. Here was a union of church and state more complete than perhaps any that had been achieved before – and the Romanov dynasty which Filaret founded would last for three centuries.

Meanwhile, Russia was continuing to expand. In the east, Ivan 'the Terrible' had waged war on the Kazan khanate and before long Russia had annexed the whole of western Siberia, an immense but sparsely populated region. The Cossacks moved in, building forts and trading posts and exacting tribute to send to distant Moscow, which derived a lot of income from Siberian furs. By the 1640s the Russians had moved sufficiently far to be clashing for land rights with the Chinese. A series of skirmishes with China, followed by peace, allowed Russian suzerainty to spread right to the Pacific coast by the end of the century.

Expansion to the west, meanwhile, brought Russia into increasing contact with western Europe. This was especially the case in the middle of the seventeenth century when Ukraine was partitioned. In Chapter 11 we shall see the effect that this had on Russian religion and culture, as western ideas, including the Enlightenment, infiltrated into the country.

SECTS AND SCHISMATICS

This period saw more divisions within the Russian Orthodox Church. The most important was the schism of the Old Believers, which we shall look at in Chapter 11. But other schisms were associated with the rise of more extremist groups on the fringes of the church.

One of the most influential of these groups were the *Khlysty*, a name meaning 'whips', referring to their supposed habit of self-flagellation. Little is really known about the *Khlysty*, a group surrounded by myth and hearsay. The group was apparently founded at the start of the eighteenth century by a man named Danila Filippovich, from Kostroma, who proclaimed himself a new messiah. No doubt Filippovich was tapping into an already-existing stream of charismatic tendencies in Russian religion, among those who emphasized the contemporary revelation of the Holy Spirit and rebelled against the imposition of the state church. The *Khlysty* were a secret society within the Orthodox Church, for Filippovich taught his followers to keep their views to themselves and not stand out. Like the Gnostics of an earlier age, they believed that the rituals, doctrines and hierarchies of the established church were all right for the common run of believers, but members of their brotherhood had gone beyond this. They alone knew the true path to God. God, they believed, was eternally incarnating in a series of messiahs (the most recent being Filippovich, although a number of other claimants appeared after him). Indeed, the Spirit of God could be invoked by any believer and made manifest in their bodies through ecstatic prayer, and in this way all participants could become Christs. The *Khlysty* therefore engaged in ecstatic mysteries and rites. It was said that these rites were essentially orgies, justified on the grounds that the Spirit of God can come in forgiveness only where there has been sin. It was also said that the *Khlysty*, zealous in their search for the spirit of Christ, would whip themselves and even that the babies resulting from their wild orgies would be sacrificed. It is striking how similar some of these charges are to those which were levelled against the very first Christians in Roman times, but it is hard now to uncover the reality behind them. Certainly it is reasonable to suppose that the *Khlysty* were simply the best-known representatives of an extremist Spirit-based movement which took many forms in early modern Russia.

Another messianic movement – although very different in outlook – was the *Skoptsy* movement, founded by a peasant from Oryel named Kondraty Selivanov. He also claimed to be a messiah, but in this case he was the only one, and the *Skoptsy* did not share the *Khlysty's* belief in perpetual divine incarnation. Instead they believed that the way to God was through extreme asceticism, most notably through castration. Selivanov had little success at first, being attacked by both the religious authorities and the *Khlysty* among whom he first preached. In the 1790s, claiming to be Tsar Peter III (the husband of Catherine the Great), he gained audience with the real Peter's son, Tsar Paul I, and tried to persuade him to castrate himself. For this Selivanov was consigned to a mental asylum. Released in 1802, he won many disciples and became extremely well known; many rich merchants were among his followers, and hundreds of thousands of people throughout Russia castrated themselves in accordance with his teachings. There was more to the *Skoptsy* than just this, of course; they also led industrious and rather earnest lifestyles, working hard and avoiding drunkenness. However, their numbers declined (perhaps for obvious reasons) throughout the nineteenth century, and after 1850 they were less significant in Russian religion.

CHAPTER 9

THE REFORMATION

Western Europe had known a thousand years of Catholic civilization, during which the church permeated every level of society. But as the Middle Ages developed into the early modern period, that hegemony was shattered in the most dramatic religious shake-up the continent had known since the days of Constantine – the Reformation.

THE RENAISSANCE

The Reformation had its roots in one of the most remarkable periods of European history, the Renaissance, which took place between approximately the fourteenth and sixteenth centuries. In some ways it represented a development of medieval thought and practices, and in other ways it was a rejection of them. The combination of these different elements meant that it was sometimes a confusing time, and sometimes a time of conflict; but also, for many, it was a time of continuity. No one was aware at the time that the Middle Ages were coming to an end, any more than their predecessors had known they were living in something called 'the Middle Ages' in the first place. Hindsight categorizes and stresses change and development which may not have been so prominent at the time.

NEW ECONOMIES, NEW SOCIETIES
Europe was changed forever by the devastating plague of the fourteenth century, which continued to kill millions in the first half of the fifteenth century. The economy was wrecked, as the population crash meant declining markets for goods and services, while despite the new labour shortage most landowners refused to increase wages. Yet the second half of the fifteenth century saw economic recovery, as the population rose again, new markets opened and the middle classes swelled dramatically.

By the end of the fifteenth century, the changes to the European economic system that we saw beginning in the fourteenth century were largely complete. It had changed from a local-based economy, revolving around the exchange of goods, to an economy driven by the movement of goods, revolving around currency. Money became not simply a medium of exchange but a commodity in itself, and new professions arose to deal in it – bankers and accountants. They were, in fact, the rising middle class. The old feudal system of society was largely superseded.

Politically, Europe was changing as well. The new movements of the Renaissance were concentrated in key trading cities which had accumulated wealth from the new trade routes that were opened up in the wake of the crusades. These cities, mostly in northern Italy, became rich and powerful. The Holy Roman empire, which had controlled much of this area, was politically weaker, and a number of wealthy cities became independent republics. Florence and Venice were the most important of these. Thus in fifteenth-century Florence we find politics being dominated by the Medicis, a family of bankers, who managed to turn the nascent republic into what was virtually a benign dictatorship. Under their rule the merchants flourished, and so did the arts.

BACK TO BASICS

With the changes in society came a conscious desire to overturn the developments of the preceding few centuries. It was during the Renaissance that the term 'Middle Ages' was invented to refer to this earlier time – a term that reflected the Renaissance belief that the reinvigoration of European culture required a return to antiquity. The word 'Renaissance' itself was coined, meaning 'rebirth' – a repeat run of the first birth, as it were, of classical Europe. The 'Middle Ages', it was felt, had been a boring period of stagnation, when the genius of antiquity had been forgotten. This basic viewpoint – that classical Greece and Rome were the template for civilization (largely ignoring the contribution of northern European culture), that the Middle Ages were, on the whole, bad, and that things were from now on going to be very different – was to a large extent a myth, but it was an extremely powerful one that continued to be highly influential into much more recent times.

Artists began to try to recreate the art of classical Greece and Rome. Sculptors such as Michelangelo Buonarroti, a Florentine of the first half of the sixteenth century, aimed to reproduce the style of sculpture of ancient Greece. But they also tried to go beyond it, consciously to celebrate the nobility of human nature. Perhaps the greatest artwork expressing this was Michelangelo's enormous statue of David, probably the most famous statue ever made, and arguably the pinnacle of perfection of the human form. Michelangelo was also a great painter – responsible for another world-famous masterpiece, the ceiling of the Sistine Chapel of St Peter's in Rome – and this period saw major developments in painting. Artists strove for greater realism in their work, discovering laws of perspective and oil paints, both of which contributed to a new visual standard.

MYSTICISM AND SCIENCE

This burst of artistic creativity reflected a new emphasis on the importance of beauty. This was also connected to the Renaissance desire to return to the classical roots of European civilization, since it accompanied a rise of interest in Platonism. New philosophers appeared who wanted to overturn the Aristotelian emphasis that the universities had been teaching since Aquinas. They felt that Aristotle's thought was rather mundane and weaker than the more divine, spiritual teaching of Plato, and they sought to strip aside the layers of scholastic Aristotelianism and return to this more primordial, purer philosophy. This philosophy was really Neoplatonism,

David, by Michelangelo Buonarroti (1475–1564). Michelangelo completed the most famous sculpture of the Renaissance in 1504, at the age of 29.

241

which had flourished in the third and fourth centuries AD, rather than the thought of Plato himself; the Renaissance sages did not see a difference between them.

A key figure in this movement was Marsilio Ficino, a fifteenth-century Florentine who believed that all the vital teachings of Christianity could be found in the works of Plato. He founded a school in Florence called the Academy, after Plato's own school, and even kept a candle burning in front of a bust of the great philosopher. Yet Ficino was also a Catholic priest. He and others like him felt that religion and pagan philosophy alike taught the affinity between the human soul and the spiritual realm, and he insisted that all

I wish that the Scriptures might be translated into all languages, so that not only the Scots and the Irish, but also the Turk and the Saracen might read and understand them. I long that the farm-labourer might sing them as he follows his plough, the weaver hum them to the tune of his shuttle, the traveller beguile the weariness of his journey with their stories.

Erasmus of Rotterdam, a major humanist scholar and influence on the Reformation, *Greek New Testament*, 1516

Humanism and the cult of the 'text'

The most important intellectual movement of the Renaissance was humanism. The term 'humanism' was coined only in the nineteenth century – contemporaries spoke rather of 'humanistic studies' (*studia humanitatis*) – but both expressions refer to a form of classical education which placed an emphasis on the study of grammar, rhetoric, history, poetry and moral philosophy. Although it developed in Italy in the fourteenth and fifteenth centuries, where it was regarded as the best way of providing the necessary oratorical skills and moral instruction for active participation in the political life of the city-states, it soon spread to northern Europe as well: by the sixteenth century, almost all universities offered a humanist education. For most, such an education served as a preparation for a career in public office or business, for instance, but for a minority the scholarship remained an end in itself.

The father of the humanist movement was the renowned poet Francesco Petrarch (1304–74). He made great efforts to build up his own library, travelling through France, Spain, Italy and Germany on the hunt for manuscripts of classical texts, many of which lay hidden in monastic houses. He also played a crucial role in changing contemporary attitudes towards classical literature from suspicion to enthusiasm. After his death the baton was picked up by numerous groups and individuals, of whom none was more influential than Coluccio Salutati, the chancellor of Florence, whose own substantial library of classical manuscripts and high political profile undoubtedly further helped to popularize and disseminate the fledgling movement.

Inevitably these manuscripts, which had generally been copied by hand by monastic scribes, contained numerous errors and corruptions; humanist scholars sought to correct these, and in doing so came to establish the principles of a new more critical method for approaching them. Different versions of the same text were compared against each other to identify divergences; great emphasis was placed on learning the languages in which they were written; and increasing attention was devoted to understanding the history and culture of the civilizations which had produced them. Rapidly, the humanists came to a more sensitive understanding of the passage of time. Crucial here was Lorenzo Valla, whose work demonstrated how the Latin language had changed over time: as a result, it became increasingly possible to identify anachronistic and therefore erroneous words and phrases in existing texts, and to suggest more likely alternatives.

While efforts to move towards definitive versions of these classical texts continued – an enterprise considerably aided by the advent of printing – scholars also turned their attentions increasingly towards the ancient sources of Christianity. These so-called 'Christian humanists', more frequently based in northern Europe, sought to apply the same critical techniques as had been applied to Greek and Roman texts, to the Bible and other early Christian writings, with a view to returning them to their original pristine condition, so that their meaning might be properly understood. In 1516 a Greek text of the New Testament was published for the first time, along with a translation into Latin by the celebrated humanist Erasmus of Rotterdam (c. 1466–1536). The publication of this and similar works by other humanists would have a profound influence on the religious developments of the sixteenth century and beyond.

KENNETH AUSTIN

religions offer their own paths to God. Others believed that this spiritual teaching had been passed down in secret traditions, which could be understood only by the initiated. There was thus almost a return to Gnosticism in some quarters. For example, Philippus von Hohenheim – who called himself 'Paracelsus' – was a doctor whose revolutionary approach to medicine and the use of herbal remedies made him the father of modern chemistry. But he also stressed the esoteric and the mystical, appealing to supposed ancient sources of wisdom such as Hermes Trismegistus (a legendary magician who was believed to have lived in ancient Egypt). Where, today, we would talk about 'science', Paracelsus talked about 'magic', and like many others he also devoted much time to the search for the 'philosophers' stone' which could grant eternal life.

The Renaissance thus saw a rise in magic and mysticism, but paradoxically it also saw a rise in what we would recognize as modern science. Figures such as Galileo and Kepler pioneered the use of the scientific method, framing hypotheses on the basis of evidence. The popular view has it that magic and superstition were the stuff of the Middle Ages, and science came later and dispelled them – but in reality magic and science both developed at the same time and from the same stable.

Yet the most significant development of the Renaissance was a mechanical one, and it occurred not in Italy but in Germany. In the 1450s Johann Gutenberg, a silversmith, developed a method of printing with movable cast type. His cast type could be rearranged to print any text quickly and efficiently. Instead of having to copy all books by hand, they could now be mass produced

A reconstruction of Johann Gutenberg's printing press.

cheaply. An information revolution was at hand, where ideas could be circulated more quickly than ever before. This information revolution would fuel the Reformation.

BACKLASHES
As all this suggests, the Renaissance involved an element of religious renewal. Christianity was reinterpreted in line with Neoplatonic mysticism. Inevitably, some

The condemnation of Galileo

The story of Galileo's defence of Copernicus's heliocentric cosmology, leading to trial and condemnation by an intolerant Catholic Church, has for many people become symbolic of a long-standing pattern of Christian hostility toward scientific conclusions that are inconsistent with a literal interpretation of the Bible. Galileo has thus come to be viewed as a martyr in a drama of perennial warfare. When the myths are stripped away, however, we find a truth far more complicated and a great deal more interesting than the myths it replaces.

In 1611 Galileo Galilei (1564–1642), professor of mathematics at the University of Padua in northern Italy, travelled to Rome to display his new telescope and the discoveries he had made using it. His discoveries were confirmed and he was acclaimed by a variety of dignitaries, including the astronomers at the Jesuit College in Rome. Contrary to myth, Galileo encountered no reluctance on the part of church officials to look at the new celestial wonders through his telescope.

Some of Galileo's telescopic discoveries contributed to the plausibility of the heliocentric model, but there were worries about its compatibility with scripture, literally interpreted. Galileo argued that the Bible is not a scientific textbook and should not be interpreted literally when it appears to address scientific matters. However, this exacerbated Galileo's problems, for here was a layman claiming the right to interpret scripture.

Galileo returned to Rome in 1615, to fight smouldering fires of resentment and backstage manoeuvring against him. There he had frequent opportunities to make his case at dinners and other social gatherings of the Roman intelligentsia. Passionate, arrogant, and quick to display his argumentative prowess, Galileo alienated some of the very people whose favour he ought to have been cultivating.

In 1616 the Holy Office (the Inquisition) completed its review of accusations made previously against Galileo and heliocentrism. He was summoned to the residence of Cardinal Robert Bellarmine (head of the Holy Office and the most powerful Catholic theologian of his day). Galileo was informed that the Copernican model had been judged false and contrary to Holy Scripture. He was admonished to abandon these opinions and forbidden to 'hold, teach, or defend' them in any manner or form, either verbally or in writing.

The ecclesiastical officials who decided the case argued (rightly) that neither Galileo's telescopic observations nor the ability of the heliocentric model to make accurate astronomical predictions constituted proof that the Copernican model represented physical reality. Against heliocentrism stood, first of all, church tradition, which the Roman theological establishment was not going to abandon without good reason. There were also biblical passages that apparently addressed the cosmological question, referring to the sun's motions rather than the earth's.

Added to this was a philosophical argument widely accepted by both astronomers and members of the church hierarchy – namely, that astronomical models were designed merely to predict planetary positions, with no pretence of describing physical reality. We cannot get up into the heavens to find out what is really going on; only God knows the mechanism that underlies the celestial motions. However, Galileo was convinced that proof was possible in the form of his theory of the tides. The tides, he claimed, could only be the result of the double motion of the earth (rotating on its axis while orbiting the sun), which caused the seas to slosh back and forth in their basins.

The ecclesiastical authorities responded that in the absence of a proof, there was no reason for them to tamper with the

traditional, common-sense interpretation of scripture. The community of scientists overwhelmingly supported the geocentric model, and it would have been an extraordinary thing for the church to abandon its traditional interpretation, common sense *and* majority scientific opinion in order to leap onto Galileo's lonely bandwagon. This struggle did not pit the church against Galileo and the scientific community, but Galileo and a small band of disciples against the church and most of the scientific community.

In 1623 a new pope was elected, Urban VIII. This was a stroke of luck, for he was considered a moderate on the subject of heliocentrism; moreover, Galileo had a history of friendly relations with him. Urban believed that humans were, in principle, incapable of achieving certainty regarding cosmological matters, but he permitted Galileo to examine the pros and cons of heliocentrism in a book, provided he did not defend its truth. Galileo set to work on his *Dialogue on the two chief world systems*, published in 1632. In the book he presented extensive, powerful arguments in favor of heliocentrism, unmistakably defending it as true. On the final page of the book, Galileo put the pope's admonition about the hypothetical character of heliocentrism into the mouth of Simplicio, the slow-witted Aristotelian laughing-stock of the *Dialogue*.

The book was an instant sensation. Urban discovered his words in the mouth of Simplicio and became convinced that Galileo had betrayed his trust and ridiculed him. Such insubordination could not be overlooked, and it was inevitable that the machinery of the Inquisition would be set in motion against Galileo.

Galileo was accused of violating the injunction of 1616, which forbade him to hold or defend the heliocentric model; and it must have been clear to everybody concerned that he was guilty. Galileo was elements within the church did not go along with it.

On the one hand, the old traditions of philosophy and spirituality were still going strong. It was in the fifteenth century that one of the best and most famous summaries of medieval spirituality was written, *The imitation of Christ* by Thomas à Kempis. This book was firmly in the tradition of Christ-centred

forced to recant. For the remaining ten years of his life, he was under house arrest, comfortably housed in a villa just outside Florence, with few restrictions on who could come and go. He was never tortured or imprisoned – simply silenced.

What can we learn from this story? The outcome of the Galileo affair was a contingent event, powerfully influenced by local circumstances. It was not merely about universal or global aspects of science and religion, but about the local circumstances impinging on individual historical actors – fear, jealousy, revenge, greed, bias, ambition, personality, rivalry, alliances and political context. Galileo's personality looms large in the story. If Galileo had learned diplomacy; if he had walked softly, been willing to compromise, and understood the value of strategic retreat, it is likely that he could have carried out a significant campaign on behalf of heliocentrism without condemnation.

Was this a battle between Christianity and science, an episode in the alleged warfare of science and religion – the view that has dominated understanding of the Galileo affair? In fact, every one of the actors called himself a Christian. Every one of them acknowledged the authority of the Bible and also had well-considered cosmological views. Bellarmine had actually taught astronomy at the University of Louvain as a young man and fully understood the issues. The battle turns out not to have been between science and Christianity, but within Christianity: between opposing theories of biblical interpretation – the one progressive, the other traditional; and within science, between the proponents of competing cosmologies. The battle lines simply did not fall along a divide separating science from religion.

DAVID LINDBERG

Galileo demonstrates his telescope to a group of Venetian noblemen.

If a man knows what it is to love Jesus, and to disregard himself for the sake of Jesus, then he is really blessed. We have to abandon all we love for the one we love, for Jesus wants us to love him only above all things. Whether you will or no, you must one day leave everything behind. Keep yourself close to Jesus in life as well as death; commit yourself to his faithfulness, for he only can help you when everything else will fail.

Thomas à Kempis, *The imitation of Christ*, 1418

mysticism which had developed in the later Middle Ages, in the hands of famous writers such as Julian of Norwich (who despite the name was an English woman of the fourteenth century). Yet Thomas had been educated at a school set up by the *Devotio Moderna* of Geert Groote, and was deeply imbued with its principles of personal integrity and devotion to Christ.

But, if medieval religion was alive and well even as the Renaissance gathered pace, others tried to turn the clock back. The most dramatic protest against the Renaissance and its influence on Christianity was that of Girolamo Savonarola (1452–98), a Dominican from Ferrara. Savonarola was a brilliant scholar, immersed in scholastic philosophy, but he had an extremely austere understanding of spirituality. He believed that Christians were under a divine injunction to live soberly and devote themselves to God alone, and that any attempt to glorify the works of man necessarily involved sinful pride and idolatry. To his mind, the flourishing of art, the cult of beauty and the interest in Platonic spirituality of the Renaissance was wholly opposed to the true spirit of the gospel. It was an attempt to dethrone God and replace him with man.

In 1489 Savonarola arrived at Florence, the cultural centre of the Renaissance, and he preached powerfully against what he denounced as paganism and self-indulgence. The cathedral was packed as

the crowds flocked to listen, many of whom shrieked or collapsed as Savonarola spoke. Such was his power over the people that after the death of Lorenzo de Medici 'the Magnificent', ruler of the city, in 1492, Savonarola succeeded in imposing a new constitution on the city according to which Christ alone was recognized as king. Whipped up by Savonarola's preaching, the city council outlawed activities such as gambling, while the punishment for homosexual acts was upgraded from a fine to death. Young men, enthused by the reforms, formed bands to travel from house to house, confiscating cards and encouraging modest dress codes.

In 1495 Pope Alexander VI banned the increasingly fanatical Savonarola from preaching, but he continued to do so, and now he called for the destruction of all that the Renaissance had achieved: the artworks, the manuscripts of the humanists, everything that in his view distracted people from God. In February 1497 Savonarola's gangs swept through Florence, confiscating paintings, books, fine clothes and cosmetics. The enthusiastic crowd hurled them onto a huge bonfire: such was the public support for the move that Sandro Botticelli, one of the most important artists of the day, threw his own paintings on the pyre to atone for his sinfulness in creating them.

Yet this 'Bonfire of the Vanities' marked the high-water point of Savonarola's campaign against the Renaissance. He began to preach against Rome itself and was excommunicated that May. In that same month there were riots against his theocratic rule, and drinking and gambling were again seen in public. Savonarola, who in the end had failed to understand that you cannot force people to reform, was overthrown, and in 1498 he was hanged in the very square where he had burned the treasures of Florence.

THE RENAISSANCE PAPACY

As Savonarola's ill-fated campaign suggests, the Renaissance was a time when – in the eyes of some – the old religious certainties were being challenged. And indeed, throughout the Renaissance, the church gradually lost much of the power it had enjoyed during the Middle Ages. The big names of the Renaissance were no longer bishops and abbots: they were more likely to be university professors.

The most prominent – and notorious – developments of this period concerned the papacy. After the failure of the Council of Florence in the 1430s and 40s to restore union with the Orthodox Church, the papacy largely lost interest in wider ecclesiastical matters like this and became concerned with improving Rome. A string of fifteenth-century popes widened streets,

You are now devoted to God and to the church, and so you should try to be a good churchman, and show that you prefer the honour and condition of the church and the apostolic see to anything else. But while you do this, it will not be hard for you to favour your family and your place of birth. On the contrary, you should be the link that binds this city more closely to the church, and our family with the city. Although we cannot foresee what accidents may happen, I do not doubt that this can be done to everyone's advantage – bearing in mind, though, that you must always favour the church's interests.

Lorenzo de Medici 'the Magnificent' of Florence, letter to his son, the future Pope Leo X, c. 1491

Vatican City, Rome, during Christmas Mass. St Peter's Square, in front of the basilica, was designed by Giovanni Bernini (1598–1680).

built palaces and generally sought to turn Rome into a modern, Renaissance city like Florence. Nicholas V, who became pope in 1447, set the tone. Sometimes known as 'the Great Humanist', he was a well-educated man who sought to promote both art and scholarship in Rome, bringing both the city and the papacy in line with humanism and the Renaissance in general.

Later in the century things became very much worse, to an extent not seen since the early eleventh century. Sixtus IV, pope from 1471 to 1484, appointed thirty-four cardinals – mostly his friends or patrons, including six nephews. And in 1492 one of Calixtus III's nephews, Rodrigo Borgia, became Pope Alexander VI. One of the most notorious popes, Alexander VI had risen through the church purely on the strength of his connections and his wealth, but still he secured the papacy only by voting for himself. One of the first things he did was install his eighteen-year-old mistress in a nearby palace, with a secret door to St Peter's so he could visit her easily. He had had several children when he was a cardinal, and he spent much of his time trying to secure good careers for them: one appalling son, Cesare, was made archbishop of Valencia at the age of eighteen within a week of his father becoming pope. Cesare was in the habit of shooting criminals with a crossbow from a balcony of the Lateran Palace, although it is unlikely that, as the rumour-mongers claimed, he was sleeping with his sister, Lucrezia. He did, however, mastermind the murder of Lucrezia's husband – which occurred when the pope was in the next room. The best thing that can be said about Alexander VI is that he managed to avoid being deposed by the French.

Nevertheless, the excesses of the Renaissance popes have often been exaggerated. For example, Pope Paul II, who reigned from 1464 to 1471, was said by his enemies to enjoy having prisoners whipped and to have died whilst engaged in an unnatural act with a pageboy. In fact, Paul II seems to have been a relatively inoffensive man who spent his time decorating churches and organizing carnivals. The Borgia family, meanwhile, were pilloried even in their own lifetime as monsters of incestuous and murderous depravity; the name of Lucrezia Borgia, in particular, is still associated with serial seductions and mass poisonings. But, although the Borgias were corrupt and often cruel, their murderous reputation was certainly exaggerated by their political enemies and later writers.

Whatever the quality of the popes' pastoral activities, uplifting changes were being made to the Vatican. The basilica that Constantine had built was found, by the mid-fifteenth century, to be leaning quite badly, and the plan was conceived to build a new one. Construction of the new church of St Peter's was begun in 1506 and continued under a succession of architects and designers – including Michelangelo – until 1615. The basilica that resulted was the largest church in the world. The sculptor Giovanni Bernini was then commissioned to decorate its interior and to design St Peter's Square, which featured two colonnades stretching around it, like the arms of the church reaching out to the world. Another remarkable development in this period was the series of discoveries of Antonio Bosio, a Maltese man who, like a Renaissance-era Indiana Jones, stumbled upon and explored the vast catacombs of ancient Rome. His book of 1629, describing what he found, provoked great interest in Christian antiquity.

Despite the increasing magnificence of the Vatican's buildings and the money that flowed through its coffers, the papacy as an institution was seeing its influence in the world at large wane. This was not due simply to the corruption or ineffectualness of many of the popes. Both theologically and politically, its position was becoming less assured. Theologically, its power was being eroded by the rise of conciliarism, the notion that the supreme authority in the church was not the pope but councils of bishops. In its weak form, conciliarism attributed this authority only to 'ecumenical councils', that is, councils of the whole church, ratified by the pope, like Nicaea. But a stronger form of the doctrine insisted that the pope's ratification was not actually necessary and at councils the bishops could act independently of him. William Ockham, for example, writing in the fourteenth century, had marshalled a battery of arguments against the notion that the pope was the supreme authority in either church and state, and insisted that the emperor had the right to depose a heretical pope. The Great Schism of the fourteenth century, and the role of the Council of Constance in ending it, had given such views greater plausibility.

Meanwhile, the papacy had lost most of its political power as the nation states of Europe became stronger. The Vatican had become simply another court, one which had lost any real influence in the world, and which was drenched in corruption. Little wonder that voices of protest were beginning to be heard. Wycliffe, Hus and Savonarola had all come and been crushed in their turn; but even as the last of these would-be reformers died in Florence, a far more significant protest against the papacy was brewing to the north, in the person of an unregarded German monk.

THE EARLY REFORMATION

The causes of the Reformation were certainly myriad and complex, and of course no single individual can really be responsible for the whole thing. But Martin Luther was the catalyst, if not the sole cause, for the remarkable religious upheaval of the sixteenth century.

MARTIN LUTHER AND THE 95 THESES
Arguably the most significant figure of the last millennium, Martin Luther, the 'German Hercules', was born in the village of Eisleben in 1483, and became an Augustinian monk as a young man. In 1508 he began to teach at a new university in Wittenberg, a small town in

Saxony, a state in the north of what is now Germany. 'Germany', of course, did not yet exist as a political entity: the Holy Roman empire was still the major power in the eastern half of western Europe. It was by this time essentially a federation of smaller states, whose princes (or 'electors') elected the overall king, who as a matter of course would then be crowned emperor by the pope in the time-honoured fashion. European politics were at this time dominated by the Hapsburg family, who ruled not only the Holy Roman empire but much of Spain as well, not to mention the Low Countries. It was here, on the convenient date of All Souls' Day in 1517, that Luther inadvertently began the Reformation.

The initial issue was simple enough. It concerned the sale of indulgences, which had developed in the later Middle Ages as an important source of revenue for the

Portrait of Martin Luther, by the German artist Lucas Cranach the elder (1472–1553).

church. They were concerned with the sacrament of confession. Normally, if you sinned, you confessed to a priest and were given a penance. The penance was necessary not to obtain forgiveness for the sin – that was guaranteed by Christ's sacrifice – but it was believed that the sinner's soul still needed to be purified before it would be able to go into heaven. Any purification that was left over at the point of death would be done in purgatory, a sort of unpleasant celestial waiting room. However, some people lived such good lives that they died with no purging still to do, and they went straight to heaven. These were the saints. They had built up a 'treasury of merit', which the church could apply to people as it saw fit: thus, you could get 'let off' a penance (or time in purgatory) by tapping into this treasury.

By Luther's day, the practice was riddled with abuse. The case which angered him concerned Albrecht of Brandenberg, who was archbishop of Magdeburg and of Mainz at the same time, as well as administrator of Halberstadt. This itself was extremely irregular (the canons of the Council of Nicaea forbade bishops from transferring from one diocese to another, let alone running several at once). However, Pope Leo X – a nepotistic member of the Medici family, already a cardinal as a teenager – allowed Albrecht to do this, provided he

paid a substantial sum of money to the Vatican for the privilege. Albrecht's means of paying was to collect revenues from the indulgences sold in his dioceses. Leo X was addicted to lavish spending, on both extravagant luxury and generous charitable causes such as hospitals and poor houses in Rome, as a result of which he exhausted the previously overflowing Vatican coffers within two years of becoming pope; so he was keen to raise money wherever possible. But Albrecht issued a document with his indulgences explaining how they worked, and in it he apparently claimed that his indulgences would not simply absolve the purchaser from the need to make penance for their sins: they would actually forgive those sins. This was a major change from the accepted understanding of indulgences.

Little wonder, then, that Martin Luther felt that it was time for a debate about the theory and practice of indulgences. He wrote a list of 95 'theses' (or short statements) questioning the ability of indulgences to forgive sins, which he planned to use as the basis of an academic debate. He sent this list to his local bishop and to Albrecht of Brandenberg, and (according to some accounts) he also put it up on the door of the university church in Wittenberg, which was used as a notice board.

Luther's intention was to have a small

The pope commissions indulgence sellers, in a propagandist woodcut by the German artist Hans Holbein the younger (c. 1497–1543).

scholarly debate, but as he later wrote, 'What I did toppled heaven and consumed earth by fire.' Albrecht sent a copy of the 95 theses to the pope, and printers began distributing pirate editions. Luther's own faculty at Wittenberg supported him, and his students burned the writings that began to appear attacking him. Luther wrote in defence of his theses, but others reacted with hostility. The Vatican prepared an official response to Luther, which stated that he was wrong, since the pope and church councils, which sanctioned indulgences, could not be mistaken.

Luther was deeply worried by all this. He had assumed that the church, including the pope, would unite against corruption – he did not expect the authorities to line up against him. He had also assumed that his theological opponents would try to defend the practice and theory of indulgences from the Bible. Instead, they ignored his arguments and even summoned him to Rome to be tried for heresy. Luther believed, however, that scripture should be the supreme authority in such matters. Could it be that the teaching of the Catholic Church and the teaching of scripture were at odds? A meeting with Cardinal Tommaso Cajetan (1469–1534), the superior general of the Dominicans, convinced him that they were. Cardinal Cajetan gave Luther a sympathetic hearing,

but insisted that his views contradicted the teachings of the pope and of the church councils. In 1519, the well-known theologian Johann Eck met Luther and his colleague and supporter Andreas Karlstadt in public debate at Leipzig. Cleverly, Eck turned the debate from a dispute over corruption and the role of indulgences into one about the authority of the pope, which he felt was the real issue at stake. Eck insisted that the pope was divinely appointed and had divine authority, and pointed out that Jan Hus had been burned for denying this. Luther, in turn, argued that Eck's view of the papacy had developed only in recent centuries and had been unknown to the early church: in particular, it was not to be found in the Bible.

Now Luther expanded his protest, attacking the doctrine of the Mass as sacrifice. For by this stage, the Catholic understanding of the Mass had made explicit the notion that the Mass was not only a sacrament (the means by which God's grace was disseminated to individuals) but also a sacrifice (a means by which Christ's sacrifice on the cross was offered to God). Instead, Luther insisted, the Mass made sense only if it was received in faith, as a promise of the gift of Christ to the believer. This meant that Masses could not be said for the dead. It was pointed out to Luther that the second book of Maccabees endorsed the saying of prayers for the dead. Luther retorted that this book, and the other deuterocanonical works, were not really part of the Bible at all. Luther was tapping into a tradition of unease with these books that had existed since the earliest Christian centuries – for, as we saw in Chapter 2, these books were in the Septuagint translation of the Old Testament that the early Christians used, but they were not in the Jewish canon as defined by the rabbis at the Council of Jamnia in the first century. Luther and his followers therefore took the radical step of abandoning the deuterocanonical works completely. This is why Catholic Bibles contain more books in the Old Testament

I began to understand that in this verse [Romans 1:17] the 'righteousness of God' means the way in which a righteous person lives through a gift of God – that is, by faith. I began to understand that this verse means that the righteousness of God is revealed through the Gospel, but it is a passive righteousness – that is, it is that by which the merciful God makes us righteous by faith, as it is written: 'The righteous person lives by faith.' All at once I felt that I had been born again and entered into paradise itself through open gates. Immediately I saw the whole of Scripture in a different light.

Martin Luther, *Preface to complete works*, 1545

It astounds me that anyone can be offended by something as obvious as this! Just tell me this. Is Christ's death and resurrection something that we do, or not? It is obviously not our work, nor is it the work of the law. Now it is Christ's death and resurrection alone which saves and frees us from sin, as Paul writes in Romans 4: 'He died for our sin and arose for our righteousness.' Tell me more! What is the work by which we take hold of Christ's death and resurrection? It can't be an external act but only the internal faith in the heart that alone, indeed all alone, takes hold of this death and resurrection when it is preached through the gospel. Then why all this ranting and raving, this making of heretics and burning of them, when it is clear at its very core, proving that faith alone takes hold of Christ's death and resurrection, without any works, and that his death and resurrection are our life and righteousness?

Martin Luther, *On translating*, 1530

than Protestant ones. Protestant Bibles sometimes print the deuterocanonical works as a separate section between the Old and New Testaments, called the Apocrypha.

And Luther attacked the very institution of the papacy itself, in the bitterest terms, as responsible for the 'Babylonian captivity' of Christianity. Some of the German princes approved, since they had no love for the power of the pope; Luther therefore wrote a work called *To the Christian nobility of the German nation*, addressed to the new Holy Roman emperor, Charles V, in which he attacked the whole ecclesiastical system, insisting that the Bible should be read by everyone, for all believers were priests. In 1520 Luther's views were condemned by the pope. The bull of condemnation ordered him to travel to Rome to deliver a recantation. Instead, Luther threw the bull on a bonfire before a crowd of his supporters. The pope responded by excommunicating him.

While the row took the form of a disagreement first about indulgences and then about the pope, at the heart of it was a doctrine that Luther had stumbled across while studying Paul's letter to the Romans at Wittenberg, and whose consequences he was still working out. This doctrine, 'justification by faith', was at the heart of his theology. Luther was convinced that the central message of Christianity was that people are saved not by what they do – whether by paying money to the church, going on pilgrimages, obeying the pope or anything else – but by a free gift, given through Christ's sacrifice and accepted by the believer through faith. This was the basic notion that drove Luther's criticisms of contemporary Catholic views and practices, and it would remain central to the whole Protestant movement after him.

In 1521 the Holy Roman empire convened a diet – or council – at the town of Worms. These were held regularly as part of the running of the empire. At this one, among many other matters addressed was the problem of Martin Luther. In the presence of Charles V himself, Luther was asked whether he would recant what he had written. Luther asked for a day to prepare his answer, but he apparently did not waver in his conviction. He replied – eventually –

Your imperial majesty and your lordships demand a simple answer. Here it is, plain and unvarnished. Unless I am convinced by Scripture or by clear reason – for I do not trust the Pope or church councils, since everyone knows that they can make mistakes and contradict themselves – I am bound by the Scriptures I have quoted. My conscience is held captive by the Word of God. I cannot and will not take back anything, because it is neither safe nor right to go against conscience.

In reply, the emperor stated that whatever arguments Luther had for his views, he must be mistaken, because it was inconceivable that he alone should be right and a thousand years of church tradition be wrong. He condemned Luther, making him officially an outlaw as well as a heretic. But Frederick 'the Wise', the elector of Saxony, protected Luther, hiding him in a castle for nearly a year.

THE NEW CHURCHES
Despite the imperial and papal edicts, a powerful reform movement was brewing. It has been said that a full third of all books sold in the German-speaking world in the 1520s were written by Martin Luther. The movement's heart was Wittenberg, where Luther's colleagues and sympathizers, including his friend Karlstadt and another colleague, Philip Melanchthon (1497–1560), led the movement. Those who were priests began to lead services in normal clothes, without vestments. They gave both bread and wine to the congregation, instead of just wine, as had been the custom previously. Statues and images were torn down as further instances of medieval superstition. Like Luther, these followers were convinced that salvation

comes through the faith of the individual, not through the mediation of the church; but some were beginning to take the principle to extremes. Prophets appeared who claimed that God had spoken to them directly.

Meanwhile, Luther himself was putting into practice the other central tenet of the reformers, which was that the authority of the Bible was greater than that of the church. While in hiding, Luther translated the New Testament into German: the work was an enormous success, selling 5,000 copies in two months – impressive, given that only one in three city inhabitants could read, and in the countryside only one in twenty.

Returning from hiding in 1522, Luther reversed many of the reforms that had been made at Wittenberg, such as the abolition of infant baptism: he felt that things were going too far. But the movement was spiralling out of his control. Thomas Müntzer (c. 1489–1525), a preacher at Allstedt, denounced Luther as too conservative, and taught that each individual can have direct access to divine revelation without needing to bother even about the Bible. Müntzer also denounced the rulers of the empire, who he believed had oppressed the lower classes. In contrast to Luther, who like Paul taught that temporal rulers should always be obeyed, Müntzer encouraged rebellion. So did other preachers, and throughout the empire peasants did rebel, attacking castles and towns as well as monasteries. An uprising at Frankenhausen was met by imperial troops. They mercilessly fired upon the peasants, who found that Müntzer's claim that God would protect them from bullets was not true after all. Müntzer himself was executed and the rebellion brutally put down.

In this affair Luther had been on the side of the princes, not the peasants, and many princes approved of his ideas. The reformers found many states protected them or even encouraged them, despite the edict of Worms. Whether or not all these princes agreed with or even understood Luther's theology, they were happy to encourage something that might enhance their own political standing over and against the emperor and the pope. In 1529 a new diet at Speyer tried to discourage this tendency. Many of the princes made a formal protest to the emperor, and it is from this protest that the word 'Protestant' comes. Soon it would be applied to the whole movement.

Luther and his circle now sought to clarify their views, in the hope of creating an agreed set of doctrines for all Protestants. In 1530 Philip Melanchthon, in consultation with Luther, revised an earlier set of doctrinal statements that had been drawn up. The resulting creed was sent to a meeting of the German princes, together with the emperor, at Augsburg in 1530. The princes accepted the creed, which became known as the Augsburg Confession. This would be one of the most important statements of Lutheran belief.

And Lutheranism spread beyond the empire. One of the first non-German-speaking regions to be influenced by the new movement was Scandinavia. Two brothers named Olav and Lars Petri, disciples of Luther, brought his ideas to Sweden: here they were lucky to find a sympathetic hearer in the person of King Gustavus Vasa. In 1527 he decreed that Lutheranism was now the official state religion. The existing Catholic hierarchy was converted, relatively painlessly, to the new version of Christianity. Denmark took a little longer. Here, King Frederick I was also sympathetic to Lutheranism, but there was considerable opposition among his churchmen. Many fled, leaving parts of the country without any effective church organization. However, Christian III, who succeeded to the throne in 1536, continued his programme of reform. He contacted Luther himself for help. Luther had only one follower who spoke both Danish and German, named Johann Bugenhagen. So he sent him to Denmark, where he proceeded to set up a brand new Lutheran church. First he crowned the king, and then he appointed new bishops.

Also [we] teach that men cannot be justified before God by their own strength, merits, or works, but are freely justified for Christ's sake, through faith, when they believe that they are received into favour, and that their sins are forgiven for Christ's sake, who, by His death, has made satisfaction for our sins. This faith God imputes for righteousness in His sight.

The Augsburg Confession, 1530

Ulrich Zwingli, by the Swiss painter Hans Asper (1499–1571).

We will test everything by the touchstone of the Gospel and the fire of Paul. Where we find anything that is in conformity with the Gospel, we will preserve it; where we find something that does not conform to it, we will put it out… Because one must obey God rather than man.

Ulrich Zwingli, *Archeteles*, 1522

Much the same thing happened in Norway and Iceland, where Danish missionaries travelled to bring Lutheranism. By the 1540s, the whole of Scandinavia was very firmly Lutheran.

THE SWISS REFORMATION

Although the most significant figure in all this, Luther was not the only catalyst for change. Another was Ulrich Zwingli, who in 1519 became the 'people's priest' of Zürich (this was the most important ecclesiastical position there). Switzerland at this time was within the Holy Roman empire, but its city-states, known as 'cantons', formed a loose and semi-autonomous federation. Zwingli was trained in humanism and knew Erasmus. He was concerned that Christianity should return to its roots in the New Testament, and he spoke out against clerical abuses at Zürich, such as the practice of priests taking mistresses. As his popularity and power in the region increased, he began to insist that the Bible alone should be the source for Christian practice and belief. In particular, he attacked the practice of fasting, which he felt was not authorized by scripture and was a solely human command. At his instigation, widespread reforms were put in place in Zürich in the mid-1520s, including the abolition of indulgences, pilgrimages, confession and extreme unction. Clerical celibacy was also abolished, and monks and nuns began to marry, as did Zwingli himself. Icons and statues, as well as altars and organs, were destroyed, and church vessels such as chalices were melted down. Even the service of the Mass was abolished, being replaced with the celebration of the Lord's Supper – for Zwingli rejected not only the idea of the Mass being a sacrifice, but even the belief that the bread and wine actually become the body and blood of Christ.

Zwingli and his reform movement were also associated with one Johann Heusegen, normally known by the Greek version of his name, Oecolampadius. He was a serious-minded humanist who had studied with Erasmus, who preached in the Swiss city of Basle, and who was an early convert to Luther's movement. He especially taught Luther's doctrine that people are saved through faith alone, not through performing any actions. Inspired by him, the people of Basle followed those of Zürich in removing all the paraphernalia of medieval Catholicism. Oecolampadius also negotiated with the Waldensians, who still had strongholds in the Alps, and encouraged them to join and merge with the new reform movement. Most did so.

The big point of disagreement between Zwingli and Oecolampadius on the one hand and Luther and his supporters on the other was the Eucharist. All agreed that the Mass was not a sacrifice, but Luther maintained the traditional belief that the bread and wine are transformed into Christ's body and blood – although he insisted that, at the same time, they also remained bread and wine. The Swiss reformers believed that they never changed at all. This was a big sticking point, and the German princes who supported the reform movement were keen for it to be resolved, since they felt that an alliance with the Protestant Swiss cantons would be politically advantageous. Philip, prince of Hesse, therefore arranged a meeting of the leaders of both factions at Marburg in 1529. The two-day discussions unfortunately failed to produce any agreement. Zwingli clung to John 6:63 – 'It is the spirit that gives life: the flesh is useless' – arguing that God works through the heart, not physical things such as bread. Luther, meanwhile, seized a piece of chalk and wrote on the table between them the words of Matthew 26:26 – 'This is my body' – and declared that Zwingli's viewpoint amounted to a denial of the incarnation itself. The meeting ended unsatisfactorily, with an agreement to disagree: Luther even refused to shake Zwingli's hand, which moved the Swiss reformer to tears.

THE RADICAL REFORMATION

The failure of the Marburg colloquy to unite the German and Swiss reformers was symptomatic of the divisions that were appearing in the Protestant movement. Radicals in the mould of Karlstadt and Müntzer continued to appear. The most significant of these radicals were the Anabaptists. The word 'Anabaptist' – which was given to them by others – meant 're-baptizer', and reflected their practice of re-baptizing everyone who embraced their ideals. Luther agreed with the Catholic Church that re-baptism was not possible, even if the original baptism had been heretical or schismatic, because Christ always works through the sacrament irrespective of who performs it. The Anabaptists, however, insisted that since salvation comes through faith alone, baptism itself could do nothing unless one already believed. Infants clearly did not believe, so their baptisms were invalid: thus everyone had to be re-baptized. Luther, for

his part, agreed that faith was necessary (and sufficient) for salvation, but he argued that God could give infants the faith necessary to receive meaningful baptism, or that they were baptized on account of their parents' or godparents' faith.

The Anabaptist movement originated in Zürich, where radical reformers tired of waiting for the council to put into practice Zwingli's ideas. They felt that Christians should meet and worship as scripture commanded, whether or not the secular authorities approved, and so they ignored the city's council when it banned them in 1525. The movement spread, as Anabaptist groups, regarding most of Europe as no longer Christian, sprang up in cities across the continent. In 1527 they held a meeting at Schleitheim, where they formed a 'Brotherly Union' or doctrinal agreement.

The Anabaptists were convinced that real Christianity involved demonstrating evidence of obedience to Christ – and the commands of scripture – rather than simply believing in a set of propositions. This worried the mainstream Protestants, as it apparently contradicted their insistence on salvation by faith alone. Moreover, the Anabaptists developed what is known as a 'congregational' form of government, where the members of the whole church, not simply the priests (and of course they denied that 'priests' had any special abilities withheld from ordinary believers), took all the decisions.

The Protestants and the Catholics alike declared war on the Anabaptists, and many were executed. The worst event occurred at Münster in 1535, where a group of radical Anabaptists had seized power, predicted the imminent arrival of Christ and declared that the Old Testament Law was still valid, including polygamy. Catholic forces crushed the movement. Yet Anabaptism continued to flourish, especially under the preaching of one Menno Simons. He travelled throughout northern Europe, strengthening and encouraging the Anabaptist groups, rather as Jacob Baradaeus had inspired the Monophysites in the sixth century. Simons was an

Baptism shall be given to all those who have learned repentance and amendment of life, and who believe truly that their sins are taken away by Christ, and to all those who walk in the resurrection of Jesus Christ, and wish to be buried with him in death, so that they may be resurrected with him and to all those who with significance request it of us and demand it for themselves. This excludes all infant baptism, the highest and chief abomination of the pope.

The Schleitheim Confession, a statement of belief by the Anabaptist Swiss Brethren, 1527

The regenerated do not go to war, nor engage in strife. They are the children of peace who have beaten their swords into ploughshares and their spears into pruning hooks, and know of no war... Since we are to be conformed to the image of Christ, how can we then fight our enemies with the sword?... Spears and swords of iron we leave to those who, alas, consider human blood and swine's blood of well-nigh equal value.

Menno Simons, Foundation of Christian doctrine, 1539

Albeit the king's Majesty justly and rightfully is and ought to be the supreme head of the Church of England, and so is recognized by the clergy of this realm in their convocations, yet nevertheless, for corroboration and confirmation thereof, and for increase of virtue in Christ's religion within this realm of England, and to repress and extirpate all errors, heresies, and other enormities and abuses heretofore used in the same, be it enacted, by authority of this present Parliament, that the king, our sovereign lord, his heirs and successors, kings of this realm, shall be taken, accepted, and reputed the only supreme head on earth of the Church of England…

The Act of Supremacy, 1534

Whereas Saint Paul would have such language spoken to the people in the church, as they might understand, and have profit by hearing the same; the service in this Church of England (these many years) hath been read in Latin to the people, which they understood not: so that they have heard with their ears only; and their hearts, spirit, and mind, have not been edified thereby.

Book of Common Prayer, 1552, preface

uncompromising pacifist and urged the Anabaptists never to meet force with force, as the leaders of Münster had. Such was his influence that the Anabaptist churches inspired by him became known as 'Mennonite'.

THE CHURCH OF ENGLAND

The English Reformation had its unlikely origins in King Henry VIII's inability to produce a son with his wife, Catherine of Aragon; they had a daughter, Mary, but the king was determined to have a male heir. He wanted Pope Clement VII to annul his marriage and allow him to marry the much younger Anne Boleyn, but the pope was reluctant – not least because Catherine was the aunt of the Holy Roman emperor, Charles V, not a man to cross. But Henry ignored the pope and in 1533 married Anne anyway. In 1534, finally deciding to side with Charles over Henry, Pope Clement declared that this marriage was invalid. Henry responded with breathtaking audacity, declaring that from now on the church in England would be under *his* control, not the pope's, and that *his* church would certainly recognize the new marriage. A series of measures during the 1530s transferred control of the existing church structures to the king.

Henry enforced this innovative approach to church–state relations with an iron fist. The Act of Supremacy, by which the king became the head of the church, was to be recognized in an oath of supremacy which all churchmen were required to swear. Many, such as Sir Thomas More, refused to do this, and they were executed. The monasteries, which were loyal to the pope, were closed down, their buildings destroyed and their goods confiscated and distributed among the aristocracy.

The brains behind much of this was Thomas Cromwell, a member of parliament who served as the king's chief minister. He drafted most of the legislation which severed the English church from Rome, and may have been responsible for the idea in the first place. Cromwell was extremely unpopular with traditionalists in England,

especially as his men began their destruction of shrines throughout the country, including that of Thomas Becket in Canterbury. In protest at his actions, there was an uprising near York in 1536 known as the 'Pilgrimage of Grace', when several thousand people marched on the city, let all the monks and nuns return home and reinstituted Catholic worship. The rebellion was crushed, the people were massacred and their leaders executed. Henry was notoriously quick to execute those suspected of treason, and Cromwell himself fell out of favour and was beheaded – without a trial – in 1540.

Henry's other chief adviser in his version of the Reformation was Thomas Cranmer, an academic who became archbishop of Canterbury in 1533. Cranmer had been influenced by Martin Luther, and he helped to ensure that the new Church of England – the Anglican Church – was essentially Protestant in character, rather than simply a smaller, copycat version of the Roman Catholic Church. Cranmer wrote the hugely important *Book of Common Prayer*, the collection of prayers and liturgies for use in English churches. The fact that this was written in English rather than Latin was radical enough, but the book also lacked many 'Catholic' features, such as representing the Eucharist as a sacrifice. The book appeared in 1549, but Cranmer was already feeling more Protestant by the time it was published, and he produced a second edition in 1552 which took the church in a still more Protestant direction.

Henry VIII died in 1547 and was succeeded by his son (by his *third* wife, Jane Seymour), Edward VI. Edward was a sickly teenager who died in 1553 and was succeeded by his older sister Mary. Mary reigned for only five years, but in that time quickly made herself into one of English history's most notorious monarchs. She was a devout Catholic and was determined to roll back the reforms of her father. Those who refused to renounce Protestantism were executed – in all, about 300 people, including Thomas Cranmer, who was burned at the stake in Oxford in 1556. For

ANNO · ETATIS ·   · SVÆ · XLIX ·

Henry VIII, by the German artist Hans Holbein the younger (c. 1497–1543).

this, the Queen became known as 'Bloody Mary' – although it is sometimes said that the epithet came not from her cruelty but from her Catholic belief that the wine of the Eucharist becomes Christ's blood. However, Mary's plan backfired. The bravery of those who died was remembered, partly through the work of John Foxe. In 1563 he published a book called *Acts and monuments* but better known as Foxe's *Book of martyrs*, which described their courage and the cruelty of their persecutors in graphic detail.

For centuries to come, Foxe's book would be widely read, and many in England developed a sometimes pathological hatred of Catholics. The earlier persecution of Catholics by Henry VIII was, apparently, largely forgotten. Even more significantly, the persecution of Catholics under Elizabeth I (after Foxe was writing) would be largely forgotten too.

Mary, having
succeeded by false
promises in obtaining
the crown, speedily
commenced the
execution of her
avowed intention of
extirpating and
burning every
Protestant. She was
crowned at
Westminster in the
usual form, and her
elevation was the
signal for the
commencement of the
bloody persecution
which followed.

John Foxe, Book of
martyrs, 1563

We are accounted
righteous before God,
only for the merit of
our Lord and Saviour
Jesus Christ by faith,
and not for our own
works or deservings.
Wherefore, that we
are justified by faith
only, is a most
wholesome doctrine,
and very full of
comfort...

The Thirty-Nine Articles,
1571

For example, one of the most famous martyrdoms under Mary was that of Nicholas Ridley and Hugh Latimer, the former bishops of Worcester and Rochester. For their Protestant faith they were burned in Oxford in 1555. The spot where they died is still marked on the road. As they stood at the stake, Latimer spoke stirring words to his friend: 'Be of good cheer, Master Ridley, and play the man, for we shall this day light such a candle in England as I trust by God's grace shall never be put out.' But Hugh Latimer himself, as bishop under Henry VIII, had in 1538 been the preacher at the execution of John Forest, a Franciscan friar who had acted as confessor to Catherine of Aragon. After his sermon, Latimer had argued briefly with Forest. Forest had insisted that if an angel came from heaven to persuade him that he was wrong to remain loyal to the pope, he would not change his mind, no matter what tortures were threatened. Latimer ended the conversation and Forest was suspended by a chain over the fire until he roasted to death. Yet in the English mind the Protestant Latimer would be remembered as a hero and martyr, while the Catholic Forest would be forgotten.

Mary died in 1558 and was succeeded by her sister, Elizabeth I, who restored the supremacy of the monarch over the church, and Edward VI's prayer book. She also oversaw further executions of Catholics to consolidate the Church of England. But still the church suffered from a poorly defined identity. Henry had insisted only that everyone recognize his authority rather than the pope's – he had not secured any doctrinal position. In 1536, he had overseen the publication of the Ten Articles, expressing his own religious views, which were little different from normal Catholicism other than the relative authority of the king and the pope. In subsequent years there were attempts to set out a definitive statement of faith for the church, but they were hampered by the fact that the Church of England had been formed out of pragmatic concerns rather than dogmatic ones and contained within itself a variety of opinions. Thus a succession of Articles appeared throughout the sixteenth century which tried to capture a basic faith that everyone could agree to. Cranmer oversaw the writing of the Thirteen Articles in 1538, showing a more Protestant direction than the Ten, but they were never published. In 1552, on the orders of Edward VI, Cranmer produced a much more Protestant Forty-Two Articles. Not until 1571 would a definitive creed be produced. This was the Thirty-Nine Articles, a revision of Cranmer's Forty-Two. Under the aegis of Elizabeth I, both convocation (the governing body of the Church of England) and the English parliament enacted them as law. Since then, every Anglican priest has been required to affirm them. Like earlier Protestant creeds, such as the Augsburg Confession, the Thirty-Nine Articles teach justification by faith alone, deny the existence of purgatory and insist that baptism and the Eucharist are the only sacraments. They also teach the predestination of the elect, but are silent on the matter of the reprobate.

This moderate Protestantism left a lot of 'wriggle room', and the church still contained considerable variety of opinion. Although everyone agreed that they were no longer *Roman* Catholics, some churchmen sought to retain a fundamentally Catholic outlook in doctrine and practice. Others, however, were more fervent Protestants. This division would remain for a long time and cause major problems for the future.

THE CATHOLIC RESPONSE

The Catholic Church was facing one of the biggest crises in its history. Even as the Protestant churches were breaking away, one of the most stalwart Catholic countries was itself lost to Europe. In 1526 the Ottoman empire – which had already absorbed the southern half of the Orthodox world – defeated Louis Jagellion of Hungary, thereby conquering that country and marching into the Catholic heartlands. In reality, this was to be the last great advance of the Muslim world into Christendom, but to the Catholic Church at the time it seemed as if the true faith was facing enemies on all sides to an unprecedented degree.

Luther had never intended to break away from the Catholic Church: he had hoped to reform it from within, but events spiralled out of his control. However, despite the fact that Luther and his followers were expelled and forced to start their own churches, their pleas did not fall on entirely deaf ears within Catholicism. Even as the Reformation gathered pace and Protestantism spread over Europe, a parallel reform movement took shape within Catholicism. This is usually called the 'Counter-Reformation', as if it were simply a response to the Reformation. The truth is slightly more complex. Both the Reformation and the Counter-Reformation had common roots in a shared desire to end the corruption and abuses of the late medieval church; those parts of this movement that broke away from the church became known as the Reformation whilst those that remained within it are known as Counter-Reformation. Sometimes it might be better to talk of the Protestant Reformation and the Catholic Reformation as two wings of a single movement of reform throughout the sixteenth century.

One major force for Catholic reform was Paul III, who became pope in 1534. One of the first things he did was make his two teenage nephews cardinals, which did not bode well for reform, but on the whole Paul was keen to reform the church and the papacy. Most of the other cardinals he appointed were also reformers, and this helped to make a big change to the way things were done. He created a commission to investigate abuse in the church and make recommendations for reform. Their report, known as the *Concilium*, was widely published and was quite damning. Abuse had been detected throughout the church, and the commission advised that the pope and the cardinals should spend more time thinking about spiritual matters and less time worrying about their position in the world. The pope put some of the recommendations into effect, such as attempting to end the selling of ecclesiastical positions, but most of its advice was ignored. Meanwhile, Paul III tried to crush Protestantism by aiding the Holy Roman emperor, Charles V, who in the mid-1540s declared war on the German Protestant states. The war was successful in largely defeating Protestantism in the southern states, but not in the north.

THE COUNCIL OF TRENT

In 1545 Paul III finally succeeded in overcoming the anti-reform party in the church and calling a council at Trent (or Trento) in northern Italy to address the whole problem of ecclesiastical abuse and Protestantism. The various sessions of the council lasted eighteen years in all, although there were long gaps and only four and a half years, in total, were spent in session. By the time it finished, both Paul III and Martin Luther had died, a further three popes had passed on and Pius IV occupied the throne of St Peter.

As far as doctrine went, the council refused to budge a fraction in the direction of the Protestants. The council agreed with the Protestants that faith is necessary to salvation, but it disagreed with them that it is sufficient. On the contrary, as James 2:24 states, good deeds are also required. The council explained that Romans 3:28, which states that faith is sufficient, means that faith is the necessary starting point. Without faith, works are useless. Again, the traditional understanding of the Mass as sacrifice was firmly upheld. That is not to say that the Mass is a supplement to Christ's sacrifice (since that sacrifice is all-sufficient) or that it is a repetition of it (since it happened once for all); rather that one, sufficient sacrifice is continually offered in the form of the Mass. The priest and the people offer a sacrifice to God, but

If anyone says that man may be justified before God by his own works... let him be anathema... If anyone says that by faith alone an impious person is justified, meaning by this that no other cooperation is required in order to obtain justifying grace, and that it is not at all necessary that he be prepared and moved by his own will, let him be anathema.

The canons of the Council of Trent, sixth session, 1547

A new spirituality: the Carmelite mystics

St Teresa of Avila (1515–82) and St John of the Cross (1542–91) represent the culmination of the rich medieval development of Christian mystical theology in western Europe. They were Spanish Carmelites who began a reform movement within the Carmelite order, linked to the wider reforms of the Catholic Reformation, but they are mainly remembered for their remarkable teaching on prayer.

Teresa and John both entered the Carmelite order in the conventional way, in early adulthood. After twenty years as a nun, Teresa experienced a life-changing 'second conversion'. Having regarded Jesus as a distant Lord and herself as unworthy of him, her discovery was that Jesus was close to her and even 'needed' her company. This led to a new sense of her vocation. Eight years later she began a reform of the Carmelite order to give more attention to prayer. She founded seventeen new houses for nuns throughout Spain, reintroducing an older, stricter version of the Carmelite Rule which emphasized enclosure and poverty against what she saw as the excessive concern in her society for wealth, family and status, which hindered the nuns from pursuing their vocations of prayer.

John of the Cross, who came from a poor background, was invited by Teresa to join the Carmelite reform, to further the reform among the male branch of the order. His academic ability had earned him a place at Salamanca University where, as a Carmelite student, he was studying theology. His gifts pointed to a high-ranking career, but he immediately accepted Teresa's invitation, drawn to the ascetic life of prayer. Twenty-seven years Teresa's junior, he helped set up monasteries in the male branch of the order and acted as confessor to Teresa's nuns.

It was a time of rapid change in the Spanish church. Teresa and John modelled their Carmelite reform on reform among the Franciscans, with an emphasis on interior prayer leading to the goal of contemplation or 'union with God'. This reform met with a reaction in the later part of the century, sparked by fears of 'illuminism' – the claim of direct revelation above the authority of the church – and of the Reformation, especially following the Council of Trent. However, Teresa and John were both intensely loyal to the Catholic Church, and though opposed by certain forces, they are best understood as working for internal reform rather than against the church.

Their originality is most visible in their writings. Teresa's main writings, her *Life*, the *Way of perfection* and her greatest work, the *Interior castle*, chart her development and teaching in prayer. The *Life* shows her early emphasis on ecstatic states, including the most famous, her 'transverberation', when she felt her heart pierced by an angel holding a golden arrow tipped with fire, and then the arrow being drawn out, carrying her into an ecstatic, 'out-of-body' state during which she was physically unable to move, but inwardly in union with God. Gradually she came to understand that ecstatic prayer states were not the goal but the transformative process of prayer. In the *Way of perfection*, she sees this transformation as the ground of community life, transforming community relationships from selfishness to mutual self-giving. In the *Interior castle*, Teresa redefines ecstasy, no longer as a state of paralysis, but as the inner working of grace which 'expands' the soul and makes it capable of God's unmediated presence. The purpose is to bring the soul to an active union, like Christ, in which action is combined with full awareness of God in union.

John of the Cross's teaching is marked by his experience of prison. As a result of an unfortunate rivalry between the Spanish monarchy and the papacy, John was put in solitary confinement for nine months before making a dramatic escape out of a window. He spoke little of the experience, but the mental anguish of feeling abandoned by God, which he called the 'dark night of the soul', runs as a theme through his writing. He first gave this expression in poems regarded as among the greatest in the Spanish language. At the request of his nuns and friars, he then expounded some of the poems in commentaries, the *Ascent of Mount Carmel*, the *Dark night*, the *Spiritual canticle* and the *Living flame of love*. In the first two, John's focal interest is in discerning the path to union with God through the experience of 'darkness', where God is felt as absent and former spiritual practices are unworkable. At the centre is Jesus' cry of dereliction ('*My God, my God, why have you forsaken me?*'), which shows that God is united with humanity even in its deepest distress. Through this perspective and by a gradual growth in the 'night', the sense of abandonment by God is discerned as a 'wound of love' which gives onto God's immediate presence in union.

The teaching of Teresa of Avila and John of the Cross has been exemplified in more recent times by the Carmelites Thérèse of Lisieux (1873–97), Elizabeth of the Trinity (1880–1906), and Edith Stein (1891–1942, killed at Auschwitz). In the terms of their time and culture, their writings focus on the way that God transforms the darkness and 'nothingness' of humanity into his presence, centred on Jesus' paradoxical loss of everything and gain of resurrection through the cross.

EDWARD HOWELLS

the sacrifice they offer is that of Christ, who, as the great high priest, offers it through them.

Similarly, the council rejected the Protestants' contention that the Bible is the sole source of doctrine and that it is more authoritative than the church. Instead, the council sought to retain the traditional view that the church and the Bible form a whole, undivided body of teaching. This means that scripture is indeed authoritative, but only when it is interpreted by the church, and in particular, the papacy. Thus, the council reaffirmed the seven sacraments, the doctrine of purgatory, the use of relics, the veneration of the Virgin Mary and other elements of Catholicism which Protestants denounced as unscriptural. The doctrine of transubstantiation was also reaffirmed. And the position of the pope was strengthened, since it was made explicit – in opposition to the wishes of the Protestants who were permitted to attend the second session in an observational capacity – that this and other councils had authority only inasmuch as the pope 'promulgated' or ratified its decisions.

But there was more room for cleaning up the corrupt practices which had sparked off the Reformation in the first place. Indulgences remained, but the trade in them was reformed considerably, with the position of indulgence-seller being abolished. The practice of one person being bishop of several places at once – like Albrecht of Brandenberg – was also outlawed. Seminaries, for training priests properly, were to be established in every diocese, and there was to be more scrutiny of candidates for ordination. The aim was to improve the moral and intellectual quality of the priesthood. Clerical celibacy was reaffirmed, again in opposition to the Protestants, but it was also to be enforced.

Pope Pius IV promulgated the decisions of Trent in 1564. After this point, Trent acted rather as the Council of Nicaea had in the latter stages of the Arian controversy over a thousand years earlier: it provided a standard of doctrine to which Catholics could point in their controversies with Protestants. Moreover, it provided for much better discipline within the Catholic Church. It marked a major point – not in the development of Catholic doctrine, since the council refused to swerve from any traditional beliefs – but in Catholic self-understanding. Conciliarism, for example, was considerably weakened after this point. Because of all this, the Council of Trent was something of a watershed in Catholic history, and historians sometimes talk of the 'Tridentine' Catholic Church to emphasize its role in determining Catholic self-understanding.

Many Catholics became more concerned to stress those elements of their faith that the Protestants rejected, such as the seven sacraments and devotion to the Blessed Virgin Mary. It was in this period, for example, that the 'Ave Maria' or 'Hail Mary' took its modern form. This prayer had come into common use in the eleventh or twelfth centuries, as a prayer to Mary based upon statements about her in the New Testament:

> Hail Mary, full of grace,
> The Lord is with you,
> Blessed are you among women,
> And blessed is the fruit of your womb, Jesus.

In the later Middle Ages, the prayer was sometimes modified so that Mary was asked for something rather than just greeted. By the end of the sixteenth century, the following conclusion to the prayer had become standard:

> Holy Mary, Mother of God,
> Pray for us sinners,
> Now, and at the hour of our death.
> Amen.

THE JESUITS

As the Catholic Church was developing this new self-understanding, a new force was appearing which would be of enormous value in the fight against Protestantism. This was the Society of Jesus, better known as the Jesuits.

Let everyone understand that real love of God does not consist in tear-shedding, nor in that sweetness and tenderness for which we usually long, just because they console us, but in serving God in justice, fortitude of soul and humility.

Teresa of Avila

Ignatius Loyola, in an anonymous seventeenth-century painting.

The Jesuits were founded by a Spanish soldier named Ignatius Loyola. In 1521, during a battle, a cannonball was fired at him and passed right between his legs, wounding him but miraculously leaving him largely intact. Recovering in hospital, unable to lay his hands on the chivalric romances he normally liked, Loyola read books on the lives of the saints and became interested in spirituality. After leaving the hospital, Loyola spent a year in prayer and meditation at a monastery, before going on pilgrimage to Jerusalem and then studying theology at a number of universities. At Paris in the 1530s, he gathered a group of like-minded friends and they vowed to dedicate their lives to Christ as revealed in the Catholic Church, through obedience to the pope. In 1540 Pope Paul III approved the new Society of Jesus.

The idea was not to create a new monastic order. As a former soldier, Loyola naturally formed his society along military lines. The principal virtue for its members – who were all priests – was obedience, to the general of the order and the pope. The society as a whole was to be put to the service of the pope in whatever capacity he saw fit. The members did not have a particular rule to follow, but they did have the *Spiritual exercises* that Ignatius wrote as a guide to disciplined meditation. They were also rigorously selected and trained: novices would train for two years before becoming 'formed scholastics', a stage which could last for up to fifteen years before becoming full members. It was only after completing this arduous training that the new member would make the vow of total, uncompromising obedience to the pope.

It seems that Ignatius particularly had in mind preaching to the Muslims, and indeed some of the first missions that he sent the early members on were to Muslims. However, the church quickly recognized the value of the Jesuits in opposing Protestantism and put them to work in this major undertaking. The Jesuits went about this in a number of ways. The first was through theological debate. Jesuit scholars began to study the arguments and the beliefs of the leading Protestants and wrote answers to them. A major figure who did this was Robert Bellarmine, an Italian Jesuit theologian with such a good reputation for preaching that Protestants as well as Catholics came to hear his sermons. He was also a deeply charitable man, who was known to clothe the poor with his tapestries, and it was said that the only reason he never became pope was that he was too honest! Appointed to the post of professor of controversies at the Jesuit college in Rome by Pope Gregory XIII, Bellarmine studied the works of the Reformers and wrote fair-minded responses to them. Bellarmine was not simply a reactionary who denied that the Protestants had said anything worthwhile: on the contrary, he aimed to defend an understanding of Christianity which was rooted in the church fathers, especially Augustine.

To engage in such scholarship, Jesuits had to be well educated, and from an early stage Ignatius Loyola was determined that education would play a key role in his society. It was, after all, supposed to be a society of elite priests, dedicated to spreading the Christian message, and this required extensive training and education. Schools and training centres were therefore opened. In 1547 Ignatius was asked to open a school for non-members of the society. He realized that this would be the perfect way of spreading the ideals and message of the society, and readily agreed. By the time he died in 1556, there were thirty-five Jesuit schools throughout Europe. These provided some of the best education on the continent. It was free, for Ignatius believed that education should be available to everyone irrespective of financial standing, and the Jesuits received enough donations to put this ideal into practice. The schools were extremely popular, especially in the southern parts of the Holy Roman empire, and this did a great deal to stem the advance of Protestantism there. A major figure in the German Counter-Reformation was Peter Canisius, the eighth person to join the Society of Jesus. Canisius spent many years preaching throughout Germany and founding Jesuit schools there. He was present at the Council of Trent and wrote a number of books explaining Catholic doctrine: the short catechisms he composed, with small explanations of each belief, were extremely popular and still used in the nineteenth century. For all this, Catholics remember Canisius as the 'second apostle of Germany', after Boniface.

A similar effect was even more evident in Lithuania and Poland, where Protestantism had become widespread – a serious threat, since Poland-Lithuania (at this time united) was the bulwark of Roman Catholicism in northeastern Europe. Everyone to the east was Orthodox. The Jesuits therefore opened a school at the Lithuanian capital, Vilnius, in 1570. This school became the most important university in north-eastern Europe, indeed, the only one at all for two

centuries. The Jesuits translated anti-Protestant or devotional works into Lithuanian, popularized the Catholic liturgy, and generally saw to it that Protestantism was successfully quashed in this important region. The same thing happened in Ukraine, at this time dominated by Poland-Lithuania. Here the official Catholicism was still struggling for dominance with Orthodoxy, and Protestantism was confusing matters even more. The Jesuits penetrated Ukraine and helped to bolster Catholicism, an effort formalized in 1596 with the Union of Brest. This declaration created a brand new church, the Ukrainian Catholic Church, which was in communion with the Roman Catholic Church but used Orthodox rites.

The latter half of the sixteenth century and the seventeenth century saw a large number of extraordinarily brilliant men emerge from the ranks of the Jesuits. Some, such as Matteo Ricci, made a major splash on the world stage; others, such as the scientist Athanasius Kircher, were content to explore volcanoes or study the causes of disease. Many Jesuits studied science, especially astronomy; by 1750 they ran thirty of the 130 observatories in the world. It was one of their number, John Baptist Riccioli, who published the first good map of the moon in 1651, and who named many of the features of the lunar surface.

One other major field in which the Jesuits opposed Protestantism was in overseas mission. Half of Europe might have apostatized, but the Renaissance explorers had revealed whole new worlds which might be amenable to Catholicism. We shall look more closely at what happened in those new worlds in Chapter 10, but for now it is important to note that the Jesuits played a major role in that story, and that the most famous missionaries of the era were all Jesuits. That made them great explorers, too – of the eight major rivers in the world, five were first charted by Jesuits.

Teach us, good Lord, to serve you as you deserve; to give and not to count the cost; to fight and not to heed the wounds; to toil and not to ask for rest; to labour and not to ask for any reward save knowing that we do your will.

Ignatius Loyola

THE LATER REFORMATION

Martin Luther died in 1546, but the Reformation did not die with him: on the contrary, it continued to develop and progress throughout the sixteenth century.

JOHN CALVIN AND THE REFORMED TRADITION

The key figure in the next phase of the Reformation was John Calvin, a man as unlike Martin Luther as one could imagine. Where Luther was large, loud and rude, Calvin was thin, quiet and scholarly. Born in 1509 in Noyon in France, Calvin studied at the University of Paris, where he became a serious-minded humanist. He also became attached to the new Protestant movement, partly because he sympathized with the French Protestants, who were persecuted by the authorities. In 1534 this persecution forced Calvin himself to leave France for Switzerland. Passing through Geneva in 1536 Calvin was waylaid by one William Farel, a follower of the now-dead Zwingli. Farel recognized the potential in the Frenchman and persuaded him to stay in Geneva and help the Protestant cause there. And – apart from a three-year period when he was temporarily expelled – there Calvin stayed for the rest of his life. Under his direction, the government of Geneva was transformed into something like a Protestant theocracy. It became known as 'the Protestant Rome' to reflect its new importance. Here, in 1559, Calvin opened a new Academy – despite being so lacking in funds that he was forced to go from house to house in person to raise the necessary cash. This Academy taught Protestant theology as well as providing a rigorous training in science and humanism – making it a Protestant answer to the schools of the Jesuits at this time springing up across Europe. Four schools were also opened in Geneva for younger students, and like the Academy their courses were later made free – thus creating, in effect, the first integrated, free, state-run education system of modern times.

The Academy was enormously popular, accepting 900 students in its opening year and increasing class sizes in subsequent uptakes. Everyone, even Catholics, could study there, since Calvin recognized that this was an excellent way of spreading Protestant ideals. And spread they did, as alumni from the Academy returned home and preached what they had learned there.

What *had* they learned there? Just as Calvin the man was very different from Luther the man, so too Calvin the theologian had quite a different spirit. Where Luther churned out vast numbers of fiery responses to his critics, Calvin was in spirit a categorizer and systematizer. Calvin believed basically the same things as Luther, especially the two prime doctrines of Protestantism – the authority of the Bible and the sufficiency of faith for salvation – but the way he presented them was quite different. His great work, the *Institutes of the Christian religion*, attempted to set out the

John Calvin as a young man, in a contemporary painting of the Flemish school.

The Protestant Rome

The Reformation in Geneva was intimately connected with the city's struggle for independence from the House of Savoy, which was achieved in 1526. The new, elected Council of Two Hundred, under the influence of the fiery Protestant preacher, William Farel, outlawed the Mass and forced either the conversion to Protestantism or exile of Geneva's Catholic clergy in 1535–36.

When John Calvin arrived in Geneva in 1536, the city was thus Reformed at least in name, but the expulsion of the Catholic Church had critically depleted the ruling elite of the city and left a political and administrative vacuum. Along with Farel, Calvin set about instituting a new church order, focused on the spiritual independence of the church from state interference, something which he was never fully to realize. Apart from an exile from 1538–41, Calvin remained the dominant ecclesiastical and political personality in Geneva until his death in 1564, though he never wielded the absolute theocratic power which later generations ascribed to him.

First, Calvin reorganized the government of the church. The pastors in Geneva were organized into the 'Venerable Company' and met quarterly for purposes of administration and mutual encouragement and discipline. The consistory, made up of the pastors and twelve elders chosen from Geneva's three ruling councils, was the primary court for church discipline and moral discipline in Geneva. Cases from insulting the French to adultery to doctrinal error were dealt with in this court; and evidence suggests that the court was, on the whole, neither exceptionally severe nor lenient. It should also be remembered that the cause célèbre of Geneva in the sixteenth century, that of the burning of the Spanish anti-Trinitarian Michael Servetus, was the result of a civil court case, and that the punishment meted out was deemed at the time universally appropriate for a heretic. The whole notion of religious tolerance was some years away.

The second significant development pioneered by Calvin was the founding of the Genevan Academy in 1559, which quickly established itself as an international centre for theological scholarship. Geneva had been a centre for refugee activity for some time, fuelled by the persecution of Protestants across Europe which created a whole population of displaced people and a consistent supply of aspiring missionaries wanting to return to their homelands with the gospel. Indeed, while Calvin was undoubtedly Geneva's most famous exile, other figures, such as the Scotsman John Knox, were also resident for periods of time. Thus, Geneva was ideal as a centre for international Reformed scholarship. The Academy's first rector was the humanist Theodore Beza (1519–1605), the teacher not only of such Reformed luminaries as Thomas Cartwright and Andrew Melville, but also of those who later deviated from the Reformed faith, most famously the Dutchman, Jacob Arminius.

With the passing of Calvin in 1564, the reins of ecclesiastical power passed to Beza, under whose leadership the city was to retain much of its theological influence. Its most famous theologian after Beza was the Italian Francis Turretin (1623–87), whose lectures formed the basis of his massive *Institutes of elenctic theology*, one of the most elaborate polemical articulations of Reformed theology. However, by the latter part of the seventeenth century, Genevan orthodoxy was under pressure both internally and externally, and the orthodox Protestant project in the city was soon to lose its intellectual and social hold over the people. In 1707, Lutherans were granted freedom to worship in the city, and the Reformed monopoly of power, held since the 1530s, was effectively brought to an end.

CARL TRUEMAN

beliefs of Protestantism – drawn from the Bible alone – thematically. Moreover, after his death in 1564, those who came after him developed the same tendency further. For example, his successor as head of the Academy was another Frenchman, Theodore Beza, who although only ten years younger than Calvin lived much longer and dominated Genevan religion for forty years. Beza was even more systematic than Calvin and, unlike him, sought in his work to set out ideas that were not explicit in the Bible but which he thought were entailed by the things that were. For example, Calvin had believed in predestination, the idea that everything people do is predetermined by God. This is suggested by passages in the Bible such as Romans 8:28–30. He had also taught *double* predestination, the idea that God determines some people towards salvation and some towards damnation. However, Beza went beyond this, to state that God planned this division of humanity into the saved and the damned even before humanity first sinned (a doctrine known by the rather abstruse term 'prelapsarianism'). Thus, Adam's sin was part of God's whole plan for humanity, which embraced the damnation of much of humanity as well as the salvation of the rest. Where Calvin had sought to restate the Bible's teachings in a more systematic way, Beza went further, seeking to answer questions that are raised but not answered by the biblical text.

The result was that 'Calvinism', a

The whole thing may be summed up like this. Christ, given to us by God's kindness, is understood and taken hold of by faith, which enables us to gain two benefits. First, reconciled to us by Christ's righteousness, God becomes, instead of a judge, an indulgent Father. Second, sanctified by his Spirit, we aspire to integrity and purity of life.

John Calvin, Institutes of the Christian religion, 1536

Reformed

Anglican

Lutheran

Roman Catholic

Roman Catholic and Lutheran

Roman Catholic, Calvinist,
Lutheran and Hussite

Roman Catholic, Calvinist,
and Lutheran

Muslim and Orthodox

border of Holy Roman empire, c.1648

0   400 km

0   300 miles

SCOTLAND

EDINBURGH

IRELAND

YORK

ENGLAND

WALES

NORWICH

LONDON

CANTERBURY

Nor
Se

U
PROV

ANTWERP

SPANIS
NETHERLA

ROUEN

PARIS

RHEIMS

Loire

FRANCE F

LA ROCHELLE

LYONS

BORDEAUX

SA

Rhône

NÎMES

MONTPELLIER

MARSEILLE

ORTHEZ

Ebro

SPAIN

SARAGOSSA

Tagus

NORWAY

CHRISTIANIA ■

SWEDEN

STOCKHOLM ■

DENMARK

■ COPENHAGEN

Baltic Sea

COURLAND

PRUSSIA

Elbe

BRANDENBURG

BRUNSWICK ■

HILDESHEIM ■ ■ ■ MAGDEBURG

OGNE

SAXONY

POLAND

SILESIA

PRAGUE ■

ainz ■

■ Heidelberg

■ Nuremberg

BOHEMIA

MORAVIA

BAVARIA

VIENNA ■

■ ZURICH

AUSTRIA

WISS
DERATION

HUNGARY

BUDAPEST ■

LAN ■

■ VENICE

Danube

FLORENCE
■

PAPAL
STATES

OTTOMAN
EMPIRE

orsica

■ ROME

The European
churches at the end
of the Thirty Years'
War.

tendency of theology stemming from Calvin but developed by his successors, became a major force within Protestantism. It was not only a theological outlook but a moral one too. Calvin himself had believed strongly in the value of hard work – not as something that could save you, of course, but as something that God demands of all believers. A year before his death, his friends had advised him to have a rest for the sake of his health; Calvin had angrily replied that he had no intention of letting God find him idle. This spirit was important to later Calvinism. Christians in this tradition distrusted what they regarded as idleness and believed that all aspects of life should be dedicated to God.

This does not mean that they thought that there should be no fun whatsoever in life or that they were all dour, Bible-quoting killjoys. Those in the Calvinist tradition have often been caricatured as such, but they were not necessarily like that, and neither were the 'Reformed' churches, a rather confusing name given to those churches that were inspired by Geneva rather than Wittenberg. Obviously all Protestant churches were 'reformed' in a broader sense, but the term has come to mean those that go back to the missions of Calvin and his followers as opposed to those inspired more directly by Luther.

In the seventeenth century, this emphasis on the moral demands of Christianity within the Calvinist tradition became important to the movement known as Puritanism. Puritanism was largely an English-speaking movement, and it represented the Calvinist influence within the Church of England. As we saw earlier, the theological status of this church was never well defined, apart from abhorring Roman Catholicism and papal control. There was a strong Puritan presence in the church by the seventeenth century, which produced figures like Richard Baxter, who wrote many theological works and even more moral ones. However, Baxter repudiated a number of typical Calvinist doctrines, including the doctrine that Christ is punished directly in the believer's place and the doctrine of predestination, partly because he felt that they discouraged good moral behaviour. Puritanism could therefore vary theologically, to some degree, from more mainstream, continental Calvinism.

EUROPE DIVIDED

At the start of the sixteenth century, there was a single Christian church in Europe. One hundred years later, there were four major ones. The Roman Catholic Church remained firm in most of the southern half of the continent, including Italy, Spain, most of France and the southern German states. The Lutheran Churches, direct descendants of Luther's initial protest, held the northern German states and Scandinavia. The Church of England remained the only legitimate church in England. The Reformed Churches – propagated as alumni from Calvin's Academy – spread the Calvinist message across Europe, dominated Switzerland, the Netherlands and Scotland and had a strong minority presence in France. Scotland had been evangelized by Calvin's student John Knox, and the Scottish became staunch Calvinists. In 1560 their parliament officially disestablished the Roman Church and ratified a confession of faith prepared by Knox. Here, the Reformed Church did away with bishops, holding this form of church government to be unscriptural; a system of 'elders' (or 'presbyters') was instituted as more in keeping with the New Testament. Scottish Calvinism is thus sometimes known as 'Presbyterianism'. It took time for this to spread, however, and the Catholic Church remained strong in the remoter parts of Scotland for some time. But the Presbyterians, now and later, always possessed particularly strong preachers; one of these, Robert Bruce, even had some sway over King James VI (later James I of England), who left him in charge of the country when he was away. Bruce spent many years in Inverness after falling out with the king, and his strong preaching helped to spread Presbyterian ideals throughout the country.

Much of the Baltic region was divided between Lutherans, Reformed and Catholics, although the Counter-Reformation had a strong impact in this region.

And then, in addition to these three main players and the Church of England, there were also minor, more diffuse groups, such as the Anabaptists.

After the remarkable period of theological creativity which had produced Luther and Calvin, things now settled down into a period of sniping between representatives of the different churches. All four major churches produced new apologists who wrote long and often very tedious attacks on each other. In so doing, the beliefs of each church became more formalized and set in stone, one reason why this period is sometimes known as 'the age of confessionalism' – so-called because different groups drew up 'confessions' or creeds to define their own positions, rather like during the Arian controversy of the fourth century.

To add to the confusion, movements appeared *within* the churches that threatened to divide them further. The most important was Arminianism, which arose within the Reformed churches after the preaching of a Dutch theologian named Jacob Arminius, who denied the doctrines of predestination and prelapsarianism, which as we saw earlier were associated with the Calvinism of Beza and his followers. In 1610 forty-two Dutch ministers influenced by Arminius signed a 'remonstrance' to the government asking for their views to be protected. The Arminians were sometimes known thereafter as 'Remonstrants' and their more conservative opponents as 'Contra-Remonstrants'. In 1618 a synod was held at Dort (that is, Dordrecht) in the Netherlands, which condemned the Remonstrants as proto-Catholics and defined the orthodox Reformed faith in five doctrines, easily remembered through

the acronym TULIP (perhaps appropriate given the Dutch provenance of the definition). These were: Total depravity (all human actions are intrinsically sinful unless grace intervenes); Unconditional election (people are saved by God's decision, not because of any merit on their part); Limited atonement (Christ's death is not efficacious for everyone, but only those who will be saved, the 'elect'); Irresistible grace (God predestines everyone to salvation or damnation and there is nothing they can do about it); and Perseverance of the saints (the elect can never become un-elect).

BAPTISTS AND QUAKERS

Finally, other new churches were founded which would play a significant role in the years to come. The first were the Baptist churches, which had their origins in Puritans who felt that the Church of England was not Protestant enough. They left to set up their own churches, becoming known as 'Separatists' or Dissenters; they would later often be known as non-conformists. There were many such groups: one large one was known after its founder, Henry Jacob, a Cambridge clergyman, as 'Jacobites' (not to be confused with either the Monophysite Jacobite Church of the Middle East or the Jacobites who would try to restore the Stuart dynasty in England in the late seventeenth and eighteenth centuries).

Another Cambridge Separatist was John Smyth, who took the unusual step of baptizing himself. A group of his followers, led by Thomas Helwys, set up the first Baptist Church in London in 1612. This group insisted that only believers should undergo baptism, so they rejected infant baptism and accepted only adult baptism – rather like the Anabaptists, although it is unclear what, if any, historical links there were between the two groups. They also rejected any notion of the state interfering with religion. The churches that emerged from this consensus became known as the General Baptists – 'general' because they believed that the benefits of Christ's death applied generally to everyone, so that salvation was available to anyone who wanted it. In other words, they rejected the doctrine of limited atonement as defined at Dort.

These Arminian views were not acceptable to everyone, and there were also Particular Baptists, who were hard-line Calvinists and believed that Christ's death worked only ('particularly') for the elect. These churches had evolved out of the Jacobites, and they generally proved to be more vigorous than the General variety. In 1644 they issued a statement of faith in which they insisted that baptism had to be performed by total immersion – that is, by literally submerging the candidate in water – and this is when the name 'Baptist' began to be applied to them. And the Baptists of both varieties proved durable – by 1660 there were some 300 churches.

Equally striking were the Quakers, founded by George Fox, a Leicestershire cobbler. Fox was a remarkable man, a blend of religious visionary and social reformer. He believed that every individual had direct access to God: indeed, there was something of God in everyone. He therefore denied that there were any special places to find God, such as churches, or people to help you find God, such as priests. These views landed him in serious trouble and he was imprisoned many times; yet he preached across the country and won many disciples. Their beliefs put them at odds not only with the Church of England, but with the accepted social order. If everyone had direct access to God, no one was more special than anyone else; Fox's followers thus refused to take off their hats before magistrates and would not swear oaths either, since Jesus forbade it in Matthew 5:33–37. Thousands were imprisoned.

By the time Fox died in 1691, there were 50,000 members of the movement and within a couple of decades twice that number again. They called themselves 'Children of the Light' or 'Friends'. But they acquired their nickname from their meetings, where they would often tremble with emotion; 'Quakers' they became, in the scathing indictment of one judge to Fox himself, and the name stuck. Their meetings were of course not church services, because they did not believe in them, and derisively called churches 'steeple-houses'. At their meetings, instead of a leader or a liturgy, everyone could take part and speak as they felt moved to.

THE WARS OF RELIGION

The late sixteenth century was not a good time for Europe. A growing population and economic problems meant that the lowest classes were much poorer than they had been a century earlier, and revolts became more common. Powerful families such as the Hapsburgs struggled for control of the dynasties of the emerging nations of Europe. In France, dynastic rivalries mixed with religion to produce the 'Wars of Religion', which devastated a generation. They began in 1562, when soldiers of the Duc de Guise fired on French Calvinists – known as Huguenots – at Vassy. In response the Huguenots mobilized under the Prince of Condé, who captured a number of cities along the Loire, bankrolled by foreign Protestants. The authorities were forced to recognize the Huguenots' gains and their rights to worship. But the Huguenots grew more powerful and less willing to settle with the Catholic authorities: Calvin himself was teaching that a government that persecuted Christians had lost the right to expect obedience. The Catholics, for their part, feared and suspected the Huguenots, who formed a social as well as a religious grouping. Huguenots stuck together and were organized in a series of local cells, regarded by outsiders as a sinister 'secret society'. Like the early Christians in Rome, they drew upon themselves suspicion, hatred and persecution.

A series of skirmishes followed until 1572, when the infamous St Bartholomew's Day Massacre took place. King Charles IX authorized the assassination of key Huguenot leaders, who were all in Paris to

Witch hunting

The most intense period of witch hunting did not occur in the Middle Ages, as many people believe, but during the sixteenth and seventeenth centuries, the period of the Reformation, Counter-Reformation and scientific revolution. Because many judicial records have been destroyed or are missing for much of western, southern and eastern Europe, it is impossible to arrive at an exact figure of the number of people executed for witchcraft, but estimates have been vastly reduced from an initial figure of nine million to approximately 35,000, of whom 29,000 were women. The epicentre of European witch hunting lay in the Germanic core of the Holy Roman empire, where it is estimated that 20–25,000 executions occurred.

During the early modern period the stereotype of the witch was significantly altered. Where previously witches could be either male or female and possessed their own magical power, now they were predominately female and entirely dependent on the devil. They congregated at obscene 'Sabbats', where they worshipped the devil and engaged in perverse anti-social activities: promiscuous sexuality, obscene dancing and cannibalism, especially of children. The witches' Sabbat did not exist in the Middle Ages; it was an invention of early modern demonologists and, in the view of some historians, represented an increased fear of disorder and female sexuality. Historians question how deeply this new, learned stereotype of the witch as the devil's disciple penetrated popular culture, where a witch was still primarily thought of as performing harmful magic (*maleficium*); but it is generally agreed that witch trials and the publicity accompanying them spread the new stereotype. Most historians agree that poor, middle-aged, widowed or single women were most likely to be accused of witchcraft, although younger women charged with sexual crimes (fornication, adultery, abortion, infanticide) were also targeted. In New England female heiresses without male kin were prominent among the accused. However, in some parts of Europe and in Russia the majority of executed witches were men.

The witch hunts were of great importance in the history of women, for they represented an unparalleled form of misogyny in which women were demonized as a group and perceived as a diabolical fifth column threatening the very existence of western civilization. Witchcraft was the most important capital crime for women in early modern history. More women were executed for this alleged offence than for all other crimes put together. Witch hunts produced an essentialist rhetoric of gender identity that polarized the sexes as never before. Indeed, the sixteenth century has been seen as one of the most bitterly misogynistic periods in western history. Literary and fictional discussions of obstreperous, disobedient wives and illustrations of women attacking and killing men proliferated. While historians have argued that Protestantism enhanced the position of women, others see this as a factor promoting witch hunts. By granting women responsibility for their own salvation, by emphasizing their importance as spiritual leaders in the home and by making marriage the norm for everyone, Protestantism increased male anxieties and exacerbated gender conflict. This is significant in light of research documenting the lenient treatment of witches by the Catholic Inquisition. This leniency has been attributed to the fact that Catholic authorities, all male, devalued women to such an extent that even witches posed no threat.

In recent years a number of historians have argued that because of their close connection with folk medicine, folk magic and popular religion, women were particularly vulnerable to witchcraft accusations. The *Malleus maleficarum* (Hammer of Witches) of 1486 considered midwives particularly likely to be witches, although this connection is not borne out in actual trials. More recent evidence does suggest, however, that women who cared for newborn children were vulnerable to witchcraft accusations because of high infant mortality rates combined with an unprecedented emphasis on motherhood.

A characteristic of newly emerging political regimes and religious authorities was their demand for a high level of control and conformity. Fear of disorder was a prevalent theme in early modern thought, and historians have recognized the special place that 'disorderly' women (prostitutes; women without male supervision; scolds) played in witch hunts. For male authorities, chaste, obedient, and, most importantly, married women were synonymous with a strong well-ordered state, while disobedient, rebellious women were suspect witches. Legal systems were increasingly used to punish wayward behavior (especially sexual) as well as wayward thought, and in this regard it is significant that witchcraft first became a criminal offence in the early modern period.

This fear of disorder reflected the very real disorders in the early modern European world, where religious wars, plagues, famines, peasant rebellions, banditry and vagabondage were endemic, and new ways of thinking threatened established systems of thought. The climate of fear engendered by political, social and intellectual turmoil led many people to embrace a pessimistic form of apocalyptic millenarianism, in which the devil assumed a position of unparalleled importance. 'Devil books' became a new genre of literature in Germany during the second half of the sixteenth century, and witches gained new prominence as the devil's most faithful and obedient servants.

There are a number of theories which seek to account for the decline of the witch hunts. One of the most persuasive holds that it was the result of 'judicial skepticism'. The acrimonious controversies of the Reformation and Counter-Reformation period about divine revelation, the accuracy of scripture and even the existence of God contributed to an increasingly critical attitude towards evidence and to the search for new methods of establishing truth. Judges and lawyers exhibited a growing concern with the credibility of witnesses and the probability of events. Judges did not stop hunting witches out of disbelief, but because they no longer knew where to find them. At a certain point – a point usually reached whenever men became a significant portion of accused witches – the excessive nature of the witch hunts made magistrates and judges have second thoughts.

ALLISON COUDERT

The St Bartholomew's Day massacre of 1572, in a painting by the French artist François Dubois (1790–1871).

attend a wedding, but somehow things got out of hand and a mob, fired with hatred of the 'heretics', spent three days murdering any Protestants they could find. The whole persecution spread throughout France and lasted months. In all some 20,000 people died, and from then on the mutual hatred between Catholics and Protestants in France was irreparable. Intermittent warfare continued until the 1580s, when Henry of Navarre, a Protestant, fought King Henry III and the Catholic League, eventually defeating them to become King Henry IV. Being a pragmatic man, he then converted to Catholicism and issued the Edict of Nantes in 1598, which permitted the Huguenots freedom of worship.

Even more devastating was the Thirty Years' War, really a *series* of wars between different European powers which raged from 1618 to 1648. On one side were the Hapsburg powers of the Holy Roman empire and Spain, while on the other were the French, English, Dutch and the Protestant German states. Ferdinand II, the

Holy Roman emperor, believed it was his duty to fight the forces of Protestantism and eradicate this heresy, whilst Maximilian I of the Palatinate, leader of the Protestant Germans, was a committed Calvinist who believed equally passionately in his cause. And so the wars raged for a whole generation, devastating Europe. At the end of it, Spain was exhausted, the Protestant states had secured the right to freedom of worship and the Catholic empire was effectively reduced to the southern and eastern region of Austria.

Finally, the seventeenth century saw one last major war along religious lines, the English Civil War. The early decades of the century saw increasing tension between those who wanted the Church of England to retain a broadly Catholic approach to worship and those who were more fervently Protestant (the Puritans). King James I (1603–25) angered many Puritans by supporting the system of bishops and refusing to persecute Catholics; the Scots were especially angered by his attempt to introduce customs such as kneeling at the Eucharist. His son, Charles I, did even worse, driving Puritans to the brink of fury. His archbishop of Canterbury was William Laud, a man who believed firmly that the Church of England should be a Catholic Church, one which, although distinct from the *Roman* Catholic Church, upheld the same traditions. In particular, he felt that bishops were essential to church organization and that priests did intercede between God and the people – contrary to the Protestant belief in the priesthood of all believers. His attempts to crack down on the Puritans meant that many fled the country for the Netherlands or the New World.

These divisions boiled over into rebellion and finally war. First the Scots rebelled and were put down by the king. Then the Irish rebelled, having been goaded by the 'plantation' policy of Charles and his father James. This brilliantly short-sighted scheme had been intended to erode the Catholicism of the Irish by importing large numbers of Scottish and English Protestants and settling them in the north of the island. Finally, political and ideological strife between the king and parliament flared into full-blown civil war in England, which lasted from 1641 to 1646. The war divided England not only politically but also in religion, since the parliamentarians were generally Puritans or Presbyterians whilst the royalists were more Catholic. Charles fervently believed that, as king, he was appointed by God to rule his subjects, whilst Oliver Cromwell, the brilliant parliamentarian general and distant relative of the reformer Thomas Cromwell, believed that he was engaged in 'God's work' and shared with the French Huguenots a hatred for all 'tyranny'.

The parliamentarians were eager to secure the aid of the Scots in fighting the royalists, but the Scots agreed to do so only if it could be guaranteed that the Church of England would move in a more Calvinist direction, in particular, abolishing bishops, just like the Presbyterians had. In 1643, accordingly, a group of Anglican divines met at Westminster Abbey and produced a new set of statements known as the Westminster Confession. It was subsequently ratified by both English and Scottish parliaments. This creed lived up to its Calvinist promise: where earlier statements of faith had begun with the nature of God, the Westminster Confession began by insisting on the divine authorship and sufficiency of the Bible. Other doctrines such as predestination and the perseverance of the saints also appeared.

In 1645 the parliamentarians executed the hated Laud for treason; in 1649 King Charles himself suffered the same fate. For nearly ten years, until his death in 1658, Cromwell acted as dictator of England, and during this time many Puritan-friendly policies were enacted. Contrary to popular myth, they did not actually ban Christmas, but the celebration of 'holy days' was strongly discouraged as 'too Catholic'.

The Commonwealth, as this government was known, did not last long; Cromwell's son proved ineffective as a candidate for lord protector and in 1660 Charles I's son, Charles II, returned from exile and was crowned king. The church's lurch towards Calvinism was reversed and the Westminster Confession was withdrawn in both England and Scotland. Nonetheless, as we shall see in Chapter 11, James II's attempt to return Catholicism to favour met determined resistance.

CHAPTER 10

A NEW AGE OF EXPLORATION

The Renaissance saw western Europeans taking a great and renewed interest in the world beyond Europe. This was partly spurred by the remarkable expedition of Marco Polo, a Venetian who, in the late thirteenth century, travelled east to Mongolian-ruled China and upon his return wrote a best-selling book about it. People across Europe were galvanized: inspired by his exploits and hoping to better them, they planned new journeys of discovery.

There were fabulous prizes to be won. India, with its riches, especially in spice, was one such. Somewhere beyond India, tales spoke of an even richer land called Cathay. Explorers were also spurred by tales of the great empire of Mali in West Africa, a Muslim state where there was so much gold that the king used a huge nugget of it to tie his horse to. In fact, Mali really did have a major gold trade, which was conducted by camel caravan over the Sahara Desert with the Maghreb (Muslim northwest Africa, that is, modern Morocco and Tunisia). Since the Maghreb also traded with Christian Europe, this meant that much of the gold current in late medieval Europe came from African mines. In 1324 the king of Mali, Mansa Musa, made a famous pilgrimage to Mecca during which he stopped off in Cairo. Travelling with a retinue of thousands, the king gave away so much gold during his stay that he flooded the market and depressed prices for some years. Europeans were entranced, and the *Catalan Atlas*, made in Spain some years later, depicts the African emperor upon his throne, holding an enormous nugget of gold.

Most intriguing of all, however, was the mysterious legend of Prester John. Dating from the twelfth century, the story concerned a Christian kingdom, ruled by a priest (or 'prester') somewhere in Asia, or possibly Africa (medieval Europeans were rather hazy about where one continent stopped and the other started). Sometimes the Christian emperor John was thought to be a descendant of the magi who visited the infant Jesus; he was briefly identified with Genghis Khan (since there were Nestorian Christians in the Mongol armies). His kingdom was said to be a perfect utopia, though surrounded by the forces of Islam or paganism. It was also thought that the Prester intended to invade Jerusalem and free it from the Muslims.

The renewal of interest in exploration that such legends fostered would lead to an explosion of Christianity beyond its traditional borders. There had, of course, already been far-flung churches in central Asia, China and Sudan, and there were still well established ones in India and Ethiopia. But now European-style Christianity was to be exported and transplanted into distant countries. It happened in two main ways. In one, missionaries went out and sought to convert the people they found. In the other, colonists went and settled in the newly discovered lands, bringing their religion with them more or less incidentally. The two methods were not mutually exclusive – missionaries travelled to colonies, and colonies sprang up around missionaries. As a rule, the 'mission approach' prevailed in most of Asia and Africa and tended to be Catholic, while the 'colonial approach' dominated in the Americas and tended to

Missionaries will convert the world by preaching, but also through the shedding of tears and blood and with great labour, and through a bitter death.

Raymond Lull, 1232–1315

This emperor, Prester John, holds full great land, and hath many full noble cities and good towns in his realm and many great diverse isles and large. For all the country of Ind is devised in isles for the great floods that come from Paradise, that depart all the land in many parts... This Emperor Prester John is Christian, and a great part of his country also. But yet, they have not all the articles of our faith as we have. They believe well in the Father, in the Son, and in the Holy Ghost. And they be full devout and right true one to another.

Sir John Mandeville, a fictitious travel writer, *Travels*, c. 1366

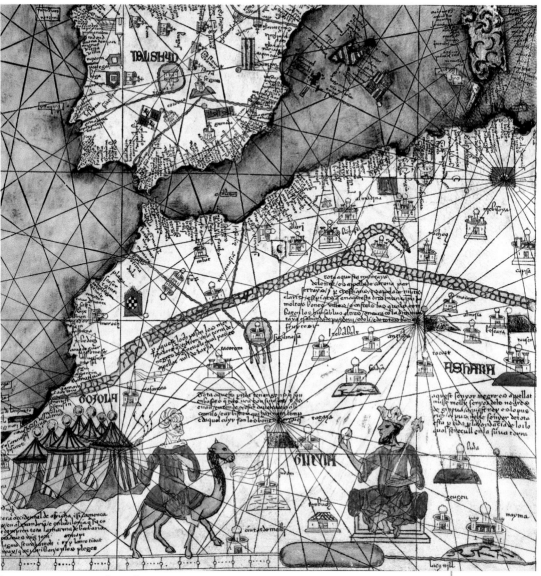

be Protestant. But, where the Europeans encountered already existing churches, different beliefs about Jesus, authority or the church itself, which had developed separately for centuries, were brought into sudden contact. When this happened, conflict was usually inevitable: the Europeans, inheriting the clear but simplistic medieval distinction between orthodoxy and heresy, sought to bring the foreign churches into line with their own beliefs, while the members of those churches naturally resisted any attempt to override their cherished traditions.

AFRICA

PORTUGAL AND 'PEPPER AND SOULS'
Portugal became independent from Spain in around 1139 when Alfonso I (1110–85) proclaimed himself king of the northern part of the modern country, before conquering most of the rest of it. Diniz (1261–1325), king from 1279, founded the University of Lisbon in 1290, negotiated his country's first commercial treaty with England, formed a Portuguese navy and in 1319 requested the pope to found the Order of Christ as the successor to the recently disbanded Knights Templar; but

A detail from the *Catalan Atlas*, made in Spain in 1375 by Abraham and Jehuda Cresques. At the bottom right is an imaginative portrait of Mansa Musa of Mali (reigned 1312–1337), holding one of the enormous nuggets of gold for which his kingdom was legendary. Such images inspired many voyages to the south and east.

Departure from Lisbon for Brazil, the East Indies, and America from Americae Tertia Pars by the Belgian cartographer Theodore de Bry (1528–98).

Portugal did not make much of a mark on the international scene and remained, essentially, Spain's little brother.

All this changed in the fifteenth century, as the Portuguese crown embarked upon a sustained period of war with the Muslim powers of Iberia and the Maghreb. The Muslims were still a lingering presence in the southern part of Spain, but vastly weaker than they had once been, although Arabian corsairs were causing havoc among Portuguese merchant shipping. Portugal therefore built a significant navy. In 1415 the Portuguese sent an invasion fleet across the Straits of Gibraltar and seized Ceuta. More Portuguese conquests in North Africa followed throughout the century, especially under Alfonso V (1432–81), known for his campaigns as 'the African'.

This African empire was expensive and subject to constant attacks from African Muslims, and it dwindled to almost nothing in the sixteenth and seventeenth centuries. At the same time new possibilities were being opened up. The key figure in this process was Henrique (1394–1460), normally known as Prince Henry the Navigator, son of King John I, who was helped by the fact that he was the apostolic administrator of the Order of Christ. This knightly order had taken over all the Portuguese possessions of the Knights Templar and Henry used these resources to finance new expeditions, ensuring that the order would have spiritual rule over any new lands that were discovered, and the Portuguese ships of discovery bore the Templars' red cross upon their white sails.

Quite how much Henry himself contributed materially to the new era of exploration is disputed: he did not personally travel anywhere apart from North Africa, nor did he found the School of Navigation traditionally attributed to him. Nevertheless, he did help to create a new atmosphere, where exploration was not done by individual sea captains as they saw fit, but was a systematic programme run by the government. Madeira and the Azores, west of Portugal, had already been discovered, but they were systematically settled during Henry's lifetime.

The first focus of Portuguese exploration was Africa. Explorers were sent further and further down its west coast, trading with native peoples as they went. Everywhere they travelled, they asked after Prester John and his Christian kingdom – for the eternal struggle with the Muslims was still uppermost in the Portuguese mind, and Prester John, should he be found, would doubtless be a valuable ally. In 1495 Manuel I decided to widen the scope of exploration to Asia as well. In 1497 Vasco da Gama (c. 1469–1525) set sail with four small ships. Stating that his goal was to find 'pepper and souls', he sailed all the way down the African coast, around the Cape of Good Hope, north up Africa's eastern coast and eventually all the way to India. He returned to Lisbon in 1499 a hero, having successfully opened up the route not only to India but to much of Africa too. Manuel I ordered the construction of the magnificent Jerónimos Monastery near Lisbon to commemorate the discovery of this route. For the explorers were not only going to spread Portuguese trade and military influence: they were also going to bring Christianity. To oversee this endeavour, Manuel created a missionary tribunal, dominated by the Order of the Cross, of which he was now the head. The tribunal, one of the earliest bodies established for the express purpose of evangelization, met every fortnight to determine the course of mission in the new lands.

But, as they explored and claimed land, the Portuguese clashed with other powers, primarily Spain. In 1479 Spain and Portugal agreed the Treaty of Alcáçovas, which allowed the Spanish to claim anything north of the Canary Islands and the Portuguese to claim anything to the south. This proved unsatisfactory, especially following Columbus's discovery, in 1492, of what was to become known as the Americas. Pope Alexander VI (who was Spanish) proposed a north-south dividing line, giving the Spanish anything to the west and the Portuguese anything to the east. This was settled in the Treaty of Tordesillas in 1494, although the Portuguese insisted on moving the line west. Together with the Papal division of the world into two hemispheres went the bestowal of the *padroado*, essentially a divine prerogative to the Portuguese to conquer and govern whatever lands lay within their half and to oversee religion there.

SETTLERS AND MISSIONARIES

As the explorers opened up the African coast, other people followed in their wake. First they built forts and trading posts and then they built settlements. Since all trade was in the hands of the Portuguese crown, and any smuggling was punishable by death, settlement was relatively slow and sparse. Clearly many people felt put off by the strict rules. However, settlements still appeared, especially around the mouth of the River Gambia. The settlers built churches, and some took local women as their wives. In 1482 a fort was constructed at São João da Mina (on the coast of what is now Ghana), which was used as a base for trading with the whole region, especially what is now Senegal, Guinea and the Ivory Coast. Gold, ivory, pepper and slaves were traded all along the coast, and missionaries from the Order of Christ arrived there and began to preach to the indigenous people. In this they were helped by a fortuitous miracle: the face of a wooden statue of Francis of Assisi which they had brought darkened in the humidity and heat. The missionaries claimed that the saint was turning black, becoming the patron saint of Africans.

The missions had some success. Many

Africans converted to Christianity, often as the chiefs or kings of tribes converted and had all their followers baptized at once. Yet it was often a rather ephemeral affair. Most of the missionaries spoke little of the local languages, and they did not explain much about Christianity to their prospective converts: instead, it was often considered enough for someone to be able to make the sign of the cross and repeat a formula about the Trinity. Inevitably, there were problems, as many Africans expected to be able to continue traditional religious practices even after Christian baptism. There was little attempt at accommodation. One slave continued to leave bread out for her dead father, who she claimed came to eat it. She was taken to Lisbon, tried before the Inquisition and imprisoned for life.

The colonists were fortunate to arrive at a time of flux in West African politics. To the north the great empire of Mali was breaking up, soon to be replaced by the even more extensive Songhai empire. Most of the vast forests and jungles of the African interior were inhabited by small tribes or statelets with no real unity. An exception was Benin, to the east, which in the fifteenth century under Oba Ewuare 'the Great' and his son Oba Ozulua 'the Conqueror' came to

dominate the south of what is now Nigeria. Benin and its client states were happy to trade with the Portuguese, but there was little progress in evangelization in this region. Christianity remained largely confined to the coastal forts and settlements, and the evangelization of Benin was sporadic at best. We know of one enthusiastic Beninite convert, called (after his baptism) Gregorio Lourenço. He worked as an interpreter and helped the few missionaries who came to Benin, but they seem to have rather neglected him: he wanted to have his family baptized, but the oba forbade it, and the missionaries, keen to win the conversion of the king and his court, complied. For people like Gregorio Lourenço, conversion to Christianity meant social marginalization.

In the seventeenth century a group of Capuchin friars (a sub-order within the Franciscans) managed to gain permission to build a chapel in the capital, Benin City, but again little came of the mission. They did manage to infiltrate a religious rite in 1665, which turned out to be a human sacrifice in the presence of the king. The friars stepped out of the crowd and tried to halt proceedings, for which they were summarily thrown out.

The Christian king of Congo welcomes a Portuguese bishop in this 1525 engraving.

CONGO AND THE SLAVE TRADE

Far more successful – at least initially – was the mission to Congo, further south. One of the first Portuguese enclaves was set up at the coastal region of Soyo, a client state of Congo – for, like Benin and indeed most African empires, Congo was essentially a federation of states dominated by the central government at the capital city, Mbanza Kongo. In 1491 Nzinga Nkuvu, the king of Congo, was baptized and took the name João (Portuguese for 'John'); one of his first acts was to command the destruction of all non-Christian idols. However, there were difficulties already. Many Congolese adopted Christianity quite enthusiastically, seeing it as an addition rather than a replacement for their traditional religion. Many others rejected it, and Nzinga Nkuvu himself subsequently returned to paganism, forcing his son, Mvemba Nzinga, who was being brought up in the Christian faith, to flee the country.

In 1506 the old king died and Mvemba Nzinga, more commonly known by his baptismal name of Afonso, returned in triumph to Congo and proceeded to stamp his personality on the country. Under Afonso churches were built and printing presses imported. He was determined to make Congo the cultural and technological equal of Portugal, and even sent two sons to Portugal to be educated: one became bishop of Uttica, the other professor of humanities at the University of Lisbon.

By the time Afonso died in 1543, there were around two million Christians in Congo – half the entire population. However, despite the apparent success of the mission there and Afonso's own attempts to Christianize the country, things were not looking good. One major problem was the slave trade, which was steadily destroying Congo's economy and its people. This was largely driven by greed for the profits to be made from sugar, which was becoming a major trade in the Atlantic islands, so great was the demand for it in Europe. Weight for weight, sugar was almost as valuable as gold, and the Portuguese wanted huge numbers of slaves to work the plantations. They found a ready supply in the 'slave rivers' of West Africa. Most slaves entered slavery when powerful states such as Benin or, to the south, Congo, captured people from weaker or client statelets and sold them on to the Europeans.

The slave trade quickly became central to the economies and burgeoning power of many European countries. One of the first English slave traders was John Hawkins, who first captured slaves on the West African coast in 1562. Two years later he had no less a backer than Elizabeth I for his next expedition. The fact that the ship he used for this cruel purpose was called *Jesus of Lubeck* reflects one of the more chilling aspects of the whole terrible business: most Christians seem not to have been bothered by the capture, sale or exploitation of slaves, or the exceptionally cruel treatment they suffered both in the slave ships and while working on the plantations. We shall see in the next two chapters how many Christians subsequently came to oppose slavery, but in the sixteenth century it seems that a love of profit overrode any moral scruples suffered by those who oversaw the trade – who all claimed, at least, to be Christians. This is despite the fact that, of course, Jesus himself not only preached about love for one's fellow human beings but warned of the dangers of wealth and avarice. Nevertheless, many Christians remained unable to see a contradiction here well into the eighteenth century: it is well known that John Newton, the author of the hymn *Amazing grace*, was a slaver before his conversion to evangelical Christianity, but it is less often reported that he continued slaving for many years afterwards as well.

It is not known how many Africans died in the Atlantic slave trade, but it was certainly tens of millions. But in the eyes of those in power in Europe, slavery was indispensable to their nations' economies and well being. Meanwhile, the economies of some African states, especially that of Congo, also came to rely quite heavily upon

I swear that such a sight would greatly astonish your highness. He says things so well phrased and so true that it seems to me that the Holy Spirit always speaks through him, for he does nothing but study, and many times he falls asleep over his books, and many times he forgets to eat and drink for talking of our Lord, and he is so absorbed by the things of the book that he forgets himself, and even when he is going to hold an audience and listen to the people, he speaks of nothing but God and the saints.

Rui de Aguiar, writing to King Manuel of Portugal, on King Afonso of Congo, 1516

Burning them by nailing them down on the ground with crooked sticks on every limb and then applying the fire by degrees from the feet and hands, burning them gradually up to the head. For crimes of lesser nature gelding, or chopping off half of the foot with an axe.

Sir Hans Sloan, a British naturalist, on the punishments inflicted on African slaves in the West Indies, 1686 the slave trade – even though it was literally destroying them from within. By 1516 some 4,000 slaves were leaving Congo every year. A single Catholic missal cost about the same as a Congolese slave. Indeed, European contact was ultimately fatal for the civilization of Congo, not just because of the slave trade, but also because the firearms which the traders sold to chieftains and kings of client states removed the military superiority which the king of Congo had previously enjoyed.

The country – and the church – survived throughout the sixteenth century, however. In 1548 a Jesuit college was founded at Mbanza Kongo, now known as Sâo Salvador, but after five years they were expelled and moved south to Angola instead. In 1596, mainly to get around the Portuguese monopoly on religion in the area, Rome gave Sâo Salvador its own bishop. However, there was still a huge lack of native priests and church structure, and political instability did not help.

THE CAPUCHIN MISSIONS

In 1640 the pope created a 'Prefecture Apostolic' of the Congo, which was put in the hands of the Italian Capuchins. Founded in the early sixteenth century in the Italian Marches by one Matteo di Bassi, these friars wanted to return to a more strict interpretation of the rule of Francis himself. They wore pointed hoods, which were believed to have been worn by Francis and his first followers and therefore symbolized this return to their roots; and they not only led very austere lifestyles, but were dedicated to preaching. This was why the Capuchins began to play an important role in foreign mission in the seventeenth century.

Italian friars began to infiltrate Congo, despite Portuguese protests that the padroado allowed only Portuguese missionaries there. War between Portugal and Spain in the 1640s allowed more Capuchins to find their way to Congo, and by the second half of the century there were enormous numbers of them, working to bring Catholicism to the indigenous people. The situation was dangerous. Many Capuchins died soon after arrival, unused to the climate, and war broke out in 1655 between Congo and Portugal, in which Portuguese forces not only wiped out the enemy but destroyed Sâo Salvador, complete with its cathedral. Slowly, the city and the church were rebuilt.

Meanwhile, the Capuchin missionaries were facing new problems with their converts. As in West Africa, the procedure was often to find a local chief or minor king, persuade him to accept baptism, and hope that he would order all his people to do the same – which he normally did. In this way, improbably vast numbers of people were baptized – some Capuchin missionaries in the late seventeenth century claimed to have baptized over 50,000 people! Little more was required of converts than the ability to repeat a Trinitarian formula and make the sign of the cross. Inevitably there were problems, as people proved unwilling to give up their traditional religions or practices; and the missionaries were equally unwilling to tolerate them. Disputes broke out between Christians and 'fetishists', as pagans were dubbed. Some fetishists claimed that baptism was fatal. Luca da Caltanisetta, a Sicilian Capuchin who worked in Congo in the 1690s, was alternately impressed by the Africans' piety and exasperated by their paganism. In his journal he wrote:

At Mbanza Zolu I sent word to the king to tell the fetishists to stop their dances and these diabolic ceremonies. They replied that they could not stop. Then I said he had to catch them and chain them or else I would come myself and catch them... I beat the heads of two idols one against the other and threw them into the fire. At that, these ignorant people showed their sadness and defiance, and almost in tears with depression they withdrew, not wishing to see their filth being burned.

Yet there were serious efforts to train the new Christians beyond the simple repetition of formulae. A catechism was translated in 1556, followed by short treatises and other educational literature. A seminary to train local priests was opened in 1682 in Sâo Salvador. Missionaries learned, however, that like most Africans the Congolese transmitted cultural and religious ideas orally, through the work of local poets and singers. The missionaries therefore did the same thing, literally singing the doctrines of Christianity to appreciative crowds. Mixed into the Bantu catechisms that were transmitted in this way were Latin phrases which the people learned to sing back during the Sunday services.

One incident testified to the power that Christian ideas held for many. It concerned a young Congolese woman named Donna Beatrice, who had a reputation for healing and miracle-working. She claimed that St Anthony of Padua had appeared to her and given her his own powers; and she called upon people to burn not only pagan idols but crucifixes. She also called upon everyone, including the royal court, to return to Sâo Salvador (the king was at that time resident in Kibangu); she predicted that the trees there would be turned into gold and silver, and jewels would appear out of the ground. In 1706 the governing council of Congo condemned her and her consort, Barro, to be burned to death. Yet her disciples still spread her message secretly for years to come.

Nevertheless, the church still did not become deeply established anywhere in the vast region of Congo. There was a shortage of priests and very little indigenous church structure: everything relied on Europeans. The church was unsustainable, and the eighteenth century saw a gradual but irreversible decline, just as the nation itself was declining under the ravages of the slave trade. Every so often a new mission would be undertaken there, and many thousands of people would be baptized; but they all seemed to have disappeared by the time the next mission came along. So it continued well into the nineteenth century.

ANGOLA
To the south of Congo lay the great plains of Angola. Here too the Portuguese lay claim, but the process of claiming and settling the land was very haphazard. When the Jesuits were expelled from Sâo Salvador in 1553, they travelled south and founded a new mission at Luanda, an island off the Angolan coast. In the absence of any other authorities, the Jesuits were soon, effectively, running a small country. Luanda grew into a city, and the Jesuits owned huge areas of coastal Angola, which they hoped to transform into a kind of benign theocracy. Schools were opened, and African clergy were trained in the kind of programme that should have been carried out in Congo. By the end of the sixteenth century, there were some 20,000 Catholics in Angola. However, the expansion of Luanda attracted royal interest and Angola became a Portuguese colony, known as Portuguese West Africa.

A similar drama played out in the Angolan interior to what had already happened in Congo: a dual process of Christianization and enslaving. The Angolan equivalent of Afonso was Nzinga (d. 1663), first a princess and later a queen of the Kimbundu and Matamba in the eastern highlands of the region. She visited Luanda to establish trading links and while there decided to become a Christian. She was baptized by the Jesuits as Aña de Souza (taking her surname from the Portuguese governor, her new godfather), but the Portuguese subsequently broke the treaty they had agreed with her. Nzinga's Catholic faith proved no hindrance to making a new treaty with the Dutch Protestants, and in 1641 she helped them to capture Luanda. In 1648 the Portuguese recaptured the city, and Nzinga was promptly re-converted to Catholicism by the Capuchin friars who were now active in Angola as in Congo to the north.

At the same time, thousands of slaves a year were being captured from the Kimbundu and Matamba. They were all baptized before leaving Luanda. The slave trade had a similar effect on Angola as on

The monks who lived there fled to an inaccessible mountain. Then a group returned to the church, saying, 'If they burn our church, which is for us like a place of pilgrimage, they will burn us too.' They went in and sat down in the middle, waiting to be set alight… A Muslim… set the place on fire… Seeing this… the monks were seized with the desire to throw themselves on the fire like moths on a lamp, and all but a very few of them did so.

The destruction of the monastery of Debra Libanos, described by Ahmad ibn Ibrahim al-Ghazi's chronicler, Arab-Faqih, History of the conquest of Abyssinia, c. 1537

It is a thing almost impossible to be believed, with what an universal joy the emperor's edict was received among the people. The whole camp, as if they had some great deliverance from the enemy, rang out with shouts and acclamations. The monks and clergy, who had felt the greatest weight of the fathers' hatred, lifted up their thankful voices to heaven. The promiscuous multitude of men and women danced and capered; the soldiers wished all happiness to their commanders: they brake to pieces their own and the rosaries of all they met, and some they burned.

The reaction to the expulsion of the Jesuits from Ethiopia, Hiob Ludolf, A new history of Ethiopia 1684

Congo, and the church itself declined much as it did in Congo. The Capuchin missions dwindled, until in 1835 the last friar left the country.

ETHIOPIA AND THE RE-CATHOLICIZATION EXPERIMENT

In 1487 a Portuguese explorer, adventurer and spy named Pero da Covilhão set off on his greatest adventure. He had already spent time in the Maghreb as a government agent learning Arabic and spying on the Muslims. Now he was going to discover Prester John himself.

Hopes of finding the mysterious Christian kingdom were renewed when King John II of Portugal sent emissaries to Jerusalem, where they met pilgrims from Ethiopia and learned the location of their homeland. Da Covilhão therefore had a fairly good idea of where he was going, and he arrived in Ethiopia in 1493 via Egypt and India, sailing up and down the east African coast in an Arabian dhow. Here he met the emperor Eskender (whom he identified, of course, with the Prester himself), and was well received – but he was not allowed to leave. Clearly a pragmatic man, da Covilhão settled down, married and raised a family. He was still there when Rodrigo de Lima, another Portuguese emissary, arrived in 1520.

The Portuguese were overwhelmed by their discovery. Prester John was real! And they seemed to have arrived in the nick of time. The Prester was under siege from the forces of Islam. The lowlands of the Horn of Africa had been united under the sultanate of Adal, and from the Adalian armies had emerged a mighty leader, Ahmad ibn Ibrahim al-Ghazi (known as 'Grañ' – 'the Left-handed One'). In the 1520s and 30s, Grañ (c.1506–43) defeated the Ethiopian armies in battle after battle, routing their generals and advancing into the previously impregnable mountain heartland of the empire. The emperor, Lebna Dengel, was forced into hiding. In desperation, he called upon his new allies, the Portuguese, to help. They arrived in 1541, shortly after Lebna

Dengel's death – a tiny force of 400 musketeers, who joined the Ethiopian army and successfully pushed Grañ back. In 1543 the great Muslim general was killed by a Portuguese bullet, and the empire he had created broke up in dissension and feuding.

The Ethiopian church had been saved, but at a terrible price. The country was exhausted by the war, which had devastated huge areas and killed hundreds of thousands. And contact with the Portuguese brought its own price too. The Portuguese had discovered that the Ethiopians might be Christians, but they were Monophysites. In Catholic eyes they were heretics, denying the two natures of Christ. The Portuguese concluded that, having saved them from the Muslims, it was time to bring them back into the Catholic fold.

The new emperor, Galawdewos (d. 1559), refused to submit to the Portuguese demands, and he wrote a Confession of faith, affirming the ancient beliefs of the Ethiopian church. However, a group of Jesuits, who had arrived with the Portuguese troops, remained in the country, at Fremona, near Adowa. Their numbers were boosted in the early seventeenth century, when the Jesuits devoted more efforts to the Ethiopian mission. The most important figure in this endeavour was the Spanish Jesuit Pedro Páez, a remarkably sensible man who believed that tact and compromise were the way forward. His kindness and good nature won him friends at the Ethiopian court and under his leadership the Jesuits prospered, building Catholic churches throughout the country. There was great suspicion in Ethiopia at large about this endeavour, since changing to Catholicism would require huge changes in the church – in its organization, its liturgy and its doctrine. More, it would mean abandoning the cherished belief that Ethiopia was special, a holy land of God where the true faith had persisted these long centuries, and submitting to the authority of a European pope.

However, the Catholic mission prospered and in 1612 the emperor himself, Susneyos, converted to Catholicism – no doubt partly inspired by his desire to secure alliances with Europe against what he regarded as the eternal Muslim threat on his coast. It looked like the dream of the Jesuits – a powerful Catholic nation in the Horn of Africa – was close to being achieved, but at this critical juncture Páez made the unpardonable error of dying and being replaced by someone desperately unsuitable. This was Afonso Mendez, another Spaniard, who arrived in Ethiopia as its Catholic bishop in 1625. He decided that Páez had been far too patient with the Ethiopians, and no further delay in their conversion could be tolerated. He immediately banned the practices of circumcision and Sabbath observance and ordered the mass rebaptism of the faithful and reconsecration of priests. Predictably there was uproar. Armed rebellions erupted and the country teetered on the brink of civil war.

The emperor Susneyos acted wisely. In 1632 he abdicated the throne in favour of his son, Fasilidas, who was not a Catholic. Fasilidas expelled the Jesuits from the country and closed its borders to Europeans. For the next two centuries, Ethiopia was closed – much like Japan during the same period. Meanwhile, Fasilidas and his successors adopted something of a siege mentality. Fasilidas established a new capital at Gonder, where he built a massive stone castle. Subsequent emperors built castles, towers and walls of their own there, until the city resembled something from a medieval fairy tale, a mighty wedding cake of a fortress. It epitomized the new Ethiopian outlook: here the true traditions were preserved, here the ancient rites were carried out, and here there was to be no further incursion from a hostile world.

THE DUTCH AND AFRICAN
PROTESTANTISM
Despite the terms of the *padroado*, the Portuguese did not quite have a monopoly over Africa. Their main competitor, both here and elsewhere, was Holland, which,

being Protestant, did not accept the papal division of the world. Indeed, by the middle of the seventeenth century, the Dutch were busy building a world empire to rival that of Portugal itself. Its West Indies Company controlled large areas of South America and its East Indies Company was challenging Portugal for control of India, Sri Lanka and much of the Malaysian peninsula. In Africa its primary possession was the Cape of Good Hope – a vital port of call on the route to India, and one which was settled in 1652. The local people, the Khoikhoi, were employed as servants by the settlers: the East Indies Company forbade slavery of the natives, although it happily imported large numbers of slaves from West Africa and also Asia. Some of the Khoikhoi did become Christians. This, though, was part of a process of 'Dutchification' rather than the result of preaching – Khoikhoi serving in Dutch households took on the language, dress and religion of their masters. Such was the rather unpromising beginning of South African Protestantism.

SOUTH AMERICA

The year 1492 was a remarkable one for Spain. In that year the last Muslim enclave at Grenada was finally captured, marking the end of the 'Reconquista' that had begun in the days of Charlemagne: Iberia was once again a Christian peninsula. Even more momentously, this was the year that Christopher Columbus (1451–1506), a sailor under commission to the Spanish crown, discovered America. He did not realize that this was what it was, mistakenly believing the world to be much smaller than it really is. He was trying to find a new route to India by sailing west and believed until the end of his life that he had discovered islands off the coast of China. It soon became apparent, however, that this was an entire continent, previously unknown to Europeans. (Although there were Scandinavian settlements in North America five centuries earlier, these had not survived, and the lands to the west had remained unknown to most Europeans.)

I entered into a hall, where the Emperor was seated upon his throne. It was a sort of couch, covered with a red damask flowered with gold. There were round about great cushions wrought with gold. This throne, of which the feet were of massy silver, was placed at the bottom of a hall, in an alcove covered with a dome all shining with gold and azure. The Emperor was clothed with a vest of silk, embroidered with gold and with very long sleeves. The scarf with which he was girt was embroidered after the same manner. He was bare headed and his hair braided very neatly. A great emerald glittered on his forehead and added majesty to him.

The emperor Iyasu of Ethiopia at Gonder in 1699, Charles Poncet, *A voyage to Ethiopia*, 1709

The São Francisco Convent at Olinda, Brazil. Founded in 1585, it was reconstructed at the end of the seventeenth century.

At 2:00 am the land was discovered, two leagues away. They took the sails in and remained under the square-sail, lying to, until day, which was Friday, when they found themselves near a small island, one of the Lucayos, called in the Indian language Guanahani. Soon they saw people, naked, and the admiral landed in the boat, which was armed... The admiral bore the royal standard, and the two captains each a banner of the Green Cross, which all the ships had carried; this contained the initials of the names of the king and queen on each side of the cross, and a crown over each letter.

Christopher Columbus's arrival on San Salvador, according to his journal, 1492

...the Indians are truly men, and they are not only capable of understanding the Catholic faith, but according to our information they desire exceedingly to receive it... the said Indians and all other people who may later be discovered by Christians are by no means to be deprived of their liberty or the possession of their property... nor should they be in any way enslaved. Should the contrary happen, it shall be null and of no effect.

Pope Paul III, Papal Bull *Sublimis Deus sic dilexit*, 1537

Under the terms of the Treaty of Tordesillas of 1494, almost all of it was claimed by Spain. A wave of explorers surged to the New World, as it was dubbed in 1494, focusing at first on Central and South America.

The discovery of America opened the door to discoveries even further west. In 1513 Vasco Nunez de Balboa crossed Panama and saw the Pacific Ocean. Six years later, the Portuguese explorer Ferdinand Magellan set off for a trip that would take his ships around the southern tip of South America and ultimately right around the world – although Magellan himself died on the way. This trip was the first to bring Christianity to the south Pacific, since the explorers were charged to preach Catholicism to all those they met. They apparently succeeded, and some Spanish ships were wrecked along the way, forcing the survivors to eke out an existence among the islanders. Intermarriage and cultural acclimatization essentially removed these little settlements from the map, but elements of Catholicism apparently survived. The Spanish sent a Jesuit mission to the south Pacific in 1668 under Diego Luis de Sanvitores. In Agana and the neighbouring islands, many people were baptized, but the conversion was ephemeral. There were revolts, harshly put down by the Spanish soldiers, and the mission ultimately came to nothing.

However, much more important in this period were the Americas themselves. Of course, the new lands were not exactly empty: the American continent contained some 57 million people when Columbus got there, an eighth of the world's total population. The native peoples were dubbed 'Indians' by Columbus and the early explorers who thought this was what they literally were. In addition to various groups in the Caribbean islands with whom Columbus dealt, there were major civilizations on the mainland, but these quickly fell to the conquistadors, who were part-explorer, part-fortune-seeker, and part-conqueror. The Aztecs, who were based in what is now Mexico,

were brought down by Hernán Cortés in 1520, who was fortunate enough to arrive at a time of political flux within the empire; the Incas, in the Andes, were brought down some years later by Francisco Pizarro.

THE COLONIES AND THE SLAVES

A system known as *encomienda* was put in place, whereby the conquistadors could claim the settlements they discovered or established for themselves. They could make the native people work for them, provided they taught them Christianity and protected them. This system had already been used effectively in the Canary Islands, and it reflected the ideology of the *padroado* that the Spanish crown was responsible for the bringing of Catholicism to the New World. But the system was generally abused by the conquistadors, who treated the natives as slaves. It largely collapsed within a few decades as the conquistadors clashed with royal representatives over who had real control, and as the native peoples themselves started dying in huge numbers from the diseases that the Europeans had unwittingly brought with them. The Spaniards then began transporting slaves from Africa to replace them, since these slaves were already immune to European diseases and were thought to be hardier. Evidence from Mexican cemeteries indicates that African slaves were already being imported by the middle of the sixteenth century at the latest.

As all this suggests, despite the high principles of some explorers and their masters in Spain, the evangelization of the Amerindians was not high on the agenda of most European fortune-seekers. One of the first attempts had been made by Ramón Pané, a layman who had accompanied Columbus and taught rudimentary Catholic doctrines to the Taino (or Arawak) people of the Caribbean islands. Unfortunately there was a misunderstanding: he gave them religious paintings, which the Tainos buried – their way of honouring them, since this is what they did in fertility rituals. Pané, however, interpreted the act as one of desecration. Things were not off to a good start, and they did not get better with the imposition of the *encomienda*. Many natives were baptized, but it was an even more cursory thing than in Africa: for example, it was a rule among some conquistadors that their men could sleep with local women only if they had been baptized. That was not a recipe for serious catechetical instruction. The Laws of Burgos, which were issued in 1512–13 in an attempt to regulate the settlements, noted that

nothing has sufficed to bring the said chiefs and Indians to a knowledge of our faith… although they are indoctrinated in and taught the things of our faith, after serving they return to their dwellings where, because of the distance and their own evil inclinations, they immediately forget what they have been taught and go back to their customary idleness and vice.

Not that the situation improved. The infamous *Requirement* was introduced in 1513, which all conquistadors had to read aloud to the Amerindians when they encountered a new group. The *Requirement* – read out, unhelpfully, in Spanish or Latin – explained that God had made the world and put St Peter and his successors in charge of everyone else, and that one of these successors had given lordship of the Amerindians' lands to the Spanish crown. If the Amerindians did not acknowledge all this, they could expect the Spanish to 'powerfully enter into your country' and 'make war against you in all ways and manners that we can'.

Some believed that the subjugation of the Amerindians was right and proper. John Major, a Scottish philosopher living in Paris, argued in 1510 that they were 'natural slaves', a notion taken from Aristotle. A Spanish lawyer and priest named Juan Ginés de Sepúlveda argued that the Amerindians were so brutish that they were good for nothing better, and should be converted to Christianity by force. After all, the Inca and Aztec civilizations had been built upon human sacrifice; any measures

Hernán Cortés goes to meet Moctezuma II, ruler of the Aztecs, in 1519, in this illustration from a contemporary Mexican manuscript.

for wiping out such practices would be justified.

There were voices of protest from a few churchmen. Unfortunately, they were largely ignored. On Christmas Day 1511 the Dominican Antonio de Montesinos preached a sermon in which he lambasted the Spanish settlers for their treatment of the Amerindians. More famous was Bartolome de Las Casas, a Spaniard who had accompanied Columbus on his third voyage to 'the New World' and who in 1510 became the first Christian priest to be ordained there. He later became bishop of Chiapas in what is now Mexico. Las Casas was desperately concerned for the welfare of the Amerindians, wrote a series of stinging attacks on the whole system and in 1550 held a major debate in person with Juan Ginés de Sepúlveda on the matter. However, Las Casas and most of those who spoke on behalf of the native Americans were concerned above all about the cruel treatment meted out to the native Americans and the slipshod way in which evangelization was done, if it was done at all. They generally did not question the institution of slavery itself or the European presence in the Americas. Indeed, Las Casas actually encouraged the importation of African slaves to relieve the burden on the native Americans, although he was concerned that they should be well treated. It would be many years before Christian criticism of Europeans' behaviour in the Americas and Africa became more radical.

There was some unhappiness in Rome with the situation. As early as the 1430s Pope Eugene IV (reigned 1431–47) had denounced the similar system in the Canary Islands, issuing a papal bull condemning the enslavement of the natives and excommunicating anyone who did not release them, but this was completely ignored. In 1537, addressing the American abuses, Pope Paul III (reigned 1534–49) insisted that the Amerindians, being human, should not be enslaved even if they were not Christians – but he too was ignored.

Tell me, by what right or justice do you hold these Indians in such cruel and horrible slavery? By what right do you wage such detestable wars on these people who lived mildly and peacefully in their own lands, where you have consumed infinite numbers of them with unheard of murders and desolations? Why do you so greatly oppress and fatigue them, not giving them enough to eat or caring for them when they fall ill from excessive labours, so that they die or rather are slain by you, so that you may extract and acquire gold every day? And what care do you take that they receive religious instruction and come to know their God and creator, or that they be baptised, hear Mass, or observe holidays and Sundays?

Antonio de Montesinos, sermon of Christmas Day 1511

THE MISSIONARIES

As the *Requirement* suggests, for many Spaniards, Christian mission in the New World was simply a part – and a fairly minor part at that – of the systematic subjugation of the Amerindians to European rule. Yet there were also missionaries who appeared with the express goal of converting the natives. Indeed, some Catholics believed that this great task was the true reason the New World had been revealed – for did it not coincide perfectly with the rebellion of Martin Luther and the mass apostasy of much of the Old World?

But there was disagreement over how it should be done. Many Franciscans, in particular, were happy to perform mass baptisms with little attempt at instructing people, since most Amerindians were slow to learn the catechism. There are stories of friars throwing water at crowds until their arms were too tired to do any more. In Xochimilco, two friars managed to baptize 15,000 people in a single day. Others opposed this method. Las Casas, for example, insisted that people should be properly instructed before being baptized. He fell out with a Franciscan friar named Fray Toribo de Benavente over this, rejecting de Benavente's view that preaching should be done quickly and, if necessary, by force. The row was ironic, given that de Benavente, like Las Casas, was a prominent advocate of the Amerindians' rights and denounced the murderous methods of the conquistadors. Many missionaries, although concerned for the state of the natives' souls, and opposing the prevalent cruelty, believed that the natives were intellectually inferior to Europeans and incapable of understanding much about Christianity. This was despite Paul III's bull of 1537 insisting that God gives everyone sufficient intellectual ability to understand the doctrines of faith.

VASCO DE QUIROGA, THE JESUITS AND THE UTOPIAN DREAM

Yet some missionaries believed that the Amerindians were capable of much more – even that they were a chosen people,

D.^r Fr. BARTOLOME DE LAS CAS.
Nació en 1474. Murió en 1566.

Bartolome de Las Casas, in an anonymous seventeenth-century painting.

selected by God to provide a new vessel for the church in a time of heresy. These views were expressed, in particular, by Vasco de Quiroga, a Spanish priest who came to Mexico in 1531, already in his sixties. First he helped to reform the administration of Mexico following the deposition and imprisonment of a particularly brutal conquistador who had been running it, and then in 1537 he was made bishop of Michoacán. Influenced by by Sir Thomas More's novel *Utopia*, which described a perfect fictional society of equality and happiness, de Quiroga determined to bring about a similar society in Michoacán. He set up communities for the native Mexicans around Lake Pátzcuaro which revolved around education, with schools in arts, industry and politics, as well as in Christian religion. Churches and hospitals were built, and the whole district was run as a sort of amalgam of More's *Utopia* – where no one had private property and everyone worked for the good of society – and the primitive church of Acts, where all possessions were pooled for the good of all. Over it all presided the elderly bishop, beloved of his people, nicknamed 'Tata Vasco' (that is, 'Father Vasco'). Most remarkable of all, the ideals that de Quiroga had instilled into his

Aztec empire, destroyed by 1521
Inca empire, destroyed by 1535
Portuguese territory, 1650
Spanish territory, 1650
Treaty of Tordesillas, 1494
⊕ archbishopric with date of foundation

0   1000 km
0   1000 miles

HAVANA
Cuba
Hispaniola
MEXICO CITY
(TENOCHTITLÁN)
1546 ⊕
VERA CRUZ
TLAXCALA
NEW SPAIN
SANTO DOMINGO
1496 ⊕

NEW GRANADA
CARACAS
Orinoco
SANTA FÈ DE BOGOTÁ
1538 ⊕

Quito
Amazon
Madeira

PERU

B R A Z I L
RECIFE
(PERNAMBUCO)

LIMA ⊕
1535
CUZCO
LA PAZ

CHILE
PARAGUAY
Paraguay
Parana
SÃO PAULO
ASUNCIÓN
RIO DE JANEIRO

S P A N I S H
P O R T U G U E S E

SANTIAGO
BUENOS AIRES

THE HISTORY OF CHRISTIANITY

utopian society endured long after his death in 1565. The Pátzcuaro area remains a centre of art and industry in Mexico to this day, and many of the regional specialities that de Quiroga encouraged are still the same.

The Jesuits achieved even more remarkable results. In 1609 the Spanish crown handed over to them control of a vast area, mostly modern-day Paraguay, though also including much of Argentina, Brazil and Bolivia. The area was inhabited by a people called the Guaraní, and the Jesuits aimed to help them live in liberty and enlightenment. An extraordinary plan was initiated, under the guidance of Diego de Torres, a Peruvian Jesuit who set out a clear and far-sighted vision for the mission stations (or reductions) that would be built. In all, over a period of forty years, thirty of these reductions were built, each housing several thousand Guaraní. In these 'Thirty Missions' the Jesuits tried to help the Guaraní better themselves as far as possible through developing their own culture rather than simply importing European ways of life. The attempt was enormously successful, and the Guaraní flourished. Each reduction was planned around a large central square with crosses at each corner, dominated by a large church, complete with living quarters for the local clergy and the town's municipal buildings. The other three sides of the square would be lined with the houses of the Guaraní, all standard, one-storey structures built of stone and clay. The church, by contrast, large enough to contain all the townsfolk, would be built of wood using traditional local methods. The people would tend their own fields and also communal fields and cattle farms, belonging to the whole community. People's lives were regulated rather like a giant monastery, with allotted hours for work, for prayer and for rest. The entire population would attend Mass every day, and the children learned to recite the catechism twice daily, as well as being taught to read and write. And the pride of every reduction was its choir and band, usually made up of thirty to forty musicians. Every church had an organ, and the Guaraní played a huge variety of traditional and European instruments, made in local workshops. They played in church and also in the fields to encourage the workers, and many travelled to Buenos Aires and other cities to perform recitals.

Although the reduction would have a mayor and a town council, it was really run by the *cura*, a Jesuit priest, and his assistant, who ran the church, organized trade and administered justice. The people's faith in these priests was absolute and their decisions were never challenged. For, fortunately, it seems that their decisions were generally wise and the people they governed were extraordinarily well behaved. In this way, in this huge but remote region, a handful of Jesuits and many thousands of Christian Guaraní succeeded in building a well-nigh perfect society, where people worked for the common good, and one which endured for nearly a century and a half. Unfortunately, the dream was shattered in 1750 when the Spanish handed much of the area over to the Portuguese, who tried to take direct control. The Guaraní rebelled with the aid of the Jesuits, but lost, and in 1767 the Jesuits were expelled for helping them.

INDIGENOUS CATHOLICISM
Despite the cruelties of the conquistadors and the inadequate evangelization methods of many missionaries, it is perhaps no surprise that the examples of people such as Vasco de Quiroga and the Jesuits did inspire genuine Christian faith and piety among many Amerindians. One remarkable example was Felipe Guaman Poma, an Incan convert to Christianity who wrote a long and detailed book in Spanish entitled *The new chronicle and good government* in which he described the drudgery of life under the conquistadors and called for more justice in the Americas. Strikingly, Poma sought to relate American history to the history of salvation as understood in traditional Catholicism, to give his people a place in God's plan just like the Europeans. He was among those who called for the possibility of an Amerindian becoming a Christian priest.

Central and South America following the European conquests.

Voodoo signifies an all powerful and supernatural being on whom depends whatever goes on in the world. But this being is the non-poisonous serpent, or a kind of adder, and it is under its auspices that all those assemble who profess the same doctrine. Knowledge of the past, realization of the present, foreknowledge of the future, all pertain to this adder, which, however, agrees to communicate its power, and make known its wishes, only through the medium of a high priest whom its devotees select, and even more so through that of the Negress, whom the love of the other has raised to the rank of high priestess.

Médéric Louis Élie Moreau de Saint-Méry, a politician of Martinique, *Description de l'isle Saint-Domingue*, 1797

Perhaps the greatest example of Amerindian piety was Martin de Porres, born in 1579 in Lima, the city established by Francisco Pizarro, the conqueror of the Incas. Porres was the illegitimate son of a Spaniard and a freed African or Amerindian slave, and like most such 'half-breeds' he had no social standing at all and was raised in poverty. Yet Martin had a remarkable Catholic faith, and from an early age would spend all night in prayer in gratitude to God for saving someone as worthless as himself. When he was eleven he begged the local Dominican friars to allow him to work as their servant; nine years later, impressed by his humility and obvious holiness, they asked him to become a friar himself. He remained in the friary for the rest of his life, running its hospital and raising money to look after the poor and sick. Martin became famous throughout Lima as a holy man, gaining a reputation for miracle-working. Regarded as a local saint almost from his death in 1639, Martin de Porres was not officially canonized until 1962.

The example of men like Felipe Guaman Poma and Martin de Porres shows how many native Americans not only accepted Christianity but identified with its central principles. Catholicism became very deeply rooted throughout much of Central and South America, to the extent that people's Catholicism would become part of their self-identity.

Yet the process of Catholicization was not perfect. As happened in many other similar circumstances, the practices or beliefs of earlier local religions persisted and mingled with Christianity. Sometimes the result could be, in effect, completely new religions. The most well-known of these were Santeria and Voodoo, both of which were created by slaves from West Africa who were converted to Catholicism but retained much of the traditional belief systems of their homeland. Santeria (the 'Way of the Saints') derived its name from Spaniards who mocked the slaves' devotion to a myriad of Catholic saints; but to the Africans, this devotion was simply a way of continuing their devotion to their own god, Olodumare, and his emissaries, the Orishas. Santeria was thus a secret religion, co-existing uneasily with Christianity; and it spread throughout the West Indies from its roots in Cuba. Even today, despite having millions of followers throughout the world, Santeria continues to be a largely secret religion.

Santeria ultimately came from Nigeria; Voodoo, by contrast, was based on the folk religion of nearby Benin, but it took the same route of disguising its Iwa spirits as Catholic saints. Voodoo developed among the slaves of Haiti, but it spread to the mainland, becoming entrenched, in particular, in the Louisiana area – even though most of the black slaves here were from Congo and its surrounding regions, rather than West Africa. These people added the magical beliefs and practices that most people today associate with the name 'Voodoo'. Despite the touristy image it has acquired in recent decades, Voodoo is still practised by many in the Americas, and it is still a remarkable mixture of African and Christian beliefs: Catholic prayers such as the Hail Mary are recited in French even as ancestral spirits are saluted.

NORTH AMERICA

Spain and Portugal, busy dividing up South America and the West Indies, seemed rather unfussed by North America, and European settlement here was relatively sporadic. The pace picked up in the late sixteenth and early seventeenth centuries, and now it was undertaken by the rising powers of the day – Britain, France and the Netherlands. But it proceeded in a rather haphazard way. Unlike the government-sponsored initiatives of Spain and Portugal, the northern European powers left settlement largely up to private individuals, and different areas were settled for different reasons.

A CATHOLIC SUPERSTATE: NEW FRANCE

The northern part of the continent was initially developed by French merchants, who traded with the native peoples in the late sixteenth century. Colonists were sent in the early seventeenth century, creating two huge – though very sparsely settled – regions called Canada (to the west) and l'Acadie (to the east). Together, these were known as New France. The main settlement was Quebec, founded near the mouth of the St Lawrence River in 1608 by the French explorer Samuel de Champlain.

Although originally settled for commercial reasons, and expanded by the French government to extend its influence, New France was developed along religious lines. Armand du Plessis, better known as Cardinal Richelieu, the chief adviser to King Louis XIII, was keen on the project and encouraged settlers to travel there. He made Champlain governor of New France, decreeing that only Roman Catholics should live there. Missionaries began to arrive to bring Catholicism to the native peoples, especially the Hurons, who were dominant in this area and who were allied with the French against the Iroquois. Although a couple of Jesuits were active in l'Acadie from an early stage, the first serious missionary efforts were carried out by the Récollets. These were a French division of the Franciscan order, which had been founded in around 1570. They got their name from the fact that they specialized in 'recollection houses', essentially monasteries where the friars withdrew for 'spiritual recollection'. But many were sent out to New France, beginning in 1615, where they began to preach to the Hurons.

The Jesuits arrived in the area in 1625 to help the Récollet missions and start new ones of their own. One of their number, Jean de Brébeuf, headed west, deeper into Huron territory, building mission stations near Lake Huron, one of the Great Lakes. The work was slow and difficult. Huron society was slowly but systematically being wrecked by alcoholism, since French traders habitually sold them alcohol in exchange for furs. The Jesuits tried to get this practice banned, eventually succeeding in 1662. It was to little avail: the Hurons were also succumbing to European diseases that the missionaries themselves were unwittingly transmitting to them. The Hurons blamed this on demonic activity associated with

Christianity. Such was the carnage wrought by smallpox and measles that in 1649 the Hurons' enemies, the Iroquois, were able to crush their forces, capture many Jesuit missionaries and kill them. Jean de Brébeuf and his assistant Gabriel Lalemant were tortured to death in an especially horrific fashion. Such was de Brébeuf's bravery – praying for his tormentors as they hacked his face to bits – that as he died they cut open his chest and ate his heart, in the hope of inheriting his courage.

Both Franciscan and Jesuit missionaries tried to educate the Hurons by building schools for their children. But these were largely unsuccessful: the Jesuits thought the boys lazy and uncivilized, preferring to play rather than learn. They did not realize that play was a traditional way of learning among the native peoples of the area; moreover, the Hurons could see no benefits from the European-style education. Discouraged, many Jesuits left Canada altogether in the 1630s, when New France fell under the ecclesiastical jurisdiction of the archbishop of Rouen.

The attempt to Catholicize the area continued with the establishment in 1642 of the settlement of Ville-Marie on an island further up the St Lawrence. The settlers

The Jesuits Brébeuf and Lallemant are martyred by the Iroquois, by the Spanish artist Francisco de Goya (1746–1828).

In recent centuries, driven by religious zeal and ablaze with piety, [the French people] have carried their weapons and the French name into the Orient and into the south, so well that in these regions, to say 'French' is to say 'Christian', and to say 'western, Roman Christian' is to say 'French'… But… if you are zealous for the Christian religion… today you must extend your piety, justice, and civility and teach these things to the nations of New France.

Marc Lescarbot, *History of New France*, 1610

The Puritan Fathers: a new theocracy?

That New England's Calvinist Puritans created theocratic governments is a stereotype that owes much to the nineteenth-century myth that Calvin established theocratic government in Geneva.

Establishing colonies outside the bounds of functioning European laws brought opportunity for innovation. New England's colonies present shifting solutions to the problem of giving structure to government. John Robinson, the Pilgrims' minister, became convinced of an obligation for mutual religious toleration (at least among Protestants) by the time Plymouth Colony began. He insisted that church officials had no authority over the magistrates except within the congregation. Guided by Robinson's writings, the colonists drew up laws intended to be 'equitable' without respect to church membership; and covenanted church membership never became a prerequisite for suffrage in Plymouth Colony.

Plymouth's 1636 constitution follows English legal precedent with few exceptions, principally in the direction of biblically warranted charity. Following advice from Roger Williams, Plymouth attempted to treat native Americans equally before the court regarding land title, as people equally possessed of the image of God. In 1645 the majority of Plymouth's magistrates favoured total

religious toleration among Protestants, but Governor William Bradford prevented the proposed vote. Dissent against Congregationalist dominance continued, leading to sympathetic support for Baptists and Quakers – but in 1660 Governor Thomas Prence disenfranchised magistrate James Cudworth (co-author of an exposé of mistreatment of New England's Quakers) and the Quaker Isaac Robinson (John's son), a punishment repealed when Josiah Winslow succeeded Prence as governor.

Although Governor John Winthrop of the Massachusetts Bay Colony might have wanted to ground laws chiefly on biblical precedent (and Reverend John Cotton provided detailed advice), competing interests represented by other colonists limited the possibility of divergence from precedents found in existing English law. Nonetheless, suffrage was long restricted to covenanted church members. Besides denying other colonists the sacraments of communion and baptism, this restriction could deny rights to distribution of common lands among the freemen.

The Plantation Covenant of New Haven Colony (1639) asserted that the Scriptures contain a 'perfect rule for the direction and government of all men in all duties, which they are to perform to God and men, as well in families and commonwealth, as in matters of the church'. Reverend John Davenport supervised the organization of the government by church members only, following the theocratic guidelines devised by Cotton but not implemented in Massachusetts Bay Colony.

Roger Williams, in Providence Plantations, was distinctly anti-theocratic,

having experienced the power of the magistrate to enforce religious conformity in Massachusetts. Williams might have been inspired by the strict separation of church and state advocated by Baptists Thomas Helwys and John Murton. The non-theocratic government in Rhode Island was stated in mutual agreements among the planters (1641, 1642), guaranteeing 'liberty of conscience' and making doctrinal disunity not actionable. These agreements received confirmation by charter in 1643.

Local towns varied in attitudes towards theocracy. Dedham (1636) attempted to reject non-covenanted residents. Controversies in Hingham and Scituate (c. 1645) focused on opposition to dominance by covenanting Congregationalists.

New England never presented sufficient unity to be 'a theocracy'; theocratic tendencies existed, but differed from England largely in asserting Congregationalist rather than Anglican dominance.

JEREMY BANGS

---

were led by Paul de Chomedey de Maisonneuve, an extremely devout soldier, who was determined to create a community that would revolve around the Catholic Church. The first thing the settlers did when they arrived at the island was to say Mass; the second thing was to build a fort, since the area was dominated by the Iroquois. Despite fears of a massacre at the hands of the Iroquois, the settlement not only survived but prospered, becoming the city of Montreal.

Still, Catholicism maintained only a tenuous hold on the country. When

François de Montmorency Laval, the new vicar apostolic of the region, submitted a report to Rome in 1660, he had found only 26 priests in New France. (A few words of explanation: the Catholic Church distinguishes between areas where there is an established Catholic hierarchy, and those without. The latter are considered mission territory. The person in charge of all things Catholic in such areas is a 'vicar apostolic', basically what would be a bishop if there were an episcopal system there. Indeed, vicars apostolic are sometimes referred to as bishops.)

Most of the settlements were still tiny, little more than villages, scratching a living in a difficult land and facing constant threats from the Iroquois and also the British, who disliked this French presence on the doorstep of their own colonies to the south. Laval worked extremely hard to create a proper ecclesiastical structure in New France, building churches and seminaries and training new priests. The work paid off, as in 1674 the Catholic hierarchy was officially set up in New France. Laval became bishop of Quebec, with the creation of the new diocese indicating the new strength of the church there. This coincided with more growth and development of New France as a whole, with the 1680s seeing vast territories in the interior of the continent to the south – 'Louisiana' – being claimed, if not settled.

However, colonial wars with the British saw New France whittled away in the eighteenth century, until by the 1760s it all belonged to Britain. The British crown hoped to impose the Church of England upon its new subjects, but recognized the difficulty of this and allowed the Catholic hierarchy to stay in place. But the Récollets and the Jesuits in the territory were not allowed to recruit and they dwindled away, both finally disappearing in the nineteenth century.

THE BRITISH COLONIES

Far to the south, the English established the colony of Jamestown in Virginia in 1607 for much the same purpose as the first colonies of New France: wealth-seeking. The fact that the first colonists devoted their time to looking for gold instead of planting crops meant that many of them died of starvation, but they soon found that growing tobacco was extremely lucrative. Plantations arose, worked first by white servants and later by African slaves. In these unpromising conditions, Christianity was a minor element of society. Most settlers were single men seeking their fortune and were uninterested in religion. As a result, there were few churches in the region. However, they did still have a part to play in daily life. Since this was an English colony, the Church of England was the official church,

The Pilgrims at Plymouth – the first sermon ashore, 1621, by the American artist Jean Leon Gerome Ferris (1863–1930).

and a priest accompanied the original colonists. The churches doubled almost as town halls: indeed, the vestry houses which accompanied most churches were apparently used for precisely that purpose, both for meetings and for storing ledgers.

In other areas, Christianity was more prominent. Maryland, to the north of Virginia, was settled in 1634, partly to give English Catholics somewhere to go. In 1649 the colony passed a toleration act which permitted freedom of religion – provided it was Christian. This made the colony a haven for Puritans fleeing Anglican Virginia, which caused great tension. Indeed, the Puritans of southern Maryland rebelled in 1650 and set up their own government, which outlawed Catholicism and Anglicanism alike. The Puritans began to persecute the Catholics in their area, burning down their churches, until the Maryland authorities wrested back control and re-instituted religious freedom.

More prominent, however, were the colonies founded by Puritans to the north. These were, in effect, communities of refugees. As we saw in the last chapter, many Puritans left the Church of England in the seventeenth century, forming new Separatist churches. Persecution led to many of these people fleeing England, often for the Netherlands, a bastion of both tolerant society and Calvinist theology. Many remained there, or in France, where they found a refuge among the Huguenots; but some dreamed of setting up a brand new society. North America seemed ideal. In 1620, the first 'Pilgrim Fathers', led by John Robinson, arrived at Plymouth in Massachusetts, having travelled from Lincolnshire via Leiden, in the Netherlands, then Plymouth in England. More arrived in the years that followed, especially after 1628, and a series of colonies sprang up along Massachusetts Bay. They were a mixture of different groups, some Anglican Puritans and others Separatists, but they made common cause, agreeing on the Cambridge Platform in 1648 as a common

statement of views and purpose. Some, however, found themselves striking out on their own. For example, Roger Williams set up a Baptist colony at Providence in 1639 after having been ejected from his settlement. The Quakers also came into conflict with other groups – three were hanged on Boston Common in 1660–61 for refusing to obey the authorities.

Meanwhile, settlers with similar views were building homes at New Amsterdam, founded by the Dutch on the River Hudson in 1626. This colony was handed to the British in 1664, and the Dutch Reformed tradition continued to be strong there.

MISSIONS TO INDIA

Unlike the Americas and much of Africa, India was not wholly unknown to Europeans of Renaissance times. After all, Europe had had profitable trade links with the subcontinent in Roman times. But no travellers went there in the Middle Ages until the thirteenth century – apart from a rather unlikely legend that an English bishop named Sijhelm travelled to India in AD 883, on the orders of Alfred the Great, to search for the tomb of St Thomas. Other than this, the first European to visit India was Marco Polo, who went to the Coromandel coast to the east and then to Quilon in the west (modern Kollam), the central region of the Malabar church. Others from the West were travelling there at this time, such as John of Monte Corvino. He was a member of the Society of Wanderers for Christ, a missionary society which had been founded by Pope Innocent III to travel east. John, and others of the society to make it to India, reported that there were Christians there, but they were in a bad way, having dwindled in numbers and abandoned important doctrines.

But it was not until the end of the fifteenth century, and the explosion in world exploration under the Portuguese, that India – and its church – became really known to Europeans. In 1498 the Portuguese explorer Vasco da Gama arrived in southern India. Bizarrely, one of the first things that this

...whatsoever person or persons within this province... shall from henceforth blaspheme God, that is curse him, or deny our Saviour Jesus Christ to be the son of God, or shall deny the holy Trinity, the Father, Son and Holy Ghost, or the Godhead of any of the said three persons of the Trinity or the unity of the Godhead, or shall use or utter any reproachful speeches, words or language concerning the said Holy Trinity, or any of the said three persons thereof, shall be punished with death and confiscation or forfeiture of all his lands and goods to the Lord Proprietary and his heirs.

The Maryland Toleration Act, setting the limits within which toleration was possible, 1649 representative of western Catholicism did was to walk into a Hindu temple and pray to an image of the goddess Kali. Apparently he thought it was the Virgin Mary.

More westerners followed, and the Malabar Christians welcomed them. They hoped that an alliance with the Catholics would strengthen their position: on da Gama's second trip to India, the Christians told him that they wanted protection against Muslims and Hindus, so that the message of St Thomas might not die out. For their part, the Portuguese recognized that an alliance with native Christians would be useful, for, as we saw in Chapter 4, the Indian Christians moved in the top circles of Indian society. And the Portuguese, as they brought over settlers and built forts along the western Indian coast, maintained good relations with Mar Jacob, the metropolitan of the Malabar church.

The principal Portuguese enclave was Goa, on the west coast of India, to the north of Malabar. Here Jesuit, Dominican, Franciscan and Augustinian missionaries jostled for elbow room, winning many conversions to Catholicism. Goa became a Catholic diocese in 1534 and it was here that in 1542 the most famous missionary of the age, Francis Xavier (1506–52), came. This remarkable Spaniard had been a friend and disciple of Ignatius Loyola and founder member of the Jesuits before moving to Portugal, where he taught and tended to prisoners of the Inquisition. He was then appointed apostolic nuncio (a representative of the pope in a particular location; the first nuncios had been appointed just a couple of decades earlier), and left for Goa, but he did not stay there long. After learning the local languages and ministering to the burgeoning missions in Goa, Xavier headed south to Cape Comorin, the southern tip of India, where he preached to the local fishermen with great success. In 1545 this human whirlwind of activity left for Malacca, leaving the Indian mission in other hands. Malacca, a port and trading centre on the western coast of the Malaysian peninsula, was a major centre of mission during this

period. Formerly the capital of a powerful sultanate which had extended its power down the whole peninsula, it had been conquered by the Portuguese in 1511 and was a convenient stopping-off point for missionaries as well as for traders.

Unfortunately, not all those entrusted with the mission were up to the task. The same situation developed in India as had occurred in Ethiopia. The Portuguese were not content with being on good terms with the Malabar Christians – they wanted them to return to the Catholic fold. Where the Ethiopians had turned out to be Monophysites, the Indians had turned out to be Nestorians. Moreover, they followed a liturgy that did not conform to the Roman one. They did not believe in priestly celibacy or make confession to priests. Trouble was inevitable. Portuguese friars started to enter Indian churches and say Latin Mass, and they accused the Indians of Nestorianism. Only the Franciscans defended the right of the Malabar Christians to use their own rites. Francis Xavier himself revered Mar Jacob, stating that in his old age the metropolitan had reverted to the Latin rites. It seems that the old man was snubbed by his flock for this, and lived out his last years being cared for by the Franciscans.

Mar Jacob died in 1549, and relations between the factions promptly deteriorated. The Malabar bishops were still sent over from Persia, rather than found among locals, and the Portuguese conspired to prevent the Persian church from sending a replacement. They felt that the Catholic bishop of Goa was the only lawful bishop of India, even though his jurisdiction officially covered only Goa, not Malabar to the south. However, one Nestorian bishop, Mar Abraham, succeeded in not only slipping through the net but also gaining the support of Pope Pius VI, having convinced him that he followed the Roman customs. Abraham therefore ruled the Malabar church until 1597, during which time Latin liturgies were translated into Syriac for the benefit of the Indian Christians. Latin seminaries were opened

They asked what he was looking for so far from home, and he told them that we came in search of Christians and spices.

Vasco da Gama's account of his arrival at Calicut (modern Kozhikode) in 1498 where people were trained in Catholic Christianity, and synods were held to bring in various reforms. The Malabar Church was being slowly conformed to the Roman Catholic Church.

When Mar Abraham died, the pace accelerated. Alexis de Menezes, the new Catholic archbishop of Goa, arrived in 1599 and felt that it was time to bring the Malabar Christians wholly under Roman rule. In particular, he was scandalized by the fact that the Malabar Christians, in their liturgy, spoke of the Nestorian catholicos as the head of the worldwide church! Clearly this would not do. His reaction was harsh: instant excommunication of anyone who failed to appreciate that the pope was the sole head of the Christian church. There was outrage, and threats were made against the archbishop's life for this grave insult to the revered catholicos.

Menezes responded by summoning the Synod of Diamper, near Ernakulam. Many refused to attend, but Menezes forced all those who did turn up to sign the decrees of the synod or face excommunication. The synod romanized the Malabar church, bringing its doctrines and rites into line with the Latin ones. In particular, the notion of the Malabar Christians that there could be one valid 'law of Peter' and another, equally valid 'law of Thomas' was condemned. So too was a belief, influenced by Hinduism, that everyone had their own way to salvation or *dharma*, no matter what religion they followed. Such relativist ideas had no place in the Roman church of this time.

Menezes ordered all Syriac books to be handed over, and many were burned. A Jesuit named Francis Roz was appointed bishop over the Malabar church, but the Indian Christians often rebelled against him. The biggest rebellion happened in 1653, when a mob at Cochin gathered under a stone cross, known as the Koonen Cross, and swore that they would never accept Catholic authority. They would recognize only their own archdeacon, and they would not rest until the Jesuits had been expelled from India. Indeed, the archdeacon himself was raised to the metropolitan throne as Mar

The miracles of St Francis Xavier, by the Flemish painter Peter Paul Rubens (1577–1640). The painting shows a number of miracles attributed to the missionary, including the healing of the sick and the raising of the dead, as if they all happened at once.

Thoma. The Malabar church was split between those who continued to accept Catholic rule and those who broke away under Mar Thoma. The Catholic Church responded by sending Carmelite missionaries to the rebels, who were sympathetically received, but completely failed to restore union with Rome. Their leader, Giuseppe Sebastiani, was made bishop in 1658; he was consecrated in secret at the Vatican to avoid offending the Portuguese authorities.

The problem was never really solved, but religious differences were overtaken by politics. The Portuguese hold over the west coast of India was increasingly precarious, being challenged by the Dutch, who had occupied Sri Lanka. In the early 1660s the Dutch moved up the Indian coast and captured the Portuguese possessions one by one. As they did so, they ordered all foreign priests to leave. Before Sebastiani left in 1663, however, he ordained an Indian named Chandy Kattanar (often known as Alexander de Campo) as vicar apostolic of the region. Kattanar was thus the first native Indian to be ordained by a Catholic – and he might have helped to bring all the Malabar Christians under Catholic rule. It was not to be. Kattanar was successful while he lived, but after his death in 1687 he was replaced by a half-Portuguese, half-Indian named Raphael. The Malabar Christians refused to recognize the authority of 'a half-caste'. Meanwhile, Mar Thoma's faction had acquired a new metropolitan, this time from the Monophysite patriarch of Antioch. Because of this, they became known as the Jacobites (after the Jacobite Church of Syria). They preferred the name Malankara Church, however. There were thus now two well-defined Malabar churches, the Jacobites (or Malankara) and the Roman. And so it was to remain for centuries, with confusion and chaos reigning among the Indian Christians.

THE FAR EAST

THE MISSIONS TO JAPAN
The mission to the Far East is most associated with one man: Francis Xavier, whom we have already met in India. He

Every Sunday I
collected them all,
men and women, boys
and girls, in the
church... Then, in the
hearing of all, I began
by calling on the
name of the most holy
Trinity, Father, Son,
and Holy Ghost, and
I recited aloud the
Lord's Prayer, the
Hail Mary, and the
Creed in the language
of the country: they all
followed me in the
same words, and
delighted in it
wonderfully. Then I
repeated the Creed by
myself, dwelling upon
each article singly.
Then I asked them
about each article,
whether they believed
it unhesitatingly; and
all, with a loud voice
and their hands
crossed over their
breasts, professed
aloud that they truly
believed it. I take care
to make them repeat
the Creed oftener than
the other prayers; and
I tell them that those
who believe all that is
contained therein are
called Christians.

Francis Xavier on his
evangelization methods in
India, Letter to the
Society of Jesus at Rome,
1543

was a brilliant and energetic man, but his approach to mission was in some ways a prime example of the kind of problems that missionaries would have to spend the next two centuries trying to correct. Barely had Xavier finished with the fishermen of Cape Comorin than, in 1545, he had left the country for Malacca. Here he met several Japanese and converted them to Christianity. Japan had become known to the West after a group of Portuguese sailors were blown there in a storm in around 1543: Xavier concluded that providence was opening up a new mission field, and became excited at the prospect of what sounded like a highly civilized country that might be open to Christianity. In 1549, travelling in a Chinese junk with his Japanese converts and a group of Jesuit colleagues, Francis Xavier landed at Kagoshima in southern Japan. Japan, at this time, had an emperor, but it was to all practical purposes ruled by a collection of warlords (daimyos) struggling for control in what is known as the Sengoku or 'country-at-war' period. The arrival of Francis Xavier in Kagoshima was thus rather like the arrival of Augustine in Kent nearly a thousand years earlier: he needed to get on the good side of the local warlord. Fortunately, he succeeded in this as readily as Augustine had: the daimyo thought that the Jesuits might encourage overseas trade and allowed him to preach. Three months later, Xavier wrote in a letter:

The people we have met so far are the best who have been discovered, and it seems to me that we shall never find among heathens another people who are the equal of the Japanese. They are a people with very good manners, generally good, and not malicious... They like to hear things explained rationally, and, although there are sins and vices among them, when you reason with them, showing that what they do is evil, they are convinced by the reasoning.

As this suggests, Xavier had great success with the Japanese. The Buddhist priests welcomed him and some befriended him, and many were greatly impressed at the distance that the Jesuits had come simply to preach their religion. In a culture where determination against the odds is a cardinal virtue, this was a point in the missionaries' favour. But Francis Xavier did not stay long. Many Japanese insisted that, if Christianity were true, the Chinese would have heard of it; he therefore decided to bring the gospel to China too. He returned to Goa in 1551 to organize this mission, and the Japanese mission – and care of the thousand or so converts Xavier had won – passed into other hands.

The mission prospered. One Jesuit, Luis Frois, had the remarkable good fortune of befriending an underling of Oda Nobunaga, one of the most powerful daimyos in Japan. Frois had several audiences with Nobunaga, who although he did not believe in any religion at all was impressed by the Jesuit and guaranteed his safety throughout the country, including the capital, Kyōto. Frois was thus able to conduct a major mission on the central and largest island of Japan, Honshu. Meanwhile, one of Xavier's companions, Cosme de Torres, directed the mission on the southern island of Kyushu, again with great success. The missionaries were also helped by a number of daimyos who became Christians themselves. The most famous of these was Takayama Ukon, an extremely cultured lord who ruled a large territory to the south of Kyōto and was renowned for his mastery of the Japanese tea rituals. His allegiance was to Oda Nobunaga, and he encouraged Christianity in his lands – even ordering the baptizing of his people.

In 1579 a man as important to Asian mission as Francis Xavier himself arrived in Japan. Alessandro Valignano (1539–1606), another Italian Jesuit, had been made visitor of the missions to the whole of Asia. He was particularly keen to start missions in China, and he travelled to Japan to study the mission there and learn from its successes.

Valignano quickly saw that mission to a foreign culture could succeed only if the missionaries understood that culture and conformed to its norms. Xavier himself had recognized this to some extent, when he discovered that the Japanese did not understand the Christian ideal of poverty, and he had ordered his missionaries to dress well. But Xavier had had no real interest in the cultures of the people he was trying to convert. He was a poor linguist and had had to rely upon interpreters. Valignano, by contrast, forced all the Jesuit missionaries in Japan to learn Japanese and fit in with Japanese culture as much as possible. In a number of writings on Japan and mission, Valignano set out the Japanese customs that Jesuits should conform to – politeness, bathing twice a day, wearing Japanese clothes and so on. He brought a printing press from Europe and used it to print edifying works for the Japanese. A special effort was made to train Japanese priests and missionaries, because Valignano recognized that the Japanese church would never thrive as long as it was led by foreigners. As part of this initiative, he arranged for a visit by four young Christians from Nagasaki – a city on Kyushu Island where Christianity was especially strong – to Europe, where they immersed themselves in Italian culture and met the pope. Valignano hoped that this would help Europeans to begin to understand Japan, a culture which he regarded as incredibly different from Europe and extremely difficult to comprehend. He also wrote a number of works attempting to explain Japan to outsiders, a project on which he collaborated with Luis Frois.

The Japanese mission appeared to be flourishing. By 1570 there were some 30,000 Christians in Japan; by the time Valignano left Japan in 1581 there were 150,000 Christians, of whom 100,000 were in Kyushu. Many lords were converts, and it was fortunate that when Nobunaga was killed in 1582, his successor, Toyotomi Hideyoshi, continued his Christian-friendly policies. Again, Takayama Ukon, the famous Christian *daimyo*, played an important role here, having transferred his allegiance from Nobunaga to Toyotomi.

Indeed, Takayama was moved to the domain of Akashi, where he again attempted to impose Christianity on the people.

Xavier had been right in his assessment of the Japanese as especially well suited to hear the gospel. They were already used to contemplating the transience of the physical life, a lesson that had been taught by the samurai culture of the *Sengoku* period, and this translated well to Christianity. The sign of the cross became common in Japan, as people wore crosses on their chests and soldiers even put it on their armour. In addition to churches, many Christian communities built simple wooden crosses, which functioned rather like traditional Shinto shrines: people could come and pray silently at them, or more elaborate processions or rituals could be performed at them.

Japanese Christianity even spread beyond Japan. In the 1590s Toyotomi invaded Korea. There were many Christians in his army, and Jesuit missionaries were allowed to accompany them. Korea was devastated by the invasion, but some Koreans were baptized, apparently mostly by the Japanese soldiers rather than the European missionaries. Some accompanied the soldiers back to Japan, and there were Korean martyrs among the Japanese Christians when persecutions began twenty years later. Nevertheless, Christianity did not become at all widespread in Korea at this time.

MATTEO RICCI IN CHINA

When Francis Xavier conceived the plan of evangelizing China, he did not realize that Catholicism had already reached the country three centuries earlier. In the thirteenth century, many in Europe had hoped that Kublai Khan and his empire might prove a useful ally against the Muslims (and that he might even be Prester John). In 1245 a Franciscan friar named John of Piano Carpini set off bearing two letters from Pope Innocent IV to the great khan. He returned two years later, having met the khan, but failed to convert him.

I have built a church in the city of Cambaliech, where the king's main palace is… I have been buying 150 boys, sons of pagans, aged between seven and eleven, who have never learned any religion. I have baptized them and taught them Greek and Latin. And I have written out psalters for them, and thirty hymnaries and two breviaries… eleven of the boys have learned our service, and they have formed a choir… His majesty the emperor loves to listen to them chanting.

John of Monte Corvino, letter from China, 1305

Matteo Ricci, in a seventeenth-century portrait from the Italian school.

Nevertheless, relations had been established. The late thirteenth and early fourteenth centuries saw a number of Franciscans, such as Willem van Rubroek and John of Monte Corvino, travelling to China, first in the hope of arranging an alliance with the Mongols and then to work as missionaries. They had relatively little success: not many missionaries were sent, it could take years to get to China, and many died on the way. It seems likely that most of the converts they did win were Mongolian or Persian Nestorians rather than indigenous Chinese. As we saw in chapter 4, the fall of the Yuan dynasty in 1368 saw the effective end of the Nestorian Church in China, and it also saw the end of the Catholic missions there – no doubt exacerbated by problems back home, including the Black Death, the 'Great Schism' of the papacy, and divisions within the Franciscan order itself.

Now, however, the mission to China would be resumed, on a far more ambitious scale and with a much more systematic approach. In 1581 Alessandro Valignano left Japan to return to Macao, a Portuguese enclave on the Chinese coast, which he hoped to use as a base to send missionaries into China itself. Francis Xavier had failed in his plans to do this: forbidden to enter the country at all, he had got no further than Shangchuan Island, where he had died in 1552, gazing across the sea to the Chinese coast. In the wake of Portuguese aggression in the area, the Chinese were extremely suspicious of westerners: any found in China were liable to be arrested as spies. Valignano therefore decided that any mission to the country would have to be extremely sensitive to its culture and native religion. Fortunately, he had the extreme good fortune to encounter in Macao one of the most remarkable men of the age, Matteo Ricci (1552–1610).

Born the year that Xavier died, Ricci was an outstanding figure even by the standards of the day. Educated by the Jesuits in Rome, where Valignano himself had been his tutor for a while, he was helped by his photographic memory to master virtually every subject he studied: he was an accomplished mathematician, geographer, musician, theologian and lawyer. Arriving in Macao in 1582, he studied – under Valignano's direction – with resident Chinese in order to learn the Chinese language and customs. He made such rapid progress that in 1583 Wang P'an, the governor of Zhaoqing, having heard of this foreigner's brilliance, sent for him. Ricci and his single companion, Michele Ruggieri, dressed as Buddhist monks and shaved their heads – in keeping with the principle of conforming to the culture of their host country – and travelled to Zhaoqing, near Canton (modern Guangzhou), where they presented themselves as refugee monks seeking sanctuary. They were granted land, and they began to build a church.

This first mission to the Chinese was not easy. For one thing, Ricci and Ruggieri found that the people here spoke a different dialect from the one they had learned in Macao, so they had to start learning it again. Moreover, after Ruggieri left in 1588,

Ricci was forced to move to Shaozhou, where he continued his efforts.

Fortunately, the Chinese were fascinated by this exotic visitor. Ricci soon learned that Buddhist monks were not respected in these parts, so he dressed instead as a scholar and tried to appear as learned as possible, for this was what the people liked to see. It also gave him access to scholars and the learned classes, whom he was especially anxious to impress. He was careful never to express disrespect for Confucius, and always told visitors that he was there to learn from the Chinese, not to teach them. But he was canny enough to bring a number of curiosities from Europe – realistic paintings, accurate maps, Euclidean mathematics – which greatly impressed the Chinese and helped to bolster his own standing with them.

At the same time, Ricci tried to explain his religion to these curious visitors. It was extremely difficult, given that there were few Chinese words to explain many Christian concepts. In Japan, the Jesuits of Xavier's original mission had translated catechisms into Japanese but simply used Latin words for all the theological terms, producing documents which mystified most readers. Ricci knew that this would not do, so he tried to find Chinese equivalents to Latin and Italian as he translated. His first effort, a translation of the Ten Commandments, was a success, as the Chinese declared that this moral code was in accord with reason. Translations of the Lord's Prayer, the Ave Maria and the Apostles' Creed followed.

At first Ricci had few converts. He continued to travel around China, meeting intellectuals and impressing them with western culture, and in 1600 he finally managed to meet the emperor in Beijing. He gave him many gifts, of which the emperor was most impressed by a harpsichord and a clock, and Ricci became close to many in the court and the bureaucracy that ran China. This enabled him to have much greater success. People at court converted to Christianity, as Ricci explained Christianity in such a way that it seemed quite compatible with traditional Chinese philosophy and culture, especially Confucianism. In particular, Xu Guangqi, a grand secretary at the court, Li Zhizao, a director of the Board of Public Works, and Yang Tingyun, a scholar, were three influential converts later known as 'the Three Pillars of Chinese Christianity'. Ricci estimated shortly before his death that there were 2,000 Christians in Beijing.

Following the style of Chinese intellectuals, Ricci wrote a number of pamphlets on philosophical and moral questions, culminating in his book *The true doctrine of the Lord of heaven*. This was a presentation of Christianity, not only written in Chinese but translated into concepts that made sense within Chinese philosophy. Indeed, Ricci was convinced that many Christian doctrines had been discovered, through the use of reason, by Confucius and his contemporaries, and so he presented his work as a contribution to the study of Confucius and the development of his ideas. He and many other Jesuits who joined him called for a return, in China, to the original values of Confucius rather than the more recent doctrines of Taoism, Buddhism and Neo-Confucianism. In *The true doctrine*, Ricci therefore focused on metaphysics, the nature of God and the soul, and the role of Jesus in salvation; subjects like the Trinity and revelation, which he thought would prove less palatable to the Chinese, he avoided. Completed in 1603, this book was received warmly by the scholars. Nearly two centuries later, it would also play a key role in the bringing of Christianity to Korea.

Matteo Ricci died in 1610, and the emperor arranged for him to be buried in a court plot. Other Jesuits, now permitted to preach throughout China, spread Catholic teachings and won many converts. They continued Ricci's policy of focusing their attention on the court and the 'literati', the highly educated elite who ran the country, on the principle that, if the elite could be converted, the rest of China or even Asia as a whole might follow. A number of Jesuits worked with the Astronomical Bureau,

According to their sayings, the service of the High Ruler is a prime duty; the protection of the body and the salvation of the soul are grand essentials; fidelity, filial piety, compassion, and love are to be universally exercised; the reformation of errors and the practice of virtue are initiatory steps; repentance and purification are the requisites for personal improvement; the true felicity of life celestial is the glorious reward of doing good; and the eternal misery of earth's prison is the bitter recompense of doing evil. All their commands and injunctions are in the highest degree compatible with the principles of Heaven and the feelings of men.

Hsu Kuang-chi, *Memorial to Fra Matteo Ricci*, 1617

assisting the Chinese astronomers and using their position as a means of access for mission. Western astronomical ideas, including the work of Galileo and the telescope, had been brought to China by Adam Schall von Bell (1591–1669), a German Jesuit. Another notable missionary was a Belgian Jesuit, Nicolas Trigault, who arrived in China in 1620 with 7,000 western books. He travelled throughout China, preaching everywhere, and wrote a book explaining the Chinese language for Europeans. However, Rome rejected his plan to conduct Masses in Chinese rather than Latin. The 1630s saw Catholic orders other than the Jesuits, especially Dominicans and Franciscans, allowed to go to China, and the numbers of missionaries increased.

By 1640 there were an estimated 60,000–70,000 Christians in China. Despite the tactics of the missionaries, very few of these – only around one in a hundred – were degree-holders. There had been considerably greater success among the minor literati, who were educated but had not passed the exams required to join the gentry; many of these held important positions in local administration or were scholars who helped to translate Christian writings into Chinese. However, the missions had had far greater success among the common, illiterate Chinese masses. Usually there were not enough priests to cater to the converts, so the missionaries arranged them into small lay congregations, where the Chinese Christians could meet and pray together in the absence of priests. In addition, many Chinese converts formed *hui*, mutual help associations, an increasingly common feature throughout China during this period, whereby people clubbed together to help the disadvantaged in their communities. Some better-off Chinese Christians founded charitable associations, known as *renhui*, whose activities ranged from providing food to the poor, paying for funerals and the upkeep of graves (very important in China with its emphasis on respect for the ancestors), and even providing education. Some provided money for printing Christian literature.

NEW MISSIONS

The appearance of the Dominicans and Franciscans in China marked a new period in Catholic mission, as the hegemony of the Jesuits was challenged by other organizations. There was a new sense of purpose to Catholic mission worldwide, marked by dissatisfaction with how things had been conducted to date. There had been no overall mission strategy, which meant that initiatives were left up to missionaries on the ground, with no coordination; and monarchs and politicians – especially, in the Americas, the kings of Spain and Portugal – were in effective control of the whole enterprise. These kings clearly could not be trusted to oversee evangelization in a disinterested way. So by the early seventeenth century, in the eyes of the Catholic Church, the case had been made for a new, centralized body in Rome to oversee both the methods and the theory of mission throughout the world. In 1622, therefore, Pope Gregory XV created the Congregation for the Propagation of the Faith. This congregation would have supreme authority, subject only to the pope himself, for worldwide Catholic mission, even in European Protestant countries such as Britain which the church regarded as mission territory. In practice, the Americas were never really under the congregation's control, because of the influence of the Spanish and Portuguese crowns; so Asia, which was subject to major mission efforts during this time, was to be the focus of the congregation's attention.

The congregation studied the mission efforts that had already been put into place, to understand how to do things better. An Italian priest called Francesco Ingoli, its secretary for two decades, carried out most of this work, making him one of the unsung heroes of Christian mission. The congregation learned what Alessandro Valignano had known fifty years earlier: mission work had been hampered by the fact that many missionaries understood little of the cultures in which they worked and cared even less. Many regarded Christianity as something to impose upon people, without seeing the need either to learn native languages or move towards the ordination of natives and the creation of proper indigenous churches. The Congregation for the Propagation of the Faith therefore began by encouraging missionaries to learn local languages and to translate the Bible and catechisms into those languages. It even set up its own printing press in 1626 to print them. In the same year, a seminary was founded to train missionaries.

In 1659, the congregation issued the following instruction to missionaries – but the advice was not always taken:

Beware of forcing the people to change their way of life, their customs and traditions, as long as these are not in open contradiction to religion and good morals. Is there anything more foolish than to transplant France, Spain, Italy, or any other European country (that is to say its customs and practices) to China! That is not what you should bring to them, but the faith which neither despises nor rejects the lifestyle of any people or their customs as long as they are not evil in themselves, but rather desires their preservation and promotion.

The setting up of this centralized mission strategy helped spur the creation of new initiatives and strategies throughout the seventeenth century. One important missionary who began his work as the congregation was set up was the French Jesuit Alexandre de Rhodes, who arrived in Macao in 1623. He made his way to what is now central Vietnam – known then as Tonkin – and arrived in Hanoi at the court of Trinh Trang, king of the northern part of Vietnam (the region being divided into two warring countries at this time). Here, de Rhodes and his companions succeeded in converting several hundred people, including Trinh Trang's sister. He was helped in this by a lunar eclipse. The Vietnamese believed this was caused by a dragon eating the moon, but de Rhodes successfully predicted the eclipse and explained its true cause, thereby securing Trinh Trang's favour and the safety

of the mission. Nevertheless, the king grew tired of the new religion and forced the missionaries out of the city. By a strange coincidence, while travelling through the countryside, de Rhodes won many new converts by predicting and explaining a *solar* eclipse. He subsequently travelled to southern Vietnam, where he again enjoyed great success in setting up new churches. While he was away, his converts proved effective missionaries themselves, and churches began to plant themselves across the country.

De Rhodes's efforts influenced the establishment of the Paris Foreign Missions Society, set up in 1660 by François Pallu and Peter Lambert de la Motte. They believed that secular priests – that is, those not belonging to a religious order such as the Jesuits or Dominicans – were better suited to mission, since they would be more adaptable. Their society therefore incorporated a seminary for training priests for mission. Pallu himself was made vicar apostolic of northern Vietnam, Laos and south-west China, while de la Motte was vicar general of central Vietnam. Here, and throughout south-east Asia, members of the society not only preached the Catholic faith but tried to encourage local converts to seek ordination. The aim of the society was always to follow de Rhodes's model of setting up a local church, with local clergy, rather than importing European priests.

PERSECUTION AND CLAMPDOWN
As the Congregation for the Propagation of the Faith was being set up in the early seventeenth century, then, things looked good in eastern Asia. However, it was not to remain so. The Vietnamese church was tested from its earliest days, partly because of the division of Vietnam into two kingdoms: each king suspected the missionaries of being spies from his rival, and they were periodically banished. There were intermittent persecutions, and many Christians were killed: throughout the seventeenth and eighteenth centuries, it is estimated that some 30,000 Vietnamese Christians died for their faith.

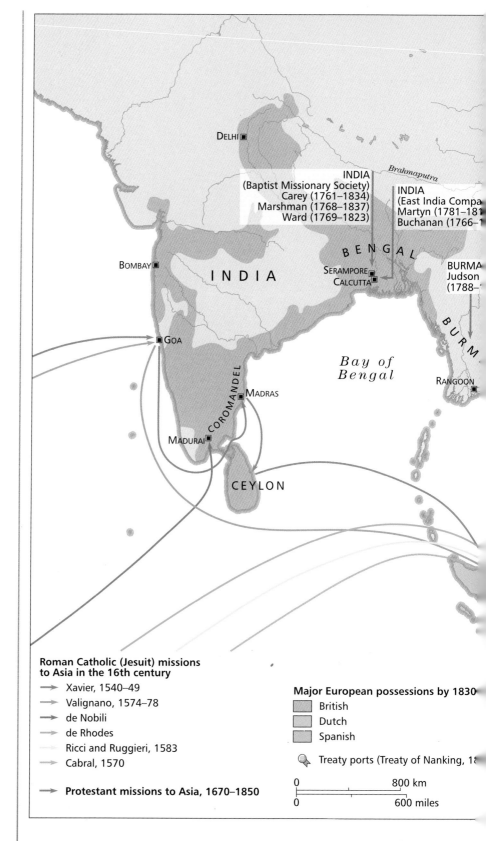

DELHI ■

INDIA
(Baptist Missionary Society)
Carey (1761–1834)
Marshman (1768–1837)
Ward (1769–1823)

INDIA
(East India Compa
Martyn (1781–181
Buchanan (1766–1

Brahmaputra

BENGAL

BOMBAY ■

INDIA

SERAMPORE ■
CALCUTTA ■

BURMA
Judson
(1788–

GOA ■

*Bay of
Bengal*

BURM

MADRAS ■

COROMANDEL

RANGOON ■

MADURAI ■

CEYLON

**Roman Catholic (Jesuit) missions
to Asia in the 16th century**

→ Xavier, 1540–49
→ Valignano, 1574–78
→ de Nobili
→ de Rhodes
  Ricci and Ruggieri, 1583
→ Cabral, 1570

→ **Protestant missions to Asia, 1670–1850**

Major European possessions by 1830
■ British
□ Dutch
■ Spanish

Treaty ports (Treaty of Nanking, 1

0   800 km
0   600 miles

PEKING ■

KOREA

KYOTO ■
JAPAN

CHINA
(London Missionary Society)
Morrison (1782–1834)
Milne (1785–1822)

(Freelance – formerly with the
Netherlands Missionary Society)
Gutzlaff (1803–51)

(China Inland Mission – founder)
Hudson Taylor (1832–1905)

NAGASAKI ■

SHANGHAI

NINGBO

C H I N A

FUZHOU

XIAMEN

CANTON
MACAO ■
HONG KONG

V
I
E
T
N
A
M

Mekong

S
I
A
M

South
China
Sea

PHILIPPINES

European missions
in Asia.

M
O
L
U
C
C
A
S

■ MALACCA

B O R N E O

S
U
M
A
T
R
A

■ BATAVIA
(JAKARTA)

In Japan, too, the initial great success of Christianity was to be tragically curtailed. The first real setback occurred in 1587, when Toyotomi Hideyoshi, the great lord who had previously protected Christians, suddenly turned against them and ordered all missionaries to leave the country within twenty days. Takayama Ukon fell from grace, ending his days in exile in Manila. Although Toyotomi's reasons remain obscure, it seems that the success of Christianity was leading to great resentment among adherents to Buddhism and the indigenous Shinto religion: many temples were being destroyed or converted to Christianity, as Christian lords cracked down on non-Christian activities. Alessandro Valignano returned to Japan at this point and pleaded with Toyotomi for leniency. Although he was allowed to stay, the lord would not rescind his order. Most of the missionaries, instead of leaving Japan, fled to Kyushu, where they were protected by local lords.

There was little persecution, however, until 1596, when a Spanish ship was stranded at Urado. Toyotomi ordered its cargo to be confiscated and its crew of 26 Christians – mostly Japanese, including some as young as twelve or thirteen – to be crucified. The order was carried out in early 1597, marking the first mass execution of Christians in Japan. Churches were burned across the country. Nevertheless, the mission continued, and the numbers of Christians swelled to 300,000. Toyotomi's death in 1598 ended this first persecution, and the subsequent civil war concluded with the victory of Tokugawa Iyeyasu in 1600. He at first permitted Christianity to be preached, but in 1614, he reversed his previous edict and ordered all missionaries out of the country, stating:

The Kirishitan band have come to Japan, not only sending their merchant vessels to exchange commodities, but also longing to disseminate an evil law, to overthrow true doctrine, so that they may change the government of the country and obtain possession of the land. This is the germ of great disaster, and must be crushed.

This order was not enforced, owing to more important political and dynastic struggles. But in 1616 Tokugawa Iyeyasu was succeeded by Tokugawa Hidetada, who was more determined to put down Christianity. Systematic searches for missionaries were now carried out, especially in Nagasaki. Those who were found were imprisoned. In Hirado, Christians tried to break a Dominican friar out of the prison, but failed. Tokugawa ordered the prisoner and a companion to be burned alive, as well as all other missionaries currently in prison; all the local Christians, their families, their hosts and their hosts' families were to be beheaded. The persecutions increased in intensity and cruelty. In August 1622 in Nagasaki, two foreign priests and the sea captain who had brought them were burned alive, and twelve ships' officers and passengers were beheaded. The following month, in the same town, 23 Christians were burned alive and another 29 beheaded. These included families and young children of the missionaries or converts.

Tokugawa Hidetada's son, Tokugawa Iyemitsu, who reigned from 1623 to 1651, completed the clampdown. There were more searches for missionaries still in the country, and all foreign ships were closely searched for hidden missionaries before they could dock. The mass burnings and beheadings continued, and the crowds, sometimes of thousands, who had gathered to watch the early ones and pray for the martyrs slowly dwindled. It is unknown quite how many people died in these extraordinarily merciless persecutions, though it was certainly thousands. Recognizing that they could not realistically kill every single Christian in Japan, the authorities tortured many thousands more into renouncing their faith. They were forced to stamp or spit on icons of Christ, known as *fumie*, and many chose to do so when told that the alternative was for their friends to be executed. Many thousands of Christians – perhaps hundreds of thousands – were driven from their homes or lost their possessions, as the remorseless clampdown continued. In 1639, Tokugawa

Iyemitsu finally decided to close Japan completely, ending all relations, even trade agreements, with the Portuguese. The only link with the West that remained was a small Dutch enclave on a neighbouring island. All missionaries who landed in Japan in the decades that followed were imprisoned and executed. Catholicism, which had seemed to start so well in Japan, had been stamped almost completely out of existence; a few hidden communities survived, but they would not make themselves known for over two centuries.

In China, too, there was persecution, but it was far more sporadic. In 1616 the government decided that missionaries were undermining traditional culture and ordered them all to leave. Some were carried to Macao in cages, but most stayed where they were and continued to work in secret. Another attempt to deport missionaries was made in 1622. A more serious setback occurred in 1644, when the Ming dynasty was overthrown by the Manchus, who invaded Beijing and set up a new dynasty. But although many Christians associated with the Ming court lost their positions, the religion was allowed to continue.

THE RITES CONTROVERSY

The 1630s, however, saw the beginning of a new problem that would severely compromise the Catholic mission to China. This was the notorious 'rites controversy'. It concerned the rituals that Chinese habitually performed in honour of their dead ancestors: the offering of prayers and food at graves and the maintenance of shrines. Confucius was honoured as a sort of general ancestor of everyone, and was given offerings on his birthday.

All of this, known generally as 'the rites', caused great division among the Catholics. Matteo Ricci had argued that the rites simply represented the natural veneration of the young to the old, and they did not constitute actual worship or involve any kind of superstition. Thus, they were not incompatible with Christianity. This was the view of most Jesuits in China. They did not allow some practices, such as praying to ancestors or offering sacrifices to Confucius, but on the whole they concluded that the rites were acceptable.

But, in 1633, a Dominican named Juan Bautista Morales arrived in China and concluded that the rites represented pagan superstition and were not acceptable for Christians. There was a general rivalry between Jesuits and Dominicans anyway at this time, even in Europe, and Morales and other Dominicans attacked the Jesuit methods ferociously. Morales left China and made a formal complaint to the Congregation for the Propagation of the Faith in 1643. The congregation concluded in favour of the Dominicans, and in 1645 Pope Innocent X banned the rites as superstitious. The Jesuits recognized that this could be a disaster for the Chinese mission, since no Chinese would convert to Christianity if it meant giving up this central element of their culture. They sent a delegation to the Inquisition in Rome to argue their case, and in 1656 Pope Alexander VII found in favour of the Jesuits. Awkwardly, Rome insisted that this did not contradict the earlier decree, because the rites were to be preserved only inasmuch as they were not superstitious or pagan. So that did not settle the question at all, because the issue at stake was precisely whether they *were* superstitious or pagan.

The controversy rumbled on. In 1693, Charles Maigrot, vicar apostolic of Fujian, ordered the rites to be discontinued in the area under his authority, stating that the decree of 1656 had been obtained under false pretences. He even banned the use of certain Chinese names for God as inherently unchristian. The missionaries – even many Dominicans – rebelled, and Rome was forced to look at the issue again. In 1704 Pope Clement XI not only upheld Maigrot's decision but went further, banning some rites that Maigrot had allowed. He sent a legate, Carlo Tommaso Maillard de Tournon, to enforce the decision: Tournon threatened excommunication for anyone who tolerated Confucianism or ancestor veneration. Many missionaries refused, since the emperor

Kangxi not only evicted Tournon but threatened those missionaries who obeyed him with the same punishment. The whole matter was settled authoritatively in 1742, at least as far as Rome was concerned, when Pope Benedict XIV stated once and for all that all rites were unacceptable and that Tournon's rules remained in force.

The mission in China faltered. The first two decades of the eighteenth century saw the Chinese authorities become increasingly suspicious of missionaries, especially those who obeyed Rome's ruling on rites, and in 1724 the emperor Yongzheng outlawed Christianity. His soldiers seized churches and banished missionaries, while many Chinese priests were forced to take new jobs. The measures were directed mainly at foreigners rather than Chinese Christians, but there was still sporadic persecution of the latter, and many Christians were martyred for their faith. The largest persecution took place in 1784–85, when there was a systematic search for missionaries and Chinese priests, and many were deported.

At the same time, many Chinese intellectuals were dismissive of Christianity. There had been such criticisms before, such as that of an official named Yang Kuang-hsien, who had campaigned against the presence of Jesuits at the Astronomical Bureau in the 1660s and published a book called *I could not do otherwise*, in which he attacked Christianity as illogical and unpatriotic. The prohibition of Christianity saw such attacks diminish, since there seemed little point in 'exposing' a religion that was already forbidden. However, Yang's work was still read, and as we shall see in Chapter 13, it became more popular with the resurgence of anti-Christian sentiment in the nineteenth century.

Still, the church's situation in eighteenth-century China was never as bad as in Japan, and there remained strong Christian communities throughout the country, descended from the *hui* and congregations that had been established in earlier years. They also had their own clerical hierarchy, which had been slowly set up following the consecration of Luo

Wenzao (sometimes known as Gregory López) as the first Chinese bishop in 1685. Luo, a poet who expressed his faith in Chinese verse, had ordained other Chinese priests, and the native priesthood had grown slowly but surely throughout the eighteenth century, ensuring that the Catholic communities had good local leadership. After a drop in the middle of the century, the numbers of Christians rose again, until by 1800 there were believed to be about 200,000 Chinese Christians, equal to the peak reached a century earlier.

INDONESIA

The vast, sprawling archipelago that is now known as Indonesia was not a single country during the age of exploration. As we saw in Chapter 4, Nestorian Christianity was known in the western part of the archipelago as early as the seventh century, but it seems to have died out by the time Portuguese explorers were opening up the area in the sixteenth century. The first Catholic baptisms were performed by a trader named Gonzalo Veloso on the island of Halmahera in 1534, and in the 1540s Francis Xavier took time out after evangelizing India and before going on to Japan to preach in the Moluccas. More Jesuits followed, as well as Dominicans, and there were successful missions spreading out from the eastern part of the archipelago throughout the late sixteenth century. The Dominicans largely ran the islands of Flores and Timor on behalf of the Portuguese, and a Dominican seminary was built at Solor in 1596. By this date there were some 40,000-50,000 indigenous Catholics in the region, perhaps one in one hundred of the population of the entire archipelago.

However, this came to an end in 1605, when the Dutch seized the island of Ambon, one of the centres of the spice trade. For the next two centuries the Dutch East India Company slowly extended its hegemony throughout the area – now known as the Dutch East Indies – and did its best to exclude all foreign interests in the area. This included the banning of Catholicism and the expulsion of most Catholic missionaries,

Having read this decree, I conclude that the westerners are really petty. It's impossible to reason with them, because they don't understand the wider issues as we understand them in China. Not one westerner is familiar with Chinese writings, and they often say incredible and ridiculous things. Judging by this decree, their religion is no different from other small, bigoted Buddhist or Taoist sects. I have never read anything so full of nonsense. From now on, westerners will not be allowed to preach in China, to avoid any more trouble.

Decree of Emperor Kangxi after hearing of Pope Clement XI's banning of rites, 1721

although some remained, especially in the Dominican heartlands of Flores and Timor. Flores, at least, remained technically a Portuguese possession. Few new missionaries were sent, though, and the Dutch East Indies followed the now-familiar story of general neglect by Rome throughout the eighteenth century. The Catholic converts were essentially left to their own devices: the Catholic European powers could no longer reach them, and the Dutch East India Company was not very interested in them. Many of the Catholics therefore simply drifted over to Protestantism, since these were the only churches now available to them. Others, however, stubbornly clung onto the faith that the Portuguese had taught them. A group of laymen was founded, called the Confreria Reinha Rosario (the Brotherhood of the Queen of the Rosary). Putting themselves directly under the protection of the Virgin Mary, the members of this society organized processions in her honour at Larantuka.

However, there were new, Protestant missionaries from the Netherlands, who had been trained at a seminary run at Leiden for ten years by the Company itself. They preached throughout the Moluccas and on Java, and by the end of the eighteenth century there were thought to be around 70,000 indigenous Protestants in the area. They were strictly regulated by the Company, whose governor-general of the region was, in effect, the head of the church as well.

THE PHILIPPINES

One of the first Europeans to visit the Philippines was Ferdinand Magellan, whose circumnavigation of the globe brought him here in 1521. His claim that the islands now belonged to Spain displeased the locals, who killed him. But 1565 saw Miguel Lopez de Legazpi establish the first permanent Spanish settlement at Cebu, and by the seventeenth century most of the islands were under Spanish control – apart from some of the southern islands, which were Muslim. The conquest and settling had strongly religious overtones. For example, one reason Legazpi settled at Cebu was that a statue of the baby Jesus was found in a hut there. This 'Santo Niño' – presumably left by Magellan forty-four years earlier – was interpreted as a divine sign and a church was built to accommodate it.

Legazpi brought Augustinian missionaries with him, who baptized a number of people, but they were not very successful. This was partly because the locals were mostly quite resentful towards their new overlords, although for the most part the Spanish in the Philippines tried to avoid the terrible behaviour of their counterparts in the Americas. Nevertheless, more missionaries followed – Franciscans, Jesuits and Dominicans – and Catholicism became more entrenched in the country. The missionaries opened schools and colleges as well as hospitals, and paid for humanitarian missions to those oppressed by their Spanish overlords. Under these circumstances, it is unsurprising that, after the initial resistance to Christianity, increasingly large numbers of Filipinos converted. Already in 1595 there was an archbishop of Manila, the administrative capital of the region. By this stage it was estimated that a quarter of a million Filipinos had been baptized.

REASON AND REVIVAL

The Reformation was a time of enormous change and creativity in European Christianity. The Enlightenment, which followed, was equally momentous. Not only did a new breed of thinker arise and, for the first time in over a thousand years, subject Christianity to sustained criticism, but the church itself saw a whole new series of awakenings. The Age of Reason was also the Age of Revival.

THE DAWN OF MODERNITY

The great wars of the late sixteenth and early seventeenth centuries – the Wars of Religion and the Thirty Years' War – left Europe devastated, and changed forever. The great powers of the sixteenth century – Spain in the west and the Holy Roman empire in the east – were exhausted. Hegemony instead passed to the centre and north of the continent, mainly to France, which arose as a new superpower. Its dynastic wars of the late sixteenth century had been settled, and France entered the seventeenth century under the firm guidance of King Henry IV. Meanwhile, the great threat to the east, the Ottoman empire, had reached its peak and was beginning to fade. Its defeat at the Battle of Vienna in 1683 would show that Europe, once lagging behind the Muslim east in power, had not only caught up but rapidly overtaken it. Hungary, which the Ottomans had conquered a century and a half earlier, was liberated and allied to Austria, which was becoming the new great power of eastern Europe. Hungary would remain part of Austria until the twentieth century,

forming once again the eastern frontier of Roman Catholicism in Europe. After the war with the Ottomans, Austro-Hungary allowed many Orthodox refugees from Serbia into the country, a migration so large that it de-Christianized much of Serbia. The Ottomans seized the chance to move many more Muslims into the abandoned areas, sowing the seeds for future discords in this part of the world. Serbia was, effectively, the border between the Austro-Hungarian and the Ottoman empires, making it the border between the worlds of Christianity and Islam and a much-contested area.

This new Europe would be built on new ideals. Politically and socially, the different ideas of the Renaissance would be developed into more extreme positions. Monarchies would become more centralized and powerful, and they would appeal to divine providence more readily. At the same time, however, trade would flourish, especially with the riches of the New World flooding into the continent. The merchants, who had begun their ascent in the late Middle Ages, would carry on rising unstoppably, and with them the middle classes. Free trade, commerce and above all tolerance would be the watchwords of the new world of the middle classes – yet the old world of autocracy and divine prerogative was still present. Religion and politics continued to be inextricably mixed, just as in the Reformation; and where some states would seek to endorse religious freedom and separate religion from politics, others would try to force a single church upon the people.

The most significant country in the forging of this new worldview was the Netherlands, which threw off Spanish suzerainty at the end of the Thirty Years'

War (1618–48). Amsterdam became the trading capital of Europe, and its merchant fleet was the largest in the world. The country was largely Reformed in religion and, as we saw in Chapter 9, the Synod of Dort had in 1618 defined the basic tenets of orthodox Calvinism. Those who rejected Dort, known as Remonstrants, were often persecuted by the authorities, but on the whole the Netherlands were remarkably tolerant for the period. Many English Puritans fled here in the first half of the seventeenth century, but when the Puritans defeated the Royalists and executed King Charles I, his son, Charles II, also found refuge in the Netherlands. Many thinkers considered doctrinally dubious worked here too, including Descartes, who was French, and his disciple Spinoza, who was Dutch, of Spanish Jewish descent – for many Jews had fled Spain and the Spanish Inquisition in earlier decades to find asylum with the Dutch.

If the Netherlands helped to make tolerance a leading theme of the Enlightenment, Britain helped to make liberalism a central concern too, although English Protestants remained united in their hatred of Roman Catholics. From 1593 people had been fined for not attending Church of England services; after the infamous plot of 5 November 1605 was foiled, when Guy Fawkes and a number of other Catholic conspirators attempted to blow up parliament while the king was inside, Catholics in general were branded as potential subversives or even what would today be called terrorists. The disenfranchisement of Catholics was made official with the Test Act of 1673, which decreed that anyone in any civil or military post must be a member of the Church of England. Roman Catholicism remained illegal until 1778, and Catholics suffered decades of discrimination. Even after membership of the church was decriminalized, they continued to be suspect in many quarters and in 1780 a Scottish aristocrat named Lord George Gordon led a mob to London to protest against the new policy of toleration. The resulting riot lasted for a week, churches and prisons were destroyed, and hundreds of people were killed. However, the English were developing a new understanding of politics and society that was based upon common consent. The execution of King Charles I in 1649 was the execution, also, of the principle of the divine right of kings and regal autocracy that he advocated.

The later seventeenth century saw a more consensual approach, one that was shown in the other constitutional crisis of the century, which occurred in 1688. James II, who came to the throne in 1685, shared the views of his father Charles I about the divine right of kings; he was also inclined

A contemporary illustration of the Catholic conspirators who plotted to blow up the English parliament. Guy Fawkes is shown third from the right.

We cannot but heartily wish, as it will easily be believed, that all the people of our dominions were members of the Catholic Church.

James II, 'Declaration of Indulgence', 1687

We forbid our subjects of the so-called Reformed religion to meet any more for the exercise of the said religion… We enjoin all ministers of the said religion… to leave our kingdom and the territories subject to us within a fortnight of the publication of our present edict.

The Revocation of the Edict of Nantes, 1685

towards Catholicism, something that was, of course, extremely unpopular. At first James promised to keep his Catholicism to himself and uphold the Church of England, which was acceptable; but as time went on he became increasingly keen to impose Catholicism on the country and overrule the Test Act. In 1687 he issued a 'Declaration of Indulgence', giving Catholics equal rights with everyone else; moreover, he favoured Catholics in filling state and military posts. A second declaration was issued the following year, which led to seven Anglican bishops – including the archbishop of Canterbury – being imprisoned in the Tower of London for not proclaiming it. The final straw was when James had a son. The people – and parliament – realized that the Catholic-friendly policies would now not end with the king's death, but would probably continue in his son, baptized a Catholic. Parliament invited the king's Dutch son-in-law, William of Orange, to take the throne. William accordingly landed with a large army in 1688, marched on London and was crowned joint ruler with his wife Mary. It became known as the Glorious Revolution, because it had been achieved without bloodshed, at least in England. (James fled to Ireland, where the people at first supported him and fought the English in his name.)

In France, meanwhile, exactly the opposite approach was taken. Here, King Louis XIV, who reigned from 1643 to 1715, enjoyed supreme power in an increasingly centralized state. The 'Sun King' is said to have commented, 'The state – that's me!' He ran the country personally, in the style of a medieval monarch, and extended the power of France through a series of aggressive wars against his neighbours. Under Louis, France was the superpower of Europe, both militarily and culturally. French became the language of scholarship and culture, and it was spoken in courts throughout the continent. The ideal of Louis XIV was 'One faith, one law, one king' (*Une foi, une loi, un roi*) and the one

faith was Catholicism. Louis promoted this and persecuted the Huguenots with increased ferocity, despite their protection under the Edict of Nantes. In 1685 Louis revoked the Edict of Nantes, thereby proscribing Protestantism. French Calvinists streamed out of France, mainly to the Netherlands and England.

The Enlightenment, then, was a time of political polarization, between trends towards what would one day become democracy and trends towards centralization. Countries that did not follow either trend fell behind – such as Poland, for example, which had lost the great power it wielded in eastern Europe in earlier centuries and was now habitually invaded or partitioned by Russia, Prussia and Sweden. However, Poland, like France, remained authoritarian in matters of religion. Since Roman Catholicism was regarded as the state religion, and most of the country's enemies or oppressors were not Catholic, to be a good patriot meant being a good Catholic. This was especially so after 1655, when the Paulite monks of the Czestochowa monastery successfully held off a far superior Swedish invasion force – a victory that was attributed to the watchful protection of the monastery's 'Black Madonna' icon which it had guarded for three centuries. After this victory, the king, John Casimir, publicly placed himself and his kingdom under the direct protection of the Virgin Mary. Membership of churches other than that of Rome was illegal.

FAITH AND REASON

CARTESIANISM

These changes coincided with major philosophical developments, principally the appearance of rationalism. The man usually blamed for this is René Descartes, who was born in France in 1596 and died in Sweden in 1650. Philosophy, in Descartes' day, was a subject for professionals, and the old medieval-style scholasticism still held sway in the universities of Europe. This was even true of the Protestant universities – for

example, Theodore Beza, the leading figure in Reformed Christianity when Descartes was a young man, was particularly keen on Thomas Aquinas. Descartes, however, was an amateur, a rich soldier of fortune with no teaching post or particular training in scholastic jargon.

Descartes sought to create a completely new way of doing philosophy, one that revolved around certainty and proof. A talented mathematician, Descartes felt that it should be possible to subject statements about the world, such as scientific or religious claims, to a burden of proof similar to that of mathematical statements. He was convinced, in particular, that the truth of a concept could be ascertained simply by analyzing it carefully; in fact, he thought that in theory this was a relatively simple exercise. In Descartes' view, human reason can never lead us astray. How, then, can it be that some people – indeed, most people – make mistakes? Descartes believed that this happens when we wilfully ignore what reason tells us. Error, in other words, is a sort of sin, a notion that betrays Descartes' religious convictions – for he was a sincere, if not very devout, Roman Catholic, and had been educated by the Jesuits.

Putting his principles into practice, Descartes sought to provide rigorous proofs of the existence and nature of the soul, the physical world and God. Where the scholastics had talked about different substances, with their essences and qualities, Descartes preferred to talk of a single physical substance – 'extension' – which is subdivided and measured mathematically. The mental realm, meanwhile, was separate from the physical, and substances here had no extension but instead had 'thought'. So, for Descartes, the world is divided into two great domains – that of unthinking extension, which simply goes mechanically through its motions, and that of unextended thought, the immaterial mind or soul.

Descartes' ideas became known as Cartesianism, and they were enormously popular – and controversial – throughout

the seventeenth century. Within Catholicism, the philosopher Antoine Arnauld was a noted advocate of Cartesianism, since he felt that its proofs of God and the soul provided a good basis for a Christian philosophy. But to some, such as the Reformed theologian Gisbert Voetius, it was all highly dubious, modern freethinking.

RATIONALISM

In the seventeenth century many people regarded Cartesian-style philosophy as something that would support Christianity. The most notable of these was the German philosopher, physicist and historian, Gottfried Leibniz. This brilliant man, whose interests covered everything from mining to Chinese history to the invention of shoes with springs in the heel for running faster, was convinced that all truth could be uncovered by the exercise of reason alone. He believed that all disagreements ultimately came down to

René Descartes, after a portrait by the Dutch painter Frans Hals (1580–1666).

It is no less impossible to conceive of a God – that is, a supremely perfect being – which lacks existence, or which lacks a certain perfection, than it is to conceive of a mountain without a valley.

René Descartes,
Meditations, 1637

315

Leibniz with the princess of Brandenburg, from a drawing by the German artist Theobald Freiherr von Oer (1807–85).

As regards the rational soul or mind… It is not only a mirror of the universe of created things, but also an image of the Deity.

G. W. Leibniz, *Principles of nature and grace, founded on reason*, 1714

logic and that, if only people could learn to see the logical structures that underlay all statements, the truth would become apparent. This would be useful to missionaries, since they could travel to the unenlightened heathen and prove the truth of Christianity with unimpeachable logic. For his own part, Leibniz devised what he felt were compelling proofs for the existence and goodness of God, the nature of the soul, the kingdom of heaven and so on.

Seventeenth-century rationalism, then, was typically concerned with supporting religion. A Catholic representative was Jacques Bossuet, the influential bishop of Meaux, who defended Roman Catholicism against the Protestants and wrote a number of books seeking to persuade them of the need to return to the true church. Indeed, some Christian thinkers thought that reason was the key to breaking down the divisions between the churches. George Callixtus, a Lutheran, and Hugo Grotius, a

Reformed theologian, devoted much energy to trying to find a way of reunion in the early seventeenth century, but they succeeded only in alienating the more intransigent members of their own churches. In 1645 Vladislav IV of Poland called the Conference of the Thorn to try to achieve reunion, but to no avail. Later, Leibniz and Bossuet conducted a long correspondence in which they tried to find common ground. But Bossuet believed that all discussions must begin with an acknowledgement of the infallibility of the Catholic Church, which Leibniz felt was unreasonable. Like all the other attempts at reunion, this one fell flat. The divisions had now existed for nearly two centuries, and were too ingrained to be reversed by intellectuals. Most ordinary believers would never have countenanced it.

SOCINIANISM AND UNITARIANISM
Rationalism carried a major risk. If you claimed that religion could be proved by

reason, and then based your religion upon reason, what happened if it turned out that your reasoning was not as good as you had thought? These problems had already been highlighted by an earlier thinker, Faustus Socinus (1539–1604), an Italian Protestant theologian. Like the later Enlightenment sages, Socinus believed that religion should be about what can rationally be proved, although he also adhered to the Protestant belief that the Bible was the prime authority in religion. But he felt that a number of traditional beliefs, such as the doctrines of the Trinity and of the divinity of Jesus, failed this test. Socinus was not very successful in his lifetime, trying, but largely failing, to spread his views in eastern Hungary and Poland, where he was associated with the Anabaptists. But many of his works were published posthumously, and he became influential in the seventeenth century. In particular, the Racovian Catechism, published at the Polish city of Racow in 1605, enshrined his most important views, and Socinianism – also known as the Polish Brethren – was a major movement in Poland until the Jesuits forced most of its adherents to flee in the 1660s.

Socinus is normally regarded as the founder of Unitarianism, the denial of the Trinity. Although Unitarianism survived – in the face of persecution – in Catholic Poland and Hungary, it did better in the English-speaking world. John Biddle, a seventeenth-century theologian, argued that Luther and Calvin had left the Reformation only half-finished: they had got rid of Romish superstition but left the pernicious doctrine of the Trinity. Some intellectuals revived the old Arian heresy, stating that the Son – incarnate in Christ – was not divine: the great mathematician and physicist Sir Isaac Newton was apparently among them, though his disciple Samuel Clarke was better known for this view. Unitarianism became popular among English non-conformists, but it was not until 1773 that the first 'Unitarian church' was opened by Theophilus Lindsey in London. The chemist Joseph Priestley, most remembered for discovering oxygen, was a notable Unitarian. The general hatred of the British public – ever-suspicious of such freethinking – forced him to flee for America in 1794, where he spread his Unitarian ideas.

DEISM
The rationalist, freethinking attitude of the Socinians and the Unitarians found its greatest expression in deism, which appeared in the English- and French-speaking worlds at the end of the seventeenth century. An important difference, though, between Unitarians and deists was that most of the members of the eastern European or English-speaking Unitarian churches adhered to a devout Protestant belief in the authority of the Bible. They rejected the doctrine of the Trinity because they felt it was unbiblical. The deists, by contrast, were an intellectual elite who rejected doctrines such as the Trinity because they believed that they failed the test of reason.

One of the most famous deists was John Toland, whose *Christianity not mysterious* was published in 1696. In it he argued that revelation had no place in religion. The Bible, similarly, has no particular authority: it is a human work, compiled over a number of centuries, not delivered from on high. People should believe only what can be rationally demonstrated. And belief in miracles, in a Trinity and in a Virgin Birth are simply superstition. Toland's ideas were taken further by Matthew Tindal, who published *Christianity as old as creation* in 1730. He insisted that religion is about living a moral life, following ethical principles which are established by reason, not by revelation, and that traditional doctrines are not very important at all.

Related to deism was Latitudinarianism, which shared deism's emphasis on the role of reason in religion and expressed doubts about some doctrines, but did not go as far. Its most important representative was John Locke (1632–1704), probably the most influential philosopher of his day. His

By natural religion, I understand the belief of the existence of a God, and the sense and practice of those duties which result from the knowledge we, by our reason, have of him and his perfections… so that the religion of nature takes in every thing that is founded on the reason and nature of things.

Matthew Tindal, *Christianity as old as creation*, 1730

anonymous *The reasonableness of Christianity* of 1695 presented his views and was very widely read. He argued that Jesus was the messiah, and that this is the essential doctrine of Christianity; less was said about Jesus' divinity or the Trinity, although Locke claimed to believe in both. Privately, he was probably sympathetic to Arianism. Very little, too, was said about revelation. In his *Essay concerning human understanding*, Locke argued that we cannot doubt that what divine revelation tells us is true, but we still have to determine whether what we are hearing *is* divine revelation. In other words, whilst he paid lip service to the role of revelation, he felt that reason must always be the final arbiter – if only because otherwise we have no means of telling true revelation from false.

English deists such as Toland and Tindal regarded themselves as reforming Christians, purging Christianity of superstitious nonsense that had accumulated over the centuries, completing the job begun by Martin Luther. The same was true in Scotland. Here, the Enlightenment was especially powerful: the country produced important philosophers such as David Hume (1711–76) and Thomas Reid (1710–96), and a growing party within the Presbyterian Church tried to apply Enlightenment ideas to Christianity. John Simpson, professor of divinity at the University of Glasgow, was put on trial for teaching deist ideas about the Trinity and Jesus, but he was treated relatively leniently. His followers were known as the 'Moderatists', and they argued that Christianity was mostly about morality.

The ideas of the British deists were extremely influential in France; but here, with a more oppressive state religion and greater persecution of minorities, the deists were far more hostile to Christianity. They presented their ideas as an *alternative* to Christianity, not a reform of it. A book called *Difficulties with religion*, published anonymously in 1710, bitterly attacked Christianity in general and the Catholic Church in particular as superstitious, contrary to reason, and arrogant. Religious claims must be proved, its author insisted, but Christianity is based upon unprovable, supposedly historical records, and therefore cannot be accepted at all. Indeed, this author characterized faith as a 'monster' which must be fought at every opportunity.

The most famous French deist was François Marie Arouet, normally known by his pen name, Voltaire (1694–1778). Voltaire was the Michael Moore of his day, venerated by many as a leading champion of reason and right-thinking, denigrated by others as a loathsome 'enemy within'. Always witty and irreverent, Voltaire specialized in writing scathing denunciations of the Catholic Church, an organization whose doctrines he mocked as all right for the ignorant lower orders but hardly standing up to objective study. Voltaire was feted by aristocrats and gathered around himself a coterie of other rationalists with similar views known, collectively, as the *philosophes*.

Yet it is important to recognize that, although today people like Voltaire are remembered as the key figures of the Age of Reason, they did not represent the religious mainstream of the seventeenth or eighteenth centuries. Deism appealed mostly to aristocrats and intellectuals. For every book that was published attacking the doctrine of the Trinity, there were innumerable replies, written by unimpeachably orthodox bishops, ministers or others whose names are today largely forgotten. And rationalism continued to be pressed into the service of orthodox Christianity – rather than used to attack it – for much of the eighteenth and nineteenth centuries.

Nevertheless, in retrospect, we can say that from a religious viewpoint the European Enlightenment represented a grand experiment: the attempt to place Christianity upon a solely rational footing. The arguments of the deists and, subsequently, the atheists, who rejected even the little that the deists retained,

The resurrection will take place to the sound of the trumpet, according to St. Paul. There will have to be several trumpets, for thunder itself can hardly be heard more than seven or eight miles around. There is a question how many trumpets will be needed: the theologians haven't yet calculated the number; but they will.

Voltaire, *The philosophical dictionary*, 1764

showed that this experiment had failed. The question of what was to replace it would be a key problem for the late eighteenth and the nineteenth centuries – indeed, it is still a question for today.

ENLIGHTENMENT IN NORTH AMERICA

The ideals of tolerance, formulated in Holland and Britain, were applied – to varying extents – in North America. One of the most successful examples was Canada, which Britain won from France in the 1760s, as we saw in Chapter 10. Faced with a strong French Catholic population, the British crown was forced – from pragmatism rather than idealism – to provide a kind of religious liberty here, with the Catholic Church allowed to retain its structures. The 1774 Quebec Act guaranteed religious liberty in Canada, provided that Catholics swore allegiance to the British crown. The bishop of Quebec even received an allowance from the government, although it was not until 1811 that the government admitted he could really be called a bishop and not simply the 'overseer of the Roman church'. The Catholics were grateful and the British were impressed, during the American War of Independence, with the Canadian Catholics' loyalty to the crown. Here, then, were the roots of the tolerance which would typify the church in Canada – born out of necessity rather than Enlightenment ideals, but curiously in line with them nonetheless.

A figure with more of an ideological commitment to religious freedom was Thomas Jefferson (1743–1826), who drafted the Declaration of Independence. While a member of the General Assembly of Virginia, Jefferson had been responsible for a bill guaranteeing 'that all men shall be free to profess, and by argument to maintain, their opinions on matters of religion, and that the same shall in no wise diminish, enlarge, or affect their civil capacities'. Ferociously attacked by those who saw it as an assault on Christianity, the bill was finally passed in 1786, making Virginia the only state in the world proclaiming complete religious liberty.

Theologically, Jefferson took a broadly deist position, rejecting the doctrines that most deists disliked – the Trinity, the virgin birth and deity of Jesus, and so on. He believed that true religion is essentially about following the moral precepts which are taught by reason alone. Indeed, while president of the United States, Jefferson somehow found the time to produce a book entitled *The life and morals of Jesus of Nazareth*. Often known as the *Jefferson Bible*, this work consisted mostly of the moral teaching of the Gospels with the miracles and eschatological material removed. It begins with Jesus' birth at Bethlehem, but not the virginity of his mother. It ends with his crucifixion, but not his resurrection. The message is clear: Jefferson regarded Jesus as a great moral

Thomas Jefferson, by the American painter Rembrandt Peale (1778–1860).

teacher, a hero and worthy exemplar, but not as a miracle-worker, not as a saviour and not as God.

Similar views were held by others among the founding fathers. John Adams, the second president of the United States, had deist leanings but was essentially a Latitudinarian: from a Calvinist background, he rejected doctrines such as original sin and divine predestination, instead holding that human beings have the potential for good and can make their own way in the world. And Benjamin Franklin – a true Enlightenment man of science, who famously flew kites in thunderstorms to see how lightning worked – rejected organized religion entirely, believing only that there was a creator God and that he was served by living a moral life.

Enlightenment in America also meant establishing education at the heart of American life. Jefferson insisted that his tombstone should record only three of his achievements: the writing of the Declaration of Independence and the Virginian law on religious tolerance, and his foundation of the University of Virginia. In fact, education had long been a concern of the religious settlers of North America. Harvard University had been established by the colony of Massachusetts in 1636, with the intention of providing a better education for ministers. Yale was founded by a Connecticut minister in 1701, moving to New Haven fifteen years later. These universities, and others like them, sought to provide a complete education, including the latest developments in philosophy and science, as did the academies and religious schools of Europe. The universities played an important role in the development of US Christianity, by producing generations of people who were deeply imbued with the ideas and aims of the Enlightenment, yet at the same time rooted in the Protestant religious outlook of the original Founding Fathers. As we shall see, Enlightenment rationalism and revivalist faith could and often did go hand-in-hand. However, the American Enlightenment, and the

I trust there is not a young man now living in the United States who will not die a Unitarian.

Thomas Jefferson, 1822

educational programme at its heart, were elements of white religion and white society only. Not only could no black American have ever had a chance of enrolling at one of the new universities, but most were illiterate – and, in the view of many slave-owners, rightfully so. As late as 1848 Virginia passed a law prescribing 39 lashes for anyone going to or teaching at a meeting where slaves learned how to read and write.

ENLIGHTENMENT IN RUSSIA

As we saw in Chapter 9, most Russians in early modern times were resolutely opposed to any influence from 'Latiny', that is, western Europe. 'Latiny' meant the Catholicism that had tried to conquer

Orthodoxy and been defeated by Alexander Nevsky in 1242. But despite the political autocracy and increasing ties of church and state in the seventeenth century, this period saw western ideas seep into Russia.

UKRAINE AND RUSSIA

Ukraine played a key role in this. The sixteenth century had seen Ukraine and Kiev – the historic centre of the Russian state and religion before the invasions of the Mongols – annexed by the united power of Poland and Lithuania. Much of Ukraine at this time was inhabited by Cossacks, semi-autonomous settlers who had fled repressive conditions in Russia, and indeed the name 'Ukraine' itself (meaning 'the borders') had emerged in the sixteenth century to reflect its liminal nature from a Russian point of view. In 1648 the Ukrainian Cossacks rebelled against Polish rule and then asked the Russian tsar, Alexis, for protection. That led to war with Poland, after which, in 1667, Ukraine was split along the River Dnieper. The west remained under Polish rule, while the east, including Kiev, was independent but subject to Moscow. From a Christian point of view, this was a major development, because it meant that the Ukrainian church was now under Russian control. As we saw in Chapter 9, Polish rule had meant that Roman Catholicism had clashed with Orthodoxy here, and in 1596 a new church, the Ukrainian Catholic Church, had been created to unite the opposing factions. The Jesuits played a key role in the attempt to Catholicize Ukraine. Now their efforts, and the wider Enlightenment which they represented, came within the Russian ambit.

The Summer Palace, St Petersburg, in an eighteenth-century painting of the Russian school. The palace was built for Peter the Great in the middle of the royal park so he could enjoy its beauty in the summer.

NIKON AND THE OLD BELIEVERS

This influx of foreign ideas was one of the factors behind the most significant incident in the seventeenth-century Russian church, the attempt by Patriarch Nikon of Moscow to reform Russian Christianity. Nikon, a pious monk from near Novgorod, was very close to the tsar, Alexis I (1629–76), and like him was a member of a movement known as the Zealots of Faith, who called for sincere devotion and the rooting out of corruption. In 1652 Alexis made Nikon patriarch and handed him immense power in the process: like Patriarch Filaret some

years earlier, Nikon called himself 'the Great Sovereign' and acted as co-ruler with the tsar. As patriarch, Nikon extended his power over not only Russia but Ukraine as well, where he dissolved the Ukrainian Catholic Church. Thus, the Ukrainians were brought back into the fold of Russian Orthodoxy.

Before becoming patriarch, Nikon had invited scholars from Constantinople and Kiev to examine the Russian liturgy and iconography. He found that the Russian church differed from the Ukrainian and Greek churches in many ways. Russian

Catherine 'the Great' and the re-Christianization of Russia

The reign of Catherine II brought public education to Russia. The few schools that functioned before her time were limited mainly to training sons of priests for following their fathers in rote performance of church services or sons of nobles for military leadership. As a reputed model of 'enlightened absolutism', Catherine inaugurated an education programme whose goal was a network of schools in cities and villages that would produce a citizenry with at least basic literacy and elementary training in Orthodox Christian piety.

Early in her reign (1762–96) Catherine asserted the need for all children to be trained in 'the fear of God as the beginning of all wisdom… the ten commandments, and our Orthodox eastern Greek religion,' in addition to 'love of their country' and reverence for 'those who by the appointment of God watch over their happiness in this world'. Sharing the deism of leading figures of the Enlightenment, Catherine did not manifest substantive, personal, Christian spirituality, but she clearly perceived the utility of Christianity for aiding the creation of a civil society ordered by enlightenment values of reason, law, and human happiness.

As Catherine reorganized the civil administration of the empire in the mid-1770s she required that local governments create schools. Her desire for general education culminated in the 'Decree for Public Schools' in 1786, which required

all provincial capitals and county seats to create two-year primary and three-year secondary schools for educating boys and girls of all social classes except serfs (who constituted about 40 per cent of the population). Pupils were to be taught 'honest and rational understanding of the Trinity and its holy law, fundamental rules of unwavering allegiance to the sovereign and true love for the fatherland'.

The first year of the primary school curriculum included, in addition to reading, writing and arithmetic, study of the shorter Orthodox catechism and sacred history. In the second year pupils studied the longer catechism. In the secondary schools they studied the New Testament alongside geometry, geography, history and classical languages.

The implementation of Catherine's programme moved slowly because of lack of resources and trained teachers, but it gradually advanced popular knowledge of the Orthodox Christian religion. By 1800 there were 315 schools empire-wide, with about 20,000 pupils. Almost all teachers were Orthodox clergymen or unordained graduates of Orthodox seminaries. Catherine required ecclesiastical educational institutions to give priority to public education by sending their best graduates into the schools instead of parishes.

Catherine's grandson Alexander I expanded on her academic programme with a substantial proliferation of the

Catherine 'the Great'.

schools, often attached to Orthodox parishes, crowned by a number of respectable universities, which continued to pursue the Orthodox goals of education. By the mid-nineteenth century Orthodox bishops reported with satisfaction a re-Christianization of urban centres where residents 'know the basic truths of the faith, the ten commandments, and the most essential prayers,' while they lamented that the picture in rural areas was much bleaker.

PAUL STEEVES

icons looked different from the Byzantine originals and had become influenced by Polish art. The *Alleluia* was being sung twice instead of three times, and Russian priests made the sign of the cross with two fingers raised instead of three. When he became patriarch, Nikon therefore ordered that all these things, and many more, were to be changed in accordance with the Greek rites. In this way he hoped to restore the Russian church to what it had once been.

Nikon's reforms were, in effect, the Russian equivalent of the Reformation, an attempt to get back to what was regarded as a more pristine version of Christianity and roll back what seemed to be undesirable developments. Of course, these reforms were far less extensive and fundamental than those enacted by Luther and his colleagues a century and a half earlier in the west – but Nikon still met enormous opposition. To an outsider it may seem strange that tempers became raised over matters such as how many fingers to use when blessing someone: however, what mattered was not the rites themselves, but the authority that lay behind them. By trying to bring the Russian church into line with the Greek one, Nikon was, in the view of his opponents, saying that the Greek church was superior. But the Russian religious mentality had, for the past two hundred years, been based on the assumption that Constantinople had lost its status as head church and Moscow had inherited it. Thus, Avvakum Petrovich, archpriest of the Kazan cathedral in Moscow, led the opposition to Nikon, arguing that the proposed reforms were actually a corruption of the true church of God.

Nikon tried to force his reforms on the church. Soldiers were sent from house to house to root out old icons and service books. Churches were razed to the ground, to be replaced by new ones in a more authentically Byzantine style. Nikon became a figurehead of hate for the *Starovery* or 'Old Believers', those who agreed with Avvakum that Nikon's innovations were unpatriotic and heretical. Yet when Nikon fell from grace in 1658, it apparently had nothing to do with any of this: for reasons that are still not really known, he fell out with Alexis I and was deposed. No successor was found, and the church limped on without a head until 1666, when a council was called in which Nikon was found guilty of various malpractices and confined to a monastery. Yet this council also endorsed his reforms, and his successor, Joasaph II, continued to enforce them. Thousands of people died, either executed for their intransigence (as Avvakum was in 1682) or committing suicide rather than submit to the reforms. Within four decades of Nikon's original decrees, some 20,000 people had been killed. Panic spread throughout Russia. The religious upheaval coincided with plague and famine, and many became convinced that the date 1666 marked the coming of the antichrist. The harvest was neglected as people gathered in cemeteries to await the end of the world, while some even torched buildings – from the inside – hoping to be purified in the flames.

The schism was never settled. The Old Believers remained separate from the main body of the Russian church, and themselves splintered into more factions: the *Popovtsy* ('with priests'), who imitated the established church with a priestly hierarchy, and the more radical *Bezpopovtsy* ('without priests'), who rejected the priesthood and all sacraments other than baptism. They were all subject to constant persecution throughout the eighteenth and nineteenth centuries, and many fled west to Lithuania or east to Siberia. In later years, fleeing further persecution, many of these Old Believers would cross the borders into China or even Japan.

PETER 'THE GREAT'
Barely had the Russian church recovered from all this before it was forcibly yanked further into the modern era by yet another domineering autocrat, Tsar Peter I, 'the Great' (1672–1725). This powerful man – a latter-day Charlemagne – became tsar in 1689 and did his best to drag Russia into the modern age, importing western customs and beliefs and building a magnificent new

capital at St Petersburg on the Baltic Sea – built of stone, not the traditional wood.

Western fashions were imposed on the Russians, and even beards – an enduring symbol of the Orthodox Church – were banned. Many old men obediently cut off their beards but kept them in boxes, convinced they could not be saved without them. At the same time, Peter was determined to end the hegemony of the church over the state: he remembered the power that Patriarch Nikon had wielded over his own father, Tsar Alexis. In 1721 he replaced the patriarchate with a 'holy synod', consisting of ten churchmen who between them would rule the church. In this way, the tsar completely eliminated the possibility of a patriarch rivalling his own power. The synod was supervised by a non-clerical government official, appointed directly by the tsar. This layman could appoint bishops as he saw fit. Thus, the hegemony of church over state, which had developed a century earlier, was reversed: now the church was essentially a state department. The church worked for the government – for example, if someone confessed treasonous activity to a priest, the priest was obliged to pass the information on. But the politicization of the church led to more splits. The upper levels of the hierarchy – the bishops and monks, known as the 'black' clergy – became involved in politics and often enjoyed lavish state support. But the lower levels – the parish priests, known as the 'white' clergy – were neglected. They often fell into poverty and had to support themselves through manual labour or charging for priestly services.

Meanwhile, western influence spread throughout the Russian church and church academies appeared along the model of those in Reformation-era western Europe. The curriculum of these schools was deeply influenced by the west, so that by the nineteenth century they were generally teaching both Catholic and Protestant theology (in order to show why both were wrong!) and they were doing so in Latin. The development of education was greatly helped later in the eighteenth century by

What is the true end of Monarchy? Not to deprive people of their natural liberty; but to correct their actions, in order to attain the supreme Good.

Catherine the Great, Proposals for a new law code, 1767

another powerful ruler, Catherine II, 'the Great' (1729–96). Catherine was actually a Prussian princess who married the heir to the Russian throne (changing her name from Sophie to Catherine as she converted to Orthodoxy). Her husband, Peter III, was weak and psychologically ill, and shortly after he became tsar in 1762 she led a coup to depose him. She ruled Russia as empress until her death in 1796, during which time she did her best to instil into the country the values of the German Enlightenment in which she had been raised.

THE ROOTS OF REVIVAL

The seventeenth and eighteenth centuries – the Age of Reason – were also a time of renewal, as new spiritual movements spread through the Protestant churches and beyond. That may seem paradoxical, as today we have become accustomed to thinking of *faith* and *reason* as opposites – even contradictories. But people did not necessarily think like that during this period. Take, for example, Benjamin Whichcote, who became a fellow of Emmanuel College, Cambridge in 1633. Whichcote was a staunch Anglican, and like many, he believed in Anglicanism as a middle way between what he saw as the degeneracy of Catholicism and the excesses of Protestantism. But he also thought that Anglicanism was based wholly upon reason and rejected the notion that faith can or should go beyond reason. Whichcote defined religion as cultivating 'a good mind and a good life', and stated, 'I oppose not *rational* to *spiritual* – for spiritual is most rational.'

Whichcote was not alone. He had a number of followers, known as the Cambridge Platonists; and the insistence that spirituality can come about through the use of reason, not in opposition to it, was a common one in this period. So whilst the seventeenth and eighteenth centuries were a time when different understandings of Christianity jostled for space, we should not overstress the conflict between them, since they sometimes had more in common with each other than one might think. In particular, we should not make a clear distinction between 'dry rationalists' such as Leibniz and Tindal and more 'evangelical' figures, concerned with piety, such as those we are about to look at. This is a distinction that has emerged since that time. In fact, many people were both rationalist and evangelical.

CATHOLIC SPIRITUALITY

It is worth noting that the revivalist or evangelical movements were largely confined to the Protestant churches. There were a number of reasons for this, but one may be that the Catholic Church had, to a greater extent, avoided the drifting away from spirituality that had occurred in the Protestant churches. As we saw in Chapter 9, the age of confessionalism had seen the Protestant churches devote more and more of their time to theological tub-thumping and increasingly esoteric scholastic speculation, with a corresponding drop of interest in the kind of spirituality that had marked the first generations of Reformers. The Catholic Church, by contrast, maintained the balance more successfully. In addition to organizations such as the Jesuits, which combined spirituality with education, there was a number of spiritual movements in the seventeenth century. One was the devotion to the Sacred Heart of Jesus, associated with a French nun named Margaret Mary Alacoque in the 1670s and 80s. Another was Quietism, a movement which was highly controversial in France in the closing years of the seventeenth century. Its most prominent representative was Jeanne Marie Guyon, usually known simply as 'Mme Guyon', a mystic who insisted that closeness to God could be attained only through total passivity and tranquillity of the soul, focusing on its own interior in silence. Indifference to all things apart from God, even the salvation of one's own soul, was essential. This teaching was, at least in part, a reaction against the rationalism of the age; and it split the French church. François de Salignac de la Mothe-Fénelon, a thoughtful

Mme Guyon, in an anonymous copper engraving from 1692.

nobleman who was also a prominent theologian and archbishop of Cambrai, defended Quietism; Jacques Bossuet, who was alarmed at the notion of disinterested love, attacked it. In the end, Rome found against Quietism; Mme Guyon was imprisoned in the Bastille for five years and Fénelon obediently banned his own books.

PIETISM

A more important movement in Europe – mainly within the Lutheran churches – was Pietism. Its godfather was a German Lutheran pastor named Johann Arndt (1555–1621), who in the first years of the seventeenth century wrote two books, entitled *True Christianity* and *The garden of paradise*. Arndt insisted that Christianity is not really about the increasingly pernickety doctrinal disputes that were raging at this time between Lutheran, Reformed and Catholic. It is about having a personal relationship with Christ that changes the way you live your life. Union with Christ is the presupposition for the Christian life rather than its goal, and Arndt recommended that the Christian should spend some time every day meditating upon the person of Christ. Here, then, we have an emphasis away from doctrine and towards lifestyle, away from a corporate concern for the church as a whole and towards the individual. Christianity is a personal way of life.

If you are in an abyss of dryness and weakness, go and bury yourself in the loving Heart of Jesus. If you are in an abyss of poverty and stripped of all things, go to the Heart of Jesus. He will enrich you. If you find yourself so weak that you fall at every step, go and bury yourself in the strength of his Sacred Heart. He will deliver you.

Margaret Mary Alacoque, *The Sacred Heart of Jesus, an abyss of wisdom and love*

Silence promotes the presence of God, prevents many harsh and proud works, and suppresses many dangers in the way of ridiculing or harshly judging our neighbour. Silence humbles the mind, and gradually weans it from the world; it makes a kind of solitude in the heart.

François de Salignac de la Mothe-Fénelon

That the holy Gospel is subjected, in our time, to a great and shameful abuse is fully proved by the impenitent life of the ungodly who praise Christ and his word with their mouths and yet lead an unchristian life that is like that of persons who dwell in heathendom, not in the Christian world. Such ungodly conduct gave me cause to write this book to show simple readers wherein true Christianity consists, namely, in the exhibition of a true, living faith, active in genuine godliness and the fruits of righteousness.

Johann Arndt, *True Christianity*, 1610

Arndt's ideas were controversial: many Lutherans argued that doctrine really did matter as much as personal piety, and that the life of the church was as important as the life of the individual. Where, in Arndt's scheme, was there a role for the sacraments? But others were inspired by his ideas. Among them was the Spener family in Alsace. Philipp Spener (1635–1705), brought up on Arndt's principles, became one of the foremost Lutheran pastors in Germany: in Frankfurt, he set up 'conventicles', small groups within the church which met for prayer, worship and discussion. These were enormously successful and in 1675 Spener published *Pious wishes*, setting out his ideas. Spener argued that Luther had left the Reformation only half completed. He had reformed the doctrine of the church, but not its lifestyle. Spener unleashed a ferocious attack upon the Lutheran orthodoxy of his day, accusing people of obsessing over points of doctrine when they should be putting Christ at the centre of their existence and living good

Philipp Spener.

lives. In particular, he argued that Lutherans' insistence upon the doctrine of salvation by faith alone led to laziness. The argument was much like that used by Pelagius against Augustine in an earlier age, although Spener did not deny that faith alone saves; rather, he insisted that

living a good life must be central to Christianity. Similarly, while Spener did accept that correctness of doctrine was important, he insisted that it was not an end in itself but a step towards cultivating a personal relationship with Christ.

'Pietism' took its name from the title of Spener's book, and it remained controversial, as the more traditional theologians insisted it undermined correct doctrine. The infighting became more bitter. In 1729, a notorious Pietist named Johann Konrad Dippel published *The true evangelical demonstration*, in which he argued that organized religion was completely opposed to true faith and called for the church structures and authorities to be dismantled so that people could follow the law of love, as taught by Christ, in peace.

At the same time, however, Pietism became a major force within not only Lutheran religion but German culture and society as well. In particular, many Pietists felt that their ideal of living in the light of Christ meant trying to improve education, for education was seen as the training not only of the mind but of the character. The greatest experiment in Pietist education occurred at Halle, near Leipzig, where a new university was founded in 1694. The professor of oriental studies was a friend of Spener's called August Francke (1663–1727), who shared his emphasis on the inner life of the individual: Francke believed that taking on the Christian life meant taking on a whole new existential attitude, one which he described as 'inner struggle'.

Like Spener, Francke dreamed of completing the Reformation. In his case, he believed this could be done only when society, like the church, had been reformed, and he recognized the key role that education could play in this. Francke therefore set about reforming the education system of the whole of Halle, not simply the university. He founded new schools, including training colleges for teachers, and sought to integrate the whole system, so that, for example, students at the university would help out at the schools for children.

At the same time, Francke was an important figure in the setting up of missionary expeditions overseas. Under the guidance of Francke and others like him, Halle became a major centre of Enlightenment thought, and Francke was joined by great thinkers such as the legal theorist Christian Thomasius (1655–1728), also a Pietist and great believer in the moral value of education, who campaigned successfully for the abolition of torture and witch trials in Germany. Here too was Christian Wolff (1679–1754), a thorough-going rationalist philosopher firmly in the mould of his mentor Leibniz. Thus, Pietism and rationalism rubbed shoulders and benefited from each other.

THE MORAVIANS

Probably the most famous Pietist group was the Moravians. This group traced its roots back to Jan Hus (d. 1415), but had dwindled greatly since his day: its last bishop died in 1671. But one man, a former Catholic carpenter named Christian David, hoped to re-establish them. Fortunately, he had powerful friends, particularly Nikolaus Ludwig, count and lord of Zinzendorf and Pottendorf (1700–60). Zinzendorf's grandmother was a friend of Francke's, and Spener was his godfather; he had even been educated at Halle in a school founded by Francke. In 1722 Zinzendorf allowed David to set up a new community on his estate called Herrnhut ('The Lord's protection').

Although David founded the community, Zinzendorf managed it full-time and became its bishop in 1737. He possessed a powerful intellect and was a strikingly original theologian, but maintained the traditional Pietist emphasis on living a Christ-like life and playing down the importance of doctrine. He felt that theology, and the discussion of theological problems, was potentially divisive and opposed to the rule of love. As he put it, 'The people should only sing, pray and talk with one another. What goes beyond the discussion of Christian experience is offensive.'

The community was based upon a shared experience of the power of God, and the whole of everyday life was to be subjugated to the will of God: they consciously tried to mimic how they thought the very first Christians had lived. Following the model of Acts 1:26, they would make decisions by casting lots; the community was governed by twelve elders, elected by all male members. People flocked to Herrnhut from all Protestant denominations, and even Catholics came too. All were welcomed, provided they followed Herrnhut's rule that, if you lived there, you worked. They believed that honest toil was intrinsically holy, for it was done for the good of the community rather than for the individual: as Zinzendorf himself commented, 'We do not work to live, we live to work.' Certainly, the community lived a rigorous lifestyle by most standards. Most people worked sixteen hours a day, slept for five, and ate and met for three – for there were three praise meetings a day, at 5 a.m. (4 a.m. in the summer), at lunchtime and at 9 p.m. Sunday was almost entirely given over to these, and they could be extraordinarily long: it was not unheard of for the congregation to meet at 6 a.m. and not finish until 3 p.m. There were no entertainers of any kind in Herrnhut, and all dancing was strictly forbidden. Drunkenness, theft, swearing, illicit sex – all were punished with immediate expulsion.

Yet the community's numbers swelled, and by the 1730s it was sending people back out again. They travelled Europe in small groups, looking for those who shared their understanding of Christianity. In 1731 Zinzendorf met a converted slave from the West Indies who spoke of the need for missionaries: within a year the first Moravian missionaries headed west to the Danish colony of St Thomas. Indeed, the community of Herrnhut took mission as one of its most important activities. Missionaries were sent everywhere, from Greenland to South Africa. They were especially successful in North America, where they preached to the native peoples. One native convert later described to the Moravians how he first heard the Christian message:

[Henry, the missionary] came into my tent, sat down beside me, and spoke nearly as follows: 'I come to you in the name of the Lord of Heaven and Earth. He sends to let you know that He will make you happy and deliver you from the misery in which you lie at the present. To this end He became a man, gave His life a ransom for man, and shed His Blood for him.' When he had finished his discourse he lay down upon the board, fatigued by the journey, and fell down into a sound sleep. 'What kind of man is this?' thought I. 'There he lies and sleeps. I might kill him and throw him out into the wood, and who would regard it? But this gives him no concern.' I could not forget his words. They constantly recurred to my mind. Even when I was asleep, I dreamed of the blood which Christ shed for us. I found this to be something different from what I had ever heard, and I interpreted Christian Henry's words to the other Indians. Thus, through the grace of God, an awakening took place before us. I say, therefore, brethren, preach Christ our Saviour, his sufferings and death, if you wish your words to gain entrance among the heathen.

THE GREAT AWAKENING

Pietism and related movements were a major influence on the most significant event in eighteenth-century Protestantism, a series of movements mostly in the English-speaking world known as the Great Awakening.

The appearance of the Moravians and others in North America coincided with the rise of movements there too, which sought to return the church to a purer, earlier kind of Christianity, the personal faith that – it was believed – had characterized the early church. It seems that by the start of the eighteenth century this call was one which the North American churches direly needed. The zeal, even extremism, of the early Protestant settlers in North America had largely died away over the preceding hundred years.

This new situation, in the second and third generations after the settlers of the early

All the doings of unconverted men not proceeding from the principles of faith, love, and a new nature, nor being directed to the divine glory as their highest end, but flowing from, and tending to, self as their principle and end, are, doubtless, damnably wicked in their manner of performance, and deserve the wrath and curse of a sin-avenging God.

Gilbert Tennent, *The danger of an unconverted ministry*, 1740

seventeenth century, was typified by the famous – or notorious – 'Half-Way Covenant' of 1662. The settlers of Massachusetts Bay had had strict criteria of entry: only the 'Visible Saints', who had publicly affirmed their faith and were not blackballed, could participate fully in the life of the church. Only they, and their children, could be baptized, although less committed people could attend services. Under the Half-Way Covenant, however, which was agreed by a number of congregations throughout the area, these entry criteria were relaxed. Children of the less committed members of the congregation could now be baptized, and full membership was available to anyone 'not scandalous in life'. Those who adopted this covenant hoped to make the church more important within their society, as they felt that the strictness of past generations risked turning it into a minority-interest club. Others opposed the innovation, regarding it as an unacceptable compromise with slackness.

The rest of the seventeenth century and the first part of the eighteenth saw increasing dissatisfaction from ministers and pastors about the state of the North American churches. The Presbyterians held a synod in Boston in 1679 at which they agreed the need for reformation, but little came of it. An earthquake in 1727 was interpreted as a sign of divine displeasure and sparked a brief resurgence in church attendance, but not a lasting one. Of course, it is hard to assess objectively what the situation was really like. Pastors and ministers in every age bewail their flock's lack of commitment and no doubt, compared to the zeal of early settlers, most congregations anywhere would appear uninspired. Still, it is undeniable that most people were no longer members of churches at all, despite the efforts of the Half-Way Covenanters, and many felt there was a more urgent than usual need for renewal.

That need was answered in the 1730s and 40s in a remarkable movement known as 'the Great Awakening'. Unlike Pietism, the Great Awakening appeared as an almost spontaneous phenomenon across a wide area, in different churches and even different countries. As this suggests, the Great Awakening was not really a single event, but a series of connected phenomena; and the relations between them were complex.

A key figure was Theodore Frelinghuysen, a Dutch Reformed minister who arrived in New Jersey in 1720. A remarkably energetic and visionary man, Frelinghuysen took control of the American Dutch Church and tried to reinvigorate it with the ideals of Pietism which, although a member of the Reformed Church, he had imbibed in Europe. By his preaching, travelling, writing, and teaching (he established what would become Rutgers University), Frelinghuysen began a process of renewal in America similar to that of the Pietists. A personal faith with Christ was the key, with a changed life, one which did not seek to conform to secular society. The message struck a chord, and people began to flock back to the churches.

Frelinghuysen inspired many beyond the confines of his own denomination. One disciple was Gilbert Tennent, a Presbyterian minister and inspiring preacher, who travelled the eastern colonies spreading the ideals of renewal as he went. He became notorious for his bitter attacks upon ministers who he felt did not live up to these ideals: his sermon on *The danger of an unconverted ministry* certainly ruffled many feathers, with its comparison of such ministers to the Pharisees who attacked Jesus. Tennent shared the old Pietist emphasis on conversion, and the distinction between the converted and unconverted; the bad ministers, in his eyes, fell into the latter category.

The greatest American figure in all this, however, was Jonathan Edwards (1703–58), one of those remarkable eighteenth-century people who combined the best of Enlightenment intellectualism with the most earnest Christian zeal. Educated at Yale, where he also taught, Edwards became a Presbyterian minister in New York and Northampton, Massachusetts. He was a brilliant man, one of the most original theologians to be born in North America, as well as a concerned and highly orthodox Calvinist. Edwards combined an emphasis on the elective grace of God with a sensitive spirituality, attuned to the beauty of nature; in his youth he was a good philosopher and amateur scientist. In 1734, while working in Northampton, Edwards found himself presiding over a remarkable revival. He described it in his *Faithful narrative of the surprising work of God*:

There was scarcely a single person in the town, old or young, left unconcerned about the great things of the eternal world. Those who were wont to be the vainest, and loosest; and those who had been most disposed to think, and speak slightly of vital and experimental religion, were now generally subject to great awakenings. And the work of conversion was carried on in a most astonishing manner, and increased more and more; souls did, as it were, come by flocks to Jesus Christ. From day to day, for many months together, might be seen evident instances of sinners brought out of darkness into marvellous light, and delivered

On January 12 1723, I made a solemn dedication of myself to God, and wrote it down; giving up myself, and all that I had to God; to be for the future, in no respect, my own; to act as one that had no right to be himself, in any respect. And solemnly vowed to take God for my whole portion and felicity; looking on nothing else, as any part of my happiness.

Jonathan Edwards,
Personal narrative,
c. 1740

Jonathan Edwards.

George Whitefield
preaching in the
open air, in a
painting by the
British artist John
Collet (c. 1725–80).

*out of a horrible pit, and from the miry clay,
and set upon a rock with a new song of
praise to God in their mouths.*

This first revival lasted no more than a
couple of years, but a more lasting one
began in 1740 when an Englishman, George
Whitefield, came to town. If Edwards was
the mind of the American revivals,
Whitefield (1714–70) was their heart. Born
in Gloucester and educated at Oxford, he
was ordained as a deacon in the Church of
England in 1736 and first visited North
America in 1738. In an age of extraordinary
preachers, he stood head and shoulders
over most. He could keep thousands
enthralled with his sermons, which were
delivered in the open air; indeed, one of his
early sermons in Gloucester was said to have
driven fifteen listeners insane with its
intensity. David Garrick, the famous London
Shakespearean actor, once remarked, 'I
would give a hundred guineas if I could say
"Oh" like Mr Whitefield.'

Whitefield went on an extraordinary
tour of North America in 1740. Vast crowds
followed him everywhere he went, and his
final sermon, in Boston, was preached to a
congregation of 20,000. Whitefield, like
Edwards, could preach fire and brimstone
when he wanted to, and he too was a strict
Calvinist, especially on the subject of
predestination. He also went determinedly
against the Enlightenment grain, insisting
that conversion was an emotional rather
than a rational phenomenon: conversion
was essential to the Christian life, but it was
an experience which transcended
denominational boundaries. In delivering
this message, Whitefield was aided by other
European missionaries and itinerant
preachers. Among the most prominent were
Moravians, sent out from Herrnhut to
spread the gospel. Even if they had
achieved nothing else, the Moravian
missionaries would have left their mark on
history when one of them, during a voyage
to North America, spoke to and left a
lasting impression upon a young John
Wesley, also going to America to preach.

The emotional religion of men like

Whitefield could be taken too far. The most
notorious extremist was one James
Davenport, who denounced the majority of
ministers in terms even more scathing than
those of Gilbert Tennent, and who
organized enormous bonfires of tracts and
books with which he disagreed. Worse,
Davenport claimed to be able to tell who
was elect and who was reprobate: he would
address the former as 'brethren' and the
latter as 'neighbours'. His antics, and those
of others like him, aroused considerable
opposition to the whole revival movement.
Charles Chauncy, a minister in Boston,
preached a famous sermon entitled
Enthusiasm described and cautioned against,
in which he attacked the movement as
inimical to order and to the churches.
Despite these attacks, though, the more
moderate revivalists were keen on founding
new seminaries and institutes of learning.
The Presbyterians founded one known as
'the Log College', which, renamed the
College of New Jersey, boasted Jonathan
Edwards as president. Today it is called
Princeton University.

As a result, American Christianity
splintered to a certain extent. The two
camps became known as New Lights (the
revivalists) and Old Lights (the
traditionalists). Moreover, the divisions were
social as well as religious. The New Lights
tended to be agricultural workers, of a
relatively low class, while the Old Lights
tended to be from the merchant classes.
This helps to explain why the Great
Awakening was a mostly New England
phenomenon, although it did occur in the
South too, laying the groundwork for the
more widespread revivals that were to take
place in that region some decades later.
Both George Whitefield and John Wesley
spent time in Georgia, and in the late
1740s, Presbyterian preachers from New
England were active in Virginia. Many
Baptists also moved into the South.
However, the social make-up of the South
was not really conducive to the New Lights:
a more aristocratic society meant that more
people had an interest in traditional
Anglicanism. By the time of the American

Revolution, around one in ten churchgoers in the South was a Baptist – a significant number, but far from a majority.

THE CARIBBEAN

To trace the history of Protestantism in the Caribbean we must go back to the 1630s, when the British and Dutch had established their first colonies there. The British colonies were organized around parishes, which became the basic unit of society and government. Each one was governed by a local council called a vestry, which was required by law to maintain a church and accommodation for a priest; thus civil and ecclesiastical duties were discharged by the same body. Yet despite the 'official' nature of the Church of England that this system encouraged, there was a strong tradition of Dissent too. The authorities were keen to encourage settlers to move to the West Indies, so they were not too fussy about their religious orientation. There were many Irish settlers, and a correspondingly strong Roman Catholic presence. But religion did not play a major part in the lives of the white population of the West Indies, and there were reports of absent clergy, half-empty churches and loose living.

Like the southern part of the North American continent, the Caribbean islands were a plantation society with large numbers of slaves, and there was great reluctance on the part of most slave-owners to allow them to be evangelized. Some attempts were made to encourage them to do so. Christopher Codrington, governor of the Leeward Islands at the start of the eighteenth century, pleaded in vain with the bishop of London (who had jurisdiction over the area) to send suitable missionaries to the slaves. When he died, Codrington left his estates to the Society for the Propagation of the Gospel (SPG) so they could build a college there to train missionaries to the slaves. The mission enjoyed some success: by 1740 it was reported that of the 207 slaves on Codrington's former estates, 67 were baptized. But the experiment was frowned upon by landowners and clergy alike throughout the rest of the Caribbean.

A different situation prevailed in the Dutch colony of Curaçao, which had previously been held by the Spanish. As we saw in Chapter 10, most of the Catholic missions – inasmuch as there had been any – had been concerned with the native Amerindians rather than with the black slaves imported from Africa. Here, however, the slaves had mostly been baptized as Catholics. Dutch hegemony therefore led to the unusual situation of white Protestants owning black Catholic slaves. These slaves retained many features of African religions in their form of Catholicism. For example, after a funeral people would gather for a sort of party held nine days after the person's death, to celebrate their 'rebirth' from the earth, corresponding to the nine months they had once spent in the womb before their first birth. At this feast, the rosary was prayed and stories were told about Nanzi, a West African mythical spider. Nanzi was a weak creature who nevertheless triumphed over the powerful Shon Arey. The subtext was clear – a resurgence of the social protest element of slave religion.

It was not until the mid-eighteenth century that real attempts were made to evangelize the slaves in the Protestant colonies, with the appearance of the evangelical missionaries. Among the most important were the Methodists, whose missionaries arrived in Antigua in 1754 and began to preach systematically to the slaves throughout the whole region. They were, as a rule, unpopular with the landowners: in 1823 a gang destroyed the Methodist chapel in Bridgetown, but no one was punished. At the same time, missionaries from North America began to appear. The most striking of these was the Baptist George Liele, a former black slave from Virginia, who came as a labourer to Jamaica. Here he held services at his home, preaching to those around him; his small mission expanded, and by the 1790s he had appointed deacons from among the slaves to assist him. Some of Liele's converts were bought by other slave-

Our possessions of the West Indies, like that of India... gave us the strength, the support, but especially the capital, the wealth, which enabled us to come through the great struggle of the Napoleonic Wars, and enabled us not only to acquire this worldwide appendage of possessions we have, but also to lay the foundation of that commercial and financial leadership which, when the world was young, when everything outside Europe was underdeveloped, enabled us to make our great position in the world.

Winston Churchill, 1956

owners, who allowed them to continue to worship; the Baptist church grew rapidly in strength throughout the British possessions. In 1814, the Baptist Missionary Society in London sent its first missionary, John Rowe, to the islands to help out.

At the same time, there were attempts on the part of the Dutch Reformed Church to evangelize the Catholic slaves of Curaçao, but these were also half-hearted. The Dutch Protestants had, as a rule, a low opinion of Catholics, who were regarded as superstitious; so they liked their black slaves to remain Catholics as this reinforced their status as slaves.

As we shall see in the next chapter, slavery in the British West Indies was outlawed with effect from 1834, to be replaced by a six-year, unpaid apprenticeship system. On the day they became free, crowds of slaves packed the churches of the West Indies. Church attendance did not remain so high in the years that followed, but Christianity was clearly deeply inculcated in many former

slaves. The Dissenting churches reported better attendance in the 1840s, and more missionaries appeared from the USA bringing the methods of the second Great Revival, including 'camp meetings'. Such missionaries were often mistrusted by the Anglican authorities, who feared that 'African' styles of worship might taint the churches with paganism.

THE BRITISH REVIVALS

Although primarily a North American phenomenon, the Great Awakening came to Britain too – indeed, we have already seen the role played by British preachers such as George Whitefield on the other side of the Atlantic. Whitefield also toured Britain, stirring up congregations with his extraordinary oratory; and so did his friend John Wesley, probably the most prominent figure in eighteenth-century English religion. Wesley had drawn inspiration from William Law, who had published *A serious call to a devout and holy life* in 1728. Like the German

An early nineteenth-century print of slaves working on a cotton plantation in the West Indies.

Pietists, Law was convinced that Christianity should be about living a new life in response to Christ, although he also felt that the benefits of such a lifestyle should be demonstrable through reason. His *Serious call* was therefore an attempt to convince readers that living a godly and moral lifestyle would make them happier. Law was one of those Enlightenment divines who believed that spirituality and reason went hand in hand: he also wrote a book entitled *The case of reason*, in which he argued that all the truths of religion should be demonstrable by reason, and revelation is simply an alternative source of these truths.

The Great Awakening, though, was a social movement rather than an intellectual one. Law may have been a harbinger of its ideals, but he was not a moving force behind their implementation. Important stirrings came from Wales, where an Anglican clergyman named Griffith Jones, rector of Llanddowror, made enormous efforts to preach a personal kind of religion, and also to educate the people of Wales. He set up informal classes throughout the country, held mainly during the winter. It has been estimated that half the population of Wales learned to read as a result of these efforts. Another Anglican priest, Daniel Rowland, had a conversion experience after attending one of Griffith Jones's sermons: during the sermon Jones had stopped speaking, looked at Rowland, and prayed specifically for him. Rowland preached throughout Wales, travelling from parish to parish – unconventional behaviour for an Anglican curate, and in 1763 he was expelled from his job. Undaunted, Rowland set up a new chapel, to which his congregation migrated. Rowland must have been an awesomely charismatic man, able to inspire both love and hatred: he was attacked by mobs, and people even tried to shoot him; yet his chapel sometimes had over 10,000 people queuing up outside to take the Eucharist because they could not all fit in at once.

Daniel Rowland could feasibly be called the Welsh John Wesley, and indeed he and Wesley alike represented a growing movement throughout Britain. In Cornwall, it was led by Samuel Walker of Truro, while in the north of England its members looked to Henry Venn of Huddersfield or William Grimshaw in Haworth. Scotland, in particular, was transformed by the movement. In direct reaction to the 'Moderatism' – essentially deism – that we saw earlier, some Presbyterians preached what they regarded as a more original and authentic Christianity, revolving around the individual's personal relation to Christ. One group, led by a pastor named Ebenezer Erskine, set up an Associate Synod in the 1730s, which turned into the Secession Church, a dissenting group which insisted that the people have the right to choose their own pastors. Within the Presbyterian Church itself, revival was ushered in by a number of preachers, none more effective – or terrifying – than Aeneas Sage, a giant of a man who became pastor in Lochcarron in the 1720s. Half a century later, Lachlan Mackenzie, writing the history of this remote Highlands parish, painted a compelling picture of the muscular methods used by this remarkable pastor, 'who did not know what the fear of man was':

He was a true soldier in every sense of the word… There was a wicked fellow in Tosgag, who kept a mistress in the same house with his lawful married wife. When Mr Sage went to see him, Malcolm Roy drew his dirk; Mr Sage drew his sword; and the consequence was, that Malcolm Roy turned his mistress off… [Sage] struck terror into vice; and by enforcing the discipline of the church, and composing differences among the people, he reduced them to a state of civilization… He laboured for 47 years among them, and his labours were eminently countenanced by his Lord and Master. Sinners were brought under a concern for their salvation and their language was that of the jailor, 'What shall we do to be saved?'… He preached the doctrines of the new birth, the corruption of human nature, and the necessity of the influences of the Divine Spirit, to break the power of sin in the soul.

Christian faith is then, not only an assent to the whole gospel of Christ, but also a full reliance on the blood of Christ; a trust in the merits of his life, death, and resurrection; a recumbency upon him as our atonement and our life, as given for us, and living in us; and, in consequence hereof, a closing with him, and cleaving to him, as our 'wisdom, righteousness, sanctification, and redemption', or, in one word, our salvation.

John Wesley, Sermon 1

John Wesley and the Methodists

John Wesley (1703–91) was the evangelist and organizer from whom most of the Methodist churches throughout the British Isles and North America later emerged. His brother Charles was a poetic genius whose hymns not only enriched the worship of eighteenth-century Methodism, but also those of many other Christian traditions since then. They remain as classic examples of evangelical spirituality, and as potent reminders of how important hymn-singing was to the early Methodist movement and the wider evangelical revival.

The Wesley brothers were the sons of Samuel Wesley, Rector of Epworth in Lincolnshire and Susanna, whose vigorous educational regimen and maternal control left a lasting impression on both of them. In 1729 they helped to form the so-called 'Holy Club' in Oxford where their severe disciplines earned them the derisory name, 'Methodists', and in 1735 they set sail as missionaries to the native Americans in Georgia. The mission ended in acrimony and failure, but the trip to North America introduced the brothers to some Moravians. It was largely under their influence that John Wesley experienced his well-known heart-warming experience at Aldersgate Street in London in 1738. A year later John Wesley, with George Whitefield's encouragement, set out as a field-preaching evangelist to the English poor.

The Methodism that Wesley and his followers preached and practised was characterized by an evangelical Arminian theology, which emphasized that Christ died for all humankind, not just the elect. Wesley viewed his mission as 'spreading scriptural holiness across the land', first in the human heart and then in the wider society. He believed it was possible to attain 'perfect love' before death, a belief that was repudiated by almost all other eighteenth-century religious traditions, but which accounts for the passionate desire for entire sanctification, which was one of the distinctive hallmarks of early Methodist spirituality.

Wesley's message proved appealing to the English lower classes. Methodism made its fastest gains in those areas least amenable to the paternalistic influence of squires and parsons including freehold parishes, proto-industrial villages, mining communities, market towns and seaports. Methodism recruited more women – especially single or widowed women – than men, a pattern that repeated itself wherever Methodism took root in the British Isles, North America and beyond. Although Methodism originated as a religious society within the Church of England, over time John Wesley's pragmatic approach to ecclesiastical governance and discipline led to growing tensions and eventual separation from the Anglican Church. Wesley remained within the Church of England throughout his life, but it came as no surprise when Methodism effectively declared sacramental independence from the established church through the Plan of Pacification in 1795. Soon after, Methodism suffered one of its many splits which characterized and sometimes disfigured the movement in the nineteenth century.

Although Methodism arose as a predominantly English movement with roots in High Church spirituality and continental Pietism, it was also part of an international 'great awakening' from the Urals in the east to the Appalachians in the west. Methodism soon spread into parts of Wales and Ireland, but it was in the United States that the movement made its most spectacular gains, emerging as the nation's largest Christian denomination on the eve of the American Civil War. Methodism's flexible and exportable structure and its egalitarian message was a good fit for a nation of free markets and democratic political aspirations. First establishing itself in the eastern seaboard cities, Methodism soon spread south and west with remarkable speed, even managing to make a substantial impact on African slaves despite the fact that preaching to slaves was discouraged by slave-owners and many church authorities at this time. African American Methodism has remained one of Methodism's most durable religious traditions.

Although primarily a movement that took root among Anglo-American Protestants, Methodism also sustained a vigorous missionary movement in the nineteenth century that led to its growth in parts of Africa, Asia and Australasia. Indeed, some of Methodism's fastest growing churches, not to mention the dramatic rise of Pentecostalism, a daughter movement of Methodism, are now located in the southern hemisphere.

How then should Methodism be interpreted and what is its place in the Christian tradition? Methodism arose as a voluntary society within the Church of England at a time when the established churches of western Europe were finding it hard to retain their traditional status and control. Next to its great hymns, the Methodist class ticket – a token of voluntary commitment and a highly prized badge of membership – is probably Methodism's most recognizable symbol. Although exaggerated claims are sometimes made about Methodism's contribution to political stability in England in the era of the French Revolution, and to the civilizing of the American frontier, Methodists across the north Atlantic region made an important contribution to the peaceful transition of societies from authoritarian control to democratic participation.

Finally then, what was it about Methodism that attracted the loyalty and commitment of so many people across the world in the eighteenth and nineteenth centuries? More specifically, is there a single compelling idea at the heart and centre of the Methodist component of the international Great Awakening? One answer would be its belief in the achievability of personal and social holiness on earth as in heaven. In that respect Methodism, by propagating religion as a means and a way to a better life for individuals and communities, could be regarded as a Protestant parallel to the Enlightenment. Crucial to the holiness experiment was the notion that pure religion was a self-adopted choice, not a state-sponsored obligation. The deceptively simple idea propagated in word and song by John and Charles Wesley was this: notwithstanding the political corruption and pastoral lethargy they identified in Hanoverian England, it was possible through divine initiative, human cooperation and the empowerment of the Spirit to promote personal and social holiness of such quality that it dared hope for perfection in the life of the believer and purification of the wider society.

What was striking about Methodism is how successfully it appealed to a wide range of social groups and people of different levels of education. It inspired trade unionists, chartists, temperance advocates, sabbatarians, anti-slavery activists, Sunday school teachers, educational pioneers, philanthropists and civic reformers. It crossed national boundaries and adapted to new environments. Its growth from a small society within the Church of England to a major international church is one of the most remarkable stories in the history of Christianity.

DAVID HEMPTON

John Wesley preaches from his father's tomb in the churchyard at Epworth, Lincolnshire.

As a result, we are told, the people of Lochcarron – who had tried to burn Sage to death on his first day in the job – became 'animated with love to God, and to their fellow men'. And the revival spread further in the 1740s when George Whitefield preached in both Presbyterian and Anglican churches. He helped to bring the revival to Cambuslang and Kilsyth, near Glasgow.

Most of these people, and many more, set up new groups intended to supplement normal church services: prayer meetings, Bible study groups and so on. They functioned much as Philipp Spener's 'conventicles' had in Germany, and indeed the first British ones had been set up by a German, Anthony Horneck, when preaching in London in the 1670s. Most were held once a week, and they operated informally, but there was a lot of variety – they could be anything from rational discussions of doctrine to opportunities to share spiritual experiences. By the middle of the eighteenth century, these 'religious societies', as they were usually called, had become the standard expression of what was becoming known as 'evangelicalism'.

FROM REVIVALISM TO EVANGELICALISM

'Evangelical', which comes from the Greek word for 'gospel', is now a much over-used and increasingly ambiguous word. In continental Europe it has traditionally been used simply as a synonym for 'Protestant', but in the English-speaking world it has been used more narrowly to refer to those who shared the theological and moral concerns of the revivalists. Thus, although these revivalists shared many concerns with other non-English-speaking groups, such as the Pietists, it is not normal to call the latter 'evangelicals', although it would not be much of a misnomer. Evangelical views were very widespread by the end of the eighteenth century; they were especially strong among the various Dissenting churches, particularly the Baptists and the Methodists – indeed, the latter had come into being as an evangelical breakaway group from the Church of England, inspired by the teachings of John Wesley

and others. But many with similar theological views remained within the Church of England, effectively a party within that church, a powerful one which had inherited the concerns of the earlier Puritan party but with more of an interest in the personal experience of each individual believer. All of these evangelicals, both within and without the Church of England, would play a major role in religious life in the years to come, especially in overseas mission, as we shall see in Chapter 13.

The rise of evangelicalism in the English-speaking world marked a new age of poetry and song. Since the Reformation, only one English hymn-book had been published that contained anything other than the Psalms; this was *Hymns and songs of the church* of 1623 by George Wither. It was not until the end of the seventeenth century that hymn-writing began in earnest. Isaac Watts, a Dissenting pastor in London, and one of the greatest of these early evangelical hymn-writers, published the enormously popular *Hymns and spiritual songs* in 1707. Probably his most famous was 'When I survey the wondrous cross', testifying to the role of personal experience, and the individual's relationship with Christ, which underlay evangelical religion.

The most famous eighteenth-century hymn-writer was Charles Wesley (1707–88), brother of John, and composer-in-chief for the Methodist movement. As the author of some 9,000 hymns, he was one of the most prolific poets of any kind in the English language, and their continued popularity attests to the major role they played in spreading and deepening evangelical ideals. Consider the first verse of one of his most famous songs:

And can it be that I should gain
An interest in the Saviour's blood?
Died he for me? who caused his pain!
For me? who him to death pursued?
Amazing love! How can it be
That thou my God, shouldst die for me?

Amazing grace! How sweet the sound
That saved a wretch like me!
I once was lost, but now am found;
Was blind, but now I see.

'Twas grace that taught my heart to fear,
And grace my fears relieved;
How precious did that grace appear
The hour I first believed.

Through many dangers, toils and snares,
I have already come;
'Tis grace hath brought me safe thus far,
And grace will lead me home.

The Lord has promised good to me,
His Word my hope secures;
He will my Shield and Portion be,
As long as life endures.

Yea, when this flesh and heart shall fail,
And mortal life shall cease,
I shall possess, within the veil,
A life of joy and peace.

John Newton

If evangelical hymns reflected evangelical experience, though, no better example could be found than John Newton. A sailor and a drifter, Newton lived a remarkable but not very edifying life, being on one occasion flogged for desertion and on another spending over a year as a slave in Africa. For years he was captain of a slave ship. But he developed an evangelical faith, nurtured partly by meeting Wesley, Whitefield and others. Eventually he became ordained as an Anglican priest, and worked with William Cowper, another evangelical poet, to produce *The Olney hymns* in 1779. Newton's most famous hymn, 'Amazing grace', remains the best-known evangelical song of all time.

CHAPTER 12

THE WEST AFTER THE ENLIGHTENMENT

The nineteenth century was a time of triumph and crisis for western Christianity. Triumph, as new movements brought spirituality to the masses, pressed for social reform and set up the most audacious mission projects to date. But crisis, as science and textual criticism threatened many cherished Christian beliefs.

NEW WARS, NEW EUROPE

The old Europe of the eighteenth century was passing away and a new world was taking its place. Much of the change was in industry and living standards, as the Industrial Revolution created a new kind of society in the west. But revolutions of another kind were also in the air. The revolt of the American colonies in 1776 set a spark that ignited in Europe, most spectacularly in the French Revolution of 1789, ending the weak and unjust rule of King Louis XVI. Three years later, the National Convention came to power under Maximilien Robespierre. He instigated 'the Reign of Terror', in which all elements of the old regime were purged, with some 15,000 people being executed.

THE JACOBINS
It was a deliberate break not only with the rule of aristocrats, but with the union of church and state that Louis XIV had perfected back in the seventeenth century. The most extreme members of the National Convention were known as the Jacobins,

because they initially met in a former Dominican friary, and the Parisian nickname for Dominicans was 'Jacobins'. This was somewhat ironic given that these politicians regarded Christianity as incompatible with being a good citizen. They attempted to 'free' the country of the religion, which they branded a tool of oppression in which the aristocrats and the priests had collaborated to keep the people silent. The result was the most thorough state persecution of Christianity in Europe since the days of Diocletian. Priests were forced to marry or face imprisonment, while churches were closed and often turned to more 'useful' functions, such as grain silos. Others were transformed into 'temples of Reason', for the Jacobins tried to promote deism as an alternative to Christianity. Many Catholics fled to Quebec, where their freedom of religion was protected by the British.

Yet the attempt to secularize France ultimately failed. In 1794 more moderate elements came to power and Catholicism, although still illegal, was tolerated. The churches quickly filled again, for most French people still felt that Catholicism was a deep-rooted part of their national culture. To be French was, to a great extent, to be Catholic, something that the Jacobins had never understood.

NAPOLEON BONAPARTE AND PIUS VII
Throughout the revolutionary period, France was at war with much of the rest of Europe, including Austria and the kingdom of Naples in southern Italy. From the ranks of the army emerged Napoleon Bonaparte,

a brilliant general who crushed France's foes, conquered both Venice and Egypt, and in 1799 brushed aside the country's constitution to become first 'consul of France'. One of his first acts was the negotiation of a concordat with the Vatican. According to this treaty, Napoleon recognized that Catholicism was the dominant religion of France, though it was not the official state religion, and tolerance was extended to minority faiths. The church had to give up any claim to its lands that had been seized during the revolution, but it did retain the right to appoint French bishops. In December 1804, in the presence of Pope Pius VII, Napoleon was crowned emperor of the French in Notre Dame cathedral in Paris. In 1806 Napoleon defeated Austria once again, forcing the resignation of the emperor Francis II, for there could be only one emperor in Europe. That was, technically, the end of the Holy Roman empire which went back to Otto 'the Great' – although it had ceased to be a political reality many years earlier as its constituent states developed into independent countries. Almost non-stop war followed with much of Europe, culminating in Napoleon's famous abortive invasion of Russia in 1812.

Napoleon's coronation as emperor in the presence of the pope invited comparisons with another all-conquering emperor who had lived exactly a thousand years earlier, and with whom he also shared a desire for collaboration with the papacy. On one occasion he wrote to Pius VII:

For the pope's purposes I am the new Charlemagne. Like Charlemagne, I join the crown of France with the crown of the Lombards… I expect the pope to accommodate his conduct to my requirements. If he behaves well, I shall make no outward changes; if not, I shall reduce him to the status of bishop of Rome.

Unfortunately from the pope's point of view, Napoleon lacked Charlemagne's piety and devotion to the Christian faith. And

The storming of the Bastille, during the French Revolution, 1789.

from Napoleon's point of view the pope did not 'behave well', failing to support him in his war against Britain. In 1809 the emperor invaded the papal states and forced the elderly Pius VII into exile in Savona and then Fontainebleau, where he was kept under constant surveillance. Not until 1814, as Napoleon was forced to fight a huge coalition to protect his conquered territories, was Pius VII returned to Rome. After Napoleon's final defeat the following year, the pope regained control of the papal states. Movingly, he wrote to the British authorities pleading for Napoleon to be better treated during his exile to St Helena, calling the fallen emperor the restorer of religion in France and forgiving him for what he had done to Pius himself.

A NEW EUROPE AND A NEW PAPACY

The restoration of Pius VII to Rome saw something of a renewal of devotion to the pope throughout Catholic Europe. In 1814 he restored the Jesuits as a papally sanctioned society (the society had been dissolved, for political reasons, by Pope Clement XIV in 1773), although they remained periodically banned in various countries, especially Spain and Russia. They and others were devoted to the papacy, in a movement known as Ultramontanism (literally, 'beyond the mountains', that is, taking their cue from Rome, the city beyond the Alps). But Ultramontanism had to jostle for elbow space with more nationally minded versions of Catholicism. In France, in the post-Napoleonic era as in the pre-revolutionary *ancien regime*, Catholic devotion often took the form known as Gallicanism. The seventeenth-century bishop Jacques Bossuet had been one of the prime architects of Gallicanism, according to which the Catholic Church is collectively infallible, but this infallibility does not apply to the pope as its head. Instead, Gallicans looked to the local French bishops as their main authorities, under the aegis of the French king (for the monarchy had been restored after Napoleon's fall). The French clergy had made a Declaration of Gallicanism in 1682, stating that pope's authority is solely

spiritual and does not extend to temporal rulers. This attitude remained strong well into the nineteenth century.

The basic attitude of Gallicanism spread beyond France. In the eighteenth century a German version was formulated by Johann Nikolaus von Hontheim (1701–90), bishop of Trier, who wrote under the pseudonym 'Justinius Febronius'. Like Bossuet, Febronius argued that the Catholic Church as a whole exercises valid authority, but the pope is only a servant of that church and has no real authority over it. All bishops are therefore equal. Febronius was condemned by Rome, but many liked his ideas, especially as he had intended them to be more amenable to Protestants, with an eye to the reunification of the churches. Joseph II of Austria (1741–90), from 1765 the Holy Roman emperor, was impressed by Febronianism and instigated a version of his own, sometimes known as Josephinism, in which the church became simply a state department. The Catholic Church in Austria was reorganized along aggressively Austrian lines: bishops were not allowed to communicate with Rome, and members of religious orders could not contact their superiors abroad. The system collapsed with Joseph's death, but Febronian ideals remained very much alive in both Austria and Germany throughout the nineteenth century. This period therefore saw something of a struggle within Catholicism, between Ultramontanism on the one hand and Gallicanism, Febronianism and related views on the other.

MANIFEST DESTINY AND NEW REVIVALS

In 1845 John L. O'Sullivan, editor of *The United States Magazine and Democratic Review*, coined a new phrase. Writing about the disputes over Oregon, he stated that the US claim to the area 'is by the right of our manifest destiny to overspread and to possess the whole of the continent which Providence has given us for the development of the great experiment of liberty and federative self-government entrusted to us'.

In his conception of the 'manifest destiny' of the USA, O'Sullivan was expressing a feeling common to many white Americans at the time that the country would – and should – naturally expand to cover the whole of North America, just as Russia, ever since early modern times, had been and still was expanding eastwards through a process of settling and enculturation. And just as Russian expansion was a complex matter involving religion, so too the US ideal of 'manifest destiny' expressed a combination of political, social and religious aims.

The nineteenth century did see the expansion of the USA to cover most of temperate North America, together with the continued flourishing of the notion that the USA was a special country, one ordained by God to bring enlightenment to the whole continent. This notion was encouraged by a new wave of religious revivals, known as 'the Second Great Awakening'.

THE SECOND GREAT AWAKENING
In contrast to Britain, where the first Great Awakening had largely died down by the latter half of the eighteenth century, revivals had never really stopped happening in the USA. They had simply become relatively low-key and localized. One important figure of the ongoing revivals of this period was Henry Alline, who embarked on a short-lived but highly influential ministry in Nova Scotia. Alline brought a powerful message revolving around God's love; he rejected many points of traditional Calvinism, especially the doctrine of limited atonement, and his message proved extremely popular. In this way, the revivals of New England spread to Canada. But Alline died in 1784 aged only thirty-five.

The revivals stepped up the pace once again at the dawn of the nineteenth century, and this time they would spread far more widely than before, beginning in two quite different locations.

At Yale Timothy Dwight, the grandson of Jonathan Edwards, became president in 1798 and preached much the same ideas as his grandfather – the need for repentance and the indwelling of the Holy Spirit – and his sermons sparked a revival that spread throughout Connecticut.

Meanwhile, in 1796, a Presbyterian minister named James McGready arrived in rural Kentucky – a frontier area that was still in the process of being settled – and his preaching was something to behold. People fainted, shook, collapsed into trances, shouted and sang. The news spread quickly and by the turn of the century there were thousands of people camped around McGready's Gaspar River Church. From this developed what became known as 'camp meetings', almost like modern-day music festivals: people would camp outdoors in tents or wagons for several days whilst attending virtually non-stop services. Barton Stone, a student of McGready's, organized a massive one at Cane Ridge in Kentucky in 1801. Between 12,000 and 25,000 people attended and listened to a number of sermons preached around the clock from different vantage points, and the crowd often degenerated into chaos as people began screaming, shouting, barking, and jumping around, sometimes for hours at a time. Meetings like this spread across the American south and were attended by people from all denominations and of all races – for, like the earlier Great Awakening, the revivals were as much a movement of the black majority as of the white minority.

Inevitably there were disputes. The hoary old problem of predestination and free will appeared again, as different groups adopted Calvinism or Arminianism. Some congregations sought to distance themselves from any kind of church or post-biblical theology and instead set up communities known simply as 'Christian'. Yet despite this, the movement created a common religious culture throughout much of the American South – that is, although the denominations remained separate, and white worshippers typically did not mix with black ones, the different congregations and preachers used similar language and ideas in a religious context. The Methodists in particular gained

The time is coming when the pressure of population on the means of subsistence will be felt [in the United States] as it is now felt in Europe and Asia... Then this race of unequaled energy, with all the majesty of numbers and the might of wealth behind it – the representative, let us hope, of the largest liberty, the purest Christianity, the highest civilization – having developed peculiarly aggressive traits calculated to impress its institutions upon mankind, will spread itself over the earth.

Josiah Strong, a social gospel leader, *Our country: its possible future and its present crisis*, 1891 enormously, being transformed from a minor sect in this part of the world to the largest Protestant church on the continent. This was in part down to the work of Francis Asbury (1745–1816), who was born in Staffordshire, England, and was sent to the USA as a missionary in 1771. He spent the next forty-five years travelling the country as a Methodist preacher, especially after 1784 when John Wesley appointed him and Thomas Coke superintendents of the American Methodist Church. Controversially, Asbury took the title of bishop, but he continued to travel and preach, maintaining tight control over all Methodist churches – a difficult task in such a huge continent. The Baptist churches also flourished during this period. As a result, evangelical Christianity became central to the culture of much of what is now the southern United States.

NEW PREACHING, NEW SECTS
The extraordinary growth of the Methodist and Baptist churches in the South occurred mostly in the first five years of the nineteenth century. The 1820s saw

An engraving of Charles Finney as a young man.

renewed revival, this time in the north again. A key figure here was a Presbyterian minister named Charles Grandison Finney who preached in upstate New York. Finney was an original and compelling preacher, who transferred the style of the 'camp meetings' of the rural South to a more urban environment, hiring halls and other venues for week-long meetings. A lawyer by training, Finney recognized the importance of rhetoric and emotional appeal in making a case: his sermons were marked by powerful reasoning and direct appeal to the listener, and his innovations included the appointment of 'ministers of music' to enliven his services. The revival spread throughout upstate New York, until Finney moved to New York City itself before accepting a teaching post in Ohio in 1835. That year saw the publication of his *Lectures on revivals of religion*, which defended his methods and was extremely influential.

The effect of the revivals upon New York state and the surrounding area was intense: it was sometimes known as 'the burned-over district', an expression that evoked the speed and fury of a forest fire as well as its devastation. Out of this religious cauldron emerged new sects and groups. The most well known was the Latter-day Saints (or Mormons), inspired by the teaching of Joseph Smith. But there were others too, such as those who followed John Humphrey Noyes, who claimed that Christ had appointed him to rule over the kingdom of God on earth. He accordingly set up a community at Oneida in New York, but it never grew very large: Noyes' followers were notorious for unusual sexual practices, such as the sharing of partners and selective breeding.

More successful was William Miller (1782–1849), a Baptist from New York who in 1835 published *Evidences from Scripture and history of the second coming of Christ about the year 1843*. Miller's book was extremely popular and many fervently believed his theory. After the 'Great Disappointment' which followed the non-appearance of Christ in 1843, Miller re-did his sums and found that Christ would

The Church of Jesus Christ of Latter-day Saints

Teenage Joseph Smith (1805–44), confused by Christian revivalism in New York state in the 1820s, asked God which church was true. The answer came through visions, in which God the Father and Jesus told him that all churches were false and promised further directions. The angel Moroni enabled Joseph to discover and translate buried metallic plates – The Book of Mormon – which described two waves of migrants from the Holy Land coming to America (around 2250 BC and 600 BC) with Jesus himself appearing in America at his resurrection.

Instructed by John the Baptist, and the apostles Peter, James and John, Joseph Smith established two priesthoods (Aaronic and Melchizedek) as the basis for the organization of The Church of Christ, founded in 1830 and renamed the Church of Jesus Christ of Latter-day Saints in 1838. The Doctrine and Covenants contains important Mormon revelations to Joseph and to later prophet-president leaders of the Saints.

Early missionaries from Joseph's new church called people to abandon the evil world ('Babylon') and gather in America ('Zion') to prepare for the Second Coming of Christ. Thousands did this, especially Europeans, often undertaking hazardous journeys. Joseph Smith was killed by a mob in 1844, but he was succeeded by Brigham Young (1807–77), who led the Saints until they settled in the Great Salt Lake Basin, now Utah. There, the Saints built temples for special rituals, especially baptism for the dead, endowments and marriages: they believed that these rites must be performed by Melchizedek priests on earth to allow the Saints to conquer death and gain other blessings in the afterlife. Genealogical work provided the identity of ancestors for these rites. The early practice of polygamy led to intense opposition from the federal government, and it was abandoned by the end of the nineteenth century. Today, some small groups, often called Fundamentalist Mormons, still practise polygamy despite opposition from the state and from their church, which prizes firm moral values supporting monogamous family life and 'sealing' together each husband and wife and their children for all eternity in the temple rites.

Today, all males who uphold Mormon values enter the Aaronic priesthhood (with its divisions of deacon, teacher and priest) from the age of twelve and the Melchizedek priesthood from nineteen.

Many young men and some women become voluntary missionaries for a two-year period. Called Elders, they lead disciplined lives involving study of sacred texts, prayer, active evangelism and teaching in the mission locality. Their church teaches that humans exist as eternal 'intelligences', as spirit children of God and, now, inhabit material bodies. God's grace guarantees resurrection because Jesus atoned for sin through his own obedient suffering. The 'degree of glory' achievable in the three major divisions of heaven (the telestial, terrestrial and celestial kingdoms) depends upon human obedience.

Mormons regard themselves as Christian, with Christ playing a major part in the Plan of Salvation reaching from eternity to eternity. Jesus is also the God of the Old Testament. But many Christian groups deny that Mormon doctrine is orthodox, and focus their criticism on its distinctive understanding of the Trinity.

DOUGLAS DAVIES

---

actually come in 1844. In that year, two followers claimed to have had a vision of Christ entering the temple of God in heaven to prepare for his return. This was taken as confirmation of the prediction, and Miller's followers therefore continued to expect the imminent (though no longer so accurately calculated) return of Christ on earth. The result was the emergence of a 'Millerite' or 'Second Adventist' church, which proved remarkably durable. The Millerites had a number of other distinctive doctrines, including the claim that the immortality of the soul is conditional upon faith; thus, unbelievers are not condemned to hell but are annihilated, whilst the faithful will be resurrected. A split occurred in this church through the preaching of Ellen Gould White (1827–1915), who among other things taught that Saturday should be observed as the Sabbath. A new group, the Seventh-day Adventists, therefore developed. In 1863 the group, now numbering 3,000, organized itself into a proper church and developed an extremely effective administrative structure, which resulted in quick growth. The Seventh-day Adventists became known for their stress on physical health, based on a holistic understanding of the body and soul as intimately connected. Their Battle Creek Sanitarium was one of the leading centres of healthy living research in the world.

MISSIONS TO THE SLAVES

As we saw in Chapter 10, vast numbers of slaves were transported from Africa – mostly West Africa – to the Caribbean and southern North America to work on the plantations there. In the seventeenth and eighteenth centuries, not many of these slaves were Christians. Few people thought

Hark! – hear those dreadful bellowings of the angry nations! It is the presage of horrid and terrific war. Look! – look again! See crowns, and kings, and kingdoms tumbling to the dust… What means that ray of light? The clouds have burst asunder; the heavens appear; the great white throne is in sight! Amazement fills the universe with awe! He comes!– he comes! Behold, the Saviour comes!

William Miller, *Letter to Elder Hendryx*, 1832

He remembers the sixty-eighth Psalm as affording numerous texts for their delectation, e.g., 'Let God arise, let his enemies be scattered'; His 'march through the wilderness'; 'The Chariots of God are twenty thousand'; 'The hill of God is as the hill of Basham'; and especially, 'Though ye have lain among the pots, yet shall ye be as the wings of a dove covered with silver, and her feathers with yellow gold.'... It is mortifying now to think that his comprehension was not equal to the African intellect. All he thought about was relief from the servitude of sin, and freedom from the bondage of the devil... But they interpreted it literally in the good time coming.

Abel McGee Chreitzberg, on a white Methodist minister running a black church in South Carolina, 1897

What enraptures the Negroes, whether they were born in Africa or America was their cradle, is the dance. There is no amount of fatigue which can make them abandon going to very great distances, and some times even during the dead of night, to satisfy this passion.

Médéric Louis Élie Moreau de Saint-Méry, a politician of Martinique, Description de l'isle Saint-Domingue, 1797

it worth preaching to them, especially in the face of opposition from landowners. Peter Kalm, a Swede, analyzed the reasons behind this in his *Travels into North America* of 1772.

It is… to be pitied, that the masters of these negroes in most of the English colonies take little care of their spiritual welfare, and let them live on in their Pagan darkness. There are even some, who would be very ill pleased at, and would by all means hinder their negroes from being instructed in the doctrines of Christianity; to this they are partly led by the conceit of its being shameful, to have a spiritual brother or sister among so despicable a people; partly by thinking that they should not be able to keep their negroes so meanly afterwards; and partly through fear of the negroes growing too proud, on seeing themselves upon a level with their masters in religious matters.

However, in 1701 the Church of England had set up the Society for the Propagation of the Gospel to send missionaries to the colonies. Their officers insisted that Christianity was quite compatible with slavery; all they sought from slave-owners was permission to preach to their slaves. Thus, it was argued that Christianity encouraged meekness and servility, and much was made of Ephesians 6:5, which instructs slaves to obey their masters. A kind of Christian defence of slavery was therefore established, in support of the main aim of evangelizing the slaves.

The missions to the slaves continued throughout the eighteenth century, enjoying some success. Many slaves were baptized because they hoped that it would improve their social status. Often the process of conversion failed in the presence of Islam, still practised by many West African slaves. At other times, Protestantism coexisted with older African religions or even mingled with them, in a process similar to the one we saw in Chapter 10, when Catholicism and African religions merged to create Santeria and Voodoo.

Thus some Christian slaves maintained the African belief in spirit-possession, insisting that true spiritual awakening came through a trance induced by a long period of prayer, known as 'seeking'.

Widespread black conversions occurred only with the two Great Awakenings. George Whitefield and Jonathan Edwards, among others, noted how many black faces there were at the revival meetings of the 1740s, and the enormous success of the Methodist and Baptist churches in the south in the opening years of the nineteenth century continued the process. The dramatic and emotional form that the second Great Awakening took in the south appealed to many black people, who saw it as similar to the rituals of their own traditional religions. By combining them, they created practices such as 'shouting', which was actually rather like dancing except that the feet never left the floor (if they had, that would really have been dancing and therefore sinful in their eyes). 'Shouting' was done to the accompaniment of spiritual songs and clapping (for drums were forbidden to slaves) and this rhythmic, somatic form of self-expression was believed to induce a state of spiritual receptivity.

Some slave-owners had by the 1830s become used to the idea of Christian slaves, and some even taught Christianity to their own slaves, giving Sunday lessons to the slaves' children. Religion, it seemed, could be a good way of controlling slaves, but it also represented a genuine concern on the part of some slave-owners for their charges' well-being and the good of their souls.

Many black people therefore began to attend the same churches as white people; others set up their own churches and worshipped alone. Most of these early black churches were Baptist, since the Baptists had the loosest organizational structure, favouring the rise of black preachers. In style, their preaching mimicked the rituals of old Africa, where the chant would be passed back and forth between leader and people. Now the preacher's 'shouting' sermon would be punctuated almost non-stop by cries of 'Amen!' or 'Yes, Lord!' from the congregation, creating an almost rhythmic call-and-response feel to the service, one which white people could not understand and often feared.

The 'black Christianity' that emerged in this way depended, above all else, upon the notion of the saving God. This basic belief was expressed in a great emphasis upon the Old Testament, especially the exodus. Just as God had led the Hebrews out of slavery in Egypt to the Promised Land, so too he would lead the African Americans out of slavery into freedom. That, at least, was the subtext. And this new understanding of Christianity as a message of liberation flourished largely independently of any white interference. Where slave-owners tried to control it, they failed. Where white ministers presided, they were often at complete theological loggerheads with their congregations, even without realizing it.

From time to time, slaves were freed, and so there developed something of a free black community, mainly in the north of the United States. Here, black Christians attended church with white Christians, but such situations tended to degenerate as the whites could not stomach it. As a result, many black congregations split away. In 1816 a completely new church organization for black Americans was established – the African Methodist Episcopal Church – with a former slave named Richard Allen (1760–1831) as its first bishop.

Many of these freed slaves or their families had fought in the War of Independence, especially on the side of the British, for they had found that, whilst the rebels claimed that 'all men are created equal', they often restricted the application of the principle to white men. As a result, many black people, especially former soldiers, moved to Canada after the war. Here, their communities revolved around the churches and charismatic leaders such as David George, a Baptist preacher, and Moses Wilkinson, a blind Methodist. Both men were from Virginia and, like their

congregations, they were free and largely autonomous. These black congregations saw their Christianity and their freedom as inextricably connected. Like other evangelical groups of the period, they read the account of the early church in Acts and sought to emulate it; they believed that their salvation by Christ from sin was also a salvation from more material bonds.

THE SOCIAL CHALLENGE

The problem of slavery was just one of many social issues that increasingly exercised Christians in the nineteenth century. This was the age of social action, when for the first time in perhaps fourteen centuries large-scale efforts were made to reform and improve European society in a real way and in line with Christian principles. In this, the English-speaking countries, and above all the evangelicals (both Anglicans and Dissenters), took the lead.

THE ABOLITION OF SLAVERY
We saw in Chapter 10 that the enslavement of native peoples in the Canary Islands had been condemned by the Vatican in the 1430s and, though again few people paid any attention, in 1537 Paul III had declared Amerindians should not be enslaved even if they were not Christians. The same situation prevailed with the African slave trade. In 1639 Urban VIII declared that enslaving *anyone* was contrary to Christianity, but he was ignored. In any case, by the eighteenth and nineteenth centuries, most of the black slaves in the Americas were in lands owned by Protestant powers.

As we have seen, in the early eighteenth century it was customary for white preachers to argue that slavery was compatible with Christianity. Opposition to slavery was generally associated with fringe Pietist or evangelical elements. Some of the earliest white opponents of slavery were the Mennonites and Quakers, who in the seventeenth century were already denouncing the practice and banning it

There were half a million slaves in the confines of the United States when the Declaration of Independence declared 'that all men are created equal; that they are endowed by their Creator with certain unalienable rights; that among these are life, liberty, and the pursuit of happiness.' The land that thus magniloquently heralded its advent into the family of nations had supported the institution of human slavery for one hundred and fifty-seven years and was destined to cling to it eighty-seven years longer.

W. E. B. Du Bois, a leading black American social activist, *The Negro*, 1915 among their members. They were generally regarded as extremist cranks, but their views gradually filtered into mainstream society. In the eighteenth century, many people involved in the evangelical revivals came out against slavery. A key figure in this process was Anthony Benezet, a Philadelphia Quaker who published several tracts attacking the slave trade and the institution of slavery – the most influential of which was *Some historical account of Guinea*, published in 1772 and widely read in Britain and America. John Wesley admired Benezet and helped to distribute his work before publishing his own *Thoughts upon slavery* in 1774, in which he uncompromisingly attacked the institution of slavery itself as fundamentally unchristian. Calls for abolition were growing in both the Americas and in Europe, especially Britain, where many people signed petitions against the slave trade – 1,900 being sent to parliament by Methodist congregations alone. The success of Dissenting churches in the

American south in the second Great Renewal of the late eighteenth and early nineteenth centuries – especially the Methodists and Baptists – helped this process. But it did not yet have an air of inevitability about it. Throughout the 1780s the Methodists held conferences which condemned slavery; but nothing came of it. British MPs were at this time elected only by wealthy men, so most had an interest in maintaining the status quo, and the Dissenters themselves largely tried to avoid the issue as too divisive and prejudicial to mission, their prime objective.

Much of the anti-slavery sentiment originated with Africans themselves. One figure in this was Ottobah Cugoano – also known as John Stuart – a Fante living in London, who in 1787 published *Thoughts and sentiments on the evils of slavery, an uncompromising attack on the whole business.* A more subtle attack was found in the autobiography of a friend of Cugoano's, entitled *The interesting narrative of the life of*

William Wilberforce as a young man, by the British painter John Rising (1753–1817).

Olaudah Equiano, or Gustavus Vassa, published in 1789. Equiano was an Igbo (from what is now Nigeria), a former slave who travelled Britain and Ireland speaking against slavery. Not only was he a dedicated and impassioned voice, but his mere existence – an articulate and intelligent, English-speaking African Christian, travelling the country and meeting many thousands of people – was itself a potent argument against the supposed justice of slavery.

Evangelical Anglicans were joining the Dissenters and the freed slaves in their views. In parliament the most eloquent was William Wilberforce, a devout MP from Hull. He introduced an Abolition Bill in 1789 – making what was said to be the best speech ever delivered in the Commons – but he still encountered great opposition. By 1807 Britain had banned only the trading in slaves. In the colonies slaves continued to rebel. John Smith, a missionary convicted of aiding a revolt in Guyana in 1823, died in prison, his conscience having led him to a decision similar to Dietrich Bonhoeffer's (see page 427). It was not until 1833 that the slaves in Britain's West Indian colonies were finally freed, with the government paying compensation to the slaveholders.

THE INDUSTRIAL REVOLUTION AND NEW SOCIAL CONDITIONS

The freeing of the slaves was, for many Christians, a great moral crusade, but for most – at least in Europe – the misery was not on their own doorstep. There were plenty of social and moral problems much closer to home. The eighteenth and nineteenth centuries were the age of the Industrial Revolution, which began with the appearance of the first factories in Britain in the 1740s. First Britain and then other countries urbanized, as people moved to the cities to find employment in the new factories. London, the greatest megalopolis in the world, saw its population rocket from one million in 1800 to seven million by 1911. Living conditions deteriorated. The German

philosopher and reformer Friedrich Engels, who spent time in both London and Manchester, reported what he saw in his famous *Condition of the working class of England*, published in 1845. In it, he quoted G. Alston, preacher at St Philip's church, in the East End of London, describing the state of his parish:

It contains 1,400 houses, inhabited by 2,795 families, comprising a population of 12,000. The space within which this large amount of population are living is less than 400 yards square (1,200 feet), and it is no uncommon thing for a man and his wife, with four or five children, and sometimes the grandfather and grandmother, to be found living in a room from ten to twelve feet square, and which serves them for eating and working in. I believe that till the Bishop of London called the attention of the public to the state of Bethnal Green, about as little was known at the West-end of the town of this most destitute parish as the wilds of Australia or the islands of the South Seas. If we really desire to find out the most destitute and deserving, we must lift the latch of their doors, and find them at their scanty meal; we must see them when suffering from sickness and want of work; and if we do this from day to day in such a neighbourhood as Bethnal Green, we shall become acquainted with a mass of wretchedness and misery such as a nation like our own ought to be ashamed to permit.

Such conditions inspired the development of communism, of which Engels himself was one of the architects; but as the comments of Alston suggest, they also inspired a new concern on the part of Christians, especially evangelicals.

There are two important points to bear in mind about Victorian Christian social activism. The first is that it was controversial – most Anglicans had little time for it, and many evangelicals believed that it was more important to worry about people's souls than it was to worry about their material circumstances. This leads into the second point, which is that social

I was soon put down under the decks, and there I received such a salutation in my nostrils as I had never experienced in my life: so that, with the loathsomeness of the stench, and crying together, I became so sick and low that I was not able to eat, nor had I the least desire to taste any thing. I now wished for the last friend, death, to relieve me; but soon, to my grief, two of the white men offered me eatables; and, on my refusing to eat, one of them held me fast by the hands, and laid me across, I think the windlass, and tied my feet, while the other flogged me severely... In a little time after, amongst the poor chained men, I found some of my own nation, which in a small degree gave ease to my mind. I inquired of these what was to be done with us? They gave me to understand, we were to be carried to these white people's country to work for them.

Olaudah Equiano describing his capture, *The interesting narrative of the life of Olaudah Equiano, or Gustavus Vassa*, 1789 concern was often mingled with evangelism. Many of these new poverty-stricken working classes had no notion of religion, and the worthy Victorians who ventured into the slums to help them were often shocked to find children and adults alike who did not know who Moses or even Jesus were. Thus began the movement to re-evangelize Britain, supposedly the heart of the greatest Christian empire the world had ever seen.

THE EVANGELICALS

Preaching and evangelism remained key concerns for evangelicals, as they had in the days of John Wesley. As we shall see in the next chapter, evangelicals played a major role in establishing societies for sending missionaries overseas. They also sought to revitalize Christianity at home. William Wilberforce, for example, published *A practical view of the prevailing religious system of professed Christians in the higher and middle classes in this country contrasted with real Christianity*, in which he exhorted the well-off to commit personally to Christ and lead more moral lives. Despite its rather off-putting title, the book was enormously successful. The moral views of the evangelicals began to filter into mainstream British society, and it became increasingly accepted that things like bear-baiting and cock-fighting (major entertainments up until that time) were wrong. Society's views of sex changed dramatically as well. Before this time, evangelicals (and Puritans before them) had disapproved of promiscuity, but it had been not at all unusual for even quite devout members of other Christian traditions to indulge themselves sexually as they saw fit. That now changed, as 'Victorian' moral standards became the norm.

The moral standards and personal devotion that were now expected of Christians were both exemplified in one issue that seems to have obsessed Victorians to a remarkable degree – Sunday observance. Evangelicals, both Anglican and otherwise, were convinced that not working on Sunday was the touchstone of

religion. This had long been a concern of Pietists: indeed, there had been laws decreeing what was permissible on Sundays since the sixteenth century. A Lord's Day Observance Society was founded in 1831 to campaign for the extension of these laws, putting pressure on parks, museums and other places that opened on Sundays. One minister at Cheltenham, in Gloucestershire, managed to prevent all trains from stopping there on Sundays for six years. A similar campaign existed in Canada, under the aegis of the Lord's Day Alliance, which in 1906 succeeded in getting the Lord's Day Act passed, regulating business activities on Sundays.

What, then, did evangelicals do on Sundays? The day was increasingly given over not simply to church services but to religious instruction. Puritans and Pietists had traditionally used Sunday for informal Bible study and teaching in the home, and now this developed into the more formal 'Sunday school', invented by a Gloucester newspaper editor named Robert Raikes in the 1780s as a way of teaching moral and religious principles to poor children. Some people mocked this Sunday-oriented earnestness, which they saw as surgically removing any fun from the day. Charles Dickens, for example, commented in his *Hard Times* of 1854 that 'there were larks singing (though it was Sunday)'.

As that suggests, many people found evangelical religion laughable or, worse, hypocritical. The Scottish Presbyterians, with their stern Calvinist theology, were particular targets. James Hogg, a Scottish poet, published a satire on them in 1824 entitled *The private memoirs and confessions of a justified sinner*, in which the devil deludes a young Calvinist into committing a series of murders, on the basis that, as a member of the elect, he cannot do anything to imperil his own soul, and the 'sinners' he kills are predestined to hell anyway. Another caricature could be found in the character of the servant Joseph in Emily Brontë's 1847 novel *Wuthering Heights*, who says things like, 'T'maister nobbut just

My religious views are not very popular but they are the views that have sustained and comforted me all through my life. I think a man's religion, if it is worth anything, should enter into every sphere of life, and rule his conduct in every relation. I have always been – and, please God, always shall be, an Evangelical.

Lord Shaftesbury, letter to Edwin Hodder

buried, and Sabbath not o'ered, und t'sound o't'gospel still i'yer lugs, and ye darr be laiking! Shame on ye! sit ye down, ill childer... and think o' yer sowls!'

SOCIAL ACTIVISM

Yet evangelical religion was still a major force behind the great efforts that were made to improve living conditions in the nineteenth century. One important group who believed that the Christian gospel should inspire social action was known as the 'Clapham Sect', led by John Venn, rector of Holy Trinity Church, Clapham, in south London. William Wilberforce and Granville Sharp (1735–1813), two of the most prominent anti-slavery campaigners, were members of this group. They were mostly evangelical Anglicans who were deeply concerned about social matters and who wrote about them in a journal, *The Christian Observer*. They were concerned about mission both at home and overseas – Charles Simeon, a major mover behind missions to India, was a member. Another was Hannah More, a member of Samuel Johnson's circle and a noted playwright in the eighteenth century, who wrote a number of tracts in which she urged the poor to rely on God. She also worked hard to improve the lives of children in the mining communities of the Mendip Hills in Somerset.

Probably the most prominent new movement for social action in Britain was the Salvation Army, created by a Methodist breakaway named William Booth (1829–1912) in the 1860s. Originally intended as a mission organization for the English inner cities, it came to mix this concern with one for social welfare. Booth organized the movement along militaristic lines, complete with uniforms and army ranks (making himself general, of course).

To many the Salvation Army was a laughable institution, its mock militarism a joke – just as the earnestness of the 'Clapham Sect' brought them ridicule in some quarters, where they were dubbed 'the saints'. But these groups, especially the Salvation Army, did play a vital role in

bringing Christianity to the poor. Booth recognized that the new working classes of the cities felt uncomfortable in traditional churches – Methodist as well as Anglican – and the services that the Salvation Army held were quite informal, with a joyful atmosphere like that of the revival meetings of an earlier age. A London survey one week night in 1882 found 17,000 people attending these meetings, compared to 11,000 in the mainstream churches. In addition to this, Salvation Army members campaigned for better wages for the workers, tried to help women out of prostitution and campaigned for the closing of pubs. An example of the way they materially helped people was the opening of a match factory in 1891, intended to help the match-sellers of London who until then had made their own matches from highly toxic yellow phosphorus. The Salvation Army factory used only harmless red phosphorus, and it paid its workers double the usual rate.

Throughout the nineteenth century evangelical voices within the Church of

Bluegate Fields in east London, one of the worst slums in Victorian Britain, in an 1870 engraving.

A population sodden with drink, steeped in vice, eaten up by every social and physical malady, these are the denizens of Darkest England amidst whom my life has been spent.

William Booth, *In darkest England and the way out*, 1890

England became stronger and social concerns were increasingly mainstream. A good example is the 'ragged schools' movement, which provided free, basic schooling to poor street children. Originating with John Pound (1766–1839), a Portsmouth cobbler who began teaching poor children in his shop in 1818, the movement grew as others were inspired by the idea. The Ragged Schools Union was founded by Lord Shaftesbury (1801–85), a high Tory Anglican and one of the most prominent Victorian philanthropists, who pushed many bills through parliament improving working conditions in factories and mines, for women and children in particular. The ragged schools mostly ran on Sundays and week nights, and they gave children a basic education, often revolving around the Bible.

Even more prominent than Shaftesbury was Thomas Barnardo (1845–1905), an Irish evangelical who taught at ragged schools and worked as a missionary, to the poor in London where he handed out Bibles, and also in Scotland, where he held rallies under Edinburgh Castle and some two hundred people every night would be converted. Most famous, though, were the hostels he opened for homeless children – 96 of them, housing 8,000 children, by the time he died.

In addition to factory reform and education, many evangelical activists fastened onto particular social evils, especially prostitution and drink. Some tried to help prostitutes off the streets, such as William Gladstone (1809–98), the dominant political figure of the second half of the nineteenth century and an extremely devout evangelical Anglican. Even when prime minister, Gladstone was notorious for wandering the streets of London looking for 'fallen women' to rescue, and he and his wife set up houses for them. Alcohol was a particular bugbear of the social reformers, who blamed public houses for many of the evils they saw around them. Many poor or working-class men squandered what money they had on drink, leading to hungry and often brutalized families. Strong government action had greatly diminished the effects of gin (the 'mother's ruin' which had almost paralyzed half of London in the mid-eighteenth century), but other forms of alcohol, especially beer, continued to have a deleterious effect on society. Many evangelicals joined the temperance movement, which was extremely widespread for much of the nineteenth century not only in Britain, but in continental Europe and the USA.

The first temperance societies, which called on their members to renounce the demon drink, appeared in New York and Massachusetts at the start of the nineteenth century, spreading to Ireland in the 1820s and then to Britain and Scandinavia. Many of the prime movers in this movement were women who saw how their family income disappeared at the taverns that their husbands passed on the way home. One American woman who campaigned vigorously for the banning of alcohol was Frances Willard (1839–98), who became secretary of the Women's Christian Temperance Union and edited the Chicago *Daily Post*. More extreme was Carry Nation (1846–1911), who believed that her campaign was divinely ordained. When mere campaigning failed, Nation tried praying in front of taverns, before attacking them single-handedly with a hatchet.

As all this suggests, for nineteenth-century evangelicals social action and preaching the gospel were closely linked. This applied to overseas missions as well. In particular, the concern about the slave trade, and the interest in Africa that it promoted, was an important factor in the rise of Protestant mission during this period, in both Britain and America. In past centuries, Protestants had been far less interested in missions abroad than Catholics had been: indeed, many of the first Protestant Reformers had regarded mission as an intrinsically Catholic undertaking and therefore suspicious. Now, however, there would be a remarkable revolution within the Protestant churches,

Talk about the questions of the day; there is but one question, and that is the gospel. It can and will correct everything needing correction.

William Gladstone

especially the socially concerned evangelicals – paradoxically triggered, in part, by the very slave trade that had helped to throttle Catholic missions to Africa in the eighteenth century. We shall see more of this important element of evangelicalism in the next chapter.

INDUSTRIAL PHILANTHROPY

Some factory owners and other industrialists recognized the great power they had over the lives of their workers and tried to use it to improve the workers' lot. Many of these patrician industrialists were Dissenters, and so they sought to create model societies for their workers run along evangelical principles. Probably the most famous of these communities was Saltaire, founded by Sir Titus Salt, a Congregationalist mill owner in Bradford. Starting in the 1850s, he laid out a new housing development surrounding his new mill, intended to provide good quality housing and other amenities, such as schools, libraries and sports facilities for his workers. The community was something of a utopia, right next door to some of the worst slums in the country – though it fell into disrepair in the 1890s as the Salt empire collapsed.

The end of Saltaire coincided with the rise of Bourneville, founded in the 1890s by the Cadbury brothers, George and Richard. The Cadburys were Quakers, involved in the temperance movement – indeed, their family had gone into chocolate-making partly in the hope of promoting hot chocolate as an alternative to alcohol. They set out to make Bourneville a model community for the people who worked in their chocolate factory. They built their village in an attractive rural location outside Birmingham and provided it with large houses (all with gardens), a hospital, a school and of course a chapel – but no pubs. Workers were offered holidays and benefits in return for pledging to avoid alcohol, and George Cadbury built a special-purpose holiday camp in his own estate to give holidays to workers' children.

ROMANTICISM

By the turn of the nineteenth century, many intellectuals had completely given up on Christianity as hopelessly outmoded, irrational and superstitious. But, even as they were doing so, a backlash against Enlightenment ideals was developing, which would produce a resurgence in religion's respectability among Europe's educated elite.

A number of philosophers and other thinkers were producing trenchant criticisms of Enlightenment ideals even by the mid-eighteenth century. David Hume (1711–76), one of the most important philosophers of the period, made a penetrating analysis of the processes of learning and induction which led him to conclude that human beings are not really rational at all: they are led by desires and use reason to justify what they do after the event. He was a major influence on Immanuel Kant (1724–1804), the greatest German philosopher, who argued that

Immanuel Kant, in an anonymous painting of around 1790.

reason is reliable but only when dealing with the world that we can sense. Things that we cannot see or hear – such as God – are beyond the reach of reason. This meant that the complex metaphysical systems of many of the Enlightenment rationalists were useless, because they tried to reason about what is intrinsically beyond reason. There could be no proofs of the existence of God. For Kant, then, Christianity is basically non-metaphysical. There can be no reliable doctrines about God or anything supernatural – all there can be is trying to lead a good life.

So alongside Enlightenment rationalism there arose a new approach which tried to escape from the tyranny of reason. This would become Romanticism, and its godfather was Jean-Jacques Rousseau

(1712–78). Where the Enlightenment sages believed in reason, order and civilization, Rousseau believed in feeling, spontaneity and nature. He thought that humanity in its natural state had once been happy – the notion of the 'noble savage' – and that history since, with the development of civilization, had been a slide downwards, not a march upwards as most people thought. People like Rousseau and his intellectual heirs therefore argued that feeling was just as important as reason.

Here, then, lay the roots of Victorian Romanticism and even sentimentality. Throughout the nineteenth century it became fashionable to idealize not the Age of Reason but the Middle Ages, now re-imagined as a time of heroism, chivalry, and

Hegel and the dialectic

G.W.F. Hegel (1770–1831), who was born in Stuttgart, was greatly influenced by the German philosopher Immanuel Kant (1724–1804), but his understanding of religion is a bit more complex than Kant's. Whereas Kant, with his emphasis on morality, was in the mainstream of Enlightenment thinking, Hegel saw that the Enlightenment's view of religion was one-sided and inadequate. For Hegel, religion was about more than morality. It was additionally and mainly about the world's union with 'absolute spirit' (Hegel's term for God). Hegel believed that all reality is characterized by rhythms of separation and union, differentiation and identification. He used the term 'dialectical' to describe these rhythms. This dialectical movement is, Hegel believed, the key to understanding the divine Trinity, which (like all reality) is a life of differentiation and oneness. In Hegel's conception, humankind and the world as a whole are simultaneously 1) different from God and 2) united with God. We experience the first as alienation (for example, the alienation due to sin). We experience the second as reconciliation (as in the Christian doctrine of redemption).

In Hegel's estimation, the world's religions constitute a history of this dialectical movement of humankind's separation from and union with God. Moreover, this history is progressive, for early religions (the religions of China and Egypt, for instance) had only a hazy grasp of our union with God. Christianity is for Hegel the ultimate religion – the religion of revelation – because here for the first time in history there is a clear notion of union. This is expressed in the doctrine of the incarnation (the union of divine and human nature) and in the doctrine of the Holy Spirit (according to which we feel this union through God's dwelling within us). But even in Christianity there remains a residue of the feeling of alienation. This takes the form of our thinking of God as a being 'out there' in heaven, separated from us on earth. In philosophy, Hegel argued, this last residue of alienation is overcome, for in philosophy we come to know our union with absolute spirit with the perfect clarity of conceptual thinking.

Hegel's influence on theology was immense. On a negative note, it was in reaction to Hegel that the Danish philosopher and theologian Søren Kierkegaard (1813–55) launched what would later be called the existentialist movement in theology and philosophy. However, Kierkegaard was not simply opposed to Hegel; he drew heavily on many of Hegel's insights. On a positive

note, Hegel's emphasis on 'the idea of revelation' helped to make this idea one of the leading theological themes in the twentieth century. Theologians such as Karl Barth (1886–1968), Paul Tillich (1886–1965) and Wolfhart Pannenberg (b. 1928) were all indebted to the prominence of the idea of revelation in Hegel's philosophy. Hegel influenced as well the doctrine of the Trinity. In Hegel's day, there was not much interest in this doctrine. But its prominence in Hegel's thought directly and indirectly led to a renaissance of Trinitarian thought in the twentieth century, with theologians such as Jürgen Moltmann (b. 1926) acknowledging their dependence on Hegel. Finally, Hegel's dialectical thought introduced into theology (and philosophy) the language of alienation and otherness. Theologians such as Barth, Tillich and Moltmann incorporated the ideas of alienation and otherness into their theologies in powerful ways.

SAMUEL POWELL

courtly love. The enormously popular 'historical' novels of Sir Walter Scott helped to create this image of the Middle Ages that remains powerful even today.

ROMANTIC THEOLOGY

For the Romantics, the love of emotion and nature was almost a religion in itself. God was no longer intellectualized and analyzed; instead he was experienced and felt through the beauty of nature. Many Romantics thus had pantheist tendencies, identifying God and nature to some degree. But others used the insights of Romanticism to approach Christianity in a new way. The most important of these was Friedrich Schleiermacher (1768–1834), who was raised by the Moravians but felt alienated by their inability to address the questions and doubts that plagued him. He then studied at the University of Halle, where he read the newly published works of Kant. Kant's insistence that God is beyond the access of reason made a great impression on him. In 1799, now working as a Lutheran minister, Schleiermacher published his famous *On religion: speeches to its cultured despisers*. In this brilliantly argued rhetorical piece, Schleiermacher insisted that the Enlightenment sages who dismissed religion as superstitious or irrational had got it all wrong. They were so obsessed with 'reason' they had forgotten there was anything else to human nature. But human beings are not just rational creatures – they have emotions and feelings too, and Schleiermacher focused on this concept of 'feeling'. Feeling, he believed, is something that accompanies every part of life, and feeling is the realm of religion, for it is through feeling that we are aware of God. So to try to lead a full human life whilst ignoring religion is impossible: religion is part and parcel of what it is to be human, because it develops the feeling side of our natures just as philosophy or science develop the rational side.

Schleiermacher's work made a huge impression upon the intellectual world. Equally significant was his later *The Christian Faith*, written in the 1820s and 30s, when its author was rector of the University of Berlin. He maintained the idea that religion is basically about 'feeling', that is, an existential sense of dependence upon God, and that in Christianity this 'feeling' revolves around salvation through Christ. Doctrines, such as those formulated by different churches over the centuries, are expressions of this feeling, rather like somebody trying to describe an emotion by putting it into words. For example, the traditional divine attributes – God's omnipotence, omniscience and moral perfection – are actually ways of describing our experience of God's action, rather than objective claims about God himself. God is that which acts upon people, not that which is described by people.

Schleiermacher's systematic rethinking of Christian doctrine would be extremely influential throughout the nineteenth century. Far less influential in his day – but more so in recent years – was a contemporary of his named Søren Kierkegaard. Unlike the pleasant and warm-hearted Schleiermacher, Kierkegaard was a rather peculiar character, melancholy and obsessed with his own unhappy love affairs. He was hardly known outside his native Denmark when he died in 1855 at the age of 42. Like Schleiermacher, Kierkegaard was deeply influenced by Kant's revolution, insisting that God is not something that can be the object of reason or knowledge: instead, God is one who acts. The key question in Christianity, for Kierkegaard, is how we respond to him. Life is about choices – not simply between different courses of action in the here and now, but between different lifestyles. And Kierkegaard suggested that the only satisfying lifestyle is the life of faith, where the individual stops trying to be rational and simply responds directly to the commands of God, just as Abraham was obeying God's command to kill his son, even though it seemed contrary to reason and morality to do so.

Although very different from each other, the work of Schleiermacher and Kierkegaard testified to a new way of thinking about Christianity, one that tried to take into

Faith means just that blessed unrest, deep and strong, which so urges the believer onward that he cannot settle at ease in the world and anyone who was quite at ease would cease to be a believer.

Søren Kierkegaard, *The gospel of sufferings*

account what it is *like* to lead a life of faith or to experience the power of God. Rather than rest content with the old formulations about doctrine and ethics, and a clear line between the two, they were trying to produce a more integrated approach to Christian faith. It was an approach with its roots partly in Kant, but it was very different from the alternative line of thought that was developing at the same time, the line of German Idealism exemplified by Hegel. For the Romantic tradition also drew its inspiration from Pietism, which remained a powerful force in German religion.

THE CRISIS OF FAITH

But even as Romanticism was gathering force and new theologians were taking stock of its insights, the Enlightenment project was still alive and well. The progress of the natural sciences was accelerating, and science itself, as opposed to philosophy, was rapidly becoming a quite distinct subject (the word 'scientist' itself was coined in the early nineteenth century by the Cambridge scholar William Whewell). In the seventeenth and eighteenth centuries, science had been used in support of religion. Isaac Newton, for example, had insisted that although the laws he had described could explain how the universe kept running, they could not explain where it came from in the first place, and one had to speak of God to do that. But by the nineteenth century, this attitude was eroding: science was getting good enough not to need God as an explanation at all. And as the intellectual world of Europe became more and more hostile to traditional religious categories, so Christianity faced what has become known as the 'Crisis of Faith'.

There was a number of elements to this crisis. One was new research in religious history, textual criticism and archaeology, which cast serious doubt over the historical reliability of the Bible. We shall look at that shortly. Far more important to the popular mind, however, was the rise of new sciences

that apparently undermined the Bible even more damningly. The early nineteenth century, for example, saw the development of the earth sciences. Scientists such as James Hutton and William Smith put forward a new understanding of geological history, according to which the age of the earth had to be drastically revised: rather than being a few thousand years old, it must be hundreds of thousands or even millions of years old.

Linked to this was the new emphasis within biology upon the development of life. The existence of different fossils at different layers in the geological strata indicated a succession of different kinds of animals and plants throughout history. Some scientists, such as Baron Cuvier, came up with the theory of 'catastrophism', according to which God had sent massive planet-wide disasters to wipe out all life before replacing it with a new set of creatures. Others, such as Cuvier's bitter rival Jean-Baptiste Lamarck, suggested 'transformism', the idea that each set of creatures had evolved gradually out of the old ones rather than replacing them in one fell swoop. From a religious point of view, the argument raised a major question, put neatly by Charles Babbage (1791–1871) in his *Ninth Bridgwater treatise* of 1837:

I intreat the reader to consider well the difficulties which it is necessary to meet. 1st. The Church of England, if we may judge by the writings of those placed in authority, has hitherto considered it to have been expressly stated in the book of Genesis, that the earth was created about six thousand years ago. 2dly. Those observers and philosophers who have spent their lives in the study of Geology, have arrived at the conclusion that there exists irresistible evidence, that the date of the earth's first formation is far anterior to the epoch supposed to be assigned to it by Moses; and it is now admitted by all competent persons, that the formation even of those strata which are nearest the surface must have occupied vast periods – probably millions of years – in arriving at their present state.

Darwinism

In 1859 Charles Darwin (1809–82), a respected English natural historian, published *On the origin of species by means of natural selection*. This book sought to account for two important phenomena: the transformation and the proliferation of species. Darwin noted that small differences, or variations, seemed to occur 'at random' among individuals within a species. He held that generally speaking, individuals that possessed variations giving them an edge in the competition for resources would be most likely to survive and leave offspring. Because the offspring would typically inherit the useful variations, they would be perpetuated and eventually become more numerous within a species. After many generations, populations of organisms that were the beneficiaries of 'natural selection' had diverged so greatly from original ancestral populations that they had become different species.

Darwin continued to refine and elaborate his theory. In 1871 he published his two-volume *The descent of man, and selection in relation to sex*, in which he traced humanity's physical characteristics to earlier species and blurred the distinction between the intellect and 'moral sense' of human beings and the mental capacities of other animals. By 1875, although few scientists were prepared to go as far as Darwin in ascribing the history of the organic world to the efficacy of natural selection, most of them did endorse the idea that species are the product of gradual change over time.

Many Christian thinkers had expressed concern about the religious implications of evolution. This was especially the case in the English-speaking world. By the middle of the nineteenth century, few exponents of Christianity in continental Europe treated the interaction of science and theology as an urgent matter. In Great Britain and North America, however, theologians and clergy had placed great emphasis on the doctrine of the 'special creation' of species. The seeming inability of natural historians to account for the periodic appearance of new species well adapted to the conditions of their existence seemed to many Anglo-American Christians to be compelling evidence that those species were artifacts of a divine designer. And many spokespersons for the Christian worldview noted that the 'development hypothesis' undermined the credibility of humanity's special kinship with God, the 'fall' of human beings in the wake of Adam's sin and other doctrines central to the biblical narrative of the scheme of redemption. If the veracity of the scriptures could not be trusted on such important issues, they maintained, there was little reason to believe that they were the product of divine inspiration.

However, it was not until about 1875, when it had become clear that the scientific community had embraced the transmutation hypothesis, that its theological implications received sustained attention. Theologians and clergy wrote numerous books and articles espousing a variety of often sharply opposed views. Many joined natural historians in endorsing the theory of evolution and sought to reformulate Christian doctrines to bring them into accord with its implications. Some 'theistic evolutionists' assumed that they could reconcile Christianity with evolution by making relatively minor adjustments in biblical interpretation, doctrinal formulations, and arguments. Others used evolution as a springboard for more dramatic revisions. At their hands, not just transmutation but all natural processes became simply the modes by which an immanent God interacted with the cosmos.

Other Christian thinkers, persuaded that a gracious God had revealed the tenets of the faith through the medium of an inerrant Bible, rejected Darwinism. Many found the rejection of the transmutation hypothesis an appropriate occasion for embracing an even more 'muscular' view of biblical authority than that which had been accepted by many of their predecessors. In this way, opposition to evolution became one of the factors that culminated in the rise of 'fundamentalism'.

During the 1920s militant anti-evolutionists in the USA sought to pass legislative measures designed to exclude the teaching of human evolution from public schools. This effort, which received nationwide publicity in 1925 with the Scopes trial in Dayton, Tennessee, proved disappointing to its supporters. Changing their tactics, anti-evolutionists focused their efforts on shaping the content of biology textbooks. Between 1925 and 1960 those efforts bore fruit; high school textbooks gave evolution less attention.

Since 1960 both 'scientific creationists' and proponents of 'Intelligent Design' have been particularly avid in seeking to show that the Darwinian theory cannot be reconciled with the data of natural history. Thus far, however, neither the vast majority of members of the scientific community, nor the sizable group of theistic evolutionists, has found those arguments persuasive.

JON ROBERTS

Yet Babbage then added:

3dly. Many of the most distinguished members of the Church of England now distinctly and formally admit the fact of such a lengthened existence of the earth we inhabit.

In other words, not everyone saw a problem here. Babbage himself argued that the findings of geology were not incompatible with Genesis, because Genesis is a difficult-to-understand text from an alien culture. It may be that it is intended to describe how life *as we know it* came to be created, rather than life or the earth itself; thus Adam and Eve could have lived in a world that was already millions of years old. Others suggested that Genesis was a metaphor, not meant to be taken literally at all. By the 1840s compromise views like this had become mainstream, and the view that geology 'disproved' the Bible (or that the Bible 'disproved' geology) was a minority one. However, the issue was put in a starker form in 1859 when Charles Darwin published *The origin of the species*, the book that more than any other polarized opinion on the matter.

LIBERAL CHRISTIANITY

In the Church of England, those who still agreed with Babbage that science and religion could happily coexist formed a small but vigorous group known as 'the Broad Church', who felt that Christians should not simply reject new ideas out of hand but engage with them constructively. In a wider context, this approach was associated with liberal theology, one of the most important trends in the nineteenth-century European churches. Doctrinally, the liberals took their cue from Schleiermacher and Hegel; but they were also greatly influenced by the remarkable rise of biblical criticism.

THE CRITICS

'Biblical criticism' does not mean 'criticism' in the negative sense of 'attacking', although to many in the nineteenth century it seemed that way. Rather, it meant looking at the Bible in the same way as any other ancient text – as something written by human beings – rather than in a purely reverential or devotional way as something inspired by God.

Modern biblical criticism really began with Hermann Reimarus (1694–1768), a teacher of oriental languages in Hamburg. Unknown to all around him, he had secretly come to reject Christianity and the reliability of the Bible. In the 1770s the German author and playwright Gotthold Lessing (1729–81) published some fragments of his writings in which it was argued that, far from being the Son of God, Jesus was actually a political revolutionary who failed in his aims; but after his death

The *Beagle* being hailed by natives in the Tierra del Fuego Archipelago, Argentina, in a painting by the ship's topographic artist, Conrad Martens (1801–78). Charles Darwin sailed with the *Beagle* on this surveying voyage between 1831 and 1836 as a companion for the captain, Robert Fitzroy, and during the trip collected much of the data on which he based his theory of evolution by natural selection.

his disciples re-invented him as a divine being who had been vindicated after all by supposedly being raised from the dead. The resurrection, on this view, was simply a fraud.

By publishing these ideas, Lessing caused a storm, and he was careful to dissociate himself from them. But it did help to start the critical study of the Bible – for what if Jesus, as presented in the Gospels, was really a theological construct invented to conceal a quite different reality?

The end of the eighteenth century saw a sudden rash of scholars intent upon putting the Bible under the most thorough examination possible, and most of them concluded that all was not as it seemed.

Johann Gottfried Eichhorn (1752–1827) of Jena and later Göttingen University pioneered the critical study of the Old Testament, arguing that most of its books were not really the work of single authors but had passed through a number of revisions over the years. In a move many found shocking, Eichhorn dealt with the stories of the Old Testament in the same way he dealt with tales from other cultures, labelling them all 'myths'. No one before had thought the stories of the Bible might be considered the same 'genre' as the stories of, say, classical Greek mythology. But the nineteenth century saw increasing acceptance of this approach among scholars, especially as advances in other fields helped to put the Bible stories into more context. A landmark advance in this was the discovery, in the 1840s, of thousands of clay tablets at Nineveh bearing an epic poem even older than the Old Testament, the *Epic of Gilgamesh*. This featured what appeared to be an alternative version of the flood story from Genesis. In this version, the man who survived the flood in a boat and released birds to check when the waters had receded was named Utnapishtim, not Noah. And this flood was sent by the Sumerian gods, not by the Lord of the Israelites. The similarities between the stories were too close to be coincidence – yet the differences were also too many simply to regard them as the same story with different names. Could it be that the biblical story was simply a variant of this pagan myth? And, if so, why believe in Noah rather than in Utnapishtim?

Ferdinand Baur (1792–1860), one of the first great scholars of Tübingen, the centre of biblical criticism, extended the critical methods to the New Testament. He argued that many New Testament books had not really been written by the authors assigned by tradition, and indeed some of them were of much later date than had been supposed: for example, the letters to the Romans, Corinthians and Galatians were the only genuine writings of Paul in the New Testament, and the letters to Titus and Timothy were actually written in the second century to attack Gnosticism. Baur also proposed the thesis that we saw briefly in the first chapter, that the first-century church was massively split between Paul on the one hand and Peter and James on the other, and that because Paul's side 'won', the New Testament was highly biased in his favour and written, in part, to conceal the earlier divisions.

Perhaps the most famous scholar was Julius Wellhausen (1844–1918), who in 1875 published his mammoth *Prolegomena to the History of Ancient Israel*. By examining the different names for God in the Pentateuch, Wellhausen argued that the Pentateuch had been compiled from four different sources, each of which not only used a different name for God but had distinct concerns and theological views. These sources had been combined by a later author. As a result, the history of the

Hebrews was quite different from how it was traditionally understood. The traditional account was that Moses came first and wrote the Pentateuch, containing the Law, which the Israelites subsequently ignored at certain periods, which is why the prophets were sent to remind them about it. Instead, Wellhausen and his followers argued that the prophets represented a more primitive stage in Israel's religious history, and the Law developed in *response* to their teaching. After all, the books of the Prophets in the Old Testament never refer to the Law or to Moses, which is very odd if those prophets were meant to be *reminding* people about the Law! It was therefore suggested that the 'history' of early Israel in the time of Moses was compiled by later writers – working after many of the prophets – in order to give the newly developed Law more antiquity. Moses, on this view, was thus something like King Arthur, a possibly historical figure, but one whose traditional image owes more to later myth-making than to real history.

At the same time, a number of scholars offered more conservative readings of the evidence. J. B. Lightfoot (1828–99), one of the leading English New Testament scholars, argued that many of the New Testament books were not really written as late as Baur had claimed. As a rule, the German scholars were more radical and the English ones far more conservative; however, the Germans were for the most part leading the field in originality and scope.

LIBERAL THEOLOGY

A number of theologians tried to use the new findings of higher criticism in their work. Probably the most famous example of this was David Strauss, who studied at Tübingen under Baur and at Berlin under Schleiermacher. In 1835, at just 27, he gave an unsuspecting world *The Life of Jesus Critically Examined*.

It was a sensation. Strauss examined the Gospels and concluded that a great deal of the events they depict had never happened, especially the miracles; they were stories that the early Christians told to 'externalize'

One cannot arrive at and maintain individual conviction of faith in isolation from the already existing community of faith.

Albrecht Ritschl

spiritual truths. For example, when we are told that Jesus fed 5,000 people with just a few bits of bread and fish, this was really expressing the idea that Jesus provides spiritual nourishment to his followers. This was an advance on the views of some earlier 'rationalist' scholars, who had suggested that the miracle stories described real events but had rational explanations – for example, Jesus had inspired the 5,000 to produce their own lunches and share them around. Strauss's view that the miracles had not happened *at all* was far more radical.

Strauss, a Lutheran deeply influenced by Hegel, intended his book to be a reinterpretation of Christianity. But many readers regarded it as an outright attack, and Strauss's career in the church was finished. The novelist George Eliot, who translated *The Life of Jesus* into English in 1846, lost her faith in the process, and it has been said that the philosopher Friedrich Nietzsche also abandoned Christianity after reading it.

A more influential figure was Albrecht Ritschl (1822–89), who became a professor of theology at Bonn in 1851 and then Güttingen in 1864. Like Schleiermacher, Ritschl believed that Christianity boils down to the experience of God, in particular the experience of justification through Christ. This is expressed communally. That is, the justified individual forms a society with others, working in a spirit of love and community. This, argued Ritschl, is what Jesus meant when he talked about 'the kingdom of God', and it is this that makes Christianity relevant to all ages. Although influenced by Schleiermacher, Ritschl also drew inspiration from Kant in his understanding of Christianity as, basically, 'about' leading a good life.

Terms such as 'liberalism' and 'liberal theology' can be very vague, much like 'evangelicalism'. Here they are used to refer to the basic position offered by Ritschl, which was shared by a number of other theologians (mostly German), especially Ernst Troeltsch (1865–1923) and Adolf von Harnack (1851–1930), who both helped to popularize liberal theology in the early twentieth century. All these theologians were happy to accept the basic findings of higher criticism as well as modern science, and either integrate them into their theology or just take them for granted. A similar movement known as 'modernism' developed in the USA at this time, which also sought to reconcile Christianity with modern science and higher criticism. Probably the most important figure in this movement was Shailer Mathews, dean of the divinity school at the University of Chicago, whose *The Faith of Modernism*, published in 1924, set out the basic principles of the movement. Mathews believed that the basic doctrines of Christianity, although essential, needed to be re-thought in the light of the new, modern worldview. In this way, Christianity could regain its relevance and its moral authority.

THE SOCIAL GOSPEL

The aims of liberal theology and modernism alike were also connected to those of the social gospel movement, which combined them with the concerns of the Christian social reformers. The godfather of the movement was John Frederick Maurice (1805–72), the son of a Unitarian who became an Anglican priest and brilliant academic. Maurice was a 'Broad Churchman', who became professor of both English and divinity at King's College, London, but lost both jobs in 1853 when the college judged his *Theological Essays* too heterodox. Despite the suspicion with which many regarded him, Maurice did not accept the more extreme kinds of German liberalism. Instead, Maurice devoted himself to improving the education of the poorer classes, setting up colleges for women and for working men. He helped to inspire the establishment of the Christian Social Union, established in 1889 with Brooke Foss Westcott, a leading biblical scholar, as its president.

The social gospel movement proper is often seen to have started with an American, Walter Rauschenbusch (1861–1918). Raised in a traditional Baptist family, Rauschenbusch found his faith shaken when he went to college and learned of higher criticism. He became

…no man shares his life with God whose religion does not flow out, naturally and without effort, into all relations of his life and reconstructs everything that it touches. Whoever uncouples the religious and the social life has not understood Jesus. Whoever sets any bounds for the reconstructive power of the religious life over the social relations and institutions of men, to that extent denies the faith of the Master.

Walter Rauschenbusch, *Christianity and the social crisis*, 1910 deeply influenced by liberal theology, especially its emphasis on the kingdom of God as a human society based on love. He felt that Christians needed to recover this emphasis in the teaching of the Bible, which had become obscured by an obsession with the salvation of the individual soul after death. This was translated into a concern for real action after he worked as a minister in New York City's notorious Hell's Kitchen area for eleven years before becoming professor of church history at Rochester Theological Seminary.

Progressive politicians such as Woodrow Wilson were deeply influenced by Rauschenbusch, and so too were later Christian leaders in the vanguard of social reform, such as Martin Luther King and Desmond Tutu. Such views were even more prominent in Canada, where they spread throughout the theological colleges. One of the most important figures was Salem Bland (1859–1950), a Methodist minister who possessed enormous charisma and (it was said) the eyes of a prophet. Bland, based at Wesley College, helped to organize those with social gospel views into a powerful lobby group within the church. He was also a popular speaker in his own right and spread these views throughout Canada.

In Britain, meanwhile, ideas like these were a major influence on the newly organized labour movement. James Keir Hardie (1856–1915), a Scottish trade union leader, who had worked since the age of seven – and in a coalmine from the age of ten – helped to found the Labour Party to promote what would become known as socialist values. Hardie, a vocal campaigner for women's rights, Indian home rule and other progressive causes in the early twentieth century, had been raised as an atheist but converted to Christianity and became a lay preacher. His concern for social justice was based in part upon his Christian convictions, which led him to steer the Labour Party away from out-and-out Marxism and also to his stand against Britain's involvement in war.

This generation has grown up ignorant of the fact that socialism is as old as the human race... When the old civilizations were putrefying, the still small voice of Jesus the Communist stole over the earth like a soft refreshing breeze carrying healing wherever it went.

James Keir Hardie, *From Serfdom to Socialism*, 1907

The volume, it is to be hoped, will be received as an attempt to illustrate the advantage derivable to the cause of religious and moral truth, from a free handling, in a becoming spirit, of subjects peculiarly liable to suffer by the repetition of conventional language, and from traditional methods of treatment.

'To the reader', *Essays and reviews*, 1860

BATTENING DOWN THE HATCHES

But many in Europe and America alike were not at all happy with the solutions suggested by the liberals. They seemed simply to be caving in to the enemy. Edward Pusey (1800–82), later to become one of the leaders of the Oxford Movement, visited Germany in the 1820s to study higher criticism. He came back astounded and convinced that the Church of England was completely unprepared for the onslaught of this 'fanaticism', as he called it. And when the more radical German ideas filtered into the English-speaking world, they were pounced upon as appalling apostasy. In 1860, for example, an Oxford academic named Benjamin Jowett (1817–93) edited a book with the unexotic title *Essays and reviews*, which contained a series of articles arguing that the Bible should not be viewed literally as a work of science and that perhaps not everything in it was true. The book was very mild by German standards of the day, but its contributors were damned in the popular press and some suffered in the church courts for heresy, since they were clergymen. The attack was led by Pusey himself, who successfully whipped up what was essentially a new witch hunt. Fifteen years later, a young Scottish minister named William Robertson Smith (1846–94) wrote an article on the Bible for the *Encyclopaedia Britannica*, in which he reproduced the basic ideas of Julius Wellhausen. As a result, Robertson Smith had to endure a storm similar to that surrounding the 'Essayists', which wrecked his health.

As these cases suggest, popular religion in the English-speaking world was almost entirely untouched by liberal developments overseas in the nineteenth century; and whenever it learned of those developments, it condemned them unequivocally. Liberals, on this view, were not Christians at all, though they might masquerade as such. In his article

Christianity and our Times, published in 1914, the American Presbyterian theologian Benjamin Warfield (1851–1921) commented that: 'Men cheerfully abandon the whole substance of Christianity, but will hardly be persuaded to surrender the name.' His target was people like the modernist Shailer Mathews. In his view and that of others like him, the 'Crisis of Faith' had a relatively straightforward solution, which was simply the rejection of the new ideas that seemed to conflict with Christianity.

THE CATHOLIC RESPONSE

On the Roman Catholic side, the rejection of liberalism and similar ideas was most associated with the indefatigable Pope Pius IX, one of the most remarkable men to occupy the throne of St Peter. In fact he occupied it for longer than any other man apart from Peter himself, from 1846 to 1878. Pius began his career as a political liberal, but he changed his views radically after 1848, when a revolution in the papal states ousted him from temporal power for eighteen months. After his return, he did not rule long over the papal states: in 1860, following his defeat in battle, the pope was forced to hand over all his territories apart from Rome to Victor Emmanuel of Piedmont. The process was completed ten years later, as Rome itself was taken and turned into the capital of the newly united Italy. The papacy's decline in temporal power since the heady days of Innocent III was complete.

Pius IX was a rather sweet and innocent soul – the revolution of 1848 had been caused, in part, by his decision to release all political prisoners upon his accession – but he was theologically highly conservative. Devoted to the Virgin Mary, in 1854 he declared as definitive the doctrine of her immaculate conception – meaning that although she was not the product of a virgin birth as Jesus was, her conception had been miraculously sinless, meaning that she did

Pope Pius IX opens the First Vatican Council on 8 December 1869, in a lithograph of the French school.

not inherit original sin. Pius insisted that this was possible because God applied to Mary's conception grace brought about by Jesus' death in the future, meaning that Mary's sinlessness was still dependent upon Jesus, even though it happened earlier. And in 1864 he published his famous *Syllabus of errors*, a comprehensive list of all the then-fashionable philosophical and scientific ideas which Pius believed attacked the faith of the church. The final 'error' which Pius condemned ran: 'The Roman pontiff can, and ought to, reconcile himself, and come to terms with progress, liberalism and modern civilization.'

In 1869 Pius called the First Vatican Council to address the crisis of faith that he perceived assailing the Catholic Church. The council was huge and dealt with an enormous amount of administrative and doctrinal matters, but it endorsed the pope's condemnation of the *Syllabus of errors*, and it went one better in endorsing the authority of the pope himself. It decreed:

> When the Roman pontiff speaks ex cathedra, *that is, when, in the exercise of his office as shepherd and teacher of all Christians, in virtue of his supreme apostolic authority, he defines a doctrine concerning faith or morals to be held by the whole church, he possesses, by the divine assistance promised to him in blessed Peter, that infallibility which the divine Redeemer willed his church to enjoy in defining doctrine concerning faith or morals.*

It is important to note that the claim was not that the pope is *always* infallible, but only when he specifically defines a definitive and binding doctrine. It is not clear precisely what circumstances are required for this to be the case, but to date, most Catholic theologians believe that it has only ever happened twice. The first time was when Pius IX defined the doctrine of the immaculate conception in 1854, and the second was when Pius XII defined the doctrine of the physical assumption of Mary in 1950. Some Catholic theologians argue that there are other instances as well, but

they are rare, at least compared to the number of binding doctrinal definitions issued by church councils over the centuries.

Nevertheless, from the moment it was defined, this doctrine was highly controversial. Gallicanism and related movements such as Febronianism were expressly opposed to it. When it became clear that the Vatican Council was going to endorse the doctrine of papal infallibility, a number of prominent Catholics attacked it: one was John Henry Newman, the most famous English convert to Catholicism. He objected not to the doctrine so much as to what he regarded as the undue haste with which it was endorsed. More virulent in his opposition was Johann Ignaz von Döllinger (1799–1890), a German professor and priest who became the figurehead for the anti-infallibility party and who used his considerable historical and theological learning to show that previous popes had disagreed with each other or even been heretics. Döllinger was excommunicated, and many others chose to leave the Catholic Church rather than accept the First Vatican Council. Known as the 'Old Catholics' (because they saw papal infallibility as an innovation), they held a council at Munich in 1871 and set up a new church structure. The Old Catholics survive today in both Europe and the USA, but their numbers are now very small.

THE PROTESTANT RESPONSE
If Pius IX's response to the Crisis of Faith was to shut and bolt the doors against it ever more tightly, a similar response was found among many Protestants, especially in the English-speaking world. On the one hand there was the 'High Church', or the Anglo-Catholics – those within the Church of England who wanted to recover what they regarded as its Catholic roots. The High Church wing was associated with the Tractarian movement in the 1830s and 40s and with the views of figures such as Edward Pusey, John Keble and (before he went all the way and converted to Roman Catholicism), John Henry Newman. High Churchers were keen on using ritual and

Without the pope there can be no church, without the church no Christianity, and without Christianity no religion and no society.

Félicité Robert de Lamennais, a French Ultramontanist who later lost his faith

If we would serve Him in His sacrament we must serve Him also wherever He has declared Himself to be and especially in His poor.

Edward Pusey

beauty in church services, and also on affirming traditional, conservative doctrines.

Added to this were the 'Low Church' or evangelical party. Many evangelicals in the Church of England became increasingly concerned to affirm traditional doctrine in the face of what they saw as the attacks of science and other modern disciplines. So, where Pius IX reacted to these attacks by emphasizing the authority of the church in general and himself in particular, the evangelicals did so by emphasizing the authority of the Bible. On this view, the Bible was infallible and supreme in authority, not simply in opposition to the church (the position of the first Protestants) but in opposition to science as well.

Some evangelicals were not keen on this, preferring a more open approach to one that simply condemned anything that disagreed with the Bible. The split between the two approaches was most apparent in the Presbyterian church in New England, which in the 1830s was divided between two groups called the Old School and the New School. The Old School, led by theologians such as Charles Hodge (1797–1878) and Archibald Alexander (1772–1851), stressed the traditional Calvinist doctrines – not only biblical authority, but total depravity and predestination. Those of the New School took their lead from Nathaniel Taylor, who emphasized instead the freedom and ability of human beings to respond to God. The schism lasted until 1870, when the New School finally satisfied the Old School that they had become more acceptably conservative, and they were reunited. By this time there was an increasing opposition on the part of many evangelicals to science and liberalism, associated with a new generation of Princeton Presbyterian theologians such as A.A. Hodge (the son of Charles) and especially Benjamin Warfield.

For Warfield, the Bible was the primary reference point for Christians. He insisted that behind the authority of the Bible stands that of the apostles, and behind them stands that of Christ himself – thus,

to doubt the New Testament is, in effect, to doubt Christ. We saw in Chapter 2 how some early theologians, such as Irenaeus and Tertullian, used a similar argument for the Bible's authority as opposed to that of 'secret traditions' and the like. Effectively, they understood the Bible's authority to be part and parcel of that of the church. But Warfield made a clear distinction between the two. The Bible is primary, and any authority that the church has comes only from the fact that it upholds the Bible.

This view characterized many theologians and churches alike at the turn of the twentieth century, especially in the USA. In 1910, for example, the General Assembly of the Northern Presbyterian Church agreed on five principles they held to be essential to Christianity: the inerrancy of scripture, Christ's virgin birth, his substitutionary atonement, his bodily resurrection and the reality of his miracles. These formed the core doctrines defended in a series of articles and essays by a wide range of authors – including Warfield – that were published in twelve volumes entitled *The Fundamentals* between 1910 and 1915. They were vehemently opposed to the conclusions of modern science, to Roman Catholicism and, most of all, to liberal theology. The name 'fundamentalism', from the title of this influential series, was soon applied to the movement. Although originally a rather mocking term, some US churches adopted the name 'fundamentalist' for themselves, since they felt that it expressed their attitude well: the doctrines in question were indeed the 'fundamentals' of the faith, to be defended against all attacks.

THE 'STRUGGLE OF CULTURES'

In the conclusion to his *Syllabus of errors*, Pope Pius IX commented that: 'for the last few years, a ferocious war on the church, its institutions and the rights of the Apostolic See has been raging'. It was a view shared

To take up the cross of Christ is no great action done once for all; it consists in the continual practice of small duties which are distasteful to us.

John Henry Newman, *Sermon 5*, 1833

In a time deeply marked by 'concession', at all events, it is worth our while to remember on the one hand that 'concession' is the high road to 'heresy', and that 'heresy' is 'willfulness in doctrine'; and on the other, that God has revealed his truth to us to be held, confessed, and defended... We are 'orthodox' when we account God's declaration in his Word superior in point of authority to them, their interpreter, and their corrector. We are 'heretical' when we make them superior in point of authority to God's Word, its interpreter, and its corrector. By this test we may each of us try our inmost thought and see where we stand – on God's side or on the world's.

Benjamin Warfield, *Heresy and Concession*, 1896

The Oxford Movement

The Oxford Movement (1833–45), led by a coterie of individuals from within or connected to the University of Oxford, was a religious and intellectual revival in defence of the Church of England as a divine institution, a branch of the wider church Catholic and a repository of apostolical succession and sacramental grace. The movement, whose acknowledged leaders included John Henry Newman (1801–90), John Keble, Richard Hurrell Froude, and (later) Edward Bouverie Pusey, soon attracted able and articulate supporters both within and without the confines of the university. The movement was sometimes known as 'Tractarianism', from the Tracts for the Times that its leaders published in the 1830s and 40s.

The movement's religious origins can be traced to a wider 'pietistic' reaction against the rationalism of the Age of the Enlightenment. The characteristic Tractarian ethos found expression in the theological notion as well as moral temper of 'reserve' which, in reaction against popular evangelical religiosity, manifested itself in an unwillingness to speak of religious experiences and sacred matters in familiar discourse and which dictated reticence when communicating religious knowledge. The movement's appeal was primarily to the ancient or early church in its practice as well as its doctrine.

The characteristic doctrinal and devotional teaching of the movement's leaders on apostolic succession, the doctrine of the church, the 'branch theory' of the undivided church, the sacraments, the principle of a Catholic Consent of Fathers and apostolic tradition and the ascetical principles represented by the duty of fasting and almsgiving, the value of celibacy and monastic retirement, found expression in a series called Tracts for the Times, published from 1833 until its closure after the publication of Newman's Tract 90 in 1841. The contemporary apologetic and polemical agenda of the movement in identifying with the doctrine and practice of both the early fathers and the seventeenth-century Anglican divines was reflected in the publication of two notable libraries of texts, the Library of the fathers (commenced in 1836) and the Library of Anglo-Catholic theology (commenced in 1841).

There was also an important practical and ethical dimension to the movement which was mediated through the preaching, sermons, homiletic literature, poetry, verse and hymns of its leaders and followers, with John Henry Newman widely recognized as a master of the homiletic art. The movement produced its poets in John Keble, Isaac Williams and others, and their verse, especially Keble's Christian year (1827), was widely read and influential even among those who rejected Tractarian doctrinal and sacramental teaching. Tractarian ideas also reached a wider social constituency through the more popular medium of novels and tales (notably those from the pens of William Gresley and F.E. Paget).

The movement soon attracted hostility from evangelicals, and it increasingly lost the initial guarded support of moderate high churchmen as it diverged from the standpoint of an older tradition of high churchmanship. Newman's conversion to Roman Catholicism in 1845 (he became a cardinal in 1879) and the secession of several of his Tractarian followers, notably W.G. Ward and Frederick Oakeley, weakened the movement but by no means heralded the 'catastrophe' that some commentators assumed. John Keble, Isaac Williams, Charles Marriott, William Copeland and many other Tractarian stalwarts remained in the Church of England and the Tractarians regrouped under Pusey's informal leadership.

It is possible to view the Oxford Movement at several different levels: as an ecclesiastical protest movement against the incursions of a liberal state; as a chapter in university and academic politics; as a theological restatement of both the corporate idea of the church and of the doctrine of the incarnation; as a restoration of patristic Christianity; as a renewal and reinvigoration of the sacramental life of the church; as a school for the pursuit of holiness and sanctity and a movement of personal religious and spiritual revival exemplified in the promotion of devotional manuals, alms-giving and fasting; as a renewal of public worship through a revival of the daily service and emphasis on liturgical forms and prayer; as a reaction against the alleged spiritual aridity and rationalism of the eighteenth century; as the championship of the notion of the quasi-medieval ideal of the Pauperes Christi against the inroads of political economy and Benthamite Utilitarianism; as a 'churching' of Romanticism, a sacralisation of the invisible world, a promoter of the concept of 'reserve' and of sacramental mysticism and typology, poetics and hymnody; as an indirect wellspring of ecclesiological and church architectural restoration; and as a 'completion' or fulfilment, rather than an outright rejection, of the earlier evangelical revival (many Tractarians were reared in evangelical households or had an evangelical early history). A balanced portrait of the movement can only be reached by recognizing each of these essentially interconnected and complementary elements.

PETER NOCKLES

by many. The traditionalists that we have just been looking at, both Catholic and Protestant, felt besieged by an increasingly hostile and secular society. At the same time, many outside the churches believed that they were taking part in the last stages of a historic struggle which had been brewing for centuries. The later nineteenth century was thus marked by increased secularism in the European heartlands of Christianity, and a new hostility towards religion among many.

SCIENCE VERSUS RELIGION
The struggle was exemplified by the famous scene at the University Museum in Oxford

in 1860, when Samuel Wilberforce, the bishop of Oxford, traded verbal blows with Thomas Huxley (1825–95), a fervent disciple of Charles Darwin. What was said at that debate has passed into legend and the truth is rather obscure: Wilberforce is said to have mocked Huxley's belief that he was descended from apes, while Huxley retorted that he would rather trace his family line to a worthy ape than to an intellectual charlatan. Huxley was not a Christian: indeed, he coined a new word to describe his religious views – 'agnostic' (or 'not knowing') – meaning that he did not know whether God existed or not.

But some who allied themselves with the new sciences were considerably more antagonistic towards religion in general and Christianity in particular. One was John William Draper (1811–82), a professor in New York, who in 1875 published *History of the Conflict between Religion and Science*. His basic thesis was clear from the title: religion was a great oppressive force which had always tried to stifle the voice of reason. Incidents such as the condemnation of Galileo were recast, not as divisions between different theologians or between different scientists, but simply as divisions between theologians on the one side and scientists on the other, and they were made to typify all relations between the two groups.

Another book making this case was *A History of the Warfare of Science with Theology in Christendom*, written in 1895 by Andrew Dickson White (1832–1918), co-founder and first president of Cornell University, where he taught history. He presented a more thorough case than Draper, arguing that in all fields, from medicine to law, the views of credulous theologians, attributing everything to miracles or divine action, had been gradually overturned by rational scientists discovering the real natural causes. In particular, White insisted that the 'scientific' understanding of the earth as a globe, known to the ancient Greek philosophers, had been suppressed by the church, which instead accepted the biblical model of the earth as flat with the sky

supported by pillars. On this view, Christopher Columbus had been a great visionary for his belief that one could sail around the world, and only in his day did the voyages of the explorers force the church to accept that it had been wrong. This was, of course, false: medieval churchmen had been well aware that the earth was spherical, and Columbus had been criticized before his voyage not for his belief that the earth was round but for his belief that it was fairly small and easy to circumnavigate – a belief that did turn out to be false. White simply distorted the evidence to fit his thesis.

As this suggests, the 'conflict theory' of the history of science and religion relied on very selective reading of the evidence, and historians have thoroughly discredited it since. It was based upon the unwarranted assumption that the then-current arguments about evolution were typical of other scientific or religious arguments of the past. Yet the remarkable thing is that, of all re-readings of history, this has proved perhaps the most durable. The notion that science and religion are inherently at odds, or that faith and reason are necessarily enemies, has become deeply entrenched in modern western culture and thought. Today, popularizers of science such as Richard Dawkins and Peter Atkins continue to repeat it, and the views of Draper and White resurface in the phenomenally popular novels of Dan Brown.

ANTI-CLERICALISM IN EUROPE
Meanwhile, attempts were afoot to secularize society itself in much of Europe. This often took the form of anti-clericalism, a rather vague term meaning general dissatisfaction with the prominence of the Catholic clergy in public life. Anti-clericalism had been nurtured in the eighteenth century under the influence of writers such as Voltaire, and it became especially strong in Portugal, despite – or perhaps because of – the strength of Catholicism there. The Marquis of Pombal, who ruled as prime minister from 1755 to 1779, not only expelled the Jesuits but

The antagonism we thus witness between Religion and Science is the continuation of a struggle that commenced when Christianity began to attain political power... The history of Science is not a mere record of isolated discoveries; it is a narrative of the conflict of two contending powers, the expansive force of the human intellect on one side, and the compression arising from traditional faith and human interests on the other.

William Draper, *History of the Conflict between Religion and Science*, 1875 broke off relations with Rome and tried to end the church's domination of education. A more sustained attempt to secularize the country began with a liberal rebellion in 1820. In 1822 a radical constitution was written, and the government largely split between the more radical elements and the traditionalists. The radicals' attempt to suppress the church failed, and in 1826 a constitutional monarchy was established. A series of dynastic wars followed, in which King Pedro IV (former emperor of Brazil) emerged as victor before abdicating in favour of his young daughter, Maria II (reigned 1826–53). Her reign saw the introduction of wide-ranging liberal reforms. The church, which had supported the conservative claimant to the throne, Pedro's brother Miguel, suffered greatly. All monasteries were abolished, and all priests in positions of authority in the army and the government were ousted. Catholicism still remained deeply rooted among the people, however – one in a hundred Portuguese was a Catholic priest – and for the rest of the century relations between the government and the church gradually improved. In 1901 many monastic orders involved in charity work were allowed to re-form. Yet only nine years later, the monarchy fell in a new revolution. The new republic was extremely anti-clerical, and the church was stripped of the property that remained to it. Wearing priestly vestments was banned, the timing of church services and bell-ringing was regulated and Catholicism was made illegal for members of the army. In 1911 church and state were officially separated. This extreme anti-clericalism was naturally repugnant to many in Portuguese society, and as we shall see in Chapter 14, the pendulum would swing back the other way within a few years.

Spain followed Portugal's lead to some degree. There, the 1830s saw the First Carlist War, a bitter civil war between two claimants to the throne – Isabel, the daughter of Fernando VII, and Don Carlos, Fernando's brother. Don Carlos represented conservative elements in Spanish society, including the church, but Isabel was progressive and anti-clerical. Don Carlos lost the war and was forced into exile, leaving the anti-clericals triumphant. Most of the monasteries were forced to close and the state seized all church property.

The year 1848 was marked by uprisings and unrest in many parts of Europe. We have already seen the political problems suffered by Pius IX in this year, and they coincided with abortive revolutions in France and Germany. In each case the revolutionaries were associated, in part, with anti-clericalism. In France, relations with the Catholic Church cooled gradually for the rest of the century. One big break came in the wake of the Franco-Prussian War of 1870–71, in which France was crushed by Prussia. A new republic was established with anti-clerical elements, which were mobilized in part by the reaction against the First Vatican Council and the proclamation of papal infallibility. Anti-Catholic resentment came to the fore in the early years of the twentieth century. In 1901 the Association Law was introduced, requiring all religious organizations to register with the state, which reserved the right to close them down. And in 1905 the Separation Act was passed, disestablishing the Catholic Church. Churches were closed down and a purge of priests in education carried out. However, complete freedom of worship was also guaranteed by the act.

But it was in Germany that the forces of anti-clericalism and the church would clash most bitterly. This was due in large part to one man, Otto von Bismarck (1815–98), the 'Iron Chancellor'. When Bismarck became prime minister of Prussia in 1860, the German-speaking states were still largely separate countries. Bismarck made their unification one of his missions, and the invasion of France which led to the fall of the monarchy there was part of this plan: he believed that the nationalist fervour this inspired would help the German states to come together. He was proved right, and from 1871 Germany was a single country, with the king of Prussia as its emperor and Bismarck himself as its chancellor.

Unity was always one of Bismarck's primary concerns, and he was especially unhappy about Roman Catholicism, which he regarded as an overly powerful segment of society with an undesirable attachment to a foreign power. This was especially so with the advent of the First Vatican Council. In the wake of this council, Bismarck began a policy he called the *Kulturkampf* (or 'struggle of culture'). He abolished the Catholic Department in the Ministry of Culture, appointing the anti-clerical Adalbert Falk minister of public worship. Falk expelled the Jesuits, put all education under state control and in 1873 he issued the 'May Laws', limiting the powers of the church. In the years that followed bishops were made subject to the state, and the state had the final word over who could be ordained. Religious orders were abolished, and priests were removed from the civil service. Pope Pius IX declared the May Laws invalid and threatened with excommunication any clergy who obeyed them.

The *Kulturkampf* was not successful. Catholicism remained just as entrenched in the southern states of Germany as Lutheranism was in the northern ones, and the Catholic Centre Party, a political organization which was one of Bismarck's primary targets, enjoyed increased popularity throughout the 1870s and 80s. His measures did create considerable bitterness, however, between Catholics and anti-clericals, which would be remembered for decades to come. In the short term, the policy was relaxed after the death of Pius IX in 1878.

It is important to remember that despite the efforts of ministers such as Bismarck, the rise of anti-clericalism and the attempts by certain governments to clamp down on Catholicism did not really make a vast difference to the faith of most ordinary people. Just as higher criticism and liberal theology were the preserve of an elite and remained almost completely unknown to most ordinary churchgoers,

Otto von Bismarck, photographed in 1890.

so too the advance of secularism was very limited during this period. It would not be until later in the twentieth century that it would bear widespread fruit throughout Europe.

REVIVAL IN RUSSIA

Russia also witnessed great social changes in the nineteenth century. Despite the efforts of the great tsars of the Enlightenment, such as Peter and Catherine 'the Great', the country still lagged considerably behind western Europe in terms of industry and general infrastructure, and it had not the income from overseas colonies and slave plantations that had provided much of the wealth of the western European nations. Its scattered, largely rural population could not raise the capital necessary to catch up with other nations, and there were fears that any attempt to do so would disrupt society too much.

There was great disruption anyway. Between 1850 and 1900 the population of Russia doubled, and industry accelerated in the western and southern regions of the country. In 1861 the conservative Tsar Alexander II authorized the emancipation of the serfs – those peasants who still lived under a medieval-style feudal system – in the hope that this would free up the agricultural system and produce more income. Unfortunately it failed to do so, and the disruption led to greater poverty for many of the former serfs and their owners alike.

THE *STARTSY*

Despite all these upheavals, Christian spirituality continued to thrive throughout Russia. This period saw the emergence of the *startsy* (or elders) as prominent figures within Russian religion. As we saw in Chapter 8, Russian Christians had a tradition of venerating holy men such as St Basil 'the Blessed', and the *startsy* were a rather less extreme development of this tradition. One of the key figures in their rise was Paisius Velichkovsky (1722–94),

Prayer, fasting, vigil and all other Christian activities, however good they may be in themselves, do not constitute the aim of our Christian life, although they serve as the indispensable means of reaching this end. The true aim of our Christian life consists in the acquisition of the Holy Spirit of God. As for fasts, and vigils, and prayer, and almsgiving, and every good deed done for Christ's sake, they are only means of acquiring the Holy Spirit of God. But mark, my son, only the good deed done for Christ's sake brings us the fruits of the Holy Spirit.

Seraphim of Sarov, to Motovilov, 1831

an eighteenth-century Ukrainian monk who was deeply versed in hesychastic mysticism. He became archimandrite (or superior) of the Niametz monastery in Moldavia, and his form of spirituality was enormously influential: he popularized the 'prayer rope', an old aid to prayer, which helped the user to count the number of times he repeated the 'Jesus prayer'. The rope remains the Orthodox equivalent of the Catholic rosary. Velichkovsky was also a scholar of note, and he researched the teachings of the church fathers: he compiled an anthology of their writings called the *Philokalia* (meaning 'love of beauty') which has been enormously popular ever since. This helped to trigger a revival of interest in patristic studies in eighteenth- and nineteenth-century Russia, which in turn led to a deeper spirituality, more in touch with the church's roots.

Another famous *start* of this period was Seraphim of Sarov, who entered the Sarov monastery, east of Moscow, in the late eighteenth century. He subsequently withdrew into the nearby forest and lived as a hermit, just as Russian monks had done for centuries, and became renowned as a spiritual teacher. A remarkable first-hand account of a conversation with this famous saint exists, written by a disciple named Motovilov. According to Motovilov, Seraphim spoke to him in the forest, sitting on a tree stump, as the snow fell around them. Towards the end of the conversation, Seraphim spoke of the need for the individual to possess the Spirit of God. Motovilov became alarmed.

Father Seraphim took me very firmly by the shoulders and said: 'We are both in the Spirit of God now, my son. Why don't you look at me?'

I replied: 'I cannot look, Father, because your eyes are flashing like lightning. Your face has become brighter than the sun, and my eyes ache with pain.'

Father Seraphim said: 'Don't be alarmed, your Godliness! Now you yourself have become as bright as I am. You are now

Russian prayer ropes made of wool.

in the fullness of the Spirit of God yourself; otherwise you would not be able to see me as I am.'

[…] I glanced at his face and there came over me an even greater reverent awe. Imagine in the centre of the sun, in the dazzling light of its midday rays, the face of a man talking to you. You see the movement of his lips and the changing expression of his eyes, you hear his voice, you feel someone holding your shoulders; yet you do not see his hands, you do not even see yourself or his figure, but only a blinding light spreading far around for several yards and illumining with its glaring sheen both the snow-blanket which covered the forest glade and the snow-flakes which besprinkled me and the great Elder.

ORTHODOXY GOES EAST

On the expansion of the Russian state, and of Russian religion, was still going on to the Far East. By the middle of the eighteenth century, settlers and missionaries had reached the Kamchatka Peninsula, jutting into the northern Pacific Ocean, and were looking beyond it. In 1741 Vitus Bering and Aleksei Chirikov sailed east and discovered the Aleutian Islands between Kamchatka and Alaska. Settlers moved in to set up fur trading stations, and in 1784 the first Russian colony in Alaska was established.

And missionaries also came, for there were people on the islands. One pioneer was Herman of Alaska, who arrived there in 1793 and preached to the islanders, also setting up schools for them. Herman ingeniously combined the role of missionary with that of *starets*, for he lived as a hermit on an otherwise uninhabited island near Kodiak Island. Here he became known as *Apa* (meaning 'Grandfather') to the locals, and he maintained his hermitage until his death in 1837. Some of the missionaries showed a remarkably tolerant attitude to the people they found. On one island, missionaries reported that the people lived in a society already so enlightened and in accordance with Christian morality that they were best left alone.

The greatest of the missionaries was John Venianimov (1797–1879), from Irkutsk in Siberia, a priest and school teacher. Like many Orthodox priests, Venianimov was married, and in 1823 he set off as a missionary to the Aleutians, taking his family with him, eventually settling on the island of Unalaska. Here, Venianimov built a hut for his family and set about erecting a church. Christianity

We will say it with the words of the Western powers. WE ARE SPREADING CHRISTIANITY AND CIVILIZATION AMONG WILD TRIBES AND PEOPLES.

A Russian steamship captain involved in the occupation of the Amur Valley, 1857

Spirituality in literature: the great Russian novelists

The great Russian novelists of the nineteenth century were all exposed to the ethos of Russian Orthodoxy, but some more deeply than others, and each was affected differently. Even those brought up in secular or atheistic households encountered Orthodoxy through their peasant nurses and servants.

Of the three most famous, Ivan Turgenev (1818–83), Leo Tolstoy (1828–1910) and Fyodor Dostoevsky (1821–81), the first became a decided if reluctant agnostic, yet gave a most sensitive portrait of a heroine imbued by a distinctively Orthodox spirituality in his Liza, the young heroine of his novel *A nest of gentlefolk* (1859), who eventually gives up her claim to human happiness and retires to a convent to pray for the world.

The great Tolstoy wrestled with religion all his life, at times experiencing acute cosmic anxiety, yet writing books and articles on theology, making his own translation of the Gospels, and eventually espousing a form of Christianity based on the ethics of the Sermon on the Mount and on Christ's injunction to love our enemies. Tolstoy attracted an international following during his own lifetime. He became a pacifist and a vegetarian, strongly opposed all forms of secular and religious authority, and was eventually excommunicated by the Orthodox Church, whose rituals he mocked in his last novel, *Resurrection* (1899). While Tolstoy's Christianity is rooted in the profound religious experience that he describes in his *Confession* (1879–81), it is to a great extent a faith of his own fashioning; it bears the marks of many of the world's great philosophical and religious traditions, among which Russian Orthodoxy plays a subsidiary role, and is conceived and presented through the lens of human reason. In his two major novels, *War and peace* (1865–69) and *Anna Karenina* (1875–77), the characters of Pierre and Levin respectively reflect Tolstoy's own unceasing, life-long search for religious truth.

Of the three, Dostoevsky's influence on religious thought has been the most enduring. Unlike his two great contemporaries, he had a pious and traditional Orthodox upbringing, but was attracted by European utopian socialism in his teens and was condemned to death by firing squad in his late twenties for a trivial political offence. His sentence was commuted at the last moment to four years in a penal fortress at Omsk and four years as a private soldier in Siberia; during the first four years he had nothing to read apart from the Russian translation of the New Testament. He experienced his escape from execution and subsequent release from captivity as a spiritual rebirth. Religion was never simply a social phenomenon for Dostoevsky: it was the very essence of life, and this fact is reflected in his novels, where what one critic has called the 'Easter motif' (of death and resurrection) structures all his major works. Some readers have stressed the atmosphere of Orthodox spirituality in his work, seeing it as the fundamental structuring principle of his world view. Deriving from the mystical traditions in Christian, and especially Orthodox theology, the Russian emphasis on '*sobornost*' ('togetherness' or 'conciliarity') and the Russian folk tradition of the holy fool, his saintly characters are admired as unique fictional embodiments of Christian life and of Russian spirituality. Such characters are Sonia in *Crime and punishment* (1866), Prince Myshkin in *The Idiot* (1868) and the novice Alesha and the *staret* (elder) Zosima in *The Brothers Karamazov* (1879–80).

However, against the Orthodox piety of Dostoevsky's later years has to be set the fact that he was prone throughout his life to moments of the most terrible doubt and unbelief. This is reflected in his novels too, and it is his ability to bring these two spiritual experiences together that constitutes the true uniqueness and glory of his major fiction. Alongside his saintly, life-enhancing characters, and in conflict with them, are atheists, agnostics and sceptics, murderers, rapists and terrorists, racked by what he called the 'accursed questions'. Some of the latter achieve spiritual rebirth; some of the former lapse into a state of confusion. Dostoevsky's world is a highly complex and modern one, which has retained its ability to speak to each succeeding generation of readers, including our own.

In seeking to set forth and embody in his last novel, *The Brothers Karamazov*, a Christianity that can lead to salvation, he confronts, and makes his characters confront, the most searching questions ever levelled at the Christian faith, questions about the suffering of innocent children, questions about whether Christ's gospel of freedom is a burden too heavy for humans to bear, questions about whether Jesus was utterly mistaken in his beliefs. Some readers have been convinced that his atheists and agnostics win the argument.

When we think of the spirituality of Dostoevsky's novels, therefore, we are not thinking of a world bathed in a tranquil spirituality and unshakeable faith, but of a world in which that spirituality is almost stifled and overwhelmed by evil, and yet constantly reborn in an infinite variety of different forms. The epigraph for *The Brothers Karamazov* is from John 12:24: 'Very truly, I tell you, unless a grain of wheat falls into the earth and dies, it remains just a single grain; but if it dies, it bears much fruit.'

Russian spirituality as expressed in the life of ordinary believers and their parish priest, steeped in superstition and folk traditions, is perhaps best depicted in the work of a Russian novelist less well known in the west, but greatly esteemed in Russia itself. This is Nikolai Leskov (1831–95), essentially a colourful short-story writer, although his novel *Minster folk* (1872) is an outstanding example of the genre. Leskov, like Tolstoy, was a voracious reader of European theology and biblical criticism. Unlike Tolstoy and Dostoevsky, he showed some sympathy for Protestant views, but ultimately he remained within the Orthodox tradition. In doing so, however, he firmly rejected the intolerance, censoriousness, political subservience and anti-intellectualism of the Russian church of his day.

MALCOLM JONES

had already reached some of the islanders, but there was still a great deal of work to do. Venianimov travelled extensively around the islands – paddling a canoe in the unpredictable storms of the northern Pacific – and learned a number of local dialects. Selecting the most widespread of these, he adapted the Cyrillic alphabet and began to translate the Bible and other Christian works, including hymns, for the islanders. His efforts met with success, and in 1829 he reached Alaska itself and began to preach there.

Venianimov's wife died while he was back in Russia publicizing the Aleutian missions, and as a result he became a monk, taking the name Innocent. But in 1840, shortly after this, he was made bishop of Kamchatka and the Aleutians, and remained there until 1867, when he became metropolitan of Moscow. As metropolitan, he not only reformed the church but helped to maintain the emphasis on missions east. He was personally much loved, and today he is remembered as one of the most important saints of the nineteenth century.

Under Innocent of Irkutsk and others like him, Orthodoxy became well established in the Aleutian Islands and western Alaska. That was shown by the bravery of a Christian islander named Cungagnaq, who took the name Peter at his baptism. In 1815 he and some companions were captured by Spanish sailors, who took them to San Francisco and tried to force them to convert to Catholicism. The Spanish cut off Peter's toes, one by one; when he still refused to convert, they cut off his fingers, joint by joint; then they cut off his hands; and finally they disembowelled him. Such a remarkable martyrdom is testament to the success of the Orthodox missions.

In 1867 Russia sold Alaska to the USA, although it did not become a state until 1959. The Russian colonies had been relatively small, but the missionaries had had considerable success among the indigenous people, which meant that, even with US ownership of the territory, the Russian Orthodox Church remained strong there. Today, there is still a much greater Orthodox presence in Alaska than elsewhere in the USA.

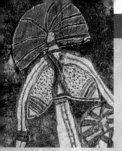

CHAPTER 13

THE AGE OF COLONIALISM

In around 1590, Cardinal Robert Bellarmine, arguing for the superiority of Roman Catholicism over Protestantism, pointed out how much more successful the Catholic missions around the world had been compared to the Protestant ones. The missions of the seventeenth century that we saw in Chapter 10 might seem to have borne out that statement. But the eighteenth century saw a gradual petering out of the Catholic missions, and in the late eighteenth and the nineteenth century their place was taken by the Protestants. A new age of mission was dawning, and it would prove to be even more wide-ranging and thorough than anything that had been seen before.

NEW WORLDS, NEW CHALLENGES

The new missionary impulse was, for the most part, organized not by the European churches themselves, but by new societies expressly founded for the purpose of mission. There was an enormous number of these, mostly set up and run by lay people, often of relatively low social status. One of the first was the Baptist Missionary Society (BMS), founded in 1792 by William Carey. More important was the London Missionary Society (LMS) a non-denominational group founded in 1795. That spurred some evangelicals within the Church of England to establish the Church Missionary Society (CMS) in 1799. While the British and German Protestants led the way in the new missionary endeavours, there was also the Netherlands Missionary Society (NZG), founded in 1797 and modelled on the LMS. This society concerned itself principally with

the Dutch East Indies, whose Christian population its members felt had been neglected by the colonial authorities there.

At least to begin with, these societies had nothing to do with secular imperialism: missionaries were sent to Europe or America as well as Africa, with the simple aim of preaching the gospel; and indeed the evangelical (and often Dissenting) nature of these societies made them suspicious in the eyes of most churchmen. Thus they were, if anything, counter-cultural rather than imperialist lackeys. This was reflected in the fact that they were also remarkably international in makeup: the CMS, for example, employed many German Lutherans. It was felt that the common faith in Protestantism – especially that kind influenced by Pietism and evangelicalism – overrode denominational boundaries. All Christians could cooperate in the spreading of the gospel. Here, then, was an important early appearance of the ecumenical spirit – although it would take a long time to spread to the leadership of the churches.

A good representative of the new emphasis on mission was Henry Venn, born in 1796 to a notable Anglican evangelical family (his father being a leader of the Clapham Sect). Henry Venn was a fierce advocate, in particular, for the rights of Africans, and he had a strong sense of their abilities: unlike many white people in his day, he believed that Africans were just as intelligent and capable as Europeans. In 1841 Venn became secretary of the CMS and sought to put his principles into action. He formulated the 'Three Selves' principle: the churches founded by the society overseas should become self-supporting, self-governing and self-propagating. This meant that a priority of missionaries should be to train local clergy to run the churches themselves, so that they could be independent of Europeans and launch missions of their own. Moreover, the churches that were founded should not be carbon copies of European churches: Venn had no interest in 'transplantation', the attempt to impose European culture upon other peoples together with European religions. Thus, although the CMS existed to send missions, those missions should ideally be temporary and end with 'euthanasia' (a 'good death'), because they were no longer needed. He likened the mission to the scaffolding, essential to the building of the church, but removed at its completion. Venn even dared to contemplate something very controversial: native bishops – even black bishops – an idea also vigorously supported by the evangelical preacher Hugh Stowell, who denounced racist attitudes wherever he found them. Thus, the CMS rejected the idea, popular with many Anglicans, of the 'missionary bishop', an Englishman sent out to be bishop of the area being evangelized.

Venn was typical of many involved in nineteenth-century mission, at least in the first half of the century. His US counterpart was Rufus Anderson, secretary of the American Board of Commissioners for Foreign Missions, and he had much the same viewpoint. Venn was influenced, in part, by the Jesuit missionaries to the Far East whom we saw in Chapter 10; and even though the advice by the Congregation for the Propagation of the Faith had not always been heeded there, the Catholic Church also maintained a similar viewpoint.

The most important Catholic missionary organization was the Holy Ghost Fathers, sometimes known as 'the Spiritans'. This group had been founded in Paris in 1703 as a seminary to provide better training for priests, and by the 1730s it was sending missionaries to New France (now part of Canada). The society was almost destroyed in the French Revolution and its aftermath, but it was effectively refounded by François Libermann (1797–1852), a French Jew who had converted to Catholicism (and been disinherited by his rabbi father for it). He founded a Society of the Immaculate Heart of Mary to evangelize former slaves, which began sending missionaries to West Africa. In 1848 this society merged with the Holy Ghost Fathers, effectively creating a new and extremely vigorous mission society. It established new seminaries throughout Europe and America for training missionaries, but the movement remained strongest in France. Indeed, the French were among the most important missionary nations in the nineteenth century: for most of the century almost all Catholic missionaries in Africa were French.

Like the leaders of the Protestant missions, Libermann was highly sensitive to the danger of imposing European culture upon other peoples. In a letter of 1847 to missionaries in West Africa, he wrote:

Empty yourselves of Europe, of its manners and mentality; make yourselves blacks with the blacks, then you will understand them as they should be understood; make yourselves blacks with the blacks to form them as they should be, not in the way of Europe, but

Henry Venn, by the British artist – and disciple of George Whitefield – John Russell (1745–1806).

Nations trespass against nations without alleged warrant. Then come the apologists with abundant political and moral arguments for the deed: finally, theology takes a hand, and provides the acceptable sanction of religion. Thus, Imperialism, from gross aggression, becomes a high political expediency or moral duty.

Nation, 66, 1898

leaving them to what is their own; behave towards them as servants would behave to their masters, adapting to the customs, attitudes and habits of their masters.

The Catholic missionaries did not always find it easy to follow this advice. In particular, it was hard to train African priests, since canon law insisted upon a mastery of Latin and a vow of celibacy, neither of which appealed to Africans. One organization that tried to find ways around this was the Society of Missionaries of Africa, known as the White Fathers, founded by Cardinal Charles Lavigerie (1825–92), archbishop of Algiers. Lavigerie was a historian, whose studies of medieval North African and European Christianity had inspired him with the dream of establishing new Christian kingdoms in Africa. Just as missionaries to European pagans had once 'converted' entire kingdoms by baptizing their kings, so too Lavigerie sent his missionaries – protected by soldiers, for these were dangerous lands – into Central Africa to attempt the same thing. Like other theorists of mission, Lavigerie hoped for a native-run church that would not be a simple copy of European Christianity, but he hit the problem of few native priests. He therefore recommended instead a system of lay, married doctors – for he believed that the task of the doctor was almost as important as that of the priest. These doctors could instruct the people in theology, even if they could not perform the sacraments. Unfortunately, the attempt to set up such a system had very little success.

THE SCRAMBLE FOR AFRICA

The story of African Christianity in the nineteenth century is enormously complicated. On the one hand, the missions and settlements of the earlier age of exploration had borne fruit, and there were Christian groups scattered throughout the continent – in addition to the much older Christianity present in Ethiopia. But at the same time, new waves of European missionaries began to appear. Thus, once again, different forms of Christianity would meet and, in many cases, clash.

THE FIRST AFRICAN PROTESTANTS

By the eighteenth century, the Protestant powers – Britain and the Netherlands, and also the Danish – had forts set up all the way down the western African coastline, especially on the 'slave coast' of West Africa and the Dutch enclave at the Cape of Good Hope. These were small settlements, existing primarily for trade. They had their chaplains, of course, whose duty was to minister to the settlers; native Africans were largely ignored. Indeed, the interior of West Africa – whose coast had the most trading forts – was mostly Muslim and often hostile to Christians.

However, the latter half of the eighteenth century saw the first Protestant missions to the Africans themselves. They were, at first, tentative. The first Anglican missionary in Africa was Thomas Thompson, sent by the Society for the Propagation of the Gospel in 1751 to Cape Coast Castle. He was no explorer, though, and he remained at Cape Coast for only five years.

More important were missions to Africa organized by black people. As we saw in the last chapter, Protestant Christianity had become widespread among slaves and former slaves in the USA and Canada, and also in Britain. Many were keen to bring Christianity to their continent of origin, and so we hear of the first black Protestant missionaries to Africa. One – the first African Protestant minister anywhere – was Jacobus Capitein, who was ordained in Holland (his dissertation, completed in 1742, was an explanation of why slavery was not contrary to Christianity). Capitein then left for Elmina, where on behalf of the Dutch Reformed Church he preached to his fellow Fante. He translated the Lord's Prayer, the Ten Commandments and a Reformed catechism into Fante. Yet

Capitein was not enormously successful. He was unable to integrate into Fante society, despite having been born into it: his Dutch masters would not allow him to marry into it, for example. His wife was white, and so he was more attached to the white community there than to the black. Capitein's ministry was therefore directed mainly at the 'mulattos' or mixed-race community which, as in all European settlements, had appeared as a result of traders taking local wives or mistresses.

The same was true of Philip Quaque, who succeeded Thomas Thompson at Cape Coast. Thompson had sent him to England to be trained, and when he returned he became chaplain to the community, in which post he remained until his death in 1816. Quaque also ministered mostly to the mulattos, opening a school for them and black Africans.

Such were the beginnings of Protestantism among black Africans. The movement received a huge boost, however, with the migration into Africa of large numbers of Christians from overseas. These were the freed slaves and their descendants, coming to start a new life in what they still saw as their home continent.

Les Colonies Françaises

Cahier nº 11.
Les Pères blancs de Monseigneur Lavigerie.

The White Fathers in Africa, in an engraving by L. Geisler from a school book, c. 1880–90.

SIERRA LEONE: AN EXPERIMENT IN AFRICAN FREEDOM

It was Granville Sharp, a dedicated anti-slavery campaigner in London, who conceived the idea of sending freed slaves back to Africa to build a new, self-governing colony. The government liked the idea, since it meant the removal of certain unpopular elements of society, and forced black beggars to take part. In 1787 the first colonists, made up of former slaves from London and a number of white prostitutes, founded Freetown on the west African coast. Things did not go well. The chosen site was close to forts used by British slavers. Soon most of the colonists either became enslaved again or began trading in slaves themselves. The local Temne people – who had not been consulted about the project – were hostile to the newcomers, and in 1789 they burnt the settlement to the ground. Ottobah Cugoano, an abolitionist campaigner in London who had himself been a slave in Grenada, suggested importing new settlers from the loyal black population of Canada. Fifteen ships full of former slaves or their descendants – from all over North America, via Canada – duly arrived in 1792, and the story of the settlement of Sierra Leone began properly.

The new settlers were, for the most part, fervent evangelicals of the kind we saw in the last chapter – indeed, the preachers David Ash and Moses Wilkinson were among them. As they marched off the ship clutching their Bibles, one group sang the hymn 'Awake and sing the song of Moses and the Lamb' – for they regarded this return to Africa as a new exodus to a promised land. As this suggests, Christianity played a central role in the life of the new colony. The Baptist and Methodist ministers who accompanied the settlers from Canada acted as 'captains' or community leaders, providing the kind of social structure which the first settlers had lacked. One striking element of this was the role that women often played in church and society. Many of their women were decidedly tough, having grown up as slaves in Virginia, and in Canada it had been common to hear the testimonies or even sermons of women in church. Now, back in Africa, women such as Mary Perth and Amilia Buxton set up their own congregations.

Barely had these energetic Christians arrived in Africa before they started taking the gospel message to the indigenous

Berwick Street, Freetown, Sierra Leone, in 1880.

Africans. There were plenty of willing listeners. When the Slave Trade Act was passed in Britain in 1807, the government tried to enforce it by policing the seas around West Africa and seizing illegal cargoes of slaves. These were all taken to Sierra Leone and given their freedom there. The population of the colony swelled dramatically, by 2,000 to 3,000 people a year – mostly people from what is now Nigeria, but some from much further down the African coast. New settlements sprang up around Freetown. The vast majority of the newcomers were mostly adherents of indigenous African religions, but many were convinced after their traumatic experiences that their old gods had abandoned them, and they were receptive to new ones.

Sierra Leone was considerably more influential than its location as a fairly small enclave on the coast of a largely Muslim part of the continent might imply. For one thing, its schools were excellent, with the college of Fourah Bay rapidly becoming the premier educational institute of West Africa, attracting scholars from Europe and students from across West Africa. Moreover, many people who had come to Freetown as rescued slaves planned to return to their homes elsewhere in Africa. By the 1830s and 40s, many were doing so. Their numbers were not huge, but they were highly significant as the bearers of the Christian message throughout Africa. Most travelled to parts of what is now Nigeria and so, for the first time, Christianity began to penetrate the west African interior. In 1840 a colony of these former inhabitants of Sierra Leone was founded at Badagry, on the Nigerian coast, and this functioned as a trading post and mission station.

Similar to Sierra Leone was Liberia, to the southeast. This coastline was settled by former slaves from the USA in the 1830s and 40s, and the country achieved independence in 1847 (hence the name 'Liberia', for its inhabitants were proud that, in their view, they were the only Africans to be both free and civilized). Mission here was a serious concern, and as in Sierra Leone it was primarily an Anglican affair. A succession of Liberian bishops established a large

Samuel Crowther.

number of mission centres in the area, with considerable success, although they did not reach as wide an area as the missions of Sierra Leone.

Other black Americans were evangelizing further along the coast, especially in Cameroon, where there was a thriving Jamaican Baptist mission overseen by the English Baptist Alfred Saker. One of his protégés was Joseph Merrick, a brilliant linguist who translated parts of the New Testament into Isubu. He was also a printer, able to print his own translations, giving a huge boost to both the Christian mission and to the spread of literacy – for, as throughout much of history, the two went hand in hand.

SAMUEL CROWTHER AND THE NIGERIAN MISSIONS

As this suggests, much of the most important mission work in Africa, especially in West Africa, was done by Africans themselves. None was more significant than Samuel Ajayi Crowther. Born in what is now Nigeria in 1806, Crowther was a Yoruba, one of a large group of people to the west of the old and declining state of Benin. Enslaved, and rescued by British government agents, he was sent to Sierra Leone where he was baptized and educated at the Fourah Bay College. He was ordained an Anglican priest in England, where his mentor was Henry Venn of the CMS. Crowther was exactly the kind of native priest whom Venn envisaged running native churches. In 1845 he returned to Yorubaland and the following year was reunited with his mother, whom, in a gesture heavy with symbolism, he baptized.

Nearby, at Abeokuta, Crowther preached to large crowds in the open air, with great success. Crowther tried hard to accommodate the Christian message to the local culture, understanding that, if the Christians went around destroying idols or condemning polygamy, they would be unsuccessful. Instead, he opened schools, something that pleased local rulers. The Christian community was boosted by more people coming from Sierra Leone – by 1851 there were 3,000 of them. These were Yoruba who had been enslaved, rescued, and mostly converted to Christianity; such was their influence that Christianity itself became, in a way, part of Yoruba culture to a greater degree than among any other African people. The main centres of Christianity were thus Abeokuta and Lagos, originally founded as a military garrison of the old Benin empire but by this time the most important city of the area.

In 1864 Crowther was made a bishop – theoretically of more or less the whole of West Africa, though in practice of a far smaller area. But instead of ministering to the Yoruba Christian community, he was sent as a missionary to the peoples of the River Niger. To the English authorities, all these peoples were pretty much the same, so it made sense to use Crowther in this way. In reality they were not the same at all, and Crowther, as a Yoruba, had much less success with the Igbo people to the east and the Hausa, who were mostly Muslim, to the north. But Crowther persevered. There was some success at the town of Brass, on the Niger Delta, where King Ockiya was baptized and the people embraced Christianity enthusiastically. But by the late 1880s the area was being largely run by the Royal Niger Company, which encouraged the alcohol trade and suppressed the missionaries. The church here largely collapsed, and the new king, Koko, a former Sunday School teacher, returned to the old religion.

FETISHISM AND SYNCRETISM

West African indigenous religion was generally referred to by Christians, both black and white, as 'fetishism' and its idols, statues and so on, as 'fetishes'. From a European point of view, all fetishism was much the same; and, while there were of course plenty of local variations, there were indeed common ideas or viewpoints. Most African peoples had a concept of a creator god, supreme above all else, but most also recognized lesser gods, spirits and other supernatural beings. There were often mediums, prophetesses and similar people who might go into trances and, it was believed, speak with the voices of some of these gods or spirits. The gods might also be given sacrifices, especially in West Africa – where even human sacrifice was sometimes practised, as the seventeenth-century missionaries to Benin City had found.

There was thus a problem for Christians, analogous to the 'rites controversy' in seventeenth- and eighteenth-century China. To what extent were fetishes permitted? Unlike the Jesuits in China, most missionaries regarded them as completely pagan and unacceptable. But the reality on the ground was complex. African religion tended to be pluralist in nature, happy to incorporate new gods alongside the old ones. Many people were therefore willing to listen to missionaries and accept their new God, and this explains the ease with which Christianity penetrated Yoruba culture. But it was often a syncretistic kind of Christianity, one which adopted traditional language or attitudes. The Yoruba referred to the Christian God as Olorun, the name of the creator god in their traditional religion. New hymns were written, in the Yoruba language, to the tunes of traditional Yoruba songs.

Such developments were welcomed by many missionaries, although they denounced 'fetishist' practices such as polygamy and the maintenance of idols. Indeed, many African converts themselves came to be among the most vociferous opponents of fetishism: William Wade Harris, whom we shall see more of in Chapter 17, was a notable example. But the

It is often asked whether Christianity or Mohammedanism is to possess Africa – as if the choice of Fate lay between these two things alone. I do not think it is so, at least it is not wise for a mere student to ignore the other thing in the affair, Fetish, which is as it were a sea wherein all things suffer a sea change.

Mary Kingsley, *West African studies*, 1899

The superstitious peasant of Germany, Ireland, and other European countries, while as at least a nominal son of the church he worships God, fears the machinations of trolls and the 'good little people,' and wards off their dreaded influence by vocal and material charms – a practice for which the African Negro just emerging from heathenism is debarred church-membership.

Robert Hamill Nassau, an American Presbyterian missionary to Gabon, *Fetishism in West Africa*, 1904 status of mission and the church as a whole in West Africa was changing enormously.

THE RENEWAL OF EUROPEAN MISSION

In the latter half of the nineteenth century, there was an explosion in European mission to far more of the African continent. There had already been stirrings earlier in the century. A major figure was Robert Moffat (1795–1883), a Scottish missionary who together with his wife was sent by the LMS to Kuruman, in the interior of what is now South Africa, in 1821. He was a guest of the king, Mothibi, and was allowed to set up a mission station – essentially a farm, with its own fields irrigated by its own canal. Moffat himself was a gardener by trade. Many people lived there, including many keen to learn at Moffat's school.

The 1840s saw the arrival of many more missionaries in the Moffat mould. From Moffat's Christian bridgehead at Kuruman, more pushed north, deeper into the previously unexplored interior: by 1847 David Livingstone (who married Moffat's daughter Mary) had reached Kolobeng. To the east, Norwegian Lutherans were starting to evangelize Zululand. And as missionaries pushed from the south of the continent, so they did from the eastern part too. The first was Johann Krapf (1810–81), a German sent by the CMS. Krapf spent several years in Ethiopia, hoping to use it as a base for further mission, but he was expelled; in 1844 he arrived in Zanzibar, the traditional focal point of trade along the East African coast. Krapf became based in Mombasa, where he spent thirty years studying the local languages and translating the New Testament into Swahili. In West Africa, meanwhile, more European missionaries, such as Alfred Saker, were appearing alongside the missions of Africans themselves.

There was a new sense among these missionaries of a great pan-African mission, with the evangelists in different countries aiming to move from village to village and eventually link up. Those in the west looked for a time when they and their eastern counterparts would shake hands in the middle of the continent.

The mission ideal was now becoming confused with a new ideal, that of the European exploration and dominance of Africa. In Britain this was partly inspired by the Scottish LMS missionary David Livingstone (1813–73), who returned home in 1856 after walking from Loanda to Quelimane. His exploration of the African interior set off an immense flurry of excitement. Livingstone described a continent ripe for exploration, one where, in his words, 'commerce and Christianity' might be imported together. Far from accommodating themselves to native customs and culture, as had been the received wisdom before, many missionaries now sought to replace them with European customs and culture. Such an attitude was not new – Robert Moffat had insisted upon English clothes for his converts, and wondered why they were reluctant to adopt them, since the English way of life was so obviously superior to the African one. But such a view was increasingly common among the missionaries. Many now believed that black people were intrinsically inferior to white ones, racist views sometimes associated with an enthusiastic but imperfect understanding of Darwinism. When he encountered missionaries like this, who patronized him and refused to recognize his authority, Samuel Crowther resigned as bishop of the Niger shortly before his death in 1882. Crowther was the symbol of an older, more sensitive approach to mission – and the times were changing.

Mission had previously been carried out almost exclusively by Baptists, Methodists and other Non-Conformists or by evangelical Anglicans; by 1850, however, it was generally accepted that mission was the responsibility of all churches. It became part of the general interest of European states in Africa, which led European powers to set out to conquer the entire continent. The 'scramble for Africa' which culminated in the Congress of Berlin of 1885, when diplomats divided the continent among themselves – mostly artificially, ignoring natural boundaries of geography or culture.

However, the European missionaries did

That we are aiming at the Missionary chain through Central Africa is no longer a question… Two good links we have already towards it – Badagry and Abeokuta and I am sure that God will give us… Ibadan… Next to that Ilorin may, by the providence of God, constitute a fourth, and a fifth will bring us to the Niger; and the same number again, if not less, to the Tchad, where we shall soon shake hands with our brethren in the East.

David Hinderer, missionary to the Yoruba, 1852

Would you like me to tell you what supported me through all the years of exile among a people whose language I could not understand, and whose attitude toward me was always uncertain and often hostile? It was this, 'Lo, I am with you alway, even unto the end of the world.' On these words I staked everything, and they never failed.

David Livingstone, 1896

In the work of elevating Africans, foreign teachers have always proceeded with their work on the assumption that the... African is in every one of his normal susceptibilities an inferior race, and that it is needful in everything to give him a foreign model to copy; no account has been made of our peculiarities; our languages enriched with traditions of centuries; our parables, many of them the quintessence of family and national histories... God does not intend to have the races confounded, but that the... African should be raised upon his own idiosyncrasies.

James 'Holy' Johnson, a West African preacher, 1873

The Hebrew could not see or serve God in the land of the Egyptians. No more can the Negro under the Anglo-Saxon.

Edward Wilmot Blyden, a black missionary from the Virgin Islands who worked in West Africa, *West Africa before Europe*, 1890

not simply 'bring' Christianity to a passive and waiting continent. The pattern of African-initiated mission was strongest in West Africa, as we have seen, but it was present elsewhere too. Missionaries brought word of Christianity, but those who heard it also took up the message and pressed on. Natural migrations of indigenous people helped to spread it far further than any European missionary could go. Christian communities which had been present since the explorations of the sixteenth or seventeenth centuries also played an important role.

Perhaps the area of Africa evangelized most in accordance with the 'European' model, where Christianity had earlier been unknown, was East Africa. Here, the missions were mostly carried out by the White Fathers and the CMS, in competition with each other, since the ecumenical spirit of mission did not extend to Protestants cooperating with Catholics. Buganda, a kingdom on the north of Lake Victoria, was evangelized by a number of missionaries, including the explorer H.M. Stanley (1841–1904), in the 1870s. Stanley and his assistant translated parts of the Bible into Swahili, so when the CMS missionaries arrived a couple of years later, King Mutesa was ready for them and very sympathetic. The leading figure was Alexander Mackay (1849–90), a Scottish CMS missionary, and he and the others enjoyed great success. The people of Buganda were very keen to learn to read – having hosted Muslim preachers in the past – and groups of 'readers' sprang up throughout the country, as people read for themselves and taught their friends. Their reading material was, of course, biblical translations and other works produced by the missionaries. In 1890 the first cathedral was built in Kampala, on the shore of Lake Victoria: it was an enormous hut made of wood and thatch.

CENTRAL AFRICA

A similar approach was used, again with considerable success, in the vast interior of the continent. Most of the immense Congo basin – Zaire – belonged to Belgium, while the French owned the areas to the north of the river and the Portuguese still held Angola, to the south. The Catholic missions in this region had largely died out by the mid-nineteenth century, but new missions were begun within a matter of decades, as different Catholic organizations competed with each other and with Protestants. The French Spiritans dominated the region from the 1870s onwards, under the leadership of Philippe-Prosper Augouard, the Catholic bishop of the region, and Charles-Victor Aubert-Duparquet, an extremely energetic missionary who travelled widely throughout Central Africa. These missionaries were well aware of the Catholic past of the region, and saw their mission as one of regeneration and a call to remembrance. They had some success, especially with the Lali and the Lari peoples of the region. Brazzaville, founded on the lower reaches of the River Congo, became an important mission centre. To the south, a Belgian missionary organization called the Congregation of the Immaculate Heart of Mary (or the Scheut Fathers, after the suburb of Brussels where they were based) was active. One of their number, Emeri Cambier, achieved a great coup by winning the friendship of Mukenge Kalamba, a powerful chief who was about to go to war with the Belgian authorities. Cambier and his companions walked through the jungle until they arrived at his palace door, whereupon the missionary produced – of all things – his ocarina (a wind instrument), which he played for the amazed guards. Eventually the king himself emerged and pledged his loyalty to the musician and to the Belgian authorities alike.

By the turn of the century more Catholic organizations were operating in the area. The Jesuits, under Emile van Hencxthoven, established a system of 'farm chapels' throughout Belgian Congo. These were small farms located near villages, which incorporated churches and catechetical schools and also housed local orphans. By 1902 there were 250 of these, caring for 5,000 children. But these farms were unpopular with many people of the area, who feared that the Jesuits were stealing children to populate the farms, and also with the Belgian authorities, who suspected the Jesuits of trying to create a state within a state, a 'new Paraguay', as they put it.

Where the Catholics led, the Protestants followed. The BMS set up a system of mission stations along the Congo itself, envisaging this as part of the 'chain' across Africa. This society, like others and like the Catholics, bought steamers to travel up and down the Congo, linking the stations together. One of the most important missionaries of this period was Henry Richards, who presided over what he called 'the Pentecost on the Congo'. Richards' simple preaching of Christ and the forgiveness of sins proved extremely popular, as did his own self-effacing character. On one occasion, his hearers asked him why he didn't obey the gospel commandment to give away his possessions; Richards therefore did exactly that, only to find that the people he gave his things to brought them back and asked for baptism instead. Meanwhile, the Presbyterians set up their mission at the town of Luebo, the centre of the Lubo-speaking area on the Zaire-Angolan border. William Morrison, the American director of the mission, planned the town carefully with squares and fenced gardens, and it grew rapidly.

SOUTHERN AFRICA

In the south of the continent, Christianity came with settlers. The Dutch colony at Cape Town had been captured by the British in 1795. Many residents – strict Calvinists who had no wish to live under British rule – fled north. These were the Boers, and their migration was known as the Great Trek, resulting in the founding of new republics, Transvaal and Orange Free State. Their Reformed faith was an essential psychological prop during such a stressful time. Boer social and religious life revolved around the family, since most lived on remote farms: every evening the head of the household would read prayers and a sermon as his family listened, as did the servants, generally 'coloured' or mixed race. Four times a year, all families in a region

would come together for *Nagmaal* (Communion), not simply a religious ceremony but a social gathering that lasted up to a week and dealt with business as well as religion.

Mission was not a priority among the Boers, who generally opposed the idea of black people being Christians. 'Coloureds' were all right, but they usually did not participate in worship with white people, and after 1857 they had to use separate chapels. Yet there was a sizeable 'coloured' population, the Griquas, who also trekked north and founded settlements of their own. The Reformed faith was strong among them, too, since culturally they were similar to the Boers themselves. And despite the lack of emphasis on mission, Christianity spread well beyond the Boers' and the Griquas' borders. For there were huge migrations of other peoples at this time as well, mostly from Zululand and Swaziland in the east of what is now South Africa. In the 1820s, for reasons that are not well understood, people began to stream out of these areas, heading in all directions, especially north. On these migrations – known as the *mfecane* – the migrants encountered Christianity, and, whether they believed in it or not, talked about it to others they met on their journeys. This phenomenon played a major role in the spread of Christianity in the whole of southern Africa, since it meant that wherever a European missionary went, no matter how remote the region, people there had probably already heard about Christianity.

For the nineteenth century did see more and more missions in southern Africa. One of the most successful was that of the Moravians, which had technically begun many decades earlier. In 1737 a Moravian missionary called Georg Schmidt had built a farm near the Dutch settlement at Cape Town and hired a small group of Khoikhoi labourers. He preached to them as they worked and, by the time he was expelled by the Dutch as a heretic seven years later, he had baptized a number of them. Not until 1792 did Moravian missionaries return. When they did, they found that Schmidt's converts had survived and taught their faith

...as Kaffir tribes have now become so thoroughly imbued with hatred to the 'white man'... as they have so resolutely and so perseveringly refused to give to the Gospel even an attentive hearing, it seems to me that the sword must first.... break them up as tribes, and destroy their political existence; after which, when thus set free from the shackles by which they are bound, civilization and Christianity will no doubt make rapid progress among them.

J. C. Warner, British government agent among the Thembu, 1856

Genadendal, the 'Valley of Grace', where Georg Schmidt established his mission station in 1738. Engraving by J. Needham, 1849.

to their children. The tiny church – without ministers – had continued to meet under the same tree where Schmidt had taught them, to read the Bible and to pray. Now it was the seed for a new Moravian mission, one which set up Christian villages or 'institutions' throughout the area, opening schools, educating the locals and winning many converts.

Missions sent by the LMS and the Wesleyans were soon jostling for space with the Moravians and they spread north, beyond the settlements and into the frontier. 'Mission stations' in the style of Robert Moffat's were the order of the day: small packages of Europe plonked in the middle of the vast African savannahs, depending on the good will of the local king. At these mission stations, locals were educated, taught English or Dutch and the principles of evangelical religion, stressing above all the importance of Sunday observance. Sundays were almost entirely devoted to Sunday school.

The Church of England arrived in South Africa after the Non-Conformists, but it made rapid strides under John Colenso (1814–83), a Cornishman who graduated from St John's College, Cambridge, and was bishop of Natal between 1853 and 1883. Colenso was a liberal-minded churchman whose studies on the Pentateuch had led him to reject the notion of biblical infallibility. The bishop of Cape Town tried to excommunicate him, but the authorities in England ruled that he had no authority over Natal. Colenso got on extremely well with the Zulus in his diocese, since he spoke their language and understood and respected their culture. Like the missionaries in West Africa, he spoke of Christianity in Zulu terms – referring to God by the Zulu name uNkhulukhulu, for example. Yet the mission was not very successful here; Shaka (c.1787–1828), the famous king of the Zulus, was never interested in Christianity.

To the south, in Lesotho, Moshoeshoe I (c. 1786–1870) was much more sympathetic to the missionaries. This area was evangelized primarily by the Paris Evangelical Mission, run by the French Reformed Church, that is, the Huguenots. Moshoeshoe's people, the

Sotho, already had some Christians among them, owing to Griqua influence. The king himself never quite converted, although he did pray in public to the Christian God, asking for forgiveness; he died on the morning of the day that he was due to be baptized. Interestingly, Lesotho was evangelized by both Reformed missionaries and Catholic ones at more or less the same time, giving the people the option of different Christianities to choose between. The Catholic missions were especially effective, as the Oblates of Mary Immaculate who organized them were very careful to respect Sotho culture and values. However, although several thousand people became Catholics, there were far more Reformed Christians in Lesotho.

AFRICA ASCENDANT: ETHIOPIA IN THE NINETEENTH CENTURY

Ethiopia had closed its borders to Europeans in the 1630s and continued on its own path. The seventeenth and eighteenth centuries had seen the Ethiopian Orthodox Church consolidate its hold on the northern part of the country in particular, even as Islam remained strong in the south. In Gonder, the capital built by the emperor Fasilidas, theologians congregated to argue about doctrinal controversies. These were in part inspired by the Catholic missions of the seventeenth century, and tended to revolve around Christology: was the church right in its ancient formula that Christ had one nature, or were the Jesuits right to say he had two? Naturally, the Ethiopian view prevailed, although new formulae were found according to which Christ was the union of human and divine natures.

The eighteenth and early nineteenth centuries were a bad time for Christianity in Ethiopia. The central power of the emperor diminished, and local lords (or *ras*) became largely independent. Even the abuna, the head of the church still sent from Alexandria, lost much of his authority, and often there was no abuna at all. The period was accordingly known as the Era of the Judges, after the period when according to the Old Testament Israel had no king; and many

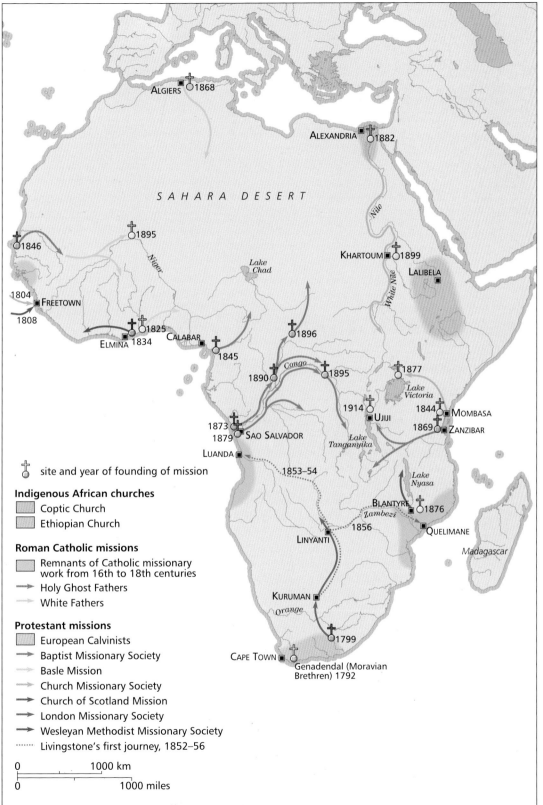

ALGIERS ◼ ✝◯1868

ALEXANDRIA ◼✝ 1882

SAHARA DESERT

Nile

✝◯1895

KHARTOUM ◼✝◯1899
LALIBELA ◼

✝◯1846

Niger

Lake Chad

White Nile

1804
◼ FREETOWN
1808

✝◯1825
ELMINA 1834   CALABAR ◼

✝◯1896

✝ 1845

✝◯1877

Lake Victoria

✝◯1895
1890 ◯

Congo

1914 ✝
◼ UJIJI

1844 ◼ ✝ ◼ MOMBASA
1869 ◼◯ ◼ ZANZIBAR

1873 ✝
1879 ◯ SAO SALVADOR

LUANDA ◼

Lake Tanganyika

Lake Nyasa

1853–54

BLANTYRE ◼ ✝◯1876
Zambezi
QUELIMANE ◼

1856

LINYANTI ◼

Madagascar

KURUMAN ◼

Orange

✝◯1799

CAPE TOWN ◼ ✝
◯ Genadendal (Moravian
Brethren) 1792

✝
◯ site and year of founding of mission

Indigenous African churches
◼ Coptic Church
▨ Ethiopian Church

Roman Catholic missions
▨ Remnants of Catholic missionary
work from 16th to 18th centuries
→ Holy Ghost Fathers
→ White Fathers

Protestant missions
▨ European Calvinists
→ Baptist Missionary Society
→ Basle Mission
→ Church Missionary Society
→ Church of Scotland Mission
→ London Missionary Society
→ Wesleyan Methodist Missionary Society
····· Livingstone's first journey, 1852–56

0   1000 km
├─────────┤
0   1000 miles

If God had allowed me, I had planned to rule all; if God prevented me, to die.

Emperor Tewodros of Ethiopia, letter to Robert Napier, 1868, two days before his death

When aroused his wrath is terrible, and all tremble; but at all moments he possesses a perfect self-command. Indefatigable in business, he takes little repose night or day... His faith is signal: without Christ, he says, I am nothing; if he has destined me to purify and reform this distracted kingdom, with his aid who can stay me: nay, sometimes he is on the point of not caring for human assistance at all.

The emperor Tewodros of Ethiopia, described by the British consul, Walter Plowden, in the House of Commons, 1868

looked to a messianic redeemer to come and help the church. Many others converted to Islam instead. Pagan religions spread throughout much of the middle of Ethiopia, leaving only the monasteries as islands of Christianity in an increasingly alienated landscape.

The early nineteenth century saw the arrival of European missionaries in Ethiopia. Samuel Gobat (1799–1879), a Swiss missionary with the CMS, came on a mission to the Ethiopian Orthodox Church itself, hoping to bring it more in line with Protestantism. This was a mission of religious reformation rather than cultural imperialism, and Gobat dressed and lived as an Ethiopian, calling for greater Ethiopian autonomy over a church which was still run by an Egyptian bishop. He tried to encourage the Ethiopians to read the Bible in Amharic – the language spoken by most people – rather than Ge'ez, and to stop venerating Mary, saints, relics and so on. Johann Krapf, by contrast, preached mainly to the Muslims and pagans in the south, hoping to create a new church that would unlock the door to Africa and create the chain of mission that so many missionaries dreamed of. His espousal of British superiority, however, led to his expulsion, and he had to transplant his ideals to Mombasa instead.

Much more successful were the Catholic missions. The hostility towards Catholicism that the seventeenth century had engendered was now mostly forgotten, and there appeared two great missionaries, Justin de Jacobis, a member of the Congregation of the Mission who worked in the north, and Guglielmo Massaja, a Capuchin, in the south. These two Italians both had great sympathy and understanding for Ethiopian traditions and stressed the similarity of the Ethiopian Orthodox Church to the Roman Catholic Church. De Jacobis, in particular, was an enormously charismatic man, who won the love of the people by travelling the country on foot, teaching as he went, and he had many converts. These even included monks, such as Ghebra Mika'el, a prominent monk of Gonder. In a kind of Ethiopian parallel to Newman's similar decision at the

same time, he converted to Catholicism in 1845. Many other Ethiopians, including the emperor Yohannes III (b. c. 1797), were sympathetic to Catholicism, which seemed to offer authority and firm doctrine in an age of uncertainty, but most did not actually convert.

Everything changed in 1855, when Kasa (1816–68), nephew of the governor of Qwara, seized the imperial throne. As emperor, he took the name Tewodros, 'Gift of God', a name already associated with the messianic elements of Ethiopian religion. This was in itself an audacious move. According to the British consul, Tewodros's aim was simple: to 'reform Abyssinia, restore the Christian faith and become master of the world'. Among his first acts was the summoning of a synod at Ambá Chará, at which he ordered the clergy to uphold the Alexandrian faith rather than the new Roman one. In this he was aided by the young abuna, Salama, something of a fanatic who, although he received the Catholic missionaries kindly, was cruel to Ethiopians who converted to Catholicism.

But the promise of Tewodros proved short-lived. Revolts against his authoritarian rule broke out, and in order to pay for crackdowns he seized church property, alienating his largest body of support. The emperor descended into destructive paranoia. The abuna, Salama, joined most of the foreign missionaries in prison. Tewodros's armies pillaged Gonder, carrying off ancient manuscripts and torching the churches. A British expeditionary force arrived in 1867 to rescue the British prisoners, easily defeating the few remaining loyal troops the following year. The emperor shot himself as the British advanced, the country in ruins.

The new emperor from 1872, Yohannes IV (1831–89), was keen to heal the divisions and rebuild his country. His magnificent coronation ceremony – involving a procession of 3,000 priests – indicated the union of church and state that he wished to restore. He set about this at the Council of Borumeda in 1878, called to resolve the Christological debates which were still raging in the church. Having settled the doctrinal dispute in favour of the traditional Alexandrian formulae, the emperor gave all Christians two years to conform to them. Some monks refused, and had their tongues torn out. The church was re-organized, and Yohannes IV had the Alexandrian church send four new bishops rather than just the one abuna, thereby creating a more manageable church structure, with himself at the top. At the same time, a mission was launched to the pagans and Muslims within the imperial borders, which had recently been enlarged by Menelik of Shewa, a sub-king in the south of the country (and next emperor). The empire and its religion expanded together. By 1880, 50,000 Muslims and 500,000 pagans had converted to Ethiopian Orthodoxy. The Ethiopian Orthodox Church, which had started the nineteenth century in such a bad way, ended it stronger than ever.

THE SECOND 'NEW WORLD'

When Europeans cast their eyes overseas in the eighteenth and nineteenth centuries, it was generally to Africa or the Americas. But another 'New World' was being opened up at the same time, in what we now call Oceania and Australasia. Here, too, missionaries came, and here too Christianity spread – often with surprising rapidity.

THE SOUTH SEAS

The islands of the Pacific presented a unique challenge to European imperialists and missionaries alike. There was a certain degree of cultural uniformity across the region, since most of the Pacific peoples had been sailing throughout this vast area for thousands of years. Many were politically advanced and different groups were allied with each other.

It is said that without the body, the soul cannot live. Therefore we have first achieved the reconciliation of the empire and arranged its affairs. From now on, we are going to turn to the matters of faith. The faith, it is said, is the foundation, all the rest is transient and perishable.

Emperor Yohannes IV, at the Council of Borumeda, 1878

A Tahitian fruit seller, c. 1880–90.

Moreover, where the Amerindians had welcomed the conquistadors as gods, the Pacific islanders were for the most part convinced of their own superiority over the Europeans. All these factors, combined with the relative density of the population in many islands, made the area unsuitable for European settlement, as those few settlements that appeared there in the sixteenth century discovered. Thus, the story of Christianity in the Pacific islands is the story not of colonization but of mission.

The abortive seventeenth-century Jesuit mission to the Pacific islands that we saw in Chapter 10 had had little success. A century later, new attempts were made to bring Christianity to these islands – but this time the religion was Protestantism, and the missionaries were British, French and Dutch. The first major mission was organized by the LMS, which in 1796 sent the *Duff* to Tahiti. The missionaries were completely overwhelmed by Tahitian culture and were unable to cope, and most of them left for Australia within a year. Yet the arrival of more missionaries kept the work going. Bibles in the local language proved very popular, for the islanders valued literacy, and in 1819 Pomare II (1782–1821), chief of much of the island, was baptized. This coincided with Pomare's victory over some of his rivals, and the people attributed much of his success to his new religion. Pomare, for his part, cleverly encouraged the spread of Christianity among his subjects, recognizing that it was associated with him rather than his rivals: thus, the more Christians there were, the stronger his hold over the people. The model for the evangelization of much of the rest of the Pacific was set: local rulers and local missionaries taking the lead, rather than Europeans.

By the 1820s there were Tahitian missionaries heading off to other islands. Auna arrived in Hawaii in 1822 and was heard sympathetically. The LMS leaders were delighted by this realization of Henry Venn's plan for self-propagating churches, but they were also expanding the work of their own missionaries. John Williams (1796–1839), who had arrived on Tahiti in 1817, bought a

ship and travelled to the Cook Islands. Many people were converted, especially through the work of Williams's assistant Aaron Buzacott (1800–64), a metalworker who divided his time between preaching and helping the islanders to build better houses. He was responsible for the new style of churches which sprang up in the Cook Islands and beyond, made of coral or stone, built to a simple style and whitewashed. Buzacott also founded the first theological college here in 1839, where the four-year course taught prospective native missionaries not just theology, but woodworking and house-building skills.

The remarkably energetic Williams travelled on, preaching in Tonga and Samoa in the 1830s. He had rivals, primarily from the Wesleyans, also enjoying great success in the same island groups. In each place, the missionaries were careful to encourage the islanders themselves to start their own missions. This they did, and the success continued, with many adopting *Lotu* – their name for Christianity.

The fact that the islanders gave Christianity a new name indicates the degree to which it became entrenched in their culture and, to some extent, adapted to it. Traditional myths and legends were used to convey Christian teaching – something that the Methodists were to ban in 1862. Stories from the Bible were adapted, so that Jesus now fed the 5,000 with breadfruit and bonito rather than loaves and fishes. The structure of the new churches often aped the structure of traditional religion. Pacific religion generally revolved around a number of gods who were closely involved in day-to-day life, and who behaved in a fairly predictable way. These gods were part of the world of *tapu*, the sacred. Their worship revolved around special feast days, and it was mediated by priests and prophets. Thus, many islanders understood the Christian system of feast days, and also the role of the minister, since it seemed similar to what they were used to. In Samoa, the Anglican minister or *faife'au* acted as the mediator between the people and the spiritual world, aided by his deacons. These ministers were greatly honoured, just as the priests had once been, and lived in fine houses and were given many gifts. The *faife'au* would pray at ceremonial occasions, but on a day-to-day level their task was to preach to the people and explain the Bible to them.

Similarly, people still believed in the world of *tapu*, but now it was a Christian *tapu* rather than a traditional one. Since they understood Christian morality and social mores as part of *tapu*, Samoans, like other islanders, were relatively willing to adopt them. Warfare and sexual promiscuity became far less of a feature of island life. Tattoos, long hair, and topless dress for women died out. That lynchpin of nineteenth-century evangelical religion, Sunday observance, replaced them. Every Sunday, Pacific islanders would dress in white – with straw bonnets for the women – and go to the newly erected stone church. And there was a new sense of social justice, with the Ten Commandments being put at the centre of law and order. Despite the introduction of Victorian morality, society was much more relaxed than before – for in the past those who transgressed Pacific social mores had been brutally punished. That was no longer the case.

The missions rolled on in a seemingly unstoppable tide. The 1840s saw Christianity come to the New Hebrides, the gateway to Melanesia, although John Williams had died here on the island of Erromanga in 1839. He and his men had come ashore as a feast was being prepared before a battle between two tribes and, unwittingly committing sacrilege by going near the food, Williams and a companion had ended up as part of the feast themselves. Hundreds of Tahitian and Samoan missionaries now descended upon Erromanga and the other islands of the area, enjoying, once again, huge success. Churches and schools were built throughout the islands and the practice of eating anyone, let alone missionaries, was ended. Touchingly, in 1859, two Erromangians of the party that had killed Williams were shown his picture and apologized for his murder: they said that they had not realized he was a man of God.

AUSTRALIA

The last great area to be discovered and colonized by Europeans was Australia, visited by the Dutch navigator Abel Tasman in the mid-seventeenth century, but first charted (and claimed for Britain) by Captain James Cook in 1770. Settling – in the form of prison colonies – began within a few years. The policy of 'transporting' criminals there ended in 1853, by which time the colonists were about half convicts and half free – for many settlers had come there in search of gold or to establish sheep farms.

Conflicts quickly arose with the native peoples of Australia, the Aborigines, of whom there were some 250,000–500,000. The settlers had very little regard for them, for they had no goods worth buying, no military capability, not even metal tools. Many settlers thus regarded them simply as a nuisance and either hoped they would die out soon or actively went out hunting

An Aboriginal rock painting, c. 23,000 BC, from Arnhem Land, Australia.

them. By 1850 there were only around 10,000 Aborigines left.

Europeans did not understand Aborigine religion – indeed, they often thought none existed. To the European mind, religion was public, easily accessible and generally written down. To the Aborigines, religion was esoteric, and it could not be communicated without complex initiation rites. There was thus mutual incomprehension, and the first Christian missionaries did not make great progress. Samuel Marsden (1764–1838), a chaplain in New South Wales, was keen on evangelizing the Aborigines, employing many as servants in the hope of converting them, but his efforts were a complete failure. Disillusioned, he concluded that missions to the Aborigines would never succeed.

The closest thing to success in the evangelization of the Aborigines was achieved, perhaps rather improbably, by a group of Spanish Benedictine monks. Led by Rosendo Salvado (1814–1900), they settled on the west coast in 1847 and built a monastery called New Norcia. Their work with the Aborigines consisted of having them live and work at the mission station, where they were taught

Convicts push the carriages of transport officers and civil servants in Australia in this lithograph from c. 1840.

new farming and craft skills as well as religion. They even put together one of the first Australian cricket teams – although the Spanish monks must have found the game as peculiar as the Aborigines did! In 1867 the monastery became an abbey, and Salvado was made bishop. In 1887 he was made protector of the Aborigines. Yet despite the flourishing of the monastery and the survival of its mission, few Aborigines converted. Salvado sent two promising converts to Italy to be ordained, but they died.

The almost complete failure of the missions to the Aborigines meant that the history of Christianity in Australia would be, for the most part, the history of the settlers' own churches. Anglicanism was the official religion of the colonies from the beginning, but there was a large Roman Catholic contingent, mainly because so many of the convicts sent there were Irish. All the settlers, whatever their background, faced a tough life in a harsh land. Many had come to seek their fortune and were not much interested in wealth of the spiritual variety. The Anglican chaplains were given few resources, so

they were pleased to welcome Presbyterians, Methodists and other Non-Conformists who sent chaplains and missionaries to the colonies. The result was that, although Anglicanism remained the only official religion of Australia, Non-Conformists were not only tolerated but welcomed, and Protestant ministers and churches generally cooperated in a remarkably ecumenical spirit, borne of circumstance. But the Protestant churches and the Catholics still greatly mistrusted each other.

NEW ZEALAND

Like Australia, New Zealand was first properly mapped by James Cook, in 1769, but substantial European settlement did not begin until the 1830s. Most settlers were Protestant, mainly Anglican but with a good contingent of Presbyterians, especially in the south, which saw many Scottish settlers. All these Protestants – and the Catholics too – had to adapt to a frontier existence. Woolsheds and courthouses were used to hold services. The pioneer communities had small chapels, built of wood or stone; but in the more remote farms and sheep stations, religious life revolved around the home, as with the Boers in South Africa. Parents would lead Sunday school for their children.

The settlers' dealings with the indigenous Maori people were wildly different from the story unfolding in Australia at this time, at least to begin with. Unlike the Aborigines, the Maori were well organized and militarily intimidating, and they had goods which the settlers wished to buy. Culturally, they were close to the Pacific islanders to the north. There were missions to the Maori from an early stage. Samuel Marsden, the Anglican chaplain in Sydney, funded some of the first. Two brothers, Henry and William Williams, arrived in the 1820s and had great success. Their wives, Marianne and Jane, were essential in their work, helping to educate the Maori women. Maori beliefs were similar to those of many Pacific islanders, and like them they spoke of *tapu* and could readily transfer their understanding of it to Christianity. They were also very keen to read, and there was a New Testament in Maori as early as 1837.

The Maori were also influenced by Roman Catholicism, which came slightly later on the scene. Jean Baptiste François Pompallier (c. 1801–71), bishop of Maronea, arrived in 1838 speaking little English and knowing little of the country. He insisted on being carried in a litter by Maori servants, but they realized that he was considered an important person by the French, and his 'chiefly' status – complete with robes, mysterious rites and sacred objects – impressed them. Pompallier succeeded in building a small Catholic Church among the Maori.

By the 1840s most Maori were Christians, at least in name. Many began to construct a new understanding of Christianity for themselves that was not so reliant on the teachings of the 'Pakeha' (or 'white people'). Like the Pacific islanders, they followed a Christian *tapu*, one that revolved around the Old Testament and the Ten Commandments. The warlike Maori were keen on the Old Testament and its rather bloody stories, and they came to understand that that the God of the Bible was the supreme *Atua* or spirit power, able to dominate lesser spiritual entities.

Quite new forms of religion, more or less influenced by Christianity, began to appear. One prophet called Papahurihia renamed himself Te Atua Wera ('The Burning God') and founded a cult in the 1830s that was a blend of traditional religion and Christianity: it involved Sunday observance, but on Saturday, veneration of a European flag and Maori sacred groves. The lizard, sacred to the Maori, was combined with the serpent of Genesis; there was baptism, but missionaries were to be excluded from heaven. This cult survived in some form until the twentieth century.

More solid, perhaps, was the church of Te Kooti (1820–91), a Maori guerrilla

In Otago, it is Presbyterian Protestantism; in Canterbury, Anglican Protestantism; and in Wellington, Protestantism of any and every kind.

Patrick Moran, Catholic bishop of Dunedin, 1873

Here I am sitting with my evil nature, thinking upon God for us and for my people. Here lives evil in the innermost part of my heart. I must think towards God for the salvation of my soul. Here I am praying daily to God for us all. Does the Word of God grow in my tribe, or does it not? My thoughts are lifted up to you every day. I am praying to God to reveal to me the hidden evils of my heart, that I may not deceive myself and lose my soul.

Paratene, a Maori Christian convert, 1834

leader who fought in the war of the 1860s against the Pakeha. In 1872 he founded a new church, Te Hahi Ringatu ('the upraised hand', originally a Maori sign of war, but interpreted by Te Kooti as a sign of worship of God). Te Kooti was regarded as a prophet, healer and miracle-worker. On one occasion he is said to have asked his followers if they believed he could walk on Ohiwa harbour. When they replied that they did, he answered that in that case he did not need to prove it. Te Kooti always preached peace and unity among the Maori, and his movement was based above all on the Bible: his ministers had little training other than immersion in the scriptures. His church had a distinctive liturgy, meeting for special services on the twelfth day of every month, but – like John Wesley – Te Kooti insisted that he had founded not a new church but a movement within the established ones.

Yet the ability of the Maori to create new, authentically Maori forms of Christianity was perhaps best illustrated by Te Whiti (1815–1905), a Maori who was converted by Methodist preachers and then became disillusioned with Pakeha religion. As the government began taking and developing Maori land in the aftermath of the wars of the 1860s, Te Whiti stood for passive, non-violent resistance. He created a new Maori settlement in South Taranaki, run on Christian lines. He and his followers saw the cause of land rights for which they stood in terms of the Old Testament history of Israel. Just as the Israelites stood firm, so too Te Whiti and his followers would, refusing to negotiate with the government, but refusing also to take up arms: instead, they simply sat on their land, refusing to move. The protest failed. Te Whiti and his lieutenant, Tohu Kakahi, were arrested and held without trial in the South Island for two years. Their community was dispersed, its land taken and sold. Even today, many Maori in South Taranaki meet every month in Te Whiti's memory, and it has been argued that his methods were an influence on Mahatma Gandhi.

I stand for peace. Though the lions rage, still I am for peace. I will go into captivity. My aim will be accomplished, peace will reign... Though dead, I shall live in the peace which will be the accomplishment of my aim. The future is mine; and little children, when asked hereafter as to the author of peace, shall say – Te Whiti – and I will bless them.

Te Whiti, 1881

INDIA

The themes we have seen so far in this chapter – of new Protestant missions, revived Catholic ones, and their effects on older local churches – were played out with the greatest intensity in India. Here, all the movements that were diffused over the vast continent of Africa were reproduced in a smaller area. We saw in Chapter 10 how Catholic missions to the subcontinent came up against the centuries-old Malabar or Thomas church, with unedifying results. Now to that mix was added a new surge of Protestantism.

THE TAMIL MISSIONS

The late seventeenth and early eighteenth centuries had seen the Portuguese presence in India largely replaced by the British, Dutch and French. Missions to the Indians by the Protestant churches began in 1706, when two German Lutherans, Bartholomaeus Ziegenbalg (1683–1719) and Heinrich Plütschau (1678–1747), arrived at the Danish colony of Tranquebar on the south-east coast of the subcontinent. Although not really Pietists themselves (Ziegenbalg believed in the importance of clerical dress and always wore black, even in the sweltering heat of southern India), both were connected to the University of Halle, at this time under the aegis of August Francke, who was especially interested in missions to India.

The mission was financially supported by the British Society for Promoting Christian Knowledge (SPCK), in another of those remarkable ecumenical efforts that characterized the early Protestant missionary movement. Ziegenbalg and Plütschau preached to the Tamil-speaking people of the area, translating the New Testament into Tamil and founding three schools – one for Tamil-speakers, one for Portuguese-speakers, and one for Danish-speakers. This alone demonstrates the diversity of the people to whom Ziegenbalg and Plütschau were ministering, as well as the centrality of education to their project. Indeed, the process was mutual, as

Ziegenbalg in particular studied Tamil writings and became an authority on Hindu philosophy and religion.

Ziegenbalg died in 1719 at the age of only 36, and leadership of the mission passed to Benjamin Schultze (1689–1760), a far less sensitive and able man. However, Schultze did extend the mission by moving to Madras, a city under British control, with the permission of the British East India Company. When he arrived, there were no Protestants in Madras at all; when he left in 1743, there were 678 Indian Christians in his congregation. In 1733 Schultze had overseen the ordination of the first Indian Protestant minister, a Christian from a high caste named Aaron. Equally important was one Rajanaikan, an Indian Catholic who converted to Lutheranism and who worked as a missionary, although he was never ordained. These attempts to make the Tamil church culturally Indian – indeed, administered, where possible, by Indians – were helped by John Philip Fabricius, another missionary who devoted himself to revising Ziegenbalg's Tamil New Testament and producing a translation of the Old. His work became one of the most popular and long-lasting Christian books of India, for his translation occupied a place in Indian Lutheranism rather like the Authorized Version in much of the USA today. It was widely admired and used, and it is still in use by some churches today.

In the latter half of the eighteenth century, the Tamil mission was dominated by Christian Frederick Schwartz (1726–98), an extraordinarily charismatic man who seems to have been loved by all who met him. In 1762 he visited the fort of Tiruchirapalli, an important base of the nawab of Arcot, the Muslim ruler of the area. The British garrison there begged him to stay and minister to them, so he did, even though he was a Lutheran; and he soon had a community of sixty soldiers who met every day for prayers. He also ran an orphanage there and preached to the Indians in the area, winning many converts, some of whom helped him with his work. Schwartz became quite famous throughout southern India, to such an extent that the British sent him as ambassador to the warlord Haidar Ali of Mysore. In the 1770s he moved to Thanjavur, a neighbouring independent kingdom ruled by King Tuljajee. Tuljajee was extremely fond of Schwartz and allowed him to preach throughout his kingdom, but despite the missionary's best efforts, Tuljajee himself never converted.

Frederick Schwartz preaches to the Hindus in this American engraving from 1852.

An English grandee of the East India Company rides in an Indian procession in this image from the 1820s.

THE EAST INDIA COMPANY AND THE RISE OF ANGLICANISM

The British East India Company was in charge of operations at the main British possessions in the early eighteenth century – Bombay, Madras and Calcutta (now Mumbai, Chennai and Kolkata). By the 1760s, however, war with France meant that the British controlled all trade with the Indian subcontinent. What followed was the gradual conquest of India by the British. Most of the subcontinent had previously been united and ruled by the Muslim Mughal empire, but by this stage the empire had largely splintered and power

had passed to local rulers. The East India Company therefore made a series of treaties with these rulers, and it became more and more involved in local government. In 1784 the British parliament passed the India Act, which meant that this system, known as 'the Raj', passed partly into the hands of the British government, as represented by a governor-general of India. In 1858 a year-long rebellion against the British led to the British government taking complete control of all British interests in India. The local princes retained their power in theory, but in reality Britain now administered India. In 1877 India became formally part of the

mission in this period tended to be associated with Anglican evangelicals or Dissenters – undesirables, in the eyes of the British authorities.

One important figure in this period was John Zachary Kiernander, another product of late eighteenth-century ecumenicalism: a Swede, trained at Halle and employed by the SPCK. He used his own money to build a substantial church at Calcutta and oversaw an energetic mission there, although this was to a large extent directed at Catholics rather than Hindus. Although Lutheran, Kiernander was supported by Anglicans in Britain and India alike. Other missionaries used Calcutta as a base, including a group of brilliant young men from Cambridge, who had been inspired by the preacher Charles Simeon; the most famous was Henry Martyn, who translated the New Testament into Urdu. After 1813, when the government permitted the sending of missionaries to the Indians, more followed, and LMS missionaries spread throughout northern India. The CMS was the most prominent missionary organization in this area, operating primarily from Calcutta and Madras. They had a particularly thriving mission at Agra, where one of the most successful missionaries was Shaikh Salih, an Indian Muslim scholar who was converted by Martyn and took the name Abdul Masih ('Servant of the Messiah'). He wrote commentaries on several biblical books, which were extremely popular, and he caused a sensation in Agra, where Muslims crowded the rooftops to hear him preach. Masih was a medical doctor, and his work among the poor also made a great impression. Of his fifty or so converts, many later reverted to Islam, but Masih represented the first real engagement between Islam and evangelical Christianity in India. He died in 1826, just a few months after being ordained as an Anglican clergyman.

His ordination came at a time of growth and consolidation of the Anglican church in India. In 1814 Thomas Middleton (1769–1822) had been consecrated as the

British empire and Queen Victoria added the title of empress of India to her already formidable CV.

British rule inevitably meant the dominance of the Church of England in India. Until the late eighteenth century, Indian Anglicanism had meant little more than chaplains ministering to traders or soldiers. Indeed, the British authorities in general, and the East India Company in particular, tended to frown on mission in the late eighteenth and early nineteenth centuries. They feared that missionaries would offend the Indians with whom they were trading. Also, as we have seen,

It will be your bounden duty vigilantly to guard the public tranquillity from interruption [by missionaries] and will impress upon the minds of the inhabitants of India, that the British faith, upon which they rely for the free exercise of their religion, will be inviolably maintained.

Instruction from the directors of the East India Company to the governor general, 1808

The Gospel recognizes no distinctions such as those of castes, imposed by a heathen usage, bearing in some respect a supposed religious obligation, condemning those in the lower ranks to perpetual abasement, placing an immovable barrier against all general advance and improvement in society, cutting asunder the bonds of human fellowship on the one hand, and preventing those of Christian love on the other.

Daniel Wilson, 1833

Under present circumstances, if a Hindu of blameless character and conduct change his faith to become Christian, he ipso facto loses all right to inheritance to the family property. Moreover, his wife and young children may be taken from him, and he cannot recover their guardianship by law.

The Bangalore Missionary Conference, 1895

first Anglican bishop in India – his immense diocese theoretically covering most of Asia and Australia! After arriving at Calcutta, he left it again for almost exactly a year while he made a grand visitation of the entire subcontinent. His successor, Reginald Heber (1783–1826), also travelled extensively and made an even greater impression. Heber loved the Indian people and they seem, on the whole, to have loved him back. He was the first Anglican bishop in India to ordain Indian priests. But his ministry was cut short after less than three years, when he suddenly died of a brain haemorrhage after plunging himself into a cold pool to escape the midday heat. Several successors lasted no longer, and so in 1833 two new dioceses were established, one at Madras and one at Bombay, subject to Calcutta. In this way, it was hoped, the workload would be lessened and bishops might live a bit longer.

The plan seems to have worked. Daniel Wilson (1778–1858), who became bishop in 1832, survived for twenty-six years and did an enormous amount of work not only to consolidate Anglicanism in Calcutta but to develop the city's missionary tradition. He donated some of his own money towards building the splendid cathedral there, consecrated in 1847, and he also directed new missions further east. It was not until 1855 that a diocese of Singapore, Labuan, and Sarawak was created, and until this time mission in south-east Asia remained the responsibility of the bishop of Calcutta. Wilson, in contrast to Middleton, was a devout evangelical, and had links to the Clapham Sect. He revitalized Anglican missions in India and the rest of Asia, helping to build a strong mission on the Malaysian peninsula that would grow even after this region was removed from Calcutta's control. Wilson also introduced a new and characteristically evangelical emphasis on addressing social ills. In particular, Wilson repudiated the old strategy, associated with the Catholic missions and also with the earlier Lutheran missions, of not challenging the caste system, which was central to Indian society.

In 1833 Wilson wrote a letter to his entire diocese in which he attacked the caste system as fundamentally unchristian; he subsequently ordered all churches to abolish segregated seating, the practice of allowing people of higher caste to take communion before those of lower, and so on. Many churches reacted angrily, and many members converted to Catholicism or Lutheranism in protest, but Wilson travelled India meeting congregations face to face and imposing 'the Wilson line', as it became known. It was highly influential. By the 1850s most Protestants in India shared this condemnation of the caste system, and by the 1860s and 70s they were reaping the rewards – for low-caste Indians were greatly attracted.

But most converts did not, on the whole, have a good time, especially in the early part of the century. They lost whatever caste status they had had under the traditional system, making them essentially outcasts from society. They might lose their families. Yet to the extent that they were still part of society, they were part of the Hindu religion. They still had to pay taxes to support Hindu temples, and the British authorities did nothing to protect them should they refuse to do so. Even after 1813 chaplains were strictly forbidden from baptizing sepoys – Indian soldiers in British service – for fear of inciting the others into rebellion. Some attempts were made to make the situation fairer: in 1832 the governor-general, Lord William Bentinck, decreed that converts to Christianity must not lose their inheritance. The following year he saw to it that religious discrimination in appointments must end, the discrimination having been in the past entirely against Christians.

Indeed, as the century wore on, the British authorities became increasingly happy with the idea of evangelizing the Indians. The idea was floated that Christian subjects would be intrinsically more satisfied with British rule and better behaved. In 1859, a year before becoming prime minister, Lord Palmerston endorsed this view. Thus the missionaries and the colonial authorities – although technically separate – tended more and more to cooperate, recognizing that they were both working towards essentially the same goals. This meant that, for many Indians, Christianity was indelibly associated with British rule. And the interest that many British scholars and administrators had shown in Indian culture, philosophy and religion in the earlier nineteenth century began to wane, as a more aggressive assertion of the superiority of all things western took hold. Thomas Babington Macaulay, president of the General Committee of Public Instruction, once wrote, 'A single shelf of a good European library was worth the whole native literature of India and Arabia.'

One striking development in Indian Anglicanism was the appearance of religious orders. A number of these quasi-monastic communities had been founded in England in the wake of the Oxford Movement, and they began to take an interest in India. One of the first was the Cowley Fathers, in Oxford, which sent several members to India. The most remarkable was Simeon O'Neill, who went to Indore in central India. O'Neill was the epitome of Victorian privilege and sophistication: a man who rowed for Oxford University and taught mathematics at Eton, who sought to live as an Indian Christian ascetic. Living a life of prayer (hampered only by the fact that he was physically unable to sit cross-legged like traditional Hindu ascetics), he translated the Psalms into Urdu and preached to Indians and European soldiers alike. Others included the Cambridge Mission to Delhi, run by Edward Bickersteth, and the Oxford Mission to Calcutta. One member of the latter, Frederick Wingfield Douglass, invited many high-caste Hindus to live in his house and learn about Christianity. He later moved south to the swamps of Behala, where he spent four decades in a small hut, living in the same conditions as the poverty-stricken Indians, who venerated him as a living saint.

These orders were typically quite Anglo-Catholic or theologically liberal, and they often came into conflict with the missionaries of the evangelical mission societies, who regarded them as crypto-Catholics or out-and-out heretics. But these evangelicals were, from the middle of the nineteenth century, also making an increasing mark on Indian Christianity.

THE BAPTIST MISSIONS

The best-known Protestant missions of nineteenth-century India were those of the Baptists, which enjoyed enormous success in the north-east of the subcontinent. The most famous Baptist missionary was William Carey, the founder of the Baptist Missionary Society. He was born in 1761 and later converted from Anglicanism to the Baptist church, becoming a minister in 1787.

In 1793 William Carey arrived in Calcutta and almost immediately lost all his money. He found a post running an indigo factory in a nearby village, but this life did not agree with Carey's family: his wife went insane and

William Carey baptizes his first Hindu convert, Kristno, in this American engraving from 1837.

one of his sons died. But Carey stuck at it for five years, mastering the Bengali language and producing the obligatory translation of the New Testament. Then in 1799 a couple more Baptist missionaries arrived in the area and proceeded to the small Danish settlement of Serampore, where they hoped to avoid the largely hostile British authorities. Carey joined them there, and the mission began to flourish.

Carey helped his colleagues to learn Bengali, and he also taught them to understand and respect the culture of the people to whom they would preach. Great care was taken not to give offence: unlike Bartholomaeus Ziegenbalg a century earlier, the Baptists did not smash Hindu gods in their temples. As a result, they had great success. Like the Anglicans under Daniel Wilson, the Baptists decided not to tolerate the caste system in their churches. As a result, many of their converts were cast out of mainstream society, lacking even a caste, and the missionaries had to help them. Many were employed in the printing works that the Baptists established at Serampore, and

others were trained as preachers. Still more were educated at the schools that the missionaries set up, which proved enormously successful. The education on offer, although elementary, was superior to that available anywhere else; and before long there were 8,000 pupils at a hundred such schools. Some of the pupils were girls, who until now had never been educated in Hindu society; the missionaries tried to encourage female education, although they made little headway against the prejudices of the society in which they worked.

Like schools founded by other missions, including those of the LMS, these were intended to provide general education and not proselytize. Indeed, fear of being accused of indoctrinating or brainwashing their charges led the missionaries to ensure that the curriculum was wholly secular. Some missionaries disapproved of this approach and wanted to teach the scriptures at the schools, although most recognized that the more cautious method was, in effect, laying the groundwork for later evangelization. Other schools were

St George's Cathedral, Madras. The church was built by Thomas Fiott de Havilland (1775–1866); it was consecrated in 1816 and became the cathedral in 1835.

founded for humanitarian reasons, such as the one opened at Sanawar by the Ulsterman Henry Lawrence to care for the street urchins who were the casteless results of unions between Indians and Europeans. Several more schools were established to continue this work, which they did well into the twentieth century. In addition to the schools, the Baptists set up Serampore College, overseen by a brilliant young Scot named John Mack.

Although the Baptist mission remained small compared to the Anglican ones, it played an important role in Indian society. The Baptists published the first Bengali newspaper, the *Samachar Durpan*, and a journal called *The friend of India*. Neither of these was overtly evangelistic and both proved very popular. William Carey, meanwhile, was committed to stamping out practices such as child sacrifice in some parts of the country, and also *sati*, the tradition of burning the widow of a dead Hindu on his funeral pyre. This was outlawed in 1829 by the governor-general, Lord William Bentick, and his promulgation was translated into Bengali by William Carey. Carey had some scruples over this, because he received the document on a Sunday, and as a good Dissenter he never worked on that day; but he consoled himself with the thought that it was never wrong to save lives on the Sabbath and duly translated it with the urgency it demanded.

ROMAN CATHOLICS AND ROMO-SYRIANS
Where, in all this, was the oldest Indian church of all? As we saw in Chapter 10, the pressure of Roman Catholicism had led to terrible divisions in the Syrian Malabar Church, between those who accepted the Roman rites and those – the Malankara Church, also known as the Jacobites – who did not. The Malankara Church was overseen by a series of bishops, confusingly all known as Mar Thomas, who claimed authority over all the Malabar Christians.

The Roman-supporting church (or the Romo-Syrians, as they are sometimes known) rejected this claim and remained

officially part of the Roman Catholic Church. Catholics were still far more numerous than Anglicans. At the start of the nineteenth century, the Catholic Church was strong in Goa and down the Malabar coast – with an estimated 750,000 Catholics in the whole of India in 1800, of whom some 100,000 were Romo-Syrians – but its missions had come to a virtual standstill. In theory, there were bishops at Cochin, who ministered to the Romo-Syrians, but this city was in the hands of the Dutch for much of the eighteenth century and they would not allow the Catholic bishops into the city. Instead, the Carmelite mission to India continued, with vicars apostolic in charge where the bishop was unable to exercise his authority. In 1777 the then vicar apostolic died, and from then on the Romo-Syrian church remained in the charge of administrators sent from Europe, none of whom was technically a bishop. This unhappy situation continued until the 1830s, when Rome decided to send new vicars apostolic from Ireland – the idea being that these English-speaking clerics would help to rejuvenate Catholicism in a country coming under British control. However, the Portuguese crown, which still held Goa and Mylapore, refused to recognize them, on the grounds that the old *padroado* still meant that only Portugal could appoint bishops in this area. A period of schism followed in Goa, with Portuguese bishops and Irish vicars apostolic at loggerheads, until 1857 when the Vatican agreed a concordat (a 'treaty' between the Catholic Church and a temporal power) which agreed boundaries between the two rival authorities.

THE MALANKARA CHURCH
Meanwhile, the Malankara Church – the Thomas Christians who did not accept Rome – was smaller, with perhaps 40,000 worshippers in 1838. In the eighteenth century it was largely ignored by the Europeans, who often did not regard it as properly Christian (its links to the Middle Eastern churches made it heretical in their

The first and primary object of my heart is the benefit of the Hindus. I know nothing so important to the improvement of their future condition as the establishment of a purer morality, whatever their belief, and a more just conception of the will of God. The first step to this better understanding will be dissociation of religious belief and practice from blood and murder.

William Bentinck, speaking on the need to abolish *sati*, 1829

We shall see churches in India raising up their spires towards heaven, Christian villages extending over whole tracts of country, churches crowded with dusky congregations and dusky communicants at the altar tables. We shall hear the native girls singing hymns in the vernacular, and see boys trooping to school or studying for the universities under missionary auspices. Those things, and many others, I have seen, and I wish to God I could fix them on the minds of my audience as they are fixed upon my own.

Richard Temple, former governor of Bombay, 1881

eyes) and who often had little respect for its priests. Jacob Canters Visscher, a Dutch chaplain at Cochin in the early eighteenth century, described in a letter the Mar Thomas who was then leading this church:

Mar Thomas… is a native of Malabar. He is a black man, dull and slow of understanding. He lives in great state; and when he came into the city to visit the Commandant, he was attended by a number of soldiers bearing swords and shields, in imitation of the Princes of Malabar. He wears on his head a silken cowl, embroidered with crosses, in form much resembling that of the Carmelites. He is a weak-minded rhodomontader, and boasted greatly to us of being an Eutychian in his creed, accusing the rival Bishop of heresy.

Some Protestant missionaries saw potential in this church, though. The Lutheran missionaries to the Tamils made contact with the Malankara Church, hoping to ally with them against the Catholics and essentially turn them into Protestants, but nothing came of this. Neither did anything come of the talks which another Mar Thomas had in the 1770s with Rome itself, seeking a reunion provided that he could remain archbishop of the Indian church: Rome refused this condition and no reunion occurred. Instead, Mar Thomas strengthened his link with the Syrian church and had himself consecrated as metropolitan by a Syrian bishop (before this, the metropolitans had not been properly consecrated). When this happened he ended the succession of Thomases by changing his name to Dionysius (often being known as Dionysius 'the Great'). Things remained confusing, though, as most of his successors would call themselves Dionysius too.

When the British took control of India, the Malankara Church found an unlikely ally. An Anglican clergyman named Claudius Buchanan (1766–1815) visited the church in 1806 and wrote a very successful travel book about it, *Christian Researches in Asia*. Many Anglicans regarded the Malankara Church much as they regarded their own church: not Protestant, not Catholic, but still ancient and legitimate. Buchanan even met Dionysius 'the Great' and discussed the possibility of the union of the two churches, although the discussions did not go far. Dionysius commented: 'I would sacrifice much for such a union, only let me not be called to compromise anything of the dignity and purity of the Church.'

More important was Colonel J. Munro, who became Resident of Travancore in 1809. A deeply pious Anglican, Munro believed that the Malankara Church needed reforming, so he set out to bring it in line with Anglicanism. He set up a college to educate its priests, which was put in the charge of Thomas Norton, and with the help of CMS missionaries such as Joseph Fenn a translation of the New Testament was made into Malayalam, the language which most of the Malankara Christians spoke (though they used Syriac in church). Although flawed, this translation proved very popular.

Munro also issued a decree permitting the Malankara priests to marry, for he knew that they had only become celibate in modern times, under the influence of Portuguese Catholicism. The priests protested that they could not afford to marry; Munro therefore arranged for the CMS to pay them large sums of money if they did. Suddenly many Malankara priests found willing brides.

Yet the hoped-for reformation of the Malankara Church did not proceed as planned. In 1830 Mar Dionysius IV became metropolitan and fell out with the Anglican missionaries. In 1836 a synod was held at Mavelikara at which Dionysius and the other authorities of the church made it clear that they would not accept any further interference from the British. Problematically, a few Malankara Christians disagreed; they liked hearing the liturgy and reading the Bible in their own language rather than Syriac. The Anglican missionaries decided to stay and help these reformers, further angering the Malankara authorities; relations became even more strained by a dispute over land owned by the missionaries which had been intended for Malankara use. Some members of the reforming party within the Malankara Church opened their own church at Mavelikara in 1840, which became incorporated into the Anglican Church.

Another group of reformers at Maramannu, led by a priest named Abraham Malpan, remained within the Malankara Church but put into practice the reforms they wanted. These involved holding services in Malayalam as well as doing away with prayers to the saints and the celebration of festivals. Other alterations were also made in line with Protestantism, such as the separate distribution of the bread and wine at the Eucharist (or *Qurbana* as it was known to the Malankara Church), rather than mixing them, as was traditional. Mar Dionysius had no time for this and excommunicated the entire congregation. Abraham Malpan reacted swiftly and shrewdly. An unwell man, he did not want to lead a new church: instead he sent his nephew, Matthew, to Mar Elias, patriarch of the Syrian Church in the Middle East. Mar Elias was impressed by Matthew and, apparently unaware of the delicate situation in India, ordained him a deacon and priest on the same day – and ended by consecrating him Mar Matthew Athanasius, the new metropolitan of the Indian church.

The larger, anti-reform sector of the church regarded Mar Matthew as an illegitimate heretic. In 1864 they had their own candidate, Mar Dionysius V, consecrated metropolitan by the new Syrian patriarch, meaning that there were two rival metropolitans. In 1875 Dionysius V invited a third Syrian patriarch, Mar Ignatius Peter III, to India to oversee a synod confirming the illegitimacy of Mar Matthew and his reforms. The synod was held in 1876 at Mulanthuruthy, and it confirmed the status of Dionysius, condemning Matthew. It also placed the Malankara Church officially under the authority of the Syrian patriarch, though it would continue to be administered by the metropolitan – something that would cause problems in the future, as we shall see in Chapter 16.

Matthew died the following year. He had failed to unite the Malankara Church under his programme of reform, but the movement did not die with him. Instead, the reformers finally split officially from the church, forming the Mar Thoma Syrian Church in 1888. Its first bishop was Mar Thomas Athanasius, the son of Abraham Malpan. Thus, in a way, the disputes of the Reformation of the sixteenth century had been replayed in miniature in India over three centuries later, and a new Protestant church had been created.

EAST ASIA

In the seventeenth century Europeans had opened up routes to Asia in search of trade. This process continued into the nineteenth century. But where, in the past, the main aim had been to secure goods from the Asian countries, such as spice, now there was an increasing desire to sell European goods to the Asian countries. The most famous incident to come out of this drive was the Opium Wars between Britain and China. But it also led to greater European involvement, interference and settlement throughout Asia. Just as in Africa and India, the main Christian influences in Asia in this century were to be Protestant.

CHINA
The nineteenth century – the late Qing dynasty – was a time of great change for China. The country had to cope with renewed interest from outside, particularly the west. Trade blossomed, especially with the British, though there was considerable tension over access to the markets. This culminated in the Opium War of 1840–42, which was fought to establish the right of British traders to conduct commerce with China. In particular, there was profit to be made from opium, which was produced in India and sold to the Chinese, around one in twenty of whom were addicted to the drug.

Into all this came the first Protestant missionaries. Christianity was still a forbidden religion. There were still many Catholics throughout the country at the

Robert Morrison, by
John Richard
Wildman, 1824.

start of the nineteenth century, and even some seminaries for training Chinese priests, but the church was something of an underground movement. That did not daunt Robert Morrison (1782–1834), who arrived in China under the auspices of the LMS in 1807. A Scottish Presbyterian minister, Morrison spent most of his time in Guangzhou (modern Canton), where he worked for the British East India Company. Thus he was torn, to some extent, between commercial and religious interests. But he regarded the latter as paramount, and produced a major translation of the Bible into Chinese. A gifted linguist, he also wrote a Chinese grammar that became standard. Like Matteo Ricci before him, Morrison wanted to act as a cultural bridge between East and West, and he set up an Anglo-Chinese School in Malacca (at this time owned by the Dutch, but shortly to fall into British hands). The school was intended to train missionaries about to head to China, but in practice most of the students were Chinese hoping to learn about the West for business purposes.

Like the Catholic missions of the

seventeenth century, the Protestant missions helped to promote greater understanding of Chinese culture back home. James Legge (1815–97), a Scottish Congregationalist, became principal of Morrison's school in Malacca. He moved the school to Hong Kong, where with his friend Ho Tsun-sheen he worked hard on problems of translating Christian terms and ideas into Chinese. Legge later became a professor of Chinese studies at Oxford, where he published many Chinese works and commentaries on them. But Legge never showed the inclination of Ricci and his heirs to try to blend in with the Chinese by dressing or living like them. Indeed, most Protestant missionaries regarded this sort of thing as rather duplicitous: instead of messing about in Chinese clothes and fraternizing with bureaucrats, they felt, missionaries should be out talking about Jesus to the common man. Unfortunately, this was not as easy as they hoped. The missionaries typically wanted not merely to Christianize but to westernize the Chinese, since it was felt that their culture was barbarous and inhumane, involving foot-binding for women, infanticide, arranged marriages and so on. Many missionaries therefore opened small schools to educate the people. Peter Parker, an American Presbyterian, opened a hospital in Guangzhou in the 1830s and pioneered the approach of mission through medicine. Missionaries had to rely on local help, but few of those they hired were Christians. Those who were Christian were known as 'rice Christians', people who converted simply to get the job. And the missions in general suffered from suspicion towards foreigners: to many Chinese, the missionaries were simply part of the western imperialism that was threatening their country, and those who converted were no longer really Chinese at all.

These tentative missions received a huge boost in the 1840s with the conclusion of the Opium War, which was fought partly to establish a new system of treaties and trade between China and the West. Missionaries were not specifically

Hong Xiuquan and the God worshippers

The Taiping Rebellion (1851–64) was one of China's most devastating uprisings, costing more than twenty million lives and wreaking ruin and misery throughout the Yangzi River heartland. The Qing dynasty's imperial forces finally suppressed the rebellion, but, weakened and exhausted by the effort, the dynasty – and the whole of the traditional empire – collapsed fifty years later.

The rebellion was also one of the most creative movements in modern Chinese history. Nowhere is this creativity more evident than in the rebel faith, which, though inspired by a Protestant missionary tract, developed into a dynamic new Chinese religion, Taiping Christianity.

The first Protestant missionary, Robert Morrison, had only recently arrived in China, in 1807. He spent many of his early years translating the Bible, and then, with the help of China's first Protestant evangelist, Liang Afa, composing and publishing evangelistic tracts. In 1836 one of these tracts, *Good words to admonish the age*, was handed to the man who would become the leader of the Taiping Rebellion, Hong Xiuquan, as he was attending the Confucian-based civil service exams in the southern port city of Canton. After learning that he had failed this exam, Hong returned home and fell ill. Delirious for several days, he envisioned himself ascending to heaven and appearing before God, who commanded Hong to return to earth and to call his fellow countrymen to repent of their sins, to forsake idolatry and to slay the demons. Upon recovering from his illness, Hong seemed a changed man.

Yet it would not be until some seven years later that Hong would understand the meaning of his vision. At this time, a cousin glancing through the missionary tract that Hong had received earlier pointed out the correspondence between the deity who had appeared in his vision and the deity who was described in the tract. Believing that this tract and the vision were signs from God, Hong and his cousin repented of their sins,

baptized themselves and began to preach the new message to their families and to their fellow villagers.

Shortly thereafter, Chinese evangelists who were distributing tracts in the area heard of Hong's efforts and invited him to Canton to study with the Reverend I.J. Roberts, a Baptist missionary. For two months in 1847 Hong studied the Bible there in Canton, becoming more familiar with the book that he had been first introduced to in the pages of the tract.

From these three sources – Hong's own vision, the missionary tract and the translated Bible, Hong began to fashion the Taiping faith. At the core of that faith was a belief in one God. The rebels' faith was a strict monotheism, reinforced by their adherence to the Ten Commandments. The Taiping understanding of the identity of this one God, however, was largely shaped by the translation of the name of God that was used in the Bible. This was Shangdi (Sovereign on High), a name which was associated with the high God of China's classical period (1050–256 BC), and a name which was also associated with the contemporary term for the imperial title. Hong Xiuquan presented this religion, Taiping Christianity, as a revival and a restoration of the ancient classical faith in Shangdi.

It was the translation of the name for God, then, that connected Hong Xiuquan's emerging faith to its Chinese cultural and religious context. In accordance with their faith in Shangdi, Hong and his followers denounced the divine pretensions of the imperial title and condemned the sacral nature of the imperial office as blasphemous. The rebel aim was not just to overturn the Qing dynasty, but, in contrast to all previous Chinese rebellions, to rise up against the entire imperial system. The rebels called for a restoration of the classical system of kingship, which prevailed before the empire, alongside the restoration of the classical worship of Shangdi. The Heavenly Kingdom would replace the empire, and the Heavenly King would replace the emperor. This was the substance of the Taiping appeal.

Hong and some of some of his early converts, many from the Hakka ethnic minority, gathered several thousand believers into a 'Society of God worshippers'. By late 1850 the society

collided with the local militia, and in January 1851 the society proclaimed the establishment of their Taiping Heavenly Kingdom at Jintian in the south-western province of Guangxi. Marching north towards the Yangzi River, the rebel forces captured the city of Nanking, the southern capital of the Qing empire, by March 1853. The Taiping christened the city 'The Heavenly Capital', and it became the capital of their Heavenly Kingdom, a kingdom which would promote some of the most egalitarian social practices and economic policies China had ever seen.

Westerners resident in China at the time had become intrigued by this rebel movement, none more so than Western missionaries. The first Western visit to the Taiping capital came in April, 1853, and what was reported, for the most part, encouraged the missionaries. They were reassured by the rebels' strong monotheism, their commitment to the authority of the Bible, and to their destruction of idols. But they felt uneasy about other reports, principally that the Heavenly King claimed to be the younger brother of Jesus.

Merchants and diplomats were more sceptical about the movement. These latter Western representatives grew antagonistic toward the rebels, especially after they won favourable trading concessions from the Qing emperor, and this, along with the rise of a revived Confucian-oriented Chinese official leadership, spelt the end of the Taiping Heavenly Kingdom. The Heavenly capital fell in 1864.

The Taiping faith transformed, nonetheless, for at least its followers, but for all Chinese to some extent, how Chinese people thought about their religion, about the imperial office and title and about the entire traditional imperial and Confucian order.

THOMAS REILLY

A Buddhist temple in Nagasaki, in about 1880.

mentioned in the treaties, but as foreigners they received new levels of protection. From 1844, Christianity was no longer illegal for Chinese. Catholic missions were resumed and stepped up, now under the protection of France, which was interested in China mainly because Britain was – and the French did not wish to be left behind. In the 1850s and 60s the French concluded a number of treaties with China which allowed missionaries to travel and preach anywhere they liked, and Chinese to practise Christianity. Waves of missionaries, both Protestant and Catholic, travelled throughout China: the number of European Catholic priests in the country rose from 250 in 1870 to 886 in 1900, while there were 1,324 Protestant missionaries (mostly British and US) by the 1890s – and 7,000 in 1920, making China during this period the largest mission field in the history of Christianity. By the early years of the twentieth century, most of the missionaries were women – not wives of male missionaries, but single women on their own. The missionary societies had (with some reluctance) realized that these women were especially effective in China. But the missionaries still encountered great prejudice and

resistance: churches were attacked and burned, and some missionaries were killed.

Yet their message did spread, largely through the education and medicine that the missionaries brought. Protestant and Catholic missions alike tended to revolve around schools, hospitals, orphanages and other social institutions which the Chinese people greatly appreciated. As a result, the religion preached at these places spread. Catholic orphanages, generally run by sisters of various religious foundations, baptized those who entered their doors and brought them up as Catholics. Peter Parker's successor, John Kerr of the American Presbyterian Mission, treated over a million patients in fifty years in China. All this was part and parcel of a wider, more official process of 'westernization': China was importing western technology during this time, and the missionaries helped to spread western culture. The Society for the Diffusion of Christian and General Knowledge among the Chinese (later the Christian Literature Society), founded in 1887 in Shanghai by missionaries, published Chinese translations of western literature of all kinds.

But Christianity still remained a

relatively minor concern in China. The famous Taiping Rebellion, inspired by semi-Christian Messianism, helped to put many people off Protestantism. More serious was the Christian attitude to Chinese culture. Missionaries expected converts to maintain Sunday observance and give up opium; more troubling was their usual demand that people give up the 'rites', still a major sticking point. But the rites were regarded as part of what it was to be Chinese: those who questioned them threatened the ideological, moral and political basis of society. A considerable anti-Christian movement developed, especially after the 1840s and the influx of foreign missionaries. The anti-Christian writings of the seventeenth-century astronomer Yang Kuang-hsien became popular once again, and his arguments had great weight for many. There were plenty of dark rumours about what Christians got up to, with popular pamphlets describing them in lurid detail. Many missionaries, for their part, hated Confucianism (and Confucius himself) as the great enemy of their faith, and had nothing but contempt for the educated classes who were steeped in its teachings – a major contrast with the attitude of the Catholic missionaries of the seventeenth century. However, the Protestant missionaries found their greatest success with the same kinds of people who had responded most to the seventeenth-century missions: the lower classes, the homeless or minor traders.

JAPAN

The Tokugawa regime, which had closed Japan to the outside world two centuries earlier, was still in power, though entering its last days. In 1854 a treaty was concluded with the USA and five years later the first missionaries – both Catholic and Protestant – appeared. One, Bernard Petitjean, was amazed in 1865 to find that the churches founded by the Jesuits in the seventeenth century were still there, but these 'Hidden Christians' had changed almost out of all recognition.

Foreigners were allowed to practise Christianity in Japan, but it was still illegal for Japanese, and there was enormous prejudice against the religion – after all, for two centuries the Japanese had been encouraged to hate it as a *jakyō*, an 'evil religion'. The government sought to control the whole of society in what was almost a totalitarian regime: Confucianism and Buddhism were used as part of this regime, as a means of underpinning and controlling society. In this view there was no room for Christianity. In 1867 the Tokugawa regime finally collapsed, and in the following year imperial rule was restored. This was a time of social flux, and the new regime had no time for foreign religions. The new emperor therefore stepped up the persecution of Christianity: notices appeared across Japan stating: 'Evil religions like Christianity are strictly forbidden. Suspicious persons should be reported to the proper office. Rewards will be granted.' The government was especially alarmed by the appearance of the Hidden Christians, now making contact with the Catholic missionaries: thousands were rooted out and removed to distant provinces. Evangelization was illegal, so, as in China, most missionaries opened schools, clinics and so on as their primary activity and used these as a foothold into Japanese society. Christian literature was illegal, so they translated other western works in the hope of preparing the ground.

But over the next few years, in the face of massive international protest, there was a relaxation of these measures. In 1873 the notice boards were removed and Christianity was effectively decriminalized, although it remained technically illegal until 1889 when freedom of worship was finally allowed. More missionaries appeared, and Christianity became more and more popular in the closing two decades of the nineteenth century. For many Japanese it went hand in hand with an increasing interest in, and desire to emulate, western culture. There was an 'enlightenment movement' in Japan at this time, whose members included most Japanese intellectuals, which insisted that Japan had to learn to copy western civilization if it was to advance. One, Nakamura Keiu, argued that this had to involve the adoption of Christianity as the root of western culture. He even pressed for the baptism of the emperor and the establishment of a Christian state in Japan. More widespread, however, was the Movement for Freedom and People's Rights, popular among working people during the same period. This movement was political in nature and called for equality and natural rights, and even democracy, in Japan. Many Christians were involved in this movement, to the extent that those who were not Christians were attacked by opponents as if they were.

The first Protestant Church for Japanese rather than foreigners was founded in Yokohama in 1872 with a congregation of sixteen. In 1873 there were thought to be 59 Japanese Protestants. Six years later there were over 2,700. By 1891 there were some 31,000 of them. Most of these were evangelized or baptized by Japanese: the European missionaries found it difficult to leave the ports, for bureaucratic reasons, and so the mission to most of the country was largely run by their converts. In 1878 the Home Missionary Society was founded, a Japanese organization for the evangelization of Japan. A striking feature of these Protestant churches was that – at least at first – they tended not to belong to any traditional denomination. The first Japanese church was founded by Presbyterian and Dutch Reformed ministers and was called simply the Church of Christ in Japan. There were also western missionaries not attached to any church. Captain Leroy Janes, for example, was a layman who lived in Kumamoto during the 1870s and taught and even baptized Japanese converts. However, the later 1870s saw this ecumenism fade away, and the traditional denominations re-asserted themselves. The congregations of the Church of Christ in Japan gradually became absorbed into the other denominations.

On the Catholic side, the first seminary for training priests was opened at Nagasaki in 1890, and the following year an episcopal system was established under the archbishop of Tokyo. At this time there were some 45,000 Japanese Catholics, although the first Japanese to become a bishop would have to wait until 1927. There was also a Russian Orthodox mission in Japan at this time, established by Ivan Kasatkin, also known as Father Nikolai. He arrived in Hakodate in 1861 and moved to Tokyo in 1872, where he set up a new branch of the Russian Orthodox Church. By 1875 there were Japanese Orthodox priests; five years later Kasatkin had become their bishop. By the time of his death in 1912, there were 30,000 Japanese Orthodox believers.

In the 1880s there was something of a revival movement throughout the country, strengthening the Protestant churches still further. 'Theatre meetings' were held, in which preachers addressed large lecture halls or crowds in the open air. Many looked forward to a day when Japan might become an officially Christian country.

INDONESIA

In Chapter 10 we saw how the rule of the Dutch East India Company over Indonesia – or the Dutch East Indies – created a sort of caesaropapism, with the governor-general acting as de facto head of the Protestant churches in the area. In 1800 the region was taken out of the hands of the company and turned into an official Dutch colony, but the condition of the churches remained the same, except that it was now the state that ran them. In 1815 the king of the Netherlands instructed the different churches in the Dutch East Indies to reorganize and unite into a single Protestant Church of the Indies and, indirectly, the king was in control of the whole thing. A Protestant missionary commented in around 1870: 'In all the ecclesiastical regulations I have come across the title Governor-General 19 times, but not once the name of Christ, not even that of God!'

Yet as the official church structures became increasingly centralized and bureaucratic, new life was to be breathed into the ailing Indonesian churches. The Netherlands Missionary Society (NZG) began sending missionaries there, convinced that the Indonesian Christians were being neglected by first the company and then the colonial administration. More and more missionaries came to the Dutch East Indies as the nineteenth century progressed. The work proceeded rather in the same manner as the missions in the South Seas, far to the east. Missionaries would bring the Christian message to a new area and then rely upon local converts to spread it further. Preaching, catechesis and further preaching was the model, and it proved successful, although not to such a striking degree as in the Pacific islands. Often, the indigenous people who took the message on had no particular relation to the European missionaries: they were not specifically hired to do mission work but did it spontaneously of their own accord. As in the Pacific, the role of village chiefs could be vital in this, and in northern Sumatra a succession of Christian Batak chiefs, beginning with Pontas Lumbantobing, were central to the establishment of Protestantism in the area.

Perhaps surprisingly, there were also many Catholic missionaries, who were now permitted to work in the Dutch-controlled areas. The first Dutch Catholics arrived in 1808 in Java, but in 1841 a vicar apostolic was appointed for Batavia (modern Jakarta), and the Jesuits once again began to take a leading role. Francis van Lith, for example, did important work in Java at the turn of the twentieth century, essentially refounding the Catholic Church there almost single-handedly. The authorities tried to prevent Catholic and Protestant missionaries from working in the same areas, which gave churches in different areas quite different flavours. For example, Flores remained strongly Catholic, while northern Sumatra became highly Protestant. As we saw in Chapter 10, a largely independent Catholic community had remained in Flores throughout the Dutch period, and the Jesuits worked hard here to reintegrate it into the wider church.

CHAPTER 14

MODERN EUROPE

If the Enlightenment challenged Christianity in its European heartlands for the first time, it is only in the twentieth century that the challenge really hit home. That century saw secularism triumph over religion as the dominant force in society throughout much of Europe. Yet Christianity remains deeply ingrained in European culture, in the west as well as in the east.

A CHANGING EASTERN EUROPE

THE OTTOMAN EMPIRE AND THE BALKANS

Ever since the fourteenth century, eastern European Christianity had been either threatened or dominated by the Ottoman empire. By the sixteenth century, the Ottomans controlled a vast territory, roughly equivalent to the eastern part of the old Roman empire and much of North Africa. But in the seventeenth century, the empire entered an incredibly long, terminal decline. The Ottomans missed out on the cultural, scientific and economic benefits of the Enlightenment. By the nineteenth century, the Ottoman empire was simply another nation state, and an ailing one at that. Dubbed 'the sick man of Europe', the old empire's failing health was a perennial concern of nineteenth-century European politicians who had no desire to see instability on the continent's borders.

This period saw the Balkan countries, which had been conquered by the Ottomans centuries earlier, gradually regain independence. It was a slow and messy process. The Serbs, in particular, had spent much of the preceding couple of centuries

periodically rebelling against Ottoman rule. They were effectively independent from the early nineteenth century onwards, as was Greece. Together with several other countries, including Bulgaria, Serbia was internationally recognized by the Treaty of Berlin of 1878, when western European politicians carved up most of the former Ottoman possessions in the Balkans.

It was a time of great uncertainty and strife. Serbia and Bulgaria went to war against each other in 1885, and the situation was muddied by religion. Serbia had been staunchly Orthodox until its annexation by the Ottomans in the fourteenth century, after which time the church had declined. Many Orthodox had fled to Austro-Hungary in the seventeenth century and many Muslims had moved in. But the church was still strong in the country, and many distrusted their old ally, Catholic Austro-Hungary. In 1908 Austro-Hungary annexed the northern area of Bosnia, leading to greater fears among Orthodox Serbs of a Catholic takeover. They began to eye the southern parts of the Balkans, primarily Macedonia and Thrace. In 1912 and 1913 the Balkans saw two brief wars: in the first, Serbia, Greece and Bulgaria allied against the Ottomans, all hoping to carve out small empires in the territory they won from their former overlords; in the second, the other two turned on Bulgaria in a squabble over that territory.

Escaping Ottoman rule inevitably brought about a rejuvenation and renaissance in the Balkan churches. Each country, as it became independent of the Ottomans politically, also wanted to become independent of Constantinople in religion: in effect, the old system of having different national churches which were either autocephalous or semi-independent, which had been wiped out by

The interior of the church of the Pantanassa monastery, Mistras, Greece, built in 1428. Mistras was founded in 1249 by the Franks, but subsequently passed to the Byzantines. It became the centre of Byzantine culture on the Greek peninsula and held out against the Turks for seven years after the fall of Constantinople in 1453.

the Ottomans and replaced with a single church answering to Constantinople, was restored. Greece was one of the first countries to gain independence, and in 1850 the patriarch of Constantinople recognized its church as autocephalous. This has led to a slight confusion in terminology ever since: the term 'Greek Orthodox Church' can refer to this Church of Greece, as well as to the older Church of Constantinople, which suddenly found itself governing a much smaller territory. Both use the Greek language, the historic language of Orthodoxy. Greece has never had a patriarch of its own, though, being administered by a synod chaired by the archbishop of Athens.

In Bulgaria, meanwhile, there was a new-found sense that to be Bulgarian was, in part, to be a member of the Bulgarian Orthodox Church. The church had suffered

In common with all the Rayah races, which have been subject to Turkish domination, [the Bulgarians] have an hereditary antipathy, partly racial, partly theological, to the rule of Islam. Whenever the Cross replaces the Crescent over the mosque of St. Sophia, the sympathies of the Bulgars will be with the victors, not with the vanquished.

Edward Dicey, *The Peasant State*, 1894

Karl Marx.

greatly under the Ottomans, who in later years had tried to regulate the Bulgarian church and declaw it as a potential agent of nationalism by importing Greek priests to run the church. By the start of the nineteenth century the Bulgarian church was not simply under the control of the patriarch of Constantinople; its role as a preserver and transmitter of Bulgarian culture had been eroded away. The Bulgarian liturgy was dying out under the pressure from new Greek-speaking schools and seminaries. Only in the monasteries were the traditions of the Bulgarian Orthodox Church preserved. A new sense of the worth of these traditions emerged in the nineteenth century, drawing in part on the work of Paissiy of Hilendar, an eighteenth-century monk who called on the church to rediscover its Bulgarian nature and end Greek dominance. By the middle of the nineteenth century, this call had resulted in most of the northern part of Bulgaria removing itself from the ecclesiastical jurisdiction of Constantinople, with its own Bulgarian priests and bishops. In 1870 the

Ottomans therefore appointed a 'Bulgarian exarch', effectively the old Bulgarian patriarch under a new name, recognizing that this was a separate church from the Greek one. Constantinople, meanwhile, denounced the new exarchate as heretical and schismatic: it would not recognize it until 1945.

Nearby Serbia became autocephalous in 1879 and Romania did in 1885. The Orthodox Church had become again what it had once been before the fifteenth century: a commonwealth of churches, all recognizing the patriarch of Constantinople as the first among equals, but each governing themselves. Nationalism, patriotism and the renewal of these ancient churches all went hand in hand. Yet nationalism and the rivalries between the Balkan states would boil over into a war that would engulf the whole of Europe and beyond. In 1914, during a period of enormous tension elsewhere in Europe, an Austrian archduke was assassinated in Bosnia by a Serb, giving the Austro-Hungarians an excuse to declare war on Serbia, whose growing power in the Balkans threatened their own influence there. Serbia was allied to Russia, and Austro-Hungary to Germany… and the Great War began.

THE COMMUNIST REVOLUTIONS

As the Ottoman empire was fading, a new force was rising which would oppress most of the Orthodox world for much of the twentieth century. Communism derived from the writings of Karl Marx (1818–83), the German philosopher who tried to analyze history in terms of the struggle between classes. Marx was influenced by Hegel's belief that history is progressive, as society moves from one form of government to another, and Marx accepted this belief, reinterpreting it in light of his understanding of class relationships as based upon material and commercial exchange. The result was an insistence that societies would naturally evolve towards a communist state, where the owners of the means of production no longer exploited the workers, but where everyone owned everything in common.

As we saw in the last chapter, there was a powerful movement towards Christian socialism in the late nineteenth and early twentieth centuries, with many arguing that the early church itself – as portrayed in Acts – had been essentially communist in nature. Marxism, however, was an atheist philosophy: Marx believed that God was a human construct and famously regarded religion as 'the opiate of the people', something invented by the ruling classes to keep people content by getting them to focus on a happy future in heaven rather than on improving their miserable present on earth.

Marxism, in various forms, spread throughout Europe in the late nineteenth and early twentieth centuries, and in 1917 the long-awaited communist revolution arrived in Russia. Tsar Nicholas II (1868–1918) was overthrown, and civil war broke out, exhausting a country that had already been fighting the First World War for three years. Industry and agriculture were in tatters, and the economy went into free-fall. The power struggle that followed the death of the communist leader Vladimir Ilyich Lenin (1870–1924) saw Joseph Stalin (1879–1953) seizing power, consolidating authority in his own hands to a degree rivalling the autocratic tsars of the past.

All of this was extremely bad news for the church in what became the Union of Soviet Socialist Republics. In 1917 the church had decided to drop the system of rule by a synod – imposed by Peter 'the Great' in 1721 – and revert to rule by a single patriarch. The man elected was Vasily Ivanovich Belavin, better known (like most Russian monks) by the name he took when making his monastic vows, Tikhon. He had spent several years as bishop of Alaska, where he had become a US citizen. The authorities regarded Tikhon (1865–1925) as a counter-revolutionary representative of tsarism, and during the civil war many priests and monks were imprisoned or killed by the Red forces. Already in 1918 church and state were officially separated, with all church involvement in education ended and all church property seized by the state.

Tikhon responded by excommunicating the government. Bishops and priests were imprisoned, as was Tikhon himself, and in the 'Great Purge' of 1936–37, in which Stalin aimed to eliminate all opposition to his rule, many more died.

Most of the newly nationalized Orthodox churches elsewhere in Europe came under Soviet influence during or following the Second World War. Ukraine was merged into the Soviet Union, and the Ukrainian Catholic Church – which was part of the Roman communion but used Orthodox liturgy – was declared illegal. The same thing happened in Romania, where, in the Transylvanian part, there was also a strong contingent of eastern-rite Catholics. The Soviets forced the Romanian government to abdicate in 1947, replacing it with a puppet communist regime. Bulgaria had become communist in 1946. Serbia, meanwhile, had been merged with Croatia and Slovenia before the war to create Yugoslavia. It was split up again after the Germans invaded in 1941, and the Nazi-influenced Croatia set up extermination camps to eliminate Jews, gypsies, socialists and Serbs. Many members of the brutal Ustase regime regarded themselves as loyal Roman Catholics and whipped up hatred against the Orthodox Church: large numbers of Orthodox Serbs who escaped death in the concentration camps were forcibly converted to Catholicism. After the war, Yugoslavia was reunited and became a socialist federal republic, modelled on the Soviet Union, under Marshal Tito (1892–1980); Serbia, Bosnia, Croatia and Macedonia, among others, were part of this country. Although not nearly as extreme as the more communist countries, the socialist government seized much church property.

The partition – communist to the east, capitalist to the west – extended right up through Europe. Hungary had had a communist revolution in 1919, but the new regime lasted only five months before being ousted and replaced by a rightist, monarchist one (headed by a regent, although there was no king). Admiral Miklós Horthy (1868–1957) ruled as an authoritarian

The communists disdain to conceal their views and aims. They openly declare that their ends can be attained only by the forcible overthrow of all existing social conditions. Let the ruling classes tremble at a communist revolution. The proletarians have nothing to lose but their chains. They have a world to win.

Karl Marx and Friedrich Engels, *The Communist Manifesto*, 1848

At a time of great struggle with an external foe… it has been God's will to visit upon Russia a grievous new ordeal… In these decisive days in the life of Russia, We have deemed it Our duty in conscience to help Our people to draw closer together… We have judged it right to abdicate the Throne of the Russian State and to lay down the Supreme Power… May the Lord God help Russia.

Tsar Nicholas II, announcement of abdication, 1917

Orthodoxy under communism

'We're not giving any information about ourselves,' said a Russian Orthodox couple to officials collecting data for the 1939 Soviet census. 'We don't need a census, we need a priest and a church.'

It was perhaps the bleakest year for the Russian Orthodox Church in Soviet history. From the very start the Bolsheviks had targeted its wealth and social influence. They seized church property, and through the late 1920s and 30s nearly all the bishops and clergy and incalculably large numbers of the faithful perished in the labour camps or were shot. By 1939 the Russian Orthodox Church had virtually ceased to exist as an institution. There were only four bishops at liberty and very few of the pre-revolutionary tens of thousands of churches remained open for worship. Theological education, monasticism and religious publications had long ceased.

Yet the ordinary people remained tenacious believers. Popular support for the church was shown when in the 1920s the Soviet authorities set up a rival 'Living Church', which professed unstinting loyalty to the communist regime and its aims. The faithful stayed away from it in droves while still flocking to their traditional churches.

Popular support for the church was also clear when Hitler invaded the USSR in 1941. For once, Stalin was wrong-footed; the first to rally the Soviet people in defence of the Motherland was Metropolitan Sergi, one of the surviving church leaders. In the territories occupied by the Germans, churches promptly reopened. In 1943 Stalin reversed his policy and restored the Russian Orthodox Church to public existence. Theological education for clergy was resumed, some monasteries reopened, and publication of religious literature, albeit in tiny quantities, resumed. The church

was systematically marginalized, however, and kept under strict state control, a situation that continued with the sudden and virulent anti-religious campaign launched by Khrushchev from 1959 to 1964. In the late 1970s the state clamped down on all dissent, and the number of Christian prisoners grew steadily. The church was prohibited by law from engaging in charitable, missionary or educational activity.

Reliable statistics were impossible to come by, but from the 1960s the impression was that the church was growing, partly as a result of increasing cynicism about the official ideology, reinforced by Khrushchev's secret speech of 1956 in which he revealed the misdeeds of Stalin, hitherto a secular deity. The Soviet 'middle class' of managers, skilled workers and technocrats remained on the whole non-religious, but growing numbers of urban intellectuals, including actors, philosophers, writers, artists and poets began to take an interest in Orthodoxy. Meanwhile the mass of churchgoers were basically of peasant stock. The survival of Orthodoxy in Russia is mainly due to the traditional self-denial and uncomplaining acceptance of suffering on the part of ordinary believers.

Easter eve, Moscow, 1975: at a church in the suburbs, police were loading young people into vans; but at a church in the centre of the city the volunteer Komsomol doorkeepers stood back as happy crowds surged in. Someone muttered, 'It's not made of rubber!'

The Russian Orthodox Church spent 70 years under communist rule. All the rest of the self-governing Orthodox churches in Europe except that of Greece endured at least 40 years. Their experiences were all variations on the interplay between the traditional identification of an Orthodox church with a particular nation and the traditional obedience of that church to the secular power. The new factor was that the secular power was for the first time militantly atheist.

The Romanian Orthodox Church has always been on the Orthodox 'front line' in Europe. It has a history of contact with other faiths and has hence developed a vigorous theological tradition which continued during communist times. This gave some resilience to a church which, particularly under Ceausescu, was at once repressed and elevated to the status of a national institution. The church funerals of Ceausescu's father and mother were major media events, with Ceausescu present while Orthodox ceremonies were performed.

The national Orthodox Church of the Bulgarians preserved the identity of the nation under centuries of rule by the Ottomans. Bulgaria gained its independence only in the late nineteenth century, and hence the church had little opportunity to develop theologically and establish a firm presence in society. This in turn meant that it had few resources to resist communist control, becoming a mouthpiece for the regime.

The Serbian Orthodox Church, although in a weak position throughout the communist period, was nevertheless prepared to oppose the government if its vital interests were at stake, and particularly when it perceived threats to the Serbian nation and culture within the multinational Yugoslav state. It was an opposition force under communism primarily insofar as it represented the national interests of the Serbs.

About one-fifth of the population of Albania were Orthodox. No manifestation of religion of any kind was permitted in Albania after it declared itself the first atheist state in the world in 1967.

PHILIP WALTERS

Stefan Wyszyński, primate of Poland, kisses the hands of Pope John Paul II during his investiture in St Peter's Square, Rome, in 1978.

regent for nearly 25 years, in a right-wing, traditionalist regime that promoted the Catholic heritage of the country much like the dictatorships of Salazar and Franco in Portugal and Spain. But after the Second World War communism was again imposed on the country. To the north, Poland, which

was of course equally Catholic, was split between the Nazis and the Soviets in 1939. After the Second World War a communist government was set up here too. Further north still, the Catholic countries of Lithuania and Estonia were absorbed into the Soviet Union itself, and Germany was divided up, with East Germany falling under the influence of the Soviet Union. This was the only Eastern Bloc country where the dominant religion was Protestantism.

In most of these countries there was limited religious freedom: the state accepted people's right to believe and practise what religion they liked. The major exception was Albania, which in 1967 banned religion completely. However, even in the other countries the state did not accept that the church, as an institution, should play a role in society. There were attempts to remove Christians from public office, to quieten bishops, close churches and so on. In Czechoslovakia, which probably saw the greatest persecution of this kind, the state controlled the appointment of ecclesiastical positions, but it was rather lax when it came to filling them. By the early 1980s a third of all parishes lacked a priest and there were only five bishops out of the thirteen the country was meant to have. At the same time, the state tried to control the church and use it as a mouthpiece for propaganda. The most notorious example was the Christian Peace Conference, based in Prague and intended as an ecumenical body of Christians from both sides of the 'Iron Curtain' to campaign on political and social justice issues. In fact, officers of the conference were expected by the authorities to campaign against injustices to the west of the Iron Curtain, and they would find themselves removed from office if they were critical of anything to the east. Throughout eastern Europe 'peace priests' became a euphemism for collaborationists.

Yugoslavia, by contrast, had relatively good relations between church and state – seminaries, monasteries and other institutions were left alone – but even here the state tried to limit the involvement of the church in national life, denying it access to radio and television broadcasts, for instance.

The Catholic Church was strongly opposed to communism. Pope Pius XI (reigned 1922–39) devoted considerable energy to denouncing it. In 1930 he called for a world day of prayer and held a Mass for Christians suffering in Russia, a call which

Lutherans and Anglicans heeded as well as Catholics. In 1937 he issued an encyclical, *Divini redemptoris*, which condemned communism and declared that, since it was a fundamentally atheistic and mistaken philosophy, it was impossible for any Christians to have anything to do with it. His successor, Pius XII (reigned 1939–58), hated communism with a real passion. The early 1940s saw him express more fear about the successes of the Red Army than about Nazi Germany, and in 1949 he decreed that Catholics who joined communist organizations must be denied the sacraments.

There were two countries where the church found itself in a more positive situation. One was Poland. Poland had identified its national interest with the Catholic Church for centuries, at least since

The Communism of today, more emphatically than similar movements in the past, conceals in itself a false messianic idea. A pseudo-ideal of justice, of equality and fraternity in labour impregnates all its doctrine and activity with a deceptive mysticism, which communicates a zealous and contagious enthusiasm to the multitudes entrapped by delusive promises.

Pope Pius XI, *Divini redemptoris*, 1937

John Casimir had placed the country's welfare in the hands of the Virgin Mary. This continued in the nineteenth century, when Poland was carved up between other countries and Polish nationalism was strongly discouraged: only the Catholic Church remained as a stronghold of Polish culture and national sentiment. With the advent of communism, this identification continued. The Catholic University of Lublin remained open, the only one in the Eastern Bloc. Cardinal Stefan Wyszyński (1901–81) led the Catholic Church here with a strong hand. For the first decade, relations were still highly strained between church and state, with seminaries being closed and priests – including Wyszyński – being imprisoned. But from the mid-1950s the pressure eased, and the state recognized the importance of the Catholic Church to Polish culture. Edward Gierek, who came to power in 1970, actively courted the church, although many restrictions remained in place.

A slightly similar situation prevailed in East Germany. In 1948 the Evangelical Church in Germany (EKD) was formed as an umbrella organization for the Protestant churches in the whole country, but in 1969 the churches in East Germany split from it to form the Federation of Evangelical Churches (BEK). This church sought to cooperate, to some degree, with the state, recognizing that neither could really function without the other. Unlike churches in other communist countries, the BEK had access to radio and television, and it could even run theological courses in universities. It ran hospitals, schools and other social services, which were often funded to a large extent by the western churches which maintained links with the BEK. This was a major reason the state tolerated its activities. Even so, the church continued to clash ideologically with the communists, and individual Christians suffered discrimination, finding it harder to get good jobs.

THE END OF THE COMMUNIST ERA
In one of the most remarkable years of recent history, 1989 witnessed the end of communism in most of eastern Europe.

The impetus came from Mikhail Gorbachev (b. 1931), president of the Soviet Union, and his policies of *perestroika* and *glasnost* ('restructuring' and 'openness'). These reforms allowed private ownership of businesses, more freedom of speech and the ending of the one-party system. In 1988 he ended the 'Brezhnev Doctrine' which had insisted that the USSR should interfere in other Eastern Bloc countries if the cause of communism seemed compromised. This left those countries

with a free hand, effectively ending the Cold War.

Poland was the first country to change: free elections were held in June 1989, and the communists were swept from power. In November 1989 the East German government collapsed and the Berlin Wall, which had divided Berlin into two halves, was broken down. The Czech government resigned shortly after, and the following month, Nicolae Ceausescu (1918–89), dictator of Romania, was overthrown and executed. The following year, Germany was reunited and Albania, Bulgaria and Yugoslavia all saw their governments become more democratic. The Soviet Union itself was dissolved in 1991. Yugoslavia, meanwhile, split into its constituent states, but disagreements over how to do this, and over the fact that the state borders did not match ethnic boundaries, led to a series of bloody wars there in the 1990s.

The end of communist rule in eastern Europe was a highly complex phenomenon,

Germans at the Berlin Wall celebrate the fall of communism in East Germany, 12 November 1989.

Mother Teresa and
Pope John Paul II in
India, February
1986.

*God in himself is a
mystery. Of his inner
experience nothing
can be said. But
through creation,
through providence
and his work of
salvation, God comes
down to the level of
man.*

Dumitru Stăniloae

but Christianity did play an important role. The mere existence of the churches in most of these countries was an implicit challenge to communism, since it meant that an alternative ideology was available, and the fact that the state tolerated it to some degree indicated that Stalin-style totalitarianism was not, in fact, in place. In Romania, an important figure who demonstrated this through his work was Dumitru Stăniloae (1903–93), a Romanian Orthodox priest who taught at a number of institutions in the 1950s, 60s and 70s. Stăniloae was deeply concerned to recover Romania's Christian heritage by redirecting Christians to their roots, the study of the church fathers. He restated for a new generation the thought of the Greek fathers, especially Maximus the Confessor, and the hesychastic mysticism of Gregory Palamas, aiming for simplicity and readability in his work. He spent several years in prison at one point, but lived to see the Ceausescu regime overthrown.

Often, the churches offered the only buildings available to non-state-sponsored societies or activities. This meant that the churches helped to foster the movement for democracy and individual rights that gathered pace in the 1980s. In East Germany, for example, the BEK was closely linked to these movements. It held immense festivals, lasting for days and with thousands of people, calling for peace, disarmament and social justice. By the end of the 1980s, and the eve of the fall of communism, the BEK was effectively the major opposition to the government in East Germany.

In Poland it had seemed to many that the Catholic Church, under Cardinal Stefan Wyszyński, offered a more credible ideology than state communism. In 1966 he had presided over the celebrations for the thousandth anniversary of Christianity in Poland, recalling the fact that, for centuries, to be Polish had meant being Catholic. It is perhaps striking that communist countries produced the two most globally recognizable faces of Catholicism in the late twentieth century – Mother Teresa of Calcutta (now Kolkata) and Pope John Paul II (1920–2005). Mother Teresa had left her native country before communism was imposed there, but Karol Wojtyla, later to become John Paul II, had struggled with it for many years. Wojtyla had known Nazi rule as a young man, training for the priesthood at an underground seminary, before the imposition of communism. He became archbishop of Kraków in 1963 and a cardinal in 1967. To begin with he said little on political matters, but this changed in 1970 when he bitterly denounced a massacre of striking shipyard workers, a denunciation which began almost a decade of attacks on the communist regime, making him a much more dangerous figure in the eyes of the regime than his superior, Stefan Wyszyński. On his frequent visits to Rome, Wojtyla reminded his fellow cardinals that there was more to the Catholic world than western Europe and South America, calling for more concern about the fate of the churches in eastern Europe.

Karol Wojtyla's surprise election to the papacy in 1978 as the first ever Polish pope energized the church in his native land and horrified the Kremlin. When the new pope visited Poland in 1979, the USSR insisted on an explanation from Polish leader Edward Gierek – how could such a thing have been allowed? Gierek, for his part, knew that he could not block the visit and did his best, without much success, to dampen the people's enthusiasm for John Paul II. At the same time, the pope's first encyclical, *Redemptor hominis*, was a sustained attack on communism, arguing that it had failed in its objective to improve the lot of humanity, and that only the church had the real potential to help people in the way that communists had dreamed. The encyclical had an extraordinary effect: a 1979 survey at Gdánsk University found that over half of the members of the Communist Party there described themselves as practising Catholics. There was not quite the massive undermining of communist atheism that this might suggest, but the pope's adroit self-presentation as champion of the people impressed many and helped to change attitudes throughout eastern Europe. Both Czechoslovakia and Hungary saw interest in Catholicism rising, as the church became associated with a principled stand against communism.

EASTERN EUROPE AFTER COMMUNISM

Since 1989 the churches of the former Eastern Bloc have found themselves in a radically new situation. There was new enthusiasm for the churches, conceived again as symbols of national pride. Romania, in particular, saw new support for the Romanian Orthodox Church, and indeed such a large majority of the population claimed membership that this church is now the largest of the Orthodox churches outside Russia. There are some 400 monasteries and 14,500 churches in the country today.

But this boost has been overshadowed by the problems which have faced the churches in this new era of uncertainty. Some of these are practical: for example, the churches were not given back their property as quickly as they hoped after the fall of communism. The Romanian Orthodox Church was given many properties which had actually belonged to the small Catholic eastern-rite community. Also, many churches had a shortage of priests, while many of those they did have were inexperienced or unsure how to lead their communities in the new era. Some churches had been run by strong bishops during the communist era, who acted as the focal point for the Christian community and stood up to the authorities: now that there were no hostile authorities, the bishops still took an authoritarian lead. Rather than replicating in their churches the national movement to democracy, these bishops tried to retain a more centralized administration.

There were internal divisions, too. One problem was with those Christians who had collaborated with the communists. In the former East Germany, the records of the Stasi, the secret police, were revealed in the early 1990s, showing that many church officials and members had cooperated with them. Many of their colleagues in the churches felt betrayed. Other problems came from ideological differences which had been fostered during the communist era. Many Christians had opposed communism because it was an atheistic, materialist philosophy that tried to create a secular state. This was especially the case in

Americans of certain ages remember where they were when Pearl Harbor was attacked, when President Roosevelt died, when President Kennedy was assassinated. Poles remember where they were when John Paul II was elected.

George Weigel

Jesus Christ meets the man of every age, including our own, with the same words: 'You will know the truth, and the truth will make you free' [John 8:32]. These words contain both a fundamental requirement and a warning: the requirement of an honest relationship with regard to truth as a condition for authentic freedom, and the warning to avoid every kind of illusory freedom, every superficial unilateral freedom, every freedom that fails to enter into the whole truth about man and the world.

Pope John Paul II, *Redemptor hominis*, 1979

Poland and in the Orthodox countries, where communism was feared as a rival ideology to Christianity. But many other Christians had opposed communism more on moral than theological grounds, because it was a totalitarian philosophy that denied basic human rights to people. This was especially the case in East Germany. After the Iron Curtain was rolled up, these different groups found themselves in profound disagreement, as the first group was associated with right-wing politics and wanted conservative social reforms, while the second group supported greater liberalizing of politics and society. In the minds of many people in eastern Europe, the conservative Christians sought to replace communist totalitarianism with a Christian version. In Poland, in particular, the immediate aftermath of the removal from power of the communists saw the Catholic Church playing a central role in the political and social reforms of the country. The church was part of discussions at every level and in every organization in the country, and when a new constitution was planned in 1990 the church tried to ensure that church and state would be re-unified. Churchmen campaigned successfully for more restrictions on abortion and birth control. As a result, the church's popularity slid dramatically within just a couple of years, and opinion polls in the early 1990s revealed that most Poles felt the Catholic Church had too much power in their country.

There was thus a basic problem over how *politically* conservative or liberal the churches should be. This was related to a division over *theological* conservatism and liberalism, spurred by the fact that these churches were suddenly engaged with the wider globe. Emerging from the insular world of the Eastern Bloc, they were forced to deal with the developments that had been going on elsewhere – the rise of new forms of liberal theology, feminism, liberation theology and so on. Many in the Orthodox and Catholic churches, in particular, shrank from these, preferring a return to conservative orthodoxy rather than movements which seemed to

them too similar to the communism they had only recently escaped. Orthodox priests and laymen alike in the former communist countries have periodically denounced not only theological liberalism but Darwinism, secularism, anything smacking of socialism and so on. In 2004 there was even an attempt by the Serbian government to make schools teach creationism and evolution side-by-side, similar to the attempts by some legislators in the USA to do the same thing.

Some people felt betrayed, to some degree, by the western churches. In 1991, as Germany reunited, so too the BEK rejoined the EKD, bringing new unity to the Protestant churches in the country – but the BEK felt it was simply being swallowed up by the EKD, losing its distinctive voice in the process. Many Orthodox leaders, meanwhile, rejected the ecumenical movement which now reached their countries, and were greatly disturbed by the appearance of Protestant missionaries.

In effect, the churches of eastern Europe faced – and still face – a crisis over their nature and function. Was their role as the voice of protest in the communist era a reflection of their fundamental nature as the voice of the people in these countries? Or was it a brief accident of history, caused by the churches' status as the only non-state-controlled ideological organization? Do the churches have a future at the heart of their national cultures, or did the communists' attempts to secularize the Eastern Bloc bear fruit? Today these countries are inhabited by a generation who know only secularism and whose parents may have done, too. Some of them remain deeply religious, such as Poland and Bulgaria, but others are largely secular, such as the former East Germany. At the same time, some of these countries are becoming more involved with the wider world. In 2004 Poland, Lithuania, the Czech Republic, Hungary and others joined the European Union, becoming united to some degree with western nations such as Britain and France, and allowing their inhabitants to move freely between them. As these nations turned more to the west, the implicit challenge to their churches became even greater. Churchmen denounced the consumerism and secularism that they feared would flood in from the west. At the same time, most church leaders came to approve of joining the EU and other west-oriented moves. The opening years of the twenty-first century thus seemed to give the promise of greater integration and cooperation between the churches of eastern and western Europe.

MODERNISM TO POSTMODERNISM: WESTERN EUROPE

THE FIRST WORLD WAR AND THE END OF THE MODERN PROJECT
After the Franco-Prussian War of 1870, western Europe enjoyed nearly half a century of peace within its own borders. This came to an abrupt end with the outbreak of the First World War in 1914, which proved to have as great an impact on the western churches as it had on the eastern.

Many welcomed the outbreak of hostilities, not simply out of patriotic fervour, but for religious reasons too. In Germany many people thought this was the next stage in Germany's struggle against its rivals towards a 'place in the sun'. Kaiser Wilhelm II (1859–1941) was not only king of Prussia but primate of the Prussian church, and he could call upon the nation to pray in the same breath as he called upon it to fight. Some liberal theologians commended the war as the means to allow Germany to dominate geopolitics and help to create the kingdom of God. Adolf von Harnack, in particular, spent much of the autumn of 1914 writing defences of German policy and even drafting speeches for the Kaiser. In Britain and America, the popularity of the social gospel movement led many to views similar to those of the German liberals, seeing the war as an unavoidable element in

A group of Canadian soldiers go 'over the top' during trench warfare in the First World War.

the establishment of the kingdom of God on earth – for such a kingdom, it was felt, required precisely the sense of solidarity and self-sacrifice that war fostered.

For some people the hostilities themselves took on religious overtones. Before the war considerable progress had been made by Protestant pacifist groups in the promotion of friendly relations between churches of different nations. There was, for example, a constant dialogue between the English and German Protestant churches:

indeed, in a disaster of timing, a conference had been planned for early August 1914. But none of that did a thing to stop the war. Everyone, it seems, forgot their pre-war principles when hostilities were announced; even Quakers queued up to enlist. The fact that Muslim Turkey fought alongside Germany and Austria was not lost on the Allies, many of whom interpreted the situation as a new crusade: indeed, after November 1914 Turkey was officially on jihad against the Allies. When the Allies

The statue of Our Lady of Fatima is paraded before hundreds of thousands of worshippers at Fatima in Portugal, before the ceremony to beatify Francisca and Jacinta, two of the children who experienced visions of her in 1917. Pope John Paul II, who presided over this ceremony in 2000, credited Our Lady of Fatima with saving his life after an attempt on his life in 1981.

captured Jerusalem in 1917, it was hailed as a new crusading success. Moreover, the different churches of the different combatants were eager to face each other in battle. Austro-Hungarians gladly went to war against the Russians, just as Catholics had warred on Orthodox in earlier ages, even seeking a papal blessing for the endeavour. When the Russians invaded Galicia, they forced Catholics to convert to Orthodoxy. When Germany captured Riga in Lithuania, they returned the favour by reconsecrating the Orthodox cathedral as Lutheran.

Meanwhile, in a war where God was supposedly on everyone's side, tales circulated of miracles. The 'angels of Mons', who supposedly saved the British from annihilation in a battle of August 1914, were so popular that to disbelieve the story was popularly interpreted as treason. Similarly, the battle of the Marne (1914), in which the French held back the German advance just a day's march from Paris, became known as 'the miracle of the Marne' and interpreted as evidence for the Virgin Mary's protection of France. Soldiers dedicated themselves to 'Our Lady of the Trenches'.

The most famous apparition during this period was of the Virgin Mary to three small children in the Portuguese village of Fatima in 1917. The Portuguese revolution had disestablished the Catholic Church and ushered in an atmosphere of rampant anti-clericalism, but the children's visions attracted attention, and 70,000 people turned up on the date of the promised final appearance of the Virgin. They did not see her, but they did report that the sun appeared to dance around the sky and even hurtle towards them. The apparitions were testament to the power of Catholicism among the people of Portugal, even as a secular government tried to stamp it out, and they helped to galvanize support for the coup of 1917 which ousted that government.

In France, meanwhile, many Catholic priests interpreted the outbreak of war as a divine judgment upon France for secularization, and as a call to it to restore its old role as defender of the Catholic faith. President Raymond Poincaré himself,

announcing the start of hostilities, called for a 'sacred union' of the nation, which took the form of many Catholic priests signing up to fight as ordinary soldiers, rather than as army chaplains, as well as previously anti-clerical intellectuals becoming more prepared to defend Catholicism as a vital part of France's cultural heritage, now under attack from Germany. The 'union' was not perfect – militant secularists condemned the Catholic Church for not being sufficiently keen on the war – but it was still quite striking. In France, as in Britain and Germany, church attendance increased dramatically in the early stages of the war, both as the national cause was identified with that of God, and as people prayed for the survival of themselves or their loved ones.

Pope Benedict XV, who was elected in September 1914, did his best to maintain some moral high ground throughout the war. He began his pontificate with a call for ecclesiastical neutrality, refusing to denounce the German invasion of Belgium. He stated instead that the church's role was to try to relieve suffering wherever it occurred and to work for peace. This he did by, for example, helping prisoners of war on all sides to contact relatives. Indeed, Benedict donated so much money to the relief of suffering – 82 million lire in all – that he almost bankrupted the Vatican, which a few years later would have to borrow money to pay for his funeral and his successor's consecration. At the same time, Benedict made a number of calls for peace, all of which were ignored: his neutral stance meant that all combatants suspected him of really being on the side of their enemies.

As the war dragged on, the patriotic fervour declined. By the time it finally ended in November 1918, much of Europe had been devastated and half a generation had been killed. Ideology, politics and philosophy in Europe would be profoundly altered by this traumatic war for the rest of the century, and this applied to Christianity as well. Many people felt that the war showed up earlier theological trends, such as liberal theology or the social gospel, as

The religion of Christ makes patriotism a law; there is no perfect Christian who is not a perfect patriot.

Désiré Mercier, cardinal archbishop of Malines, Belgium, 1914

The soldier has got Religion; I am not so sure that he has got Christianity.

The Church of England's study of soldiers' beliefs, 1919

inherently flawed. They had actually promoted the war, when Christians should be working for peace. Most famously, Karl Barth (1886–1968), later the most important theologian of the twentieth century, but at that time a provincial Lutheran pastor, washed his hands of liberal theology in August 1914 and began a search for something better. At the same time, others saw in the post-war period an opportunity for that pre-war liberalism to flower, as the need for reconstruction and the rebuilding of bridges between nations seemed to offer the hope of building the kingdom of God on earth.

THE AGE OF THE DICTATORS

The rise to power in 1920s Italy of Benito Mussolini (1883–1945) – and in 1930s Germany of Adolf Hitler (1889–1945) – marked the emergence of fascism as a real power in western Europe. Just like communism, though in different ways, fascism not only meant the establishment of a totalitarian state, but also the construction of an ideology that was opposed to Christianity on many points.

Where, in all this, were the churches? Strikingly, they were playing a larger role in everyday life and politics than they had before the First World War. It is tempting to assume that the 'modernization' of society throughout this period must have involved 'secularization', as in France in the early years of the century, but that is not necessarily so. One reason for this was that, in an age of what seemed to be increasing secularization (as in Germany's Weimar Republic, the democratic regime that preceded Hitler) and uncertainty, the churches provided not simply stability but a fixed point around which people could order their lives. A church might be associated with a school, a sports club, social events and so on. And the appearance of new ideologies, such as fascism, often had the effect of driving people back to the established ideologies, such as Catholicism. This meant that, in many places, the churches and their associated groups acted almost as the glue

that held society together or, in a more common metaphor, as the pillars that held it up. This phenomenon is therefore known as 'pillarization', and it was common throughout Europe in the 1920s and 30s, especially in Catholic countries or regions.

Politically, this was reflected in the strength of explicitly Christian political parties in many countries, such as the Centre Party in Germany, which was Catholic, and the Christian Social Party in Austria. Since these parties offered a third way between socialism and fascism, they often occupied the political centre ground and played a vital role in parliaments across Europe, which were mostly moving to a proportional representation system that encouraged coalition governments. Many people felt that secular politics had failed – as proven by the slaughter of the Great War – and that explicitly Christian politics might provide a better way. Some of these political parties were therefore quite radical or countercultural, such as the Anti-Revolutionary Party in the Netherlands, which was Calvinist, or the Christian People's Party in Norway, which was Lutheran.

Nevertheless, explicit opposition to the dictators was not always forthcoming from the churches. For one thing, there were non-fascist dictators who approved of Christianity. One such was General Francisco Franco (1892–1975), who emerged as dictator of Spain in 1936 following the civil war. Officially known as 'Leader of Spain by the grace of God', Franco was not really a fascist, despite his imposition of a one-party state and the banning of all dissent – indeed, he had no particular governing ideology at all, and therefore sought support from the Catholic Church to provide one. Catholicism thus flourished under Franco. The same situation held in Portugal, governed from 1932 onwards by a former student of the Jesuits, António Salazar (1889–1970). Like Franco, Salazar was a dictator who presided over a one-party state, but he offered primarily stability and conservative values rather than any fascist ideology. His 'New State' therefore endorsed Catholicism as part of Portugal's cultural heritage, and even

I stand by my word. I will protect the rights and freedom of the church and will not permit them to be touched. You need have no apprehensions concerning the freedom of the church.

Adolf Hitler, to representatives of the Catholic Church, 1933

Dialectical Theology

Dialectical theology, sometimes called 'Crisis theology', arose in the crisis of the European First World War. Karl Barth (1886–1968) is the theologian most deeply linked to this movement in German theology as its primary inspiration, notably through his famous commentary on the epistle to the Romans (1922). This was not only a commentary on the text of St Paul's letter, but a radically new theological manifesto or summons to reject liberal Protestantism, for a long time dominant in German academic theology. Such was its impact that one Roman Catholic theologian of the time, Karl Adam, called it 'a bombshell in the playground of the theologians'.

Liberal Protestantism was felt by Barth and others to have been revealed as bankrupt in its attitude to the catastrophe of the 1914 War. Barth's *Commentary on Romans* set out to sound the alarm against 'cultural Christianity' by emphasizing again the transcendence, unknowability and sheer holiness of God, and the danger of 'domesticating' God into morality, aesthetical sense or any other human cultural or psychological activity. God for Barth is 'wholly other', of 'infinite qualitative' distinction from the created order, which is deeply fallen. Indeed we cannot speak of God with our merely human capacities. God's being eludes human concept and speech, and theology must therefore be 'dialectical' in constantly negating what it affirms. Conservative biblicism is rejected as seeking to capture truth about God; liberalism is even more roundly criticized for identifying God with human ethics; Roman Catholicism is rejected for identifying the divine with the

institution of the church. Barth does wish to return to the Bible, but in its capacity to point us to God, as someone might point to a moving bird in flight.

Dialectical theology also sought to recover a Christian eschatology for theology, by which was meant the inbreaking of God into history. This note was struck by the title of the journal carrying the message of the movement, 'Between the Times'. Besides Barth, other theologians writing under this banner included Rudolph Bultmann, Friedrich Gogarten, Emil Brunner and Eduard Thurneysen.

The movement contained different emphases and interests within itself. Barth criticized Brunner for suggesting that the human being had a capacity for God, a point of contact, whereas Barth believed that God alone could supply that by grace. Bultmann's path took a radically subjective turn, perhaps showing that dialectical theology itself was subject to dialectical polarization. For Bultmann, we can know by faith only that God exists and that the message of the gospel is that Jesus himself had authentic faith. Barth developed his dialectical theology in a much more objective and traditional direction, with Jesus revealed to faith, and not to some dispassionate historical investigation, as the Trinitarian Son of God made flesh.

Some of the cultural influences shaping dialectical theology included Kierkegaard's writings, and also the novels of Dostoevsky exploring the reality of sin and evil. The pessimistic side of human nature and history was pitted against liberal optimism, an optimism killed off on the barbed wire of the Somme. Artistically, this inter-war era was one of radical questioning. T.S Eliot's poem *The Waste Land* portrayed a pessimistic bleak European culture, adrift from its moorings. Expressionism in art, with its fractured and broken imagery, disturbing the

conventional and establishment views, notably Picasso's *Guernica* on the Spanish Civil War, echoes dialectical theology. Indeed, Barth's *Romans* is full of the imagery of lightning splintering trees, of mountain rivers gushing headlong downwards, of the crater left by the meteorite.

Dialectical theology was overwhelmingly a German theological movement, and an attack on liberal theology which proved extremely successful. It also swept away the conservative evangelical tradition of such theologians in Germany as Adolph Schlatter, a scholarly biblical theologian. Roman Catholic theologians, too, acknowledged Barth as their greatest critic and dialogue partner. The movement never really found favour in England, but Scotland proved far more receptive. Today, however, there has been a considerable renewal of interest in Barth in English-speaking theological circles, as liberal theology has lost touch with grassroots Christianity and fundamentalism is regarded as verging on bibliolatry. Dialectical theology declines any claim of human enlightenment or rationality to define God; it also refuses to allow a deification of any text or institution, whether scripture or church – they may 'become' witnesses to God as the Spirit acts. Dialectical theology tried to find a way of affirming God's reality and sovereign holiness as disclosed in the narratives of 'the strange new world of the Bible', while preserving divine freedom from capture by human language and concept.

TIMOTHY BRADSHAW

partly based its economic policy upon papal encyclicals. Finally, the dictator Engelbert Dollfuss (1892–1934) came to power in Austria in 1932 and offered a similar right-wing, conservative agenda based in part around Catholic principles – although he was killed by Nazi assassins just two years later.

Even the fascist dictators, though, were not only welcomed by many Christians but actively supported, to varying degrees. Pope Pius XI, who succeeded Benedict XV in 1922, praised Mussolini as a 'man sent by providence', words he would later regret. Notably, it was Mussolini's regime that concluded the Lateran Pacts with the papacy in 1929, resulting in the establishment of Vatican City. Before that date, ever since Pius IX had lost the papal states in the nineteenth century, the papacy had been a stateless

Whoever exalts race, or the people, or the State, or a particular form of State, or of the depositories of power, or any other fundamental value of the human community – however necessary and honourable be their function of worldly things – whoever raises these notions above their standard value and divinizes them to an idolatrous level, distorts and perverts an order of the world planned and created by God; he is far from the true faith in God and from the concept of life which that faith upholds.

Pope Pius XI, *With deep anxiety*, 1937

A Hitler Youth rally at Nuremberg in 1933.

institution, independent of Italian law but without any legal territory of its own. The Lateran Pacts remedied this situation by making Vatican City an independent country, an enclave within Rome and the smallest sovereign nation in the world, with the pope as head of state.

Pius XI also negotiated a 'concordat' with Hitler in 1933, the terms of which meant that the Catholic Church and the Nazi state would leave each other alone; after all, they had a shared interest in blocking the spread of communism. Hitler completely ignored the concordat, however, and in 1937 began arresting dissident Catholic priests and clamping down on opposition within the Catholic Church.

Hitler found greater compliance in Ludwig Müller (1883–1946), a Lutheran with outspoken anti-Semitic views who supported the Nazis. The Nazis unified the Protestant churches of Germany into a single Reich church, and put it in the charge of Müller as Reich bishop. Müller enthusiastically began re-organizing the

church along Nazi lines. Instead of the Bible, *Mein Kampf*, Hitler's autobiography, was placed in churches, and only Nazi party members could preach. 1933 saw the adoption of the 'Aryan paragraph', which forbade baptized Jews or anyone descended from or married to non-Aryans from holding ecclesiastical positions. In a kind of horrible resurrection of Marcionite theology, one Reinhold Krause called for the elimination of anything Jewish in the church, from the Old Testament to the writings of the man he called 'Rabbi Paul' in the New. Here was a new kind of caesaropapism, making the church not only a state department but a vehicle of state ideology. These changes reflected the views of the 'German Christians' ('Deutsche Christen' or DC), a movement within the Protestant churches which was essentially Nazism in a Christian guise. With the slogan 'the swastika on our breasts and the cross in our hearts', the DC worshipped Christ as an Aryan superman who had defeated the Jews, and they idolized Hitler as a Germanic messiah. The

striking thing is that this travesty of Christianity was not imposed upon the church by the Nazis – indeed, Hitler himself apparently thought it rather silly.

Many other religious groups had less truck with the Nazis. The Jehovah's Witnesses in Germany refused to have anything to do with Nazism and were mercilessly persecuted as a result, some 2,000 losing their lives in concentration camps. In 1937 Pope Pius XI published an encyclical entitled *With deep anxiety* – very unusually, written in German rather than Latin, and intended to be read in all German churches. It attacked Nazi ideology, especially its militarism and racism. However, the pope's objection to Nazism was theological rather than humanitarian. Thus, he rejected racism because it was a form of idolatry – raising a race to the position of worship properly exclusive to God – rather than because it harmed people. But the pope did express solidarity with those being persecuted in Germany: in 1938 he made the famous statement 'Spiritually, we are all Semites.'

There was also resistance to Nazism among the Protestant churches, but it similarly tended to focus on theological rather than humanitarian issues. The most important vehicle of this protest was the Confessing Church ('Bekennende Kirche' or BK), established in 1934 by Martin Niemöller (1892–1984), a First World War submarine commander before becoming a Lutheran pastor in Dahlem, a suburb of Berlin. Niemöller was a German nationalist who had condemned the decadence of the Weimar Republic and initially welcomed Hitler's rise to power, but he quickly became disillusioned. The BK was essentially a form of unarmed resistance movement, which opposed the infiltration of Nazi racist and nationalist doctrines into Christianity. It was based, doctrinally, on the Barmen Declaration of 1934, which was drafted by Karl Barth and which rejected any notion of the state's authority over the church. Here, then, was another *theological* rejection of Nazism, rather than a *moral* one. Barth did denounce the Nazis' anti-Semitism, declaring

it a sin against the Holy Spirit, but most of his colleagues in the BK were more worried about the state's claim of authority over the church. At a rally held in Dahlem in late 1934, which was attended by 20,000 people, Niemöller declared, 'It is a question of which master the German Protestants are going to serve, Christ or another.'

Many of the activists in the BK were persecuted or imprisoned. Niemöller was arrested in 1937 and sent to Sachenhausen and Dachau concentration camps, not freed until the end of the war. Karl Barth lost his professorship in Bonn when he refused to swear an oath to Hitler, but from 1935 was able to continue work at Basle in his native Switzerland. A younger theologian, Dietrich Bonhoeffer (1906–45), tried to take things further. He felt that theological opposition to the presence of Nazi propaganda in the church needed to translate into moral opposition to racism and anti-Semitism as well as militarism. So Bonhoeffer dedicated himself to the resistance movement, and set up an out-of-town seminary for ministers,

which was run almost like a monastery. He also used his international church connections – especially in the USA and Britain – to raise awareness of the situation in Germany and the BK's opposition to Nazism. In 1939, as war loomed, Bonhoeffer was in New York; but he chose to return to Berlin rather than remain in safety on the grounds that, if Christians were to play a part in the reconstruction of Germany after

We reject the false doctrine, as though the state over and beyond its special commission should become the single and totalitarian order of human life, thus fulfilling the Church's vocation as well. We reject the false doctrine, as though the Church over and beyond its special commission should and could appropriate the characteristics, the tasks, and the dignity of the state, thus itself becoming an organ of the state.

The Barmen Declaration, 1934

Dietrich Bonhoeffer in 1932, with a group of young people soon to be confirmed.

the war, they would be needed there during it. In 1943 Bonhoeffer was linked to a plot to help Jews to escape Germany and imprisoned. The following year he was implicated in the July Plot, a nearly successful assassination attempt on Hitler made by senior army officers. Bonhoeffer had struggled with his conscience, believing that trying to kill anyone was incompatible with Christianity, but eventually concluded that in Hitler's case the consequences of not doing so weighed more. For this Bonhoeffer, together with his brother and two brothers-in-law, was hanged in 1945, even as the Red Army approached Berlin itself. He has generally been regarded not simply as a victim of political oppression but as a martyr, for his opposition to Hitler was part and parcel of his Christian faith.

AFTER THE HOLOCAUST

The end of the Second World War in 1945 brought arguably even greater social and cultural changes than the end of the first in 1918. There was, to some degree, an increase in church attendance and general piety in Europe and in the USA in the fifteen years or so following the end of the Second World War. The war had, in many quarters, been seen as a Christian crusade against pagan Nazism, and this not only helped to rejuvenate the churches but in some countries led to the introduction of legislation of a Christian nature. England and Wales made religious education and services in schools compulsory in 1944, and West Germany outlawed capital punishment and abortion as part of the reaction against Nazism.

Yet if there was a resurgence in Christianity during these years, it was also a time of crisis and the rethinking of traditional attitudes. This was caused partly by the revelations from eastern Europe, where it became increasingly apparent what the Nazis had been doing, even as they fought off the Allies and the Red Army. Approximately six million Jews had been systematically murdered in the extermination camps of the eastern territories, a figure amounting to two-thirds of the Jews in Europe and a third of all

the Jews in the world. The several million non-Jewish victims included Slavs, gypsies, homosexuals, disabled people, and others. The Holocaust (or *Shoah*) would be in many ways the defining event of the twentieth century – the paradigm case of humanity's capacity for evil and for genocide.

The response of the Christian churches to this in the immediate aftermath of the war was complex. Many Christians still held more or less anti-Semitic views themselves and, shameful though it is to report, many throughout Europe had a residual feeling that Hitler had not been entirely wrong in addressing the 'Jewish question' – although few approved of mass murder. In eastern Europe, as the Iron Curtain descended, some churches regarded those who had collaborated with the Nazis relatively

benignly – such people were, after all, not communists.

The Catholic Church has been accused of running schemes to try to help former Nazis escape justice at the Nuremburg trails, although the Vatican denies the claims. Nevertheless, some church officials were certainly complicit. Alois Hudal, who during the war ran a seminary for German priests in Rome, stated that he thought most of the accused were innocent and that in any case Christians had a duty of love and forgiveness. Others had a less high view of his motives, branding Hudal a pro-Nazi. After the war he helped many of the worst Nazi criminals escape justice, including Adolf Eichmann, one of the architects of the *Shoah*. At the same time, Pope Pius XII claimed that most Germans had opposed the Nazis, and he

tried to have the sentences passed against Nazi war criminals reduced. Pius XII has become something of a bogeyman for those concerned by the Catholic Church's failure to speak out as much as it could have done at this time. When he became pope in 1939, he had failed to publish an encyclical that his predecessor, Pius XI, had prepared, denouncing anti-Semitism and racism. It has been argued that the pope saved thousands of Jews through personal intervention and through providing channels by which church officials could help them, and that he did not speak out publicly against the persecutions for fear of making the situation worse. But, it seems, his hatred of communism did dull the edge of his opposition to Nazism.

If this was not the Vatican's finest hour, other Christian groups did take a more

Auschwitz-Birkenau, Poland, the most notorious of the Nazi extermination camps, photographed in 1996.

We say this with great pain: by us, infinite wrong was done to many peoples and countries.

The Stuttgart Declaration of Guilt, 1945

So be on your guard against the Jews, knowing that wherever their synagogues are, you will find nothing but a den of devils, where sheer self-glory, conceit, lies, blasphemy, and slander of God and men are practiced in the most malicious way... And where you see or hear a Jew teaching, remember that all you are hearing is a poisonous basilisk, cheerfully poisoning and killing people – and with all this, they claim to be doing what is right. Be on your guard against them!

Martin Luther, *On the Jews and their lies* 1543

decisive stand from a very early stage. In late 1945 German Protestant leaders issued the Stuttgart Declaration of Guilt, in which – without explicitly mentioning the Jews – they expressed remorse for not standing up more robustly against the Nazis' crimes. Throughout the world, but especially in Europe, Christians felt compelled to rethink their historic attitudes towards the Jews. Certainly the history of Christianity's relations with the Jews had not been a good one from the end of the second century onwards: to mention just a couple of well-known instances, the Fourth Lateran Council of 1215 had compelled Jews to wear identifying badges much as the Nazis had done, and Martin Luther had written of his hatred for the Jews, even stating that it was not a crime to kill one. It's worth stressing that the anti-Jewish sentiments of Luther and certain other theologians of the past, such as John Chrysostom, were typically theologically rather than racially based. They objected to the Jewish *religion*, not to the Jewish *race*. The Nazis, by contrast, hated the Jewish *race*, and insisted that anyone descended from Jews was a Jew no matter what they believed. But religious prejudices can easily feed racial ones, so Christians now tried to find more positive ways to relate to Judaism, in particular by finding new theological formulations that positively took account of Judaism's continued existence as a religion, rather than seeing it simply as a prelude to Christianity that had unaccountably not ended with the coming of Jesus.

Roman Catholicism, too, soon moved to a similar position. The Second Vatican Council, which we shall look at shortly, called for greater understanding of those of other faiths, particularly Judaism. Pope Paul VI set up a Commission for Religious Relations with Jews, which in 1975 issued a set of guidelines stating that the Holocaust and its memory should be the starting point for relations with Jews today. In 1979 Pope John Paul II visited Auschwitz, and on that occasion and a number of others he condemned as strongly as possible the Holocaust and the anti-Semitism which had produced it. The 1990s saw a number of conferences and declarations from Catholic bishops apologizing for not doing enough to prevent the Holocaust, and deeply regretting the Christian anti-Semitism of the past which had made it possible. Indeed, the late twentieth and early twenty-first centuries have seen a number of statements from the leaders of different churches expressing regret for actions in past centuries or apologising to the victims and their descendants. In 2000 John Paul II held a 'day of forgiveness' Mass at which, on behalf of the Catholic Church, he asked forgiveness for past atrocities against Jews, heretics, women, Protestants and people of other religions – although he did not explicitly apologize for the crusades, as many had hoped he would. And in 2006 the general synod of the Church of England, led by Rowan Williams, archbishop of Canterbury, apologized for its benefiting from slavery up to 1834, including the maintenance of the Codrington estate in Barbados.

If the Holocaust forced Christians to rethink their relations with Jews, it also forced them to rethink their own faith. For the twentieth century was not only the century of two world wars – it was a century in which genocide and mass killings seemed to proliferate throughout the world, whether it was the atrocities committed by Japanese troops in Manchuria in the 1930s, the dropping of atomic bombs on Hiroshima and Nagasaki in 1945, the killings of the 'Cultural Revolution' in China of the 1960s or of anti-communist sympathizers in Cambodia in the 1970s, or the 'ethnic cleansing' of ethnic Albanians carried out by Serbs in Kosovo in the 1990s. How can Christians speak of a loving, all-powerful God in the light of such things? As the Jewish theologian Richard Rubenstein asked in his 1996 book of that title, how can there be theology 'after Auschwitz'? Such questions had been asked before – famously, after the Lisbon earthquake of 1755, in which hundreds of thousands of people died and which shook the faith of many in Enlightenment Europe. Yet the question was now asked in a more penetrating and sustained way. One result, in philosophical theology, was the rise of interest in the issue of 'theodicy' (literally, 'justifying God'), the attempt to show how belief in God is compatible with the existence of suffering. Where, once, Christians had believed that humankind is in the dock, being judged by God, now the situation seemed to have reversed itself. The years after the Second World War would be marked by a radical questioning in many quarters of the traditional understanding of what 'God' really means at all.

THE 1960S AND A POST-CHRISTIAN EUROPE

After the resurgence of the late 1940s and the 1950s, the 1960s represented something of a crisis period for Christianity in the west. It was now that church attendance really began to fall, and fewer and fewer people identified themselves as Christians at all. The laws protecting what were regarded as Christian principles or values – such as the anti-abortion and anti-homosexuality laws in most countries, and laws forbidding or limiting divorce, especially in Catholic countries such as Italy and Ireland – were questioned.

It is uncertain to what extent this represented the culmination of a trend that had been brewing for decades, or whether it was a really new shift in people's attitudes. It was a complex phenomenon with a number of causes. One was the growth of interest in other religions, partly as a result of immigration into Europe: many Muslims from North Africa migrated to France, for example. Indeed, such was the influx that it has been suggested that there are now more practising Muslims in France than there are practising Catholics. At the same time, pop culture encouraged interest in eastern religions. The Beatles famously travelled to India in 1968 to seek enlightenment at the feet of the Maharishi Mahesh Yogi. Hinduism, Buddhism and vaguer eastern mystical trends became well known in Europe and the USA alike. Even among those not interested in these 'new' options, a sense developed of religion as a personal thing, something that each individual should

choose and follow for themselves. To put it another way, many people felt that instead of following a 'religion' they should develop a 'spirituality'. The word 'spirituality' came to refer to a non-traditional approach to the divine, one which eschewed notions of authority and instead encouraged individual experimentation. Its rise coincided with the rise of the New Age movement and neo-paganism, which began in the 1950s and became popular in the 1960s and afterwards. Neo-pagan religions such as witchcraft and Wicca offered an alternative and more individualist 'spirituality', which contrasted with what was perceived as the more rigorous, inflexible 'religion' offered by the traditional churches.

In addition to the encroachment of other religions and 'spirituality' upon the traditional Christian heartlands, the 1960s saw secularism make serious inroads, now in the realm of popular culture rather than politics. For the first time, significant numbers of people claimed to have no religion at all, identifying themselves as either atheists or agnostics. Religion in general, and Christianity in particular, held little interest for many people, especially the young. Indeed, Christianity was often identified as part of the oppressive establishment against which many young people of the time were rebelling: Daniel Cohn-Bendit, one of the leaders of the Paris students who took to the streets in 1968, called for a dismantling of the Christian religion and its ethics. The feminist movement of the 1970s took up the call, branding Christianity an irredeemably patriarchal religion. Yet perhaps more significant than these clarion calls against religion was a more subtle shift of focus away from it altogether. The 1960s saw the beginnings of the ideal of the consumer lifestyle, when people were encouraged to buy all kinds of labour-saving devices and when new levels of prosperity promised more holidays. Television meant that people could stay at home for entertainment. As a result, many people lost interest in movements beyond the immediate family circle. Membership of political parties fell,

The world is ready for a mystic revolution, a discovery of the God in each of us.

George Harrison

as well as of churches. Ultimately, people just weren't very interested in religion any more. Perhaps that, rather than an active opposition to religion, was more fatal to Christianity's role at the centre of European culture than any other factor.

The disillusionment with Christianity among many young people in the 1960s meant that, when they had children, they were raised with very little awareness of the religion: as a result, within a generation Christianity was not simply a minority interest but was no longer very familiar. In France in 1966 some 23 per cent of people claimed to attend Sunday Mass regularly; by 1990 only 12 per cent did. As we shall see in the next chapter, Christianity in the USA underwent a similar crisis during the same period, but this was not so sustained and Christianity remained a dominant factor there into the 1980s and beyond. In Europe (and Canada), by contrast, the crisis of the 1960s simply kept on going, with fewer and fewer people knowing or particularly caring much about Christianity.

Even so, the 'post-Christian' culture now found in Europe should not be over-emphasized. The most popular pilgrimage sites in Europe, such as Lourdes in France, still attract millions of visitors every year. The 2001 census in Britain found that 71 per cent of people still identified themselves as Christian, compared to only 14 per cent claiming to have no religion. It may be questioned what the majority of that 71 per cent understood 'being Christian' to mean, given that at this time only around one in ten of the population attended church regularly. Yet Christianity still remains central to much of western European culture. The Church of England, of course, is the official religion of Britain, with its bishops sitting in the House of Lords. Germany and Italy both have church taxes, meaning that those who give their religion as Catholic or Protestant on their tax form automatically support their church financially (in contrast to Britain, where the Church of England gets no financial help from the state). In Belgium the state pays the salaries of Catholic priests.

An interesting situation prevails in Scandinavia, where Lutheranism still plays a large but declining part in national life. Finland has a state church – the Evangelical Lutheran Church – and its leaders are closely involved in political debates. In Sweden the privileged position of Lutheranism was eroded after the war by increasing pluralism and secularism, helped by the country's liberal immigration laws which helped to foster other religions. The Lutheran Church of Sweden was therefore disestablished as the national church in 2000, but it and other churches still receive government money funded by a national church tax. In Denmark, church and state are officially separated too, but there are still extremely close ties between them. The Evangelical Lutheran Church in Denmark (the Danish national church) is supported by the state, which funds two theological faculties for training ministers. The state imposes a church tax, as in Germany, and gives the church direct financial help. In Norway, the Church of Norway is the state church, with the monarch as its head (as in the Church of England). It is divided, to some extent, between liberals and traditionalists and the post-war period has seen some tension between church and state over how liberal the state should be. There was a famous occasion in the 1950s when Ole Kristian Hallesby preached a sermon on the radio in which he warned non-Christians of eternal damnation, causing anger among many, including among more liberal-minded Christians who felt that this did not reflect God's loving nature.

RADICAL MOVEMENTS

The anti-Christian sentiment which built up in many parts in the 1960s and 70s was reflected in the concerns of many Christians themselves, who felt that the secularists had some good points which Christians should accept. The approach had been anticipated in the 1940s by Dietrich Bonhoeffer, who, while in prison in Germany, had mused on how the church could respond to 'a world come of age' which no longer accepted the mythological garb in which Christianity had

It took several centuries... to convert Britain to Christianity, but it has taken less than forty years for the country to forsake it.

Callum Brown, *The death of Christian Britain*, 2001

dressed since antiquity. What did God mean to people today, and could the church reinvent itself to be relevant? Bonhoeffer talked of 'religionless Christianity', and his concerns came to seem more and more relevant in the 1960s, when his views began to gain wide currency.

Rudolf Bultmann (1884–1976), an extremely influential biblical scholar and theologian, believed that the New Testament offered many insights of existential philosophy hidden beneath mythological language. The task of theology was therefore to uncover the basic message and discard the outdated myths. A similar programme was attempted by Paul Tillich (1886–1965), another German, whose most important work was done in the USA after he was barred from teaching at German universities in 1933 and fled the Nazi regime. Tillich believed that the New Testament was essentially a set of 'symbols' which could be decoded to produce an account of the individual's experience of God, now understood simply as 'Being itself'.

Ideas such as these remained largely the preserve of scholars and specialists, but in 1963 they were introduced to the unsuspecting wider public by John Robinson (1919–83), the Anglican bishop of Woolwich, London. In 1963 he published a small book entitled *Honest to God*, mostly a study of ideas from Bultmann, Tillich and Bonhoeffer. It was fairly tame compared to the ideas of the German theologians who inspired it, but it became one of the most remarkable Christian phenomena of the 1960s. The notion that an Anglican bishop could write a book which people interpreted as denying most of the important elements of the Christian faith was unheard of. The book sold by the hundred thousand. Commuters read it on the bus and talked about it in the pub, and it was discussed to death on television. Robinson became an instant celebrity, denounced in pulpits throughout the English-speaking world. But many people felt inspired by his book: dissatisfied with what they had heard in church, they had been unaware that any alternative views existed.

More extreme was the 'Death of God' movement of the 1960s. This was never really a coherent movement at all, more the popular perception of the more radical ideas of some theologians who argued that 'God' should refer to part of human nature, not to a being with its own objective existence. Indeed, its very name came from *Time* magazine, which on Good Friday 1966 asked on its front cover, 'Is God dead?' – thereby linking the movement irrevocably to journalistic image and presentation. In an age of pop politics, pop philosophy and pop art it was the first movement of pop theology. A key figure was Thomas Altizer, who argued that Christianity had to drop the old idea of God as 'out there' if it was to survive.

By the 1970s the 'Death of God' movement had passed from the scene, both in popular culture and in theology. But the concerns of the radical theologians of the 1960s would be echoed in the decades to come as Christians sought different ways to make Christianity relevant in a 'post-

Christian' world – leading to more conflict within the churches, as we shall see.

Roman Catholic theology saw the influx of similar ideas. Two theologians came to represent this general approach in the popular mind: Hans Küng (b. 1928), and Edward Schillebeeckx (b. 1914). Küng became a professor at Tübingen in 1960

Shall we retain the ethical preaching of Jesus and abandon his eschatological preaching? Shall we reduce his preaching of the Kingdom of God to the so-called social gospel? Or is there a third possibility? We must ask whether the eschatological preaching and the mythological sayings as a whole contain a still deeper meaning which is concealed under the cover of mythology. If that is so, let us abandon the mythological conceptions precisely because we want to retain their deeper meaning.

Rudolf Bultmann, *Jesus Christ and mythology,* 1958

Hans Küng, photographed in 1978.

and two years later Pope John XXIII made him an official theologian at the Second Vatican Council. Küng became increasingly critical of John's successor, Paul VI (reigned 1963–78), and in particular he questioned the doctrine of papal infallibility, which led to the withdrawal of his licence to teach as a Catholic theologian. During the pontificate of John Paul II (reigned 1978–2005) Küng maintained a continual and often bitter attack on the Vatican for its increasing authoritarianism and centralizing of power, while at the same time offering a liberal Catholic theology which questioned many traditional church teachings.

Schillebeeckx, a Belgian who was educated by the Jesuits before becoming a Dominican, is often mentioned in the same breath as Küng. Like the Swiss theologian, he was prominent at the Second Vatican Council but subsequently endured considerable criticism for his increasingly liberal views. He set out these views in two books that became phenomenally popular – *Jesus: an experiment in Christology*, published in 1979, and *Christ: the experience of Jesus as Lord*, which appeared the following year. Unexpectedly, these books flew off the shelves as soon as they came out. They presented an understanding of Jesus' divinity that took into account the most recent scholarship on the New Testament. On this conception, Jesus' divinity should be understood not in a dry, dogmatic way but as part of the story of Jesus' life and death. An element that many found shocking was Schillebeeckx's insistence that faith in Jesus' resurrection did not depend upon belief that his tomb was really found empty: just as Paul never mentioned the empty tomb, but spoke about what it means to live and die 'in Christ', so too faith in the resurrection means that the story of Jesus' life and death has an impact on us here, now. That is what the resurrection is really about, and from that point of view it does not really matter what happened to Jesus' body many centuries ago.

God (and this is a definition) is the sum of our values, representing to us their ideal unity, their claims upon us and their creative power... Values do not have to be independently and objectively existent beings in order to be able to claim our allegiance.

Don Cupitt, *The sea of faith*, 1984

What I have tried to say, in a tentative and exploratory way, may seem to be radical, and doubtless to many heretical. The one thing of which I am fairly sure is that, in retrospect, it will be seen to have erred in not being nearly radical enough.

John Robinson, *Honest to God*, 1963

BONES AND COUNCILS: A REVITALIZED ROMAN CATHOLICISM

In the midst of this ferment, two movements helped to give the Catholic Church a greater sense of identity. The first was a series of archaeological excavations on the site of the Vatican, from the 1930s to the 1960s, which uncovered some of the early crypts and even the original graveyard on which the Vatican had been built. The crypts were put back into service for papal burials, and some of the bones that were found from the early Christian period were cautiously identified with those of St Peter himself. In 1968 Pope Paul VI announced that the relics of the first pope had officially been discovered.

As this was going on, the Vatican was hosting one of the most important church councils in modern history, the Second Vatican Council. It was announced by Pope John XXIII (1881–1963) just a couple of months after his election in 1959, in a move that took the church by surprise: John XXIII was nearly 77 when elected and many expected him to be a 'safe pair of hands' who would not do much as pope. Moreover, many had assumed that the doctrine of papal infallibility at the First Vatican Council had meant the effective end of conciliarism. However, the Second Vatican Council – technically a continuation of the first, which had never officially ended, but really a completely new event – opened in 1962 with the aim of updating the church's structure and practices. It met over several periods until late 1965 and, with over 3,000 participants in total from all over the world, it was the largest church council in history, ten times larger than Nicaea itself.

Like all councils of the Catholic Church, its aim was to elucidate the faith established at previous councils, including the Council of Trent and the First Vatican Council. But Vatican II did represent something of a new spirit of openness. For example, the liturgy was revised so that it could be said in vernacular languages as well as Latin, and the priest would no longer turn away from the congregation.

The ecumenical movement

The 'ecumenical movement' as a term embraces a large number of initiatives, bodies and structures dedicated to the quest for the visible unity of the body of Christ. We must understand ecumenism not only in terms of questions of church doctrine, authority and structure, but also in relation to the calling of all Christians to common mission. During the twentieth century, the ecumenical agenda broadened to include questions of peace and justice, stewardship of the environment, globalization and interfaith relations. By the beginning of the twenty-first century, the ecumenical movement could be said to be well established, diverse and yet also facing difficult questions regarding its future identity, goals and resourcing.

The classic theological foundation of ecumenism derives from faith in the persons of the Trinity and the values intrinsic to the triune relationship now applied to the church. The common duty of believers is defined in the prayer of Christ for his disciples, 'that they may all be one. As you, Father, are in me, and I in you, may they also be in us, so that the world may believe that you have sent me' (John 17:21).

The 1910 World Mission Conference in Edinburgh marked the growing awareness that churches needed to work together in common mission 'to evangelize this world in this generation'. Despite the chaos of war and reconstruction in the next few years, contacts between churches at international level grew rapidly, and national councils of churches were founded in various parts of the world, numbering twenty-three by 1928. A US-inspired initiative to found an ecumenical Faith and Order Movement was followed in the 1930s by world conferences on Life and Work in Stockholm (1925) and Oxford (1937). The two strands were to form the foundation of the World Council of Churches (WCC), of which the provisional committee was constituted in 1938. The first Assembly of the WCC gathered in Amsterdam in 1948 as 'a fellowship of churches which accept our Lord Jesus Christ as God and Saviour'.

Since 1948 the WCC has embraced not only Protestant, Anglican and other post-Reformation churches in its membership, but also most of the Orthodox churches. The Roman Catholic Church remains outside the WCC, but sends observers to the Assembly and is a member of the Commission on Faith and Order. The WCC programmes cover a wide range of areas for the joint action of member churches, such as human rights, ecology, race and gender issues, and the Faith and Order foundations of ecumenism. The Faith and Order work resulted in the seminal document *Baptism, Eucharist and ministry* (Lima, 1982), and eventually the unity formula of Canberra (1991) which more clearly defined the search for full communion on the basis of unity in diversity. By the end of the century, however, the WCC faced new problems with funding and Orthodox dissatisfaction with ecumenical liturgies.

In every continent and nation, diverse patterns of ecumenical agreement and co-operation emerged in the second half of the twentieth century. The Church of South India (1947) was a pioneering ecumenical venture, and by the end of the century Anglicans and Lutherans in the USA had concluded an agreement of full communion, the Concordat of Agreement, inspired by earlier agreements in Europe (Meissen 1990, Porvoo 1996). After many years of unsuccessful attempts at unity, Anglicans and Methodists in the British Isles agreed to covenant together on the way to eventual full organic unity. Lutherans and Roman Catholics signed a Joint Declaration on Justification in 2000, but the ecumenical climate cooled with conservative statements on the nature of the church from Rome and the Russian Orthodox Church in the same year. Throughout the last few decades a number of initiatives, local and international, have brought together Reformed and Lutherans in united Protestant churches and in the Community of Protestant Churches in Europe.

The ecumenical challenges of the early twenty-first century reflect a context very different from that of the pioneering decades of the movement. The churches now have to contend with a world of new tensions and contrasts – north/south, wealth/poverty, local/global, inter-faith – and of constantly developing new technologies and of unforeseen political flash points.

It is also clear that the circumstances of the churches themselves are radically changing as many, particularly in Europe and North America, face declining membership and income, the challenge of government policies on ethical and sexual questions and the rise of new religious networks and fresh expressions of church. Fewer resources and energy are available to sustain ecumenical bodies and structures. Key issues to be faced now include how to involve within existing structures those growing churches (Pentecostal and Free Evangelical, particularly in the southern hemisphere) which have not hitherto been active in ecumenical organizations; how to define the relationship of these structures to the largest global Christian denomination, the Roman Catholic Church; and how to simplify the different ecumenical 'levels of belonging' in which churches of widely differing size and resources are engaged. Inevitably, the churches are giving attention to issues of good stewardship, seeking to avoid duplication of effort and over-ambitious programmes which cannot be adequately resourced.

In the next crucial decades, the churches urgently need to enthuse new generations for the cause of Christian unity, and to ensure that local congregations and people at all levels of the church own this cause as a focus for their understanding of mission, discipleship and their accountability to God and each other.

CHARLES HILL

More important, perhaps, was the new openness towards non-Catholic faiths. The council confirmed the traditional view that the Catholic Church was the only legitimate Christian church, but it also stated that Christ might be found outside it. Evidently there were pious Christians in other churches as well, and the council recognized that the history of Catholicism and Protestantism was one where mistakes had been made on both sides, causing unnecessary mutual bitterness. The Orthodox churches, meanwhile, were interpreted as very closely allied to Catholicism, with their ordinations recognized as valid. Even more striking was the council's assessment of non-Christian religions. Unlike many theological liberals, the council did not go so far as to suggest that non-Christian religions could offer the hope of salvation. But it did acknowledge that there was much in those religions that was good or worthy, and it recognized that non-Christians might have much to teach Christians. Their religions were not to be seen simply as the work of the devil. On the contrary, God works in the world and through the minds of human beings, who are able to grasp at least some of the truth through their own capacities.

The Second Vatican Council did not offer any easy answers. It did not prescribe how Catholics should pursue relations with other Christians or with members of other religions, but it did set out the programme calling on them to do so. This made it one of the most important milestones in the ecumenical movement. Today papal encyclicals and other official Catholic documents cite the council and its decrees constantly, and in many ways its teachings are only slowly being unpacked and acted upon. It also remains controversial. Some Catholics believed that the council had effectively been hijacked by liberals, citing the presence of Hans Küng, Edward Schillebeeckx, Karl Rahner (1904–84) and others at its sessions. In France, Marcel Lefebvre (1905–91), archbishop of Tulle and head of the Holy Ghost Fathers,

denounced Vatican II and the liberalism that he believed had infected the Catholic hierarchy from the pope downwards. In particular, he opposed the attempt to update the liturgy, which he argued represented a betrayal of the faith of the Council of Trent, and insisted upon sticking to the old forms and ordaining new priests who shared his views. He was excommunicated in 1988.

A NEW SOCIAL AGENDA

The 1960s saw many churches becoming increasingly politicized. Harvey Cox, a Harvard theologian, commented in 1965 that politics had replaced metaphysics as the language of theology. In 1961 Pope John XXIII issued an encyclical entitled *Mater et magistra* which modified the hard-line anti-communist stance of his predecessors to accept that there were some elements of communism which were actually laudable.

On the whole, though, the Catholic Church has tended to side with conservative political elements. In Spain the coming of democracy and the election of a socialist government in 1982 was welcomed by the Catholic Church, but the government's moderately anti-clerical agenda led to a cooling of relations between the two. The church there has spoken out against secularization and what are perceived to be liberal, anti-Christian laws, particularly the legalization of abortion, the introduction of sex education in schools and so on. Spain remains one of the most firmly Catholic countries of western Europe, as does Italy, but in Italy too the church has found its influence over public and political life slowly slipping. It campaigned vigorously in a referendum on abortion in 1981, but it lost. In 1984, the Catholic Church was officially disestablished. In countries such as these, then, the Catholic Church has tried to act as the guardian of traditional values and morals, which has led it to oppose liberal reforms and take a politically conservative stance. As we shall see in the next chapter, this has also been the case in the USA,

...the separated [non-Catholic] Churches and Communities as such, though we believe them to be deficient in some respects, have been by no means deprived of significance and importance in the mystery of salvation. For the Spirit of Christ has not refrained from using them as means of salvation which derive their efficacy from the very fullness of grace and truth entrusted to the Church.

The Second Vatican Council, *Unitatis redintegratio*, 1964

Inside St Peter's Basilica, Rome, during the Second Vatican Ecumenical Council of the Roman Catholic Church.

despite the fact that the church also opposes capital punishment and denounced the US invasion of Iraq in 2003, putting it more in line with liberal politics.

Examples like this show why it is wrong to assume, as many people do, that the church's concerns coincide simply with those of right-wing or conservative elements in secular politics. The complexity of the situation is illustrated by the experience of the French church. Here, the 1960s saw many Catholics associating with the protest movements and arguing that Christianity should be a force for reform in France. This Marxist-influenced group was bitterly opposed by others who felt that the church should be an agent of stability, order and the preservation of traditional society and morals, not one of change. In 1972 the French Conference of Bishops produced a remarkably broad-minded document entitled *Politics, Church and Spirit* which tried to provide guidance on the matter. They suggested that Christianity was compatible with a number of different political stances, and that the church should not try to ally itself with any one political group.

The European Protestant churches have tended to be much more politically left-wing than the Catholics. In keeping with the spirit of the times, the World Council of Churches held an important assembly at Uppsala in 1968 which addressed problems of politics and social justice. Martin Luther King was to have given the opening sermon to the assembly: his assassination shortly beforehand helped to give a sense of urgency to the proceedings. The assembly voted to give money to a number of organizations in the world fighting for social justice, which caused something of a scandal when their names were revealed in 1970 – they included liberation movements and even black nationalist guerrilla organizations in various African countries. Many pointed out that using church money to fund armed struggles was not the right direction to take.

In another example, the 1980s saw the Church of England take quite an outspoken stand against the right-wing Conservative British government and the then prime minister, Margaret Thatcher (b. 1925). At a service to mark the end of the Falklands War with Argentina in 1982, the archbishop of Canterbury, Robert Runcie (1921–2000), called for peace and reconciliation and prayed for the families of Argentines who died as well as British servicemen. For this, the archbishop was branded a traitor and bitterly attacked in the popular press. Thatcher was further incensed three years later, when the church produced a report entitled *Faith in the City* which consisted of a sustained attack on the government. Thatcher's policies, the church claimed, had led to an increasing gap between rich and poor, and terrible deprivation in inner-city areas.

It is extremely hard to tell what the future holds for the churches in Europe. For one thing, most of them show no signs of recovering from the post-war decline. In some areas, to be sure, there is growth. In the English-speaking world, evangelicalism has made great strides, as we shall see in more detail in the next chapter, but this has not helped to redress the balance greatly. As a result, there is increasing emphasis in the churches on mission within Europe, and the evangelization of those who know little of Christianity. In Protestantism this is associated especially with evangelicalism, while in Catholicism the task is sometimes known as 'the new (or second) evangelization'. Pope John Paul II often used this term to refer to the fact that the secularized society of western Europe had created, in effect, a new mission field, one where Christianity *had* flourished but was now being forgotten. In contrast to the great missionaries of the 'first evangelization', who had brought Christianity to cultures that did not know it, there was now a need to remind cultures of what they had forgotten.

Another element that may become increasingly important is the influence of

Christianity from overseas, partly from America, but even more so from Africa. As we shall see in more detail in Chapter 17, Africa has seen Christianity flourish even as it declines in the west, and in a dramatic reversal of the nineteenth-century situation, African forms of Christianity are now being imported to Europe.

And many of the churches remain split – between political liberals and conservatives, between theological liberals and conservatives, between those who support Vatican II and those who do not, and so on. The ecumenical movement, which for the past century has worked to break down barriers between the churches, sometimes seems to be mirrored by a fragmentation within each church and the erection of new barriers. Perhaps the key to the churches' future role in European society lies in how these internal debates will be played out.

CHAPTER 15

MODERN AMERICA AND OCEANIA

If the churches apparently faltered in Europe in the twentieth century, that was not the case in most of America and Oceania. In the Pacific and in South America, Christianity has continued to grow and develop, while in the USA, virtually alone of western nations, Christianity has retained a central role in national life. But the churches' unusual position here has given rise to problems and divisions of its own.

UNITY OUT OF DIVERSITY

THE CANADIAN CHURCHES

An unusual situation prevailed in British-run Canada from the 1760s onwards. Here, the Church of England was, naturally, the dominant church, but the French-speaking regions of Quebec and Acadia were predominantly Catholic, and the Catholics enjoyed a guarantee of freedom of worship. Meanwhile, the mid-nineteenth century saw increasing protests on the part of the other Protestant churches against the Church of England's privileged position. We saw in Chapter 12 how the revivals of New England had spread to parts of Canada, under the influence of preachers such as Henry Alline, and this movement had helped the Baptist and Methodist churches in the country. Moreover, the latter half of the eighteenth century had seen many people, loyal to the British Crown, flee the fledgling USA for Canada, bringing with them the non-conformist religions of New England and beyond. As a result, by the middle of the nineteenth century, the Protestant scene in Canada was extraordinarily diverse. Anglicans, Presbyterians and Methodists each accounted for about a quarter of all

Protestants, with the rest divided between the other churches. In 1854 the anti-Anglican protest movement, led by the Methodist Egerton Ryerson, succeeded in having all special privileges removed from the Anglicans. Since then, there has in practice been no established church in Canada.

In 1867 Canada achieved self-government, becoming a confederate dominion of four provinces (later expanded to ten). All but one of these provinces were deeply Protestant in nature, with all the major churches represented. The exception was Quebec, still staunchly Catholic. Indeed, in an age of uncertainty within the Catholic Church, the Catholics of Quebec were strongly Ultramontanist, contrasting with the Gallican attitude of the French themselves. There was something of a revival within the Canadian Catholic Church in the middle part of the

nineteenth century, led in part by Ignace Bourget, the bishop of Montreal. Large houses acquired altars, crosses were erected at roadsides and people streamed into churches to listen to long meditations on the sorrows of Jesus. The sacrament became a special object of devotion. Congregations vied with each other over how long they could venerate it for. Some adopted the practice known as the Perpetual Adoration of the Blessed Sacrament, in which members of a group venerated the host non-stop in shifts. While such practices were perhaps extreme, it was very common for people to keep shrines at home or use special disciplines in their private prayers. Catholic piety was, at this time, a major element in mainstream culture.

The strong position of Catholicism in French-speaking Canada remained firm in the first part of the twentieth century. Many societies were founded in the 1920s to promote Catholic morality and social values, and images of the Sacred Heart of Jesus became popular. They proliferated in parks and other public areas and were even found in buses. Most spectacular was the four-day National Eucharistic Congress of 1938, organized by Rodrigue Villeneuve, cardinal archbishop of Quebec. It was an event of truly national significance: train companies put on extra services at special rates, and a hundred thousand people at a time stood in the Plains of Abraham for the open-air services. Great processions were held as the sacrament was paraded past tens of thousands of worshippers.

The vigour of Catholicism in Quebec was matched by that of Protestantism in the rest of Canada – there were, throughout the country, three Protestants for every two Catholics. The legacy of the revivals was powerful, and the nineteenth century had seen evangelicalism become very strong throughout Canada, to a much greater extent than in England, where the Anglo-Catholic movement provided a counterbalance. Protestantism in Canada resembled, to some extent, Protestantism in Wales and Scotland, where the revivals had proved especially influential. Churches were important institutions in the growing cities of Canada, and their preachers were major figures in society. In 1891 the Toronto *Daily Mail* held a poll – inconceivable today! – in which people were asked to vote for their favourite preacher. The winner was Joseph Wild of Bond Street Congregational Church, who managed to poll 160,494 votes – remarkable given that there were under 150,000 inhabitants of the city at

The National Eucharistic Congress, Quebec, 1938.

The Superior now informed me... that one of my great duties was, to obey the priests in all things; and this I soon learnt, to my utter astonishment and horror, was to live in the practice of criminal intercourse with them... She gave me another piece of information which excited other feelings in me, scarcely less dreadful. Infants were sometimes born in the convent; but they were always baptized and immediately strangled! This secured their everlasting happiness; for the baptism purified them from all sinfulness...

Maria Monk, author of an anti-Catholic, fabricated account of life in a Canadian nunnery, *Awful disclosures*, 1836

this time. No doubt Mr Wild, like most other ministers of this time, preached evangelical doctrine and morals to his enormous congregation. Social morality was a major concern of the churches, as was mission: indeed, in the early twentieth century, Canada sent out more missionaries per head of population than any other country.

This was an age of increased cooperation between the Protestant churches, who because of the dominance of evangelicalism shared many views and concerns. This culminated in the formation of the United Church of Canada, one of the most remarkable exercises in church union of modern times. The negotiations began in 1902 between the Presbyterians and the Methodists. A Basis for Union was agreed in 1908, but disagreements about details meant that the new church was not created until 1925. It consisted of the Methodists, the Congregationalists and about two-thirds of the Presbyterians. Union with the Anglicans was impossible because of their insistence upon maintaining the episcopate, something that the others could not agree to. The new church became the largest Protestant church in Canada, one especially marked by concern for social issues (showing the continued influence of the social gospel movement).

PROTESTANTS AND CATHOLICS IN THE USA

In the USA, by contrast, Protestantism was highly dominant from an early stage. If the 'manifest destiny' of the USA was to dominate its continent as a Christian republic, it was also to protect Protestantism. In 1830 a country of 13 million contained about 300,000 Catholics, mostly in Maryland. They had been given their first bishop in 1789, John Carroll, who like most of his flock was an aristocratic Marylander.

But this situation was challenged later in the nineteenth century, as new immigrants arrived in the country. Many were Protestant, and so German and Scandinavian Lutherans and Dutch

Reformed congregations began to appear. But many others were Catholics. In particular, the 1840s and 50s saw Irish immigrants appear by the hundred thousand, fleeing the potato famine back home. Many German Catholic immigrants also appeared during this time. By 1860 the USA's population had increased to 31 million, of whom over three million were Catholics. There were now more Catholics than Methodists or Baptists and far more than Episcopalians (the name that the Anglican Church had adopted after the revolution). Many Protestants were extremely alarmed, especially in the cities of the east coast where the immigrants mostly settled. Books and pamphlets appeared denouncing Catholics, and there were riots. In 1840 the American Society to Promote the Principles of the Protestant Reformation was formed in New York, its members insisting that Catholicism was irreconcilable with being a good American. Another, more famous organization began life in 1849 as the Order of the Star-Spangled Banner, later renamed the American Party: as such it proved very successful in the 1850s. But the organization became known as the 'Know Nothings', after members' typical responses to questions about the group. The organization was, in part, opposed to immigration per se: it was felt that the new arrivals threatened the supposedly Anglo-Saxon stock of the USA, a belief that reflected the 'nativism' or opposition to immigrants that was common in the eastern USA at this time. But the immigrants' Catholic faith was also a cause for concern among the 'Know Nothings', who believed that their devotion to the pope would undermine their allegiance to their adopted country.

OLD-TIME RELIGION: THE AMERICAN CIVIL WAR

If there was religious turmoil on the east coast, that was nothing compared to what happened shortly afterwards when the country was plunged into civil war. As in so many other wars, religion played an important factor in the war of 1861 to 1865. This was, in part, due to the tremendous success of the second Great Awakening in the southern states, which we saw in Chapter 12. Most people in the south were Baptists or Methodists, though there were also many Presbyterians; the aristocratic families, meanwhile, tended to be Episcopalian. All of these churches were largely evangelical, which meant that there was far more religious uniformity in the south than there was in the north, even after the influx of the Lutherans and Catholics. There was a strong sense of regional identity, based around conservative moral values and chivalric codes of behaviour, which were associated with the agrarian economy and landscape that distinguished the area from the north. By the 1850s, many in the south had come to regard themselves as a culturally uniform group, distinct from the north, and one which might seek political independence. The issue over which the two would go to war was slavery; for the

white southern Christians, in contrast to most in the north and most in Europe at this time, were still convinced that slavery was quite compatible with Christianity and indeed part of the stable world order that this religion promoted. But this was part of a more general cultural divide, one which was played out at the religious level too. Thus, in the 1840s the white Baptist and Methodist churches both split off from their colleagues in the north over slavery, and the Presbyterians followed some years later.

When war broke out in 1861, then, many southerners believed they were on a crusade for the protection of the Christian civilization they had built, one which was morally superior to the more degenerate and fragmented north. Nine times during the war, Jefferson Davis, the president of the Confederation, called for a day of national fasting. There were frequent religious revivals in the Confederate army itself, generally erupting when the troops rested between active campaigning, and

I do order and declare that all persons held as slaves within said designated States, and parts of States, are, and henceforward shall be free; and that the Executive government of the United States... will recognize and maintain the freedom of said persons.

Abraham Lincoln, *Emancipation proclamation*, 1863

General George Pickett leads the Confederates on a disastrous charge at the Battle of Gettysburg, 3 July 1863, in this illustration from *The story of our country*, 1920, by American writer and illustrator Elmer Boyd Smith (1860–1943).

MODERN AMERICA AND OCEANIA

443

these were fostered by the large network of army chaplains that the churches set up. Of course, the great irony was that while white southerners believed they were fighting for Christian religion, the north believed exactly the same thing, convinced that destroying the wicked rebels was a divinely ordained task.

The irony was not lost on the participants themselves. When Union troops occupied Confederate towns, many of the soldiers attended churches presided over by southern ministers. In the Episcopalian churches, the set liturgy demanded that, at one point, the minister pray for the president. The Yankees were horrified when they heard prayers for Jefferson Davis being read from a pulpit, and intervened to ensure that Abraham Lincoln was commended to the Lord instead. And many soldiers on both sides, taken prisoner by the enemy, were amazed to find that their 'wicked' opponents appeared to pray and read the Bible just as they did themselves.

Defeat in 1865 might have brought a period of soul-searching for the south, but in fact it brought what one might call cultural defiance. Many people were concerned to assert southern culture and religion all the more vehemently, for fear of being overwhelmed by Yankee culture. Attendance at the Methodist and Baptist churches, still in schism from their northern counterparts, increased. The war was understood as a great martyrdom for the sake of Christianity, a crusade that became known as the 'Lost Cause', one that had passed through a 'baptism of blood'. Ministers identified themselves with this 'Lost Cause', none more so than the famous J. William Jones of Virginia, Baptist preacher and former army chaplain. He edited journals and wrote school textbooks to perpetuate this understanding of the south and of the war, and of the northerners as undisciplined, immoral rabble. He and others like him sought to hold before the eyes of their congregations the examples of the war's 'heroes'. Monuments were erected to many of them, such as the deeply religious general Thomas 'Stonewall' Jackson, and their names

appeared in stained-glass windows of churches. Robert E. Lee, the great Confederate general, was hailed as a new Moses who had led his people on a righteous struggle and portrayed as the perfect southern gentleman, virtuous and chivalrous in every way. Every 3 June (Jefferson Davis's birthday), southern women would place wreaths on the graves of the war dead in a ceremony that explicitly linked the cause for which they had died with Christianity. And the living veterans held regular rallies where they sang hymns and looked forward to meeting their fallen comrades in heaven. Less savoury elements of the 'Lost Cause' phenomenon appeared in the racist Ku Klux Klan, which also took inspiration from the 'Know Nothings', and which flourished in the 1860s and 70s before dying out. A new Klan, whose members styled themselves as Christian knights fighting for white America and traditional morals, appeared in the 1920s and was briefly powerful enough to organize great parades in Washington, DC.

The retrenchment of southern culture and Christianity continued well into the twentieth century as the South became the celebrated 'Dixieland'. As Elvis Presley put it, 'old times there are not forgotten', for the Christianity of the 'Lost Cause' would become the 'old-time religion' of the deep south.

THE LEGACY OF THE AWAKENINGS

PREACHERS, REVIVALS AND A NEW EVANGELICALISM

We saw in Chapter 12 that, in the USA, the revivals of the eighteenth century never really went away. Instead, they entered a pattern of ebb and flow, with great new preachers appearing in each new generation to preside over local revivals of varying intensity. In the late nineteenth century, for example, the greatest was Dwight L. Moody (1837–99), a New England shoe salesman who worked hard for the churches in Chicago. In 1873 he went on a preaching tour of Britain with Ira

---

In the beauty of the lilies Christ was born across the sea,
With a glory in His bosom that transfigures you and me:
As He died to make men holy, let us die to make men free,
While God is marching on.

'The Battle Hymn of the Republic', by Julia Ward Howe

Lord, we acknowledge Thee as the all-wise author of every good and perfect gift. We recognize Thy presence and wisdom in the healing shower. We acknowledge Thou had a divine plan when Thou made the rattle snake, as well as the song bird, and this was without help from Charles Darwin. But we believe Thou wilt admit the grave mistake in giving the decision to the wrong side in eighteen hundred and sixty-five.

J. William Jones

Sankey (1840–1908), a hymn-writer, which proved enormously successful. The tour lasted two years, after which Moody and Sankey returned to the USA and travelled across the country, addressing enormous rallies. Moody preached a simple message of individual redemption, one which contrasted with the interest in social reform that was developing at this time, and he inspired many missionaries. In the next generation, the greatest evangelist was Billy Sunday, who began his career as a professional baseball player but started preaching in the 1890s and didn't stop until his death in 1935. Sunday was a far more passionate speaker than Moody, capable of hurling abuse upon his theological opponents, and he spoke in the slang of his audience.

And so the chain has continued. Since Sunday, the most famous US evangelist has been Billy Graham (b. 1918), who began preaching in the 1940s with the 'Youth For Christ' movement. Graham combined a mainstream evangelical faith, which consciously avoided traditional doctrinal controversies and sought to tolerate minor differences of opinion, with a heartfelt plea to the individual to come to Christ. The 1950s saw Billy Graham begin his preaching tours of other countries, which continued for the rest of the twentieth century, ensuring his record as the man to have preached to more people than anyone else in history – over 80 million in person, and countless others through broadcasts and books. Remarkably, Graham even managed to preach throughout eastern Europe in the late 1970s and 80s, encouraging the churches there and denouncing their communist governments.

It is hard to measure the effect of great preachers like this, but certainly, from Moody to Graham, they have helped to maintain evangelicalism as the dominant form of Christianity in the USA. Local preachers, too, have played their part and have helped to create vibrant evangelical communities within the wider society. Many of these emerged between the two world wars, a time when the Methodist and Baptist churches in particular enjoyed great success.

Dwight L. Moody.

The Bible without the Holy Spirit is a sundial by moonlight.

Dwight L. Moody

One influential leader was J. C. Austin, a Baptist minister from Virginia who enjoyed enormous success in Pittsburgh, building up a congregation 5,000-strong. In 1926 he moved to Chicago to run the Pilgrim Baptist Church and oversaw an extraordinary revival there. The church was already large – its building seated 2,500 people – but it would be full two hours before the service began, and Austin had to preach several times each Sunday to give everyone a chance to listen. Under Austin the church became almost a city within a city. It built its own community centre and gymnasium, and, perhaps more importantly, organized its congregation into a hundred smaller groups to ensure that nobody got lost within its vastness. These groups dealt with social welfare as well as religion, for example by teaching families how to look after their children: thus we see a parallel to the 'pillarization' in European society that was occurring at this time. And

I have one message: Jesus Christ came; He died on a cross; He rose again. He asks us to repent of our sins and receive Him by faith as Lord and Savior. And if we do, we have forgiveness of all our sins.

Billy Graham

445

[We believe in]:

The only true God, the almighty Creator of all things, existing eternally in three persons – Father, Son, and Holy Spirit – full of love and glory.

The unique divine inspiration, entire trustworthiness and authority of the Bible.

The value and dignity of all people: created in God's image to live in love and holiness, but alienated from God and each other because of our sin and guilt, and justly subject to God's wrath.

Jesus Christ, fully human and fully divine, who lived as a perfect example, who assumed the judgment due to sinners by dying in our place, and who was bodily raised from the dead and ascended as Savior and Lord.

Justification by God's grace to all who repent and put their faith in Jesus Christ alone for salvation.

The indwelling presence and transforming power of the Holy Spirit, who gives to all believers a new life and a new calling to obedient service.

The unity of all believers in Jesus Christ, manifest in worshiping and witnessing churches making disciples throughout the world.

The victorious reign and future personal return of Jesus Christ, who will judge all people with justice and mercy, giving over the unrepentant to eternal condemnation but receiving the redeemed into eternal life.

The 'Doctrinal basis' of the Inter-Varsity Christian Fellowship of the United States

yet the Pilgrim Baptist Church was not even the largest Baptist church in the city – that honour went to the Olivet Baptist Church across town, which with a congregation of 12,000 in the 1930s was the biggest Protestant congregation in America.

Modern US evangelicals share many views and concerns with their forebears: in particular, devotion to the Bible and to Christ as a direct influence on the individual. The idea of a conversion experience remains central, and many of the more hardline evangelicals use the conversion experience as a way of distinguishing between 'true' and 'nominal' Christians. The idea is that those who have not had the conversion experience, who have not had a moment when they acknowledged Christ as their personal saviour, are not really Christians at all. This emphasis on personal salvation revolves around the cross, and the belief that Christ died in the place of the sinner.

And the great preachers, with their vast congregations, are still to be found. The post-war period saw more preachers using the latest technology to reach audiences greater than their predecessors could have dreamed of. Radio preaching was pioneered by Charles Coughlin (1891–1979), a Catholic priest from Michigan, in the 1920s, until the church ordered him to stop in the 1940s, partly because of his increasingly outspoken anti-Semitism and admiration of Hitler. It has been estimated that a third of all Americans listened to his broadcasts. However, in subsequent decades, and especially in the South, most of the great broadcast preachers have been evangelical Protestants. In the 1950s Billy Graham pioneered the use of prime-time television to reach audiences who might otherwise not have heard a Christian message. At the same time, Oklahoma's Pentecostal preacher Oral Roberts (b. 1918) and Ohio's Rex Humbard (b. 1919) were doing the same thing. However, the real 'televangelists', as they were dubbed, were a phenomenon of the 1970s and 80s. Using the highest production values, preachers such as Robert Schuller (b. 1926) and Jimmy Swaggart

(b. 1935) reached enormous audiences and made enormous amounts of money: *The Jimmy Swaggart telecast*, for example, made over $150 million each year and was watched by eight million people every week. However, the age of the televangelists ended in the late 1980s with a series of highly publicized financial and sexual scandals, culminating in 1988 when it emerged that Jimmy Swaggart habitually slept with prostitutes. Moreover, many conservative evangelicals attacked some of the preachers, especially Roberts and Schuller, for preaching not authentic, evangelical Christianity but self-help therapy dressed up as religion. The industry – even those preachers not touched by the scandals – suffered a crippling public relations disaster, and although US evangelists have continued to preach on television, they have done so in a more low-key way.

But if flamboyant mass-audience preachers have become less fashionable, there are still enormous evangelical churches which show no signs of decline. The largest congregation in the USA today is Lakewood Church, Houston, where some 30,000 people turn up each week to listen to the preaching of the pastor, Joel Osteen (b. 1963). Osteen offers a positive, joy-filled interpretation of evangelicalism which stresses God's love, the value of the individual and the ability to improve oneself with positive thinking. Such has been the popularity of this message that in 2005 his church opened a new and enormous building – a former basketball arena – capable of seating 16,000 people at once.

STUDENTS AND FREE DINNERS:
EVANGELICALS WORLDWIDE
If evangelicalism is by far the most widespread and prominent form of Protestantism – indeed, of Christianity – in the USA, this is also true elsewhere in the English-speaking world. Britain and Australia have both seen the movement become extremely prominent in the post-war years. Just as in the USA, evangelicalism in these countries became stronger in the late nineteenth century, underwent a period of

crisis in the early twentieth century as it grappled with liberalism and modernism, and became much more entrenched and prominent after the Second World War. But where evangelicalism's success in America is associated with (though not necessarily wholly attributable to) the great preachers we have just been looking at, in the other English-speaking countries it has been more associated with grass-roots movements.

Of these, none has been more significant than student organizations. This trend goes back at least to the Student Volunteer Movement (SVM), which was formed in Britain in response to the preaching of Dwight L. Moody in the 1870s. Some 100,000 students signed cards pledging to become involved in overseas mission, the main aim of this society. The SVM helped to mobilize students in the cause of evangelical mission, but more significant in renewing evangelicalism at home was the Inter-Varsity Christian Fellowship, which originated at Cambridge University in 1877. A major figure in this was Howard Guinness, vice-chairman of the organization, who set up similar organizations in Canada, the USA and Australia in the 1920s and 30s. All of these movements, together with branches in other countries, joined the International Fellowship of Evangelical Students in 1947.

The existence of these organizations testifies to one of the strengths of the modern evangelical movement, which is to combine large-scale organization with local-level support. Typically, each university has its own Christian Union, which is affiliated to the national organization, but which is further subdivided into smaller units, perhaps one for each hall of residence or college on its campus. These groups meet regularly for Bible study and prayer, led by students; but a measure of control is maintained by the university-wide organization. The Christian Unions often cooperate with local evangelical churches: the students are likely to attend one of these churches and its ministers may be invited to speak at Christian Union meetings. One of the principal aims of the student evangelical movement is evangelism among other students, and there can be few students at English-speaking universities who have not seen posters advertising outreach events or been invited by an earnest friend to attend one.

Some evangelicals have used similar methods beyond the universities. One of the most successful in recent years has been the Alpha course, developed by Nicky Gumbel of Holy Trinity Brompton, a large evangelical Anglican Church in London.

Nicky Gumbel leads an Alpha Course meeting at Holy Trinity Brompton.

PLEASE KEEP OFF

American evangelist Billy Graham preaches at the annual 'Singing on the Mountain' event on Grandfather Mountain, North Carolina in 1962.

Originally a course explaining basic evangelical beliefs to church members, Alpha quickly became an introduction to that faith for outsiders, who were invited to talks by members. The idea spread, and now churches throughout the world use the Alpha course. Each week, those on the course are invited to a meal, a talk on the subject of the week and period of discussion. The course is strictly regulated by Holy Trinity Brompton and each participating church must follow the set pattern of which subjects to teach each week; books and videos by Gumbel are prominently used. The course has been extraordinarily successful, transcending its evangelical and Anglican roots to such a degree that even Pope John Paul II commended it. Some churches, unhappy with the strict evangelical theology that it teaches, have imitated it with courses of their own, though none has enjoyed the same remarkable success.

Despite this basic uniformity of emphasis, there are still important divisions within evangelicalism, especially in the USA. They are part of the new controversies and debates that threaten to split the English-speaking churches today.

NEW MOVEMENTS, NEW CONTROVERSIES

The post-war period, especially the 1960s, saw something of a low-key crisis in many churches in America, especially the Catholic Church. The effects of this were felt particularly strongly in Canada. In the 1950s the proportion of priests in the country peaked, and the end of that decade saw the beginning of the 'Quiet Revolution', in which French Canadians sought to reintegrate themselves into Canada as a whole more successfully. The 'Quiet Revolution' saw Quebec becoming more secular, a development that many Catholics did not resist. Many felt the church might be more effective as a countercultural voice in a secular state,

rather than as an organization devoted to organizing immense rallies and processions of thousands of people, as in the first half of the twentieth century. Although less dramatic than in Quebec, the same process of secularization took place over the rest of Canada. There has emerged a situation similar to that in western Europe that we saw in the last chapter: while a majority of the population retains some attachment to Christianity (over 80 per cent of Canadians identified themselves as Christians in the 1991 census), Christianity plays little active role in most people's lives (only a fifth of Canadians go to church regularly).

A similar crisis hit the USA in the 1960s. In 1965 there were 180,000 Catholic nuns there; five years later there were only 160,000. The rise of Catholic Pentecostalism during this period indicated that, even among those loyal to the church, there was a sense of disillusionment with traditional structures and institutions and a desire to find new ways to express their faith.

Yet the churches of the USA, more than in any other country, weathered the crisis of the 1960s extraordinarily well. We saw in the last chapter how in Europe the loss of faith in traditional Christianity has continued in a more or less uninterrupted fashion ever since, and this has happened in Canada. In the USA the trend was halted or even reversed in many places. The reasons are complex, but one element may be the role of the countryside in the USA. In contrast to western Europe, where the majority of the population is urban, and Canada, where the churches' loss of influence was commensurate with the shifting of populations to the large cities, the USA has retained a huge rural or provincial hinterland in the interior of the country, bordered by the areas of high population density along the east and west coasts. This divide between the city and the country is felt at many levels – in politics, for example, the Mid-west and the South are conservative, while New England and California are liberal – and one of these is the religious level. The coasts have become largely secular societies, much like urban western Europe, but in between, small-town America remains deeply religious. The reasons are too complex to tackle here, but they include the fact that more rural communities retain traditional social structures and values much more readily than ever-changing urban ones do. As a result, Christianity has retained a prominence in US American life unmatched in any other western country. Political leaders still speak of their personal faith, and use the language of traditional evangelicalism to do so, in a way that would be considered deeply embarrassing in most western countries. Yet Christianity in modern America is certainly not uniform. The twentieth century has seen new movements, new controversies, and new divisions at the deepest levels.

THE AFRICAN AMERICAN EXPERIENCE
In Chapter 12 we saw the role that Christianity came to play in African American culture and society in the nineteenth century, and it continued to do this well into the twentieth. Although slavery had been abolished in the 1860s, most black people in the South continued to live in very poor conditions, virtually indentured to wealthy white landowners. Under these conditions, Christianity continued to offer the hope of worldly salvation. In fact, more is known of the aspirations of twentieth-century African American Christians than that of their forebears, because of the rise of the music industry in those early decades. Enormous numbers of 'race records' were recorded, featuring early jazz and blues compositions, as well as 'spirituals' and even sermons. As we saw in Chapter 12, black Christianity often featured little distinction between singing and preaching, since the congregation was expected to participate in both; many preachers were singers and vice versa, and on their records, popular figures such as the Reverend Gary Davis (1896–1972) – a blind, Baptist guitarist –

might alternate between the two forms. They continued to hold before their listeners the times when God intervened in the past on behalf of the oppressed, above all the Israelites in Egypt, and the figure of Moses recurs constantly in sermons and spiritual songs. The River Jordan, too, is a common theme – for to cross the Jordan is to pass into the promised land. It also implicitly refers to the Ohio River, the border dividing the slave states from the free states.

In the Depression and its aftermath, the 1930s and 40s saw vast numbers of black Southerners travel north in search of better living conditions and jobs. In reality, many of those who moved simply found themselves living in new ghettoes and working in menial jobs. But the great migration did change the face of black American Christianity, since the northern black churches tended to be more restrained and less 'African' in style than the southern ones, in part because their members were generally more affluent. Thus new churches sprang up in the northern industrial cities such as Chicago and Detroit, sometimes known as 'storefront' churches because, although generally better off than they had been in the South, the black congregations were generally too poor to construct their own buildings and so they simply converted old premises such as shops. The 'storefront' churches were enormously varied – sometimes they were fairly standard Pentecostal churches in the southern style, sometimes they were more exotic cults.

PENTECOSTALISM
However, black American Christianity has been closely connected with another major movement, Pentecostalism, one of the most important developments in world Christianity of the twentieth century. It had its roots in the Holiness movement, a trend that spread through the churches of the USA – especially the Methodists – in the second half of the nineteenth century. This movement harked back to the revivals of the

I am told that tens of thousands of prayer meetings are being held on this day, and for that I am deeply grateful. We are a nation under God, and I believe God intended for us to be free. It would be fitting and good, I think, if on each Inauguration Day in future years it should be declared a day of prayer.

Ronald Reagan, *First inaugural address*, 1981

The dove descended on my head just as it descended on the heads of those who got happy at camp meeting. The only difference was that instead of singing about the New Jerusalem my dove began to moan about high-brown women and the men they tied to their apron strings.

W.C. Handy, the 'father of the blues'

eighteenth century. Its members stressed that the evangelical life involves not one but two conversions. The first involves repentance and the forgiveness of sins, but the second involves full sanctification, the dedication of oneself to God and the living of a holy life. The Holiness preachers and congregations therefore stressed moral living, and were known for their austere lifestyles. By the 1880s, many of these groups had broken away from the Methodists to form splinter denominations of their own.

One of these Holiness Methodist preachers, Charles Parham (1872–1929), ran a Bible school in Topeka, Kansas. Here, on 1 January 1901, his student Agnes Ozman started speaking 'in tongues', strange languages that made no sense. It began when Parham had his students study what the New Testament said about the blessings of the Holy Spirit, and Parham became convinced that those blessings were being suddenly bestowed upon his group. He believed that the coming of the Spirit indicated a 'second baptism' in the Holy Spirit, and that speaking in tongues was the 'Bible evidence' of this baptism. Parham's movement really made its mark in 1906, when one of his students, William Seymour (1870–1922), began preaching at 312 Azusa Street, Los Angeles. His preaching had an extraordinary effect of a kind not witnessed in the USA since George Whitefield. People shrieked and shouted, danced, fell over and, most of all, babbled incomprehensibly in tongues. This happened at three services a day, seven days a week, for three years. Miracles were attested, and the crutches of those who had been healed soon covered the walls of the church.

The movement spread, as Azusa Street worshippers travelled across the USA. Gaston Barnabas Cashwell took the message to the Holiness churches of the South in 1906, while Charles Harrison Mason took it to Memphis, forming a new church, the Church of God in Christ, and William Durham took it to Chicago,

where he helped set up the Assemblies of God in 1914. Since they all believed that the defining moment for all Christians was the coming of the Spirit to the apostles on the Day of Pentecost, they became known as Pentecostalists. Before the first decade of the twentieth century had finished, the movement had spread to Europe, South America and Africa.

Those early days were a time of enormous enthusiasm and excitement. Many people believed that the 'tongues' in which they babbled were real languages, such as Hindi or Chinese. Parham himself was convinced that from now on missionaries could travel the world without having to learn foreign languages. Some enthusiastic missionaries really went to countries such as India with this expectation, only to be sadly disappointed.

Although Pentecostalism was connected to evangelicalism – most Pentecostalists would have regarded themselves as evangelicals, and they believed much the same things – it was far less doctrinally rigid. However, Pentecostalism became still more open in the years after the Second World War. During this period a tendency known as Neo-Pentecostalism removed the stress on the 'two baptisms' theology of the earlier period and became more ecumenically minded. Pentecostalism spread beyond the traditional evangelical churches into the Anglican (Episcopal) and even Catholic churches. It helped to inspire what became known as the Charismatic movement within these and other churches. Members of this movement share the Pentecostalists' belief that manifestations of the Holy Spirit should play a major role in the life of the church, although they typically have less emphasis on speaking in tongues. But they are typically a voice for reform within the larger denominations, without seeking to start new denominations, as the early Pentecostalists did.

The Charismatic movement, as opposed to broader Pentecostalism, is

Christianity and equality: Martin Luther King

Martin Luther King, Jr (1929–68) was born in Atlanta, Georgia, into a middle-class black Baptist family. King's call to the ministry led him to Crozer Theological Seminary in Chester, Pennsylvania. His graduate education continued at Boston University, where he received his PhD in systematic theology in 1955.

After being offered several positions by academic institutions, King decided to return to his native South and became pastor of Dexter Avenue Baptist Church in Montgomery, Alabama. In 1960 he became co-pastor with his father of Ebenezer Baptist Church in Atlanta. He held this position – as well as indispensable leadership in the civil rights movement – until his assassination in Memphis, Tennessee in 1968.

King's understanding of non-violence was based on the Christian teaching of love found in the Sermon on the Mount, as well as Mahatma Gandhi's method of *ahimsa* (non-injury).The spirit and content of non-violence were from Jesus, the path and method from Gandhi. The core of this philosophy was that non-violence is not passive non-resistance, but an active non-violent resistance to evil. King's leadership for civil rights in campaigns from Montgomery to Memphis saw the practice of this principle evolve with integrity and effectiveness.

His first campaign found its catalyst in the refusal by Rosa Parks (1913–2005) to stand for a white man who wanted her seat in a bus in 1955, although the law segregating blacks from whites on public transport required her to do so. A year-long bus boycott was started, protesting successfully against segregated public transport in Montgomery. The next major campaign, in 1963, was to integrate public accommodations in Birmingham, Alabama. The method used was no longer a non-cooperating boycott, but non-violent direct action by way of several forms of civil disobedience. During this campaign, King served an eight-day jail sentence during which he wrote *Letter from Birmingham Jail*, one of the most significant Christian documents of the twentieth century. All of these efforts were to result in the Civil Rights Act, passed by congress in 1964.

Before that, in the summer of 1963, King led a massive march on Washington, DC, and delivered his famous 'I have a dream' speech, in which he laid out in detail his vision of the 'beloved community', the centrepiece of his life and thought. The ideals found here were based on the Judeo-Christian vision of the messianic era and the kingdom of God, as well as the political ideals of the USA's founding documents with their ideal of a 'holy commonwealth'. In 1964 King became the youngest person to receive the Nobel Laureate for peace, but his work was not finished. A successful campaign in Selma, Alabama, in the spring of 1965 prompted Congress to pass the Voting Rights Act a few months later.

King took a public stand in 1967 against the Vietnam War, in which he saw an interrelationship among what he called the three basic evils in the USA – racism, poverty and war. This brought him severe criticism from black and white leaders alike, who charged him with 'mixing politics and civil rights'. His response was simple: 'justice is indivisible'.

In the spring of 1968 he shifted his emphasis to human rights and issues of class, such as housing, education, jobs and health. But the success of this Poor Peoples' Campaign was seriously qualified by King's assassination while he was calling for a higher standard of living for garbage workers in Memphis. From then his widow, Coretta King (1927–2006), kept alive his dream of the 'beloved community' as one where 'barriers that divide and alienate humanity, whether racial, economic, or psychological' would be removed. This ideal was not limited to America. He often spoke of 'the world house', a world where 'we must transcend our races, our tribe, our class and our nation'.

His passion for social justice and peace was rooted in the central themes of the Protestant liberalism he encountered at Crozer and Boston. But these themes of religious experience, the humanity of Jesus, a strong ethical orientation, confidence in human reason and the dynamism of history easily found their place in King's mind and heart because he had heard much of them, in one form or another, from the black church and at Morehouse College in Atlanta, where he was educated. It was this liberal theology, validated by the prayers, sermons and spirituals of the black church, that fuelled King's desire to resist injustice. By word and deed King showed how the Christian gospel of love could be used to transform a racist and unjust society into one on the way to racial harmony and social justice.

IRA ZEPP

often seen to have begun with Dennis Bennett, the Episcopalian rector of St Mark's Church in Van Nuys, California. In 1960 he told worshippers that he had experienced a new outpouring of the Holy Spirit. Pressure from church members who were unhappy with this led to his resignation, but he subsequently moved to Seattle and ministered there, inspiring many with his preaching about the Holy Spirit.

One of the first figures in this movement within Catholicism was Kevin Ranaghan (b. 1940), a Notre Dame student of liturgy, who in 1967 started speaking in tongues at a service at Duquesne Catholic University in Pittsburgh. A group gathered at Notre Dame, and within a few years tens of thousands of people were attending meetings there. Leo Joseph Suenens (1905–1996), the cardinal archbishop of Mechelen-Brussels and primate of Belgium, was also a major figure behind the spread of the movement. He was one of the four moderators of the Second Vatican Council and leaned towards liberalism, calling for a re-examination of issues such as the ban on contraception and married priests. He was also enthusiastic about the Charismatic movement, defending it in the Vatican in the 1960s and 70s. And Charismatic-style worship has even spread to some Orthodox churches, mainly in America – although the traditional Orthodox emphasis on stillness, order and beauty, as well as the set liturgy, means that Pentecostalism has not made great inroads into these churches and has been severely denounced by many Orthodox.

It is essential to appreciate the role that not only evangelicalism but also African American Christianity played in Pentecostalism's development. Two of the key figures in its early years, William Seymour and Charles Harrison Mason, were the sons of freed slaves, and Mason's congregation was mostly black. There are obvious parallels between the Pentecostalists' worship and that of black

Americans that we looked at in Chapter 12, such as 'shouting' and the call-and-response of black preaching. This caused problems: the South, where Pentecostalism spread most quickly, was still a highly racist society where segregation was the law, and Charles Parham himself was a segregationalist. Seymour's meetings in Los Angeles were mixed-race, but the churches that were founded as his disciples spread around the USA were mostly either black (like Mason's) or white (like William Durham's). So there developed white Pentecostalism and black Pentecostalism. However, the black influence remained strong; it is no coincidence that Pentecostalism has become the most prevalent form of Christianity throughout Africa.

Today, Pentecostalism remains controversial, especially among more conservative evangelicals who are often unhappy with what they regard as its excessive emotionalism and doctrinal looseness. They often charge that it overlooks the seriousness of sin and does not sufficiently stress the importance of accepting key doctrines such as the role of the cross in salvation. Charles Parham himself believed in universal salvation, rather than the usual evangelical belief in the eternity of damnation for non-believers. Many American Pentecostalists today are Unitarians.

One development, controversial even among Pentecostalists themselves, is the Toronto Blessing. This phenomenon began in 1994 at Toronto Airport Vineyard Christian Fellowship in Canada, as congregations began to laugh uncontrollably, shout out and fall over. The manifestation appeared to spread from person to person like a virus sweeping through the room. The revival spread, as people travelled to Toronto to see it for themselves: similar outbreaks have occurred elsewhere in the world, inspired by the Toronto church. Many Christians, however, have denounced the Toronto Blessing as a work of the devil, insisting that disorderliness and apparently pointless things such as babbling or falling over cannot come from God. But supporters argue that the Toronto Blessing is a new work of the Holy Spirit like that of the Day of Pentecost itself, and it is a gift to the faithful.

Despite the controversies, Pentecostalism's remarkable rise has assured it a key place in the history of twentieth-century Christianity. We shall encounter it repeatedly in the final chapters of this book, from Brazil to South Africa to Japan. The independent Pentecostal churches are major players in the world ecumenical scene. By the mid-1990s, the Church of God in Christ had 5.5 million members in the USA, while the Assemblies of God Church – now the largest independent Pentecostal church –

decades has been that between conservative and liberal, and this is a split that can be seen at every level in the churches.

In Chapter 12 we saw how this division came about in the face of the 'crisis of faith'. Modernists such as Shailer Mathews found themselves bitterly at odds with fundamentalists such as Benjamin Warfield. In the middle were the majority of evangelicals, who on the whole agreed with the fundamentalists in matters of doctrine but were less insistent on breaking off relations with those who disagreed. Thus there was division not only between liberals on the one hand and evangelicals on the other, but also between fundamentalist evangelicals and more accommodating ones. This latter division can be seen in the furore surrounding Harry Fosdick in the 1920s. Fosdick (1878–1969) was a Baptist preacher in New York City, a pious

The Bible is not an infallible Book, in the sense in which it is popularly supposed to be infallible.

Washington Gladden, *Who wrote the Bible?*, 1894

had 25 million members throughout the world.

CONSERVATIVES AND LIBERALS
The twentieth century has seen Christianity in the USA splinter. Many divisions were there already, above all that between Protestant and Catholic, as well as that between North and South which we saw earlier. But the primary division in recent

evangelical, complete with the obligatory conversion experience as a child, but he achieved notoriety with a sermon in 1922 entitled *Shall the Fundamentalists win?*, in which he argued for openness to liberal theology, science and scholarship. Supporters sent copies of this sermon to every Protestant minister in the country, and he followed it up with books defending the same position. Fosdick moved to the

Worshippers at the Apostolic Outreach Center in New Orleans, 1993.

My brother, if the Bible is not also scientifically accurate, it is not, to me at least, the Word of God. I have a very plain reason for that. The Lord God who made this world and all the scientific marvels which we are now discovering in it – that same Lord God knew all these things from the beginning... Now if the Bible is the Word of God, and if God inspired it, then it cannot contain any scientific mistakes because God knew every truth and fact of science from the beginning.

W. A. Criswell, pastor of First Baptist Church, Dallas from 1944–95

For the church and theology as a whole, fundamentalism constitutes an ecumenical problem rather than an intellectual problem... The root of it is the fact that fundamentalists deal with the real difficulties of differences in faith and life by deeming non-Christian the bodies and the persons who do not agree with them.

James Barr, *Fundamentalism*, 1977

Riverside Baptist Church, built by the Rockefellers, where he preached to immense congregations until his retirement in 1946. He was opposed by a new generation of conservative theologians, such as John Gresham Machen of Princeton, whose *Christianity and Liberalism* of 1923 stated that liberals simply were not Christians.

The tension between the two wings of evangelicalism has been evident in the number of organizations founded to represent their views. Two of the most important have been the American Council of Christian Churches (ACCC) and the National Association of Evangelicals (NAE), both established in the 1940s. The former was founded by Carl McIntire, a fiery fundamentalist radio preacher. It was vehemently opposed to political and theological liberalism alike, as well as to Roman Catholicism. The NAE, by contrast, was created in deliberate opposition to the ACCC and, whilst upholding conservative evangelical doctrines, sought to be more open and more involved in national life. It was this organization, for example, that set up the 'Youth For Christ' movement which was associated with Billy Graham.

The fundamentalist churches have continued to exist as a small but vocal minority within American evangelicalism. The main distinguishing feature of fundamentalist churches is not their doctrine so much as their refusal to associate with what they regard as heretical groups, such as liberals and Catholics: indeed, they typically refuse to associate with other *evangelicals* who associate with these undesirables. Billy Graham has been a bête noire for many fundamentalists, for, although they agree with him on most doctrinal matters, they find his openness to non-evangelicals and even non-Protestants unacceptable. This has been a concern of fundamentalists from the start. So in 1936, for example, John Gresham Machen led a group of Presbyterian fundamentalists who split with their wider church to form the Orthodox Presbyterian Church – a group which itself divided the next year, spawning

the Bible Presbyterian Church. This illustrates the tendency of fundamentalists to keep splitting into smaller and smaller groups, contrasting with the large organizations and international cooperation usually mounted by mainstream evangelicals. Issues over which fundamentalists have often split include disputes over the interpretation of the book of Revelation – for an emphasis on the end times is common in fundamentalism – and also over whether Pentecostalism is acceptable. Thus, fundamentalists are rather cut off from the broader evangelical world, as well as from the still broader Christian world beyond that. This is not always the case, and there have been calls from within fundamentalism to try to engage more with other Christians. The 1940s, for example, saw the foundation of the Fuller Seminary in California in an attempt to bring fundamentalism back into the academic theological world, and thence into mainstream evangelicalism.

Yet despite these divisions within evangelicalism, the division between doctrinally conservative evangelicals and non-evangelical liberals is still deeper, and it is found throughout the English-speaking world. It is perhaps most fierce in Britain, since here the Church of England is still a coalition of different groups. Where Puritans and Anglo-Catholics (or Low, Broad and High) once coexisted in an uneasy tension, today the main division is between evangelicals and liberals, with Anglo-Catholics added to the mix. Of these, the evangelicals are the most vocal group. Many find a voice in the organization Reform, which calls for the church to change in a more evangelical direction. The Anglican Church also faces the problem that its daughter churches in different countries are quite different theologically. The African Anglican churches – such as the Church of Nigeria, the largest Anglican church of all – are doctrinally highly conservative and evangelical or Pentecostal in liturgical style. But the Episcopal Church of the United States is far more theologically liberal and Anglo-

Catholic in liturgical style. The church lacks a central authority analogous to the Vatican, for the archbishop of Canterbury, although considered 'first in honour' among the Anglican primates and their spiritual leader, cannot interfere in the internal affairs of other Anglican churches. Some see this as a blessing – ensuring a variety of voices within the Anglican communion – but others have disagreed, since it makes it hard to ensure that the various voices sing in harmony.

In the 1980s and 90s the main point of dispute within the church was the ordination of women. Historically, the Anglican churches agreed with the Roman Catholic and Orthodox that only men could be priests, but in the twentieth century this view was gradually whittled away. In 1944 Florence Li Tim-oi in Hong Kong became the first female priest. However, it was not until 1976 that the Episcopalian Church of the United States authorized female priests. The first female bishop was ordained in 1989. The Church of England, meanwhile, ordained the first female priests in 1992, but it was not until 2005 that it passed a motion allowing for the future consecration of female bishops. The issue was enormously divisive. The evangelical group Reform campaigned against women priests on the grounds that they are forbidden by 1 Timothy 2:12, 'I permit no woman to teach or to have authority over a man; she is to keep silent.' The Anglo-Catholics also opposed them, and their organization, Forward In Faith, campaigned even more vigorously on the issue. In 1992 some left the Church of England for Rome. Many others remained behind but refused to accept the authority of bishops who ordained women. In a splendid example of the Anglican ability to compromise, the church solved this problem by appointing 'flying bishops', Anglo-Catholic bishops with no set dioceses, to travel around the country overseeing these churches.

The dispute over female priests has died down considerably in recent years, although it was reignited in 2006 when Katharine

A female priest gives Communion to a member of her congregation.

Jefferts Schori was elected presiding bishop of the US Episcopal Church, making her the first woman to lead an Anglican church. The primary issue now dividing the church, however, is homosexuality. Here the divisions are more clear-cut. Not all evangelicals were opposed to female priests – on the contrary, many moderates welcomed the move. But virtually all evangelicals agree that homosexual activity is wrong, since it is condemned in Leviticus 18:22. They therefore oppose any notion of the church sanctioning homosexual relationships or ordaining gay clergy. The evangelical voice on this has therefore been much stronger and more united than on the female priests issue, and it has had more of an effect.

In 2003 a gay priest named Jeffrey John was nominated as the bishop of Reading, 60 km (38 miles) west of London. Vocal opposition from evangelicals there and abroad persuaded the archbishop of Canterbury, Rowan Williams, to withdraw his acceptance of the nomination; John was subsequently appointed to a less prominent post as dean of St Alban's. Although John was celibate, many evangelicals had wanted him to condemn homosexuality explicitly before taking up his post, something not normally required of new Anglican bishops. A much bigger row broke out later in 2003,

Jerry Falwell preaching at Thomas Road Baptist Church, Lynchburg, Virginia, in 1980.

The idea that religion and politics don't mix was invented by the devil to keep Christians from running their own country.

Jerry Falwell

when Gene Robinson was elected bishop of the US state of New Hampshire. Unlike Jeffrey John, Robinson was not only gay but in an active, long-term relationship. His election was opposed by many within the Episcopal Church, but – since the liberal side of this church is relatively strong – he was successfully elected and installed. The incident has threatened to bring irreconcilable schism to the Anglican communion, with evangelicals in both England and Australia bitterly criticizing Williams for not overruling Robinson's election. Peter Akinola, the outspoken archbishop of Nigeria, declared his church not fully in communion with that of the USA. In Canada, by contrast, there is more support for their fellow North Americans, for the Anglican church here is similarly liberal – the diocese of New Westminster, for example, approves the blessing of same-sex partnerships.

The division between evangelicals and theological liberals cuts right through Protestantism, but it is felt most keenly in the Anglican communion because both form such large groups within it. It seems almost impossible to see a way for them to be reconciled, given their very different viewpoints: evangelicals insist that the Bible must be the final authority on all matters, while liberals argue that the Bible is only one authority among some, none of which is really final or infallible, and that Christians must let go of outdated moral norms which they consider unjust or unloving.

THE 'RELIGIOUS RIGHT'

There has also been renewed controversy between Christians and non-Christians in the USA over the role of the former in secular politics. Until the late 1970s there was no particular Christian lobby group within US politics, although many individual Christians were politically active. This changed in 1979 when the televangelist Jerry Falwell (b. 1933) formed the Moral Majority, a pressure group which campaigned on conservative social issues. Although theoretically bipartisan, the Moral Majority had far more influence in the Republican Party than the Democrats, and its formation coincided with the rise to the presidency of Ronald Reagan, who supported many of its policies. It disbanded in 1989 and was replaced by the Christian Coalition, led by the Baptist minister, Pentecostal televangelist and conservative politician Pat Robertson. Under Falwell, Robertson and others, the 'Religious Right', as this general movement has been dubbed, has become extremely powerful in American politics, to a degree beyond its size. Reliable figures are hard to come by, but it has been estimated that there are perhaps 200,000 active members of the Religious Right, with ten or twenty million sympathizers.

The Religious Right campaigns for socially conservative policies, often dubbed 'pro-family' policies and 'pro-life' issues. Probably the biggest concern is abortion, which is denounced as murder, but the Religious Right is also generally opposed to euthanasia, anything to do with homosexuality, sex education in schools and the teaching of evolution in schools unless it is accompanied by the teaching of the literal truth of Genesis. It typically strongly supports the Zionist movement and pro-Israeli policies. Many members of the Religious Right are also opposed to the separation of church and state in the USA, and campaign for prayers to be said in school. Many political liberals – whether Christian or not – are disturbed by these campaigns, not simply because they oppose the individual policies, but because they regard the campaigns as an attempt to overturn an officially secular state and replace it with a theocracy.

As a rule, the Religious Right is still associated with the Republican Party, contributing to its campaign funds and sometimes even distributing its literature in churches. Shortly before the 2004 presidential election, one Baptist church in North Carolina threatened to expel anyone who voted against President George W. Bush (b. 1946), a threat that it acted upon after the election. A remarkable thing about the Religious Right is that it has transcended its 1980s condition as a movement primarily of evangelical Protestants, and it has succeeded in uniting non-evangelical Protestants who share many of its concerns and even Roman Catholics. Again before the 2004 election, Cardinal Joseph Ratzinger (b. 1927), then prefect of the Congregation for the Doctrine of the Faith in Rome and soon to become Pope Benedict XVI, wrote to US bishops warning them against a Catholic politician who was pro-abortion, and stating that anyone who voted for him must be denied access to the Mass. Although unnamed, his target was George W. Bush's Democrat challenger. The fact that one of the most significant policy-makers in the Vatican had apparently supported a Protestant candidate over a Catholic one was significant, since it implied that the one issue of abortion overrode other concerns. For example, the Vatican had vehemently condemned George W. Bush's recent invasion of Iraq, but it still intervened on his behalf. So some people have observed that the rise of the Religious Right has seen the Catholic Church in the USA apparently function as a single-issue lobby movement, campaigning on abortion and largely overlooking other matters. Of course that is an exaggeration, but still many people, both inside and outside the Catholic Church, find the trend worrying.

THE AMERICAN CATHOLIC CHURCH AND SEXUAL ABUSE

Another serious controversy which has dogged the North American Catholic Church in recent years has been the problem of paedophile priests. A series of cases gained great publicity in the late 1990s, although it emerged that some went back much earlier than that. One priest in Ireland was found to have been abusing children in the 1940s, while Canada had seen the scandal of the Duplessis Orphans, children in Catholic-run orphanages who between the 1940s and the 1960s were wrongly categorized as mentally ill and subjected to unsuitable treatment or even direct abuse.

The main focus of public outrage was not against the original abusers so much as the hierarchy of the Catholic Church, which was accused of not trying to bring the abusers to justice, or even covering it up. In 2002 Brendan Comiskey, bishop of Ferns in Ireland, resigned over these allegations; the following year, Bernard Law, cardinal archbishop of Boston, followed suit. However, Cardinal Law was then appointed to a post in the Vatican curia, before being made archpriest of Santa Maria Maggiore, leading to more claims that the Vatican did not take the situation seriously.

Only very few priests were found to have been involved in abusing children, and there is no evidence that, proportionally, there are any more paedophiles among the priesthood than in society at large. But the scandals, and the allegations of cover-ups, proved extremely damaging to the church, especially in the USA, where Cardinal Law was widely denounced. The term 'paedophile priest' entered the popular vocabulary, and the church suffered a very serious public relations crisis. Its finances were also greatly hit, partly by a drop in donations and partly because of lawsuits and fines. Law's archdiocese, Boston, lost millions of dollars in this way. In 2004, after settling over a hundred compensation claims, the archdiocese of Portland, Oregon filed for bankruptcy, the first Catholic diocese ever to do so. Joseph Ratzinger, as head of the Congregation for the Doctrine of the Faith in Rome, wrote to bishops insisting that they could not reveal to the police details of the church's internal investigation on

When there is no vision of God, when there's no vision of God's law, when there's no vision of right and wrong, where there's no vision of ultimate reward and ultimate punishment, when there's no vision of decency, when there's no standard of values, society breaks apart and everybody does what he wants to do.

Pat Robertson, 1985

This vision of the United States of America as a nation that needs only a strong, God-fearing leader to establish it as the world's democratic 'defender of the faith' is not a delusion that will pass with Reagan's retirement from the White House. Greater than any present danger is the prospect that the US public will continue to look for leaders who will sustain the promise of tough, indomitable leadership and will not compromise what are mistakenly conceived to be American traditions and morals.

Wilbur Edel, *Defenders of the faith*, 1987

the matter. However, he did not instruct bishops not to cooperate in other ways with any police investigation.

THE LATIN AMERICAN EXPERIENCE

At the start of the twentieth century, 90 per cent of the population of South America identified themselves as Catholic. To many, Catholicism was part and parcel of their cultural or national identity. In Mexico, the revered 'father of the nation' was Miguel Hidalgo y Costilla (1753–1811), a Catholic priest who had helped inspire the revolution of 1810–11. In practical terms, however, the picture was not so rosy from a Catholic viewpoint. For example, the fact that in many areas few people got married in church indicates that, for them, Catholicism was a matter of national identity more than of practising religion. This was especially so in more rural areas, where many people still maintained elements of the old pagan religions and combined them with Catholicism – or with elements of African religions, brought over by African slaves and settlers. In Brazil, slavery had only been abolished in 1888, and Africans and their descendants now made up a significant proportion of the Brazilian population.

At the same time, the urbanization and industrialization of much of the continent in the late nineteenth and early twentieth centuries made for social change and upheaval, and many in the cities were questioning the role of the church or of European-style doctrines and practices. That was perhaps hardly surprising in the light of a number of political developments over previous years, such as the 'French intervention' of 1861 when British, Spanish and French forces landed in Mexico after the government defaulted on debts, and the French actually occupied Mexico City for several years. Little wonder, given both this and intermittent US interference in Mexican politics and borders, that many Latin Americans felt dissatisfied with 'western' culture. Between 1880 and 1930, the population of Latin America doubled to 100 million, creating huge changes in society; this period also saw new aspirations, as countries sought to catch up with the USA, an enormously successful industrial nation practically on their doorstep. Part of this involved encouraging immigration, and this also brought instability to both society and religion. Some states sought to reassert their authority in the face of this change and instability: Brazil, for example, became a constitutional democracy in 1889, but the following years saw fewer people being entitled to vote, not more, and the military-dominated government failed to prevent frequent outbreaks of violence in the country.

'RED MEXICO'

Some states were increasingly hostile to church influence. Mexico, for example, had seen the church endorsed by the dictator Porfirio Díaz (ruled 1884–1911), but this came to an end with the revolution of 1910. The armed phase of the revolution lasted for seven years, during which churches were liable to be burned by the aggressively secular revolutionaries. The revolutionaries had many internal disagreements, but they all agreed that the country had no place for 'priestcraft'. The constitution of 1917 laid out that all education was to be secular, monastic orders were banned, foreign priests deported, and Mexican priests not only had to be registered with the government but could not vote. In some areas, anyone wearing a Catholic badge or insignia might face jail.

Fortunately, Alvaro Obregón, president of Mexico from 1920 to 1924, recognized that it was important not to alienate the church too much, and he enforced these harsh measures only selectively. Nevertheless, the campaign against Catholicism continued via less 'official' avenues: churches were vandalized and their contents thrown onto bonfires. In some cases the vandals held mock services in which they 'consecrated' bulls as bishops

Mexican rebels
shooting from a
boulder overlooking
a valley, c. 1911.

and shouted to God to strike them down. Catholics responded by denouncing everything to do with the new regime and its perceived lax morals (even the new interest in the tango), and they posted guards around the churches, who sometimes found themselves engaged in running street battles with the anti-clericals. In the countryside, though, the church continued to play a major role in everyday life. Where people were used to seeing their local priest act as a doctor, teacher, engineer or social worker, it was not easy for them to forget their allegiance to the church.

Obregón's successor, Plutarco Elías Calles (president from 1924 to 1928), was an anti-clerical extremist, determined to eradicate Catholicism from Mexico completely. In 1926 he introduced laws forcing priests to register or face heavy fines, and public religious acts were banned. Church property was to be nationalized, and all Catholic organizations and publications were outlawed. Catholic protest organizations sprang up around the country, and in 1926 the church declared that it could not operate under such conditions. Priests continued to minister to the faithful in private, but there were no more church services. As priests found themselves often on the run from the authorities, protected, hidden or fed by their loyal parishioners, lay Catholics were authorized to fill in for them. They presided over prayers and even performed baptisms and heard confessions if necessary. Some priests commented that the state of ecclesiastical emergency seemed to have made their congregations *more* devout, as the siege mentality strengthened their resolve. A boycott of all governmental institutions was begun. Catholics no longer used buses, sent their children to state schools or went to cinemas.

On 1 January 1927, René Capistrán Garza, leader of the national League for the Defence of Religious Liberty, declared armed rebellion. Throughout the staunchly Catholic state of Jalisco, militants armed with ancient rifles or clubs seized control of villages. The government sent troops to put down the Cristero Rebellion, as it was known, but clever guerrilla tactics on the part of the revolutionaries saw several defeats inflicted upon government troops. One of the most effective generals of the rebellion was Victoriano Ramírez, known popularly as El Catorce ('The Fourteen') because he had once broken out of jail, killed fourteen men ordered to recapture him and sent a message to the mayor asking him to send more men in future.

The rebels held out for over two years, until a peaceful solution was reached in 1929. The new president, Emilio Portes Gil, agreed to permit worship and allow anyone, even priests, to criticize the law – provided they followed it. The rebels went home, and for the first time in three years, church bells rang across Mexico.

Still, it was not until the 1940s that the tension really eased. Manuel Avila Camacho, president from 1940 to 1946, made an effort to woo the church back into national life, recognizing that the anti-clericalism of the past had brought only disunity and chaos. From this time on, although many of the anti-Catholic laws remained on the statute books, they were not enforced.

THE RENEWAL OF LATIN CATHOLICISM
The problems in Mexico were certainly an exception in their intensity, but they reflected growing anti-clericalism across Latin America in the early twentieth century. The church itself was becoming disestablished – first in Brazil in 1891, and then in Cuba and Uruguay in the 1910s and Chile in 1925. This period saw new religious movements which tried to reassert an enthusiastic if flawed understanding of Catholicism in reaction to anti-clericalism and capitalism that they believed to be spreading throughout South American society. For example, in the 1890s a lay preacher, Antônio Conselheiro, established a religious community at Canudos in Brazil. A huge makeshift town of mud huts grew around the church of Bom Jesus, and vast numbers of people flocked to it, convinced that this town and its opposition to governmental liberalism and capitalism was the start of the kingdom of God on earth. Stories spread that the houses were made of food or that the nearby desert would be transformed into sea. But in 1897 the

federal government declared war on the settlement, brutally destroyed it and killed many thousands of people.

The church's official response to all these problems associated with the liberal or revolutionary states was to try to reassert orthodoxy and traditional practices – a sometimes heavy-handed approach that did not always have the desired effect. The effort had, in a sense, begun with Pope Pius IX. As a young man, the then Mastai Ferretti had spent two years in South America. When he became pope he was therefore the first one ever to have visited the continent, and in 1859 he had blessed the foundation of a Latin American college in Rome, the Jesuit-run Pio Latino, with the aim of tightening the links between Rome and the Latin American churches. Ten years later, forty Latin American bishops had attended the First Vatican Council, and during the discussions there every one of them had supported the doctrine of papal infallibility from the start.

So there was already an Ultramontane tendency, at least within the church hierarchy, in South America. This provided the background for the Plenary Council for Latin America, called by Pope Leo XIII (reigned 1878–1903) and held at the Vatican in 1899. It was the first major council of Latin American bishops, presided over by their own archbishops, but it was intended as the response of the church as a whole to the problems of South America. The council was especially concerned to continue and extend the process of evangelization of the continent, recognizing that Catholic values were only skin-deep in many areas. To this end, the council planned to make the Catholic Church more independent throughout the continent. In many places, the church was too dependent on the secular states, and the council hoped to reinvigorate the church's own hierarchy, partly through a call to standardize the Latin American doctrinal, moral and liturgical mores in line with the universal church. New catechisms were compiled, with a special eye to rural farm workers. Equally

May there be presented ever more clearly in Latin America the countenance of a Church authentically poor, missionary and paschal, freed from all temporal power and boldly committed to the liberation of the whole man and of all men.

The Latin American Bishops Council at Medellín, 1968

importantly, there was a call for a greater spiritual engagement with people throughout their lives. In the past, many people had regarded Catholicism as a matter of being baptized; there was now an effort to make them think of Catholicism as a matter of attending Mass. The practice of first communion for children was encouraged.

The council represented a programme of 'Romanization': a call to return to the church's roots to face a new era. It was not simply about purity of doctrine and liturgy, but obedience: the bishops had to follow the lead of Rome, and the priests had to follow the lead of the bishops. Those who resisted were excommunicated, and there were even book-burnings. Yet on the whole, the attempt was successful. By the 1920s the church hierarchy was stronger and better disciplined, and there was indeed more uniformity in doctrine and practice, at least in Argentina and southern Brazil. To the north, however, in northern Brazil and in Cuba, things had changed less.

SOCIALISM AND LIBERATION

Changing social conditions in South America meant hardship for many. Slavery had been replaced by wage labour, but the living conditions of millions in the great cities were increasingly appalling. And in the early years of the twentieth century, the Catholic Church remained strangely silent on such issues. Most of the campaigns for social welfare or better working conditions had nothing to do with the church. The main exception to this was in factories, where Pope Leo XIII ordered the church to try to smooth relations between workers and bosses, appealing to bosses to provide good conditions for their employees. Much of the motivation for this was the fear of communism, which the pope thought might be fostered by poor industrial relations.

But after the Second World War, a number of highly prominent Catholic bishops began to speak out on behalf of the people of their countries and basic human rights. For example, Hélder Câmara, who in 1964 became archbishop of Olinda and

Recife in Brazil, criticized the Brazilian government so much that it sent a number of assassins against him – but they could not bring themselves to kill such an obviously saintly man. Four times nominated for the Nobel Peace Prize, Câmara was denounced by the authorities as 'the Red Bishop' and even spent nine years officially not existing, all references to him in the media scrupulously removed.

When Hélder Câmara died in 1999, the president of Brazil declared three days of national mourning. But not all activist bishops were reconciled to the state in this way. Even more famous than Câmara was Oscar Arnulfo Romero (1917–80), who became archbishop of San Salvador in El Salvador in 1977. The country at this time was suffering between an oppressive right-wing government and left-wing terrorist protests, undergoing continual political chaos and intermittent civil war. Romero

> *When I give food to the poor, they call me a saint. When I ask why the poor have no food, they call me a communist.*
>
> Hélder Câmara

Oscar Romero celebrates a wedding, 18 March 1980, six days before his assassination.

denounced the government and its oppressive measures, and wrote to President Jimmy Carter of the USA, begging him to stop sending the government aid and weapons. His weekly radio broadcasts were the most popular in the country. But in 1980 he was assassinated while saying Mass.

The protests of bishops such as Hélder Câmara and Oscar Arnulfo Romero represented a growing sense that the church did not simply stand up for the rights of the poor – it actually identified with them. In his personal lifestyle, Câmara had demonstrated this by living in a small room at the back of his church instead of the archiepiscopal palace, sleeping in a hammock and hitch-hiking instead of using an official car. Another bishop who insisted on the same principles was Samuel Ruiz García (b. 1924), who in 1959 became bishop of San Cristóbal de Las Casas in southern Mexico. After spending much of his time with the poverty-stricken native people of the area, he came to believe that the poor are actually the reason for the church's very existence. It is there to help the poor.

This basic conviction – that the church does not simply have a *duty* to help the disadvantaged, but is in some way *identified* with them – became the basis for the famous movement known as liberation theology. The movement was named after the 1971 book *Theology of Liberation* by Peruvian theologian Gustavo Gutiérrez (b. 1928), in which he insisted that theology – and the church – must be concerned at all times with the suffering of the poor, or they fail to be true to the God revealed in the Bible. For God himself, according to the liberation theologians, closely identifies with those who suffer – an idea that has its roots in the doctrine of the incarnation and the suffering of Christ. Gutiérrez and others like him argued that instead of thinking simply about the church and its role, Christians must focus on society, and think about how the church fits in with society and can transform it. Capitalism, on this view, has failed, and the church must join the protest against it, offering instead the hope for the future that

is bound up in the Christian expectation of the return of Christ. Anything else is idolatry. Faithfulness to Christ is shown not simply in what one believes, but in what one does – hence the call to stop focusing on 'orthodoxy' ('right belief') and start thinking about 'orthopraxy' ('right practice').

Liberation theology became enormously influential. In 1968 the Latin American bishops met at Medellín in Colombia, where they issued a number of declarations which helped to spread these concerns. This conference almost eclipsed the Second Vatican Council, as far as South America was concerned. But liberation theology was controversial. In particular, Pope John Paul II, seeing in its theology a kind of Christian Marxism, warned against its excesses in a statement of 1984 entitled *On certain aspects of the theology of liberation*. In this document, and in the visit to South America that he made a couple of months later, the pope insisted that the Catholic Church does uphold the rights of the poor and speak up for them, but not to the exclusion of all other groups. Thus he rejected what amounted to the class warfare of some kinds of liberation theology, which suggested that because God is 'for' the poor, he is 'against' the rich. Mainstream Catholicism aims to be more inclusive.

Nevertheless, the influence of liberation theology extended well beyond Latin America. In North America, for example, it influenced the development of black theology, which in the hands of writers such as James Cone (b. 1938), professor of theology at Union Theological Seminary in New York, argued that, because God is intrinsically on the side of those who suffer, we can say that God is on the side of black people where they have been mistreated by whites, and even say that God is black, if by this we mean that he identifies with suffering peoples. Feminist theologians such as Rosemary Radford Ruether (b. 1936) have used similar ideas to talk of the femaleness of God. In the next two chapters we shall also see how forms of liberation theology have emerged in both Asia and Africa.

...if Christ is present among the oppressed, as he promised, he must be working through the activity of Black Power. This alone is my thesis.

James Cone, *Black theology and Black Power*, 1969

PROTESTANTISM

In the nineteenth century, immigration from Europe began to transform the religious character of South America. There was an Anglican church in Rio de Janeiro in 1819, and a thriving community of German Lutherans in southern Brazil. However, these churches remained tiny for many decades. Protestant missions to the South Americans themselves began in the mid-nineteenth century, but they were fairly half-hearted compared to missions elsewhere; the dominance of Catholicism on the continent made many Protestants feel that mission there would be fruitless, or pointless as everyone was already Christian. Nevertheless, the more anti-Catholic churches, especially in the USA, persisted, with the result that revivalist, evangelical Protestantism from the south of the USA did begin to filter into South America. The major denominations there – the Presbyterians, Methodists and Baptists – built churches in Brazil and Argentina in the latter half of the nineteenth century, and by the twentieth century, many left-wing governments promoted them as part of their anti-Catholic propaganda.

The Protestant churches remained a very minor element of South American Christianity until the early decades of the twentieth century. The main factor which helped them grow after this was the arrival of Pentecostalism from the USA. The first Pentecostal churches were founded in Chile and Argentina in 1907 – only a year or two after the first ones in North America – and they spread gradually throughout the continent. Unlike the earlier Protestant missions, these Pentecostal churches were typically new, home-grown denominations, rather than overseas plantations from established, foreign churches. As a result, there is a vast number of Pentecostal denominations in South America, most of which are quite small or confined to only one country. The main exception is Peru, where Pentecostal churches have not dominated Protestantism to such an extent, and where those that do exist are mostly part of the US-based Assemblies of God.

Nevertheless, it is perhaps only since the 1970s or 80s that the Protestant churches have been able to claim significant minorities of the population. At the end of the twentieth century Uruguay had the fewest Protestants – some 5 per cent of the population – while Guatemala had the most – some 20 per cent. Most of Latin America hovers around 15 per cent, of which some two-thirds are Pentecostalists. However, the importance of these churches is greater than these relatively modest statistics might suggest. South American Protestants typically have much higher church attendance rates than Catholics, suggesting greater commitment; their numbers are also growing in much of the continent. In particular, indigenous peoples and the more socially disadvantaged classes are disproportionately drawn to Protestantism, suggesting that the Protestant churches have been more successful at identifying with the poor even than the Catholic liberation theologians. All this has led some people to wonder whether South America, which has been so closely identified with Roman Catholicism for so long, might be on the verge of becoming a Protestant continent. That, perhaps, is still some way off, if it ever happens: many countries still do not give Protestants quite the same rights as Catholics, although freedom of worship is usually guaranteed now. Also, the Protestant churches have typically not cooperated with each other as much as in other continents, which weakens their voice: only Peru has a National Evangelical Council to act as a united front for the Protestants. Today Bolivia, Argentina and Costa Rica are the only Latin American countries to remain officially Catholic, but Catholicism is still so deeply entrenched in the culture of most of South America that it is hard to see it being displaced just yet.

THE PACIFIC

THE ANTIPODES

From a religious point of view, Australia and New Zealand, in the early part of the twentieth century, were largely a copy of Britain. In both countries the Church of

England predominated among the white settlers. The southern part of New Zealand had seen many Scottish settlers, and so Presbyterianism was strong here. In Australia, there was a larger Catholic contingent (partly because of the many Irish settlers in the nineteenth century), making it the largest rival to the Church of England.

These countries had not been settled with religious aims in mind, compared to much of the Americas, and religion therefore played a correspondingly smaller role. In the second half of the twentieth century the churches faced the same crisis of secularization and loss of interest in Christianity as Europe. The developing antipodean obsession with sport did not help, as young people found more enjoyable things to do with their Sundays than go to church.

Even before this, though, the tough frontier life endured by many settlers did not encourage theological speculation. Worship was conducted in relatively small churches and chapels in the more remote areas and in brick cathedrals, much like those 'back home', in the larger towns such as Melbourne, Auckland or Christchurch. However, religion remained important as a social or cultural marker. Anglicans still did not like Catholics, and indeed Australian Catholics were almost a society within a society for many years, shunned by the Protestant denominations.

Nevertheless, Christianity played an important role in the spur to social and political action, especially in New Zealand, where various church groups were formed to campaign for a better society. The Committee on Temperance and Public Morals, for example, formed by the Methodists in 1902, sounds rather archaic today, but it was concerned with matters as diverse as workers' living conditions, the state of the League of Nations and anti-Semitism. Another group with similar concerns was the Public Questions Committee of the Presbyterians. Indeed, social questions overcame denominational differences in 1942 to create the Inter-church Council on Public Affairs. These groups were not simply talking shops, but were the focus of real concern about

issues in New Zealand society and beyond. Christian social action influenced national politics: Joseph Archer, who led the Labour Party in the 1920s, was a Baptist minister.

New committees and groups continued to be set up for decades to come, such as the Presbyterian Race Relations Committee in 1974. In 2000 the Churches' Agency on Social Issues was created by merging several of these groups and adding Quakers to the Methodist- and Presbyterian-dominated mix.

And this kind of interdenominational cooperation has been even stronger in Australia, which saw the birth of the Uniting Church of Australia in 1977, created by merging the Methodist and Presbyterian churches with the Congregational Union. This important step in ecumenism was made possible by agreeing a Basis of Union, a doctrinal statement expressing the basic principles of the Protestant faith. Given that the Presbyterians were rather strict Calvinists, where the Methodists, like John Wesley, generally did not believe in predestination, this doctrine and similar 'hardline' Calvinist issues were simply left out of the statement. The church is run by a system of councils and synods, with presbyters at the coalface – no bishops, of course.

For the indigenous people of Australia and New Zealand, things were quite different. Christianity played an important role in the struggle for indigenous rights throughout the twentieth century. Both Australian Aborigines and New Zealand Maori appealed to Christian values in their campaigns, and indeed a shared Christian faith did help to commend their appeals to some. The church has seen distinctive and vibrant forms of Christianity develop among the indigenous communities. By the twentieth century, the evangelical Protestant missions had finally proved fairly successful among the Aborigines, and today some two-thirds of Aborigines identify themselves as Christian. The indigenous religion of the Aborigines can no longer be practised as it was, but many Aborigines have transferred their traditional spiritual concerns and some practices to Christianity. For example, Aborigines traditionally use smoke as a symbol of

You have lived your lives in spiritual closeness to the land... through your closeness to the land you touched the sacredness of man's relationship with God. The silence of the bush taught you a quietness of soul that put you in touch with another world, the world of God's Spirit.

Pope John Paul II, speaking to the Aborigines at Alice Springs, 1986

Artwork from Kutjungka Catholic Church in traditional Aboriginal style representing scenes from the Last Supper. In the top left, Jesus washes the feet of the disciples. The lower left represents Peter's refusal to have his feet washed, and in the lower right his later acceptance. At the top right, Jesus and the disciples are seated at the table, while Judas turns away from the others.

purification, and so it is often used at baptisms in addition to water. The last couple of decades of the twentieth century have also seen the emergence of Aboriginal Christian art. This beautiful tradition is especially associated with the Kutjungka Catholic Church in the Balgo Hills, where the Jesuit priests have worked closely with the local community and with Aboriginal groups in the community. The Jesuits encouraged them to create and preserve new artworks, which combined the traditional abstract dots, swirls and other Aboriginal motifs with the cross. Other paintings depict subjects such as Christ's Passion or Pentecost, done in the Aboriginal style – for example, seated figures

May the peace of the Father
Son, Holy Spirit too
And the Faithful Angels
Protect us all.

May the Faithful Mouthpiece too
Guide us all
To Truth, to Righteousness,
To the Throne of Jehovah.

'Ma te marie', Ratana prayer

are represented by crescents, and sacred animals or birds find their way into the Christian scenes.

In New Zealand, Maori forms of Christianity have prospered and continued to develop along interesting and unusual lines. The movement founded by Te Kooti, Te Hahi Ringatu, survived and today claims around 8,000 adherents. More important today is another movement called Ratana, named after Tahupotiki Wiremu Ratana (c. 1873–1939), who in 1918 had a series of visions and became a preacher and healer. By 1925 his movement had become both a new church – the Ratana Church – and a political party, which gained its first seat in parliament in 1932. Ratana himself was part political activist and part spiritual leader: he called for a new recognition of the rights of the Maori on the basis of the Treaty of Waitangi (1840), but at the same time he denounced Maori cultural traditions that he believed were incompatible with Christianity. Nevertheless, the theology of his church was not exactly orthodox. His followers augmented the traditional Trinity with two new elements – the angels and Ratana himself (known as the 'Mangai' or mouthpiece of God), who often took the place usually reserved for Jesus in the prayers of the church. The symbol of Ratana is therefore a five-pointed star. Today the Ratana Church is still strong, and it is the largest Maori denomination, claiming nearly 50,000 adherents.

THE PACIFIC CHURCHES

By the start of the twentieth century, the Polynesian societies of the central and eastern Pacific had been well Christianized. Just as in early medieval Europe, people had copied their rulers in adopting the new religion. Methodism from Britain and Catholicism from France were especially well established. Local missionaries continued to operate in the area, bringing Christianity to the as-yet unconverted on their own cultural terms and enjoying great success.

The 1940s interrupted this happy picture, as war enveloped the Pacific. Many missionaries left to fight; others were imprisoned as the Japanese advanced from island to island. The arrival of US forces in many areas disillusioned many indigenous people, for these supposed representatives of Christian civilization were not necessarily any more benign than the pagan cannibals of the past.

To the west, by contrast, the Melanesians had converted more slowly, and the process was still going on well into the second half of the twentieth century. The dominant figure here was Maurice Leenhardt (1878–1954) of the Paris Missionary Society, who arrived on the island of New Caledonia in 1902. Its Kanak people had been evangelized a few years earlier entirely by *natas* (or messengers) from the nearby Loyalty Islands, led by one missionary named Haxen, who died shortly after Leenhardt arrived. Leenhardt had enormous respect for these native missionaries and the churches they founded, noting that the French colonial authorities had brought only alcohol and destruction to the Kanak, whereas the *natas* had brought Christ and life. He believed that to override their work with a European mission would be profoundly wrong. Instead he saw himself as a servant, not the leader, of these native-led churches and he travelled around the island encouraging them and training new missionaries.

Leenhardt's fascination with the Kanak led him to write voluminously about their culture even as he was translating the Bible for their use, and he insisted that such indigenous peoples must be allowed to create their own understanding of Christianity, even if this was tinged with pre-Christian religious elements. After all, he pointed out, even European Christianity is full of hangovers from pagan days, so it would be unreasonable to expect anything other from the Kanak. In everything, the belief that white missionaries knew better than indigenous ones was Leenhardt's constant bugbear. His views made him unpopular with both the French authorities in New Caledonia and his fellow Protestants back in Europe. In 1920 he returned to France permanently and became a prominent anthropologist. Many white missionaries in New Caledonia promptly forgot his advice and continued their tendency to dominate the Kanak churches and pastors; others were deeply influenced by him. One of them, Leenhardt's nephew Philippe Rey-Lescure, later went to Tahiti and helped to spread his ideas there.

By the time of the Second World War, Leenhardt's principles had become accepted by many missionaries throughout the western Pacific. That war saw a general halt to mission, but after the 1940s it not only resumed but accelerated. The western Pacific became one of the key areas for missionaries to travel to in this period – by 1960 about 4,500 European missionaries were active there. The opening up of the region to air travel enabled more to come, and to go to more remote regions, than ever before: the mountains of New Guinea, for example, were explored more fully, and Christianity was brought to the people there.

However, across the Pacific, the post-war era saw new questions being asked about Christianity. In particular, the experiences of the war had shown almost everyone that Leenhardt had been right: it was not acceptable for Europeans to be in charge of the missions and churches throughout the region. The indigenous people had proved to be perfectly capable of running these things themselves when there had been a shortage of foreigners during the war, so why should they not continue during peace time? A call for religious independence went hand-in-hand with one for political independence.

This issue was addressed at a conference held at Malua, in Western Samoa, in 1961. Representatives of all the Protestant churches in the region attended, and the concern for indigenous leadership that it sparked led to the formation in 1966 of the Pacific Conference of Churches. These developments coincided with the Second Vatican Council, and the Catholic Church joined the Conference in 1976.

CHAPTER 16

MODERN ASIA

Throughout this book, we have traced the development and spread of Christianity to new lands and new cultures. We have seen that the spread of Christianity has always, to some degree, necessitated the development of Christianity, because the religion has had to 'translate' itself into a form that the new culture can understand. Establishing the degree to which such 'translation' is valid – and the point at which it becomes unacceptable compromise – has always been a major problem for missionaries and others, as we have seen above all in the notorious 'Chinese rites' controversy in Chapter 10. But the past century has seen an acceleration in the move towards 'indigenization', the creation of authentically Christian forms of belief and worship that are nevertheless equally rooted in cultures quite alien from the religion's European and Middle Eastern heartlands. In Asia, the stamp of Christianity remains evident in areas that were owned by Europeans in an earlier age: Goa, Malacca and Singapore, for example, all feature splendid old churches from the colonial eras. But the times have changed since then, within the churches as well as in the wider world. If the story of Christianity in Asia before the twentieth century was, to a considerable extent, the story of missionaries, then development during and after the twentieth century has been dominated by indigenization.

INDIA

Indigenization of Christianity in India has, in the past century and a half, been closely tied to the growth of the nationalist movement. Ironically, the rise of this movement in the latter part of the nineteenth century was made possible, in a way, by the very imperialism against which it protested. The British had successfully united India in a way that no empire before, even the Mughals, had managed. A political unity had been imposed upon a collection of semi-autonomous states, and more than that, railways and telegraph systems had been built connecting the furthest points of this vast region. Ideas as well as people could travel swiftly, and there was a new sense of 'India' as a country and 'Indian culture' as a recognizable tradition which deserved to be free. Alexander Duff (1806–78), a bluff Scottish missionary who had little more than contempt for Indian culture and religion compared to the West, introduced British-style higher education to India in the 1830s. He helped to found the University of Calcutta, which gave an enormous boost to education in India – although Duff remained convinced that only education in the English language, following a western curriculum of western history, mathematics and classics, would help the Indians to escape what he regarded as the drag of their own inferior languages and culture.

But nationalism was also a backlash against the anti-Indian, pro-western propaganda that was increasingly spread by the British in the latter stages of the nineteenth century. As we saw in Chapter 13, the colonial authorities had become more and more interested in the evangelizing of the Indians. They taught the intrinsic superiority of western culture over Indian, especially the superiority of Christianity over Hinduism and Islam. But there was a growing middle class of well-

Behold, [Jesus] cometh to us in his loose flowing garment, his dress and features altogether oriental, a perfect Asiatic in everything. Watch his movements, and you will find genuine orientalism in all his habits and manners, in his uprising and down-sitting, his going forth and his coming in, his preaching and ministry, his very language, style and tone. Indeed, while reading the Gospel, we cannot but feel that we are quite at home when we are with Jesus, and that he is altogether one of us.

Keshab Chandra Sen

educated Indians who reacted strongly against this and became determined to reassert Indian culture and Indian religion. Writers such as the swami Vivekananda (1863–1902) and the poet Bankim Chandra Chatterjee (1838–94) praised the virtues of Hinduism, and in response to the missionary claim that those who rejected Christ would go to hell, they retorted that Hinduism encompassed all religions and needed no influx of western gods.

Yet some took exactly the opposite approach. For them, Indians could best recover their sense of national pride and cultural strength – paradoxically – by importing the best of western culture and, in particular, Christianity. They were part of a remarkable dialogue between Hinduism and Christianity that had already been going on for nearly a century.

CHRISTIAN HINDUISM AND THE NATIONALIST MOVEMENT

The great-grandfather of the constructive partnership of Christianity and Hinduism was Ram Mohan Roy (1774–1833), a well-educated Bengalese of high Brahmin ancestry, who was made a raja in 1830. He argued that all religions were basically the same and, like the Enlightenment sages, he believed that the use of reason should lead people to put aside their differences. It was in this spirit that he published *The precepts of Jesus: the guide to peace and happiness* in 1820, in which he praised the moral teachings of the New Testament. But Roy's insistence on the basic agreement of Christianity and Hinduism on monotheism, and his attempt to examine Christian ethics apart from Christian doctrines such as the incarnation, led to controversy with missionaries in India. Roy argued that Jesus had taught that living a moral life is the way to salvation, something that angered some missionaries, and he endorsed Unitarianism as a more rational doctrine than Trinitarianism. He founded a society named the Brahmo Sabha, dedicated to the worship of the one true God, and it often took rather an anti-

Christian tone in the early years.

A more inclusive approach was taken by Keshab Chandra Sen (1838–84), who joined the Brahmo Sabha in 1858 and who greatly increased its appeal beyond the rather narrow group of Bengali intellectuals who had previously dominated. In 1866, however, disagreements within the movement led to Sen founding a more liberal version of his own. Sen believed that the moral values of Christianity summed up everything that was good in Hinduism or elsewhere. Identifying the twin directives of forgiveness and self-sacrifice as the heart of Christianity, he argued that nothing could be a better model for Indians in the modern world. This did not mean adopting western-style Christianity (as some Indians feared), but attempting to take the best of all religious traditions and on their basis build a platform for social and political reform. Sen tried to make the Brahmo Sabha a universal religion, centred on Jesus understood as the interpreter and corrector of true Hinduism.

Although controversial, Keshab Chandra Sen represented a growing feeling among many Indian intellectuals by the end of the nineteenth century that Christianity offered a new way forward for India. Some tried to follow him in taking a non-denominational approach, rejecting the traditional churches as either too western or too fragmentary in

I am reminded of the passage in the Gospel in which he says, 'I am not come to destroy, but to fulfil'. The Mosaic dispensation only? Perhaps the Hindu dispensation also. In India he will fulfil the Hindu dispensation.

Keshab Chandra Sen

Ram Mohan Roy, by the Bangladeshi artist Atul Bose (1898–1977).

their approach: an example was the sadhu Sunder Singh, a mystic who in the first three decades of the twentieth century tried to transcend the different religious traditions whilst holding fast to the ideal of Jesus.

At the same time, there was great interest in more traditional forms of Christianity. Just as the mystics and scholars were pioneering an intellectual encounter between Hinduism and Christianity, so too a quieter encounter had been brewing for many years. As we have seen in earlier chapters, Christianity appealed in particular to members of the lower castes in Hindu society – even to those with no caste at all – and many people began to dwell on the fact that Christianity apparently offered a different model of society, one where individuals were welcomed and honoured irrespective of where they came from. This in itself was a powerful incentive to many to become Christians themselves. All of the churches found new members turning up, and many looked to European history, and especially the Reformation, as a model for what might happen to India. Samuel Satthianadhan, a prominent Christian in the 1880s, spoke of the invariably positive effects of Christianity on society such as education and social reform. Leading reformers such as Charan Banurji and Pandita Ramabai Saraswati – the first real champion of women's rights in India – shared this view. Little wonder, then, that when the Indian National Congress was formed in 1885, Christians took a leading role in its affairs. The same was true of the Home Rule League, formed in 1916 under the presidency of Joseph Baptista, a Roman Catholic lawyer.

In fact, the first half of the twentieth century was a time of increasing cooperation between both different religions and different churches. A major event in this was the formation in 1914 of the National Christian Council of India (NCCI) as an umbrella group for all of the Protestant churches in the country. Meanwhile, the 1920s saw the 'Round

Table Conferences', organized by the Baltimore-born missionary E. Stanley Jones (1884–1973), which involved dialogue with Hindus, Sikhs and Buddhists.

In the 1920s and 30s, C. Dandoy and P. Johanns, two Belgian Catholics, produced a journal called *The light of the east*, which was intended to promote mutual understanding between Christians and non-Christians in India, with a view to the evangelization of the latter. In it, Johanns argued at length that Vedantic philosophy, if systematized, turned out to be quite similar to Thomism, the school of philosophy based on the thought of Thomas Aquinas. At the deepest philosophical level, therefore, there was an affinity between Hinduism and Catholicism, and the former could be understood sympathetically as a precursor to the latter rather than a rival. Such an approach was mirrored by a new generation of Indian theologians who aimed to continue the programme of Keshab Chandra Sen in spelling out a Hindu Christianity. These included Vengal Chakkarai, whose *Jesus the avatar* was published in 1927 and set out a new vision of Jesus as the new 'avatar' (in Hindu terminology an incarnation of God). His brother in law, Pandipeddi Chenchiah, also used the Hindu concept of the avatar, but in the opposite way, contrasting the permanence of Christ's incarnation with the temporary and ephemeral nature of Hindu avatars.

THE MALANKARA CHURCH BEFORE NATIONAL INDEPENDENCE

As these new Christian movements were gathering pace in India, its oldest Christian group was not doing so well. This was especially unfortunate given that it was blessed at the beginning of the twentieth century with the leadership of an especially gifted new bishop. Vattasseril Mar Dionysius VI (1858–1934) was by any standards a remarkable man, who had already made a name for himself as an outstanding preacher and theologian. Unfortunately, he was not to preside over

Christianity, by its history, its services to the State and to society has earned the right of citizenship in India. Only a false nationalism can [prevent] Christianity and Christians [from being] part of the people and the country. The Nationalism that is going to prevail in this country will be neither Hindu nor Muslim but Indian.

M. Ruthnaswamy, speaking to the Catholic Congress in Bangalore, 1933 a glorious period in his church's history. Having been wracked with dissension in the seventeenth century over Roman Catholicism, and in the nineteenth over Anglicanism, the church was to suffer yet another damaging split, this time over a squabble about authority.

Dionysius VI was consecrated metropolitan (in waiting) in 1908 by the Syrian patriarch, Mar Abdullah. He took over the reins the following year when the old metropolitan died. At this point, things went downhill. Mar Abdullah arrived in India but unexpectedly refused to confirm Mar Dionysius as head of the Malankara Church. Instead he wanted control of the church's temporal possessions to pass to him, the patriarch. This was not acceptable to Dionysius and his party, but many others – with various grudges against Dionysius – supported the patriarch. The result was schism, formally begun in 1911 when Mar Abdullah excommunicated Mar Dionysius and his supporters. The church was split down the middle and continued to be split even after Abdullah died in 1915. The bickering over property rights continued in the law courts and reconciliation proved impossible. The party that had supported Dionysius, who died in 1934, retained the name Malankara Orthodox Syrian Church, whilst the patriarch-supporters became the Syrian Orthodox Jacobite Church.

THE POST-INDEPENDENCE CHURCHES
India finally gained its independence in 1947. This year was also a momentous one for the churches, since it saw the formation of the Church of South India (CSI). This new denomination was formed by the merging of the Anglicans, the Methodists, the Presbyterians and the Congregationalists. In 1970 the same groups in the north of the country, together with some smaller denominations, merged to form the Church of North India (CNI). As a result, most Indian Protestants are now members of one of these two large churches – apart

Traffic congestion in Calcutta as India celebrates independence from British rule, 15 August 1947.

from the Baptists, Lutherans and American Methodists, all of whom remained separate. The union of the different traditions into these two large churches represents one of the greatest achievements of the modern ecumenical movement.

Strikingly, the movement has encompassed parts of the Syrian church as well. As a result of all the splits in that church, there are today no fewer than eight churches in India all claiming descent from the original community of Syriac-speaking Thomas Christians. Yet the internal divisions have led to closer links to the other denominations. The Romo-

Syrians, whom we saw in Chapter 13, are now known as the Syro-Malabar Catholic Church, and are not only the largest of the eight groups but remain in full communion with Rome. At the other end of the spectrum, the reforming Mar Thoma Syrian Church, which split off from the Malankara Church in the late nineteenth century, has always enjoyed good relations with the larger Protestant churches already in India, which regard it as a sort of newcomer to the Protestant fold. After independence, these relations became closer. In 1958 the Mar Thoma Syrian Church established intercommunion with the CSI, meaning that, while they

Mother Teresa in Calcutta, with children from her orphanage, 1979.

remained separate churches, they regarded each other's ministers and sacraments as valid. The CNI subsequently joined this accord, and in 1978 all three churches established a Joint Council which was to oversee what was in effect a federation of the three churches, known collectively as the Bharat Christian Church. Today, there are efforts under way to merge them into a fully unified Church of India.

The Catholic Church, meanwhile, continued to consolidate its position. The only part of India in which a sizeable proportion of the people were Catholics was Goa, a Portuguese possession until 1961 and still technically under the old *padroado* system, meaning that the Portuguese authorities were responsible for the administration of the church there. Even after being merged with the rest of India, Goa remains the most important Catholic area in the country, with churches and secular buildings still having a remarkably 'Portuguese' feel even today.

But the most famous figure in Indian Catholicism of recent years lived on the other side of the subcontinent, in Calcutta. Mother Teresa was born Agnes Gonxha Bojaxhiu in Macedonia to Albanian parents in 1910, and as a teenager she joined the Sisters of Loreto, hoping to become a missionary. She worked in their schools in Calcutta until 1948 when, after feeling a vocation to work directly with the poor, she left the order to found the Missionaries of Charity, who took vows not simply of poverty, chastity and obedience, but also to help the poorest of the poor. She and her companions opened hospitals, leper colonies, and other institutions to help the most disadvantaged in the vast slums of Calcutta. The Missionaries of Charity became a global order, working in countries around the world, and Mother Teresa herself became one of the most famous faces of Catholicism in the world until her death in 1997. Indeed, to many she represented the uneasy relationship of the Catholic Church with the modern world. On the one hand she dedicated herself to helping the less fortunate and received the Nobel Peace Prize in 1979. On the other, her fidelity to conservative Catholic views made her highly controversial, particularly among those who argued that, by forbidding contraception, she actually worsened the living conditions of the very same poor to whom she dedicated her life. The fact that such arguments tended to coalesce around the figure of Mother Teresa is perhaps testament not so much to any especially controversial character of her work or personality as to her remarkable prominence as *the* most visible and famous representative of Christian 'good work' in the modern world.

Today around 2.5 per cent of India's one billion inhabitants are thought to be Christians, meaning that there are more Christians in the country than there are Sikhs. This large Christian community – which can trace its roots back further than any other in Asia – continues to make major contributions to Christianity on the continent. For example, the 1980s saw the emergence of *dalit* theology, India's answer to liberation theology. *Dalit* means an 'untouchable' person in the caste system, and the new breed of Indian theologians seeks to draw upon the experience of such low-caste people within the churches to explore how God relates to the oppressed and marginalized, and to reject the more liberal rapprochement between Christianity and Hinduism that typified the first half of the twentieth century.

CHRISTIAN ASHRAMS

However, a striking feature of this rapprochement, which gathered pace after independence, has been the development of Christian ashrams in India. An ashram is a traditional feature of Hindu culture, a community of disciples of a particular guru or spiritual teacher. In antiquity, ashrams formed spontaneously but operated as centres of scholarship and philosophy as well as religion. Their inhabitants sought to follow the way of *Sannyasa*, that is, renunciation of the world and turning to the divine.

At the start of the twentieth century, a

There are some churches in this diocese where any Sunday morning Christians of from five to twelve different castes kneel side by side in one row to receive the Sacrament of the Body and Blood of our Lord.

V. S. Azariah, bishop of Dornakal, 1935

Nuns celebrate the Eucharist at the Shantivanam ashram, Tamil Nadu, 1993.

number of Indian Christian leaders sought to transform the ashram tradition into a Christian movement. One of the first to do so successfully was an Anglican priest named Jack Winslow, who founded an ashram in Pune in 1921 called Christa Seva Sangha. Winslow had studied Hindu mysticism and asceticism, and sought to use their insights in Christian service to others. Influenced by Winslow, E. Forrester Paton (a Scotsman) and Savarirayan Jesudason (an Indian) set up another ashram called Christukula at Tirupattur. This ashram promoted evangelism and also the provision of medical facilities (both Forrester Paton and Jesudason were doctors).

The first Catholic ashram was Shantivanam, founded by Jules Monchanin in 1950 at Tamil Nadu, with the help of Henri Le Saux, a Benedictine monk who had visited Hindu ashrams to learn from the gurus. They sought to follow traditional Indian forms of meditation and discipline, even taking Indian names. Although many were deeply suspicious of the notion of a Catholic ashram, the movement was encouraged in the 1960s by the Second Vatican Council. In 1969, a seminar was held at Bangalore which encouraged the development of Catholic ashrams as centres of prayer, meditation, and mission.

Like the Hindu ashrams, the Christian ashrams revolve around the three poles of action, knowledge and devotion. Action means both evangelization and social work, while prayers and meditation are done in the traditional Hindu style, but with Christian content. The Christuluka ashram, for example, has a large stone prayer hall called the *Jebalayam*, built in the style of a Dravidian temple. The members of the ashram meet here every morning and evening for meditation and reading of the Gospels – the same times of day that Hindu followers of Sannyasa would meet. The Christavashram, a non-denominational ashram near Kottayam, meanwhile, has a conical chapel in the style of a Hindu temple, where, again, the members meet every morning and evening. There are Bible studies and prayers at other times of the day. The first Catholic ashram, the Shantivanam, is even more Hindu in form. At the meetings for prayer and meditation, there are readings from the Vedas, the Upanishads and the Bhagavad Gita as well as from the Bible, and even from the Qur'an too. Members apply purple kumkumm powder between the eyebrows at noon, to symbolize wisdom, and ashes in the evening to symbolize moral purification.

Most of these ashrams are extremely small, often with only a few individuals, or (where celibacy is not the rule) a few families, in residence. There are often visitors passing through, and some ashrams operate only for a few months of the year. Yet they remain as a remarkable manifestation of the attempt to find a form of Christianity native to India – indeed, a Hindu Christianity.

CHINA

NEW CHALLENGES

The opening years of the twentieth century were years of crisis for Christians in China, since the interventions by western powers in China and its interests had resulted in widespread resentment against the west and Christianity, often perceived as a mere tool of foreign imperialism. In 1900 such feelings boiled over into the violence of the Boxer rebellion, led by anti-foreign fanatics in Beijing. The 'Society of Harmonious Fists' (usually called 'the Boxers') was a kind of guerrilla sect that combined traditional religious and magical cults of the Shantung area into a new movement that had initiation ceremonies, spirit possession and the like. They especially hated Christians, and their uprising was directed above all at churches and missionaries. Chanting 'Kill the foreign devil' and brandishing 'magic weapons', the terrifying Boxer guerrillas met stiff resistance from the Christians, but they were finally defeated when foreign troops arrived in Beijing and wiped them out in what proved to be an even more brutal massacre. In the uprising, 231 foreigners were killed, but tens of thousands of Chinese Christians – Catholic and Protestant – also died. Among them were also Chinese Orthodox Christians.

Little better was to follow. In 1911 there was a revolution and the first Chinese republic was established, but it was soon turned into a dictatorship under General Yuan Shihkai (1859–1916). This culturally conservative regime sought to discourage new and foreign ideas and reinstate

Confucianism. In opposition to this, many intellectuals, mainly in Beijing, founded the 'New Culture' movement, which argued for intellectual and religious freedom. However, the 'New Culture' movement was deeply influenced by Marxism, and most of its adherents had a very negative view of religion – including Christianity – as intrinsically superstitious. The 1920s saw widespread anti-Christian feeling among university students. Indeed, the rise of the nationalist movement brought with it great suspicion of Christianity as a foreign religion: during the civil war of 1926–27 most foreign missionaries fled China or moved to the coasts, and after this period their numbers were always greatly reduced.

And despite the status of Christians as national scapegoats during this period, there were still not very many of them. Their numbers were growing, but by the end of the 1930s there were half a million Protestants and three million Catholics out of a national population of 500 million.

THE SEARCH FOR AN INDIGENOUS CHRISTIANITY
Little wonder, then, that during these years Chinese Christians faced something of an identity crisis. In what sense could they be

During the night, a crowd passed by, led by a woman Boxer… who asked me my name, my business, and where I was going. As I seemed to satisfy them with my answer, they went about their business, which was the destruction of a Catholic village, and the murder of the Christians. The next morning I continued on my way, being early joined by a Boxer who invited me to dine with him, after which we separated. That night I heard the keeper of the inn at which I stopped say to a Boxer, 'We have no Christians here,' and I spent the night in peace. The following day a child warned me not to go through a certain village, saying that the Boxers were taking everyone they suspected, and I saw the fire kindled at which they burnt twenty Christians, while I at the same time thanked the Lord for putting it into the mind of a child to warn me, and thus save me… from a like horrible fate.

Yao Chen-yuan, a Chinese Christian, recounting his experiences during the Boxer rebellion

Commandos of the Marine Infantry execute Boxer rebels in 1900–1901, in this contemporary painting.

both Chinese and Christian? The 'indigenizing movement' – really a collection of different movements with similar aims – sought to answer this question, and in doing so defuse the attacks on Christianity by showing that the religion was not simply a stooge of foreign imperialism. Its rather unlikely godfather was Karl Gützlaff (1803–51), a maverick but charismatic German Pietist missionary who in the 1820s had been sent by the Netherlands Missionary Society to south-east Asia. He broke with the society and went to China instead, where in 1844 he founded the Chinese Union. This body was based upon Gützlaff's conviction, developed after years of little success in China, that the Chinese church could grow only under the leadership of the Chinese. He travelled Europe whipping up support for his project of training Chinese missionaries, but allegations of corruption undermined his efforts and the Chinese Union collapsed shortly after Gützlaff's death.

Despite the scandals associated with the Chinese Union – many other missionaries refused to believe that any of its members were Christians at all – it left an important legacy to the Chinese church. It succeeded in preaching to many villages and towns throughout the country, and in subsequent years many missionaries to these areas found the ground already prepared. These missionaries included many associated with the China Inland Mission (CIM), an interdenominational organization founded in 1865 by James Hudson Taylor (1832–1905). Hudson Taylor stressed the role of lay people as missionaries, and his society operated on the 'faith principle', according to which missionaries would receive no salaries but instead rely upon the providence of God. Like Gützlaff, Hudson Taylor was extremely optimistic about the Chinese capacity for the gospel and looked for a day when the entire country might be converted. He was lucky to have able lieutenants and successors, including Dixon Hoste and Benjamin

Broomhall, who helped to make the CIM more respectable. Throughout the first half of the twentieth century, it was the largest Protestant mission in China.

Yet there was still the dream of a truly indigenous church, one not reliant upon foreign missionaries. There were signs of hope, with, for example, the preaching of Ding Limei, one of the most prominent missionaries in China in the 1910s. This Chinese preacher, who travelled the country in the style of the great US evangelists, had great success – though he did not represent truly independent Chinese Christianity, being affiliated with the YMCS.

Meanwhile, the Catholic ideal of indigenous churches had been revitalized by Pope Pius XI (reigned 1922–39), who was extremely keen to eradicate any trace of colonialism or cultural imposition from mission, and who believed that overseas churches would never prosper unless they were led by local people. In Rome in 1926 he ordained the first six Chinese bishops of modern times. And a similar movement was taking place in the Protestant churches. By now, and for the first time, there were more Chinese Protestant ministers in China than there were foreign ones. A number of these ministers and also lay people set up churches on their own, which were expressly to be free of foreign interference. There was a general desire to get away from the kind of Christianity of the foreign missionaries, popularly regarded as crass boors who did not understand Chinese culture and did incalculable harm by suppressing the veneration of ancestors. It is also possible to see this movement as part of the more general 'nationalizing' movement that gripped China in the years following the revolution of 1911: the churches, like other Chinese institutions, wanted to be authentically Chinese and free of the West.

Already in 1906, in Shanghai, there was the Chinese Independent Church, which subsequently split into two factions, each ignoring all foreign Christians. Twenty years later there appeared an even more determinedly non-denominational church, the Little Flock, founded by Ni To-sheng, usually known as Watchman Nee (1903–72). This congregation did not even call itself a church or have a name ('Little Flock' was actually the title of its hymn book, written by Nee himself). There were no ministers and no sacraments. Members could be baptized if they wanted, but it was not compulsory. The Eucharist was a simple re-enactment of the events of the last supper, as presented in the New Testament. Nee insisted upon the importance of a personal conversion and the presence of Christ within the individual believer, and the basing of one's life upon the teachings of the Bible. His movement was perhaps as de-institutionalized as Christianity could be, and it proved popular: in 1949 there were several hundred churches in the movement, with some 70,000 members.

Churches like these were popping up all over China during this period. Most remained quite small, localized movements, but some became more widespread. Many were known as *ling-en* churches, after a comment by a Methodist minister named Wu in Beijing in 1932, who said during prayers that he had been 'moved by *ling-en*'. The term means 'blessings of the Spirit' and Wu's circle began to seek spiritual 'movement' just as he had experienced it. They, and similar groups, stressed the physical and spiritual experience of the Holy Spirit and the changes it brings in the believer. A complete and radical change in lifestyle was called for, and mystical experiences during prayer sessions were expected. Spontaneous prayer and improvised hymn-singing were practised, as well as Spirit-inspired dancing and jumping, and speaking in tongues – the Chinese version of Pentecostalism.

One of the most remarkable movements which had some of these characteristics was the Family of Jesus, founded by Ching Tien-ying in 1922 in Shantung province. It was a sort of commune, which on the basis of Mark 3:33–35 insisted that its members break all ties with their families (a rule that was later relaxed). Members lived together and had all their property in common, and everyone worked for the good of the community. The movement spread, with more communities being set up; the industriousness of their members meant that the movement became quite wealthy, something that drew the adverse attention of the government. In response, the movement gave away most of its property, and from then on members lived in poverty. The Family of Jesus therefore represented a kind of Chinese monasticism. Members lived simple lives, sleeping on beds of straw, rising at dawn to sing hymns and devoting most of their time to agriculture or craftwork. They also preached in the surrounding areas, rather like latter-day Franciscan friars. Members would travel in groups of three or four, taking no money or spare clothes (in accordance with Mark 6:8–9), and they would often prove remarkably successful. In 1950 it was estimated that there were some 300 communities, with a total of 15,000 members, and the movement continues to be strong today.

Other churches, meanwhile, rather than splitting off from the existing denominations, preferred to try to join together with the aim of creating a single Chinese (Protestant) church. Various small-scale unions took place, and committees were set up to try to plan the creation of a genuinely national church. The unions coalesced into the Presbyterian-dominated Church of Christ in China, which was officially founded in 1927, although it had already had a de facto existence in some places for a decade. However, some churches, including the Lutherans, Baptists and Methodists, did not join it. Instead, they worked with the National Christian Council – the NCC – founded in 1922 as a sort of umbrella organization for all Protestant churches.

The indigenizing movement was both a populist movement and an intellectual one. A leader such as Watchman Nee, with his emphasis on getting back to biblical teachings and a Christ-centred lifestyle, represents the more populist side.

On the other side were the intellectuals, who were more concerned with problems of social justice and politics, as well as with creating a 'Chinese theology'. In his *Rooting the Christian church in Chinese soil* of 1945, Wei Cho-min would express this idea like this:

> As Christianity becomes embedded in Chinese culture, further emphasis on things Chinese will no doubt bring about renewed support for our religion. Then a Chinese theology will be added to the Greek, Latin and Euro-American theologies. This will not separate the Chinese church from those of other countries, but will rather add to the Christian tradition the best qualities handed down from our past, thus enriching it further.

One major element of this programme in the 1920s was the National Christian Literature Association of China (also known as the Wenshe), founded in 1924 in association with the NCC. The president of the association was Chao Tzu-chen, or T.C. Chao, a young theologian who had studied in Holland and was then teaching at Suzhou University. The association's journal, the *Wenshe Monthly*, quickly made a name for itself with its controversial articles attacking the role of foreign missionaries in Chinese Christian life and arguing that Christian literature in China should be produced only by Chinese. The journal's outspokenness was its undoing, since it was bankrolled largely by the Institute of Social and Religious Research in New York, which took a dim view of these ideas. The *Wenshe Monthly*'s brief but dazzling existence accordingly ended in 1928. Another organization which took something of a radical line, questioning the traditional norms of Christianity and seeking a new Chinese 'Christian renaissance', was the Life Fellowship, which published the journal *Life* throughout the 1920s. The journal sought to offer a non-partisan, non-denominational, scholarly forum for thoughtful Christians. In particular, it

published articles calling for a radical reorganization of society along Christian lines, similar to the views of the social gospel movement. Many leading Christian intellectuals were involved in this, including T.C. Chao and Cheng Ching-I (or C.Y. Cheng), another leading theologian and (from 1927) the first president of the Church of Christ in China.

The social concerns of these theologians helped to inspire the great efforts made by many Christians in the 1920s and 30s to help with the 'national project' of re-thinking and re-building China. In particular, the Christians set up many new schools, a programme especially associated with James Yen, who had worked with poor Chinese immigrants in France and come to believe that the future of the church lay with helping the poor. Like many well-educated and liberal-minded Chinese during this period, he was concerned for the quality of education and life in general in rural China. So in 1923, back in China, he founded the National Association of Mass Education Movements, or MEM, which established adult education programmes in rural villages as well as medical clinics and other institutions. The movement was a great success, and Yen travelled not only Asia but the world, visiting poor countries and setting up similar programmes. He had particular success in the Philippines.

RUSSIAN ORTHODOXY IN CHINA
While this was going on, there was a quiet influx of Christians elsewhere in the country. The heartlands of Protestant and Catholic churches alike were the large coastal cities. But the nineteenth and early twentieth centuries saw Christians streaming into China from the opposite direction, from over the border with Russia. The Cossacks, semi-independent groups seeking a new life outside tsarist control, had been settling in the east since the seventeenth century. Skirmishes between Russia and China had led to some Cossacks being absorbed into the Chinese empire, and in the early eighteenth century there

were abortive attempts on the part of the Russian Orthodox authorities to send priests and missionaries to them.

The process continued throughout the nineteenth century, as the encroachment of tsarist control eastwards led to more Cossacks fleeing over the border. Missions were now organized to China, culminating in 1897 with the arrival of Innokentii Figurovskii (c. 1863–1931). This energetic missionary set up new schools and churches in China, as well as printing presses, and he enjoyed great success. In 1902 he became bishop of Beijing, and by 1914 there were over 5,000 Chinese Orthodox Christians, worshipping at sixteen churches and two monasteries.

In the aftermath of the 1917 revolution, many thousands of Russian refugees streamed into China. Most found new homes in Manchuria, which became a centre of Russian Orthodoxy in exile. As a result, there were some 200,000 Orthodox Christians in China by the end of the 1930s, divided between five dioceses, with a metropolitan at Beijing overseeing them.

THE CHRISTIAN MANIFESTO AND THE THREE-SELF MOVEMENT

The 1920s saw not only the mobilization of the anti-Christian movement, the rise of Christian intellectualism and the establishment of interdenominational churches, but also the founding of the Chinese Communist Party (CCP). After the Second World War, and civil war in the aftermath of the Japanese withdrawal from China, the CCP took power in 1949. China was now a communist country, ruled by the party's chairman, Mao Zedong (1893–1976).

The CCP was not as anti-religious as one might have expected, at least officially. Indeed, before forming the new government in 1949, it invited religious leaders – Buddhist and Christian – to a consultative conference. The official line was that, since religion was false, the establishment of a communist state should see it naturally decline. This was reflected in the 1954 constitution of the People's

Republic of China, which guaranteed its citizens the freedom to practise whatever religion they chose. However, this did not mean the state was neutral. Atheism was to be encouraged and, of all religions, Christianity was most distrusted, because of its association with the West and with capitalism. One large segment of the Christian community was removed immediately following the seizing of power by the CCP, since all Russians were ordered out of China, cutting the numbers of the Russian Orthodox Church in the country to some 20,000.

Little wonder, then, that many Protestant churches hoped to persuade the government of their utility by supporting the communists, at least in their aims of improving manufacturing and agriculture, and in purging the country of undesirable foreign influences. A meeting of the National Christian Council in 1949 concluded that the indigenizing movement should be stepped up, with all efforts made to ensure that all Chinese churches were as free as possible from dependence upon foreign churches. This view was strongly endorsed by the government, and negotiations between government officials and church leaders produced, in 1950, a document known as the 'Chinese Christian Manifesto'. The document was drawn up by Wu Yao-tsung, or Y.T. Wu (1895–1980), a leading Christian intellectual, and it was ratified by about half the Protestant churches in China. It called for the churches to get back to what Wu regarded as the roots of Christianity, by helping the poor and disavowing foreign imperialism.

Wu's manifesto was an important influence on the Three-Self Patriotic Movement (TSPM) that appeared in its wake. The TSPM sought to make all Chinese churches self-governing, self-supporting and self-propagating, and Wu himself was its guiding light. In 1954 the NCC was abolished, together with the traditional Protestant denominations, and the TSPM imposed on the churches as the sole politically acceptable Protestant

The idols were set up by the peasants, and in time they will pull down the idols with their own hands; there is no need for anybody else to throw away prematurely the idols for them. The agitational line of the Communist Party in such matters should be: 'Draw the bow full without letting go the arrow, and be on the alert.'

Mao Zedong, 'Report of an investigation into the peasant movement in Hunan' 1927

Christian churches and organizations in China should exert their utmost efforts, and employ effective methods, to make people in the churches everywhere recognize clearly the evils that have been wrought in China by imperialism; recognize the fact that in the past imperialism has made use of Christianity; purge imperialistic influences from within Christianity itself; and be vigilant against imperialism, and especially American imperialism, in its plot to use religion in fostering the growth of reactionary forces.

The Chinese Christian Manifesto, 1950

A Three-Self Patriotic church in Xining, Qinhai province.

organization. Many Protestants welcomed the move, reflecting the calls for Christian unity that had been heard in China for many years, but others opposed the TSPM and the communist-sanctioned union that had been forced upon them.

As a result, many churches organized 'denunciation meetings', at which 'imperialist' – foreign – elements were denounced. Anyone could be a victim of such denunciations, which were usually quite unjustifiable. T.C. Chao, a theological ally of Y.T. Wu, was denounced and lost his university post. Ching Tien-ying, the founder of the Family of Jesus movement, was arrested for being a landlord, and his Christian communes were closed. Watchman Nee was arrested for being unpatriotic and anti-revolutionary. More well known was the case of Wang Ming-tao, whose independent Protestant church in

Beijing was self-supporting, but who believed that the TSPM and associated elements were too theologically liberal, and that Christians should not meddle in politics. In the 1950s he was denounced more than once, arrested (on 'political' charges), released and re-arrested, wrecking his health in the process, and finally left in a cell for twenty-two years before his eventual release in 1979. Meanwhile, the TSPM Committee, under Y.T Wu as its chairman, took over the management of most of these churches. This actually meant the closing of many churches, because ministers were increasingly required to spend more time in productive labour; congregations were therefore combined and met at a smaller number of bigger churches with fewer ministers. The ministers who remained were required to preach about the struggle of good and evil in the physical

churches; little wonder, then, that by the 1950s the evangelicals were extremely mistrustful of Wu personally and the TSPM in general. The main journal of Chinese Protestantism, *Tianfeng*, which Wu set up in 1946 and edited throughout this period, regularly carried articles attacking evangelical leaders and even offering advice on how to run an effective denunciation. Yet Wu was always guided by a passionate concern for the welfare of the church and of the Chinese people, and a conviction that Christianity and communism had many values in common and should cooperate for the good of society. The consequences of his beliefs, both positive and negative, are still being felt in the Chinese churches today.

CATHOLICISM UNDER COMMUNISM

Indigenization, of the kind directed by the TSPM, was impossible for Catholics. The very nature of their church meant that they were not only linked to, but subject to foreign churchmen. Given that there were more than twice as many Roman Catholics in China as there were all the Protestants put together, this was a major problem. Nor did it help that the Vatican continued to recognize the pre-communist nationalist regime, which after the civil war had fled to Taiwan and set up a government in exile.

Before 1949 the Roman Catholic Church had been growing quite rapidly, helped in part by a historic Vatican decree of 1939 which stated that veneration of Confucius and ancestors was, in fact, an acceptable custom and not religious in nature. Thus the hoary old 'rites controversy' was finally laid to rest. By 1949 there were nearly three and a half million Chinese Catholics, but they lagged behind the Protestants when it came to indigenization. Although the leading dioceses such as Beijing and Shanghai had Chinese bishops, around half of all priests and two-thirds of all bishops in China were foreign.

Following the coming to power of the CCP, some Catholics hoped to emulate the

world and the role of hard work and patriotism in this struggle. References to other-worldly things, such as the return of Christ and the end of the world, were discouraged.

As all this suggests, Wu was as controversial as he was significant, and the controversy continued after his death in 1979. In 1983 Ting Kuang-hsun, who succeeded Wu as leader of the TSPM, likened him to the apostle Paul for his role in energizing Christianity in China. But others regarded him as a traitor to Christianity for his cooperation with the communist government, or even as a heretic for his liberal theological views and positive evaluation of communist ideals. The denunciations, which Wu did not instigate but which happened under his leadership, were often directed against more evangelical elements within the

Protestant indigenizing movement. In 1950 a priest named Wang Liang-zuo published a manifesto similar to that of Y.T. Wu, calling for an end to imperialism and political independence from the Vatican (whilst maintaining a 'religious connection' with it). Similar ideas lay behind the Chinese Catholic Patriotic Association (CCPA), set up in 1957. However, most Catholics wanted to have nothing to do with any of this and the bishops agreed, insisting that a Chinese Catholic Church truly independent of Rome was impossible. One who insisted upon this most strongly was an Italian, Archbishop Antonio Riberi (1897–1967), the apostolic nuncio. He continued to recognize the nationalist government in exile rather than the new CCP regime, and he exhorted foreign missionaries to stay where they were, even in the face of persecution. He helped to set up the Legion of Mary, a lay organization which encouraged personal discipline in prayer and in helping others.

Many more Catholics than Protestants were denounced by the authorities and arrested. Their property, including schools and hospitals, was confiscated – for in the CCP's eyes freedom to worship meant freedom to conduct services in churches, not freedom on the part of religious organizations to own and run other property. Increasingly, the Catholic Church was driven underground, but, as so often before in the face of persecution and pressure, its members became more determined. It was a time of martyrs, such as Father Beda Chang (1905–51), director of the Bureau of Chinese Studies in Shanghai. Chang was arrested in 1951 and died in prison shortly after, apparently after maltreatment. The churches of Shanghai were packed with mourners for his requiem Masses, and his example encouraged those who remained loyal to the pope. Shanghai was a centre of this resistance, and on one terrible night in 1955 around 300 Catholics, including a number of priests and nuns and the bishop himself, Gong Pinmei (or Ignatius Kung), were arrested. The bishop was accused of espionage and flung into prison, where several hundred more Catholics followed after another purge a couple of weeks later.

Students and teachers march through Tiananmen Square, Beijing, in support of Mao Zedong in August 1966. Their banners read 'Raise high Mao Zedong's thought and the great red flag.'

The CCPA still existed, and persecution meant that its approach became more attractive to many Catholics. As a result, the Catholic Church became split in two – not a formal schism, but a de facto one. The CCPA was acceptable to the authorities, but not to most bishops, and not to the Vatican. The CCPA bishops began to ordain 'patriotic' bishops of their own without Vatican approval. Pope Pius XII condemned this practice, leading the Chinese government to ban Catholics from having anything to do with the Vatican. The de facto schism deepened, and by the 1960s there were more 'patriotic' bishops than there were Vatican-appointed ones (and far fewer in total than there had been before 1949).

THE CULTURAL REVOLUTION
The uneasy alliance between the CCP and the 'patriotic' movement within Protestantism and Catholicism came to an end in 1966 with the Great Proletarian Cultural Revolution. Initiated by Chairman Mao himself, this was a reaction to what was seen as an infiltration of the government, bureaucracy and party itself by bourgeois and elitist elements. Students were encouraged to spearhead the 'Red Guards', who, armed with the 'little red book' of Mao's writings, marched throughout the country seeking the forces of the bourgeoisie wherever they might lurk, from taxi drivers to the most high-ranking members of the CCP itself. The riots and purges lasted into 1969, but the Cultural Revolution itself continued beyond this. Mao became the centre of a new cult: pictures of him appeared everywhere, oaths of loyalty were sworn to him personally, and quotations from the 'little red book' were seen and heard wherever one went. Intellectuals, including teachers and scientists, were persecuted: hundreds of thousands were arrested, and tens of thousands killed.

The churches suffered terribly during the Cultural Revolution. The Red Guards marched into the church buildings and stripped them of Christian symbols and Bibles, burning them on huge street bonfires. In their place, posters appeared ridiculing Christian belief and insisting that only fools believed in God. Every single church in the country was closed and locked or turned into warehouses or other, more 'useful' purposes.

Across China, Red Guards battered down the doors of private homes and extracted 'confessions' from known Christians, who might be arrested, beaten up or forced into new, menial jobs. Many were pressed into service at the work camps in the countryside. Even members of the TSPM or the CCPA suffered just as their counter-revolutionary co-religionists: to the Red Guards, all Christians were tarred with the same brush.

All the churches now existed completely underground. In place of church buildings, private homes were used for services, creating the movement known as 'house congregations'. In a remarkable reversion to a form of worship not unlike that of the Christians of the first and second centuries AD, small groups of friends would meet in each other's houses to read the Bible and pray. As they did so, they would copy by hand the passages being studied, thereby creating new copies of parts of the Bible. Printed Bibles were almost impossible to find, and these hand-written texts were the only way most Christians could read the Bible at all. When in public, Christians would still pray together, keeping their eyes open, and laughing as if in normal conversation.

There were travelling preachers who sometimes visited these house congregations, but each group was autonomous, since all official church organization had been destroyed. Perhaps most striking of all was the fact that the churches not only survived in this way, but actually spread. In some rural communities Christians were in the majority, and many people joined them, struck by their commitment to each other and their capacity for hard work.

There is no God; there is no Spirit; there is no Jesus… We are atheists; we believe only in Mao Zedong.

Poster on a YMCA building in Beijing, 1967

AFTER THE REVOLUTION

The Cultural Revolution finally ended in 1976 when Mao died. Religious leaders were freed and a more tolerant atmosphere prevailed. It had already begun in 1972, when some African and Indonesian diplomats in Beijing had asked why there were no churches available for their use: as a result, two churches, one Protestant and one Catholic, were allowed to open there. Now, in the late 1970s and the early 1980s, freedom to worship once again became a reality in China as a whole. Deng Xiaoping (1904–97), a moderate within the CCP, rose to power after Mao's death and instituted major reforms to loosen the government's grip on the economy and industry. He also adopted a much more open foreign policy, especially with the USA, and this helped to relax the pressure on the Christians within China.

Indeed, there was a renewal of interest in Christian literature and thought among many intellectual and academics. There was a movement known as the 'Cultural Christians', where people read the Bible and studied Christian philosophy and theology, but without joining a church or becoming baptized. This important movement led to the increased availability of major theological works of the past. In 1980, meanwhile, the China Christian Council (CCC) was set up under the leadership of Ting Kuang-hsun, Y.T. Wu's successor as head of the TSPM. The emphasis on theological liberalism and the social gospel, which Wu had overseen, was diminished. The CCC now exists as the umbrella organization of all Protestant churches in China, which since the 1950s have had no separate denominational structures and been officially 'post-denominational'. That said, different groups within this church do often still have the same theological or organizational characteristics of their old denominations.

Today there are thought to be some 55,000 Protestant churches and smaller 'meeting points' within the aegis of the CCC, with 16 million believers, as well as vast numbers of more informal groups, the successors to the 'house congregations' of the Cultural Revolution era. Some of these groups are connected to CCC churches and have a supplementary role. But others do not recognize the CCC and exist almost as rival churches. Such groups are still illegal under Chinese law, which recognizes only the CCC (and the TSPM) as the acceptable face of Protestantism. Members of the house churches therefore live under the fear of arrest. In particular, the students' revolt in Tiananmen Square in 1989, and the brutal methods used by the government to suppress it, coincided with more attempts on the part of the state to clamp down on Christian opposition. The CCC itself had supported the student protesters, and now the government introduced new laws requiring the registration of all places of worship, with greater state control over membership of religious organizations. Since then, many religious groups who do not enjoy state recognition have suffered state attacks, which have even increased since 1999: the Falun Gong ('the practice of the wheel of dharma') are perhaps the best known victims of this policy, but unofficial Protestant churches have suffered too. In particular, some evangelical congregations have been regarded, not as unofficial Protestant groups, but as non-Christian cults, a designation carrying more severe penalties.

As for the Roman Catholics, the split that occurred in the 1950s and 60s still remains in place today. There are, in effect, two Catholic Churches in China – one known as the Open Church, which is linked to the CCPA and is officially recognized, and the Underground Church. The Open Church came into being when, after Mao's death, bishops and clergy returned to their posts. Most were now willing to cooperate with the government, especially after 1981 when the government no longer forced bishops to swear independence from Rome. The following year, congregations were allowed to pray for the pope. Nevertheless, many priests felt that the Open Church was an apostate church and refused to collude with an atheist government. Fan Xueyan, bishop of Baoding, led this movement, and in 1981 he secretly ordained a number of bishops.

Every citizen has the freedom of religious belief and the freedom of nonbelief.

Statement of government policy, Renmin Ribao, 1980

The Kakure Kirishitan

The story of the group of elderly women emerging from the shadows in 1865 to confess a shared faith with French Catholic priest Fr Bernard Petitjean has long since passed into folklore. Petitjean was surprised and delighted to discover that the flame of Christianity had, against all the odds, been kept alive in secret since the expulsion of the missionaries in the early seventeenth century. He believed that they and the ensuing waves of believers who emerged (their number is usually given as 50,000), should immediately be reassimilated into the Catholic fold. But about half of them chose, instead, to remain faithful to 'Kakure' (Hidden) Christianity.

Forced to perpetuate the faith in secret, without a vernacular Bible or those sacraments that required the presence of the priesthood, they had perpetuated a tradition based on devotional books (containing the main Catholic prayers in Japanese) and a calendar of rituals. Consequently, these Kakure communities chose to adhere to the faith, and the memory, of their ancestors, whom they saw, in turn, as having remained faithful to the original Jesuit message over some ten generations of torture and martyrdom.

These Kakure communities persist to the present day, in ever-dwindling numbers, confined to the vicinity of Nagasaki and some neighbouring islands. It is only in the past few decades that scholars have sought to study their beliefs, inspired by the realization that, with no attempt at outreach, the faith is destined to disappear altogether with the death of the current generation of almost exclusively elderly Kakure. Central to these investigations has been the question of the relationship between the form of Christianity transmitted to Japan by the earlier Jesuit missionaries during the so-called 'Christian century' (1550–1649) and the contemporary Kakure faith. The similarities are highlighted in their core text, *Tenchi hajimari no koto* (*The Beginnings of Heaven and Earth*), which reads as a crude, often corrupted, synopsis of selected parts of the Bible, heavily overlain with elements of the Christian mystery play and Japanese folk tales. For all the similarities, however, the *Tenchi* points heavily in the direction of accommodation with the Japanese religious environment, with the core tenets it embodies enveloped in the language of the native Shintō tradition, as well as Buddhism and Taoism. At the heart of such comparisons lies the polytheistic nature of the Kakure tradition: the focus of worship is a vast pantheon of *kami* (divinities usually associated with Shintō), which includes, not just God the Father, Jesus Christ and the Virgin Mary, but also a series of inanimate objects into which a spirit has entered and which consequently require constant attention.

All of this poses the fundamental question whether this tradition represents a preservation, transformation or denial of the Christian faith first transported to Japan some 450 years ago. The first scenario sees the Kakure prayers and traditions as representing a kind of time capsule, the study of which provides fascinating insights into the nature of sixteenth-century Jesuit theology; the second sees the original forms and beliefs overlain with elements from a series of other religious traditions in Japan; the third takes this one step further, suggesting that the Kakure have departed so fundamentally from the Catholic orthodoxy that they should be seen as a new religion. The reality would appear to encompass all three of these models. The Kakure have clearly evolved and digressed considerably from the secret beliefs of their ancestors. But this could represent less a blatant rejection, more an attempt to replace their earlier exclusivism with an approach more acceptant of other elements of Japanese religiosity.

MARK WILLIAMS

Within ten years, there were fifty Underground bishops. The movement continues to exist, though like the illegal Protestant congregations it is coming under increased governmental pressure. Yet the situation remains unusual: when news of Fan Xueyan's ordinations reached the ears of Pope John Paul II, he ratified the ordinations and recognized the legitimacy of the new bishops and their successors. Thus, with the Open Church and the Underground Church both united to the Holy See, there is no official schism; yet they do not recognize each other.

The Orthodox Church in China, meanwhile, has been autocephalous since 1957. Based around Harbin, the Orthodox Christian community remains small but thriving.

JAPAN

The 'glorious 1880s' had seen church membership in Japan grow exponentially. Protestants, Catholics, and Orthodox alike had had incredible success, and many hoped – or even assumed – that Japan would be a Christian nation by the start of the twentieth century. That dream would never be fulfilled – but the Japanese churches did have many remarkable years ahead of them.

THE IMPERIAL RESCRIPT ON EDUCATION
The enthusiastic adoption by of the government and the intellectuals of all things western which, in the 1880s, had benefited the churches, changed in the 1890s. The Meiji government operated a

rather contradictory policy of restoration (*fukko*) and renovation (*ishin*). This meant adopting western industrialization and technology (*ishin*) whilst maintaining traditional culture and religion (*fukko*). This approach was enshrined in the *Imperial rescript on education*, issued in 1890 by the prime minister, Yamagata Aritomo. The rescript was a restatement of traditional values, such as loyalty and hard work, and it encouraged the Japanese to adopt these values, seen as part of the 'Japanese national character', in the service of their nation and their emperor. The rescript was sent to all schools, where it was to be memorized by all students, who would also read long commentaries on it, a practice that continued until after the Second World War. As a result, there was far less enthusiasm for western culture in general and Christianity in particular.

Yet this was no blanket ban such as had been seen in the early Tokugawa years. In fact, the first decades of the twentieth century saw growth among the churches – not as spectacular as during the 1880s, certainly, but impressive enough. The industrialization of Japan meant radical new social conditions for many, much as had been experienced in western Europe a century earlier; and this had similar effects to that earlier Industrial Revolution. Socialism and even communism grew in popularity, but so did the Protestant churches, which especially appealed to the working classes. There were 51,000 Japanese Protestants in 1901 – in 1930 there were 194,000. By then there were also 93,000 Catholics in the country. As these figures suggest, Christianity remained a growing, but numerically very minor, presence in Japan. Buddhism, Shintōism and Confucianism remained far more prominent in society. In fact, Shintō, the traditional indigenous cult of Japan, was officially regarded as central to Japanese culture, and participation in its festivals and rituals was seen as a patriotic duty for all Japanese, irrespective of their religious beliefs. Naturally, many Christians refused to have anything to do

with Shintō, and the authorities would monitor such dissenters carefully. The Religious Organizations Law of 1939 gave the government the power to close down any religious organization whose activities were believed to be counter to the 'Imperial way'.

THE UNITED CHURCH OF CHRIST
Under these circumstances, Japanese Christianity itself changed. The Religious Organizations Law stated that the government would recognize only a single Protestant Church. It therefore forced all the Protestant Churches in the country to re-organize into a body known as the United Church of Christ. Formed in 1941, this church was a new organization that absorbed and replaced all the Protestant groups with the exception of some Anglicans, Seventh-day Adventists and a few others who refused to join.

In their eyes, and in those of many foreign observers at the time, this church was a compromise church, tainted by officialdom almost as the Reich Church in Nazi Germany was. Certainly, it did not look good when, in early 1942, the leaders of the new church visited Ise Jingū, the main Shintō shrine, to ask for the blessings of the Shintō gods. Church services including bowing towards the emperor's palace and singing a hymn to the emperor. The government ensured that the church encouraged the war effort, removing all hymns about peace from the hymn books. By 1944 ministers were being given the topics for their sermons from the government, and they were told that a new date had to be chosen for Christmas, since 25 December clashed with the anniversary of the emperor's accession.

THE NONCHURCH MOVEMENT
If this was one face of 'Japanese Christianity', there was another, which was more spontaneous and more concerned to preserve the real teachings of the church. The indigenizing movements within Japanese Christianity grew out of dissatisfaction with the forms of Christianity

Protestantism institutionalized was a return back to the discarded Roman Catholicism. We need another Reformation to bring Protestantism to its logical conclusion. The new Protestantism must be perfectly free without a trace of ecclesiasticism in it – a fellowship, not an institution – free communion of souls, not a system or an organization. Practically, it will be a churchless Christianity, calling no man bishop or pastor, save Jesus Christ, the Son of God.

Uchimura Kanzō, 1928

that Japanese converts learned from foreign missionaries. In particular, they felt that these missionaries did not understand Japanese culture or value it sufficiently. Instead, they followed 'displacement theology', according to which Christianity could flourish only by displacing – that is, eradicating – Japanese religion and culture. To put it another way, the Japanese, rather like the Hindus in India, were used to syncretizing. Japanese religion and morality was already a mixture of Buddhism, Shintōism and Confucianism. The missionaries' insistence that Christianity had a monopoly on truth did not make sense from this point of view. The founders of the different indigenizing churches wanted to strip Christianity of what they saw as western culture and return to its roots in a Japanese way.

One of the pioneers of the indigenizing movement was Uchimura Kanzō (1861–1930). Born in Edo (renamed Tokyo in 1868), he was converted to Christianity while studying at the Sapporo Agricultural College. He visited the USA in 1884 and stayed for four years. He lived with Quakers and was enormously impressed by them, and studied at Amherst College, where he underwent a profound religious experience, gaining a new sense of Jesus' sacrifice and personal relationship with himself. This was a moment of conversion to a truly evangelical form of Christianity, for Uchimura felt that everything he had done up to that point had been an attempt to earn salvation, something he now realized was impossible.

Returning to Japan in 1888, Uchimura began to preach the evangelical message that he had learned in America – but he removed from it any American or non-Japanese cultural elements. He argued that real Christianity could not be divided between different churches, as had happened in Europe – each one claiming to be 'the' Christian church, when in fact none of them was.

In 1897 Uchimura became editor of the *Yoruzu chōchō*, which he turned into the

A group of Japanese samurai and officers study a map in the 1860s.

largest newspaper in Japan. At the same time, he started his own journal, *Seisho no kenkyū* (*Study of the Bible*). In this, Uchimura developed an understanding of Christianity as a Japanese religion, not a cultural import. He was strongly patriotic, and he backed the government in its war with China at this time – but he later became a pacifist and resigned from his newspaper over the pro-aggression stance he was required to take. Despite his own conversion under the influence of westerners, Uchimura hated what he regarded as the cultural imperialism of the missionaries. Instead, Uchimura sought to find traces of Christianity within Japanese culture itself. He pointed to the similarities in ethics between Christianity and Buddhism and Confucianism, seeing here an indication of God's activity in Japanese culture even before the arrival of Christianity. In *Bushidō*, the 'way of the warrior' in which samurai were traditionally trained, Uchimura believed Japan had produced the finest ethical system in the world, emphasizing loyalty, service and selflessness. From a Japanese point of view, the apostle Paul was a samurai *par excellence*, and Uchimura looked to a time when Christian religion and *Bushidō* principles might be joined together. Similarly, in 1926, Uchimura wrote an article in which he likened Buddha to the moon and Christ to the sun, commenting:

I love the moon and I love the night; but as the night is far spent and the day is at hand, I now love the Sun more than I love the Moon; and I know that the love of the Moon is included in the love of the Sun, and that he who loves the Sun loves the Moon also.

Many people were deeply inspired by Uchimura and his writings, and *Mukyōkai* – the 'Nonchurch' movement – became stronger, especially in Tokyo. Uchimura did not wish to set up yet another church – rather, he wanted to avoid institutionalizing Christian faith altogether. That meant having no priests or ministers, and no

sacraments either, since in his view these were simply part of the man-made institution that served only to obscure the teaching of Christ. Instead, Uchimura hired lecture halls to speak to audiences of several hundred people every week. He set up a society called the *Kyōyūkai* ('Society of Friends') to provide pastoral support to the non-denominational Christian movement.

The Nonchurch movement was the biggest and best-known form of indigenous Christianity to emerge in Japan, but it never became hugely popular. One potential problem was that it inherited from Confucianism a strict understanding of the relations between the sexes – so men and women would sit on opposite sides of the lecture hall to hear Uchimura preach, for example. More fundamentally, there was no form of training for ministers and preachers: people were expected to rely upon their own understanding of the Bible, as developed through personal reading, and upon their own charismatic abilities. Anything else would have been a betrayal of the Nonchurch principle.

After Uchimura Kanzō's death his movement remained strong. In the mid-1950s it was thought to have anywhere between 50,000 and 100,000 members. The nature of the movement makes it very hard to be accurate, but it is thought that since then membership has declined. The lack of leadership, other than local leaders of Bible study groups, has made it hard for the Nonchurch movement to organize any kind of effective membership drive, and it seems that young Japanese Christians simply do not find it so interesting.

Yet, although the Nonchurch movement is the most famous form of indigenous Japanese Christianity, it is by no means alone. There are dozens of churches, sects and other groups that – as the Christian novelist Shusaku Endo (1923–96) put it – have sought to dress Christianity in a kimono, rather than in ill-fitting western clothes. We can look at just a couple of examples.

Worshippers at Urakami cathedral, Nagasaki, 2005. The cathedral had been the oldest and largest Christian building in Japan until the atomic bomb was detonated right above it in 1945. It was rebuilt in 1959.

THE CHRIST HEART CHURCH

Uchimura Kanzō's slightly younger contemporary, Kawai Shinsui (1867–1962), founded a version of Christianity that was heavily influenced by Buddhism. Kawai was converted by Methodist missionaries as a young man, but he came to feel that their form of religion lacked a major element of Buddhism as understood in Japan: the emphasis on self-improvement and personal struggle as a path to strength and enlightenment. Kawai studied the Gospels intensely, combining this academic rigour with meditation, which he did for five hours every day in a field. The religious experiences that this brought him convinced Kawai that Christ and his teaching should be understood not simply as the fulfilment of Judaism, but as the fulfilment of Shintōism, Buddhism and Confucianism as well.

Kawai therefore founded the Christ Heart Church in 1927 to teach this new understanding. Kawai insisted that, while we must accept Jesus as a saviour who removes our sins without any effort on our part, we must also accept him as a master who expects responsive effort from us. Moral striving and self-improvement must therefore be central to the Christian lifestyle, something that Kawai did not see in the western Protestant churches. He therefore had his disciples follow what he called the fourfold path of Bible study, prayer, meditation and practice. Meditation followed the Zen Buddhist style, often focusing on the text of Romans 12:1, or on an image of Christ (Kawai himself carried one in the sleeve of his kimono at all times). There was also the physical training known as *kyōjenjutsu*. As a result, the church's buildings were generally referred to as *dōjōs*, that is, places of spiritual training rather than of worship.

Kawai Shinsui died in 1962 in his mid-90s, but his church survives today,

...a sudden idea came to me: What if Buddha, Confucius, Socrates should meet Christ?... I am sure they would discover something in addition to what Peter, James, John, and Paul had found. This being so, some greater truth beyond the Christianity conveyed from the West may be revealed by embodying the minds of these saints, and thus providing the West with the secret of truth found also in Japan.

Kawai Shinsui

although it has declined. Like the Nonchurch movement, it has had difficulty recruiting younger people, and today has perhaps only a thousand members. Kawai had always envisaged his church as a minority interest organization, a kind of Japanese-style monastic movement rather than something for everyone.

JAPANESE PENTECOSTALISM

The names may be similar, but nothing could be more different from the Christ Heart Church than the Spirit of Jesus Church. It was founded by Murai Jun (1897–1970), the son of a Methodist minister, who in 1918 was about to commit suicide on a ferry. At the critical moment, he suddenly found himself speaking in tongues. Murai became a preacher and evangelist, and in 1941 he founded the Spirit of Jesus Church, whose name appeared in a vision that his wife experienced. The church had a very emotional and dramatic form of worship, with speaking in tongues and faith-healing playing a major role. The table at the front of the church would feature simply a Bible and a flask of oil, used to anoint people during the healing part of the service. The mainstream Protestant churches were alarmed and attacked Murai as a servant of Satan, as well as a Unitarian, for his congregations worshipped 'Jesus only'. Murai, for his part, maintained he was getting back to the form of worship of the first Christians and obeying the injunctions of Jesus himself.

Most of this is not so dissimilar from western Pentecostalism. But one difference was the way in which the church adopted traditional elements of Japanese culture. For example, the church condemned the traditional veneration of ancestors associated with Shintō. But it did offer baptism for the dead, effectively replacing the 'pagan' practice with a Christian one. Similarly, it developed services for the purification of land or buildings, to protect people from the spirit world, just as traditional Shintō practices do. In this way, the Spirit of Jesus Church managed to move into the cultural ground occupied by Shintō whilst still condemning anything to do with the traditional folk religion.

The church did not prosper at first. But in the 1950s and afterwards its membership rocketed. In 1958 it had some 28,000 members. In the early 1990s it claimed 420,000 members, in 200 churches and 400 house churches. Such large figures were possible because the church counts as a member anyone who attends a service and receives baptism by water and by Spirit. The latter experience comes about through the repetition of the word 'Hallelujah', which is thought to bring on the gift of speaking in tongues. The church claims only 23,000 *active* members, although this is still a significant number – the Spirit of Jesus Church has more churches in Japan than any other indigenizing movement.

Another Pentecostal movement is the Holy Ecclesia of Jesus, founded in 1946 by Ōtsuki Takeji, who had had a moving religious experience while working as a missionary in China. A key distinctive doctrine of this church was 'the name of the Lord', which Ōtsuki found in Romans 10:13 and Acts 9:21. Believing that calling on this name was a distinctive feature of primitive Christianity, Ōtsuki listed the names of God from throughout the Bible, from 'God almighty' in Genesis 17:1 to 'love' in 1 John 4:16. His followers would recite the names in unison, in almost a Buddhist-style mantra. Ōtsuki was dissatisfied with Protestantism's rather bleak church interiors, and he was inspired instead by Roman Catholicism in making his churches 'sacred spaces'. Altars, crucifixes and stained glass windows were therefore to be found in his churches, as well as statues of the saints.

The Holy Ecclesia of Jesus had a thousand members by the end of its first decade, but it has grown ever since. Today it has some 10,000 members – smaller than the Spirit of Jesus Church, but unlike there, its numbers are not declining.

THE WAY

These versions of Japanese Christianity are all more or less recognizable as Christian churches. A far more syncretistic approach was founded by Matsumura Kaiseki (1859–1939). In 1876, he had a religious experience that convinced him that the Christian God was identical to Tentei, the god of Confucianism, and he was baptized soon after. He entered a missionary college run by Presbyterian and Dutch Reformed missionaries, but he left as he felt the missionaries did not understand Japanese culture.

Eventually, in 1905, Matsumura founded a new church of his own, known first as the One Heart Association, then the Church of Japan, and finally simply The Way. Like the deists, Matsumura argued that most of the metaphysical doctrines of traditional Protestantism – such as the divinity of Christ, the objectivity of the atonement and the authority of the Bible – were really man-made notions that had become attached to Christianity through historical accidents. Instead, he hoped to get back to what he regarded as the basic principles (*shi kōryō*) of all religions, especially Christianity and Confucianism. In 1917 a headquarters for the movement was built in Tokyo called the Hall of Divine Worship, modelled after traditional Shintō temples. Worshippers would hear readings from the Bible or Confucian writings, sing hymns and meditate. The altar would feature a hanging scroll with the name of God in Chinese characters, and followers of The Way had similar scrolls at home to act as small shrines.

After the Second World War, The Way became more explicitly Christian. The Hall of Divine Worship now looks more like a western church, and services feature far more Bible readings and Christian hymns. Although still only a small group even within the small world of Japanese Christianity, The Way represents quite a dynamic understanding of fairly extreme theological liberalism.

CHRISTIANITY IN JAPANESE SOCIETY

As all these different movements suggest, Japanese Christianity today is remarkably diverse. More than that, it is a complex pattern where foreign influences and 'indigenizing' tendencies are not simply alternatives to each other but influence each other quite profoundly. A church such as the Spirit of Jesus Church mixes influences from Western Pentecostalism with the concerns of Shintō, while The Way has one foot in Western liberalism and the other in Confucianism. Today, Japan is a largely secular society. Government surveys regularly show improbably large percentages of the population as followers of Shintō, but this is achieved by counting as a believer anyone who lives near a shrine or attends Shintō festivals, which is virtually everyone. Approximately 1 or 2 per cent of Japanese identify themselves as Christian, but another 10 per cent or more say they empathize with Christianity, suggesting that the religion has achieved a degree of cultural assimilation greater than church attendance figures might imply. Also, Christianity in Japan tends to be far more of an individual affair than elsewhere in the world. That is, typically, individual Christians understand their faith as lying between themselves and God; it is not so important to express and nurture that faith in a church community or even within the family. Most Japanese Christians are converts, rather than having been brought up in a Christian household. It can be rather a lonely faith, and Christians may find themselves ostracized.

However, Christianity has become associated with certain elements of life, such as romantic love. The notion of love as existing between two equals was rare before the Meiji restoration; the Japanese word *ai* meant the love of a superior for an inferior. But Christian missionaries used it to refer to both God's love for humanity and humans' love for God, suggesting it was a two-way thing. Thus the re-invention of *ai* to fit something like a Western notion of romantic love has associations with Christianity even today – and around a third of all weddings in Japan are Christian weddings, even though so few people are practising Christians. Many ministers of all the Christian denominations take special care in their 'wedding ministry', recognizing that this is a key area where they can reach potential new members.

KOREA

The one Asian country where Christianity has become a really major religion is Korea. This success story is all the more remarkable for the fact that instead of relying on European missionaries, the Korean church effectively evangelized itself.

THE BEGINNINGS

In Chapter 10 we saw that the first Korean Christians were – rather improbably – converted by Japanese soldiers who invaded Korea in the 1590s. However, no church seems to have been established at this time; and foreigners, including missionaries, were not allowed into the country.

As a result, Christianity did not return to Korea for nearly two centuries after those initial conversions, and it returned in a rather unusual way. As in China, religion here was dominated by Confucianism and Buddhism, with Korean intellectuals deeply interested in the philosophy of these two traditions, much of which was imported from China. By the eighteenth century, Korean scholars possessed some of the Chinese works written by missionaries to China in the seventeenth century, and many found them highly intriguing. In 1783 one of these scholars, Lee Sung Hoon, travelled to Beijing on a diplomatic mission and took the opportunity to seek out more of the books and also some Christian missionaries. He found Jean de Grammont, a former Jesuit missionary, who baptized him. Lee Sung Hoon returned to Myongdong with a collection of Chinese Christian literature, including *The true doctrine of the Lord of heaven* by Matteo Ricci. The books proved

enormously popular among his intellectual circle, and Lee Sung Hoon baptized several of them himself. In the absence of any priests, the new Christians enthusiastically not only baptized each other, but began to celebrate Mass in their homes. Not until 1794 did they have a priest, when the bishop of Beijing sent them a Chinese one, James Chou Wen-mu. He found an estimated 4,000 practising Christians waiting for his ministry.

THE PERSECUTIONS

Chou had to enter Korea in secret, because even at this early stage there was an immediate crackdown on the new church by the Korean Chosŏn dynasty. The reason was much the same as the Chinese persecutions earlier in the eighteenth century: Christianity threatened Confucianism and the veneration due to ancestors. Many Christians were killed, including James Chou himself, martyred with 300 others in 1801. That was not the end of it: a brilliant young scholar named Hwang Sa-yong escaped into the mountains, where he wrote to the bishop of Beijing in China describing the cruel persecutions and pleading for help in the form of a western army to protect the Korean church. Unfortunately, his letter was intercepted by government agents, who concluded that it simply proved that Christianity was in league with unfriendly foreign elements and intrinsically treacherous. The crackdown was stepped up.

The persecutions, although cruel and systematic, failed to prevent the incredibly rapid growth of the church. When Chou died, his flock had increased to some 10,000 people. A prominent Catholic named Chŏng Ha-sang acted as one of the de facto leaders of the movement, and he made many trips to Beijing to plead for priests. But the Catholic Church there was not in very good shape either, and no more priests were sent. More help was forthcoming from the Paris Foreign Mission Society, which continued to specialize in south-east Asian mission. Indeed, in 1831, the Korean church was put under the direct control of a vicar apostolic, who would answer to the society. The first one died on his way to Korea; the next two were martyred when they got there. Priests were smuggled into the country to minister to the church, often entering towns in improbably secret ways, such as through the drains. There was nothing glamorous about their fate, though, which was generally to be found by the authorities, tortured and executed. Even groups who seemed similar to Christians were persecuted. An example is Choe Che-u, who founded a new cult based partly upon Catholicism but also upon Confucianism, Buddhism and Shamanism. Calling it the Eastern Learning to distinguish it from Catholicism (the Western Learning), Choe failed to convince the authorities that it was sufficiently distinct, and he was beheaded in 1864.

The desperate shortage of priests continued. In 1866 there were 23,000 Catholics with only twelve priests between them. That year saw the outbreak of particularly cruel persecution, when a Russian warship appeared off the Korean coast. Believing an invasion to be imminent, and branding all Christians as potential traitors, the government ordered a complete extermination. Siméon-François Berneux, who had acted as bishop to the Korean Catholics for ten years, was beheaded. In the next three years 10,000 Christians lost their lives. Many others are thought to have died of starvation or deprivation as they fled into the countryside. Despite it all, the church continued to grow, and it developed an especially apocalyptic, world-denying character. A number of spiritual classics from the West was translated and circulated, including Thomas à Kempis's *The Imitation of Christ*, and Korean Christians stressed the need for discipline and asceticism in personal life, as well as the impending judgment of Christ. Earthly things would pass away, they believed, in the face of God's spiritual authority. Devotions revolved around Christ's passion or Mary's sorrows, and believers longed for the future happiness of heaven. The stress

seems to have been on the discipline and spiritual teaching of the church, rather than that of the Bible. There were some translations of the Bible into Korean – one was made by Luke Hwang Sok-tu, who was beheaded in 1866 – but they seem not to have been widely disseminated.

KOREA OPENS UP

In 1873 the young King Ko-jong deposed his father as regent and began his personal rule of Korea. A new era of change was afoot. Ko-jong was keen to import western learning and modernize the country, although he had to struggle against the conservative reactions of most of his scholars. In 1883 the 'Hermit Kingdom' opened its doors to foreigners and finally granted religious freedom to its subjects. Catholic missionaries began to return, and the vicar apostolic, Felix Ridel, began building the cathedral at Seoul. By 1911 there were 77,000 Catholics in the country. Meanwhile, Protestant missionaries also appeared. Again, Koreans themselves took the initiative in this: in 1884 one Yi Sujŏng, who had become a Christian whilst visiting Japan, asked western Protestant churches to send missionaries. They were coming anyway, of course. The first, John Ross, had already begun the process, whilst acting as a Scottish Presbyterian missionary in China. While there he had learned Korean and made a translation of the New Testament. He helped to bring Protestantism to communities at the Korean border, in the hope that they would spread the religion south of their own accord – and indeed his translation proved very popular and did spread.

From the 1880s onwards, missionaries from all the usual denominations poured into Korea, following the cautious approach of setting up schools and hospitals, still unsure how serious the government was about allowing evangelization. Many converts were won. With the Chosŏn dynasty entering its last phase, earnest Korean intellectuals were keen to find alternative ideologies with which to invigorate their country, especially in the face of Japanese aggression. Many felt that the adoption of western culture and religion might provide an answer to the ideological crisis, and so the churches filled rapidly.

In 1907 the missions were boosted by an event known as the 'Great Revival' at P'yŏngyang, which spread throughout Korea and even into China. This encouraged further efforts at evangelization by Korean Protestants. By 1914 there were 196,000 Korean Protestants, about 1 per cent of the country's total population.

FROM THE JAPANESE OCCUPATION TO THE DIVIDED NATIONS

In 1910 the Japanese invaded and established colonial rule over Korea, during which there were attempts to single out Christians as potential trouble-makers. In 1912, 124 people – including 98 Christians – were accused of trying to murder the governor-general. Most were acquitted, but their trial helped to create a strong link in the popular mind between the national movement and Christianity. In 1919 the

March First Movement began, based around a declaration of independence signed by thirty-three people, including fifteen Christian leaders. The movement was based around the principle of non-violent protest and demonstration, and the Japanese authorities clamped down on it harshly, killing or injuring thousands of people. Churches were destroyed, and in one incident villagers were forced into a church which was then burned down.

The clash between Japanese imperialism and Christian resistance coalesced around the establishment of Shintō shrines, where the Japanese expected people to participate in the traditional rites. Most Christians refused, for both religious and patriotic reasons. Pressure was stepped up, until in 1938 the General Assembly of the Presbyterian Church was forced to pass a resolution stating that Shintō worship was not incompatible with Christianity. The other churches followed. Two thousand people were arrested for refusing to go along with this.

A service at the Yoido Full Gospel Church, Seoul, South Korea, in 1990. This Pentecostal church currently has some 800,000 members, making it the largest Christian congregation in the world.

The end of the Second World War saw new problems for the Korean churches. The country was liberated from the Japanese but divided into two spheres of influence, the north under the Soviets, and the south under the USA. In the north, the churches quickly came to grief under the Soviets, who regarded them as bourgeois. Indeed, there were more Christians in the north than in the south at this time, making the problem all the more serious. Many fled to the south before the onset of the Korean War in 1950. Those who remained suffered an uncertain fate: certainly all Catholic priests found in the country after the outbreak of hostilities were thrown into prison, where many died. The war came to a de facto end in 1953, though technically it never ended and the two sides remain in a state of suspended hostilities.

In the north, little has been heard from the Christian churches for half a century. Biblical translations have been made there, and Christian leaders have emerged for talks with their counterparts in the south and elsewhere, but these are representatives of groups endorsed by the government and probably not really representative of the churches in the country. Only one Catholic church building and two Protestant ones officially exist there. Today, North Korea is probably the world's most secretive country, as well as the most hardline communist state in the world, and it suffers under an exceptionally totalitarian and militaristic dictatorship. The fate of Christians under such circumstances remains very hard to determine. Yet nothing can be predicted in the topsy-turvy world of North Korea. The dictator, Kim Jong Il (b. 1942), was reportedly impressed by the Orthodox Church on a visit to Russia, and decided he wanted one too; so in 2003 work began on the Church of the Holy Trinity in P'yŏngyang. Yet it is hard to see this as anything more than a publicity stunt, rather than a genuine move towards religious freedom.

In the south, meanwhile, the churches found themselves divided over the degree to which different congregations or individuals had collaborated with the Japanese, particularly over the issue of Shintō worship, and also over the question whether to retain the Japanese-imposed single Protestant church. These squabbles simply led to more divisions, which did not help the main task of reconstructing church buildings and the ecclesiastical structures that had been wrecked by the Japanese.

THE REJUVENATION

Not for some fifteen years did the situation change. The Catholic Church continued to grow steadily, reaching membership numbers of nearly three million by the end of the century. In 1968 the Korean Catholic Church acquired its own cardinal, and in 1984 Pope John Paul II performed the first ever canonization ceremony outside Rome at Seoul, where he canonized 103 Korean martyrs – more people than had ever before been canonized at one stroke. It was something of a vindication of the extraordinary struggle from which the Catholic Church had emerged a century earlier.

But it was dramatically overtaken by the Protestant churches, which at the end of the 1950s saw a new movement known as 'Church Growth'. This was a complex phenomenon with a number of different elements. On the one hand, it was a social movement, concerned to improve living conditions of labourers and others; on the other, it was an explicitly evangelistic movement with the aim of bringing more people to the churches. Structures known as *kido-wŏn* ('prayer halls') were built, normally just outside the towns and villages, for prayer retreats and revival meetings, often involving faith-healing. As this suggests, the 'Church Growth' movement was closely associated with the rise of Pentecostalism within Korean Protestantism.

The movement was incredibly successful, mirroring the economic boom the country enjoyed after partition. Between 1957 and 1967 membership of the Protestant churches doubled, and the rate of increase was maintained. By the

…we are commanded by God to overcome today's reality of confrontation between our divided people – who share the same blood but who are separated into south and north… our mission is to work for the realization of unification and peace.

Declaration of the churches of Korea on national reunification and peace, 1988 end of the twentieth century, between a quarter and a third of the 48 million South Koreans were Christians, mostly Presbyterians and Methodists, representing a growth rate unparallelled anywhere else in the world during this time. Their growth was accompanied by the rise of new sects that combined Christianity with other faiths, including Buddhism, Confucianism and older shamanist elements. These included Chŏndo-gwan, the Evangelist Hall Movement, which was popular in the 1950s and 60s, founded by an enormously charismatic Presbyterian preacher called Pak T'aesŏn who claimed to work miracles. Churches of his movement sprang up throughout South Korea, but a number of scandals in its leadership led to a decline in the 1970s. More well known is T'ongil-gyo, the Unification Church, founded in 1954 by Mun Sŏnmyŏng (b. 1920) and later renamed The Family Federation for World Peace and Unification (FFWPU). The church was based upon a strange reinterpretation of Christian theology, according to which Jesus came to save souls but failed to save bodies because he never had any children. That task falls to 'the Lord of the Second Advent', Mun himself, who in the 1970s moved to the USA. The Unification Church (or the 'Moonies', after their leader) became more successful there than in Korea itself, but has suffered continual criticism of its methods: it is accused of using cult-like techniques to 'brainwash' converts, and there have been frequent allegations of corruption and excessive affluence on the part of its leaders.

This Pentecostalism-fuelled rise in mainstream Protestantism and marginally associated cults was accompanied by a resurgence in more liberal-minded concern for social and political action. The 1970s saw the development of the Korean equivalent to liberation theology, known as Minjŭng sinhak, or 'theology of the people'. This approach stresses that history is basically about people and the

obstacles that they face, and the work of God in helping them to overcome them. Yet this attempt to create a distinctive Korean theology has been unmatched by the emergence of equally distinctive Korean hymns, church architecture and so on. How the Korean churches may develop in the next fifty years – and how they will build upon the great advances of the last few decades – is one of the most intriguing questions in Christianity today.

SOUTH-EAST ASIA

South-east Asia offers perhaps the most diverse picture of Christianity in a relatively small area. On the one hand there is modern, materialistic Singapore, which has not only religious freedom but a number of huge, US-style 'megachurches' such as the City Harvest Church, with some 19,000 members, and a charismatic leader, Kong Hee (b. 1964). This evangelical church not only has an immense, titanium-clad central building, but is the first church in the world to have been awarded an ISO 9000 certificate for the quality of its management: it has almost become a brand in its own right, helped by the fact that Kong's wife, Ho Yeow Sun, is a pop star with her own line of boutiques. But like some of the huge American churches on which it is modelled, the City Harvest Church's slickness is a point of contention for some critics, who accuse it of turning Christianity into a brand and preaching a materialist 'prosperity gospel'.

Yet in nearby countries, the story is as different as it could be. Just over the border with Singapore, Malaysia combines religious tolerance and control in a rather exasperating fashion. The country is officially Muslim, and although anyone can practise their own religion, it is illegal for non-Muslims to proselytize Muslims, and for Muslims to change religion. This is especially tricky, given the large Christian minority, especially in eastern Malaysia, on the island of Borneo. Many indigenous people were converted to Catholicism here after the Second World War, as waves of

We receive no financial help from outside sources. Our churches were built by the contributions of our members… Our resources are in God's hands and the generous heart of our people.

Vergis George, on the Indian Mar Thoma Christians in Malaysia, in *Christianity in Malaysia*, 1992

missionaries travelled the island, even to previously inaccessible areas. The vigorous church which sprang up suffered persecution under Tun Mustapha Harun, the chief minister of the state of Sabah, in the 1960s and 70s. He expelled foreign missionaries and even prevented the vicar apostolic – a Malaysian citizen! – from entering the state. In response, a group of lay Catholics created a council called the PAX to run the church and its missions in the area. In 1976, following the relaxation of the persecution, Pope Paul VI (reigned 1963–78) recognized the achievement of this unusual body by creating a new

diocese in northern Borneo, which, uniquely, was to be run jointly by the bishop and by PAX.

A similar situation of cautious optimism – in this case after a long history of persecution – pervades the churches elsewhere in the region. For example, we saw in Chapter 10 how the seventeenth and eighteenth centuries were marked by persecutions of the emerging Catholic Church in Vietnam. This situation continued into the nineteenth century, and there are many remarkable stories of the 'martyrs of Vietnam'. Ignatius Delado, vicar apostolic of East Tonkin, worked in the area

The City Harvest Church, Singapore. The massive building extends for four storeys below the ground as well as eight above it; the fountain alone cost over half a million Singaporean dollars.

for half a century before finally being captured in 1838 and locked in a cage, where he answered all questions about himself but refused to inform on his fellow Christians. He died of exposure and starvation, still in the cage. One of his successors, Valentine Berriochoa, was betrayed by a friend in 1861 before being tortured and killed by the usual method of decapitation. Neither were the martyrs all Europeans: most were Vietnamese, mainly leaders of local churches or missionaries. A typical example might be Andrew Dung An Trang, who became a Christian after being taught by a lay Catholic catechist and later became a priest. He worked in a number of parishes and was arrested more than once, each time being ransomed by his parishioners. Despite this, and sometimes travelling in disguise or under false names, he was eventually caught, tortured and beheaded in 1839. Merely between 1857 and 1862, it is thought that some 5,000 Vietnamese Christians suffered the same fate. Many fled to Cambodia or Thailand. Thailand had had a small but thriving Catholic mission since the seventeenth century. The Cambodian Catholic community was even tinier, numbering only a few hundred, and it was swamped by the Vietnamese refugees. Indeed, even today there are only a few tens of thousands of Christians in Cambodia, and most are ethnically Vietnamese.

The French captured the southern part of Vietnam in 1852, and gradually over the next thirty years took the rest of the country. This meant an end to persecution of the church, and the Vietnamese Catholic Church grew accordingly. There were few Protestant missions here compared to elsewhere in Asia, since Catholicism was promoted as part of the French culture which the Europeans, despite the resistance to French rule on the part of many Vietnamese, were keen to inculcate. In 1933 Nguyên Bá Tòng became the first indigenous Vietnamese bishop. By the Second World War, there were about two million Vietnamese Catholics. However, the Japanese invasions during the war weakened the French hold on the country, and in 1954 Vietnam was divided into two. This was a disaster for the church in the northern half, which became communist: fully half its members fled south to avoid communist rule. Those who remained suffered the usual restrictions from the communist government, with priests and bishops closely monitored or even placed under virtual house arrest, so that the faithful had to visit them for services rather than the other way around. Bibles and other Christian books were branded 'counter-revolutionary propaganda' and were smuggled into the country by well-wishers. This situation was extended to the south of the country after the communist victory in the Vietnam War of the 1960s and 70s, and the church there was also put under strict state control, with church property being seized and seminaries closed down. This coincided with even worse persecution of the Vietnamese Christians' co-religionists in Cambodia, where two military dictatorships – first of General Lon Nol and then of Pol Pot of the Khmer Rouge – cracked down on Catholicism, seizing or destroying much of its property and expelling Christians, mostly to Vietnam. Many Cambodian monks were rounded up en masse and tortured, worked to death or directly executed.

The situation in Vietnam only lightened in the 1980s and 90s, as the government relaxed its controls, and church membership is now increasing. In Cambodia, meanwhile, Catholicism was legalized in 1990. Today it is still considered mission territory, but it has its own vicar apostolic, who produced a Khmer translation of the Bible in 1997.

Things are similar in Thailand, where there were also Catholic missions from the seventeenth century onwards. In the late nineteenth century, Thailand had a particularly effective vicar apostolic named Jean-Louis Vey, who organized new missions in previously unreached parts of the country. Since then, the Catholic community – and to a lesser extent the Protestants, who make up about a quarter of Thai Christians – has played a small but important role in Thai society, establishing schools and hospitals and working to improve the lot of the poor.

Despite the modest successes in these countries, however, two areas in south-east Asia have seen particularly remarkable achievements, mostly by the Catholic Church. These are the Philippines and Indonesia.

THE PHILIPPINES

The late nineteenth century was a time of great upheaval in the Philippines. In 1896 revolution broke out against Spanish rule, which ended in 1898 through the intervention of the USA, which took over control of the country and fought a brutal war to impose its rule there. This had major implications for Christianity, since until this point Protestant missions had still been banned. Protestantism had managed to infiltrate the Philippines to some extent, and there were even underground churches; but now they could flourish as never before. US missionaries arrived in force. Five hundred and forty of them disembarked from the *USS Thomas* in 1901, after which they were all nicknamed 'Thomasites'.

The Catholic Church, meanwhile, was suddenly stripped of its state support and much of its money and was plunged into crisis. This was exacerbated by a priest named Gregorio Aglipay (1860–1940), who during the revolution urged all Filipino Catholics to break away from the Roman Catholic Church and form a new, national Catholic Church instead. He was sponsored in this by the revolutionaries, and he even acted as chaplain to the revolutionary armies, leading guerrilla attacks on Spanish forces. Rome excommunicated Aglipay and in 1902 he set up his own church, the Philippine Independent Church, with himself as head bishop. It proved extremely popular: by 1905 a quarter of all Filipino Christians were 'Aglipayans', and it was especially strong in the north of the country. Apart from being independent, the church was doctrinally and liturgically very

similar to Roman Catholicism, but gradually things changed. Aglipay himself became more theologically liberal, and eventually he came to reject the doctrine of the Trinity. The result was schism within his church, coming to a head in 1938. Isabelo de los Reyes, an elderly layman and prominent politician, led a breakaway group which would later become united to the American Episcopal Church.

Nevertheless, despite the serious problems caused by the end of Spanish rule and the Aglipay movement, the Roman Catholic Church remained deeply entrenched in Filipino culture, and the Protestant churches made only a tiny impression. No more than 3 or 4 per cent of the Christian population were Protestant in the inter-war period, and the figure has not changed much since. The Aglipayans, meanwhile, did not recover from their schism over the Trinity, and they also stabilized at about 4 per cent of the Christian population. Twentieth-century church history in the Philippines, therefore, was still mostly Catholic history.

And that history has been one of considerable social action. This was necessary after the Japanese occupation of the islands during the Second World War, and the church was involved in helping farmers, setting up schools and so on. A number of priests became highly politicized, particularly after the election of Ferdinand Marcos (1917–89) as president in 1965. Marcos's rule became increasingly authoritarian, with the imposition of martial law in 1972. Many in the church spoke out against it. Marcos's spoliation of the country caused massive problems of poverty, unemployment and corruption, leading to increased protests from churchmen. The Catholic Church became, in effect, the conscience of the country, a role it has continued to play ever since. The Christians for National Liberation, set up by a priest named Edicio de la Torre, were affiliated to the country's Communist Party and advocated revolution as the only solution to the worsening human rights

It is a Filipino movement. It throws off the yoke of the pope... It is altogether of the soil, and therefore he who does not support it is not a good Filipino.

Homer Stuntz, a Methodist leader in the Philippines, on the Aglipay movement, 1904

Demonstration in the Philippines during the Marcos versus Aquino presidential campaign.

situation in the country. In 1981 Pope John Paul II tried to persuade the 3,000 or so members of the movement to leave it, but to no effect.

More famous as a central figure in what was in effect Filipino liberation theology was Jaime Sin (1928–2005), who became archbishop of Manila in 1974 and a cardinal in 1976 (at which he commented, 'Now there is an eighth cardinal sin!'). Sin was a major opponent of the Marcos regime. In 1986, Corazon Aquino, the widow of a murdered opposition leader, won the popular vote in the presidential election, but the national assembly declared Marcos the winner. The people took to the streets in protest, and Sin played a leading role, making radio broadcasts urging people to particular locations to block the troops from preventing the coup. Such blocking, Sin insisted, should be done non-violently, and his intervention helped to prevent loss of life as the troops were held back and Aquino successfully took the presidency. Indeed, many in the church were deeply involved in the protests. News footage of the protests, beamed around the world, showed nuns, in full habits, brandishing rosaries from the barricades.

INDONESIA

In the first decades of the twentieth century, the missions to the Dutch East Indies carried on much as they had in the late nineteenth century. The Catholic and Protestant missionaries alike continued to consolidate their position in different parts of the archipelago. A particular success was the conversion of many of the Batak people of northern Sumatra, where there was something of a mass movement to Protestantism, creating the Batak Protestant Church. The Lutheran and Reformed missionaries here, led by the redoubtable Ludwig Ingwer Nommensen, were careful to respect the indigenous culture of the Batak. As a result, many older religious customs were preserved in the new Christian communities, such as the standard problem confronting

Christians in Asia, the veneration of ancestors.

The 1940s were a time of crisis for Indonesia in general and the Christian population in particular. First the region was occupied by the Japanese, who officially protected the Christians but in practice confiscated churches and schools; and then many Muslims took the opportunity to persecute Christians. But the fact that most foreign churchmen were expelled or imprisoned during this period forced Indonesians themselves to run their churches, thereby demonstrating that they were well able to do so without foreign help. There thus developed a strong drive towards independence from foreign churches that paralleled the drive to national independence that followed the expulsion of the Japanese.

In 1945, the nationalist leaders Ahmed Sukarno (1902–70) and Mohammad Hatta (1902–80) declared independence. Neither was a Christian, but many Christians were involved in the nationalist movement, and one, a Batak named Amir Sjarifuddin, was prime minister during the war of independence. As a result, both Protestant and Catholic churches enjoyed high prestige in the post-war period. New theological colleges and seminaries multiplied, and an Indonesian Council of Churches was established.

Today, there are some five million Catholics in Indonesia, concentrated on Flores and Timor, although there are also many in central Java. Protestantism is stronger, with 13.5 million people; and the Batak Protestant Church today has three and a half million members, making it the largest Protestant denomination based in south-east Asia. It founded its own university at Pematang Siantar and Medan in 1954, acquiring a separate theological institute in 1978. But Protestantism is also strong in eastern Indonesia, where in Irian (western New Guinea) some 85 per cent of the population are Christian. The further west you go, the fewer Christians (and the more Muslims) there are, apart from northern

Sumatra and Jakarta itself – for up to a quarter of the population of the capital city today is Christian. Christianity in Indonesia now, both Catholic and Protestant, is typically engaged in something of an ideological struggle with Islam: where either religion predominates, the other is discriminated against. The fact that there are more Muslims than Christians overall means the churches have tended to come off worse in this struggle, which is typified by poor understanding on both sides and which sometimes boils over into violence. In 1999, for example, war broke out in the Moluccas and Sulawesi between the two sides, with hundreds of churches and mosques destroyed. Today, therefore, despite their considerable success over the past two centuries in one of the most populous countries on earth, the Catholic and Protestant churches of Indonesia are at something of a crossroads, and their future is uncertain.

CHAPTER 17

MODERN AFRICA

The twentieth century saw the Christian world turned upside down. At the start of the century, most Christians lived in the northern hemisphere, particularly in Europe and North America. But the decline of Christianity in many parts of the northern hemisphere, coupled with its extraordinary growth in Africa, meant that by the end of the century there were more Christians in the southern hemisphere. Today, the place once called 'the dark continent' has become the centre of gravity of the Christian world, and the worldwide church, not just its representatives in Africa, is having to change.

An 'Askari' – or East African soldier – on Mount Kilimanjaro, Tanzania, November 1914.

THE END OF THE COLONIAL PERIOD

COLONIALISM, WAR AND THE MOVE TO AUTONOMY

On the whole, colonialism meant stability for Africa. The Europeans suppressed the previously perennial rivalry or warring of many tribes and kingdoms. Yet this ended in 1914, as war Europe-style came to the continent. Suddenly, the vast territories that the European powers had claimed in Africa were at war with each other, and this meant Africans fighting as well as Europeans. The worst of the fighting was in eastern Africa, where Germany controlled Tanzania and the area around Lake Tanganyika, including Rwanda. The British and French sent troops from Uganda, Kenya and other nearby countries, while the Germans advanced west; all of them used locally raised troops, as well as vast numbers of 'porters', Africans employed to help the troops but not fight themselves. The porters suffered much higher losses than the soldiers, partly through disease and starvation. Millions of Africans found themselves moving from one end of Africa to the other, and hundreds of thousands died on the way or in combat.

If the Great War meant great hardship and social change for Africa, it also meant new circumstances for the churches. Many missionaries were forced to evacuate, to help with the war effort or because they were in enemy-controlled territory. As we saw in Chapter 13, mission in Africa was often achieved through international, ecumenical effort, and so war meant enormous disruption as people of different nationalities could no longer work together. Many churches now found themselves operating without European help. In the late nineteenth century a more patrician model of mission had developed, where missionaries sought to impose European civilization and culture on Africans together with Christianity. The old ideals of self-governing churches, run by people like Samuel Crowther, had become less popular. Now, with the onset of war, those ideals were suddenly being thrust upon people whether they liked it or not.

Some churches foundered without missionary support. These were small missions that had only recently been founded or which had had little success. Most moderately well-established churches, by contrast, prospered during the war. Some European missionaries had time to ordain African pastors or ministers before they left, but in many cases – especially in the Catholic churches – this was not possible, and lay members of the congregations led the churches in the absence of ministers or priests. Just as in the Pacific during the Second World War, they generally did a good job – but unlike that parallel situation, it was not always recognized by the Europeans.

Nevertheless, after the war there was a major drive to help the African churches become more self-governing. This was especially so in the Catholic Church, and the movement owed a great deal to two great 'missionary popes'. The first was Benedict XV, who in 1919 issued an encyclical called *Maximum illud*, calling for the training of indigenous clergy in churches throughout the world, who could take over from European missionaries. Benedict believed that mission had become too mixed up with national colonial interests, and he denounced those missionaries who, during the war, had put national interests before Christian ones. New colleges in Europe, and local seminaries in Africa, were to be set up for the training of native clergy.

These far-sighted policies were endorsed by Benedict's successor, Pius XI. His encyclical *Rerum ecclesiae* of 1926 called for much the same things. In 1925 he had authorized an exhibition of African art at the Vatican, reflecting his insistence on the value of African culture in its own right. In 1926 the pope put his principles into action by ordaining the first six modern indigenous Chinese bishops; the following year he ordained the first Japanese bishop. Such moves were popular, but many Catholics wondered if they could really be replicated in the 'less civilized' Africa. Some referred to the pope's desire for an African clergy as his 'pious wish', implying that he was just being idealistic. Pius responded, 'No, it is our will and command.'

LEADING THE WAY: CATHOLICISM IN EAST AFRICA

The explosion in African Roman Catholicism that resulted took place mostly in central and eastern Africa, above all in Uganda, the region to the north of Lake Victoria, which was based around the central kingdom of Buganda. We saw in Chapter 13 how this area, one of the last to be visited by Europeans, was evangelized quite quickly in the late nineteenth century by both Protestant and Catholic missionaries. By the early twentieth century, this British-administered territory was dominated by Anglicanism: the king, the *kabaka*, was crowned by the Anglican bishop, and during the upheaval of the First World War the people laboured to build a great Anglican cathedral in the capital, Kampala. Even Sir Apolo Kagwa, the prime minister, had personally carried bricks up the hill every morning to help construct this monumental building, so different from the large thatched hut of twenty-five years earlier. Nevertheless, the British governor refused to make a formal union of church and state to mirror that back home in Britain: the Anglicans had to share their territory not only with the Muslim minority in the north but also with the Catholics, who had two cathedrals of their own in Kampala. The Catholic Church here had been overseen by the French missionary Henri Streicher (1863–1952),

It is a matter of genuine sorrow that there still exist countries to which the Catholic Faith was brought centuries ago but where, in spite of that fact, one does not find even now native priests except possibly those occupying minor posts…

Pope Benedict XV, *Maximum illud*, 1919

Before everything else, We call your attention to the importance of building up a native clergy. If you do not work with all your might to attain this purpose, We assert that not only will your apostolate be crippled, but it will become an obstacle and an impediment to the establishment and organization of the Church in those countries.

Pope Pius XI, *Rerum ecclesiae*, 1926

who in the 1880s and 90s helped to build a strong Catholic community in the kingdom of Buddu, where the chiefs wore crucifixes and, every morning, people would wave rosaries from their doors to invoke the power of the Virgin over their household. In 1897 Streicher was made the first Catholic bishop of Uganda. By 1905 there were 86,000 Catholics in Uganda.

By the time Pius XI was calling for indigenous clergy, the Catholic congregations in Uganda had swelled even more massively. There were 375,000 Ugandan Catholics in 1923, and the first native priests had been ordained ten years earlier before a vast crowd. The process of indigenization was slow, but it was relentless. By 1934 all mission stations in Uganda were headed by Africans. And in 1939 Joseph Kiwanuka became bishop of Masaka, the first indigenous African Catholic bishop of modern times.

In this way, Uganda became something of a model for Catholic churches throughout Africa – and indeed for Anglican ones too. For, although there were African assistant bishops in the West African Anglican churches by the 1930s, this generation had not yet produced a successor to Samuel Crowther. The work of Henri Streicher had embedded Catholicism deeply within Ugandan culture and daily life, and both his churches and the Anglican congregations were closely bound up with Ugandan society. These were churches that, although initiated by European missionaries, were now increasingly self-running and identified with local culture: they spoke Bantu rather than English, and the British governor did not interfere in them. Another striking element of the assimilation of Christianity was the fact that Ugandan Christians wore traditional Ugandan clothes, instead of dressing like Europeans as had been the norm elsewhere. The churches were also closely associated with the local civil government: Uganda was a kind of confederation of monarchies, each with its own strict hierarchy from the king downwards. The Anglican Church had

To get one indigenous priest is for me more important than converting ten thousand people.

Henri Streicher, 1929

cleverly matched these hierarchies to its own ecclesiastical hierarchy, so that each official from the king downwards was matched by a cleric, from the bishop downwards. Monarchy, Bantu culture and Catholic or Anglican Christianity were thus seamlessly matched together to create an African Christian civilization – in a land where Europeans had not even arrived until half a century previously.

Similar growth emerged in neighbouring countries. To the south, in Rwanda and Burundi, which was now a Belgian mandate, there were successful missions among the Tutsi people. Most of the aristocracy of this region were Tutsi, while the farmers were Hutu (although these were not exclusive castes). Until this point, Christian missions had been more successful among the Hutu. But now many Tutsi began to convert, keen to incorporate Catholicism into Tutsi culture just as had been done in Uganda. Much of this was connected to the desire to improve literacy and education, and the schools filled with eager Tutsi converts, ready to be taught in their own language by Christian Tutsi teachers. In Burundi, it was said that there were 1,000 baptisms a week in 1935, but the missions remained disciplined, with the catechumenate lasting the standard four years. This was in part due to Julien Gorju, the bishop of the area, who was extremely concerned to maintain proper procedure at a time when enthusiasm could easily have led to the neglect of sufficient instruction. But although the White Fathers, who were active in the Rwandan missions, called it a 'tornado' of conversion, the process was slower than in Uganda. In particular, neither Musinga, king of Rwanda, nor Mwamabutsa, king of Burundi, converted to Christianity – although the Belgians deposed Musinga in 1931 and replaced him with his son, Mutare IV. This king was baptized in 1941, and five years later, with great pomp, he dedicated the country to Christ. By 1940 there were some 300,000 Christians in Rwanda.

CENTRAL AFRICA: NEW MISSIONS, NEW GROWTH

The successful missions in East Africa showed just what kind of church growth was possible in a remarkably short period of time under colonial rule. At the same time, a similar story was unfolding in neighbouring Central Africa. Both Catholic and Protestant (mostly Baptist) missionaries had good results in the immense Congo basin in the nineteenth century. This continued into the twentieth. However, the various colonial powers took quite different attitudes towards mission. The early twentieth century was the time that anti-clericalism was strongest back in France, and as a result, the authorities in French Congo were quite cool towards mission. But they did not, on the whole, interfere with the Catholic missionaries, either here or in Cameroon to the west, which after the First World War was divided between the French and British.

This provided an immense mission field to the French and Belgian Catholics. In Cameroon, François Xavier Vogt, a Spiritist who was vicar apostolic of the region between 1922 and 1943, oversaw a period of extraordinary growth. Vogt recognized the importance of encouraging Africans to spread the word, rather than import missionaries, and he was lucky that the Ewondo people of the area produced a large number of extremely enthusiastic teachers. Hundreds of these well-trained catechists travelled the area, armed with a catechism in the Ewondo language written by one of their number, Joseph Ayisi. They would disappear into the forest and return to the mission station leading a band of dozens of people, sometimes whole villages who had responded to the message and walked for days to be baptized. And this success was almost matched by the Protestants. Modi Din, one of the native Duala people, became an extremely charismatic preacher, winning many converts though worrying the European missionaries, who feared his enthusiasm and possible lack of discipline. In the south, the Presbyterians had great success among the Bulu, where some 70,000 people were baptized in 1925.

It was a similar story to the east, in the huge territory known variously as Belgian Congo or Zaire (now the Democratic Republic of the Congo). Just as in Cameroon, Catholicism advanced thanks

Yao tribespeople attend a class on Christian beliefs at Mangoche, Malawi, c. 1907.

We asked them why they had become Christians. It was because the missionaries were white. The whites are strong. They have the guns and the aeroplanes and the motor-cars, all the things in the black man's book of marvels… What they teach must be right. This seems to be the main argument of the missionaries, whether they employ it consciously or not.

F. C. Egerton, a traveller in French Cameroon, on Christianity at the court of King Nana of Bazou, *African Majesty*, 1938

We all received these three great thoughts: the thoughts of life-force, of fecundity, and of love. Because God is Father, he is child, and he is unity. In other words, through his being Father, since he is Father, he gave us life-force. Because if a man is full of life he resembles his God. When we are full of life, truly full of the life of the spirit, then we resemble God, the Father. And through his being child, God gave us fecundity. Through his being one, because of his being unity, we receive love. Therefore we all receive these three great thoughts. Truly all of us.

Baba Nkondo, a Jamaa leader, 1966

to a veritable army of local catechists: in 1923 there were 7,660 of them, rising to an incredible 163,000 by 1961. By this time, thanks largely to their efforts, there were nearly six million Catholics in the country. Much of the brilliance of the Catholic missions lay in the discipline with which these grassroots missionaries were coordinated from above. Despite the criticisms they had suffered in earlier decades in this region, for example, the Jesuits were still here, led by Joseph van Wing. He not only helped to coordinate the missionaries but drove for social reform in matters such as opposing the destruction of widows' property when their husbands died. And in contrast to the French-administered territories, the Belgian government encouraged Catholic missions and gave them generous land grants. Through the efforts of people like van Wing, and through this governmental help, much of society in Zaire became Catholicized. For example, in the city of Lubumbashi in the south-east of the country, the powerful bishop, a Benedictine monk named Jean Félix de Hemptinne, set up schools, associations and other organizations to this end. Like van Wing, de Hemptinne understood the need to respect and preserve local culture: his institutions were run by Africans and organized along ethnic lines.

A more innovative approach, taking this idea much further, was 'Jamaa', a kind of Christian society or church within a church. Jamaa was the brainchild of a Belgian Franciscan friar named Placide Tempels, who while working in Zaire came to believe that Christianity should be preached within the framework of existing Luba culture and society, not as a replacement for them. He made an extensive study of this culture – publishing his findings in *Bantu Philosophy* in 1945 – and within a few years Jamaa emerged at his mission near Kolwezi. Tempels believed that the central Luba value was loving union, as found in that of husband and wife, and so he organized Jamaa around married couples and their close relationship

with a priest. Together, these three could hope to experience Christ in their midst, just as Christ is also known through his close union with Mary. Jamaa was thus about loving union, but also priestly instruction, private devotion and discipline. In organization it resembled traditional Luba societies, but with many of the Franciscan ideals that Tempels brought to the area. For example, it shared the value that the Luba traditionally placed on dreams. In each couple, it was hoped that the husband would develop a mystical union with 'Bikira Maria', while the wife would develop one with 'Bwana Yezu Kristu', in what were almost parallel marriages; and these were experienced through dreams. Some priests regarded all this with great suspicion, and the movement sometimes came close to being condemned. But in the 1950s and 60s it spread through the area, developing almost into a secret society: there were initiation ceremonies and strange jargon to preserve its mystique.

Protestant missionaries, by contrast, were only tolerated and received little help. The Protestant churches were therefore less successful than the Catholics, although by any normal standards they were still remarkable. For example, Lewis Brown, an American Baptist missionary at Vanga, had the bright idea of decentralizing the mission station system. This meant that converts no longer had to traipse for days to be baptized or to receive instruction, and the mission prospered. By 1960 there were nearly two million Protestants throughout the country, mostly Baptists.

Thus we see the church advancing through a complex interplay of European and African initiatives, with cooperation between white and black missionaries proving most fruitful. However, the most dramatic episode in Central African Christianity during this period was opposed by the European powers. That was the preaching of Simon Kimbangu, and we shall see more of him later in this chapter.

GROWTH AND CONFLICT IN WEST AFRICA

Throughout this period, Islam was expanding and consolidating its position in Africa just as Christianity was. Much of this was a conscious reaction to the spread of Christianity and the partition of Africa by Christian European powers: those areas that were traditionally Muslim naturally sought to entrench and reaffirm their historic faith in response. As a rule, the British and French authorities – who governed most of the Muslim areas – were suspicious of Islam, although they generally tolerated it. As a result, the religion became more attractive to people in these regions who still practised traditional African religions, and many converted to Islam. So regions that had been only partially or superficially Muslim became much more strongly Muslim.

There were four areas of Africa, in particular, where Christianity was in close contact with Islam. We have already seen one – East Africa, where Islam came to be a minority concern following the remarkable expansion of Catholicism and Anglicanism in Uganda and the surrounding region. The other three were Ethiopia and its environs, North Africa (including Egypt), and West Africa. We shall look at Ethiopia and North Africa later in this chapter. How did the church respond to the challenges of Islam in West Africa?

In Chapter 13 we saw how Christianity became well established along the West African coast, in areas such as Sierra Leone, Liberia and Yorubaland. The early twentieth century saw it consolidate this success. In Ghana and Nigeria, for example, the churches formed an unlikely association with cocoa farming, an industry which was introduced into these areas at the end of the nineteenth century. Most of the cocoa workers were members of the churches, and they prospered, which made Christianity appear attractive to others. As society changed to reflect the new industry and new conditions, Christianity became more closely bound up with local culture. This was especially so in Yorubaland, in western Nigeria, which saw a process of accelerated urbanization during this period. Its leading city, Lagos, grew dramatically in the first half of the century from 42,000 people in 1901 to 665,000 in 1963. There were more Muslims here than Christians, at least during this period, but the Christians tended to be richer and better educated. Most of the schools were church-run: some Muslims sent their children to these schools, but others denounced this as inviting conversion.

This was a time when the initiative in the churches was passing – very gradually – to Africans themselves. As we have seen, the episcopate remained European, but a kind of distinctly West African Christianity was developing. The most dramatic side of this phenomenon was the extraordinary Prophet Harris and his imitators, whom we shall meet shortly; but there were others too, such as the Yoruba novelist Daniel Olorunfemi Fagunwa. His books, including his first and most famous, *The forest of a thousand demons*, were written in the local language and presented Christian faith and ideals in opposition to the traditional indigenous religion – a religion of which his own grandfather had been a priest. In Fagunwa's world, God's love encounters and overcomes traditional magic and fetishes, offering new hope to the Yoruba. His books were very widely read, finding their way onto the syllabuses of church schools.

Meanwhile, Christianity was spreading further east and north. The Igbo people, who lived to the east of the Yoruba, had been evangelized by the missions of Samuel Crowther in past decades, and they began to migrate west to cities such as Lagos, where they came into further contact with the churches. The Tiv, to the north, saw their society fragment and change radically with the coming of the railway in the 1920s: there was more work and more money, which fuelled a dissatisfaction with traditional religion and a remarkable movement towards Christianity. And around the Niger Delta lived the Isoko, who had never seen a

Come, let us go home, do you hear me? Will you not go yet? Come.

Agore Iwe (1906–79), the first Anglican bishop of Benin, from a 1930s primer in Urhobo missionary before 1910 when Edda Otuedo, a court clerk, arrived in the area and preached informally there. Another West African, Bevebolo Bribina, picked up where he left off, but soon encountered persecution. Undaunted, Bribina took her converts to the Isokoland countryside and founded a Christian settlement called Obhodo ('New Town'). It grew rapidly, becoming the centre of Christianity in the area. People thronged enthusiastically to the churches, throwing their old 'fetishes' onto bonfires in the manner now traditional for African Christian converts. Unlike many other African Christians, the Isoko disapproved of syncretism, to the extent of rejecting the traditional local name for God, Oghere: instead he became Egode or Ijohiva, known through his son, Jesu Kriti. Yet they still retained their belief in traditional gods and spirits, now understood as enemies of Egode, and many people kept Bibles under the pillows as a charm against them.

The conversion of the Isoko was, in a way, the shape of things to come. It was done almost entirely by West Africans –

and, moreover, by lay people, ordinary grassroots Christians who moved to a new country and felt called to witness to their new neighbours. There were, after all, so few black ministers and priests, so it is no wonder that African-led mission tended to be a lay development. The success of this makeshift mission amazed European missionaries who arrived in Isokoland shortly afterwards.

As Christianity became better established along the West African coast, it inevitably crept ever further into the interior of the continent, where it came into closer contact with the Islam that had dominated this part of the world for many centuries. This happened in northern Nigeria, where the Hausa people were traditionally Muslim; they largely resisted Christianity, but many of the peoples of the area and slightly to the south, who had for centuries been oppressed by the powerful Hausa, were more than happy to convert to the rival religion. A traditional feature of Islam here, as throughout West Africa, was the Qur'an school – usually held not in a school building but in the

Voodoo dolls in a fetish market in Lome, Togo, in 1991.

open air, around a bonfire, symbolizing the presence of Allah as the teachers instructed children in the Muslim faith. Now the evangelical missionaries to this area cleverly copied the institution, setting up large numbers of Bible schools which proved very successful.

The two religions also met in Burkina Faso, west of Nigeria, a plateau lying between the coastal regions to the south and Mali to the north. Burkina Faso had been administered by the French since 1897: confusingly, it was first treated as part of Mali, which was known at this time as French Sudan; later it was separated and called Upper Volta. As soon as the French arrived, Catholic missionaries followed, especially the White Fathers, who were having such success in East Africa at this time. The first baptisms were performed in 1905, and moderate success was found among the Mossi people, who made up around half the population, and who until this time had been largely Muslim.

The missionaries had to fight on two fronts in Burkina Faso and Mali alike. On the one hand, they were greatly outnumbered by the Muslims. Ougadougou, the capital of Burkina Faso, had hardly any Christians, apart from the missionaries, until the 1920s. They adopted the methods that many Catholic missionaries had used with success in the past, especially in Asia – becoming part of the local society and culture, hoping to use non-religious institutions to spread their faith. The White Sisters, for example, set up a carpet factory which employed young Mossi women: the hope was that these girls would convert, marry Mossi men, and spread Catholicism. The plan was a moderate success. Here, the missionaries were fortunate in having one of the best mission directors of the period, Johanny Thévanoud, who arrived at Ougadougou in 1903 and became its first bishop in 1921, serving until his death in 1949. For over forty years, Thévanoud took charge of the missions to the Mossi – but he also fought on the other front, against French anti-clericalism. Just as in French Congo, the administration in Mali and Burkina Faso was, as a rule, quite hostile to the missionaries. There were fears that missionaries' attempts to reform local society – pressing for more opportunities for Mossi women, for example – would lead to instability. Mission schools were discouraged. However, Johanny Thévanoud worked hard to establish good relations with the authorities, and he often succeeded. Under his far-sighted leadership, the Catholic Church prospered in Burkina Faso: by the Second World War, about a third of the population of Ougadougou was Catholic.

Indeed, the Catholicism of Burkina Faso spread outwards into the surrounding areas. In 1906, expecting to be expelled from the country by the anti-clerical administration, a group of White Fathers decided to pre-empt the order and left Ougadougou, ending up in northern Ghana, to the south. They did not do much better here, since the British authorities did not admit foreign, non-English-speaking missionaries. They were expelled after a few years, but the mission they began at Navrongo continued under the leadership of Canadian White Fathers. Here, twenty years of labour brought the missionaries almost no results. In 1929, when it seemed the mission would die out, a new opportunity arose: the British authorities designated a new mission sphere in the north-west of Ghana, where the Dagarti people lived, for the Anglicans, but the Anglicans were unable to find missionaries to go there. The authorities therefore allowed the White Fathers to preach there instead. Suddenly, the White Fathers found success. The Dagarti were highly receptive to Christianity, something which was helped by a dramatic incident in 1932. A terrible drought had gripped the region, and the Catholics held a service at Jirapa, attended by the local chiefs, to pray for rain. Almost immediately the clouds opened, and the people came streaming in from the local countryside to revere the men who had wrought this miracle.

NEW PROPHETS, NEW MOVEMENTS

We have seen how the initiative in the churches was passing to Africans themselves – most prominently in Uganda and the surrounding area, and more slowly in West Africa. The most dramatic aspect of this phenomenon was the rise, in the early twentieth century, of a number of extraordinarily charismatic Christian prophets. Together, they not only helped to swell the ranks of the various churches to a remarkable degree, but also represented a new and highly African understanding of Christianity.

The most famous of these people was the man often referred to as the Prophet Harris (c. 1865–1929). His full name was William Wade Harris, and he was a Grebo – one of the indigenous peoples of Liberia – who had been brought up as a Methodist but converted to the Church of England. He had tried to organize a revolution to turn Liberia over to the British crown; upon its failure he had been thrown into prison. Here, every night, he had a vision of the Archangel Gabriel, who instilled in him an unshakeable faith in himself as the divinely appointed Prophet of Africa. He gained a new sense of his African identity, and gave up the European-style clothes he had worn before and his American shoes. Instead, upon his release in 1913, Harris crossed the border into Ivory Coast to preach. He was barefoot, dressed in a white cloak, he carried a six-foot cross made of bamboo, and he was accompanied by two or three of his wives.

Harris was one of the most remarkable preachers in African history. Like a latter-day John Wesley, he spoke to crowds thousands strong, imploring them to turn away from idols to God. Harris's message was uncompromising, and he had no time for accommodation to traditional African religions (apart from polygamy). Instead, all 'fetishes' were to be burned upon the great bonfires that he lit. The people responded in their hordes: some 100,000 people were converted in little more than a year. Many were baptized by Harris himself with a small bowl he carried for the purpose;

many more were baptized when the clouds opened and Harris cried out the Trinitarian formula, using the rain itself as the sacrament. Whole villages were converted at a stroke – and, even more remarkably, the Christian communities that were founded in this way proved surprisingly durable. Harris's message was fairly simple, revolving around the need to turn to Jesus, who he believed would return imminently; he did not much mind which church people joined, provided they joined one. Church attendances swelled dramatically – even the Catholic churches found huge numbers of new recruits.

In 1915, the French authorities in Ivory Coast had had enough of this extraordinary but potentially volatile phenomenon, and they expelled Harris back to Liberia. He stayed here until his death in 1929, still preaching, but never with the same impact. But his assistant, John Swatson, continued to preach in the area, with continued remarkable success.

Harris had his imitators. One was Garrick Sokari Braide (c. 1880–1918), who appeared in 1915 far to the east, in the region of the Niger Delta. Like Harris, he was an Anglican and a fiery preacher, who inspired people to burn the 'fetishes' and turn to God instead. Many thousands turned to him, but James Johnson, the local bishop, was displeased. Braide claimed to be a second Elijah, and he also tolerated polygamy. He was arrested and died soon after. Elsewhere in the region one could hear the preaching of Moses Orimolade and a female visionary called Abiodun Akinsowon and, in the 1930s, Joseph Babalola, who led a revival among the Yoruba. Yet another African prophet was Sampson Oppong (d. 1965), who preached to the Asante people in Ghana in the early 1920s. Like Harris, Oppong travelled simply, bearing a cross, and wore a white robe (although he changed into a khaki one for travelling and a black one for preaching). Oppong also won vast numbers of converts – some 20,000 in a couple of years – although in his case they were mostly Methodist.

514

And the phenomenon was not confined to West Africa. The most famous prophet in the Congo region was Simon Kimbangu (c. 1887–1951), who managed, if anything, to make an even greater impact than Harris in a shorter period of time. Born at Nkamba, Kimbangu became a Baptist at a young age and taught in a mission school. In 1918 he became a lay preacher, but he was disturbed by dreams or visions in which Jesus seemed to appear to him. In 1921 he visited a family where a woman was ill. He laid hands on her and she was healed. Immediately there was uproar. People flocked from the whole region to see this new prophet and healer, and he quickly acquired disciples, including an inner cadre of twelve 'apostles'. Stories of healings and even resurrections spread, as Kimbangu told the people to burn their fetishes and turn to God. There were wild demonstrations of the divine power, including speaking in tongues.

Although the Baptist church in the area considered Kimbangu's ministry legitimate, the Belgian authorities did not and they arrested him and his immediate followers after only a few months. Kimbangu was sentenced to death, but the sentence was commuted to life imprisonment in Lubumbashi. However, his movement did not die. On the contrary, the 'Kimbanguists' flourished and spread, though they continued to revere Nkamba as a holy place. There were periodical rumours that the 'Absent Prophet' would return. He never did – dying in prison in 1951 – but the movement remained a major element of Christianity in the Congo region, despite periodic clampdowns from the government and the mainstream churches alike. Not until 1958 were the Kimbanguists officially recognized as a legitimate church, and two years later Kimbangu's body was returned to Nkamba, the Kimbanguist Jerusalem, for burial.

Even as the Kimbanguists were receiving belated recognition, another prophetic movement was beginning hundreds of miles to the south, in Northern Rhodesia (now Zambia). Alice Lenshina Mulenga (1920–78) had been brought up as a Presbyterian, but in 1953 she had an experience which she interpreted as one of death and resurrection, and she became a popular preacher. Like the other prophets, she attacked traditional religion, or as she regarded it, 'witchcraft'; she also fiercely denounced the drinking of beer. Her message was extraordinarily successful, with whole villages joining the 'Lumpa Church' en masse and singing the hymns that Mulenga herself wrote.

The sheer numbers of people converted through the preaching of these 'prophets' testify to the charisma and power they must have wielded. And they made a huge impact on the churches of the area. In Harris's case, he cared nothing for denominations, and so all the churches in the Ivory Coast area found unprecedented numbers of converts. Indeed, European missionaries coming to the area in the wake of Harris's preaching were overwhelmed with the unexpected size of their congregations: the Catholic churches in Ivory Coast, for example, swelled from just a few hundred at the start of the century to 20,000 in 1922. The numbers kept rising, too, for many years after the prophets had left, suggesting that this was not simply a shallow fad but a major development in African Christianity. Indeed, a new denomination appeared in Ivory Coast, the Harrists, who followed roughly orthodox Protestant theology but who were proud of the African origin of their church and of its founding prophet. The Harrists were closely associated with the Ebrie people, around Abidjan.

The Kimbanguists, Harrists and others represent the first major new Christian denominations that were formed in Africa. In many ways, the teaching of these prophets – and innumerable other, less well-known ones – was quite orthodox from a Protestant point of view. They were not doctrinally innovative. But they all had much in common which was drawn from

Through Simon Kimbangu, who was obedient to God, the promises of Jesus have been fulfilled and the Name of the Father and the Son has been glorified. Through him the Congolese realized that God and Jesus had turned to us in mercy. The sorrow and suffering of our fathers had been heard by God the Father, and our tears were wiped away.

Joseph Diangienda, Simon Kimbangu's son and successor as head of the church traditional African religion. The emphasis on a 'prophet', a charismatic preacher, often with great healing powers, was typically African. In the Congo region, for example, such people were called *ngunza* and believed to be possessed by spirits. Simon Kimbangu was, in effect, a Christian *ngunza*. And, like traditional prophets, the Christian prophet would generally carry a staff, which represented his authority. Indeed, Kimbangu passed his staff on to his sons, who even retained the title *Mvwala* or 'Staff' as leaders of his church. So William Wade Harris's bamboo cross was a sign not simply of Christ but of his own power to preach and heal; for healing was central to the ministry of the prophets, just as it was important to much indigenous African religion. Africans generally expected their gods to work for the health of their followers, and to do it through these charismatic wonderworkers. Little wonder, then, that where Jesus was preached, Jesus was seen to heal. This was especially so in the years immediately following the Great War, when Africa, even more than Europe, was gripped by the terrible flu epidemic that cost millions of lives.

Most of these prophets and their followers did not see themselves as mingling Christianity and traditional religion – on the contrary, a call to burn the fetishes was standard for all Christian prophets. They believed that what they taught and practised was entirely in keeping with the Bible, for the Protestant missionaries had taught their converts to believe what the Bible said. But they could never have anticipated some of the consequences of this – consequences that came from reading the Bible in an African context rather than a European one. In the Bible, the African converts read of events that seemed familiar to them: dreams and visions in which God taught his people, and great apostles and prophets who did mighty works and healed the sick. They expected to see this happen now. They also expected the biblical prophecies, especially those relating to the coming of God's kingdom on earth, to be fulfilled in their

time: thus Kimbangu's village of Nkamba was hailed as the New Jerusalem, while Mulenga's village of Kasomo became 'Zioni'.

Most European missionaries had believed in the miracles described in the Bible, but they thought of them as special 'biblical era' events and did not expect to see them replicated. But many Africans did not distance themselves from the text in this way, and this led to quite new problems. For example, was polygamy permissible? The missionaries were emphatic that it was not, but the Africans saw that the Old Testament patriarchs apparently had many wives, just as they were accustomed to do themselves. Again, to what extent were dreams to be considered valid revelation alongside the Bible? After all, many people in the Bible received revelations from God in dreams. This was a question that no European missionary had even considered, and it was one to which they had no answer.

INDEPENDENT AFRICA

The Second World War, like the first, caused great upheaval throughout Africa. Once again, Africans were pressed into service to fight a 'white man's war', and this time they travelled not only throughout Africa to fight it but to Europe and Asia too. And the years that followed brought even greater changes to African society. The success of the missions and their schools meant that many Africans were now not only Christian but better educated than their parents had been, and they felt more of a connection with the European powers for which they had fought. A trend developed of Africans travelling to Europe to visit the colonial powers and study there, and also to the USA and the USSR. The drive to independence accelerated, fuelled by a number of complex factors, including the natural resentment that many of these well-educated Africans felt at the continuing failure of the colonial powers to recognize that Africans were capable of

...the missionary has made the African soil fertile for the growth of imperialism... [but] he has equally helped to lay the foundations for the present spirit of nationalism... When African historians come to write their own account of the adventure of Africa with imperialism, they will write of the missionaries as the greatest friends the Africans had.

Dennis Osadebay, a Nigerian politician, 1947

self-government. The Pan-African congresses, held at a number of locations at irregular intervals, called for Africans to be allowed to govern themselves; the fourth congress, held in 1945 at Manchester, was especially influential. Ghana was the first country to achieve independence, under Kwame Nkrumah in 1957. The successful handover of power led to independence for most African countries in the 1960s: Nigeria, Gabon, French and Belgian Congo (which took on a variety of names but are now the Republic of the Congo and the Democratic Republic of the Congo) in 1960, Tanzania in 1961, Kenya in 1963, Zambia in 1964 and so on.

It was, naturally, a time of enormous change and uncertainty. In some cases, independence itself did not come easily: Angola suffered what was in effect civil war between the Portuguese forces and nationalists between 1961 and 1975, when it finally gained independence; but then the setting up of a Marxist government was followed by further violence and guerrilla action. Other countries, which had gained independence more easily, found further chaos down the line. In 1965, for example, Rhodesia (formerly Southern Rhodesia, now Zimbabwe) declared independence under the white minority government of Ian Smith, but the racist constitution he set up in 1969 helped the situation to degenerate into civil war throughout the 1970s between government forces – backed by a white mercenary army and supported by the white South African government – and guerrillas. Uganda, granted independence in 1962, seemed all right to begin with, but in 1971 a coup brought the brutal dictator Idi Amin to power, resulting in both government-led purges and guerrilla resistance.

Many of the problems were a legacy of colonial times, when borders had been determined without any thought for traditional ethnic boundaries. Most countries therefore contained several different groups who might have little love for each other, while some peoples found

international borders passing through the middle of their traditional lands. In Nigeria, tribal tensions led to many Igbo setting up an independent state, Biafra, in 1967. The extremely bitter civil war that resulted lasted for three years, and a million people died – largely because of the tactic of destroying farmland to starve the enemy. In Rwanda and Burundi, meanwhile, war between the Hutu and the Tutsi led to thousands of Hutu fleeing into Tanzania and other neighbouring countries.

Religious differences could be an exacerbating factor in this. Again in Nigeria, some in the Muslim-dominated north regarded the civil war as a holy war against the largely Christian Igbo. There was a series of massacres of Igbo in the north. For the most part, Christians and Muslims have lived fairly peacefully with each other in West Africa, but the atrocities in Nigeria were one occasion when the tolerance broke down.

And the churches could also represent stability and continuity. Many of the first generation of political leaders, the founding fathers of the independent African nations, were Christians: Kwame Nkrumah of Ghana, for example, was a Catholic, while Kenneth Kaunda of Zambia was a Presbyterian.

SOUTHERN AFRICA

Perhaps the most bitter struggles in post-colonial Africa have been in those countries where white rule meant segregation, discrimination or subjugation of the black majority. The history of the churches in southern Africa was, for the first part of the century, largely the history of the churches of the white settlers and their descendants, and in many ways this history mirrored that of their counterparts back in Europe or the United States. For example, the controversy between fundamentalists and modernists in the USA was replayed in the Afrikaner churches of South Africa in the early years of the twentieth century. Figures such as Johannes du Plessis, a theologian and patron of mission in the 1920s, argued for

Lead, kindly light, amid the encircling gloom
Lead Thou me on!
The night is dark, and I am far from home;
Lead Thou me on!
Keep Thou my feet; I do not ask to see
The distant scene: one step enough for me.

A hymn by John Henry Newman, sung by members of Kwame Nkrumah's Convention People's Party during the drive for independence

John Mbiti and the development of African theology

John Mbiti (b. 1931), a Kenyan scholar, has pioneered the articulation of African Christian theology. He has made an enormous impact in African academy and church life, interpreting Africa to the universal church and academy.

In his doctoral dissertation at Cambridge University in 1963, he used the concept of eschatology to reveal the underlying task of African theology. He distinguished between the layers of what the New Testament taught, what missionaries conveyed to the Akamba people (of Nigeria), how the Kikamba (of Kenya) conceptualized life after death in their indigenous worldview, and, therefore, how they decoded missionary teachings, by appropriating some elements and reconfiguring these through the prism of their worldview. In culture contacts, despite the efforts by hegemonic forces to implant certain doctrines, hearers appropriate the gospel from their own worldviews. The bearers brought the gospel repackaged with western culture and an enlightenment worldview. They privileged literacy to people who emphasized orality, narrative theology, maximum participation in liturgy, inclusion of visions, dreams and a relationship between body and mind manifested through healing and prayer. The question is: what did the hearers hear and say about the relationship of God to human beings and the world of nature?

Mbiti refused to castigate missionaries while rejecting the denigration of indigenous religions and cultures. He argued that the sources of 'doing theology' comprise the Bible as the source of divine revelation, the indigenous worldviews, religions, cultures, oral reflections by the people of God, the existential forces in their environments, the heritage of Christian traditions and the presence of other religious faiths. African Christianity results from the encounter of the gospel with these factors. Mbiti's conclusion is that African religions and cultures embody a preparation for the gospel because Christ is in every culture and judges all cultures. African Christianity is a continuum with dimensions of African religions such as the celebration of life and corporate sense of existence. God is one and has been known and worshipped in various ways by African peoples before the missionaries arrived. This explains the wide areas of resonance between African and biblical worldviews: a charismatic perception of reality; three-dimensional perception of space; the dynamic relations of 'here and now' to the 'not yet' period; the power in the blood, name and words; the reality of miracles and supernatural interventions in daily lives. However, there are differences. The African perceives time as an event (*kairos*); life flows in a cyclical fashion from birth through death to reincarnation. The New Testament perceives time as something abstract (*kronos*) that moves in a linear fashion from the past through the present to the future.

Mbiti studied African religions and cultures (focusing on shared elements), concepts of God, prayers, love and marriage and the use of the Bible. Combined with his vernacular poems and anthropological studies, he rehabilitated Africa's rich cultural heritage and religious consciousness, and brought them into Christian theology, and thereby removed the veil of strangeness of the gospel among African communities. He showed that prayers, libations, sacrifices, dance music, rites of passage and festivals were means of weaving covenants with the supreme being, spirits and ancestors and to ward off evil. He showed how these could be redirected towards God in a conversation process.

Mbiti recognized that the core of gospel-culture encounter is the role of Christ. Other scholars canvassed the notion of Christ as ancestor. Mbiti argued that Christ answers the search for meaning and wholeness in every culture, including African religious life. Christ completes the sacralization of the whole of life that removes the veil between the sacred and the profane. In Africa, the human world is a mirror of the spirit world. So Christ is the crowning completion of all quests, the brilliance of the flickering light in world religions. Other scholars have tried to image the face of Jesus in Africa as a chief, king, ancestor and guest. These imageries fail to capture the full Jesus. Mbiti focused on Christ's meaning and lordship over life, reconciling the whole of creation to God.

OGBU KALU

the need to understand the Bible in the light of modern science. For this, du Plessis was fired from his university in 1930, in a case that went all the way to the country's Supreme Court. Du Plessis won, but he did not get his job back. The Dutch Reformed Church in the country remained suspicious of modernism – almost to the point of paranoia – for many years.

At the same time, the remote mission stations were still operating in the sparsely populated northern expanses. Alston May, Anglican bishop in what is now Zambia (but in the 1920s and 30s was Northern Rhodesia), was said to have no permanent home. Instead he spent his entire life on the road, first on a bicycle and then in a succession of vans, which all wore out as he drove from village to village visiting his flock. Maurice Leenhardt, the great missionary of New Caledonia, visited the French Protestant missions in the area in 1923 and concluded that they were in a very bad way – entirely run by white missionaries, without any degree of native involvement or leadership. As a result, they had no depth or staying power. Yet African-initiated movements did arise, almost as an alternative. In the late 1920s a notable church appeared at Ndola, entirely run by local people, and thirty years later Northern Rhodesia also saw the movement of the prophet Alice Lenshina Mulenga.

To the south lay what is now Zimbabwe but was then Southern Rhodesia, and beyond that was South Africa. In both of these British-administered countries, a white minority ruled a black majority in a fundamentally racist society. In Southern Rhodesia, Anglicanism and Methodism were the majority churches, with Anglicanism in particular catering to both black and white communities with its large numbers of church schools. There was also a significant Catholic minority, although this did not become a major factor until after the 1950s.

South Africa, meanwhile, had become a unified colony of Britain in 1910, and gained its independence in 1961. The presence of the Boers meant that the Dutch Reformed Church (NGK) was still the major church, together with a significant Anglican presence. Catholicism existed only as a small minority concern until the 1920s, when a Dominican friar named Bernardus Jordanus Gijlswijk became apostolic delegate in the country. He and his subordinates worked extremely hard to bring Catholicism to the people, especially the black Africans, and enjoyed considerable success in what had for centuries been an almost completely Protestant country.

In both Southern Rhodesia and South Africa there was a de facto colour bar in most of the churches, just as in most of society. There were white congregations and black ones, but they did not mix – usually not because of any explicit rules, but because that was simply how things were done. In South Africa, however, the situation intensified after the Boer nationalists took power in 1948. A series of legislative measures was passed in the 1950s enforcing the segregation of blacks and whites. Many in the churches supported this system of apartheid. The NGK, for example, had for some years been campaigning for greater racial segregation, on the basis that mixing the races had undesirable social consequences. Mixed marriages, in particular, were condemned as unbiblical and contrary to nature. This was defended theologically by appealing to the Calvinist doctrine of predestination: the hierarchy of the races, with white people 'naturally' superior to blacks, was part of the natural order that was created and predestined by God. The drive to equality, by contrast, was perceived as part of the iniquitous movement of modernism, humanism and communism.

But many other Christians disagreed. The English-speaking churches in South Africa, dominated by the Anglicans, all opposed apartheid to varying degrees. However, these churches were still mostly white-dominated in the 1950s and had segregated congregations, in fact if not in

Equalization leads to the deterioration of both nations. Mixed marriages between higher, civilized and Christianized nations with lower races militate against the Word of God... This is nothing less than a crime... The Voortrekkers constantly guarded against such admixture and through their act of faith our nation was saved as a pure Christian race in this our land.

Philippus J.S. de Klerk, a Reformed Church minister, 1939

Trevor Huddleston, photographed in 1959.

In opposing the policies of the present Government… I am not prepared to concede that any momentary good which might conceivably emerge from them is good… For both the acts and the motives are inspired by a desire which is itself fundamentally evil and basically un-Christian: the desire to dominate in order to preserve a position of racial superiority, and in that process of domination to destroy personal relationships, the foundation of love itself. That is anti-Christ.

Trevor Huddleston, *Naught for your comfort*, 1956

theory. There was disagreement over how actively they should oppose apartheid. Geoffrey Clayton, Anglican archbishop of Cape Town, felt that the church should stay out of politics. But Ambrose Reeves, bishop of Johannesburg, disagreed. A major activist at this time was a white priest named Trevor Huddleston, who in 1955 published a diatribe against apartheid entitled *Naught for your comfort*, which made a great impression and led to Huddleston's expulsion from the country. The mood among the English-speaking churches turned increasingly anti-apartheid: in 1960 Clayton's successor, Joost de Blank, called for the World Council of Churches to expel the NGK. It did not do so, but in that year it did hold a consultation in Johannesburg, opposing apartheid and calling for equal rights for all South Africans. And many in the NGK supported its resolutions. The result was a kind of witch hunt within the NGK, at the instigation of the prime minister, Hendrik Verwoerd; all delegates to the consultation were punished. The NGK became a pariah church both internationally and within South Africa, despite its dominance there. But some within the NGK did not toe the party line. Christiaan Frederick Beyers Naudé,

moderator of the Southern Transvaal Synod, spoke out against apartheid: he was expelled from the NGK, and set up the Christian Institute of Southern Africa to support others in the same position. Because of his work with the anti-apartheid movement, Naudé was closely watched by the government; between 1977 and 1984 he was officially a 'banned person', virtually under house arrest.

After the 1960s, leadership of the anti-apartheid movement within the churches, as in South Africa as a whole, passed from concerned whites to black people themselves. Not only were the English-speaking churches predominantly black by this stage, but liberation theology and its equivalents among African Americans in the USA made a great impression upon many black South African Christians. Tensions increased within the NGK, and with the NGSK, the black wing of the church. In the 1980s the moderator of the NGSK was Allan Boesak, who helped to persuade the World Alliance of Reformed Churches to suspend the NGK in 1982; he also oversaw the drafting of the Belhar Confession, which stressed the unity of the church and its tendency to reconciliation rather than domination, and which condemned apartheid as a heresy. The illegal opposition party, the African National Congress (ANC), set up a department of religion. Meanwhile, Desmond Tutu (b. 1931), the first black general secretary of the South African Council for Churches, was also a major figure. He had become the Anglican bishop of Lesotho in 1976, and in 1984 he received the Nobel Peace Prize for his advocacy of non-violent resistance to apartheid. Two years later, he became archbishop of Cape Town. Tutu preached what was known as contextual theology, the South African equivalent of liberation theology, so-called because it sought to speak to the 'context' of South African Christianity and to change it. Its advocates believed that the problems of South Africa in general and its churches in particular could be addressed only when the underlying injustices of society as a whole began to change.

In 1985, the Institute for Contextual Theology issued its famous *Kairos Document*. Signed by 150 church members, this contrasted the 'church theology' of institutional racism and its idolatrous God of segregation with the '*kairos*' of reconciliation. '*Kairos*' is Greek for an event or moment of opportunity: the authors of the document were therefore calling upon the church to make the most of this moment when reconciliation might be possible, to create a 'prophetic theology' of reconciliation. This could be done by working for the oppressed and under-privileged.

Those who took this view were often subject to persecution. A number of anti-apartheid activists, such as Diliza Matshoba, were assassinated. Hundreds more were imprisoned and often tortured. In 1988, the headquarters of the South African Council of Churches in Johannesburg was blown up, and the Catholic Bishops' Conference building in Pretoria was burned down.

The campaign, escalating on both sides, ceased only after F.W. de Klerk became president in 1989. He legalized the ANC and other forbidden parties, and he released ANC leader Nelson Mandela from prison after twenty-seven years. A national conference of church leaders was held at Rustenburg. Here, in a historic declaration,

the South African churches – including even the NGK – agreed that apartheid had been a sinful institution. Those who had been party to it repented and asked forgiveness from God and from South Africa. In so doing, the South African churches moved into a new era, one of uncertainty, where their own role in the reconstruction of South African society was unclear.

For throughout this whole period, the Christian centre of gravity was shifting in South Africa from the traditional, institutional, largely white-led churches to a new kind of church – spontaneous, local, and black-dominated. These were the 'AICs' – African Initiated (or, sometimes, Indigenous or Independent) Churches – and their rise in South Africa presaged a Christian revolution throughout the continent.

THE SPIRIT AND THE LAW: PENTECOSTALISM AND THE AFRICAN INITIATED CHURCHES

As we have seen, the story of African Christianity in the twentieth century is, rather like that in other parts of the world, one of control gradually passing from white missionaries to indigenous peoples. That has happened in two ways – first, the passing of authority within the established churches to Africans, as pioneered in the nineteenth century with the Anglican Samuel Crowther and in the twentieth with the Catholic Joseph Kiwanuka in Uganda. But we have already seen something of the second way – the establishment by Africans of new churches of their own. These are usually known as AICs. The term is perhaps slightly insulting – as if it were surprising or noteworthy that churches in Africa should be initiated by Africans – as well as rather artificial. For example, it is common to distinguish between the 'prophetic' churches of the 1920s and 30s and the true AICs of the post-World War II era, but in fact it may be equally valid to see them as parts of the same movement. Indeed, the more durable of the prophetic churches, such as the Harrists or the Kimbanguists, were in effect the first AICs. The main difference is that AICs do not, as a rule, derive from great

God does have a sense of humor. Who in their right minds could ever have imagined South Africa to be an example of anything but the most ghastly awfulness, of how not to order a nation's race relations and its governance? We South Africans were the unlikeliest lot and that is why God has chosen us... God intends that others might look at us and take courage.

Desmond Tutu, *No future without forgiveness*, 1999

Throughout the Bible God appears as the liberator of the oppressed. He is not neutral. He does not attempt to reconcile Moses and Pharaoh, to reconcile the Hebrew slaves with their Egyptian oppressors or to reconcile the Jewish people with any of their late oppressors. Oppression is sin and it cannot be compromised with, it must be done away with. God takes sides with the oppressed.

The *Kairos Document*, 1985

prophets like those of the pre-war era. They may have charismatic founders, such as John Chilembwe of the Providence Industrial Mission in Malawi who led an abortive uprising in 1915; but these figures are not idolized as William Wade Harris or Simon Kimbangu were. In fact, there is currently considerable disagreement about how to categorize or even identify AICs.

Whatever one calls them, there is no denying the impact and importance of the AICs. By 1985 it was estimated that there were some 12,000 of them throughout the continent, with some 33 million members. But what are they exactly? The essential characteristic is that they are new churches, founded by Africans to serve their local communities, as opposed to new congregations within the established denominations. But attempts to find common characteristics other than that have not always borne fruit – hardly surprising given the vast number of churches in question. A useful distinction with AICs is between 'Ethiopian' and 'Zionist' churches. 'Ethiopian' churches are so-called, not because they have anything to do with the Ethiopian Orthodox Church, but because like that church they are indigenous: that is, they differ from the 'mainstream' churches only in their origins. A good example might be the Moshoeshoe Berean Bible Readers Church, founded in Lesotho in 1922 by the charismatic evangelist Walter Matitta. This church followed orthodox Reformed doctrine.

'Zionist' churches, by contrast, are not simply indigenous but have quite a different flavour from the mainstream churches. It is a distinction recognized by the churches themselves: in Lesotho, for example, the Zionist churches refer to themselves as the *Dikereke tsa Moya* (churches of the Spirit) as opposed to the *Dikereke tsa Molao* (churches of the Law). The tension between them that this suggests is a little like that between Pentecostals and evangelicals in the USA – and indeed, African Zionism owes a great deal to American Pentecostalism.

The movement goes back to a South

African named P.L. Le Roux (1865–1943), whose commitment to what he believed to be the promptings of the Holy Spirit apparently overrode his fidelity to any ecclesiastical organizations. In the early years of the twentieth century he worked as a Dutch Reformed missionary to the Zulus. But he became deeply influenced by a recently founded church in Chicago called the Christian Catholic Apostolic Church, and in 1903 he left the Dutch Reformed Church to found a new one, the Zionist Apostolic Church. This church had much in common with the Pentecostal movement which was just beginning to emerge in the USA. Like the Pentecostal churches, the Zionist church emphasized the power of the Holy Spirit within the congregation: there was speaking in tongues and healing. Indeed, Le Roux himself became more deeply involved in Pentecostalism and left the Zionist church in 1908 to join the Apostolic Faith Mission, leaving his earlier experiment in the hands of his follower Daniel Nkonyane. However, the Zionist church expanded rapidly to become a network throughout South Africa. As we saw in Chapter 15, Pentecostalism was itself deeply influenced by African American Christianity to begin with. Its emphasis on the power of God through the Holy Spirit, and the subjection of the life of the community to that power, was extremely attractive to the Africans, especially the Zulus, the Swazi and the Sotho. In the 1920s, it spread to northern South Africa under Ignatius Lekhanyane and to Zimbabwe under Andreas Shoko and others.

It is something of an irony that the archetypal African Initiated Church should have been founded by a white South African inspired by an American movement, but Le Roux's abdication from the church, and its massive success with the black people of southern Africa, ensured that its origins were quickly forgotten. Zionism was a movement, rather than a single church, and leaders such as those already mentioned founded their own groups based upon their own 'Zions' or holy cities, usually near a river or lake which would be

Man has two natures in one person – the human nature and divine nature. When you are talking of healing, you are talking of divine holiness. Divine holiness comes from God Almighty. The gift was given to me, not for the work of righteousness, which I have done. The gift of healing is given to me according to his grace.

T. P. Joshua, pastor of the Synagogue Church of All Nations, Lagos, on his healing and exorcism ministry renamed 'Jordan' and used for baptisms. Typically, these leaders believed themselves to be divinely called: they would often have dreams or visions, perhaps of God or Jesus, or of their own ancestors, calling them to found a new holy city. Often this would be associated with a period of illness, during which the visionary drew close to heaven. Thus again we see similarities to the great prophets of the inter-war period.

The most important of these leaders was Isaiah Shembe (1867–1935), who was very similar to those prophets. In 1911 he established the Church of the Nazarites (or the Amanazaretha) at Ekuphakameni near Durban, where he soon became regarded as a true prophet of God – indeed, more than this, for the people would sing of him:

> Our Liberator,
> We Dingaan's people
> We have heard him,
> He has come,
> The Liberator has arrived
> You, Zulus, we have heard him.

This was one of the songs in the Amanazaretha hymn book, which was mostly written by Shembe himself, suggesting a certain genius for self-promotion on the part of this prophet. Indeed, after Shembe's death he continued to be revered as the revealer of Christ to the Zulu, and the church was run by his family.

Today, the Zionist churches and related movements continue to be of major importance in South Africa; the country has far more than its fair share of AICs (some 4,000, accounting for a third of the black population), as though they had somehow drifted down and collected at the tip of the continent. Yet they are found throughout Africa, and they really came into their own in the independence era. Before this, they were the object of considerable suspicion on the part of the colonial authorities and the established churches alike. But once African nations became independent, the AICs often became the source of considerable pride. After all, people reasoned, if the country deserved its own

Worshippers at the Victory Army Church of God, Kinshasa, Congo, in 2002. This AIC has rocketed in popularity to such an extent that during services hundreds of people stand outside, unable to fit in the building.

African church music

Africans naturally love music. Most festivities are accompanied by one kind of music or another. The music varies from celebration to celebration. Only the best music is considered good enough for the celebration in order to give it the grandeur it deserves. This natural tendency flows into the African worshipping forms. Music gives sweetness to the expression of prayer, promotes the union of minds and makes the celebration more vibrant. Music in African worship is not something that looks like an appendix – it springs rather from the very nature of the celebration. For Africans, worship is always a sort of feast, a means of glorification of God, a commemoration of the Easter victory of Christ. Profound participation in such a celebration is quite inconceivable apart from its joyful expression in music.

Actually, worship assumes a very noble character when it is celebrated with music. With such melodious music, prayers assume a very high joyous expression, while unity of hearts is rendered most profoundly from the unity of voices. With music in worship, minds are raised more easily to the heavenly realities by means of the splendour of sacred signs and symbols, and the whole celebration prefigures, more clearly, the worship which is performed in the heavenly Jerusalem.

Remarkable achievements have taken place in the area of church music in Africa. Today more than ever, the efforts of various choirs, choir masters and composers have become evident especially in the area of compositions. One cannot fail to admire and appreciate the beautiful, soul-searching and often hair-raising songs composed by these exceptionally talented people in the local languages and vernacular. One sees already a great potentiality in the African music treasury, which is a clear indication that there will

be no limit to the greater achievements Africans can attain in church music.

In most local churches in Africa the music at worship comprises predominantly local compositions, well rendered in beautiful rhythm through local musical instruments, as well as hand-clapping, dancing, swaying and so on. At times church music is accompanied with a gospel band. All these add in no small measure to making African worship very active and lively and enhancing participation a great deal. Local compositions are to a very large extent preferred to the other chants composed in foreign languages.

The Holy Spirit occupies a prominent role in African church music. There is hardly any worship that commences without the invocation of the Holy Spirit in songs of various types. Theologically, it is the Spirit of God that brings the worshipping community together from the various corners of their world to worship God. The Spirit enables the worshipping community even to pray and to call God 'Abba' (father). Jesus Christ is central in the worshipping form of the Africans. So a lot of songs are composed in the name of Jesus. Then to God the Father is directed all worship, honour, majesty, power, glory, wisdom and thanksgiving from the people of God through Christ in the unity of the Holy Spirit.

When it comes to praising God, the typical African in worship hardly checks time, for any amount of time spent in worship to God is time well invested. Africans are very exhaustive in enumerating God's attributes, as in this chant, which is a typical example of a popular hymn that cuts across all denominations in most African worship:

Glory be to God in the highest!
Response: Alleluia! (twice)
We adore you!
We honour you!
We thank you!
We praise you!
We glorify you!

Glory be to God in the highest!
Response: Alleluia! (twice)
To the Father!
Lord Jesus!
Holy Spirit!

Glory be to God in the highest!
Response: Alleluia! (twice)
Everybody shout Alleluia!
For his Anointing!
For his Blessings!
For his Bounty!
For his Fidelity!
For his Glory!
For his Goodness!
For his Grace!
For his Greatness!
For his Healing!
For his Kindness!
For his Love!
For his Mercy!
For his Presence!
For his Wisdom!
He is EMMANUEL!

Church music in African celebration forms part and parcel of worship. Each piece of music underscores the aspect of the mystery of Christ being celebrated and the liturgical season in question. Against this backdrop, the music plays an important role towards a deeper understanding of the mystery celebrated and facilitates the appropriation of the mystery into the personal and communal life of the worshipping community.

PATRICK CHUKWUDEZIE CHIBUKO

government, then it should have its own churches, too. Indeed, membership of such a church acquired a certain social cachet: many churches have uniforms, and their members wear them even in everyday life; and many companies prefer to employ AIC members, since they have a reputation for

hard work and honesty. Tobacco and alcohol are usually forbidden for church members. As the number of AICs suggests, most are small, with only local appeal. But some have transcended their origins to become major factors in their own nations, such as the Aladura Church in Nigeria.

Even in these cases, however, one of the defining features of AICs is their local flavour. There may be large rallies or dramatic festivals, but most of the time they meet in groups of perhaps a couple of dozen people.

Another common feature of AICs is the way in which they incorporate traditional indigenous religious beliefs or customs. We have already seen how the African Christian prophets were, in many ways, similar to traditional African prophets, and we can see the same sort of similarities in the AICs. These churches typically stress the power of God and his active intervention on behalf of his people, just as indigenous religions regarded their gods, and this is often demonstrated by the prominence of healing ceremonies. These are not just for physical ailments. They can also be performed for spiritual or mental malaise, or as reconciliation ceremonies where relationships have broken down. In each case, the sufferer is presented to the community and the divine power is invoked. Holy objects may be used – a staff, the Bible or holy water – in a Christian counterpart to the 'fetishes' of old.

But such 'Africanizing' of Christianity remains controversial among the AICs and indeed African Christians in general. Consider the case of the Swazi, whose worldview was traditionally dominated by the spirits of the dead (*emadloti*). The living would pray to the *emadloti* to intercede with the divine on their behalf, and remember them with sacrifices and other rituals. The *emadloti*, for their part, would watch over the living and often help or warn them, perhaps through dreams. Today the *emadloti* remain a major element of Swazi culture, and they are therefore a highly controversial topic among Christians. Some simply regard them as demons. Others believe that veneration of the *emadloti* is compatible with Christianity. Emmanuel Milingo (b. 1930), for example, the former Catholic archbishop of Lusaka, argues that an authentic Swazi theology can present Christ himself as the greatest *emadloti*, a figure of the past who is with us today and

intercedes with God on our behalf. On this conception, instead of opposing the traditional spiritual world with a new Christian one, the traditional spirits can simply be Christianized. Milingo himself is a controversial figure – the Vatican's concerns about his large healing and exorcism services led to his being removed from Lusaka in 1983, and he subsequently became involved with the 'Moonies' and even briefly married before returning to the Catholic fold. Throughout it, he remained committed to the ideal of the church existing to minister to the people, for which he insisted that it had to become genuinely African. This meant becoming open to the uniquely African spiritual experience, and to the spiritual world that had always been central to African beliefs. Debates of this kind are still highly prominent among churches throughout Africa today, whether AICs or established denominations: to what extent can the church legitimately take on the forms or even the beliefs of pre-Christian faiths?

The AICs remain on the move. Much of Africa has been conquered by either them or Pentecostal elements within the traditional churches, and now they are spreading overseas. As we saw earlier, many young Africans in the post-war years began travelling to Europe or America, and this trend has continued, with large numbers of Africans either visiting or moving permanently to the old colonial powers. They have brought their religions with them. In south London, for example, where there are many West Africans, there are AICs practically everywhere one looks – some in large and fancy-looking buildings, others wedged in between small shops on busy thoroughfares. These churches have successfully transplanted African-style Pentecostalism to Europe, and they have started outreach and missions to white Europeans – in a kind of reverse replay of the coming of European Christianity to Africa, which came first with settlers and then with missionaries. These churches, like their parent communities in Africa, offer a mixture of Pentecostal-style worship, conservative doctrine and great emphasis on the Bible and the miraculous.

And even where African Christianity has not yet arrived, its influence is felt. We saw in Chapter 15 how the conservatism of African Anglicans has clashed with the liberalism of British and American Anglicans: although the archbishop of Nigeria is lower in the pecking order than the archbishop of Canterbury, there are more active Anglicans in Nigeria now than there are in England, which gives him considerable power within the worldwide Anglican communion. The success of the traditional denominations in Africa, and the spread overseas of the AICs and related churches, both mean that Christians in Europe and America are being forced (whether they like it or not) to take account of African Christianity in a more fundamental way than ever before. The leadership of the traditional denominations is still based in Europe and the USA, but their real power bases, and with them their character and direction, are increasingly to be found in Africa.

THE ANCIENT AFRICAN CHURCHES

If the twentieth century was the century in which Africa became largely Christian, the exception, by some irony, was that part of the continent that had known Christianity for the longest. North Africa – including the Maghreb and Egypt – remained very predominantly Muslim. But here too the church continued to survive, if not to thrive, much as it had ever since the seventh century. Tunisia and Algeria gained their independence in 1962, after which most Europeans left and Christianity – primarily Catholicism – became a very small but resolute minority interest there. Despite the often brutal measures that the French had taken to try to prevent Algeria gaining its independence, the years since have seen good relations between the Catholics and Muslims in these countries, especially under Cardinal Léon-Étienne Duval, the archbishop of Algeria, who was so concerned for interfaith relations that he was sometimes dubbed 'the bishop of the

Muslims'. In Egypt, meanwhile, the Monophysite Copts still formed the largest Christian community, and the early twentieth century found them concentrated in the city of Asyut, which formed almost a Christian enclave in the country. However, conditions were improving for them. The inter-war years saw modernization not only of industry but of society as well. In the 1920s, laws restricting women's role in society were relaxed, such as the ending of compulsory veil-wearing, and Muslims and Christians alike shared a growing sense of Egyptian nationalism. In this climate, relations between the two groups were perhaps better than they had ever been. In a remarkable display of interfaith cooperation, priests preached in mosques while imams addressed congregations in churches.

The situation deteriorated in the later twentieth century, however. In 1956, President Gamar Abdel Nasser declared that Islam was the state religion, leading many Christians to leave Egypt – something which explains, in part, the two million Coptic Christians who are today scattered throughout the western world. And in the 1970s and 80s, President Anwar Sadat became increasingly suspicious of Christian ambitions within Egypt, even accusing the Copts' leader, Shenoudah III (reigned from 1971), of planning to set up an autonomous Christian state at Asyut. In 1981 he effectively outlawed the Coptic Church, arresting Shenoudah III and a number of other bishops and priests. Yet the persecution ended almost as soon as it had begun: a month later, the president was assassinated and Coptic Christianity once again recognized.

Yet throughout all this, the church underwent a number of renewals. One of the most remarkable occurred in 1968, when for nearly a year the Virgin Mary appeared to worshippers at a church in Cairo. Miracles and healings abounded and were even found to occur among Muslim visitors – something that helped interfaith relations no end. Perhaps no less surprising, and more important for the

long-term survival of Coptic Christianity, has been the resurgence of monasticism in the closing decades of the twentieth century. The ancient monasteries of Egypt – oldest of all Christian monasteries, and the prototypes for all that followed – have been there ever since the beginning, surviving even the fall of Rome and the long centuries of Muslim dominance. Inevitably, their inhabitants had dwindled in number, and by the middle of the twentieth century the monasteries were a shadow of their former selves. But since the 1970s, there has been a great deal of interest in the monasteries from a new generation of Egyptian Christians. In particular, students began visiting the monasteries for extended periods – perhaps a couple of months, perhaps longer – during their studies, either to study Coptic Christianity or as a spiritual retreat. Many stay on and become monks, leading to a rejuvenation of the monastic communities, but most return to their secular lives, taking knowledge of and

interest in the ancient Coptic traditions with them.

The monasteries also acted – and continue to act – as one of the major links between the Egyptian and the Ethiopian churches. Indeed, the Ethiopian church certainly had its ups and downs in the twentieth century. As we saw in Chapter 13, a strong king, Yohannes IV, brought order and unity to the country and to the church at the end of the nineteenth century; he was aided in this by Menelik of Shewa (1844–1913), who succeeded him as Menelik II in 1889. This emperor was a strong leader who founded a new capital, Addis Ababa, and kept up vigorous military campaigns to extend Ethiopian power in the south while building diplomatic and trade relations with Europe and the USA. He also, in an age of colonialism, struck a major blow for African independence when in 1896 he defeated an invading Italian army at Adwa. The Italians had established a colony at neighbouring Eritrea, on the coast, and had ambitions to extend their

St Antony's monastery, Al Zaafarana, Egypt. This monastery was founded in AD 356, just after the death of Antony of Egypt, making it the oldest active monastery in the world.

O Lord, almighty in whom there is no weakness, eternal in whom there is no transience; in admiring Your work as well as Your judgements, a created being, even after much searching, cannot fathom them – except to a limited extent. It is a subtle secret which a creature, even after much exploring, cannot know but which You alone do know: why in the immediate past as well as now You have made the Ethiopian people, from the ordinary man to the Emperor, sink in a sea of distress for a time, and why You have made the Italian people up to its King swim in a sea of joy for a time.

Emperor Haile Selassie of Ethiopia, *Autobiography*, preface, 1937

power into what they regarded as its natural hinterland. Indeed, there was considerable cultural crossover between the two regions. The Eritreans of the highlands, who were mostly Christian, regarded themselves as Ethiopian. And many Eritreans, fed up with Italian colonial policy, moved to Ethiopia in the early decades of the twentieth century. In the coastal lowlands, however, most people were Muslim and felt little sympathy for Ethiopia.

Menelik was also keen to extend the influence of the Ethiopian Orthodox Church throughout the country, and he ordered his priests to evangelize the pagan areas of Ethiopia – often encouraging quick baptisms with relatively little preparation. The policy was quite successful, however, and Ethiopia saw a gradual increase in monasticism and many new churches being built. Indeed, many Muslims converted to Christianity too: the most dramatic conversion was that of Sheikh Zakaryas of Begemdir, who in the 1890s had a series of visions of Jesus which led him to try to reform Islam in a Christian direction. Eventually, in 1910, he and 3,000 of his followers were baptized, creating a culturally distinct minority within the Ethiopian church.

Ethiopia was plunged into crisis when, after a long illness, Menelik fell into an intermittent coma in 1909. The great emperor's end was protracted and undignified: as he lay sick and incapacitated, his wife and his nobles squabbled over the succession. When he finally died in 1913, his grandson, Lij Iyasu, took power, but he alienated the nobles and in 1916 was deposed and replaced by Zewditu, daughter of Menelik and the first empress to rule in her own right since the queen of Sheba. However, the power behind the throne was an ambitious and extremely able noble named Tafari Makonnen, ras (or duke) of Shewa. In 1930, after already having ruled the country with a strong hand for a decade, Ras Tafari became Emperor Haile Selassie (his baptismal name, meaning 'Power of the Trinity').

Haile Selassie (1892–1975), the last Lion of Judah, was one of the most remarkable rulers of the twentieth century. He reformed the government, built up relations with other countries and generally did his best to modernize Ethiopia as far as possible. He gained the sympathies of much of the world in 1935, when Mussolini finally ordered an Italian invasion of the country. As the Italians advanced in April 1935, Haile Selassie, fleeing before them, prayed for several days, without food or drink, in the great rock church of Medhane Alem at Lalibela. The prayers came to nothing, and the emperor was forced to leave for Europe, to plead unsuccessfully for international intervention.

There was intermittent guerrilla resistance for the five years during which Italy held Ethiopia. The church was involved in much of this. In July 1936, for example, the archbishop of Dessie, Petros, was suspected of implication in an attack on Italian troops at Addis Ababa, and he was shot. The following year, during a general purge of the Ethiopian elite following an attempt on the Italian administrator's life, the ancient monastery of Debre Libanos was destroyed; 297 monks and 23 others were shot, and hundreds more sent to concentration camps. The resistance was maintained until, in 1941, British forces liberated Ethiopia. Returning from his exile in the English provincial town of Bath, Haile Selassie spoke from his palace to the crowd beneath, imploring them to act as Christians and not to avenge themselves against the Italians.

While the emperor consolidated his power and successfully restored peace and prosperity throughout Ethiopia, things were very different in Eritrea, which the Allies had seized from Italy. No one could agree what to do with the country. In 1949 there was considerable violence between Christians, who wanted to be merged with Ethiopia, and Muslims, who did not. In 1952 the United Nations gave Eritrea its own federal government, under the

sovereignty of the Ethiopian emperor.

Tensions between Christians and Muslims in Eritrea were mirrored by similar problems in the Ogaden, in the south of Ethiopia itself. Here, most people were Muslim. However, much of the land was underpopulated, and in the 1960s the Ethiopian government, as part of its plan to improve agriculture throughout the country, settled large numbers of people here, including many retired soldiers. Most were Christian, and inevitably, problems arose. Many indigenous people rebelled, forming the Ogaden Liberation Front in 1963, which had links to neighbouring Somalia. Indeed, many people fled to Somalia, which provided asylum to these refugees and also arms to the insurgents within Ethiopia. This situation continued until 1971, when Ethiopian forces largely subdued the province.

Through it all, the Ethiopian Orthodox Church remained strong. A major event occurred in 1959, when the Coptic Church finally upgraded the abuna to full patriarch status. Abuna Basilios became the first

Ethiopian patriarch of the Ethiopian church, finally ending the centuries-long dependence upon Egypt. However, there were trying times ahead. In 1974 there was a Marxist coup, and a military junta known as the Derg seized power. The aged Haile Selassie was imprisoned, to be (probably) murdered the following year. A period of terror was instigated, as the Derg sought to purge the country of its political and ideological opponents. Among these were leading churchmen; for, like other communist regimes, the Derg proclaimed 'equality of faith' but in reality tried to oppose Christianity as much as possible. The patriarch, Tewophilos, was executed in 1977. His government-approved successor was a hermit named Tekle Haimanot, but the Coptic Church refused to recognize him on the grounds that Tewophilos's death had not been formally announced. There was therefore a complete split between the Egyptian and Ethiopian churches. Meanwhile, Tekle Haimanot proved less cooperative than the Derg had hoped: he was a highly disciplined ascetic

The emperor Haile Selassie of Ethiopia inspects the Grenadier Guards in London, 1954, during a state visit to the country that had housed him during his exile two decades earlier.

and theological conservative who had no inclination to compromise with the communists. When Tekle Haimanot died in 1988, a more amenable character named Merkorios was installed.

The Derg period was one of disaster for Ethiopia. Their attempts to create large nationalized farms, involving the movement of huge sections of the population from one place to another, backfired, causing the notorious famine of the mid-1980s, in which an estimated seven million people died. In 1991 the Derg were toppled and the church was re-established as the national religion of Ethiopia. Patriarch Merkorios was forced to abdicate, being replaced by Paulos; Merkorios went into exile, where he claimed that his abdication had been made under duress. Some bishops went with him and formed a synod in exile, which is still recognized by some Ethiopian Orthodox today, in a schism that remains unresolved.

Yet despite all these upheavals, Ethiopian faith and spirituality have remained remarkably resilient. The church's official title today is the Ethiopian Orthodox Tewahido Church, ('*tewahido*' being a Ge'ez word for 'union'). This title reflects the church's adherence to its ancient Monophysite faith and refusal to compromise with the Chalcedonianism of the larger Catholic, Orthodox and Protestant churches; it is, today, the largest of the Monophysite churches. Since 2000, and the granting of independence to Eritrea, it has also recognized (not always willingly) the independence of its smaller sibling, the Eritrean Orthodox Church.

The church retains not only its distinctive doctrine but also the distinctive appearance of its buildings. The early churches in Ethiopia were built in the Roman style, long and rectangular. As time passed, Ethiopian churches became rounder. They are sometimes regarded as inspired by the Ethiopians' understanding of the Temple of Solomon, remembering their strong belief that their nation and

Ethiopia, the land located in North East Africa with her many thousand years of history, is the land of God... the histories of almost all the countries in the world were written only by men of the world, whereas the history of Ethiopia, in addition, has been written, in the Holy Scripture, by the guidance of the Holy Spirit.

Kessis Kefyalew Merahi, *The contribution of the Orthodox Tewahido Church to the Ethiopian civilization, 1999*

their faith in God derived from Solomon's son. But it has also been suggested that round churches evolved from round houses, typical of medieval Ethiopia.

Whatever their origins, typical Ethiopian churches are round or octagonal, normally built on a hill, often with a thatched roof. In a western long church, the sanctuary is at the eastern end; in an Ethiopian church it is in the middle, and is called the *mäqdäs*. This represents the holy of holies, which was at the heart of the Temple of Solomon. Just as the holy of holies contained the famous ark of the covenant, so too the *mäqdäs* contains the tabot or wooden replica of the ark.

The *mäqdäs* is screened, and only priests – or the king – can enter. Around it is the area known as the *qddist*, which is for those who will receive the Eucharist. Around that is the *kine mahlet*, which is for everyone else. During the divine liturgy, the priests circulate among the congregation throughout this area, praying, blessing them, and perfuming the air with incense. This outer area also contains the choir: thus, the congregation is surrounded by music, and all face inwards towards the representation of the place of God. The Ethiopian church is nothing less than a symbolic representation of the Christian heaven: not for nothing is its service called the divine liturgy.

The Ura Kidane Mehret church on the Zeghe peninsula, Lake Tana, Ethiopia. The late medieval church is filled with tapestries and other artefacts that are even older, providing a link between the modern, living community and its revered past.

GLOSSARY

Words marked in italics provide a cross-reference to head-words in the Glossary.

Apostle   from a Greek word meaning 'one who is sent', referring to the main leaders of the first Christian communities. The most important apostles were Peter, James the Just, and Paul.

Archbishop   the term usually used in the West for a *metropolitan*.

Arianism   a *heresy* of the fourth century, which denied that *Christ* is really the second person of the *Trinity*, that is, that he was God. Arianism was condemned at the Council of Nicaea in AD 325, but survived for many decades afterwards, and has been revived on a number of occasions since.

Arminianism   named after Jacobus Arminius, a Dutch Calvinist who denied the doctrine of *predestination*. Arminianism was condemned at the Synod of Dort in 1618, and was subsequently regarded as a *heresy* by many Calvinists.

Atonement   the *doctrine* that *Christ* saves, a central belief of the *New Testament*. Different Christians have had different views on what salvation means and how Christ brings it about.

Baptism   a ceremonial washing with water, signifying that the person's sins have been forgiven. Baptism is the historic initiation ceremony of Christianity, and is traditionally regarded as one of the *sacraments*.

Bible   a collection of *scriptures* that Christians consider authoritative. The Bible consists of two parts, the *Old Testament* and the *New Testament*. Different *churches*, and different individuals within each church, disagree on how authoritative the Bible should be considered, and on what it means to call it 'inspired' by God. The *canon* of the Bible was established at two African councils in the AD 390s.

Bishop   from a word meaning 'overseer', a bishop is the person in charge of the Christian community in a particular area. Originally, a bishop would have run a single congregation, but as more people became Christians a single city could contain a number of *churches*, each run by their own *priests*, all of whom were subject to the bishop. The area in the control of a bishop is his *see* or *diocese*, and the main church in his diocese is a *cathedral*. An especially important bishop is called a *metropolitan* or *archbishop*, or even a *patriarch*. Some churches, such as the Presbyterian Church, reject the system of bishops.

Bull   after the eleventh century, a pronouncement by the *pope*; after the fifteenth century, the word referred only to those documents signed by the pope and accompanied by his seal.

Caesaropapism   literally, treating the emperor as the *pope*. Where Christianity is the official religion of a state, there has often been a tendency for the secular ruler to try to extend his authority over the church. This began with the emperor Constantine and has been seen, in particular, in medieval Makuria and Byzantium, and early modern Russia and England.

Canon   from the Greek for 'measuring stick', the word 'canon' was used by early Christians to refer to the 'rule of faith', the basic *doctrines* and practices inherited from the *apostles*. Those churches who deviated from this 'canon' were judged *heretical*. The word 'canon' subsequently came to be applied to the *Bible* and the books that compose it: a 'canonical' work is part of the Bible, while a 'deuterocanonical' book is part of the 'secondary canon' or Apocrypha.

Cardinal   a very senior cleric within the Catholic Church. The word was used from the fifth century onwards to refer to certain important priests, but later in the Middle Ages came to refer mostly to leading *bishops* and *archbishops*. Since the twelfth century, the cardinals have had the responsibility of electing each new pope.

Catechumen someone who has converted to Christianity, but has not yet been baptised and is being instructed in the *doctrines* of the faith first.

Catharism a medieval *heresy*, indeed almost a rival church with its heartlands in what is now southern France. The Cathars seem to have been rather like latter-day *Gnostics*, believing the physical world to be evil. The Cathars were defeated and dispersed in 1242.

Cathedral from the Greek word for 'seat', a cathedral is a *church* where a *bishop* presides (and, in antiquity, literally had a seat). The cathedral is therefore the main church in any city, and probably the largest.

Catholicos the *patriarch* of Ctesiphon (later Baghdad), and head of the Church of the East. A dispute over the succession in the sixteenth century resulted in two rival lines of patriarchs: today, one is resident in Baghdad, and the other in the United States. The head of the Armenian church is also called 'catholicos', and his *see* is Etchmiadzin.

Christ the Greek translation of 'messiah'. From an early stage, Christians believed that Jesus was the Christ, a belief that gave them their name. The word 'Christ' soon came to apply to Christ rather like a name, although it was really a title.

Christology *doctrines* about *Christ*, either his person (who he was) or his work (what he did, also known as the *atonement*).

Church this can mean a number of things. First, it can mean a single Christian community. Second, it can mean the building in which they meet. Third, it can mean the organization (or *denomination*) to which the community belongs. Fourth, it can mean all Christians everywhere.

Congregation this means two things. First, it is the group of people who worship at a particular *church*. Second, it is an organization within the *curia* of the Catholic Church with a defined authority and purpose, rather like a ministry within a secular government.

Council a group of *church* leaders, meeting to address some particular issue (also known as a *synod*). Councils often issue *creeds* which set out their decisions. In Roman Catholic and Orthodox thinking, when a council represents the whole Catholic and Orthodox churches, it is called ecumenical. There have been only seven ecumenical councils in history (although Catholics and Anglicans recognize only the first four of these).

Creed a list of *doctrines*, usually issued by a *council* or other group representing a *church*, as their official faith. This is a standard way of establishing the *orthodox* faith of a church. The most important creeds in Christian history include the Nicene Creed and the Apostles' Creed.

Curia effectively the government of the Catholic Church, made up of various *congregations*.

Denomination a Christian organization. For example, the Catholic Church is one denomination, while the Church of England is another. Different denominations are usually completely independent of each other, although sometimes they may cooperate, through the ecumenical movement.

Diocese sometimes called a 'see', the area under the control of a *bishop*.

Dissenter in England, a member of a church other than the official Church of England.

Docetism from the Greek word for 'seeming', the *doctrine* that *Christ* only appeared to be human. Docetism emerged in the first century and was quickly condemned as a *heresy*.

Doctrine a belief, often defined officially or semi-officially in a *creed*. When a doctrine is part of the official faith of a *church* or group, it is part of *orthodoxy*; if it is at variance with orthodoxy, it is *heresy*.

Dominicans together with the *Franciscans*, the most well-known mendicant order of *friars*. The Dominicans were founded by Dominic de Gusmán in 1216.

Easter the most important festival in the Christian calendar, the commemoration of Jesus' resurrection.

Elect in Calvinist theology, those people who, through God's *predestination*, will be saved.

Eucharist one of the central Christian rites, in which believers consume bread and wine in memory of Jesus' Last Supper before his death. Traditionally, the bread and wine are believed to become Jesus' body and blood, although different churches have had different interpretations of what this means, especially among the Protestant denominations. The Catholic Church normally calls the Eucharist the *Mass*.

Fetish a missionaries' name for the indigenous religions of Africa, and for the objects used in those religions.

Franciscans together with the *Dominicans*, the most well-known mendicant order of *friars*. The Franciscans were founded by Francis of Assisi in 1210.

Friar often confused with *monks*, friars are in fact a different kind of order. The most well known are the *Franciscans* and the *Dominicans*, both founded in the early thirteenth century. Unlike monks, the friars were meant to go out into the world and preach, rather than stay in *monasteries* contemplating God – hence the term 'mendicant' orders.

Gnosticism a major religious and philosophical movement that flourished in the second century AD. Gnosticism came in many varieties, but typically involved a belief that the physical world is evil and that secret teachings provide the key to salvation. Gnosticism seems to have existed mainly as a variant of Christianity, and possibly as a semi-independent movement in its own right, but many Christians regarded it as *heretical*. Later, Gnostic ideas resurfaced in Paulinianism, Bogimilism, and Catharism.

Gospel a word meaning 'good news', used in two ways. First, it can mean the Christian message itself. Second, it can refer to one of the four books describing Jesus' life and teachings, which are found in the *New Testament*.

Heresy from a word meaning 'choice', a *doctrine* that is not considered *orthodox*. Often, a heresy is officially defined as such, perhaps in a condemnation by a *church* leader or at a *council*. There have been many movements and doctrines throughout Christian history that have been regarded by others as heretical, notably *Arianism*, *Pelagianism*, *Nestorianism*, *Monophysitism*, *Catharism*, *Arminianism*, and others. But what one church considers heresy, another church may consider orthodoxy, and many modern Christians prefer to avoid such terms in favour of a more tolerant attitude towards different versions of Christianity.

Hermit from the Greek word for 'desert', a hermit is someone who lives entirely alone in a secluded place, in order to focus on God alone. The first great Christian hermit was Antony of Egypt, but the ideal goes back to Jesus himself, who fasted in the desert for forty days after his *baptism*. In the fourth century, many hermits began to live together, becoming *monks*.

Huguenots in the sixteenth and seventeenth centuries, French Protestants. It is not certain where the name came from.

Icon an image, usually of Jesus, the Trinity, or a saint. Icons are traditionally painted in a beautiful but highly stylized manner, intended to lead the mind to God. They are most important to the Orthodox Church, where they have played a central role in worship since the sixth and seventh centuries AD, but some other Christians, especially Protestants, regard their use as potentially (or even actually) idolatrous or superstitious.

Incarnation the *doctrine* that *Christ* was literally God made flesh.

Jesuits see *Society of Jesus*.

Kingdom of God in Judaism and the *Old Testament*, the kingdom of God usually meant the time when God would intervene dramatically in history and establish his personal rule on earth. In later Christianity, the concept would sometimes be reinterpreted to mean the *church*, or an ideal human society.

Lent a period of forty days before *Easter*, when Christians traditionally fast. The forty days commemorate the forty days that Jesus spent fasting in the desert after his *baptism*.

Liberalism in theology, a term that has a wide range of meanings. It usually involves a relatively questioning attitude towards traditional authorities and a desire to use contemporary worldviews and attitudes to restate Christianity.

Liturgy the sequence of hymns, prayers, and other elements that make up a service in *church*.

Mass the Catholic term for the *Eucharist*. Traditionally, the Catholic doctrine of the Mass differs from the Protestant Eucharist in that it is understood as a sacrifice, made by the *priest* to God, in which *Christ's* sacrifice on the cross is presented anew.

Messiah meaning 'anointed one', a figure described in some Jewish *scriptures*, associated with the coming *kingdom of God*. Different groups had different expectations of the Messiah – some believed he would be a warrior–king, others a sort of priest. The first Christians believed that Jesus was the Messiah. 'Christ' is the Greek equivalent of 'messiah'.

Metropolitan the *bishop* of a particularly important city, who has authority over nearby bishops. In the West, metropolitans are usually called *archbishops*.

Monastery a community of *monks*.

Monk from the Greek word for 'alone', indicating that a monk is someone who aims to be alone with God. Monks first emerged in the fourth century AD, inspired by great *hermits* such as Antony of Egypt, but monks typically lived together in communities (or *monasteries*) governed by a 'rule'. Monasticism became a major element in the medieval church in both East and West, with 'rules' by figures such as Basil of Caesarea and Benedict of Nursia proving very influential. Monasticism is still

central to the eastern Orthodox and non-Chalcedonian churches, but has waned in influence in Catholicism and especially in the Protestant churches, which have typically placed much less importance on it.

Monophysitism the *doctrine* that *Christ* had only one nature, not two. Monophysitism was condemned as a *heresy* at the Council of Chalcedon in AD 451, but many Christians refused to accept this and formed the Monophysite churches, which became dominant in Egypt, Ethiopia, and Armenia.

Nestorianism from the teaching of Nestorius, *patriarch* of Constantinople, who was charged with distinguishing between the human and the divine in *Christ* so much that he made Christ into two different people. Nestorianism was condemned as a *heresy* at the Council of Ephesus in AD 431. However, many Christians, especially in Mesopotamia, refused to accept this and split away from the church, creating the 'Nestorian Church' or Church of the East.

New Testament a collection of writings from the early church, which later generations of Christians took to be holy *scriptures*. The *canon* of the New Testament as we know it was first specified by Athanasius of Alexandria in AD 367, and confirmed in the AD 390s.

Old Testament a collection of Jewish *scriptures*, which the early Christians also took to be holy writings. The Old Testament is made up of the *Pentateuch*, the Prophets, and a number of other works, but not all Christian churches agree on the *canon*, that is, which books it contains. Together with the *New Testament*, the Old Testament makes up the Christian *Bible*.

Orthodoxy from the Greek meaning 'right belief', a *doctrine* is considered orthodox if it conforms to what a *church* or group officially believes. Orthodox doctrines may be officially defined in a *creed*. A doctrine that is not orthodox may be condemned as *heresy*.

Patriarch   the *bishop* of one of the most important *dioceses* in early Christianity. After the Council of Chalcedon in AD 451, there were five patriarchs, at Rome, Alexandria, Constantinople, Antioch, and Jerusalem. The Church of the East, however, recognized the bishop of Ctesiphon (later Baghdad) as patriarch instead of the bishop of Jerusalem. The patriarchs of Rome and Alexandria have also been known as *popes*, while the patriarch of Baghdad is the *catholicos*.

Pelagianism   the *doctrines* associated with Pelagius, who in the early fifth century denied the doctrine of original sin and insisted that human beings are free to choose good or evil. Pelagianism was condemned as a *heresy* in AD 417.

Pentateuch   the books of Genesis, Exodus, Numbers, Leviticus, and Deuteronomy, which make up the first five books of the Christian *Old Testament*. Jews traditionally call these five books the Torah. They are traditionally believed to have been written by Moses himself, although most modern scholars date them much later than this. They contain the Jewish Law.

Pilgrimage   a journey to a location considered holy, undertaken for spiritual reasons. The custom of making pilgrimages arose in the fourth century, and was an important element of Christian life in the Middle Ages. Famous pilgrimage sites included Canterbury and Jerusalem. The Protestant *churches* have placed much less emphasis on pilgrimage, but many Catholics continue to practise it, with locations such as Lourdes remaining popular.

Pope   from the Latin for 'father', the title 'pope' was applied to important *bishops* in the early church, above all those of Rome and Alexandria. After the fall of Rome in the sixth century, the pope of Rome became more important in the West, since there were no other Latin-speaking *patriarchs*; already regarded as the head of the church, he grew in authority throughout the Middle Ages. The patriarch of Alexandria is still officially called 'pope', but the title is usually reserved for the Roman patriarch.

Predestination   the belief that everything that happens, including the apparently free actions of human beings, are actually predetermined and controlled by God. This doctrine was developed by Augustine, and later was associated in particular with Calvinism; its denial was associated first with *Pelagianism* and later with *Arminianism*.

Priest   the person in charge of a congregation. A priest is also someone who mediates between God and the people, so many Protestant *churches* do not call their ministers 'priests', because they reject the idea that any member of the church has closer access to God than anyone else.

Relic   an object considered to be particularly holy. Typically, relics are parts of the bodies of saints, but they may also be other items, such as the piece of the 'true cross' discovered by Constantine's mother in the fourth century. In late antiquity and the Middle Ages, Christians believed that these objects could channel God's power. But after the Reformation, the Protestant churches rejected such views as superstitious.

Resurrection   in Christianity, this can refer to the resurrection of Jesus after his death, or to the general resurrection of all people at the end of time. Christianity traditionally regards both resurrections as bodily, contrasting with the belief of some ancient philosophers in the survival of the soul after death.

Revival   a renewal of interest in Christianity, often in a society where other concerns have taken precedence. The term is especially used for the revivals that took place in Britain and America in the eighteenth and nineteenth centuries.

Sacrament   a ritual which has special significance within Christianity. According to the Catholic Church, there are seven sacraments, but most Protestants accept only two, *baptism* and the *Eucharist*. Different *churches* also have different understandings of the nature of the sacraments – whether they are simply signs of God's grace, or actually convey it.

Scriptures   a general term for holy writings, or, in the case of Christianity, another word for the *Bible*.

Secularism   this can mean either a trend in society in which religion becomes less widespread or significant, or a conscious effort or programme to reduce the influence of religion in a society.

See   another word for *diocese*.

Seminary   a college for training *priests*.

Social gospel   a movement in the late nineteenth and early twentieth centuries that sought to use Christian values to improve the living conditions of the poor. The social gospel was usually politically left-wing and allied to theological *liberalism*.

Society of Jesus   often called the 'Jesuits', the society was founded by Ignatius Loyola in 1540 as a society of *priests* dedicated to the service of the Catholic Church. Controversial in many quarters, it was officially disbanded in all countries except Russia in 1773, but restored by the Vatican in 1814.

Synod   a church *council*, either one that meets temporarily to settle a particular issue or a permanent one that meets regularly.

Trinity   according to *orthodox* Christian *doctrine*, God is three persons – Father, Son, and Holy Spirit – but one God. The doctrine developed during the first four centuries of Christianity, but has been denied by various groups, including the *Arians* and *Unitarians*.

Unitarianism   the denial of the *Trinity*, and insistence that God is simply a single person. Modern unitarianism developed during the Enlightenment.

Vatican   the governing authority of the Catholic Church, located in Rome. The Vatican contains St Peter's basilica and St John Lateran, the leading churches of Catholicism, as well as the *pope*'s apartments and the *curia*. Since 1929, Vatican City has been an independent country, the smallest in the world.

CONTRIBUTORS

Lesley Abrams,
Colyer-Fergusson Fellow and Tutor
in Medieval History, Balliol College,
University of Oxford, England

Nigel Aston,
Reader in Early Modern History,
School of Historical Studies,
University of Leicester, England

Kenneth Austin,
Lecturer in Early Modern History,
University of Bristol, England

Jeremy Bangs,
Director of the Leiden American
Pilgrim Museum, USA

Timothy Bradshaw,
Senior Tutor and Tutor in Christian
Doctrine, Regent's Park College,
University of Oxford, England

Patrick Chibuko,
Liturgical Commission Chairman,
Catholic diocese of Enugu, Nigeria

Justin Clegg,
Curator of Medieval Literary
Manuscripts, The British Library,
England

Allison Coudert,
Professor of Religious Studies,
Department of Religious Studies,
UC Davis, USA

Richard Cross,
Tutor in Theology, Oriel College,
University of Oxford, England

Douglas Davies,
Professor in the Study of Religion,
Department of Theology,
University of Durham, England

Dr Mark Edwards,
Fellow of Christ Church College,
University of Oxford, England

Arthur Freeman,
Professor of the New Testament,
Moravian Theological Seminary, USA

Thomas Graumann,
Senior Lecturer in Early Church
History, Faculty of Divinity,
University of Cambridge, England

John Healey,
Professor of Semitic Studies,
Department of Religions and Theology,
University of Manchester, England

David Hempton,
Professor of Church History, School
of Theology, Boston University, USA

Charles Hill,
European Secretary of The Council
for Christian Unity, England

Edward Howells,
Lecturer in Christian Spirituality,
Heythrop College, England

Malcolm Jones,
Professor Emeritus, Department
of Russian and Slavonic Studies,
University of Nottingham, England

Ogbu Kalu,
Professor of World Christianity,
McCormick Theological Seminary, USA

Andrew Knowles,
Canon Theologian at Chelmsford
Cathedral, England; associate of St
John's College, Nottingham, England

David Lindberg,
Hilldale Professor Emeritus of the
History of Science, Department of
the History of Science, USA

Andrew Louth,
Professor in the Department of Theology,
University of Durham, England

John McGuckin,
Professor of Early Church History,
Union Theological Seminary, USA

Peter Nockles,
Lecturer in Church History,
John Rylands University Library
of Manchester, England

Thomas O'Loughlin,
Reader in Historical Theology,
Department of Theology and
Religious Studies, University of Wales,
Lampeter, Wales

Edward Peters,
Henry Charles Lea Professor of History,
Department of History, University of
Pennsylvania, USA

Stephen Platten,
Bishop of Wakefield, England

Samuel Powell,
Chair and Professor of Philosophy
and Religion, School of Theology and
Christian Ministry, Point Loma Nazarene
University, USA

Thomas Reilly,
Associate Professor of Asian Studies,
Seaver College, Pepperdine University,
USA

Jon Roberts,
Professor of History, Department of
History, Boston University, USA

Michael Robson,
Dean of St Edmund's College,
University of Cambridge, England

Paul Rorem,
Benjamin B. Warfield Professor of
Medieval Church History, Princeton
Theological Seminary, USA

Constantine Scouteris,
Professor of the History of Christian
Doctrine, Department of Theology,
University of Athens, Greece

Elina Screen,
Research Associate, Department of
Coins and Metals, Fitzwilliam Museum,
University of Cambridge, England

Paul Steeves,
Professor of History and Director of
Russian studies, College of Arts and
Sciences, Stetson University, USA

Paul Thomas,
Professor at the Department of English,
Brigham Young University, USA

Carl Trueman,
Professor of Historical Theology,
Westminster Theological Seminary, USA

Peter Walker,
Tutor in New Testament and Biblical
Interpretation, Wycliffe Hall, Oxford,
England

Philip Walters,
Director of Research, The Keston
Institute, Oxford, England

Thomas Weinandy,
Honorary Fellow of Greyfriar's College,
Oxford, UK; Executive Director of the
Secretariat for Doctrine and Pastoral
Practices of the United States
Conference of Catholic Bishops

Mark Williams,
Professor and Head of the Department
of East Asian Studies, University of
Leeds, England

Ira Zepp,
Professor Emeritus in Religious Studies,
McDaniel College, USA

BIBLIOGRAPHY

GENERAL

Ahlstrom, S. *A religious history of the American people* New Haven, CT; London: Yale University Press 2nd ed. 2004

Belitto, C. *The general councils: a history of the twenty-one general councils from Nicaea to Vatican II* New York: Paulist Press 2002

Bokenkotter, T. *A concise history of the Catholic Church* rev. ed. New York: Doubleday 1990

Breward, I. *A history of the churches in Australasia* Oxford: Oxford University Press 2001

Constantilos, D. *Understanding the Greek Orthodox Church* 3rd ed. Brookline, MA: Hellenic College Press 1998

Duffy, E. *Saints and sinners: a history of the Popes* 2nd ed. New Haven, CT; London: Yale University Press 2002

Fernando, L. and Gispert-Sauch, G. *Christianity in India: two thousand years of faith* New Delhi: Viking 2004

Ferngren, G., ed. *Science and religion: a historical introduction* Baltimore, MD; London: John Hopkins University Press 2002

Gritsch, E. *A history of Lutheranism* Minneapolis, MN: Fortress 2002

Hastings, A., ed. *A world history of Christianity* London: Cassell 1999

Isichei, E. *A history of Christianity in Africa: from antiquity to the present* London: SPCK; Grand Rapids, MI: Eerdmans 1995

Küng, H. *Christianity* London: SCM 1995

McBrien, R. *Catholicism* 3rd ed. London: Geoffrey Chapman 1994

McManners, J., ed. *The Oxford history of Christianity* Oxford: Oxford University Press 1990

Noll, M. *A history of Christianity in the United States and Canada* Grand Rapids, MI: Eerdmans; London: SPCK 1992

Pospielovsky, D. *The Orthodox Church in the history of Russia* Crestwood, NY: St Vladimir's Seminary Press 1998

Sundkler, B. and Steed, C. *A history of the church in Africa* Cambridge: Cambridge University Press 2000

Thompson, R. *Religion in Australia: a history* Melbourne; Oxford: Oxford University Press 2002

CHAPTER 1

Barrett, C. K. *Paul: an introduction to his thought* London: Continuum 2001

Brown, R. and Moloney, F. *An introduction to the Gospel of John* New York: Doubleday 2003

Burkett, D. *An introduction to the New Testament and the origins of Christianity* Cambridge: Cambridge University Press 2002

Carroll, J., ed. *The return of Jesus in early Christianity* Peabody, MA: Hendrickson 2000

Chilton, B. and Neusner, J., eds. *The brother of Jesus: James the Just and his mission* Louisville, KY: Westminster John Knox Press 2001

Crossan, J. and Reed, J. *In search of Paul: how Jesus' apostle opposed Rome's empire with God's kingdom* London: SPCK 2005

Davidson, I. *The birth of the church: from Jesus to Constantine*, AD 30–312 Oxford: Monarch 2005

Donfried, K. *Paul, Thessalonica, and early Christianity* Grand Rapids, MI: Eerdmans 2002

Ehrman, B. *Lost Christianities: the battle for Scripture and the faiths we never knew* New York; Oxford: Oxford University Press 2003

Ehrman, B. *The New Testament: a historical introduction to the early Christian writings* 3rd ed. New York; Oxford: Oxford University Press 2004

Grant, R. *Paul in the Roman world: the conflict at Corinth* Louisville, KY; London: Westminster John Knox Press 2001

Hurtado, L. *Lord Jesus Christ: devotion to Jesus in earliest Christianity* Grand Rapids, MI: Eerdmans 2003

Hyldahl, N. *The history of early Christianity* Frankfurt am Maine: Lang 1997

Lampe, P. *From Paul to Valentinus: Christians at Rome in the first two centuries* London: T&T Clark 2003

Lapham, F. *An introduction to the New Testament apocrypha* London: T&T Clark 2003

Nanos, M. *The irony of Galatians: Paul's letter in first-century context* Minneapolis, MN: Fortress 2001

Nanos, M. *The mystery of Romans: the Jewish context of Paul's letter* Minneapolis, MN: Fortress 1996

Painter, J. *Just James: the brother of Jesus in history and tradition* Minneapolis, MN: Fortress; Columbia, SC: University of South Carolina Press 1999

Patzia, A. *The emergence of the church: context, growth, leadership and worship* Downers Grove, IL: InterVarsity Press 2001

Perkins, P. *Peter: apostle for the whole church* Minneapolis, MN: Fortress 2000

Rowland, C. *Christian origins* 2nd. Ed. London: SPCK 2002

Sanders, E. *The historical figure of Jesus* London: Penguin 1993

Shanks, H., ed. *Christianity and rabbinic Judaism: a parallel history of their origins and early development* Washington, DC: Biblical Archaeology Society 1992

Skarsaune, O. *In the shadow of the Temple: Jewish influences on early Christianity* Downers Grove, IL: InterVarsity Press 2002

Slee, M. *The church in Antioch in the first century CE: communion and conflict* London; New York: Sheffield Academic Press 2003

Stegemann, E. and Stegemann, W. *The Jesus movement: a social history of its first century* Edinburgh: T&T Clark 1999

Theissen, G. *Fortress introduction to the New Testament* Minneapolis, MN: Fortress 2003

Theissen, G. *The religion of the earliest churches: creating a symbolic world* Minneapolis, MN: Fortress 1999

Tomkins, S. *Paul and his world* Oxford: Lion 2004

Vermès, G. *The changing faces of Jesus* New York; London: Penguin 2002

White, J. *Evidence and Paul's journeys: an historical investigation into the travels of the apostle Paul* Hilliard, OH: Parsagard 2001

Wright, N.T. *The resurrection of the son of God* London: SPCK 2003

CHAPTER 2

Bradshaw, P. *Eucharistic origins* London: SPCK 2004

Chadwick, H. *The early church* rev. ed. London: Penguin 1993

Clark, G. *Christianity and Roman society* New York; Cambridge: Cambridge University Press 2004

Dively Lauro, E. *The soul and spirit of scripture within Origen's exegesis* Leiden; Boston, MA: Brill 2005

Donovan, M. *One right reading? a guide to Irenaeus* Collegeville, MN: Liturgical Press 1997

Dunn, G. *Tertullian* London: Routledge 2004

Edwards, M. *Origen against Plato* Aldershot: Ashgate 2002

Ehrman, B., ed. *The Apostolic Fathers* Cambridge, MA: Harvard University Press 2003

Esler, P., ed. *The early Christian world* London: Routledge 2000

Ferguson, E., ed. *Christianity in relation to Jews, Greeks and Romans* New York; London: Garland 1999

Frend, W. H. C. *The early church: from the beginnings to 461* new ed. London: SCM Press 2003

Grant, R. *Irenaeus of Lyons* London: Routledge 1997

Griggs, C. *Early Egyptian Christianity: from its origins to 451 CE* rev. ed. Leiden; Boston, MA: Brill 2000

Guy, L. *Introducing early Christianity: a topical survey of its life, beliefs and practices* Downers Grove, IL: InterVarsity Press 2004

Hargis, J. *Against the Christians: the rise of early anti-Christian polemic* New York: Lang 2001

Hinson, E. *The early church: origins to the dawn of the Middle Ages* Nashville, TN: Abingdon Press 1996

Klauck, H.J. *The religious context of early Christianity: a guide to Graeco-Roman religions* Edinburgh: T&T Clark 2003

Marjanen, A. and Luomanen, P., eds. *A companion to second-century Christian 'heretics'* Leiden; Boston, MA: Brill 2005

Markschies, C. *Gnosis: an introduction* London: T&T Clark 2003

Mitchell, M. and Young, F., eds. *The Cambridge history of Christianity: 1. Origins to Constantine* Cambridge; New York: Cambridge University Press 2006

Osborn, E. *Clement of Alexandria* Cambridge: Cambridge University Press 2005

Osborn, E. *Irenaeus of Lyons* Cambridge: Cambridge University Press 2001

Osborn, E. *Tertullian: first theologian of the West* Cambridge: Cambridge University Press 1997

Pagels, E. *The Gnostic Gospels* London: Penguin 1990

Pearson, B. *Gnosticism and Christianity in Roman and Coptic Egypt* New York: T&T Clark 2004

Rankin, D. *Tertullian and the church* Cambridge; New York: Cambridge University Press 1995

Roukema, R. *Gnosis and faith in early Christianity: an introduction to gnosticism* London: SCM 1999

Rousseau, P. *The early Christian centuries* London: Pearson 2002

Rutgers, L. *Subterranean Rome: in search of the roots of Christianity in the catacombs of the Eternal City* Leuven: Peeters 2000

Salisbury, J. *The blood of martyrs: unintended consequences of ancient violence* New York; London: Routledge 2004

Trevett, C. *Montanism: gender, authority and the New Prophecy* Cambridge: Cambridge University Press 1996

Trigg, J. *Origen* London: Routledge 1998

Wilken, R. *The Christians as the Romans saw them* 2nd ed. New Haven, CT: Yale University Press 2003

CHAPTER 3

Ayres, L. *Nicaea and its legacy: an approach to fourth-century Trinitarian theology* Oxford: Oxford University Press 2004

Barnes, T. *Athanasius and Constantius: theology and politics in the Constantinian empire* Cambridge, MA: Harvard University Press 1993

Bentley-Taylor, D. *The apostle from Africa: the life and thought of Augustine of Hippo* Fearn: Christian Focus 2002

Brown, P. *Augustine of Hippo* 2nd ed. London: Faber & Faber 2000

Coakley, S., ed. *Re-thinking Gregory of Nyssa* Oxford: Blackwell 2003

Curran, J. *Pagan city and Christian capital: Rome in the fourth century* Oxford: Clarendon 2000

Drake, H. *Constantine and the bishops: the politics of intolerance* Baltimore, MD; London: Johns Hopkins University Press 2000

Ehrman, B. and Jacobs, A., eds. *Christianity in late antiquity, 300–450 CE: a reader* New York; Oxford: Oxford University Press 2004

Frend, W.H.C. *The Donatist church: a movement of protest in Roman North Africa* Oxford: Clarendon 2000

Goehring, J. *Ascetics, society, and the desert: studies in Egyptian monasticism* Harrisburg, PA: Trinity 1999

Hanson, R. *The search for the Christian doctrine of God: the Arian controversy 318–381* Edinburgh: T&T Clark 1988

Harmless, W. *Desert Christians: an introduction to the literature of early monasticism* Oxford: Oxford University Press 2004

L'Huillier, P. *The church of the ancient councils: the disciplinary work of the first four ecumenical councils* Crestwood, NY: St Vladimir's Seminary Press 1995

Lieu, S. and Montserrat, D., eds. *Constantine: history, historiography and legend* London: Routledge 1998

Matthews, G. *Augustine* Oxford: Blackwell 2005

McGuckin, J. *St Cyril of Alexandria: the Christological controversy: its history, theology, and texts* Crestwood, NY: St Vladimir's Seminary Press 2004

Meredith, A. *Gregory of Nyssa* London; New York: Routledge 2003

Meredith, A. *The Cappadocians* London: Geoffrey Chapman 1995

Moorhead, J. *Ambrose: church and state in the late Roman world* London: Longman 1999

O'Donnell, J. *Augustine: a new biography* New York: Ecco 2005

Odahl, C. *Constantine and the Christian empire* London; New York: Routledge 2004

Pelikan, J. *The Christian tradition: A history of the development of doctrine 1. The emergence of the Catholic tradition (100–600)* Chicago; London: University of Chicago Press 1971

Pettersen, A. *Athanasius* London: Geoffrey Chapman 1995

Pohlsander, H. *The emperor Constantine* 2nd ed. London: Routledge 2004

Rapp, C. *Holy bishops in late antiquity: the nature of Christian leadership in an age of transition* Berkeley, CA: University of California Press 2005

Rebenich, S. *Jerome* London: Routledge 2001

Rees, B. *Pelagius: life and letters* Rochester, NY: Boydell 1998

Rousseau, P. *Pachomius: the making of a community in fourth-century Egypt* rev. ed. Berkeley, CA; London: University of California Press 1999

Rubenstein, R. *When Jesus became God: the struggle to define Christianity during the last days of Rome* San Diego, CA; London: Harcourt 1999

Russell, N. *Cyril of Alexandria* London: Routledge 2000

Samuel, V. *The Council of Chalcedon re-examined: a historical and theological survey* Philadelphia, PA: Xlibris 2001

Wessel, S. *Cyril of Alexandria and the Nestorian controversy: the making of a saint and of a heretic* Oxford: Oxford University Press 2004

Williams, D. *Ambrose of Milan and the end of the Arian-Nicene conflicts* Oxford: Clarendon 1995

Williams, R. *Arius: heresy and tradition* 2nd ed. London: SCM 2001

CHAPTER 4

Alfeyev, H. *The spiritual world of Isaac the Syrian* Kalamazoo, MI; Spencer, MA: Cistercian Publications 2000

Baum, W. and Winkler, D. *The Church of the East: a concise history* London; New York: RoutledgeCurzon 2003

Brock, S. *The luminous eye: the spiritual world vision of Saint Ephrem the Syrian* Kalamazoo, MI: Cistercian Publications 1992

Brock, S. ed. *The Syriac Fathers on prayer and the spiritual life* Kalamazoo, MI: Cistercian Publications 1987

Cahillot, C. *The Ethiopian Orthodox Tewahedo Church tradition* Paris: Inter-Orthodox Dialogue 2002

Cragg, K. *The Arab Christian: a history in the Middle East* London: Mowbray 1992

Davis, S. *Early Coptic papacy: the Egyptian church and its leadership in late antiquity* Cairo: American University in Cairo Press 2004

Frend, W. *The rise of the Monophysite movement* Cambridge: Cambridge University Press 1972

Gabra, G. *Coptic monasteries: Egypt's monastic art and architecture* Cairo: American University in Cairo Press 2002

Garsoian, N. *Church and culture in early medieval Armenia* Aldershot: Ashgate 1999

Gillman, I and Klimkeit, H.J. *Christians in Asia before 1500* Richmond: Curzon 1999

Hacikyan, A. ed. *The heritage of Armenian literature* Detroit: Wayne State University Press 2000

Kaegi, W. *Heraclius: emperor of Byzantium* Cambridge: Cambridge University Press 2002

Kamil, J. *Christianity in the land of the pharaohs: the Coptic Orthodox Church* Cairo: American University in Cairo Press 2002

Louth, A. *Denys the Areopagite* London: Continuum 2001

Marcus, H. *A history of Ethiopia* Berkeley: University of California Press 2002

Meinardus, O. *Two thousand years of Coptic Christianity* Cairo: University of Cairo Press 2002

Palmer, Martin *The Jesus Sutras: rediscovering the lost religion of Taoist Christianity* London: Piatcus 2001

Regan, G. *First crusader: Byzantium's holy wars* New York: Macmillan 2003

Tang, L. *A study of the history of Nestorian Christianity in China and its literature in Chinese* rev. ed. Frankfurt am Maine: Peter Lang 2004

Thomas, D., ed. *Christians at the heart of Islamic rule: church life and scholarship in Abbasid Iraq* Leiden; Boston, MA: Brill 2003

Welsby, D. *The medieval kingdoms of Nubia* London: British Museum Press 2002

CHAPTER 5

Angold, M. *Church and society in Byzantium under the Comneni, 1081–1261* rev. ed. Cambridge: Cambridge University Press 2000

Bathrellos, D. *The Byzantine Christ: person, nature and will in the Christology of Saint Maximus the Confessor* Oxford: Oxford University Press 2004

Browning, R. *Byzantium and Bulgaria: a comparative study across the early medieval frontier* London: Temple Smith 1975

Chadwick, H. *East and West: the making of a rift in the church, from apostolic times until the Council of Florence* Oxford: Oxford University Press 2003

Chryssavgis, J. *John Climacus: from the Egyptian desert to the Sinaite mountain* Aldershot: Ashgate 2004

Cunningham, M. *Faith in the Byzantine world* Oxford: Lion 2002

Dagron, G. *Emperor and priest: the imperial office in Byzantium* Cambridge: Cambridge University Press 2003

Evans, J. *The Emperor Justinian and the Byzantine Empire* Westport, CT: Greenwood 2005

Giakalis, A. *Images of the divine: the theology of icons at the Seventh Ecumenical Council* Leiden: Brill 1994

Giuzelev, V. *The adoption of Christianity in Bulgaria* Sofia: Sofia Press 1976

Gregory, T. *A history of Byzantium: 306–1453* Oxford: Blackwell 2004

Hamilton, J. and Hamilton, B. *Christian dualist heresies in the Byzantine world, c.650–c.1450* Manchester: Manchester University Press 1998

Herrin, J. *The formation of Christendom* London: Phoenix 2001

Herrin, J. *Women in purple: rulers of medieval Byzantium* London: Phoenix 2002

Hussey, J. The Orthodox Church in the Byzantine Empire Oxford: Oxford University Press 1986

Limberis, V. Divine heiress: the Virgin Mary and the creation of Christian Constantinople London: Routledge 1994

Louth, A. Maximus the Confessor London: Routledge 1996

Meyendorff, J. Byzantine theology: historical trends and doctrinal themes 2nd ed. New York: Fordham University Press 1979

Meyendorff, J. St. Gregory Palamas and Orthodox spirituality Crestwood, NY: St Vladimir's Seminary Press 1997

Morris, R. Monks and laymen in Byzantium, 843–1118 Cambridge: Cambridge University Press 1995

Norwich, J. J. Byzantium: the apogee London: Viking 1991

Norwich, J. J. Byzantium: the decline and fall London: Viking 1995

Norwich, J. J. Byzantium: the early centuries London: Viking 1988

Parry, K. Depicting the Word: Byzantine iconophile thought of the eighth and ninth centuries Leiden: Brill 1996

Pelikan, J. Imago Dei: the Byzantine apologia for icons Princeton, NJ: Princeton University Press 1990

Pelikan, J. The Christian tradition: A history of the development of doctrine 2. The spirit of Eastern Christendom (600–1700) Chicago; London: University of Chicago Press 1974

Simeonova, L. Diplomacy of the letter and the cross: Photios, Bulgaria and the Papacy, 860s–880s Amsterdam: Hakkert 1998

Tachiaos, A.E. Cyril and Methodius of Thessalonika: the acculturation of the Slavs Crestwood, NY: St Vladimir's Seminary Press 2001

Whittow, M. The making of Orthodox Byzantium, 600–1025 Basingstoke: Macmillan 1996

CHAPTER 6

Blair, J. The church in Anglo-Saxon society Oxford: Oxford University Press 2005

Brown, P. The rise of western Christendom: triumph and diversity 200–1000 AD 2nd ed. Oxford: Blackwell 2003

Carver, M., ed. The cross goes north: processes of conversion in northern Europe, AD 300–1300 York: Boydell 2003

Chapman, J. Saint Benedict and the sixth century Westport: Greenwood Press 1971

Christys, A. Christians in al-Andalus, 711–1000 Richmond: Curzon 2002

Collins, R. Visigothic Spain, 409–711 Oxford: Blackwell 2004

Cusack, C. Conversion among the Germanic peoples London: Cassell 1998

Daniel-Rops, H. The church in the Dark Ages London: Phoenix 2001

Dunn, M. The emergence of monasticism: from the Desert Fathers to the early Middle Ages Oxford: Blackwell 2000

Fletcher, R. Moorish Spain London: Weidenfeld & Nicolson 1992

Fletcher, R. The barbarian conversion: from paganism to Christianity Berkeley, CA: University of California Press 1999

Gameson, R., ed. St Augustine and the conversion of England Stroud: Sutton 1999

Hillgarth, J., ed. Christianity and paganism, 350–750 rev. ed. Philadelphia, PA: University of Pennsylvania Press 1986

Houwen, L. and MacDonald, A., eds. Alcuin of York: scholar at the Carolingian court Groningen: Forsten 1998

Hylson-Smith, K. Christianity in England from Roman times to the Reformation 1. from Roman times to 1066 London: SCM 2001

MacMullen, R. Christianity and paganism in the fourth to eighth centuries New Haven; London: Yale University Press 1997

Markus, R. Gregory the Great and his world Cambridge; New York: Cambridge University Press 1997

McKitterick, R., ed. Carolingian culture: emulation and innovation Cambridge: Cambridge University Press 1994

Moorhead, J. Theoderic in Italy Oxford: Clarendon 1993

Olsen, T. Christianity and the Celts Oxford: Lion 2003

De Paor, L. Saint Patrick's world: the Christian culture of Ireland's Apostolic Age Blackrock: Four Courts 1993

Pelikan, J. The Christian tradition: A history of the development of doctrine 3. The growth of medieval theology (600–1300) Chicago: University of Chicago Press 1978

Richards, J. The popes and the Papacy in the early Middle Ages 476–752 London: Routledge and Kegan Paul 1979

Wallace-Hadrill, J. The Frankish church Oxford: Clarendon 1983

Watt, J. The church in medieval Ireland 2nd ed. Dublin: Macmillan 1998

Webster, L. and Brown, M., eds. The transformation of the Roman world AD 400–900 London: British Museum Press 1997

Wood, I. The missionary life: saints and the evangelisation of Europe Harlow; New York: Longman 2001

CHAPTER 7

Aers, D. Sanctifying signs: making Christian tradition in late medieval England Notre Dame, IN: University of Notre Dame Press 2004

Barber, M. The Cathars: dualist heretics in Languedoc in the high Middle Ages Harlow: Longman 2000

Barber, M. The new knighthood: a history of the Order of the Temple Cambridge: Cambridge University Press 1994

Berman, C., ed. Medieval religion: new approaches New York; London: Routledge 2005

Biller, P. The Waldenses, 1170–1530: between a religious order and a church Aldershot: Ashgate 2001

Blomkvist, N. The discovery of the Baltic: the reception of a Catholic world-system in the European north (AD 1075–1225) Leiden: Brill 2005

Brooke, C. The age of the cloister: the story of monastic life in the Middle Ages rev. ed. Stroud: Sutton 2003

Christiansen, E. The northern Crusades rev. ed. London: Penguin 1997

Davies, B. Aquinas London: Continuum 2002

Dickson, G. Religious enthusiasm in the medieval west: revivals, crusades, saints Aldershot: Ashgate 2000

Elliott, D. Proving woman: female spirituality and inquisitional culture in the later Middle Ages Princeton, NJ; Oxford: Princeton University Press 2004

van Engen, J. Religion in the history of the medieval West Aldershot: Ashgate 2004

Evans, G. R. Bernard of Clairvaux New York; Oxford: Oxford University Press 2000

Evans, G. R., ed. The medieval theologians Oxford: Blackwell 2001

France, J. The Crusades and the expansion of Catholic Christendom, 1000–1714 London: Routledge 2005

Frassetto, M., ed. The year 1000: religious and social response to the turning of the first millennium New York: Macmillan 2002

Galli, M. Francis of Assisi and his world Oxford: Lion 2002

Glick, L. Abraham's heirs: Jews and Christians in medieval Europe Syracuse, NY: Syracuse University Press 1999

Hamilton, B. Religion in the medieval West 2nd. Ed. London: Arnold 2003

Heffernan, T. and Matter, A., eds. The liturgy of the medieval church Kalamazoo, MI: Medieval Institute Publications 2001

Hopper, S. To be a pilgrim: the medieval pilgrimage experience Stroud: Sutton 2002

Hylson-Smith, K. Christianity in England from Roman times to the Reformation 2. 1066–1384 London: SCM 2000

Jotischky, A. Crusading and the Crusader states Harlow: Pearson Longman 2004

Kamen, H. The Spanish Inquisition: an historical revision London: Weidenfeld & Nicolson 1997

Kroll, J. and Bachrach, B. The mystic mind: the psychology of medieval mystics and ascetics New York; London: Routledge 2005

Leff, G. Heresy, philosophy and religion in the medieval West Aldershot: Ashgate 2002

Linehan, P. and Nelson, J., eds. The medieval world London; New York: Routledge 2001

Logan, F. A history of the church in the Middle Ages London; New York: Routledge 2002

Morris, C. The papal monarchy: the Western church from 1050 to 1250 Oxford: Oxford University Press 1991

Mundy, J. Europe in the high Middle Ages, 1150–1300 3rd. ed. Harlow: Longman 2000

Pick, L. Conflict and coexistence: Archbishop Rodrigo and the Muslims and Jews of medieval Spain Ann Arbor, MI: University of Michigan Press 2004

Rex, R. The Lollards New York: Palgrave 2002

Riley-Smith, J. Hospitallers: the history of the order of St John London: Hambledon 1999

Robinson, I., ed. The papal reform of the eleventh century: lives of Pope Leo IX and Pope Gregory VII Manchester: Manchester University Press 2004

Russell, J. A history of medieval Christianity: prophecy and order New York: Lang 2000

Sayers, J. Innocent III: leader of Europe 1198–1216 London: Longman 1994

Scott, R. The Gothic enterprise: a guide to understanding the medieval cathedral Berkeley, CA: University of California Press 2003

Shinners, J. *Medieval popular religion, 1000–1500: a reader* Peterborough, ON: Broadview 1997

Stouck, M.A. *Medieval saints: a reader* Peterborough, ON: Broadview 1999

Thomson, J. *The Western church in the Middle Ages* London: Arnold 1998

Volz, C. *The medieval church: from the dawn of the Middle Ages to the eve of the Reformation* Nashville, TN: Abingdon 1997

Webb, D. *Medieval European pilgrimage, c.700–c.1500* Basingstoke: Palgrave 2002

CHAPTER 8

Bushkovitch, P. *Religion and society in Russia: the sixteenth and seventeenth centuries* New York; Oxford: Oxford University Press 1992

Engelstein, L. *Castration and the heavenly kingdom: a Russian folktale* Ithaca, NY; London: Cornell University Press 1999

Fennell, J. *A history of the Russian church to 1448* London: Longman 1995

de Hartog, L. *Russia and the Mongol yoke: the history of the Russian principalities and the Golden Horde, 1221–1502* London: British Academic Press 1996

Klokzowski, J. *A history of Polish Christianity* Cambridge; New York: Cambridge University Press 2000

Korpela, J. *Prince, saint and apostle: Prince Vladimir Svjatoslavic of Kiev, his posthumous life, and the religious legitimization of the Russian great power* Wiesbaden: Harrassowitz 2001

de Madariaga, I. *Ivan the Terrible: first tsar of Russia* New Haven, CT; London: Yale University Press 2005

Martin, J. *Medieval Russia, 980–1584* Cambridge; New York: Cambridge University Press 1995

Murray, A. *Crusade and conversion on the Baltic frontier, 1150–1500* Aldershot: Ashgate 2001

Pavlov, A. and Perrie, M. *Ivan the Terrible* London: Longman 2003

CHAPTER 9

Adair, J. *Puritans: religion and politics in seventeenth-century England and America* Stroud: Sutton 1998

Allen, M. and Rees, V., eds. *Marsilio Ficino: his theology, his philosophy, his legacy* Leiden: Brill 2002

Bernard, G. *The king's Reformation: Henry VIII and the remaking of the English church* New Haven, CT; London: Yale University Press 2005

Cottret, B. *Calvin: a biography* Grand Rapids, MI: Eerdmans; Edinburgh: T&T Clark 2000

Duffy, E. *The stripping of the altars: traditional religion in England c.1400–c.1580* 2nd ed. New Haven, CT: Yale University Press 2005

Gordon, B. *The Swiss Reformation* Manchester: Manchester University Press 2002

Grell, O. *Calvinist exiles in Tudor and Stuart England* Aldershot: Scolar 1996

Helm, P. *John Calvin's ideas* Oxford: Oxford University Press 2004

Holt, M. *The French Wars of Religion, 1562–1629* 2nd ed. Cambridge: Cambridge University Press 2005

Hylson-Smith, K. *Christianity in England from Roman times to the Reformation 3. 1384–1558* London: SCM 2001

Ingle, H. *First among friends: George Fox and the creation of Quakerism* New York; Oxford: Oxford University Press 1994

Johnson, M. *The Borgias* London: Penguin 2001

Kolb, R. *Luther's heirs define his legacy: studies on Lutheran confessionalization* Aldershot: Ashgate 1996

Kyle, R. *The ministry of John Knox: pastor, preacher, and prophet* Lewiston, NY: Mellen 2002

Lane, A. *John Calvin: student of the church fathers* Edinburgh: T&T Clark 1999

Lindberg, C. *The European Reformations* Oxford: Blackwell 1996

Louthan, H. and Zachman, R. *Conciliation and confession: the struggle for unity in the Age of Reform, 1415–1648* Notre Dame, IN: University of Notre Dame Press 2004

Maag, K., ed. *Melanchthon in Europe: his work and influence beyond Wittenberg* Grand Rapids, MI: Baker 1999

MacCulloch, D. *Reformation: Europe's house divided, 1490–1700* London: Penguin 2004

Mannermaa, T. *Christ present in faith: Luther's view of justification* Minneapolis, MN: Fortress 2005

Marins, R. *Martin Luther: the Christian between God and death* Cambridge, MA; London: Harvard University Press 1999

Marshall, R. *John Knox* Edinburgh: Birlinn 2000

McGrath, A. *A life of John Calvin* Oxford: Blackwell 1990

Muller, R. *After Calvin: studies in the development of a theological tradition* Oxford; New York: Oxford University Press 2003

Mullett, M. *Martin Luther* London: Routledge 2004

Mullett, M. *The Catholic Reformation* London: Routledge 1999

Murdock, G. *Calvinism on the frontier, 1600–1660: international Calvinism and the Reformed Church in Hungary and Transylvania* Oxford; New York: Oxford University Press 2000

Naphy, W. *Calvin and the consolidation of the Genevan Reformation* new ed. Louisville, KY: Westminster John Knox Press 2003

Nischan, B. *Lutherans and Calvinists in the age of confessionalism* Aldershot: Ashgate 1999

O'Malley, J., Bailey, G., Harris, S., and Kennedy, T. F., eds. *The Jesuits: cultures, sciences, and the arts 1540–1773* Toronto: University of Toronto Press 1999

Parsons, J. *The church in the republic: Gallicanism and political ideology in Renaissance France* Washington, DC: Catholic University of America Press 2004

Pelikan, J. *The Christian tradition: A history of the development of doctrine 4. Reformation of church and dogma (1300–1700)* Chicago; London: University of Chicago Press 1983

Polizotto, L. *The elect nation: the Savonarolan movement in Florence, 1494–1545* Oxford: Clarendon 1994

Pettegree, A., ed. *The Reformation world* London; New York: Routledge 2000

Steinmetz, D. *Reformers in the wings: from Geiler von Kaysersberg to Theodore Beza* Oxford: Oxford University Press 2001

Tomlin, G. *Luther and his world* Oxford: Lion 2002

Williams, G. *The radical Reformation* 3rd ed. Kirksville, MO: Truman University Press 2000

Wright, A. *The Counter-Reformation: Catholic Europe and the non-Christian world* 2nd ed. Aldershot: Ashgate 2005

Wright, J. *God's soldiers: adventure, politics, intrigue, and power: a history of the Jesuits* London: Doubleday 2004

Wright, S. *Our sovereign refuge: the pastoral theology of Theodore Beza* Carlise: Paternoster 2004

CHAPTER 10

Agbeti, J. *West African church history 1. Christian missions and church foundations, 1482–1919* Leiden: Brill 1986

Bremer, F. *The Puritan experiment: New England society from Bradford to Edwards* Hanover: University Press of New England 1995

Caraman, P. *The lost empire: the story of the Jesuits in Ethiopia 1555–1634* London: Sidgwick & Jackson 1985

Cheriyan, M. *Orthodox Christianity in India: a history of the Malankara Orthodox Church AD 52–2002* Kottayam: Academic Publishers 2002

Costelloe, M., ed. *The letters and instructions of Francis Xavier* St Louis, MO: Institute of Jesuit Sources 1992

Cronin, V. *The wise man from the west* London: Harvill 1999

Engeman, T. and Zuckert, M., eds. *Protestantism and the American founding* Notre Dame, IN: University of Notre Dame Press 2004

Fernández Olmos, M. and Paravisini-Gebert, L. *Creole religions of the Caribbean: an introduction from Vodou and Santeria to Obeah and Espiritismo* New York; London: New York University Press 2003

Greer, A., ed. *The Jesuit relations: natives and missionaries in seventeenth-century North America* Boston, MA: Bedford/St Martin's 2000

Hall, D., ed. *Puritans in the New World: a critical anthology* Princeton, NJ; Oxford: Princeton University Press 2004

Hanke, L. *All mankind is one: a study of the disputation between Bartolomé de Las Casas and Juan Ginés de Sepúlveda in 1550 on the intellectual and religious capacity of the American Indians* De Kalb, IL: Northern Illinois University Press 1994

Hastings, A. *The church in Africa, 1450–1950* Oxford: Oxford University Press 1996

Higashibaba, I. *Christianity in early modern Japan: Kirishitan belief and practice* Leiden; Boston, MA: Brill 2001

Hilton, A. *The kingdom of Kongo* Oxford: Clarendon 1985

Kwantes, A., ed. *Chapters in Philippine church history* Colorado Springs, CO: International Academic Publishers 2002

Lippy, C., Choquette, R., and Poole, S. *Christianity comes to the Americas, 1492–1776* New York: Paragon 1992

Murphy, T. and Perin, R. *A concise history of Christianity in Canada* Toronto; Oxford: Oxford University Press 1996

Neill, S. *A history of Christianity in India: the beginnings to 1707* Cambridge: Cambridge University Press 1984

Pardo, O. *The origins of Mexican Catholicism:*

Nahua rituals and Christian sacraments in sixteenth-century Mexico Ann Arbor, MI: University of Michigan Press 2004

Phan, P. *Mission and catechesis: Alexandre de Rhodes and inculturation in seventeenth-century Vietnam* Maryknoll, NY: Orbis 1998

Postma, J. *The Atlantic slave trade* Westport, CT; London: Greenwood 2003

Reiter, F. *They built Utopia: the Jesuit missions in Paraguay, 1610–1768* Potomac, MD: Scripta Humanistica 1995

Ronan, C. and Oh, B., eds. *East meets west: the Jesuits in China, 1582–1773* Chicago: Loyola University Press 1988

Ross, A. *A vision betrayed: the Jesuits in Japan and China, 1542–1742* Edinburgh: Edinburgh University Press 1994

Spence, J. *The memory palace of Matteo Ricci* London: Penguin 1984

Standaert, N., ed. *Handbook of Christianity in China vol. 1: 635–1800* Leiden: Brill 2001

CHAPTER 11

Barnett, S. *The Enlightenment and religion: the myths of modernity* Manchester: Manchester University Press 2004

Bergin, J. *Crown, church and episcopate under Louis XIV* New Haven, CT; London: Yale University Press 2004

Brockway, R. *A wonderful work of God: Puritanism and the Great Awakening* Bethlehem, PA: Lehigh University Press; London: Associated University Presses 2003

Byrne, J. *Religion and the Enlightenment: from Descartes to Kant* Louisville, KY: Westminster John Knox Press 1997

Cameron, E., ed. *Early Modern Europe: An Oxford History* Oxford: Oxford University Press 2001

Cracraft, J. *The revolution of Peter the Great* Cambridge, MA; London: Harvard University Press 2003

Dayfoot, A. *The shaping of the West Indian church, 1492–1962* Barbados: Press University of the West Indies; Gainesville, FL: University Press of Florida 1999

Freeman, A. *An ecumenical theology of the heart: the theology of Count Nicholas Ludwig von Zinzendorf*, Bethlehem, PA; Winston-Salem, NC: The Moravian Church in America 1998

Heitzenrater, R. *Wesley and the people called Methodists* Nashville, TN: Abingdon 1995

Hempton, D. *Methodism: empire of the Spirit* New Haven, CT: Yale University Press 2005

Hill, J. *Faith in the Age of Reason* Oxford: Lion 2004

Lambert, F. *Inventing the 'Great Awakening'* Princeton, NJ; Oxford: Princeton University Press 1999

Lindberg, C., ed. *The pietist theologians: an introduction to theology in the seventeenth and eighteenth centuries* Malden, MA; Oxford: Blackwell 2005

Marsden, G. *Jonathan Edwards: a life* New Haven, CT; London; Yale University Press 2003

Marshall, J. *John Locke: resistance, religion and responsibility* Cambridge: Cambridge University Press 1994

Michels, G. *At war with the church: religious dissent in seventeenth-century Russia* Stanford, CA: Stanford University Press 1999

Noll, M. *The rise of evangelicalism: the age of Edwards, Whitefield, and the Wesleys* Leicester: Inter-Varsity Press 2004

Outram, D. *The Enlightenment* Cambridge: Cambridge University Press 1995

Pearson, R. *Voltaire almighty: a life in pursuit of freedom* London: Bloomsbury 2005

Price, J., ed. *History of British deism* London: Routledge 1995

Stout, H. *The divine dramatist: George Whitefield and the rise of modern evangelicalism* Grand Rapids, MI: Eerdmans 1991

Turner, J. *John Wesley: the evangelical revival and the rise of Methodism in England* Peterborough: Epworth 2002

Walters, K. *The American deists: voices of reason and dissent in the early republic* Lawrence, KA: University Press of Kansas 1992

CHAPTER 12

Aston, N. *Religion and revolution in France, 1780–1804* Basingstoke: Macmillan 2000

Baird, W. *History of New Testament research: 1. From Deism to Tubingen* Minneapolis, MN: Fortress 1992

Bebbington, D. *The dominance of evangelicalism: the age of Spurgeon and Moody* Leicester: Inter-Varsity Press 2005

Beiser, F. *Hegel* London; New York: Routledge 2005

Burleigh, M. *Earthly powers: the clash of religion and politics in Europe, from the French Revolution to the Great War* London: HarperCollins 2005

Chandler, M. *An introduction to the Oxford Movement* London: SPCK 2003

Chapman, M. *Ernst Troeltsch and liberal theology: religion and cultural synthesis in Wilhelmine Germany* Oxford: Oxford University Press 2001

Clements, K., ed. *Friedrich Schleiermacher: pioneer of modern theology* Minneapolis, MN: Fortress 1991

Davies, D. *An introduction to Mormonism* Cambridge; New York: Cambridge University Press 2003

Dawes, G., ed. *The historical Jesus quest: landmarks in the search for the Jesus of history* Louisville, KY: Westminster John Knox Press 2000

Desmond, A. and Moore, J. *Darwin: the life of a tormented evolutionist* New York: Warner 1991

Dorrien, G. *Soul in society: the making and renewal of social Christianity* Minneapolis, MN: Fortress 1995

Gross, M. *The war against Catholicism: liberalism and the anti-Catholic imagination in nineteenth-century Germany* Ann Arbor, MI: University of Michigan Press 2004

Hankins, B. *The second Great Awakening and the Transcendentalists* Westport, CT; London: Greenwood 2004

Hannay, A. *Kierkegaard: a biography* Cambridge: Cambridge University Press 2003

Holland, J. *Modern Catholic social teaching: the popes confront the industrial age* New York: Paulist 2003

Hope, N. *German and Scandinavian Protestantism 1700–1918* Oxford: Oxford University Press 1995

Knight, G. *Millennial fever and the end of the world: a study of millerite adventism* Boise, ID: Pacific Press 1993

Lewis, D. *Lighten their darkness: the evangelical mission to working-class London, 1828–1860* Carlisle: Paternoster 2001

de Mattei, R. *Pius IX* Leominster: Gracewing 2004

Mattingley, C., ed. *Water drops from women writers: a temperance reader* Carbondale, IL: University of Illinois Press 2001

McKivigan, J. and Snay, M., eds. *Religion and the antebellum debate over slavery* Athens, GA: University of Georgia Press 1998

McLeod, H. *Religion and society in England, 1850–1914* Basingstoke: Macmillan 1996

Mitchell, H. *Black church beginnings: the long-hidden realities of the first years* Grand Rapids, MI: Eerdmans 2004

O'Dwyer, M. *The papacy in the age of Napoleon and the Restoration: Pius VII, 1800–1823* Lanham, MD: University Press of America 1985

O'Regan, C. *The heterodox Hegel* Albany, NY: State University of New York Press 1994

Pelikan, J. *The Christian tradition: A history of the development of doctrine 5. Christian doctrine and modern culture (since 1700)* Chicago; London: University of Chicago Press 1989

Raboteau, A. *Canaan land: a religious history of African Americans* Oxford: Oxford University Press 2001

Roberts, J. *Darwinism and the divine in America: Protestant intellectuals and organic evolution, 1859–1900* Notre Dame, IN: University of Notre Dame Press 2001

Steer, R. *Church on fire: the story of Anglican evangelicals* London: Hodder & Stoughton 1998

Valliere, P. *Modern Russian theology: Bukharev, Soloviev, Bulgakov: Orthodox theology in a new key* Edinburgh: T&T Clark 2000

CHAPTER 13

Agbeti, J. *West African church history 2. Christian missions and theological training, 1842–1970* Leiden: Brill 1991

Ballhatchet, K. *Caste, class and Catholicism in India, 1789–1914* Richmond: Curzon 1998

Cheung, D. *Christianity in modern China: the making of the first native Protestant church* Leiden; Boston, MA: Brill 2004

Davidson, A. *Christianity in Aotearoa: a history of church and society in New Zealand* 3rd. ed. Wellington: Education for Ministry 2004

Fyfe, C. *A history of Sierra Leone* Aldershot: Ashgate 1993

Garrett, J. *To live among the stars: Christian origins in Oceania* Fiji: University of the South Pacific 1982

George, T. *Faithful witness: the life and mission of William Carey* Leicester: Inter-Varsity Press 1992

Gilley, S. and Stanley, B., eds. *World Christianities c.1815–1914* Cambridge: Cambridge University Press 2005

Hudson, D. *Protestant origins in India: Tamil evangelical Christians 1706–1835* Grand Rapids, MI: Eerdmans 2000

King, M. *God's farthest outpost: a history of Catholics in new New Zealand* Auckland; London: Penguin 1997

Laamann, L. *Christian heretics in late imperial China: the inculturation of Christianity in eighteenth- and early nineteenth-century China* New York; London: RoutledgeCurzon 2003

Lodwick, K. *Crusaders against opium: Protestant missionaries in China, 1874–1917* Lexington, KY: University Press of Kentucky 1996

Munro, D. and Thornley, A., eds. *The covenant makers: islander missionaries in the Pacific* Suva: University of the South Pacific 1996

Neill, S. *A history of Christianity in India: 1707–1858* Cambridge: Cambridge University Press 1985

O'Connor, D. *Three centuries of mission: the United Society for the Propagation of the Gospel 1701–2000* London: Continuum 2000

Palmer, B. *Imperial vineyard: the Anglican Church in India under the Raj from the mutiny to partition* Lewes: Book Guild 1999

Park, E. *White Americans in black Africa* New York; London: Garland 2001

Peel, J. *Religious encounter and the making of the Yoruba* Bloomington, IN: Indiana University Press 2003

Porter, A. *Religion versus empire? British Protestant missionaries and overseas expansion, 1700–1914* Manchester; New York: Manchester University Press 2004

Pulford, C. *Eating Uganda: from Christianity to conquest* Banbury: Ituri 1999

Rubinstein, M. *The origins of the Anglo-American missionary enterprise in China, 1807–1840* Lanham, MD; London: Scarecrow 1996

Stanley, B. *The history of the Baptist Missionary Society, 1792–1992* Edinburgh: T&T Clark 1992

Stenhouse, J. and Thomson, J., eds. *Building God's own country: historical essays on religions in New Zealand* Dunedin: University of Otago Press 2004

Stevens, C. *White man's dreaming: Killalpaninna Mission, 1866–1915* Melbourne; Oxford: Oxford University Press 1994

Suberg, O. *The Anglican tradition in South Africa: a historical overview* Pretoria: University of South Africa 1999

Ward, K. and Stanley, B., eds. *The Church Mission Society and world Christianity, 1799–1999* Grand Rapids, MI: Eerdmans 2000

CHAPTER 14

Alberigo, G. *A brief history of Vatican II* Maryknoll, NY: Orbis 2006

Altizer, T. *The new gospel of Christian atheism* Aurora, CO: Davies Group 2002

Baird, W. *History of New Testament research: 2. From Jonathan Edwards to Rudolf Bultmann* Minneapolis, MN: Fortress 2002

Bethge, E. *Dietrich Bonhoeffer: a biography* rev. ed. Minneapolis, MN: Fortress 2000

Bowden, J., ed. *Thirty years of honesty: Honest to God, then and now* London: SCM 1993

Brown, C. *The death of Christian Britain* London: Routledge 2001

Bruce, S. *God is dead: secularization in the West* Oxford: Blackwell 2002

Chadwick, O. *The Christian church in the Cold War* London: Penguin 1992

Coppa, F. *The modern Papacy since 1789* London; New York: Longman 1998

Cupitt, D. *The sea of faith* London: BBC 1984

Davis, N. *A long walk to church: a contemporary history of Russian Orthodoxy* 2nd ed. Boulder, CO; Oxford: Westview 2003

Diskin, H. *The seeds of triumph: church and state in Gomulka's Poland* Budapest: Central European University Press 2001

Fergusson, D. *Rudolf Bultmann* London: Continuum 2000

Ford, D., ed. *The modern theologians* 2nd ed. Oxford: Blackwell 1997

Hebblethwaite, P. *John XXIII: Pope of the century* rev. ed. London: Continuum 2000

Helmreich, E. *The German churches under Hitler* Detroit: Wayne State University Press 1979

Heron, A. *A century of Protestant theology* Cambridge: Lutterworth Press 1980

Hockenos, M. *A church divided: German Protestants confront the Nazi past* Bloomington, IN: Indiana University Press 2004

Hoover, A. *God, Germany, and Britain in the Great War: a study in clerical nationalism* New York; London: Praeger 1989

Knox, Z. *Russian society and the Orthodox Church: religion in Russia after communism* New York; London: Routledge 2005

Madges, W., ed. *Vatican II: forty years later* Maryknoll, NY: Orbis 2006

Mangina, J. *Karl Barth: theologian of Christian witness* Aldershot: Ashgate 2004

Michel, P. *Politics and religion in Eastern Europe: Catholicism in Hungary, Poland and Czechoslovakia* Oxford: Polity 1991

O'Connor, G. *Universal father: a life of Pope John Paul II* London: Bloomsbury 2005

Pelton, R., ed. *Monsignor Romero: a bishop for the third millennium* Notre Dame, IN: University of Notre Dame Press 2004

Plant, S. *Bonhoeffer* London: Continuum 2004

Pollard, J. *The Vatican and Italian fascism, 1929–32: a study in conflict* Cambridge: Cambridge University Press 1985

Roslof, E. *Red priests: renovationism, Russian Orthodoxy and revolution, 1905–1946* Bloomington, IN: Indiana University Press 2002

Sánchez, J. *Pius XII and the Holocaust: understanding the controversy* Washington, DC: Catholic University of America Press 2002

Scholder, K. *A requiem for Hitler: and other new perspectives on the German church struggle* London: SCM; Philadelphia, PA: Trinity 1989

Webster, J. *Barth* 2nd. Ed. London: Continuum 2004

Weigel, G. *Witness to hope: the biography of Pope John Paul II* updated ed. New York: Harper 2005

Wynot, J. *Keeping the faith: Russian Orthodox monasticism in the Soviet Union, 1917–1939* College Station, TX: Texas A&M University Press 2004

CHAPTER 15

Aguilar, M. *A social history of the Catholic Church in Chile: the first period of the Pinochet government* Lewiston, NY; Lampeter: Mellen 2004

Anderson, A. *An introduction to Pentecostalism: global Charismatic Christianity* Cambridge: Cambridge University Press 2004

Baldwin, D. *Protestants and the Mexican revolution: missionaries, ministers, and social change* Urbana, IL: University of Illinois Press 1990

Baldwin, L. *To make the wounded whole: the cultural legacy of Martin Luther King, Jr.* Minneapolis, MN: Fortress 1992

Barr, J. *Fundamentalism* 2nd ed. London: Xpress 1995

Bruns, R. *Billy Graham: a biography* Westport, CT; London: Greenwood 2004

Clifford, A. *Introducing feminist theology* Maryknoll, NY: Orbis 2001

Clifford, J. *Person and myth: Maurice Leenhardt in the Melanesian world* Durham, NC; London: Duke University Press 1992

Erskine, L. *King among the theologians* Cleveland: Pilgrim 1994

Garrett, J. *Footsteps in the sea: Christianity in Oceania to World War II* Fiji: University of the South Pacific 1992

Garrett, J. *Where nets were cast: Christianity in Oceania since World War II* Fiji: University of the South Pacific 1997

Hart, D. *That old-time religion in modern America: evangelical Protestantism in the twentieth century* Chicago: Dee 2002

Hollenweger, J. *Pentecostalism: origins and developments worldwide* Peabody, MA: Hendrickson 1997

Jacobsen, D. *Thinking in the Spirit: theologies of the early Pentecostal movement* Bloomington, IN: Indiana University Press 2003

Kay, W. and Dyer, A., eds. *Pentecostal and Charismatic studies: a reader* London: SCM 2004

Kaye, B., ed. *Anglicanism in Australia: a history* Carlton South, Victoria: Melbourne University Press 2002

Kessler, J. *Conflict in missions: a history of Protestantism in Peru and Chile* Denver, CO: Academic Books 2001

Lehmann, D. *Struggle for the Spirit: religious transformation and popular culture in Brazil and Latin America* Cambridge: Polity 1996

Lewis, D., ed. *Christianity reborn: evangelicalism's global expansion in the twentieth century* Grand Rapids, MI: Eerdmans 2004

Lincoln, C. E. and Mamiya, L. *The black church in the African American experience* Durham, NC; London: Duke University Press 1990

Massam, K. *Sacred threads: Catholic spirituality in Australia, 1922–1962* Sydney: University of New South Wales Press 1996

Miller, R., Stout, H., and Wilson, C., eds. *Religion and the American Civil War* New York; Oxford: Oxford University Press 1998

Numbers, R. *The Creationists* New York: Knopf 1992

O'Toole, J., ed. *Habits of devotion: Catholic religious practice in twentieth-century America* Ithaca, NY: Cornell University Press 2004

Piggin, S. *Evangelical Christianity in Australia: spirit, word and world* Melbourne; Oxford: Oxford University Press 1996

Rawlik, G. and Noll, M., eds. *Amazing grace: evangelicalism in Australia, Britain, Canada, and the United States* Montreal; London: McGill-Queen's University Press 1994

Shipps, J. *Sojourner in the Promised Land: forty years among the Mormons* Chicago, IL: University of Illinois Press 2000

Smith, C. *Christian America? What evangelicals really want* Berkeley, CA: University of California Press 2000

Smith, C. and Prokopy, J., eds. *Latin American religion in motion* New York; London: Routledge 1999

Stackhouse, J. *Canadian evangelicalism in the twentieth century: an introduction to its character* Toronto; London: University of Toronto Press 1993

Thomas, L., ed. *Living stones in the household of God: the legacy and future of Black theology* Minneapolis, MN: Fortress 2004

Tombs, D. *Latin American liberation theology* Boston, MA; Leiden: Brill 2002

Westmeier, K.W. *Protestant Pentecostalism in Latin America: a study in the dynamics of missions* Madison, NJ: Fairleigh Dickinson University Press; London: Associated University Presses 1999

CHAPTER 16

Anderson, K. *Bold as a lamb: Pastor Samuel Lamb and the underground church of China* Grand Rapids, MI: Zondervan 1991

Bays, D., ed. *Christianity in China: from the eighteenth century to the present* Stanford, CA: Stanford University Press 1996

Brown, G. T. *Christianity in the People's Republic of China* Atlanta, GA: John Knox Press 1983

George, K. *Church of South India: life in union, 1947–1997* Delhi: ISPCK 1999

Goh, R. *Christianity in Southeast Asia* Singapore: Institute of Southeast Asian Studies 2005

Grayson, J. *Korea – a religious history* London: RoutledgeCurzon rev. ed. 2002

Han, G. *Social sources of church growth: Korean churches in the homeland and overseas* Lanham, MD: University Press of America 1995

Harvey, T. *Acquainted with grief: Wang Mingdao's stand for the persecuted church in China* Grand Rapids, MI: Brazos 2002

Hayford, C. *To the people: James Yen and village China* New York: Columbia University Press 1990

Hunt, R., Kam Hing, L., and Roxborogh, J., eds. *Christianity in Malaysia: a denominational history* Petaling Jaya: Pelanduk 1992

Kayal, K. *Keshub Chunder Sen: a study in encounter and response* Calcutta: Minerva 1998

Kinnear, A. *Against the tide: the story of Watchman Nee* rev. ed. Eastbourne: Kingsway 1990

van Klinken, G. *Minorities, modernity and the emerging nation: Christians in Indonesia, a biographical approach* Leiden: KITLV 2003

Miura, H. *The life and thought of Kanzo Uchimura, 1861–1930* Grand Rapids, MI: Eerdmans 1996

Mullins, M. *Christianity made in Japan: a study of indigenous movements* Honolulu: University of Hawaii Press 1998

Park, C.S. *Protestantism and politics in Korea* Seattle, WA: University of Washington Press 2003

Preston, D. *The Boxer Rebellion: the dramatic story of China's war on foreigners that shook the world in the summer of 1900* New York: Berkley 2000

Raj, S. and Dempsey, C., eds. *Popular Christianity in India: riting between the lines* Albany, NY: State University of New York Press 2002

Ralston, H. *Christian ashrams: a new religious movement in contemporary India* Lewiston, NY: Mellon 1989

Reid, D. *New wine: the cultural shaping of Japanese Christianity* Berkeley, CA: Asian Humanities Press 1991

Sahu, D. *United and uniting: a story of the Church of North India* Delhi: ISPCK 2001

Sebba, A. *Mother Teresa: beyond the image* London: Orion 1998

Tian, R. *Peaks of faith: Protestant mission in revolutionary China* Leiden; New York: Brill 1993

Turnbull, S. *The Kakure Kirishitan of Japan: a study of their development, beliefs and rituals to the present day* Richmond: Japan Library 1998

Wi Jo Kang *Christ and Caesar in modern Korea* Albany, NY: SUNY Press 1997

Williams, P. *The life and work of Mother Teresa* Indianapolis, IN: Alpha 2002

Yamamoto, S. *History of Protestantism in China: the indigenization of Christianity* Tokyo: Gakkai 2000

Yu, C.-S., ed. *Korea and Christianity* Berkeley, CA: Asian Humanities Press 2002

Yu, C.-S., ed. *The founding of Catholic tradition in Korea* Berkeley, CA: Asian Humanities Press 2002

CHAPTER 17

Anderson, A. *African reformation: African initiated Christianity in the twentieth century* Trenton, NJ: Africa World Press 2001

Asamoah-Gyadu, J. K. *African charismatics: current developments within independent indigenous Pentecostalism in Ghana* Leiden: Brill 2005

Bailey, B. and Bailey, M. *Who are the Christians in the Middle East* Grand Rapids, MI: Eerdmans 2003

Besier, G., ed. *The churches, Southern Africa and the political context* Atlanta, GA; London: Minerva 1999

Blakely, T., van Beek, W., and Thomson, D., eds. *Religion in Africa: experience and expression* London: Currey; Portsmouth, NH: Heinemann 1994

DomNwachukwu, P. *Authentic African Christianity: an inculturation model for the Igbo* New York: Lang 2000

Eide, O. *Revolution and religion in Ethiopia: the growth and persecution of the Mekane Yesus Church, 1974–85* Oxford: Currey 2000

Elphick, R. and Davenport, R., eds. *Christianity in South Africa: a political, social and cultural history* Oxford: Currey; Cape Town: Philip 1997

Gifford, P. *Ghana's new Christianity: Pentecostalism in a globalizing African economy* Indianapolis: Indiana University Press 2004

Gish, S. *Desmond Tutu: a biography* Westport, CT: Greenwood 2004

Hansen, H. and Twaddle, M., eds. *Christian missionaries and the state in the Third World* Oxford: Currey 2002

Hasan, S. *Christians versus Muslims in modern Egypt: the century-long struggle for Coptic equality* Oxford: Oxford University Press 2003

Hege, N. *Beyond our prayers: Anabaptist church growth in Ethiopia, 1948–1998* Scottdale, PA: Herald 1998

Hinfelaar, H. *History of the Catholic Church in Zambia 1895–1995* Lusaka: Bookworld 2004

Katongole, E., ed. *African theology today* Scranton, PA: University of Scranton Press 2002

Kitshoff, M., ed. *African independent churches today: kaleidoscope of Afro-Christianity* Lampeter: Mellen 1996

Kuperus, T. *State, civil society and apartheid in South Africa: an examination of Dutch Reformed Church-state relations* Basingstoke: Palgrave 1999

Lockot, H. *The mission: the life, reign and character of Haile Selassie I* London: Hurst 1992

McGrandle, P. *Trevor Huddleston: turbulent priest* London: Continuum 2004

Mockler, A. *Haile Selassie's war* rev. ed. Oxford: Signal 2003

Molyneux, K. *African Christian theology: the quest for selfhood* Lewiston, NY: Mellen 1993

Rasmussen, A. *Modern African spirituality: the independent Holy Spirit churches in East Africa, 1902–1976* London; New York: British Academic Press 1996

Sanneh, L. *Piety and power: Muslims and Christians in West Africa* Maryknoll, NY: Orbis 1996

Sanneh, L. and Carpenter, J., eds. *The changing face of Christianity: Africa, the West, and the world* Oxford: Oxford University Press 2005

Shank, D. *Prophet Harris, the 'black Elijah' of west Africa* Leiden: Brill 1994

Thomas, D. *Christ divided: liberalism, ecumenism and race in South Africa* Pretoria: Unisa 2002

Tutu, D. *No future without forgiveness: a personal overview of South Africa's Truth and Reconciliation Commission* London: Rider 1999

Verstraelen, F. *Zimbabwean realities and Christian responses: contemporary aspects of Christianity in Zimbabwe* Gweru: Mambo 1998

INDEX

Bold entries indicate
main section on topic

People

Places

A

Subject index

(including biblical books)

PICTURE ACKNOWLEDGMENTS

Picture research by Zooid Pictures Limited and Lion Hudson plc

pp. 2 (detail) and 496 Bohemian Nomad Picturemakers/Corbis UK Ltd; p. 3 Tibor Bognar/Alamy; p. 5 (detail and) 131 Archivo Iconografico S.a/Corbis UK Ltd; p. 13 Erich Lessing/AKG-Images; pp. 14–15 Michael S Yamashita/Corbis UK Ltd; pp. 14 (detail) and 35 Araldo De Luca/Corbis UK Ltd.; p.18 Charles & Josette Lenars/Corbis UK Ltd; p. 19 Lion Hudson Plc; p. 21 Rabatti Dominigie/AKG-Images; p. 23 Lion Hudson plc; p. 27 Erich Lessing/AKG-Images; p. 33 AKG Images; p. 36–37 Museum voor Schone Kunsten, Ghent, Belgium/Giraudon/Bridgeman Art Library; p. 40 AKG-Images; p. 42 Michael S Yamashita/Corbis UK Ltd; pp. 44 (detail) and 59 Archive Iconografico; S.a/Corbis UK Ltd; p. 47 Archivo Icongrafico, S.a/Corbis UK Ltd; p. 51 Art & Immagini Srl/Corbis UK Ltd; p. 53 AKG-Images; p. 54 Araldo de Luca/Corbis UK Ltd; p. 45 Nick Rous; p. 61 © Stapleton Collection/Corbis UK Ltd; p. 63 Mary Evans Picture Library; p. 66 Charles & Josette Lenars/Corbis UK Ltd; p. 68 Lion Hudson plc; p. 73 Electa/AKG-Images; p. 74 Andrea Jemolo/AKG-Images; pp. 72 (detail) and 77 Elio Ciol/Corbis UK Ltd; pp. 78–79 © 1992. Photo Scala, Florence. courtesy of the Ministero Beni e Att. Culturali; p. 80 Archivo Iconografico, S.a/Corbis UK Ltd; p. 83 Erich Lessing/AKG-Images; p. 86 Reza Webistan/Corbis UK Ltd; p. 90 AKG-Images; p. 92 Jean-Louis Nou/AKG-Images; p. 97 Scala Art Resource; p. 102 Archaeological Museum Aleppo Syria/Dagli Orti/Art Archive; pp. 100 (detail) and 108–109 Gianni Dagli Orti/Corbis UK Ltd; p. 104 Visual Arts Library, London/Alamy; p. 106 Robert Preston/Alamy; p. 107 Andrew Holt/Alamy; p. 112 Tristan Lafranchis/AKG-Images; p. 115 Eddie Gerald/Alamy; pp. 116–17 Gian Berto Vanni/Corbis UK Ltd; p. 119 Gerard DeGeorge/AKG-Images; p. 123 Roger Wood/Corbis UK Ltd; pp. 126–27 Michael S. Lewis/Corbis UK Ltd; p. 130 Erich Lessing/AKG-Images; pp. 130 (detail) and 155 Mimmo Jodice/Corbis UK Ltd; p. 132–33 Adam Woolfitt/Corbis UK Ltd; pp. 136–37 Schmitz-Snigen/Zefa/Corbis UK Ltd; p. 141 AKG-Images; p. 143 British Museum; p. 146 Biblioteca Nacional, Madrid, Spain/ Bridgeman Art Library; p. 147 Gianni Dagli Orti/Corbis UK Ltd; p. 148 Biblioteca Nacional; p. 156 © Richard and Kailas Icons; London; UK/Bridgeman Art Library; p. 159 AKG-Images; p. 158 (detail) and 160 Cameraphoto/AKG Images UK; p. 162 Cameraphoto/AKG-Images; p. 163 British Library; p. 165 Pirozzi/AKG-Images; p. 166 AKG-Images; p. 167 Homer Sykes/Corbis UK Ltd; p. 169 Tristan Lafranchis/AKG-Images; p. 170 Bodleian Library; Oxford/Art Archive; p. 173 Elizabeth Dizney/AKG-Images; p. 175 Bibliotheque Muncipale; Castres; France/Giraudon/Bridgeman Art Library; p. 179 Werner Forman/Corbis UK Ltd; p. 181 Enzo & Paolo Ragazzini/Corbis UK Ltd; pp. 182 (detail) and 198 Museo Civico, Bologna; Italy/Giraudon/Bridgeman Art Library; p. 184 Musee Conde, Chanilly, France/Giraudon/Bridgeman Art Library; p. 185 Bibliotheque Nationale, Paris, France; Lauros/Giraudon/Bridgeman Art Library; p. 186 AKG-Images; p. 187 Corbis UK Ltd; p. 189 Nick Rous; p. 190 ArkReligion.com/Alamy; p. 193 Nick Rous; p. 197 Topfoto; pp. 200–201 Nick Rous; p. 202 Christie's Images/Corbis UK Ltd; p. 203 Dean Conger/Corbis UK Ltd; p. 205 Biblioteca Nazionale, Palmero/Dagli Orti/Art Archive; pp. 208–209 Francis G. Mayer/Corbis UK Ltd; p. 210 Superstock Ltd; p. 212 AKG Images; p. 214 Sean Burke/Alamy; p. 216 Chris Hellier/Corbis UK Ltd; p. 217 Michael Nicholson/Corbis UK Ltd; p. 218 AKG-Images; p. 220 British Library; pp. 220 (detail) and 228 Jeff Greenberg/Lonely Planet Images/Getty Images; p. 221 Jon Arnold/Jon Arnold; p. 223 Bibliotheque Nationale, Paris, France/Bridgeman Art Library; p. 227 David Alexander; p. 230 Private Collection/RIA Novosti/Bridgeman Art Library; pp. 232–33 Peter Turnley/Corbis Uk Ltd; p. 234–35 Viennaphoto/allOver photography/Alamy; p. 240 (detail) and 272 AKG-Images; p. 242 Arte & Immagini Srl/Corbis Uk Ltd; pp. 244–45 Gianni Giansanti/Sygma/Corbis UK Ltd; p. 246 Erich Lessing/AKG-Images; p. 247 Mary Evans Picture Library/Alamy; p. 249 David Lees/Corbis UK Ltd; p. 250–51 AKG Images; p. 254 AKG-Images; p. 257 Gianni Dagli Orti/Corbis UK Ltd; p. 262 Giles Mermet/AKG-Images; p. 264 Erich Lessing/AKG-Images; pp. (274 (detail) and 276 Theodore de Bry/Visual Arts Library (London)/Alamy; p. 275 Courtesy of the Museum of Martimo (Barcelona), Ramon Manent/Corbis UK Ltd; p 278 Mary Evans Picture Library; pp. 284–85 Mireille Vautier/Alamy; p. 287 AKG-Images; p. 289 AKG-Images; p. 293 AKG-Images; p. 295 Bettmann/Corbis Uk Ltd; p. 299 Erich Lessing/AKG-Images; p. 302 Gesu, Rome, Italy/Bridgeman Art Library; pp. 312 (detail) and 337 City Temple, London/Eileen Tweedy/Art Archive; p. 313 Mary Evans Picture Library/Alamy; p. 315 Achivio Iconografico S.a./Corbis UK Ltd; p. 316 AKG-Images; p. 319 Bettmann/Corbis UK Ltd; p. 320–21 State Russian Museum, St. Petersburg, Russia/Giraudon/Bridgeman Art Library; p. 322 Adam Woolfitt/Corbis UK Ltd; p. 325 AKG-Images; p. 326 Mary Evans Picture Library; p. 329 Corbis UK Ltd; pp. 330–31 Bridgeman Art Library; p. 334 Historical Picture Archive/Corbis UK Ltd; pp. 340 (detail) and 358–59 Bibliotheque des Artes Decoratifs, Paris, France/Archives Charmet/Bridgeman Art Library; p. 341 Leonard De Selva/Corbis UK Ltd; p. 344 Bettmann/Corbis UK Ltd; p. 348 © Wilberforce House, Hull City Museums and Art Galleries UK/Bridgeman Art Library; p. 351 Mary Evans Picture Library; p. 353 AKG-Images; p. 358 AKG-Images; p. 369 AKG-Images; p. 371 Fortean/Topfoto; pp. 374 (detail) and 391 Charles & Josette Lenars/Corbis UK Ltd; p. 375 National Portrait Gallery; p. 377 Archives Charmet/Bridgeman Art Library; p. 378 Hulton Archive/Getty Images; p. 379 © The Stapleton Collection/Corbis Uk Ltd; pp. 384–85 © The Stapleton Collection/Bridgeman Art Library; p. 389 Michael Maslan Historic Photographs/Corbis UK Ltd; p. 392 AKG-Images; p. 395 Granger Collection; pp. 396–97 TopFoto; p 399 Granger Collection; p. 400 TopFoto; p. 404 National Portrait Gallery; p. 406 Historic Picture Archive/Corbis UK Ltd; p. 410 (detail) And 416–17 Peter Turnley/Corbis Uk Ltd; p. 411 Vanni Archive/Corbis Uk Ltd; p. 412 Bettmann/Corbis UK Ltd; p. 415 Bettmann/Corbis UK Ltd; p. 418 Sipa Press/Rex Features; p. 421 Bettman/ Corbis UK Ltd; p. 422 Reuters/Corbis UK Ltd; p. 426 © Stapleton Collection/Corbis Uk Ltd; p. 427 Ullstein Bild/AKG-Images; pp. 428–29 Michael St. Maur Sheil/Corbis UK Ltd; p. 433 Sophie Bassouls/Sygma/Corbis UK Ltd; p. 436 Hank Walker/Time & Life Pictures/Getty Images; p. 440–41 Turcotte & Gousse; Québec/Archidiocèse de Québec; pp. 440 (detail) and 467 Patricia Lee/Gracie Greene/Gracie Mosquito/Joan Nagomara/Lucy Gill/Balgo-Kutjungka Catholic Church; p. 443 Blue Lantern Studio/Corbis UK Ltd; p. 445 TopFoto; p. 447 Alpha International; p. 448–49 Hulton Archive/Getty Images; p. 453 Flip Schulke/Corbis UK Ltd; p. 455 Bob Sacha/Corbis UK Ltd; p. 457 Christine Osborne/Corbis UK Ltd; p. 458 Wally McNamee/Corbis UK Ltd; p. 461 Corbis UK Ltd; p. 463 Christian Poveda/Corbis Uk Ltd; p. 471 TopFoto; p. 473 Associated Press/Empics; p. 474 Kapoor Baldev/Sygma/Corbis UK Ltd; p. 476 Ian Berry/Magnum Photo; p. 477 AKG-Images; p. 482–83 Paolo Pellgrin/Magnum Photos; p. 484 Bettmann/Corbis UK Ltd; p. 489 Alinari Archives/Corbis UK Ltd; p. 491 Franck Robichon/Epa/Corbis UK Ltd; p. 499 City Harvest Church; p. 502–503 Greg Smith/ Corbis UK Ltd; p. 506 AKG-Images; pp. 506 (detail) and 527 Shawn Baldwin/Corbis UK Ltd; p. 509 Mary Evans Picture Library; p. 512 Caroline Penn/Corbis Uk Ltd; p. 520 TopFoto; p. 523 Per-Anders Petterson/Getty Images; p. 529 Bettmann/Corbis UK Ltd; p. 530–531 Roger Viollet Collection/Getty Images

All maps by Richard Watts (Total Media Services).

Lion Hudson

Commissioning editor: Morag Reeve
Editorial team: Catherine Sinfield, David W. Bygott (*freelance*), Liz Evans (*freelance*), Alison Brown (*freelance*)
Book designer: Simon Emery (Aqua Design)
Jacket designer: Jonathan Roberts
Picture researcher: Kate Leech
Production manager: Kylie Ord